A-Z SUPER SCALE
GREAT BRITAIN
NORTHERN IRELAND

Journey Route Planning maps

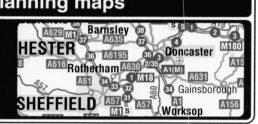

Airport plans

Access maps to principal
Airports in Britain......205

Britain & Northern Ireland Road maps

Over 32,000 Index References

A	Aberkenfig. B'end .....
	Aberlady. E Lot ......
Abbas Combe. Som 4C 22	Aberlemno. Ang .....
Abberley. Worc 4B 60	Aberllefenni. Gwyn ...
Abberley Common. Worc ...4B 60	Abermaw. Gwyn ......
Abberton. Essx 4D 54	Abermeurig. Cdgn ...
Abberton. Worc 5D 61	Aber-miwl. Powy .....
Abberwick. Nmbd 3F 121	Abermule. Powy .....
Abbess Roding. Essx 4F 53	Abernant. Carm .....
	Abernant. Rhon .....

Including cities, towns,
villages, hamlets and
locations 206-238

Detailed Main Route maps

Index to Places of Interest

Full postcodes to easily
locate popular places of
interest on your SatNav
.........................239-242

City and Town centre maps

Motorway Junctions

Junction	M1	
2	Northbound	No exit, access from A1 only
	Southbound	No access, exit to A1 only
4	Northbound	No exit, access from A41 only
	Southbound	No access, exit to A41 only
6a	Northbound	No exit, access from M25 only
	Southbound	No access, exit to M25 only

Details of motorway
junctions with limited
interchange..............243

Sea Port & Channel Tunnel plans

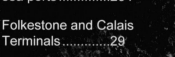

EDITION 31 2022

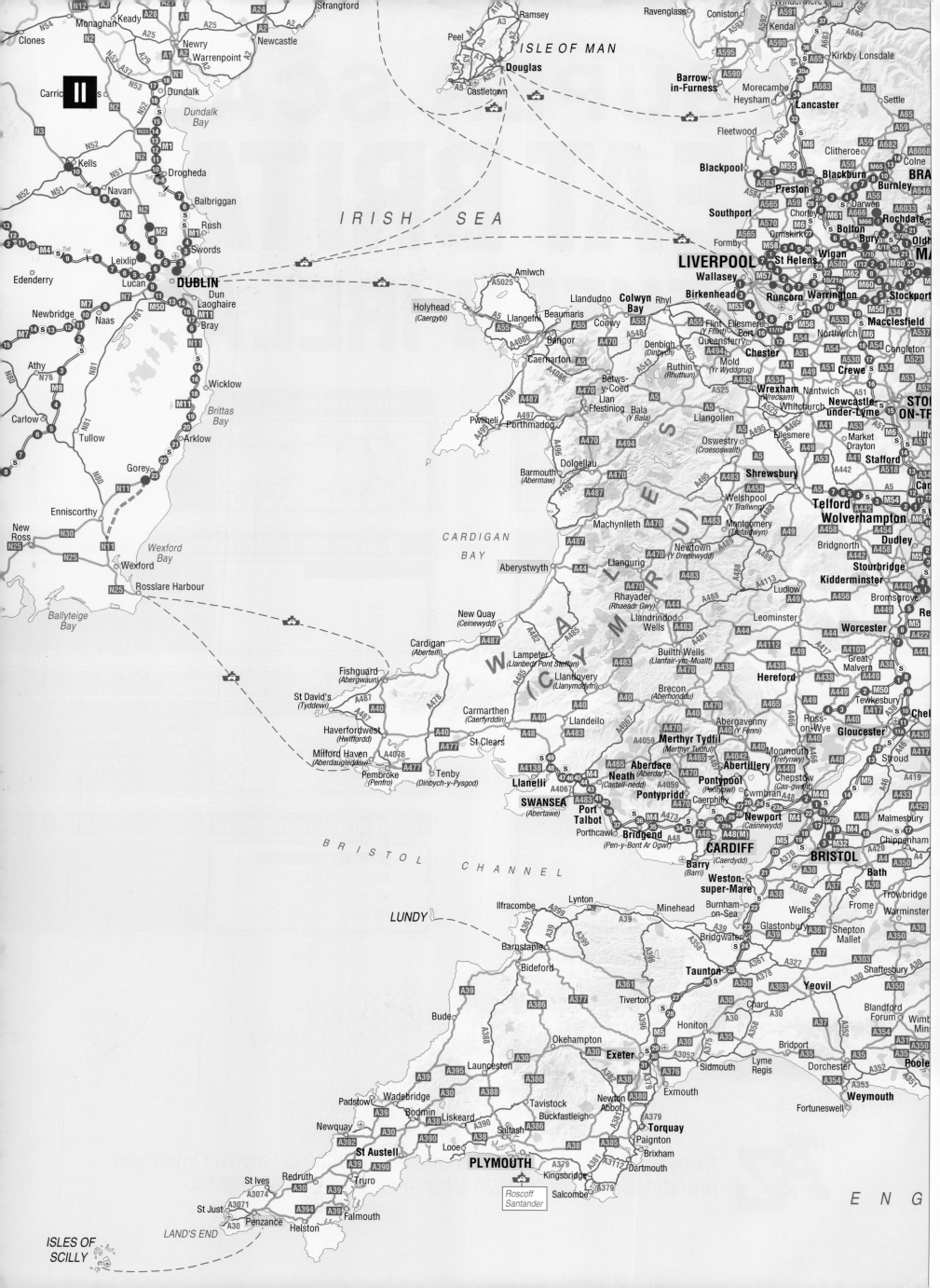

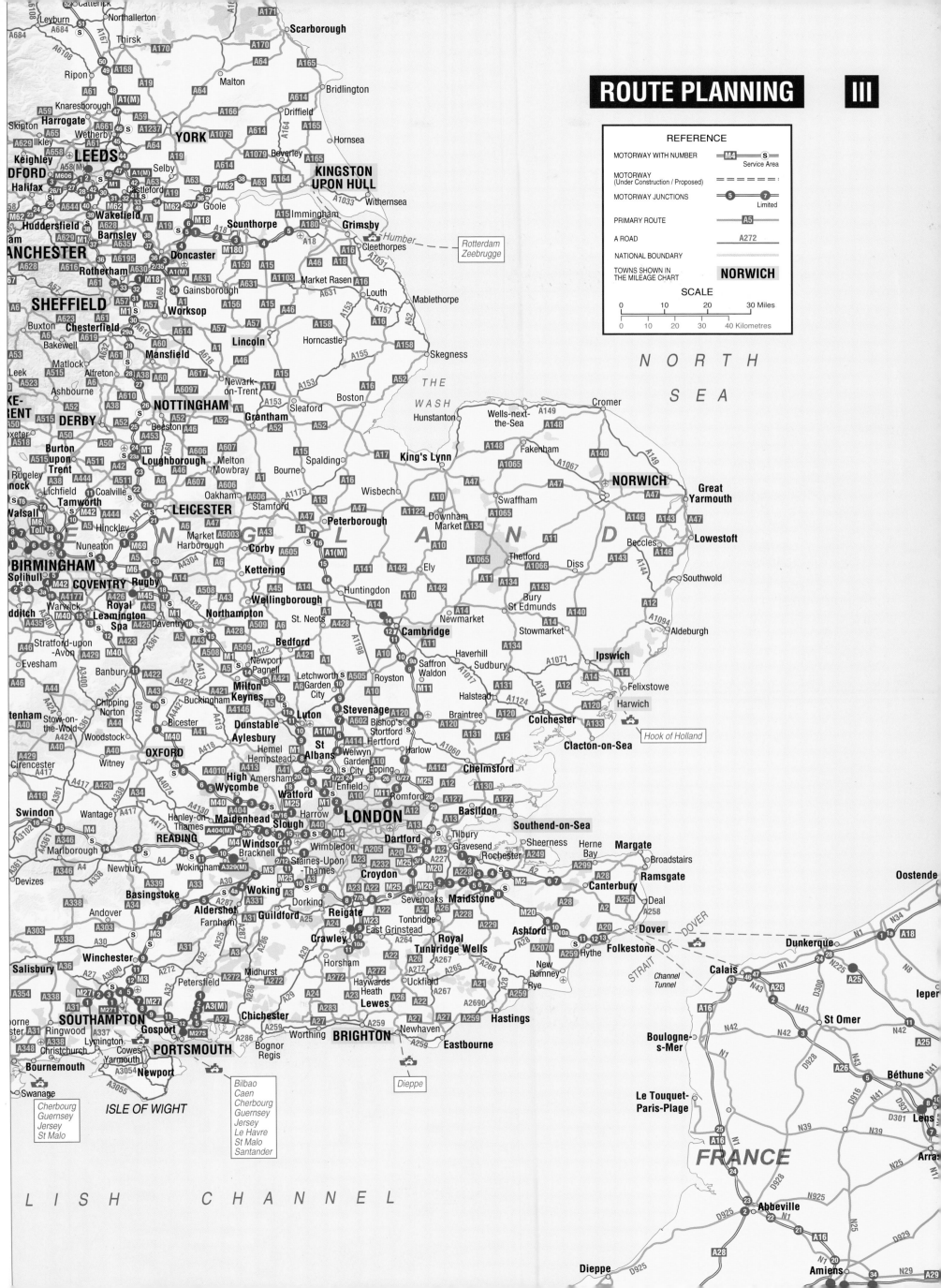

ROUTE PLANNING   III

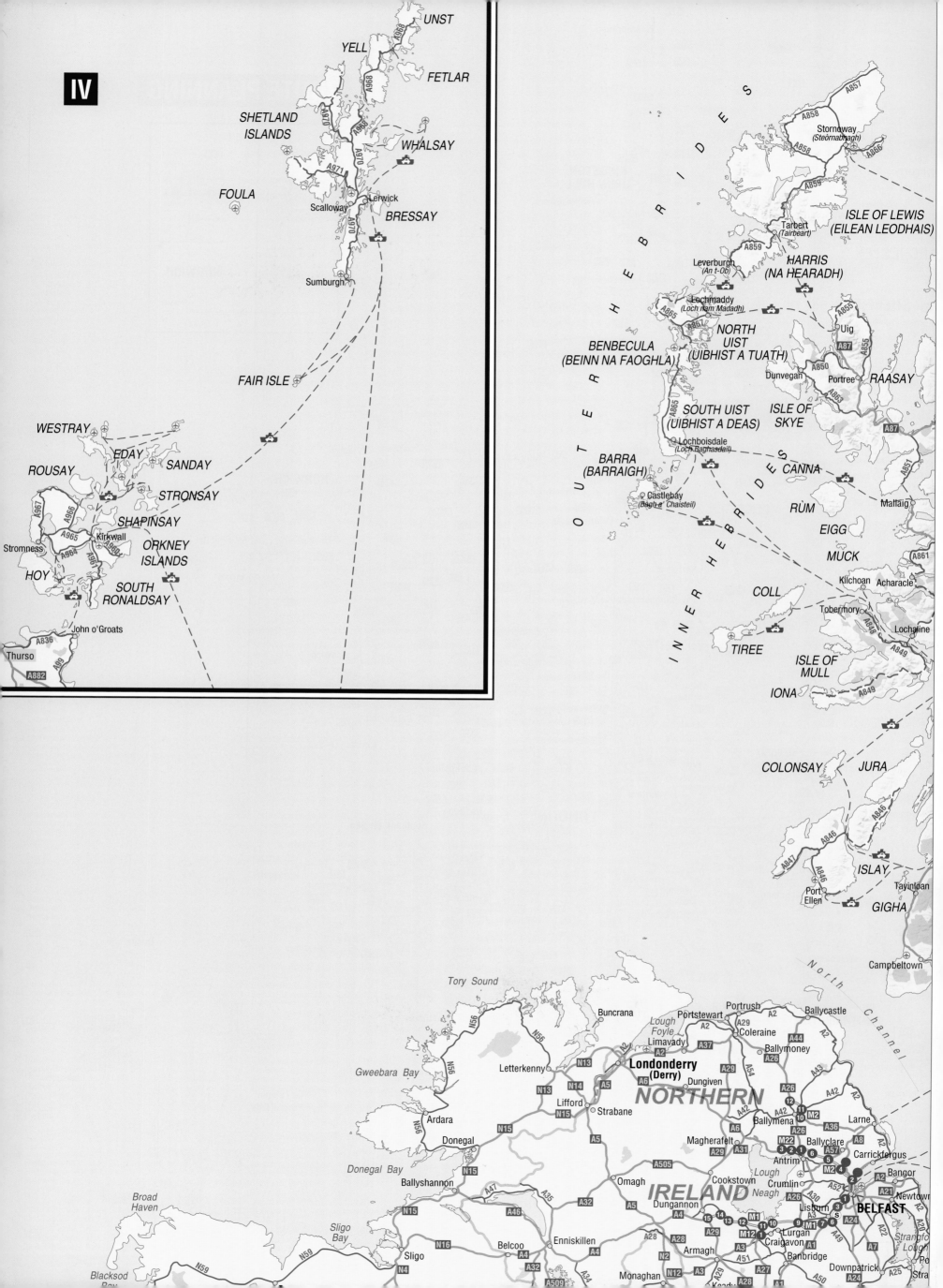

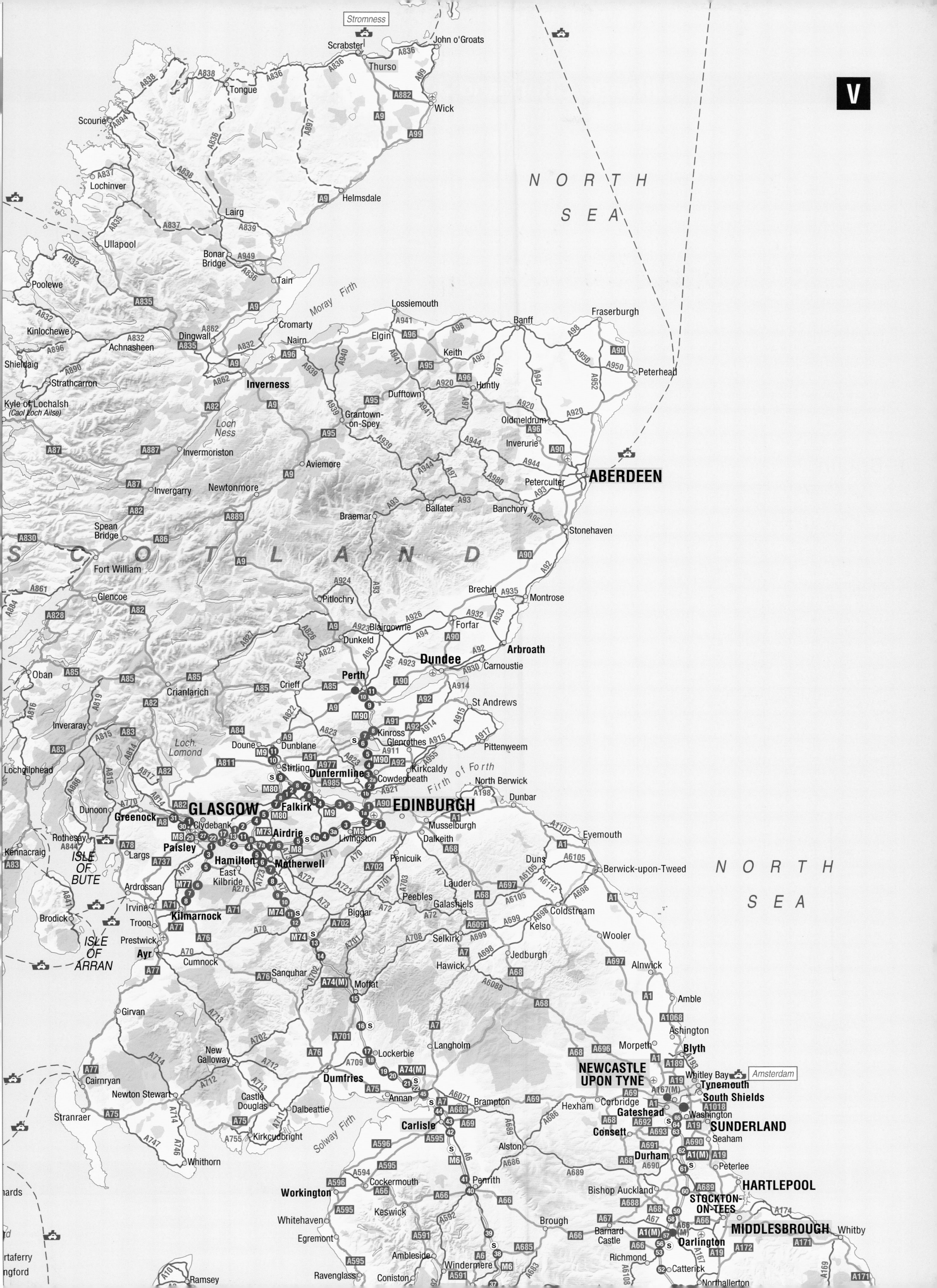

V
NORTH SEA
NORTH SEA
SCOTLAND
Stromness
Scrabster
John o'Groats
Thurso
Tongue
Wick
Scourie
Lochinver
Helmsdale
Lairg
Ullapool
Bonar Bridge
Tain
Poolewe
Moray Firth
Lossiemouth
Fraserburgh
Cromarty
Banff
Kinlochewe
Dingwall
Achnasheen
Nairn
Elgin
Keith
Shieldaig
Peterhead
Strathcarron
Inverness
Huntly
Kyle of Lochalsh
(Caol Loch Ailse)
Dufftown
Grantown-on-Spey
Loch Ness
Oldmeldrum
Inverurie
Invermoriston
Aviemore
ABERDEEN
Invergarry
Newtonmore
Peterculter
Ballater
Banchory
Braemar
Stonehaven
Spean Bridge
Fort William
Glencoe
Pitlochry
Brechin
Montrose
Blairgowrie
Forfar
Dunkeld
Arbroath
Dundee
Carnoustie
Oban
Perth
Crianlarich
Crieff
St Andrews
Inveraray
Kinross
Glenrothes
Loch Lomond
Doune
Dunblane
Pittenweem
Stirling
Kirkcaldy
Lochgilphead
Dunfermline
Cowdenbeath
Firth of Forth
North Berwick
Dunoon
Falkirk
Dunbar
Greenock
GLASGOW
EDINBURGH
Clydebank
Musselburgh
Rothesay
Airdrie
Livingston
Dalkeith
Eyemouth
Kennacraig
Paisley
Largs
ISLE OF BUTE
Hamilton
Motherwell
Penicuik
Duns
Berwick-upon-Tweed
East Kilbride
Lauder
Ardrossan
Peebles
Galashiels
Coldstream
Irvine
Brodick
Troon
Kilmarnock
Biggar
Kelso
ISLE OF ARRAN
Prestwick
Selkirk
Wooler
Ayr
Cumnock
Hawick
Jedburgh
Alnwick
Sanquhar
Moffat
Amble
Girvan
Ashington
New Galloway
Langholm
Morpeth
Blyth
Lockerbie
NEWCASTLE UPON TYNE
Whitley Bay
Amsterdam
Cairnryan
Tynemouth
Dumfries
South Shields
Newton Stewart
Castle Douglas
Annan
Brampton
Hexham
Corbridge
Gateshead
Washington
Dalbeattie
Stranraer
Carlisle
Consett
SUNDERLAND
Kirkcudbright
Solway Firth
Alston
Seaham
Whithorn
Durham
Peterlee
Penrith
Cockermouth
Workington
HARTLEPOOL
Bishop Auckland
STOCKTON-ON-TEES
Whitehaven
Keswick
Brough
MIDDLESBROUGH
Barnard Castle
Darlington
Whitby
Egremont
Ambleside
Richmond
Ravenglass
Windermere
Catterick
Coniston
Northallerton
Ramsey

This chart shows the distance in miles and journey time between two cities or towns in Great Britain. Each route has been calculated using a combination of motorways, primary routes and other major roads. This is normally the quickest, though not always the shortest route.

Average journey times are calculated whilst driving at the maximum speed limit. These times are approximate and do not include traffic congestion or convenience breaks.

To find the distance and journey time between two cities or towns, follow a horizontal line and vertical column until they meet each other.

For example, the 285 mile journey from London to Penzance is approximately 4 hours and 59 minutes.

Northern Ireland

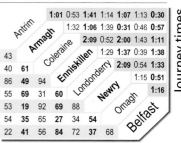

Journey times

	1:01	0:53	1:41	1:14	1:07	1:13	0:30
Antrim		1:32	1:06	1:39	0:31	0:46	0:57
	Armagh		2:09	0:52	2:00	1:43	1:11
		Coleraine		1:29	1:37	0:39	1:38
43			Enniskillen		2:09	0:54	1:33
40	61			Londonderry		1:15	0:51
86	49	94			Newry		1:16
55	69	31	60			Omagh	
53	19	92	69	88			Belfast
54	35	65	27	34	54		
22	41	56	84	72	37	68	

Distance in miles

Belfast to London = 440m / 9:46h (excluding ferry)
Belfast to Glasgow = 104m / 4:46h (excluding ferry)

Britain

Distance in miles

Journey times

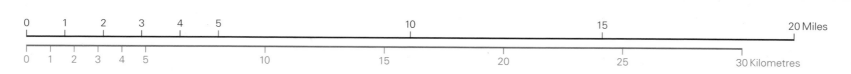

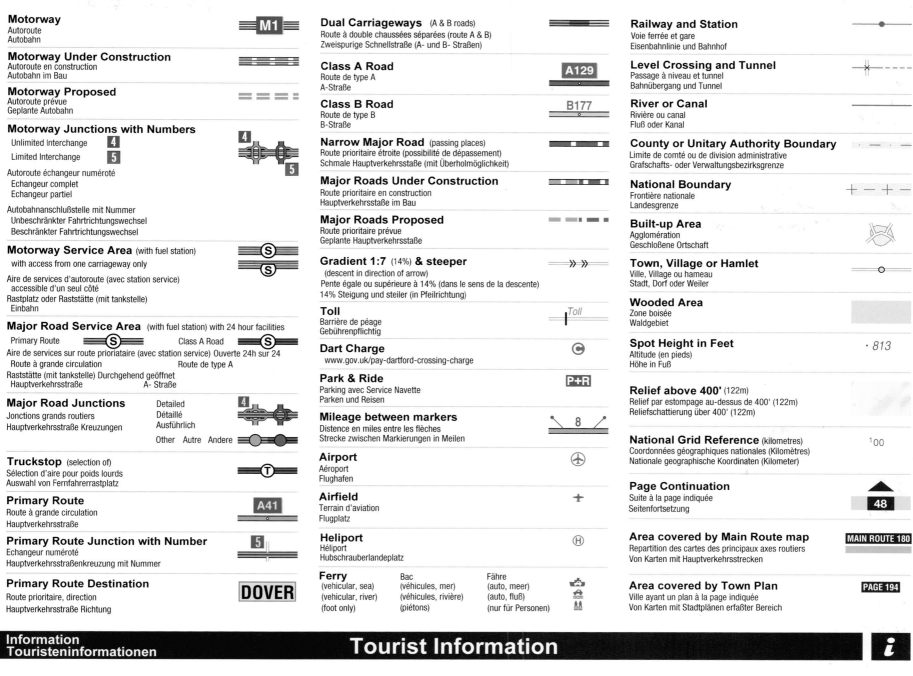

Motorway
Autoroute
Autobahn — **M1**

Motorway Under Construction
Autoroute en construction
Autobahn im Bau

Motorway Proposed
Autoroute prévue
Geplante Autobahn

Motorway Junctions with Numbers
Unlimited Interchange **4**
Limited Interchange **5**

Autoroute échangeur numéroté
Echangeur complet
Echangeur partiel

Autobahnanschlußstelle mit Nummer
Unbeschränkter Fahrtrichtungswechsel
Beschränkter Fahrtrichtungswechsel

Motorway Service Area (with fuel station)
with access from one carriageway only **S**

Aire de services d'autoroute (avec station service)
accessible d'un seul côté
Rastplatz oder Raststätte (mit tankstelle)
Einbahn

Major Road Service Area (with fuel station) with 24 hour facilities
Primary Route **S**   Class A Road **S**
Aire de services sur route prioritaire (avec station service) Ouverte 24h sur 24
Route à grande circulation   Route de type A
Raststätte (mit tankstelle) Durchgehend geöffnet
Hauptverkehrsstraße   A- Straße

Major Road Junctions
Jonctions grands routiers   Detailed / Détaillé / Ausführlich **4**
Hauptverkehrsstraße Kreuzungen

     Other   Autre   Andere

Truckstop (selection of)
Sélection d'aire pour poids lourds
Auswahl von Fernfahrerrastplatz — **T**

Primary Route
Route à grande circulation
Hauptverkehrsstraße — **A41**

Primary Route Junction with Number
Echangeur numéroté **5**
Hauptverkehrsstraßenkreuzung mit Nummer

Primary Route Destination
Route prioritaire, direction
Hauptverkehrsstraße Richtung — **DOVER**

Dual Carriageways (A & B roads)
Route à double chaussées séparées (route A & B)
Zweispurige Schnellstraße (A- und B- Straßen)

Class A Road
Route de type A
A-Straße — **A129**

Class B Road
Route de type B
B-Straße — **B177**

Narrow Major Road (passing places)
Route prioritaire étroite (possibilité de dépassement)
Schmale Hauptverkehrsstaße (mit Überholmöglichkeit)

Major Roads Under Construction
Route prioritaire en construction
Hauptverkehrsstaße im Bau

Major Roads Proposed
Route prioritaire prévue
Geplante Hauptverkehrsstaße

Gradient 1:7 (14%) & steeper
(descent in direction of arrow)
Pente égale ou supérieure à 14% (dans le sens de la descente)
14% Steigung und steiler (in Pfeilrichtung)

Toll
Barrière de péage
Gebührenpflichtig — *Toll*

Dart Charge
www.gov.uk/pay-dartford-crossing-charge

Park & Ride
Parking avec Service Navette
Parken und Reisen — **P+R**

Mileage between markers
Distence en miles entre les flèches
Strecke zwischen Markierungen in Meilen — 8

Airport
Aéroport
Flughafen

Airfield
Terrain d'aviation
Flugplatz

Heliport
Héliport
Hubschrauberlandeplatz — Ⓗ

Ferry
(vehicular, sea)   Bac (véhicules, mer)   Fähre (auto, meer)
(vehicular, river)   (véhicules, rivière)   (auto, fluß)
(foot only)   (piétons)   (nur für Personen)

Railway and Station
Voie ferrée et gare
Eisenbahnlinie und Bahnhof

Level Crossing and Tunnel
Passage à niveau et tunnel
Bahnübergang und Tunnel

River or Canal
Rivière ou canal
Fluß oder Kanal

County or Unitary Authority Boundary
Limite de comté ou de division administrative
Grafschafts- oder Verwaltungsbezirksgrenze

National Boundary
Frontière nationale
Landesgrenze

Built-up Area
Agglomération
Geschloßene Ortschaft

Town, Village or Hamlet
Ville, Village ou hameau
Stadt, Dorf oder Weiler

Wooded Area
Zone boisée
Waldgebiet

Spot Height in Feet
Altitude (en pieds)
Höhe in Fuß — · 813

Relief above 400' (122m)
Relief par estompage au-dessus de 400' (122m)
Reliefschattierung über 400' (122m)

National Grid Reference (kilometres)
Coordonnées géographiques nationales (Kilomètres)
Nationale geographische Koordinaten (Kilometer) — ¹00

Page Continuation
Suite à la page indiquée
Seitenfortsetzung — **48**

Area covered by Main Route map
Repartition des cartes des principaux axes routiers
Von Karten mit Hauptverkehrsstrecken — **MAIN ROUTE 180**

Area covered by Town Plan
Ville ayant un plan à la page indiquée
Von Karten mit Stadtplänen erfaßter Bereich — **PAGE 194**

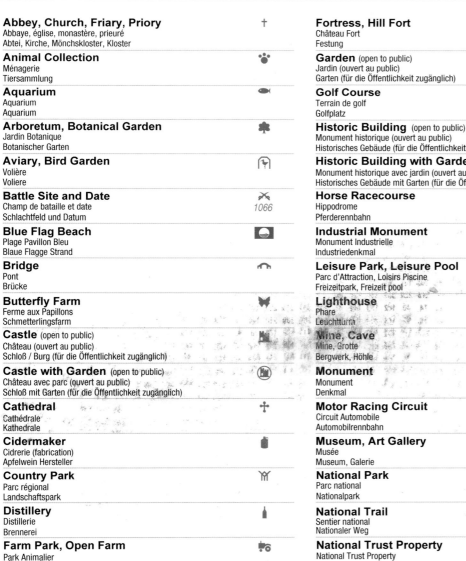

Abbey, Church, Friary, Priory
Abbaye, église, monastère, prieuré
Abtei, Kirche, Mönchskloster, Kloster — ✝

Animal Collection
Ménagerie
Tiersammlung

Aquarium
Aquarium
Aquarium

Arboretum, Botanical Garden
Jardin Botanique
Botanischer Garten

Aviary, Bird Garden
Volière
Voliere

Battle Site and Date
Champ de bataille et date
Schlachtfeld und Datum — ⚔ 1066

Blue Flag Beach
Plage Pavillon Bleu
Blaue Flagge Strand

Bridge
Pont
Brücke

Butterfly Farm
Ferme aux Papillons
Schmetterlingsfarm

Castle (open to public)
Château (ouvert au public)
Schloß / Burg (für die Öffentlichkeit zugänglich)

Castle with Garden (open to public)
Château avec parc (ouvert au public)
Schloß mit Garten (für die Öffentlichkeit zugänglich)

Cathedral
Cathédrale
Kathedrale — ✝

Cidermaker
Cidrerie (fabrication)
Apfelwein Hersteller

Country Park
Parc régional
Landschaftspark

Distillery
Distillerie
Brennerei

Farm Park, Open Farm
Park Animalier
Bauernhof Park

Fortress, Hill Fort
Château Fort
Festung

Garden (open to public)
Jardin (ouvert au public)
Garten (für die Öffentlichkeit zugänglich)

Golf Course
Terrain de golf
Golfplatz

Historic Building (open to public)
Monument historique (ouvert au public)
Historisches Gebäude (für die Öffentlichkeit zugänglich)

Historic Building with Garden (open to public)
Monument historique avec jardin (ouvert au public)
Historisches Gebäude mit Garten (für die Öffentlichkeit zugänglich)

Horse Racecourse
Hippodrome
Pferderennbahn

Industrial Monument
Monument Industrielle
Industriedenkmal

Leisure Park, Leisure Pool
Parc d'Attraction, Loisirs Piscine
Freizeitpark, Freizeit pool

Lighthouse
Phare
Leuchtturm

Mine, Cave
Mine, Grotte
Bergwerk, Höhle

Monument
Monument
Denkmal

Motor Racing Circuit
Circuit Automobile
Automobilrennbahn

Museum, Art Gallery
Musée
Museum, Galerie — Ⓜ

National Park
Parc national
Nationalpark

National Trail
Sentier national
Nationaler Weg

National Trust Property
National Trust Property
National Trust- Eigentum

Natural Attraction
Attraction Naturelle
Natürliche Anziehung — ★

Nature Reserve or Bird Sanctuary
Réserve naturelle botanique ou ornithologique
Natur- oder Vogelschutzgebiet

Nature Trail or Forest Walk
Chemin forestier, piste verte
Naturpfad oder Waldweg

Picnic Site
Lieu pour pique-nique
Picknickplatz

Place of Interest
Site, curiosité
Sehenswürdigkeit — *Craft Centre* •

Prehistoric Monument
Monument Préhistorique
Prähistorische Denkmal

Railway, Steam or Narrow Gauge
Chemin de fer, à vapeur ou à voie étroite
Eisenbahn, Dampf- oder Schmalspurbahn

Roman Remains
Vestiges Romains
Römischen Ruinen

Theme Park
Centre de loisirs
Vergnügungspark

Tourist Information Centre
Office de Tourisme
Touristeninformationen — **i**

Viewpoint
Vue panoramique   (360 degrees) (360 degrés) (360 Grade)   (180 degrees) (180 degrés) (180 Grade)
Aussichtspunkt

Vineyard
Vignoble
Weinberg

Visitor Information Centre
Centre d'information touristique
Besucherzentrum — **V**

Wildlife Park
Réserve de faune
Wildpark

Windmill
Moulin à vent
Windmühle

Zoo or Safari Park
Parc ou réserve zoologique
Zoo oder Safari-Park

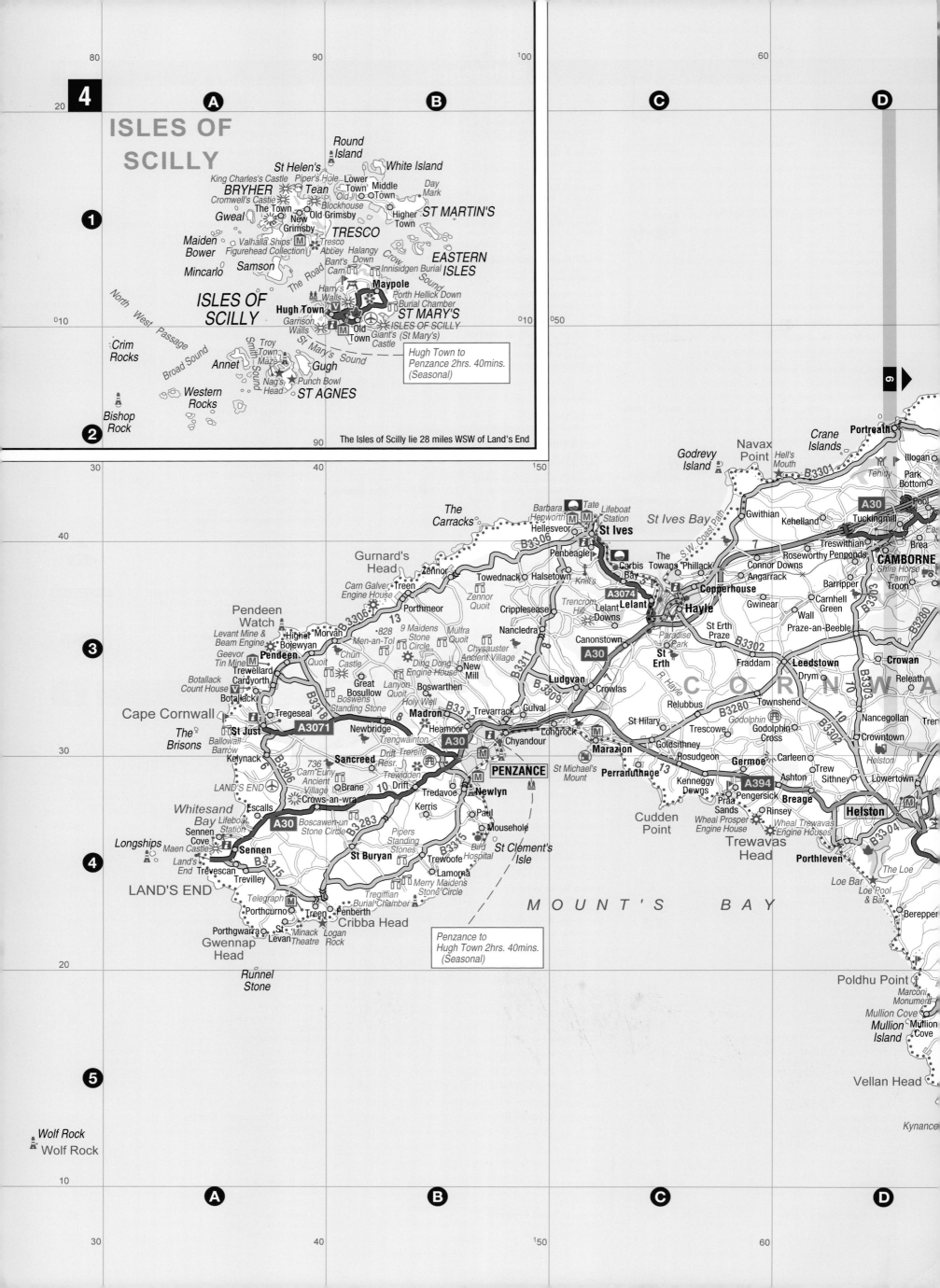

ISLES OF SCILLY

4

Round Island

St Helen's
Piper's Hole

White Island

King Charles's Castle
BRYHER
Cromwell's Castle
Lower Town
Tean
Old Town
Middle Town
Day Mark

ST MARTIN'S

Gweal
The Town
New Grimsby
Old Grimsby
Higher Town

Maiden Bower
Valhalla Ships'
Figurehead Collection
Tresco Abbey
Halangy Down
Innisidgen Burial Ground

TRESCO

EASTERN ISLES

Mincarlo
Samson
Bant's Carn
Crow Sound

Maypole
Porth Hellick Down Burial Chamber

ISLES OF SCILLY
Harry's Walls
Hugh Town
Garrison Walls
Old Town
ST MARY'S
ISLES OF SCILLY
(St Mary's)
Giant's Castle

1

Crim Rocks
North West Passage
Broad Sound
Troy Town Maze
Annet
Smith Sound
Gugh
Nag's Head
Punch Bowl
ST AGNES

Bishop Rock

2

Hugh Town to
Penzance 2hrs. 40mins.
(Seasonal)

The Isles of Scilly lie 28 miles WSW of Land's End

The Carracks

Godrevy Island
Navax Point
Hell's Mouth
Crane Islands
Portreath

Gurnard's Head
Barbara Hepworth
Tate
Lifeboat Station
St Ives Bay
S.W. Coast Path
Gwithian
Tehidy
Illogan
Park Bottom
Pool
A30

Zennor
Hellesveor
St Ives
Penbeagle
Carbis Bay
The Towans
Phillack
Kehelland
CAMBORNE
Tuckingmill
Brea
East
Treswithian
Roseworthy Penponds
Shire Horse Farm

Carn Galver Engine House
Treen
Porthmeor
Towednack
Halsetown
Knill's
Zennor Quoit
Cripplesease
Trencrom Hill
Lelant Downs
Lelant
Hayle
Copperhouse
Connor Downs
Angarrack
Gwinear
Barripper
Troon
Carnhell Green

Pendeen Watch
Levant Mine & Beam Engine
Higher Bojewyan
Morvah
Men-an-Tol
·828
9 Maidens Stone Circle
Mulfra Quoit
Nancledra
Canonstown
Paradise Park
St Erth Praze
Fraddam
Praze-an-Beeble
Wall
Crowan
Releath

Geevor Tin Mine
Pendeen
Chûn Castle
Quoit
Ding Dong Engine House
Chysauster Ancient Village
New Mill
A30
St Erth
Relubbus
Drym
Leedstown
Townshend
Nancegollan
Crowntown

3

Trewellard
Carnyorth
Great Bosullow
Lanyon Quoit
Boswarthen
Holy Well
Ludgvan
Crowlas
Trescowe
Godolphin Cross
Godolphin
Helston

Botallack Count House
Botallack
Boswens Standing Stone
Madron
Trevarrack
Gulval
St Hilary
Goldsithney
Rosudgeon
Relubbus

Cape Cornwall
Tregeseal
St Just
Newbridge
Heamoor
Trengwainton
Longrock
Chyandour
Marazion
Perranuthnoe
Kenneggy Dewas
Pengersick
Breage
Carleen
Trew
Ashton
Sithney
Lowertown

The Brisons
Ballowall Barrow
A3071
Sancreed
Drift Trereife Resr.
Trewidden
PENZANCE
St Michael's Mount
Helston

Kelynack
736
Carn'Euny Ancient Village
Brane
Drift
Tredavoe
Newlyn
Cudden Point
Wheal Prosper Engine House
Praa Sands
Rinsey
Wheal Trewavas Engine Houses
Porthleven
Loe Bar

LAND'S END
Crows-an-wra
10
Kerris
Paul
Trewavas Head
Loe Pool & Bar
The Loe

Whitesand Bay
Escalls
Boscawen-un Stone Circle
Mousehole
Bird Hospital
St Clement's Isle

Longships
Sennen Cove
Maen Castle
Sennen
St Buryan
Trewoofe
Lamorna
Merry Maidens Stone Circle

4

Land's End
Trevescan
Trevilley
Pipers Standing Stones
B3315

LAND'S END
Telegraph
Porthcurno
Treen
Penberth
Cribba Head

Porthgwarra
St Levan
'Minack Theatre
Logan Rock
Tregiffian Burial Chamber

Gwennap Head

M O U N T ' S   B A Y

Penzance to
Hugh Town 2hrs. 40mins.
(Seasonal)

Poldhu Point
Marconi Monument
Mullion Cove
Mullion Island
Mullion Cove

Runnel Stone

5

Wolf Rock
Wolf Rock

Vellan Head

Kynance

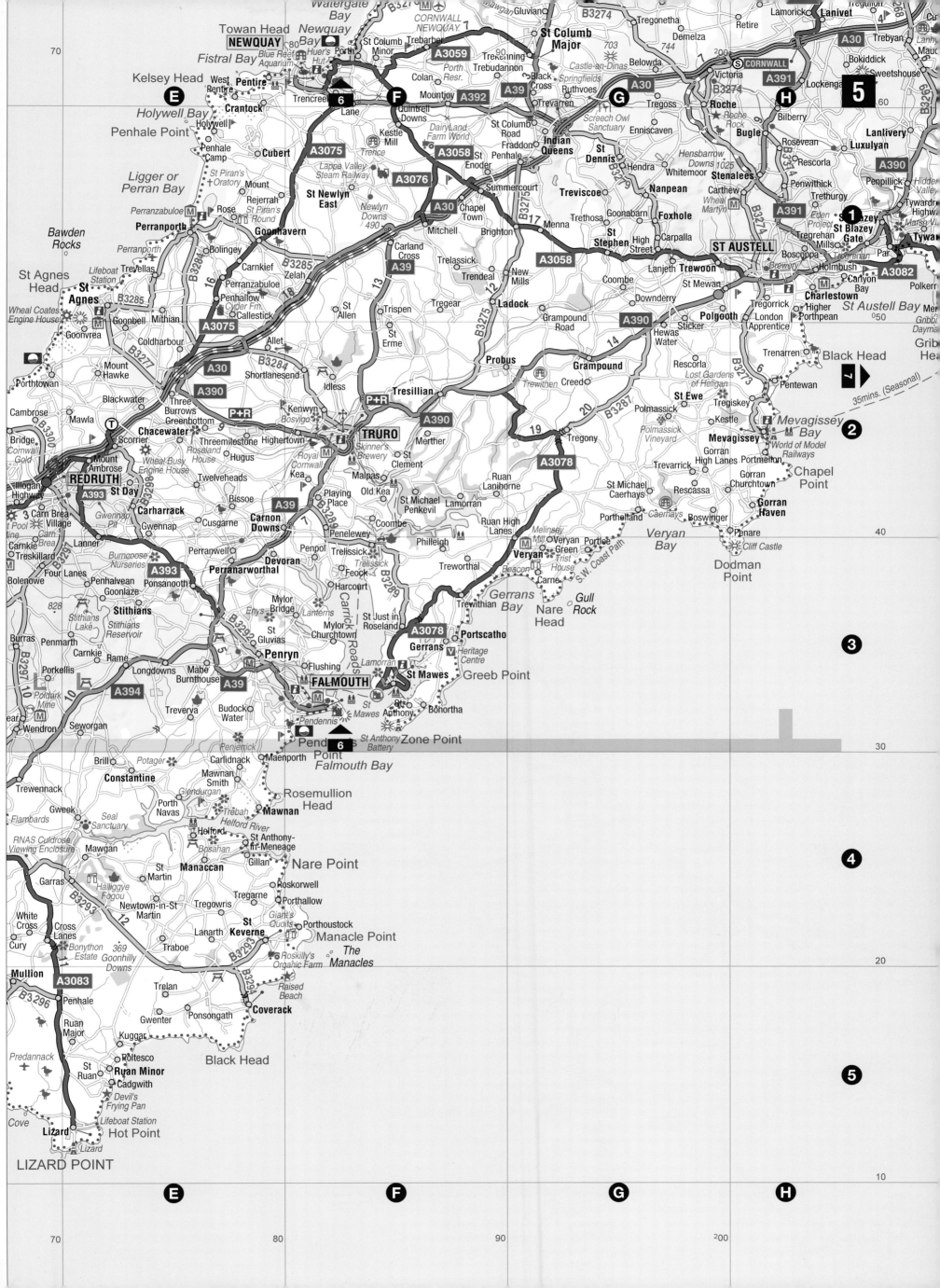

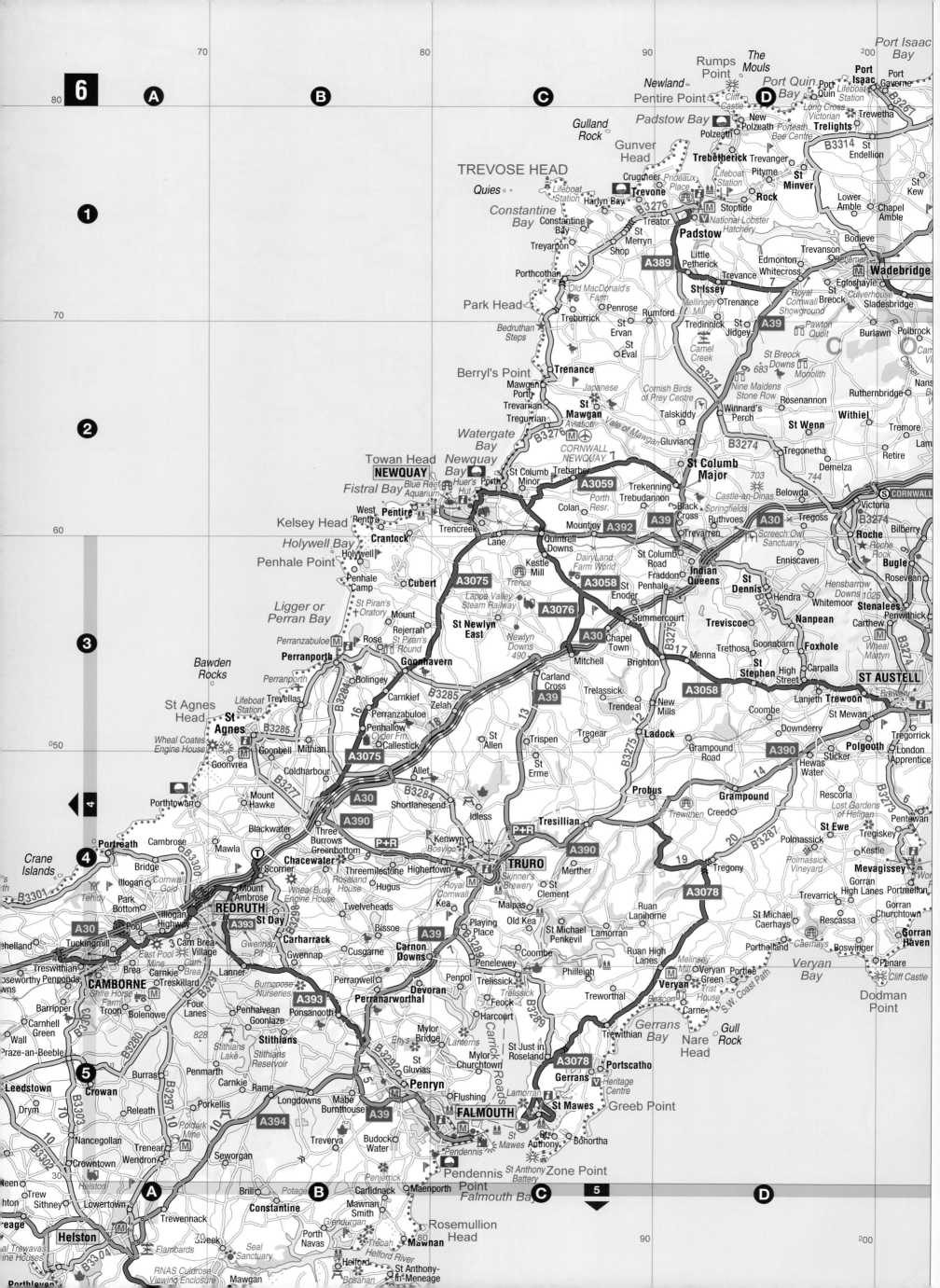

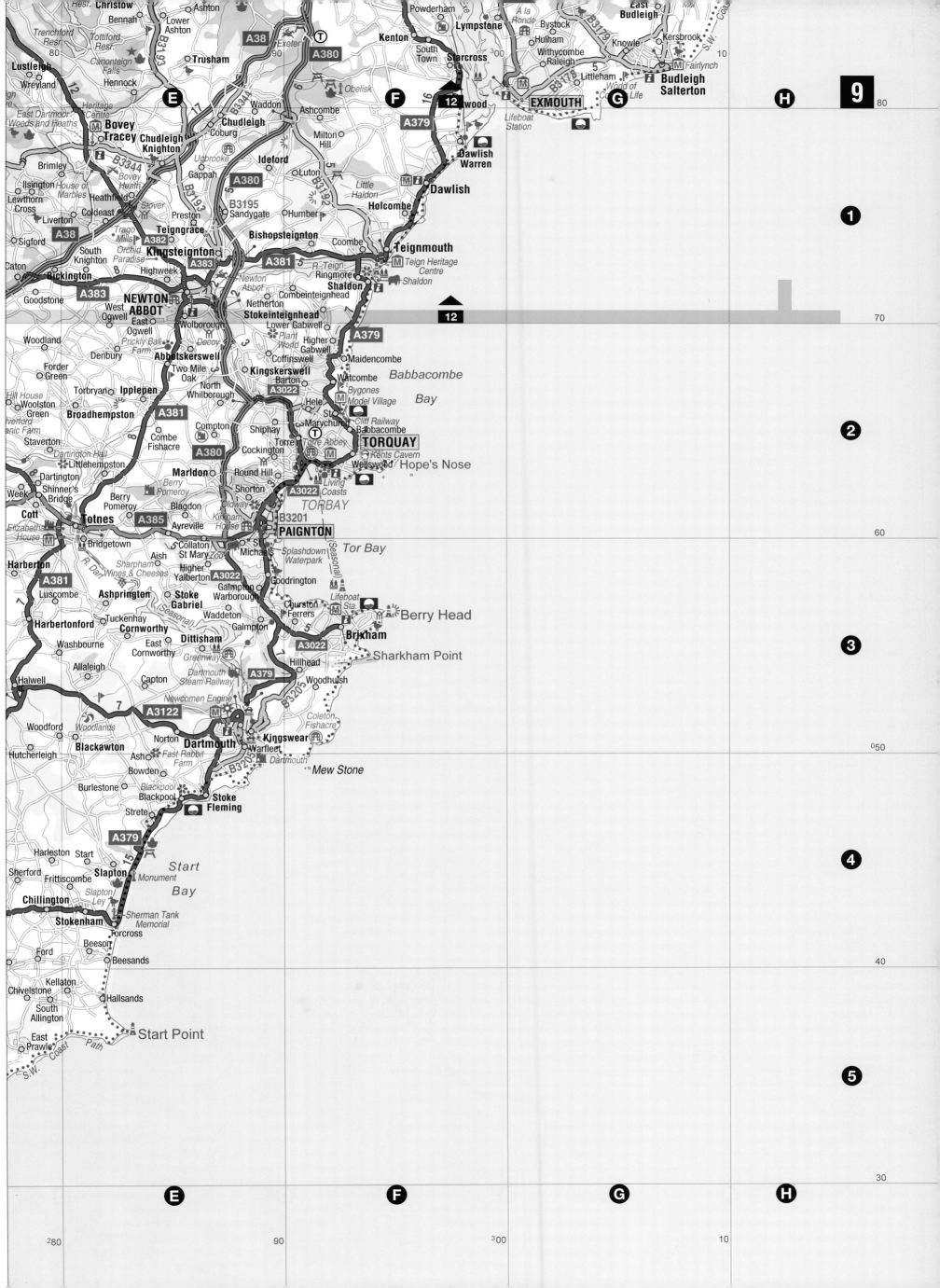

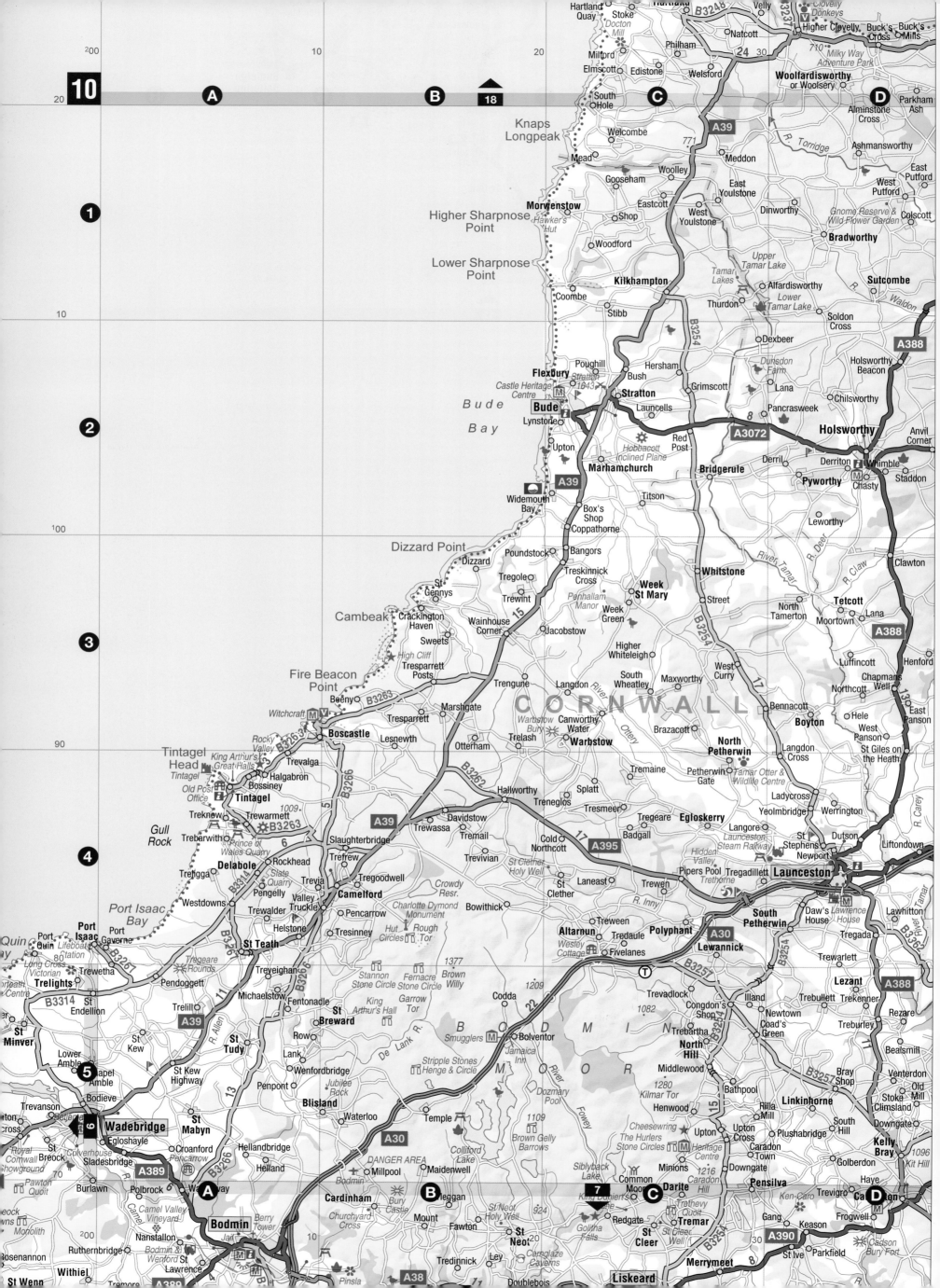

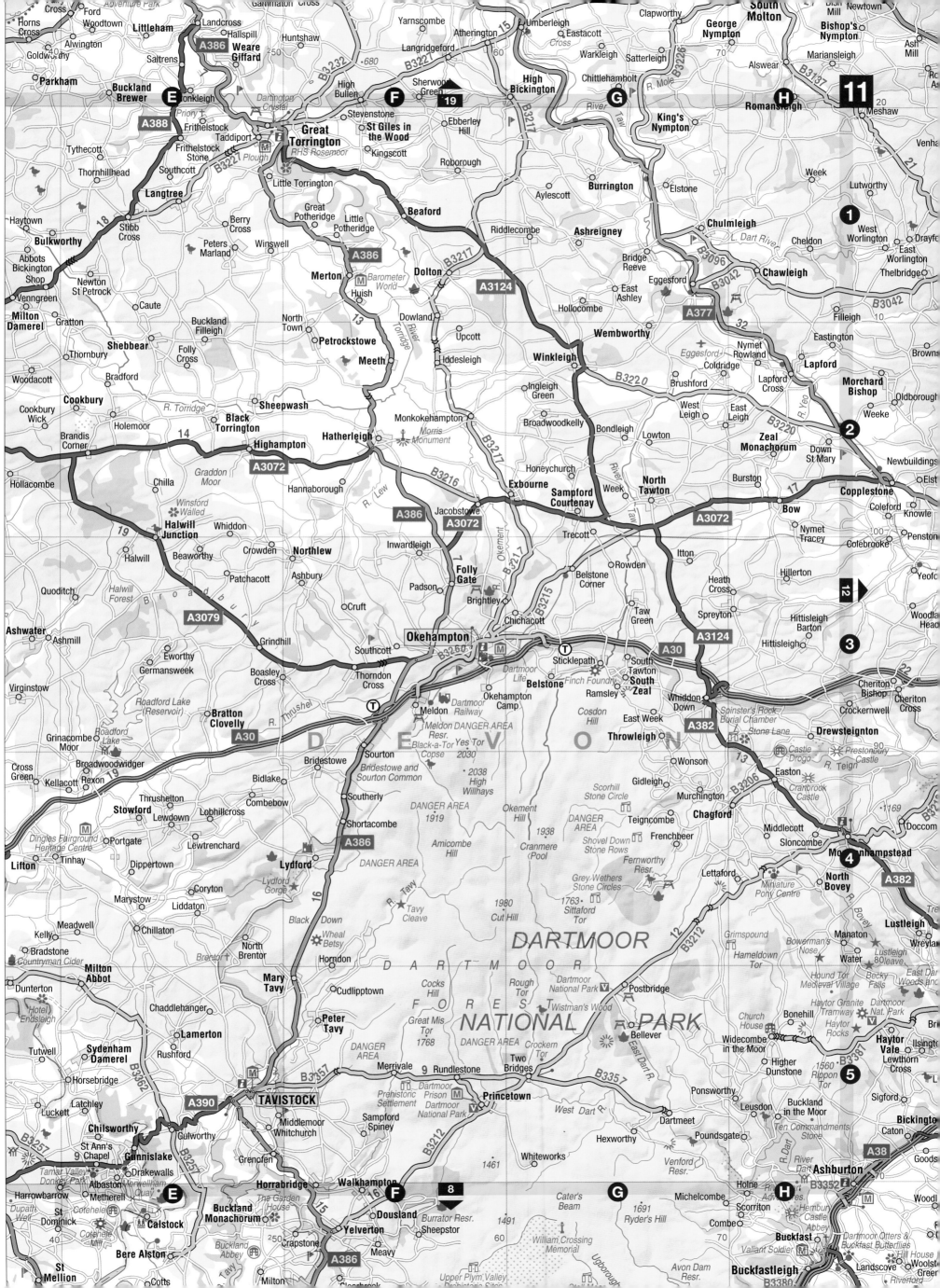

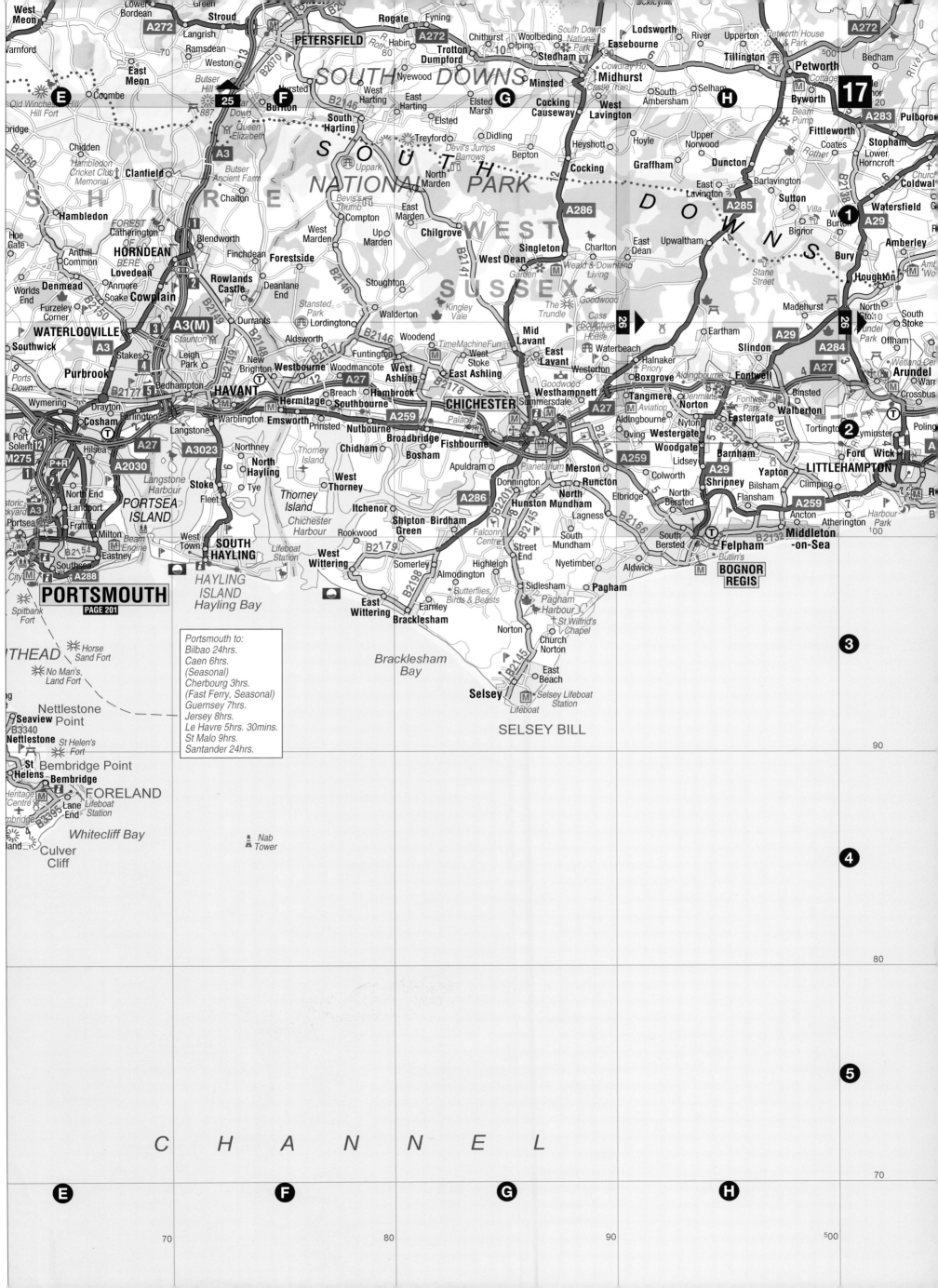

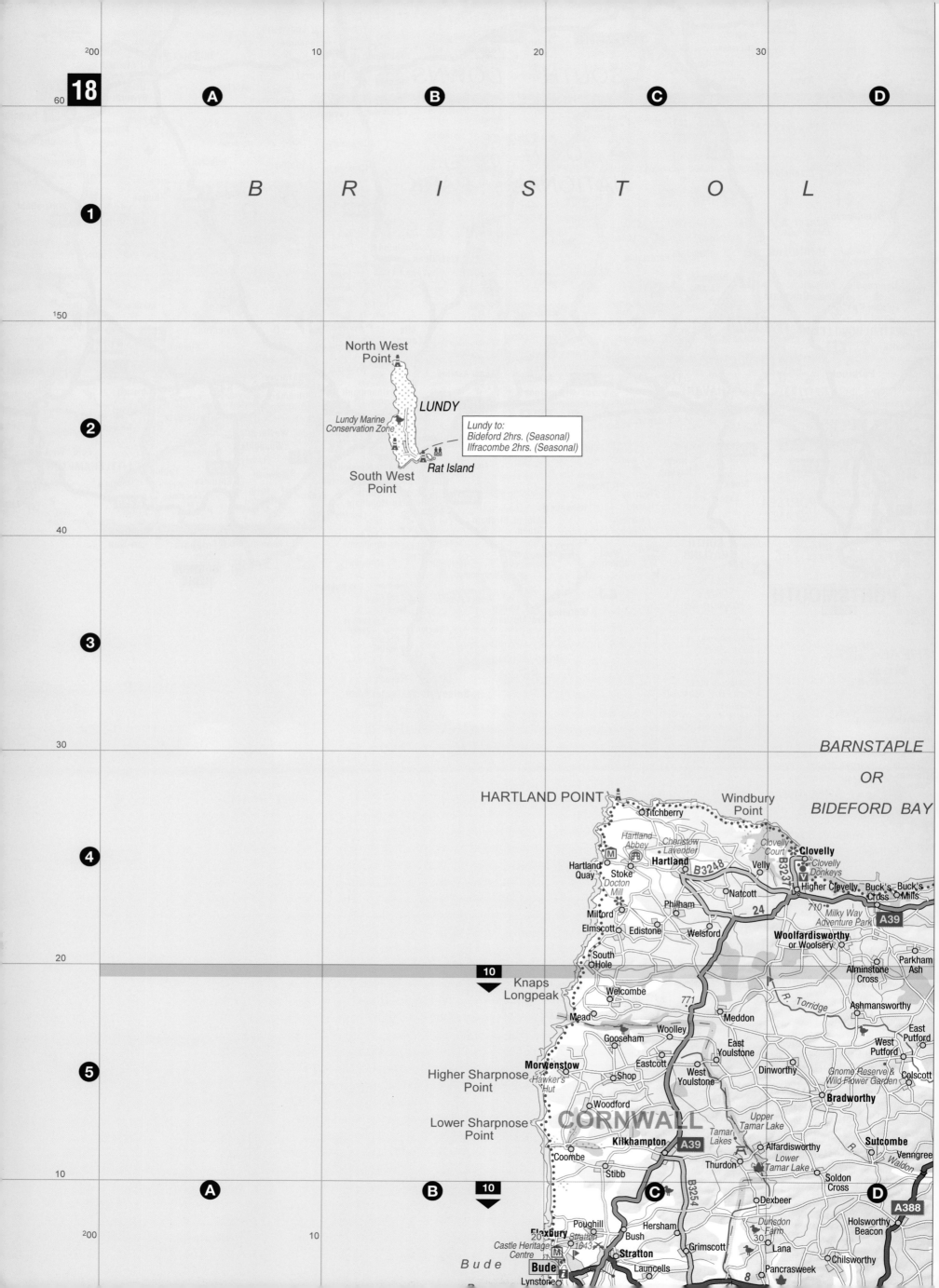

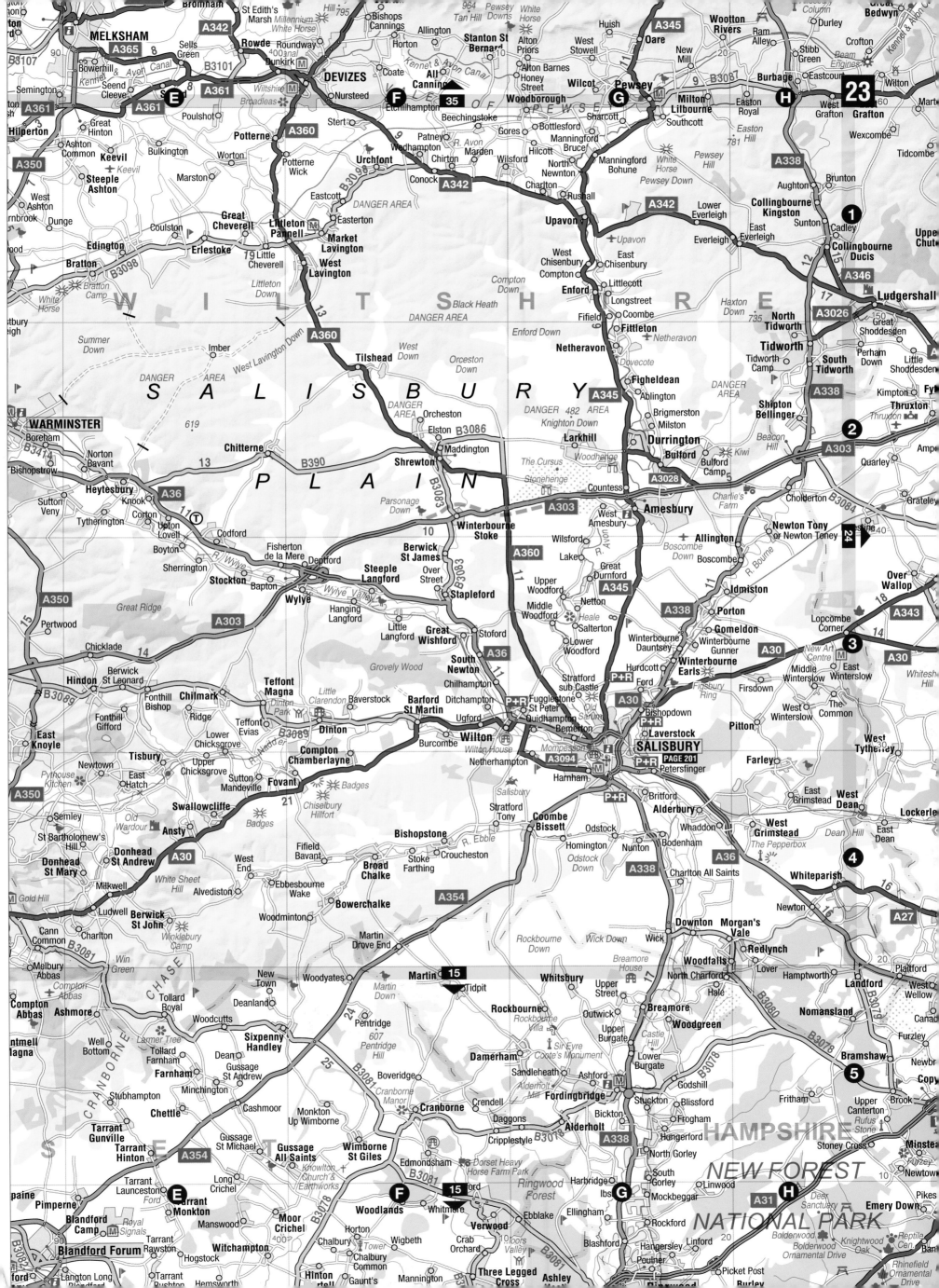

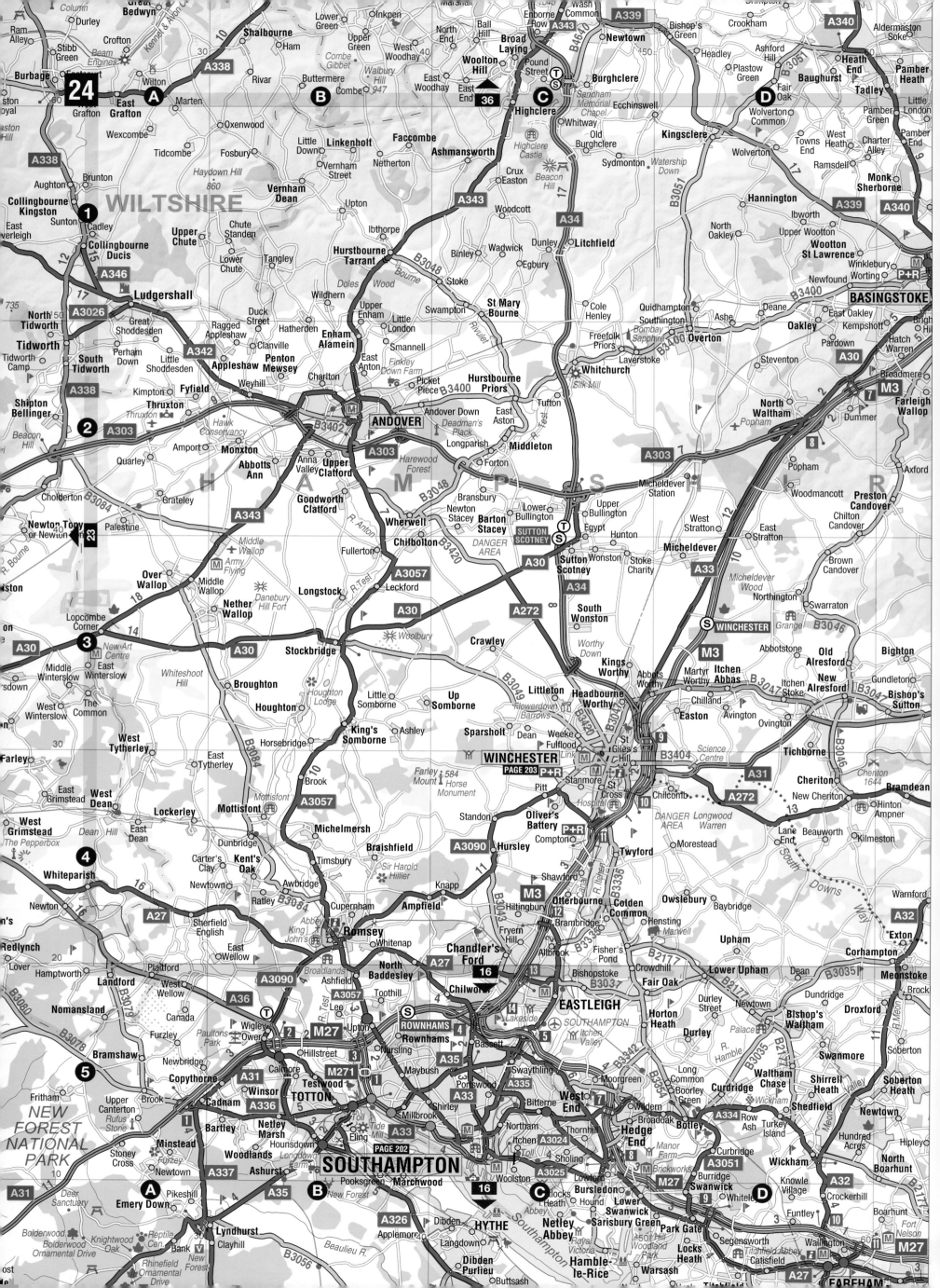

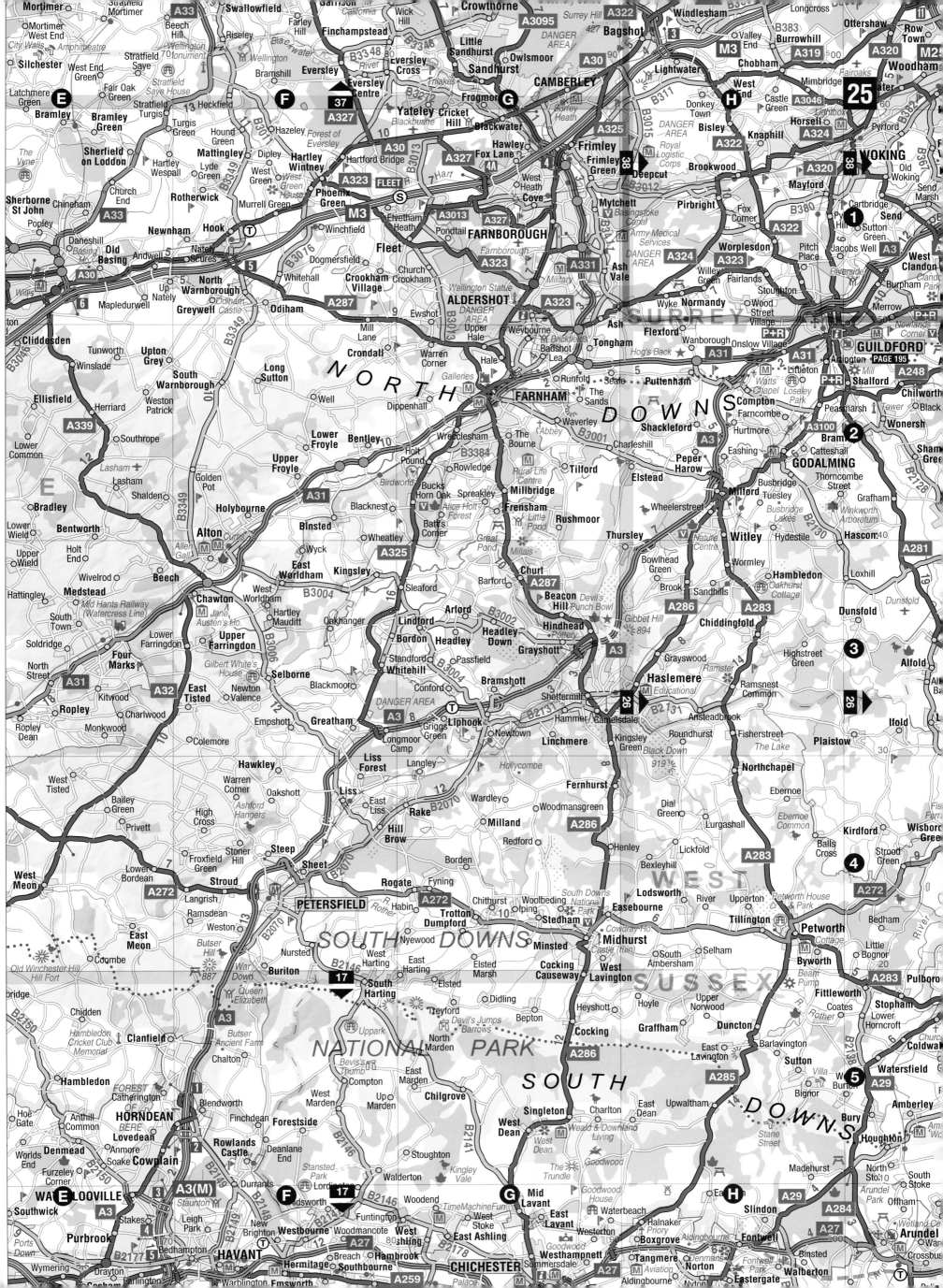

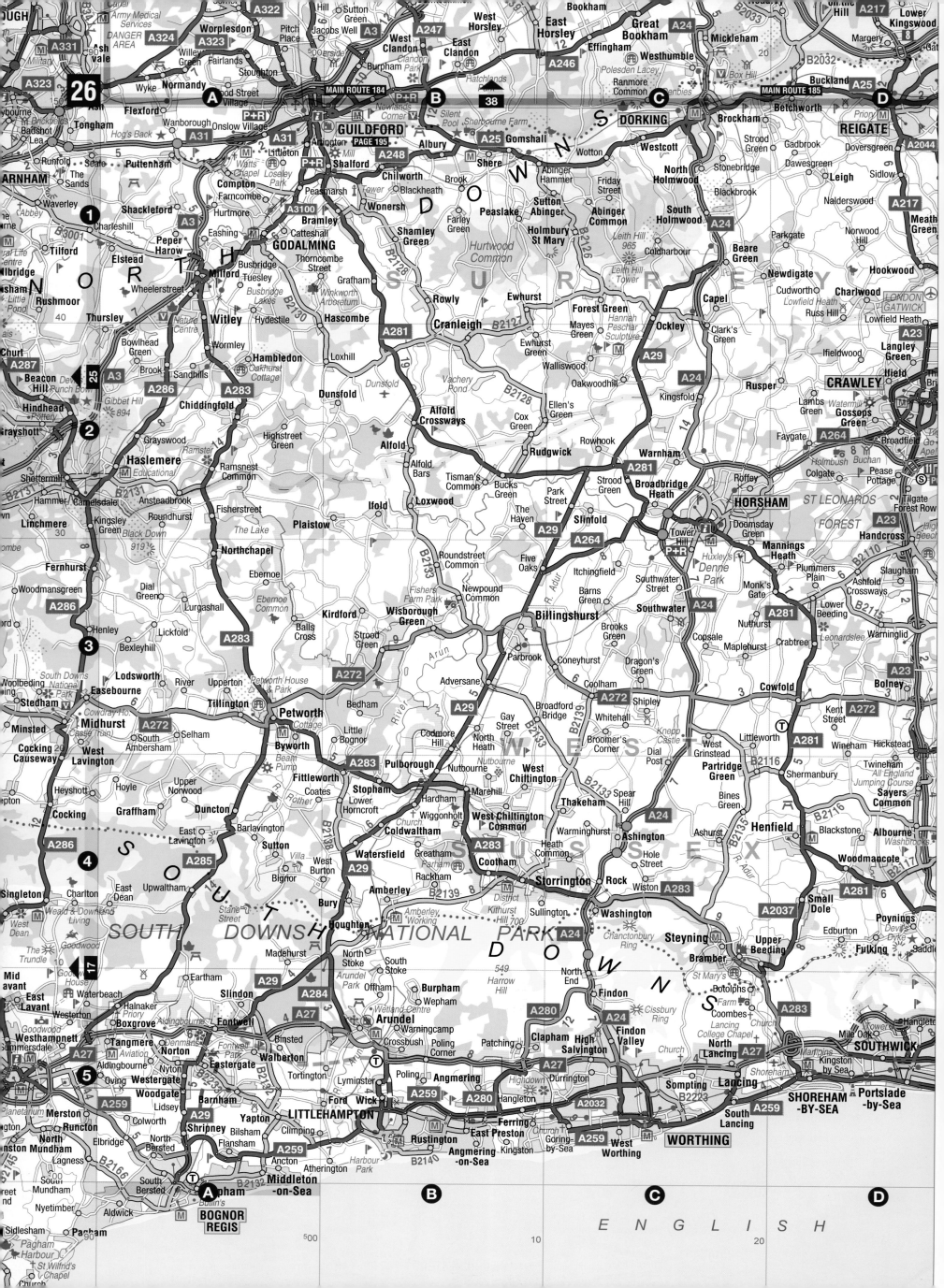

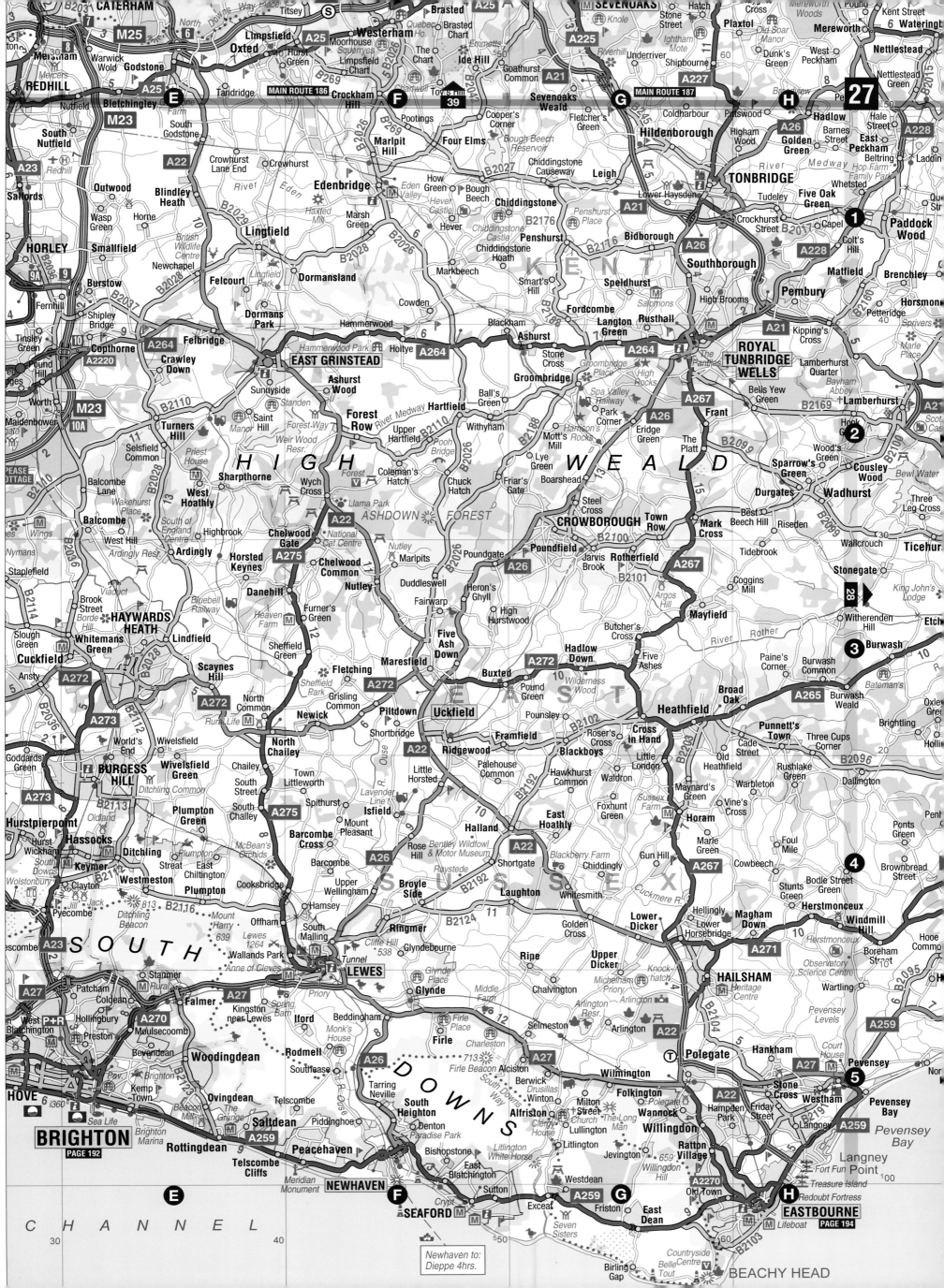

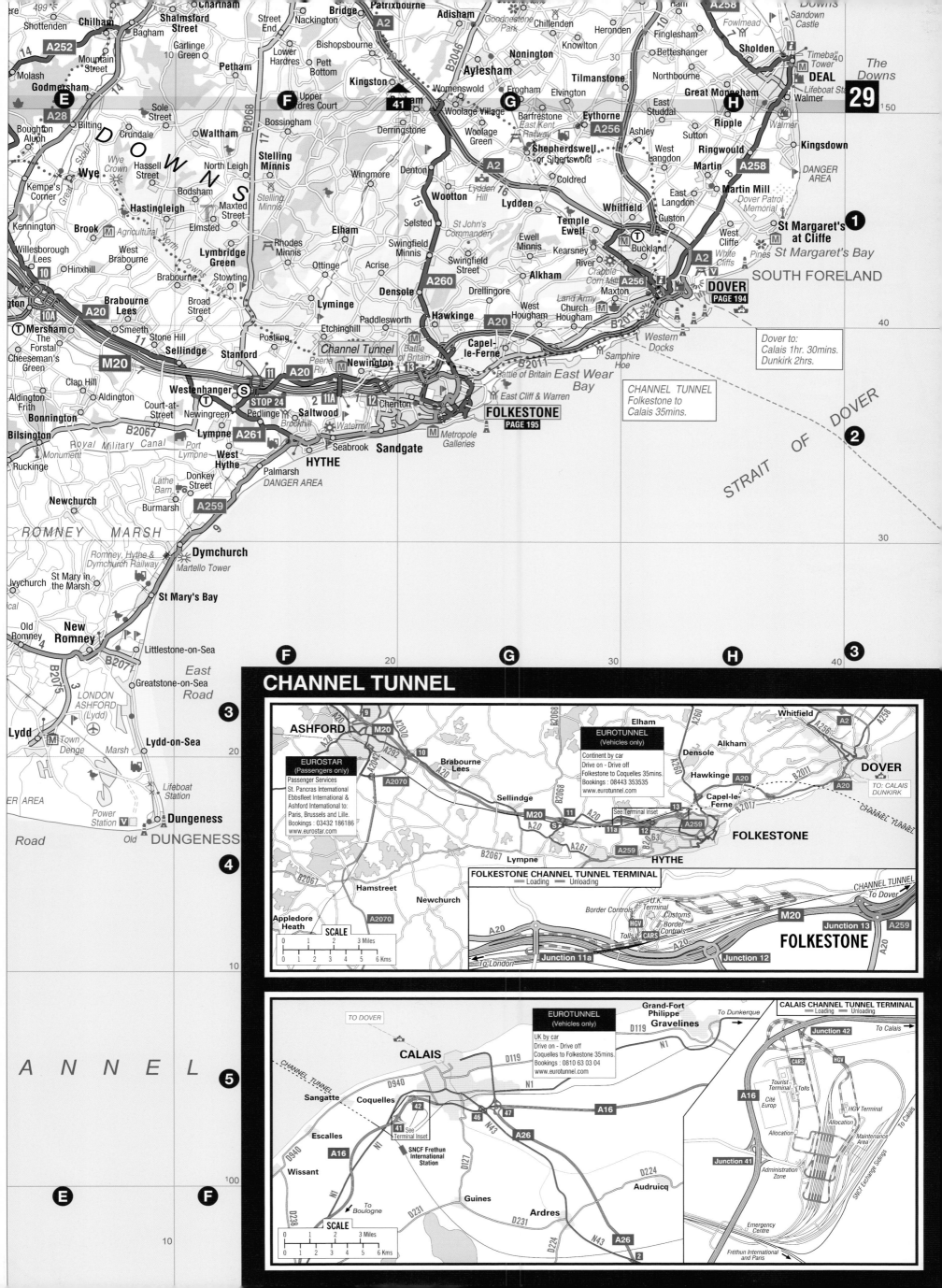

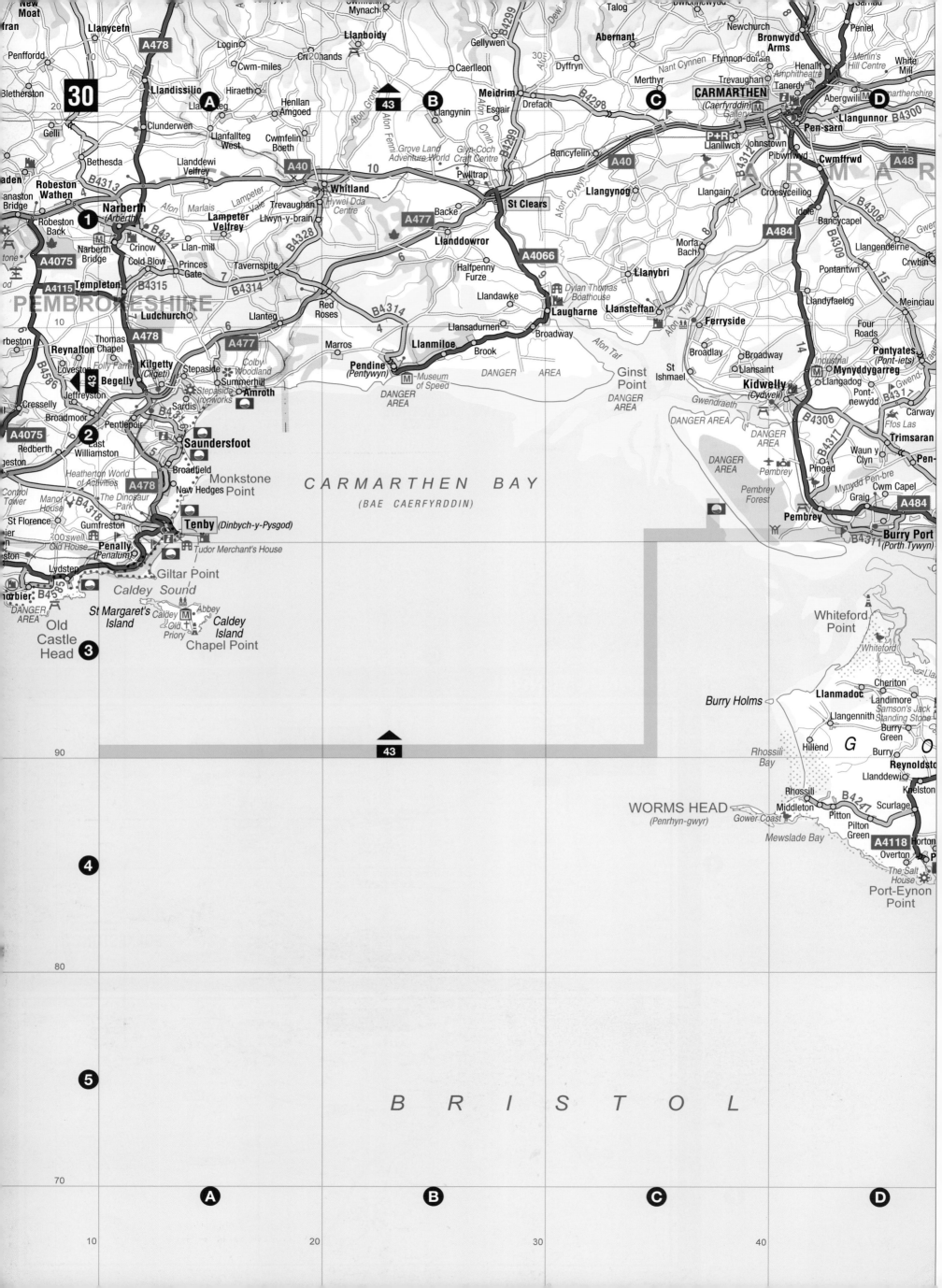

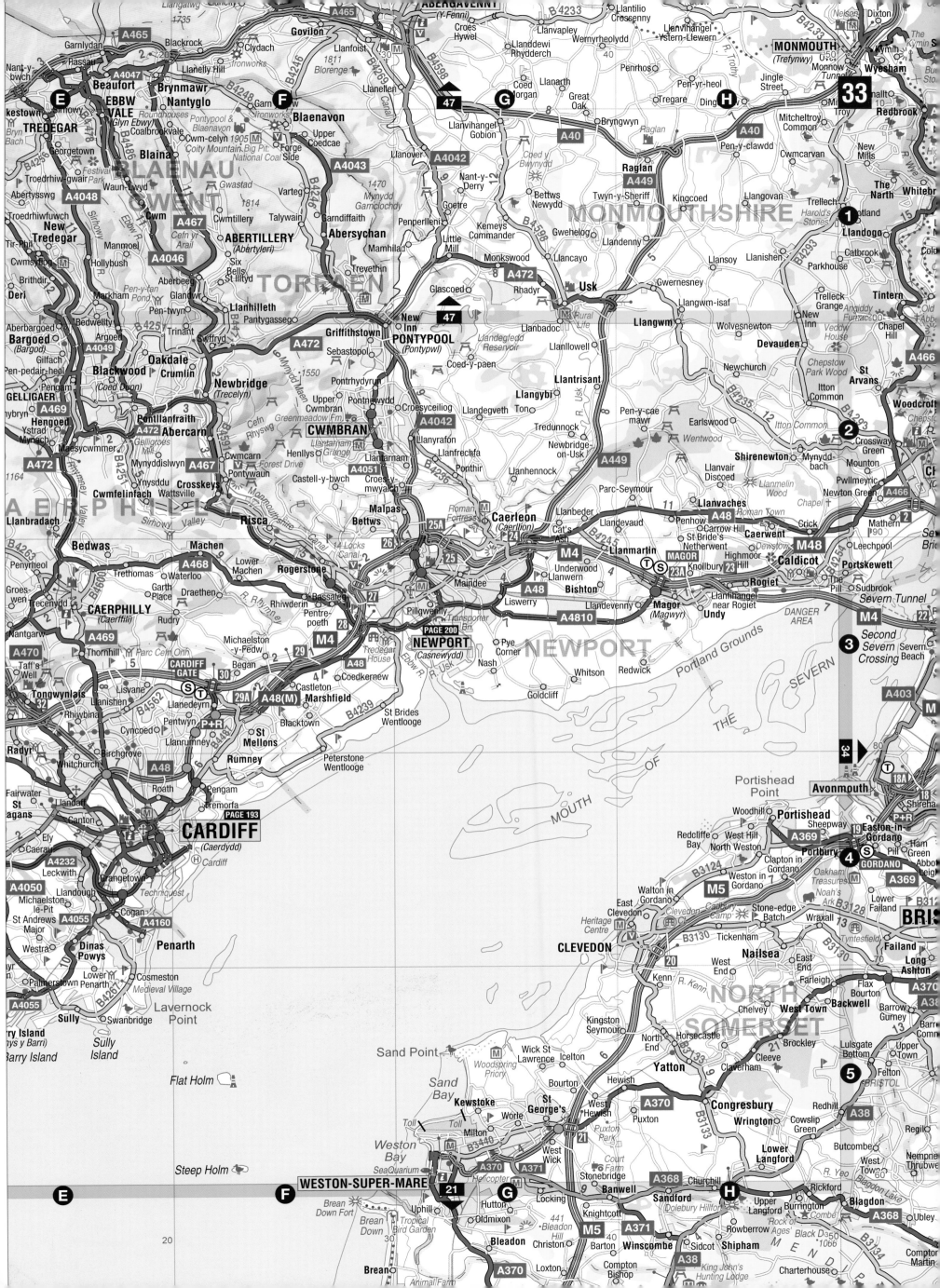

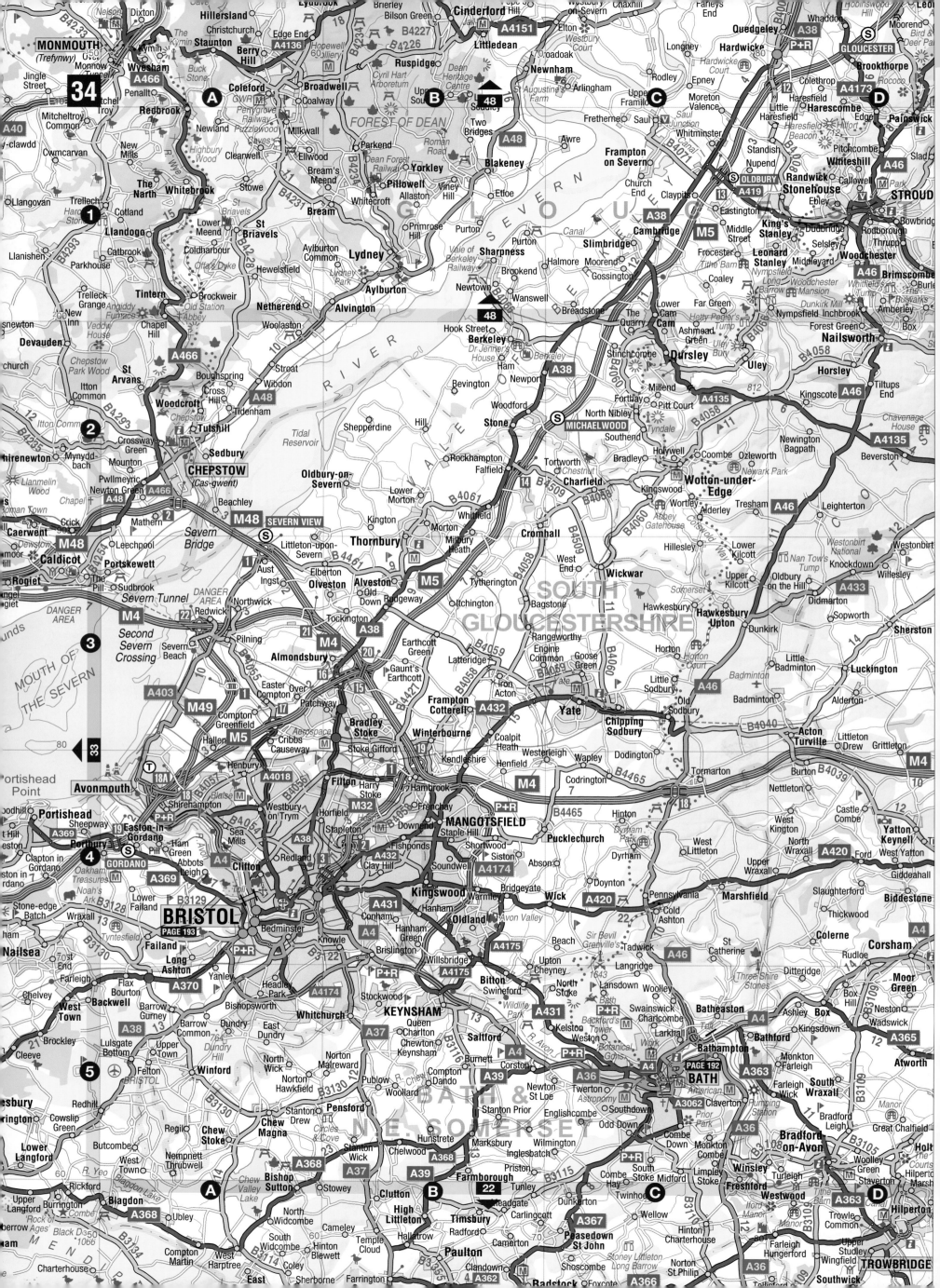

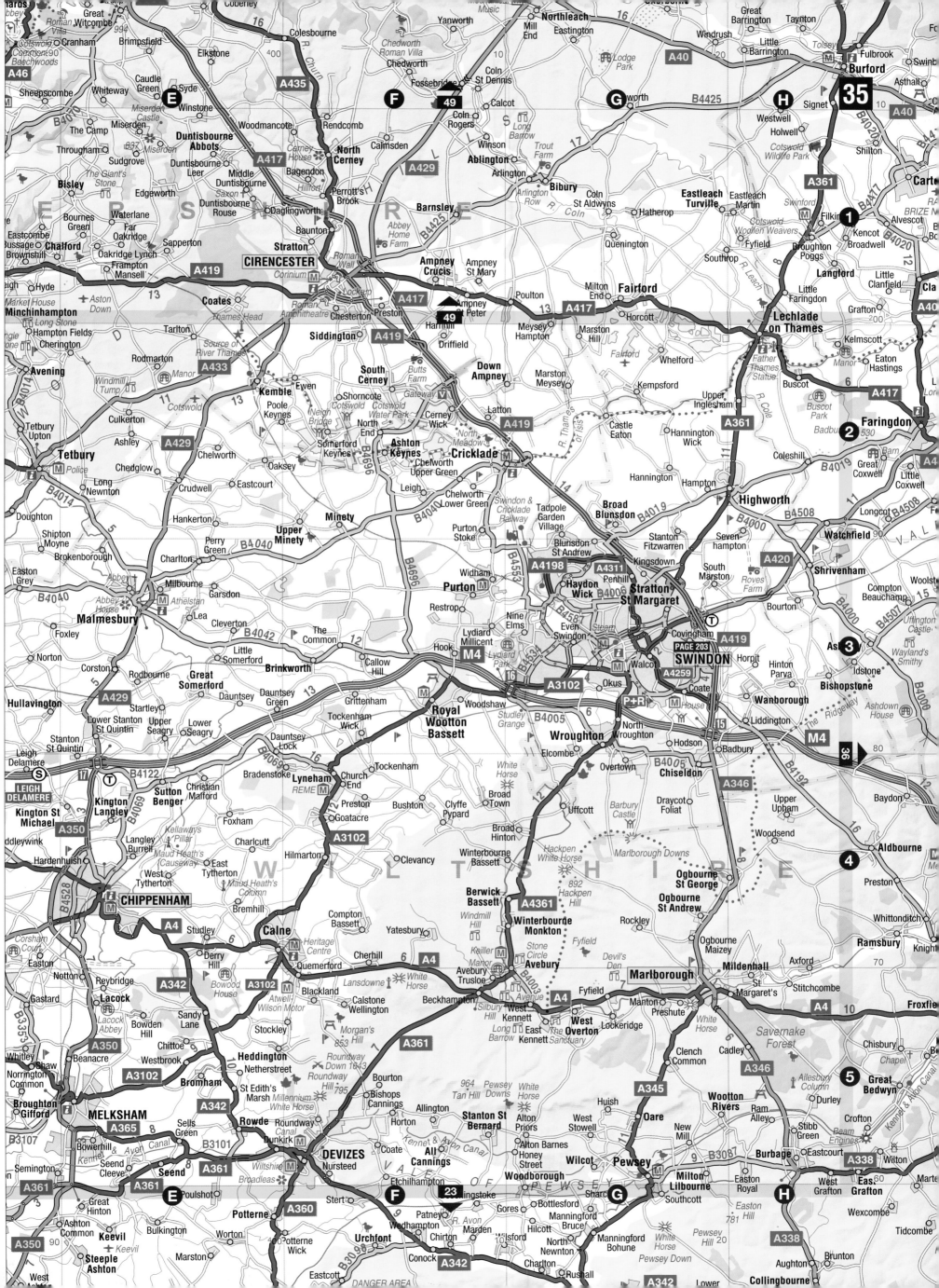

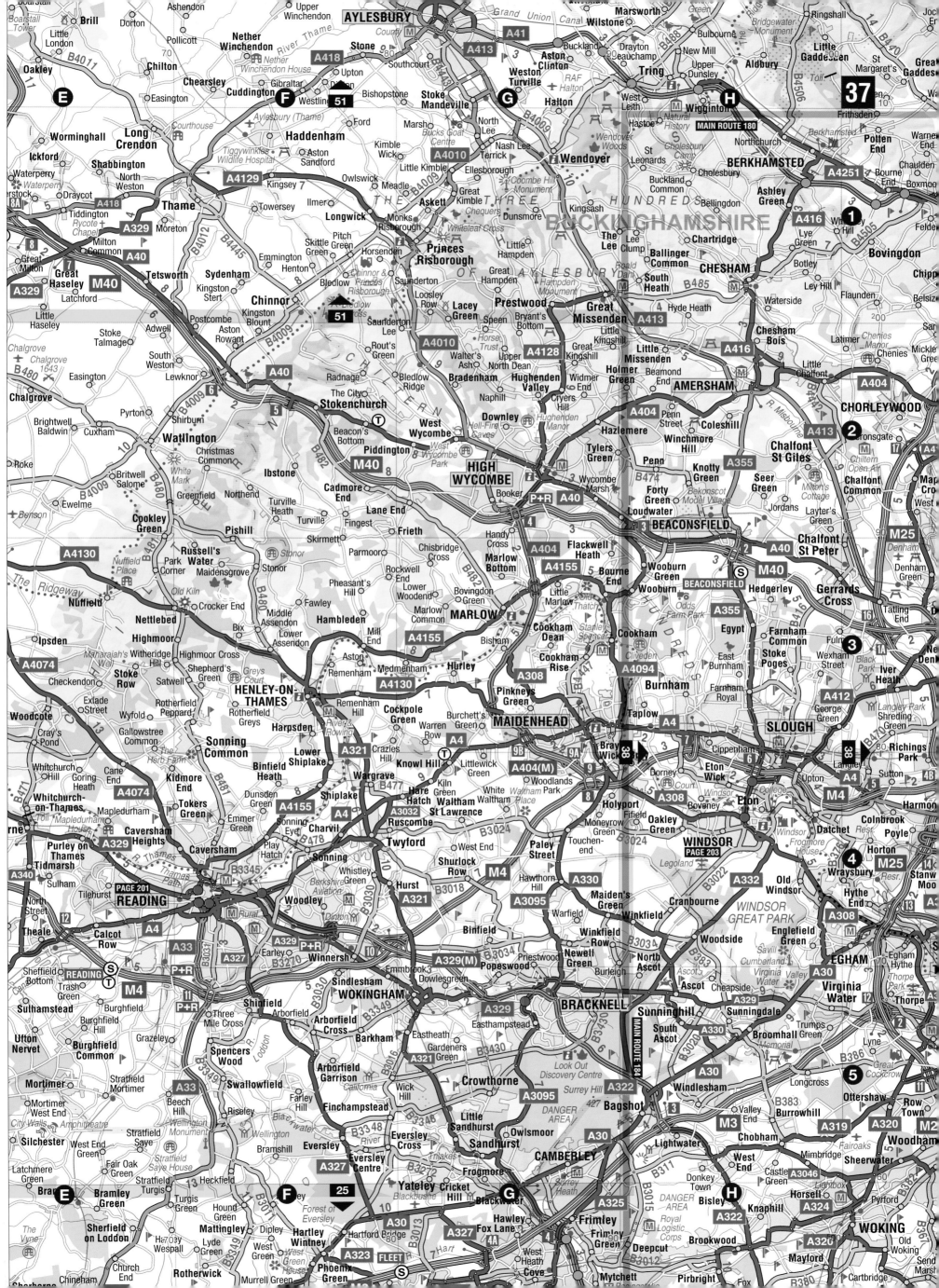

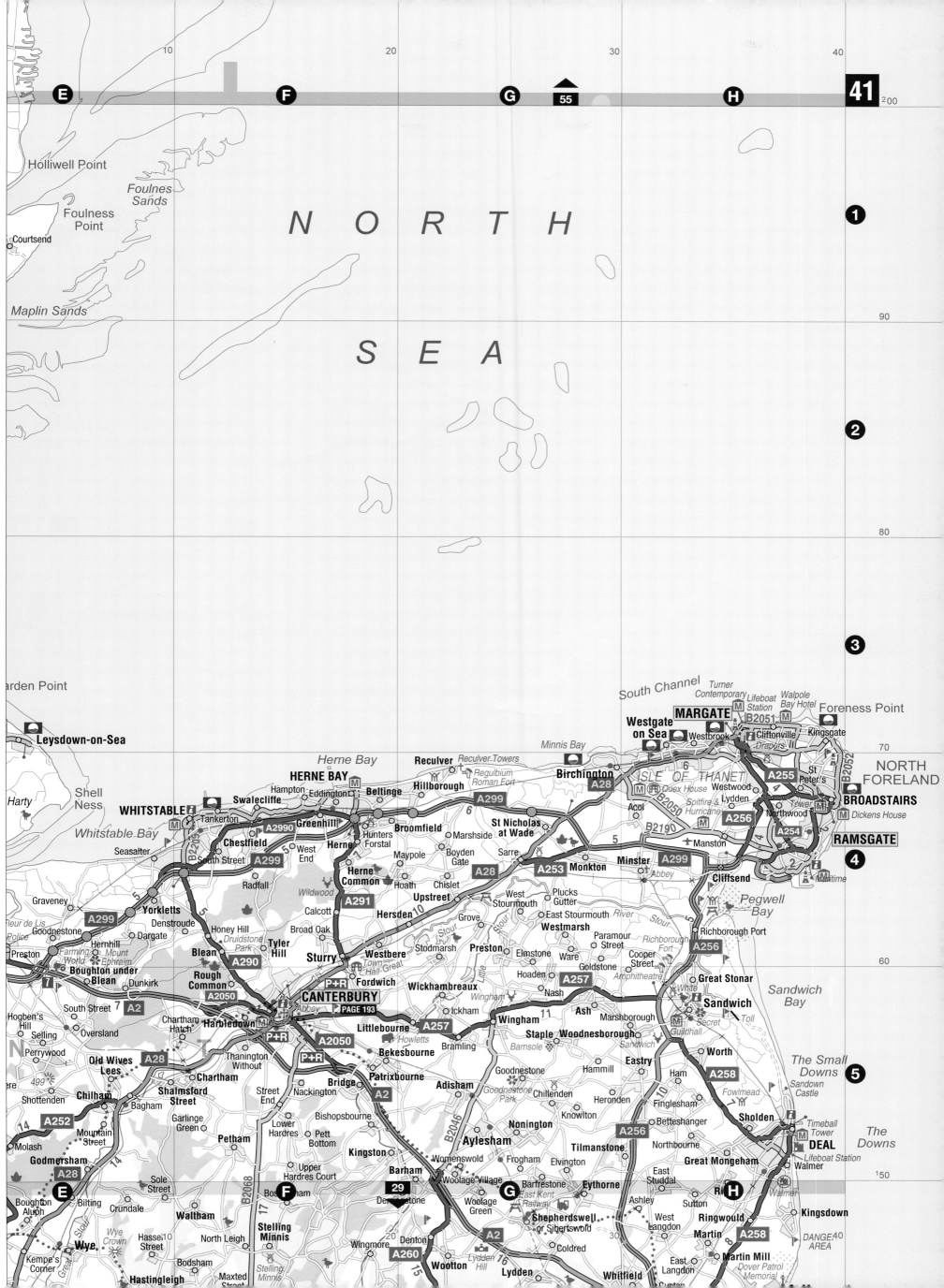

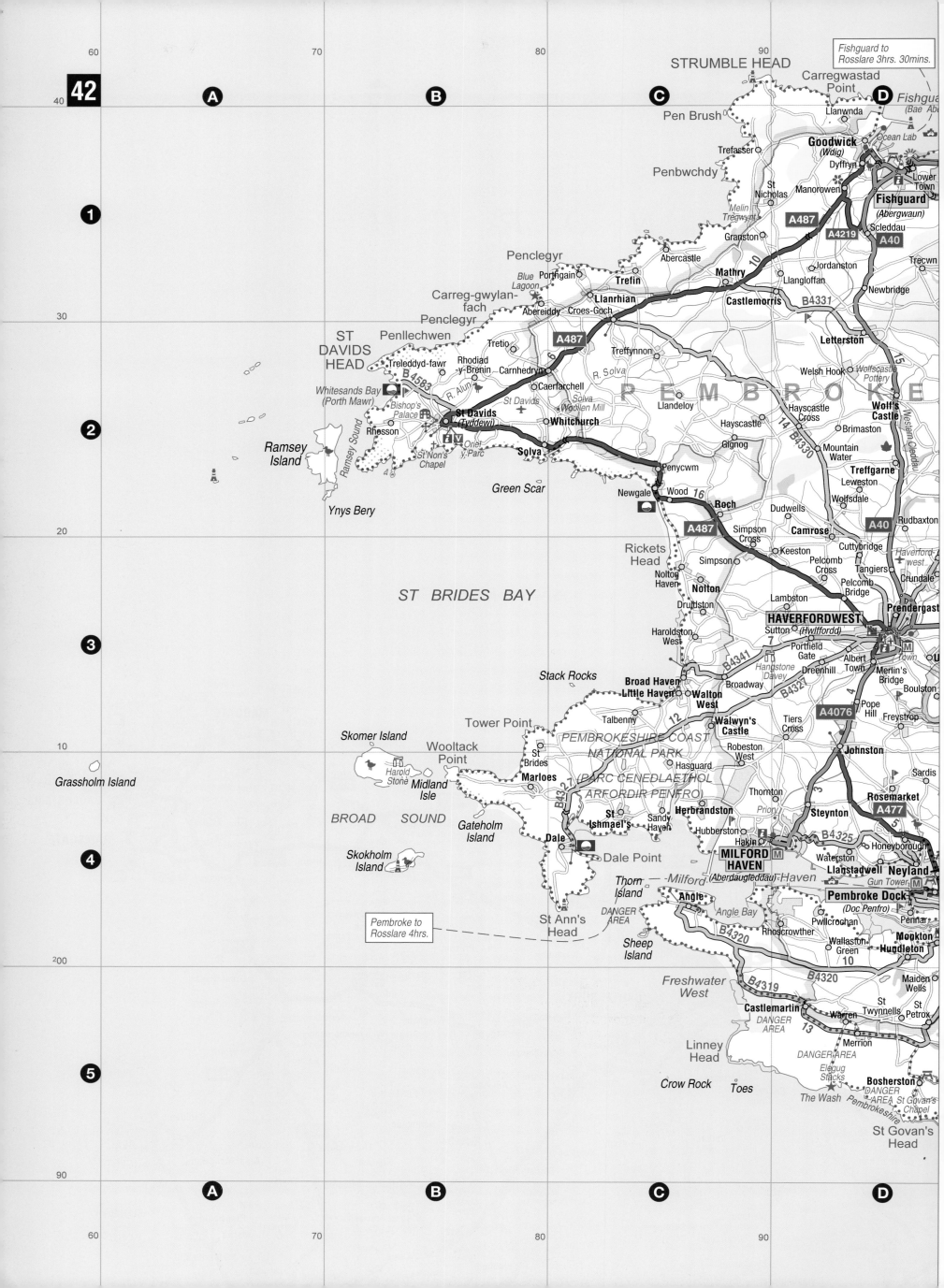

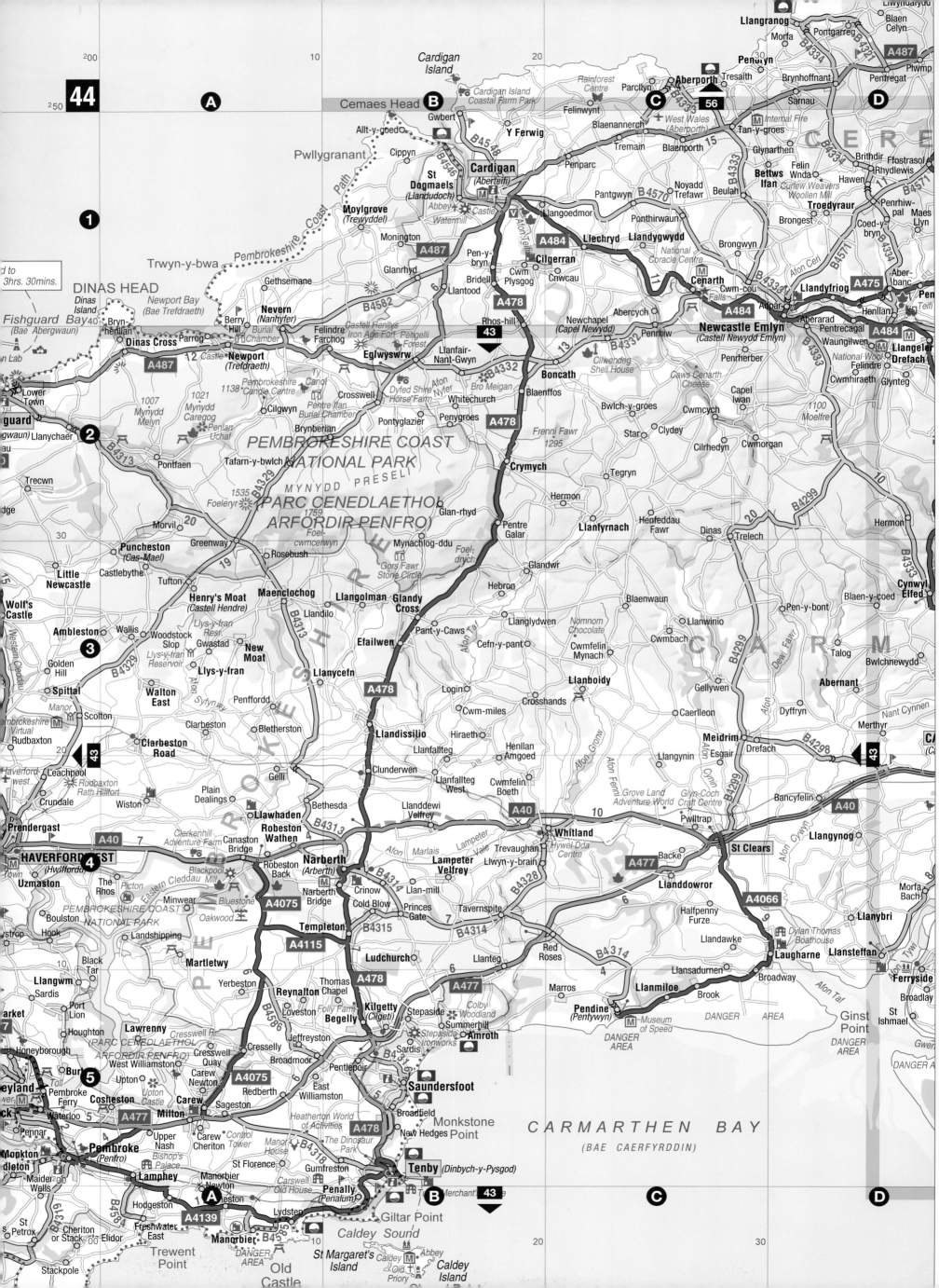

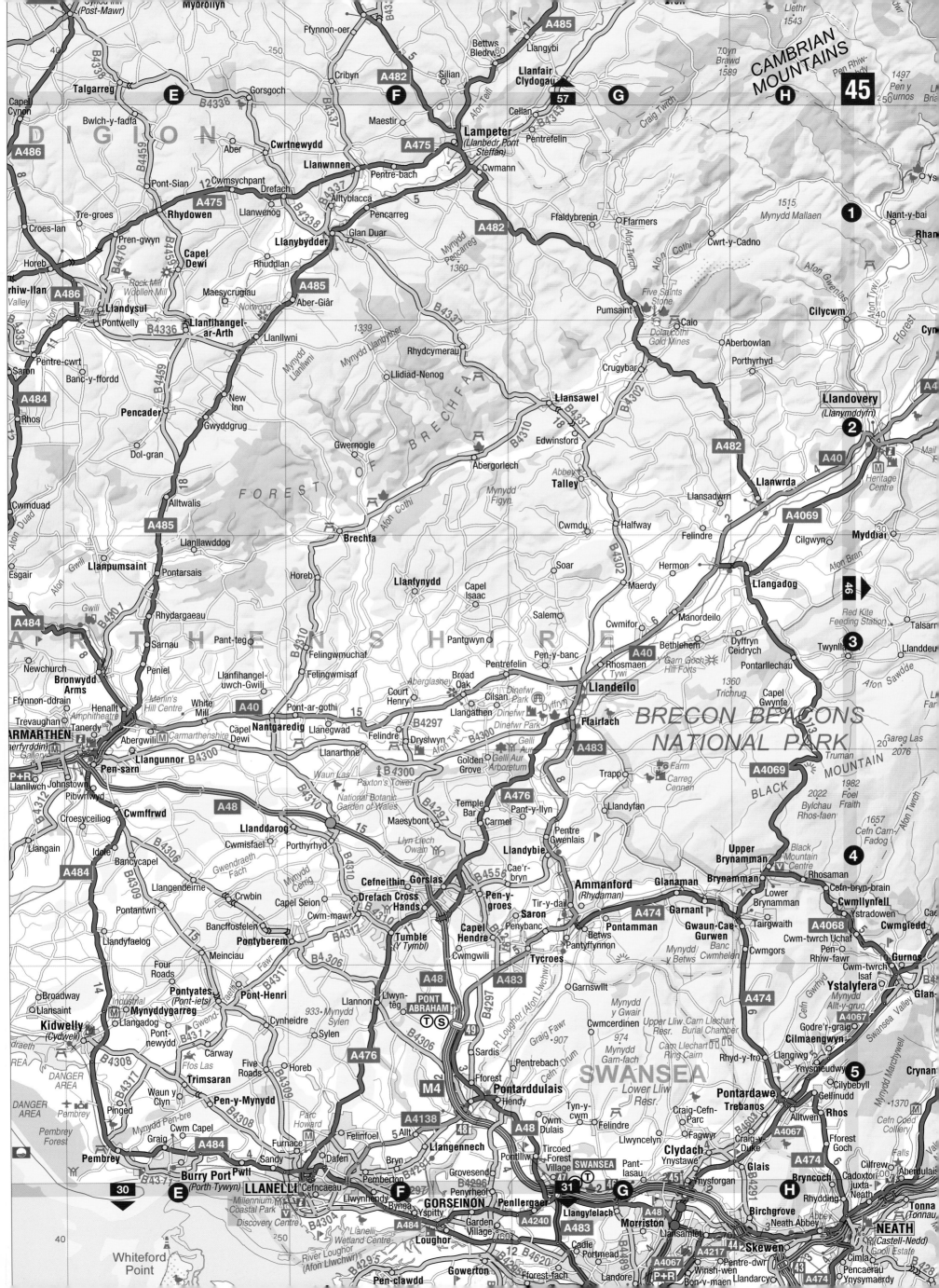

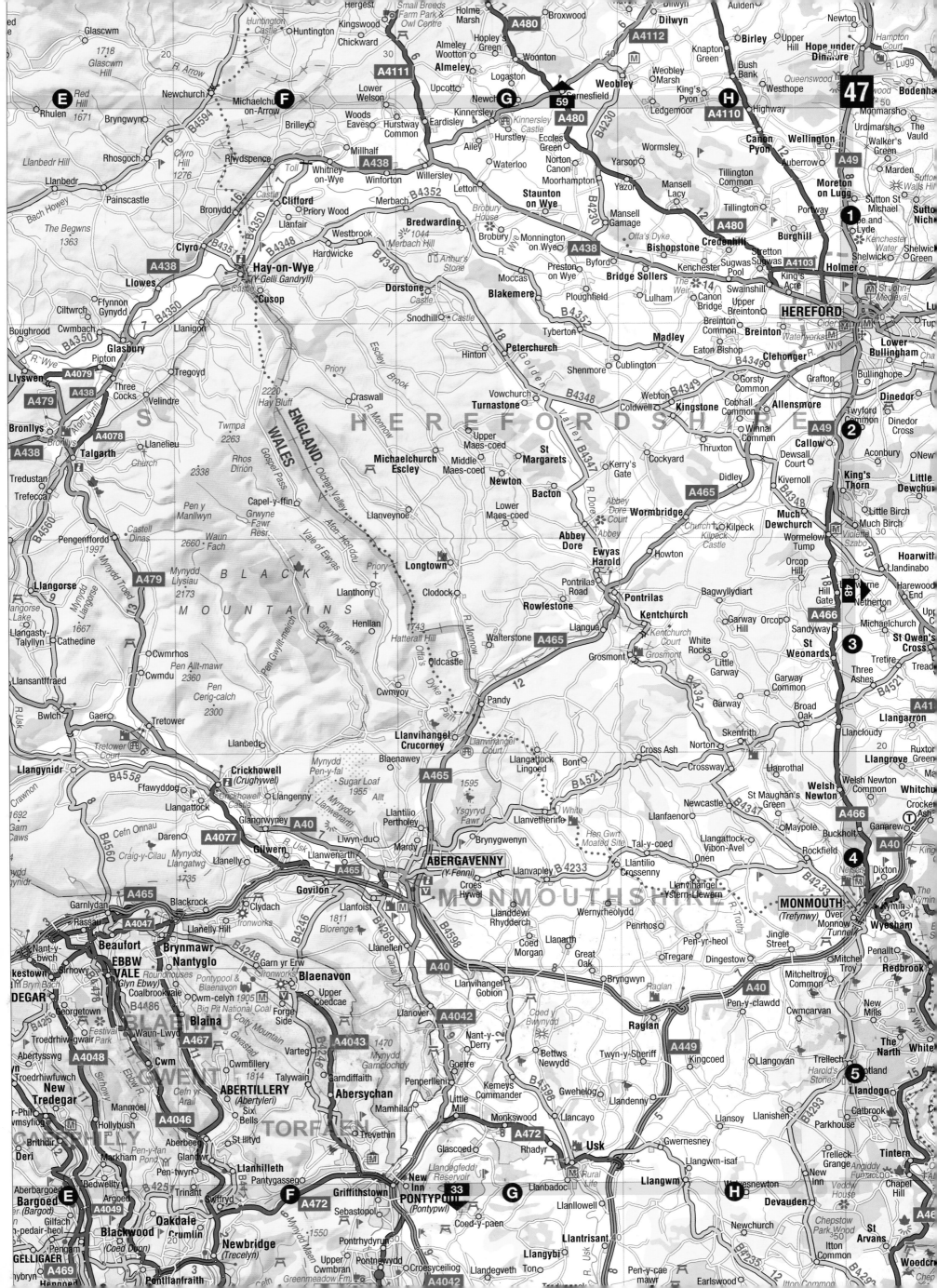

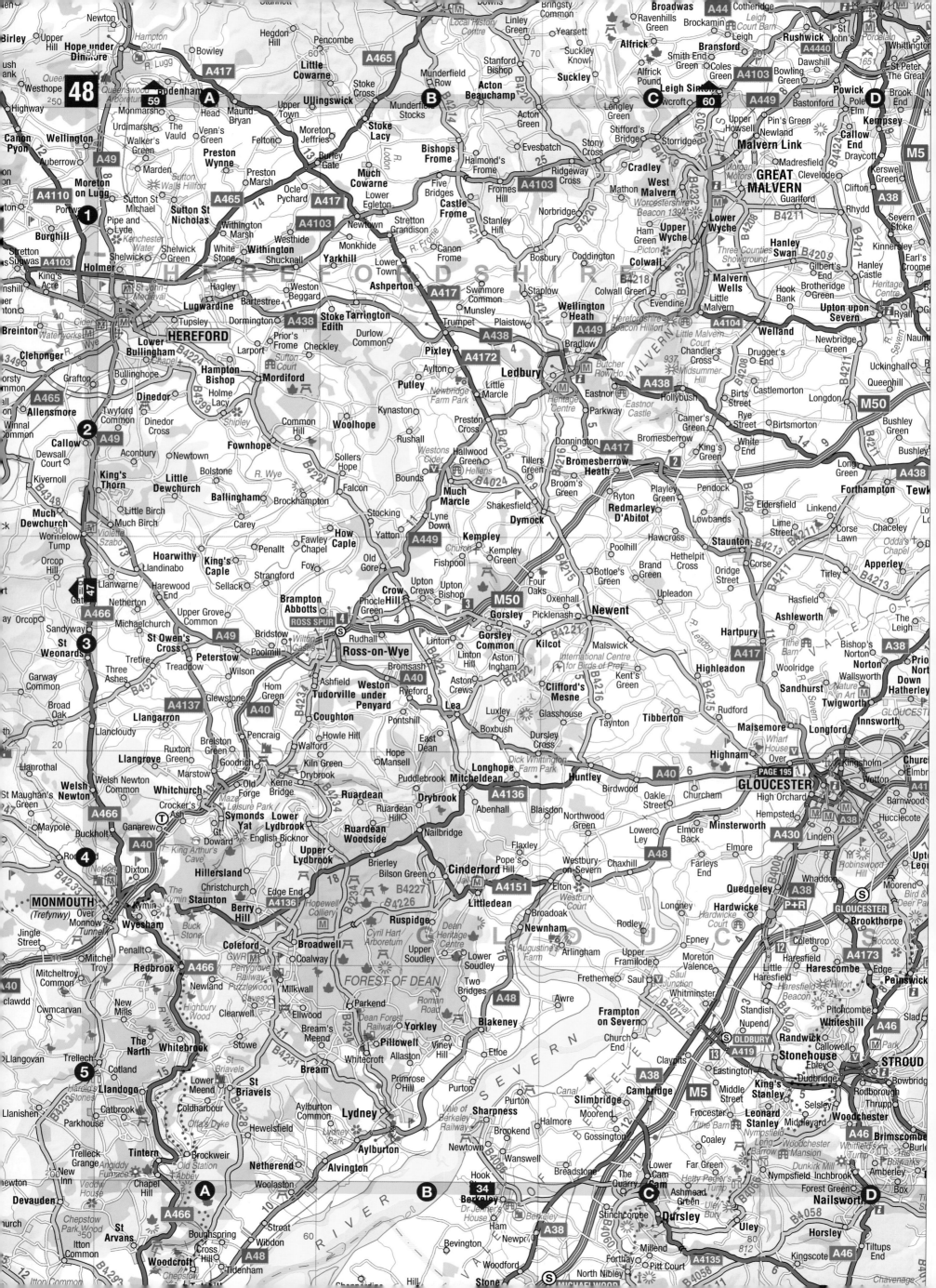

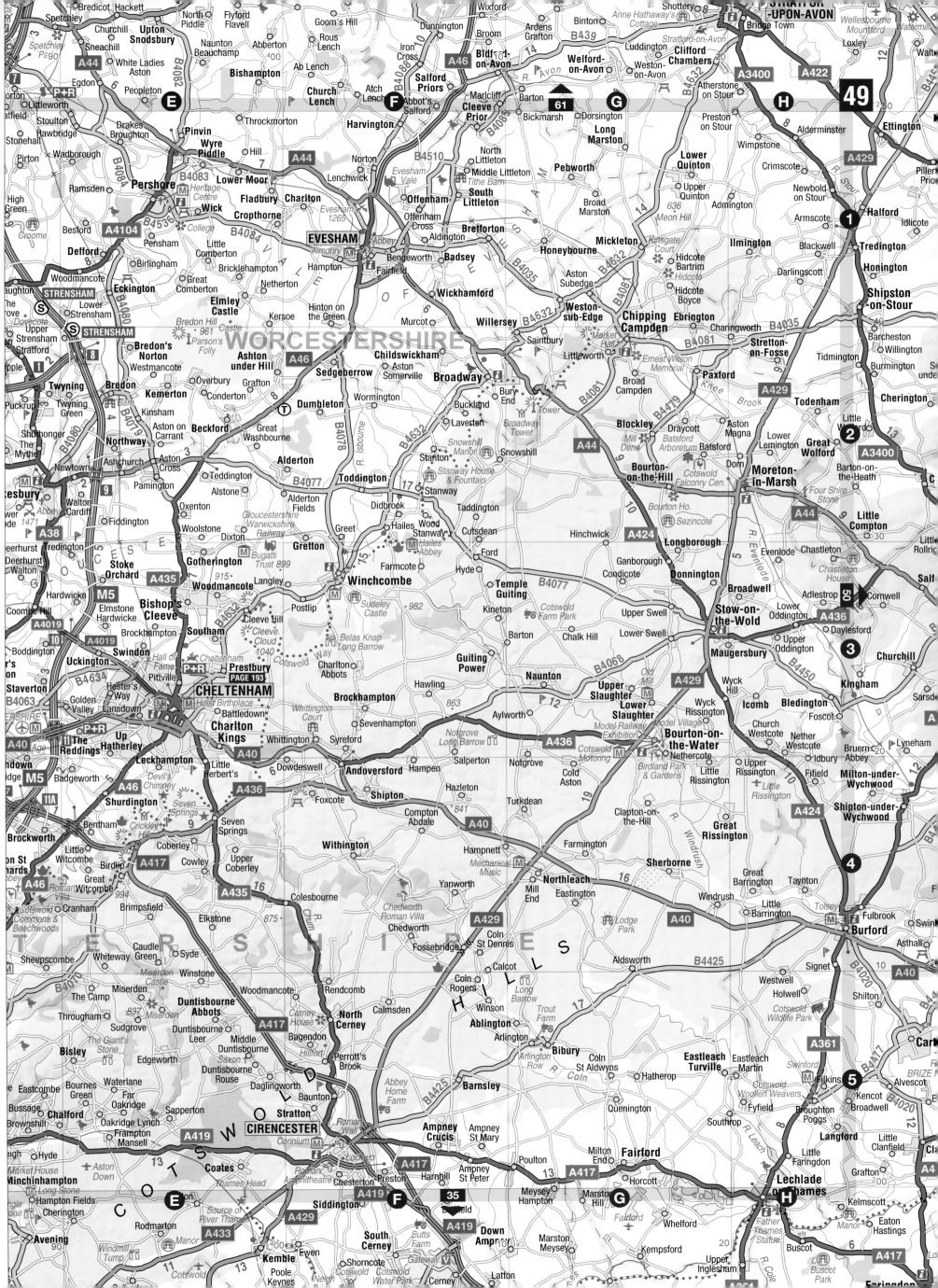

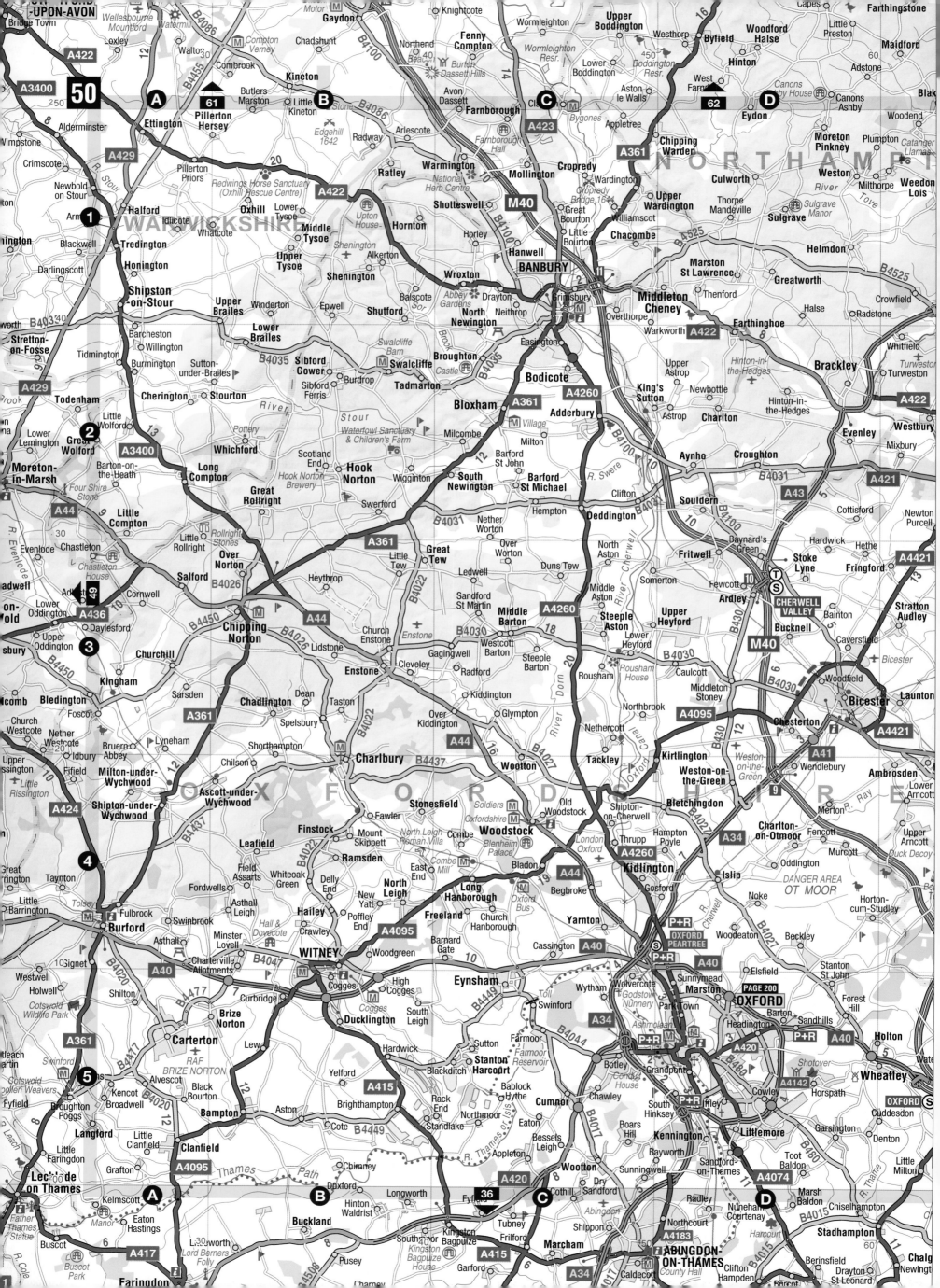

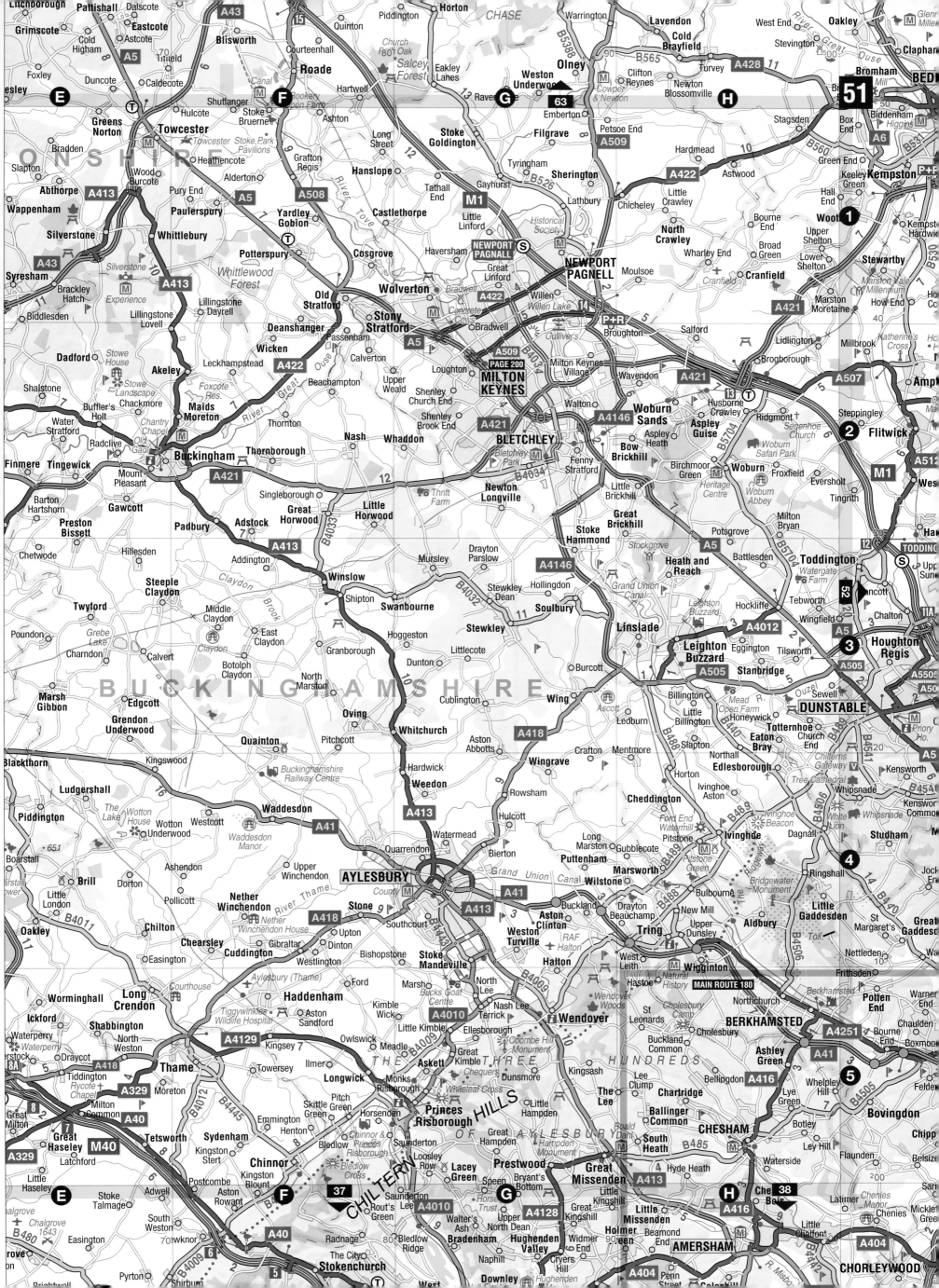

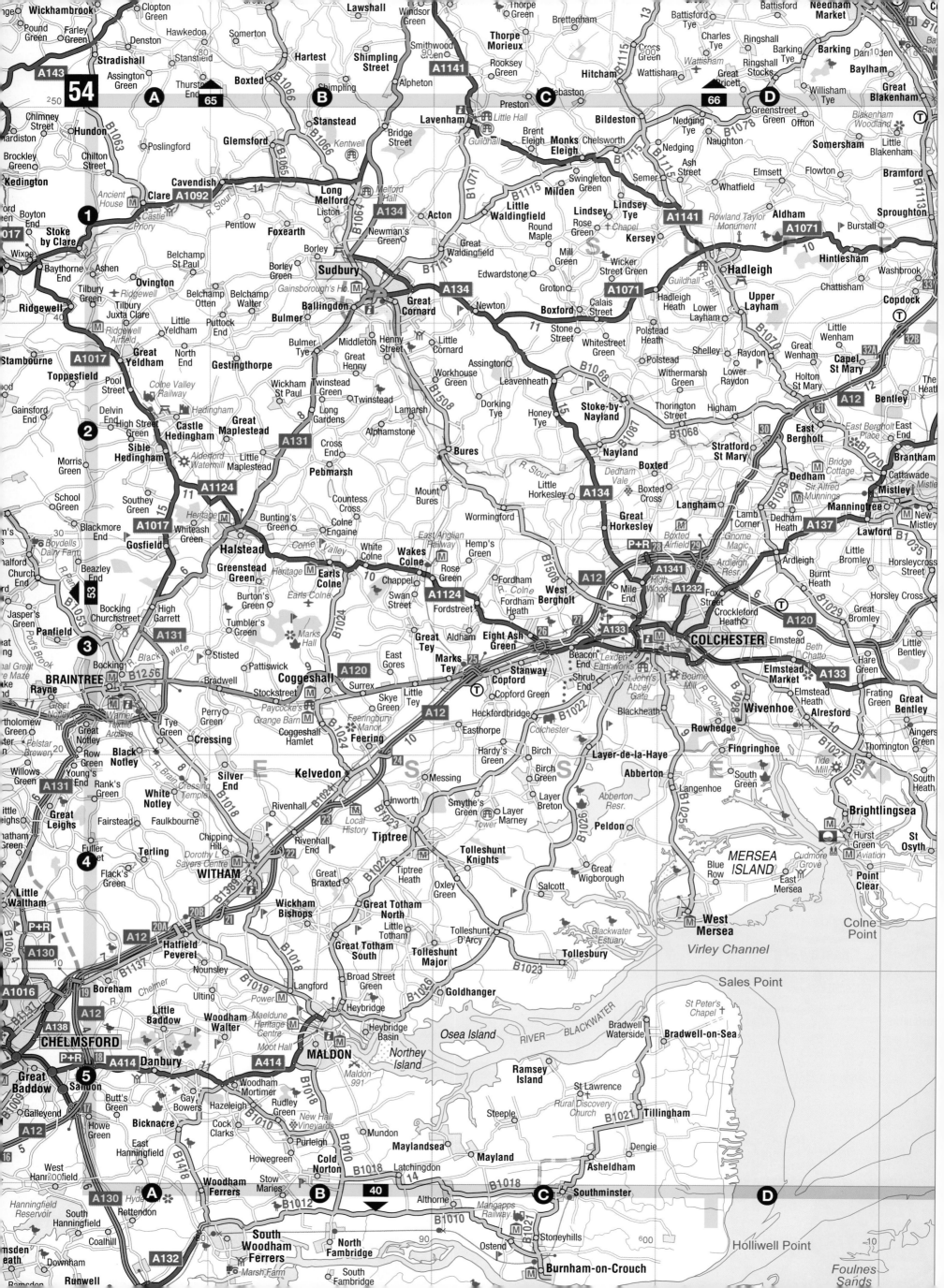

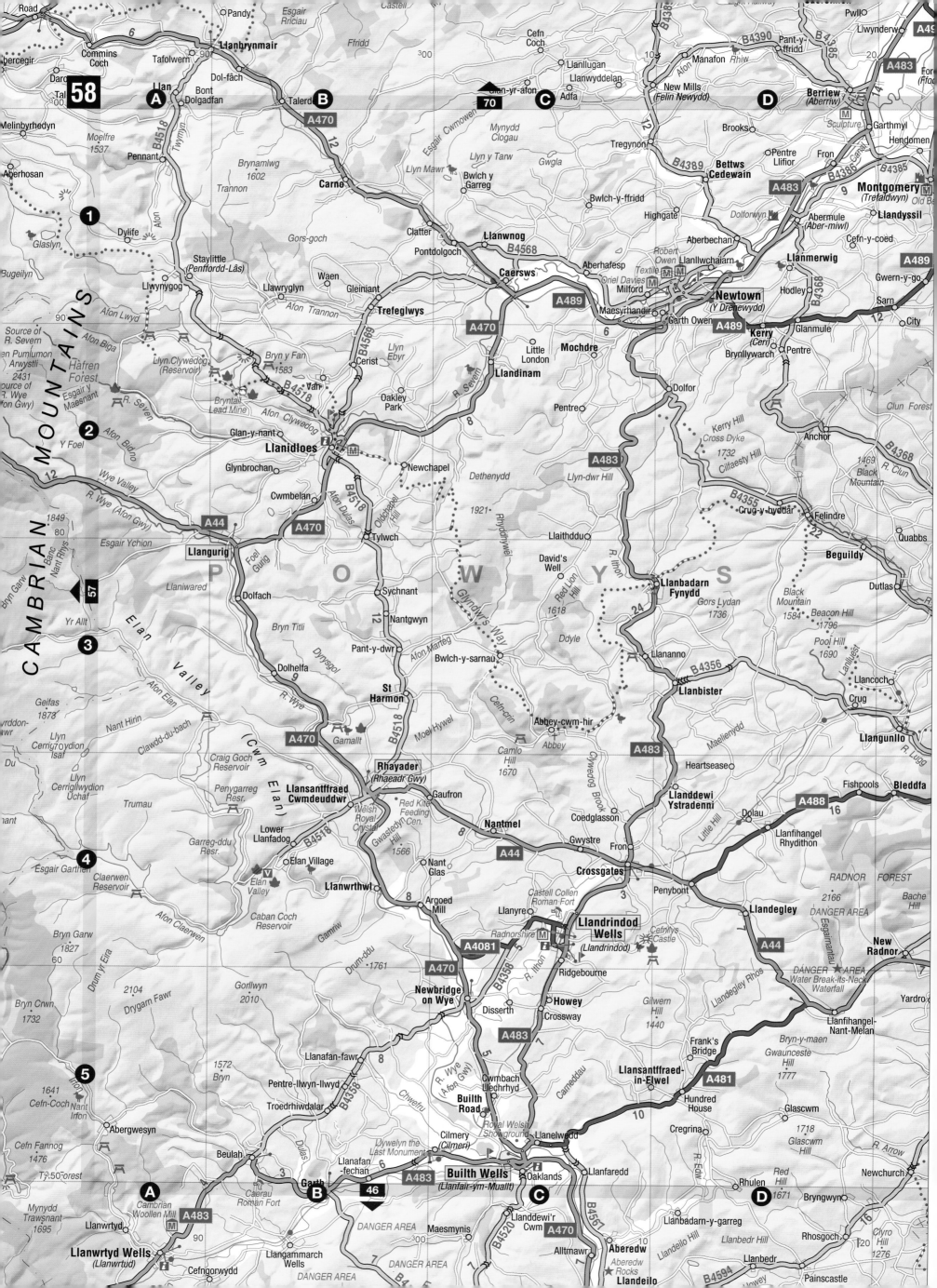

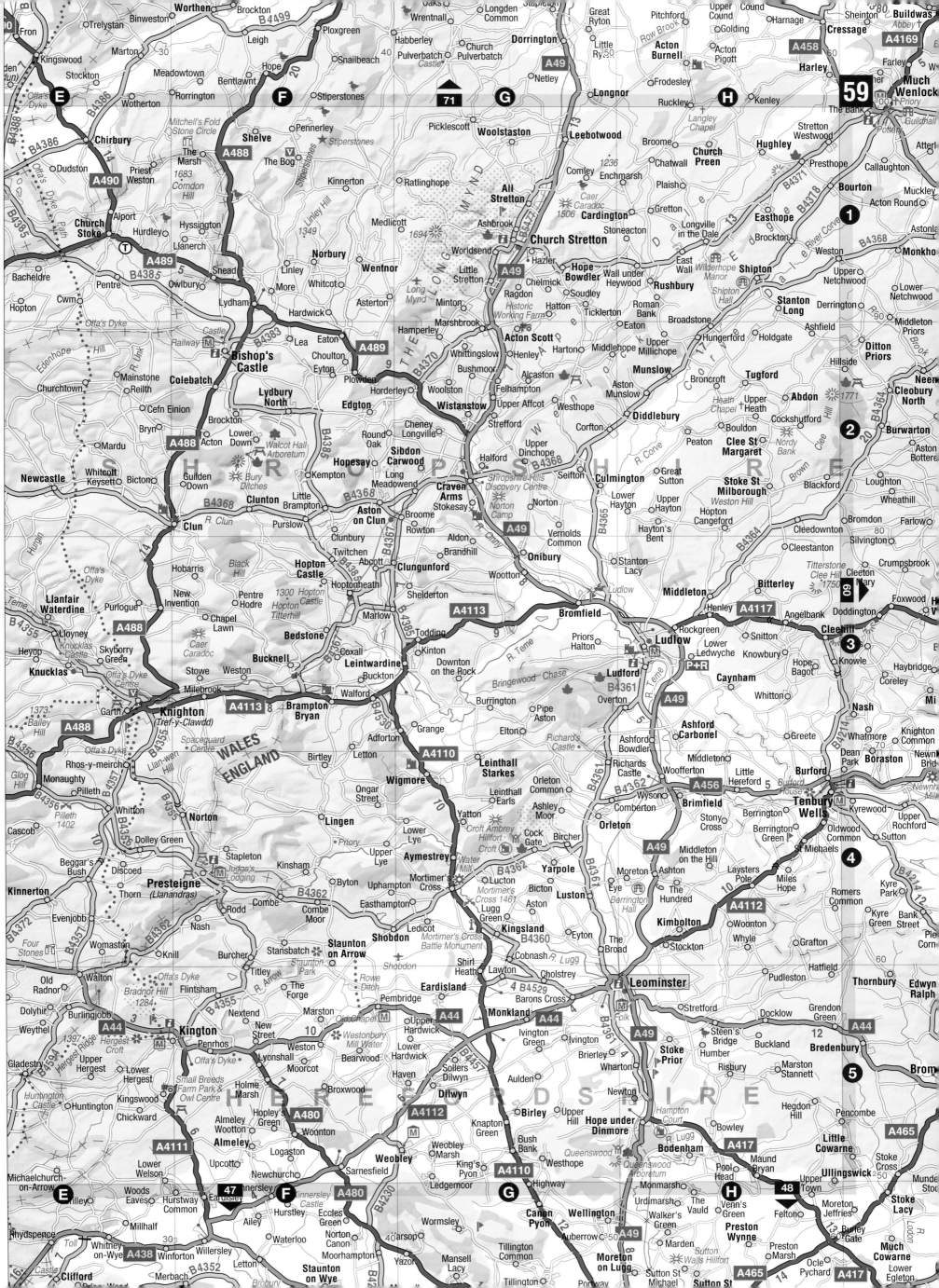

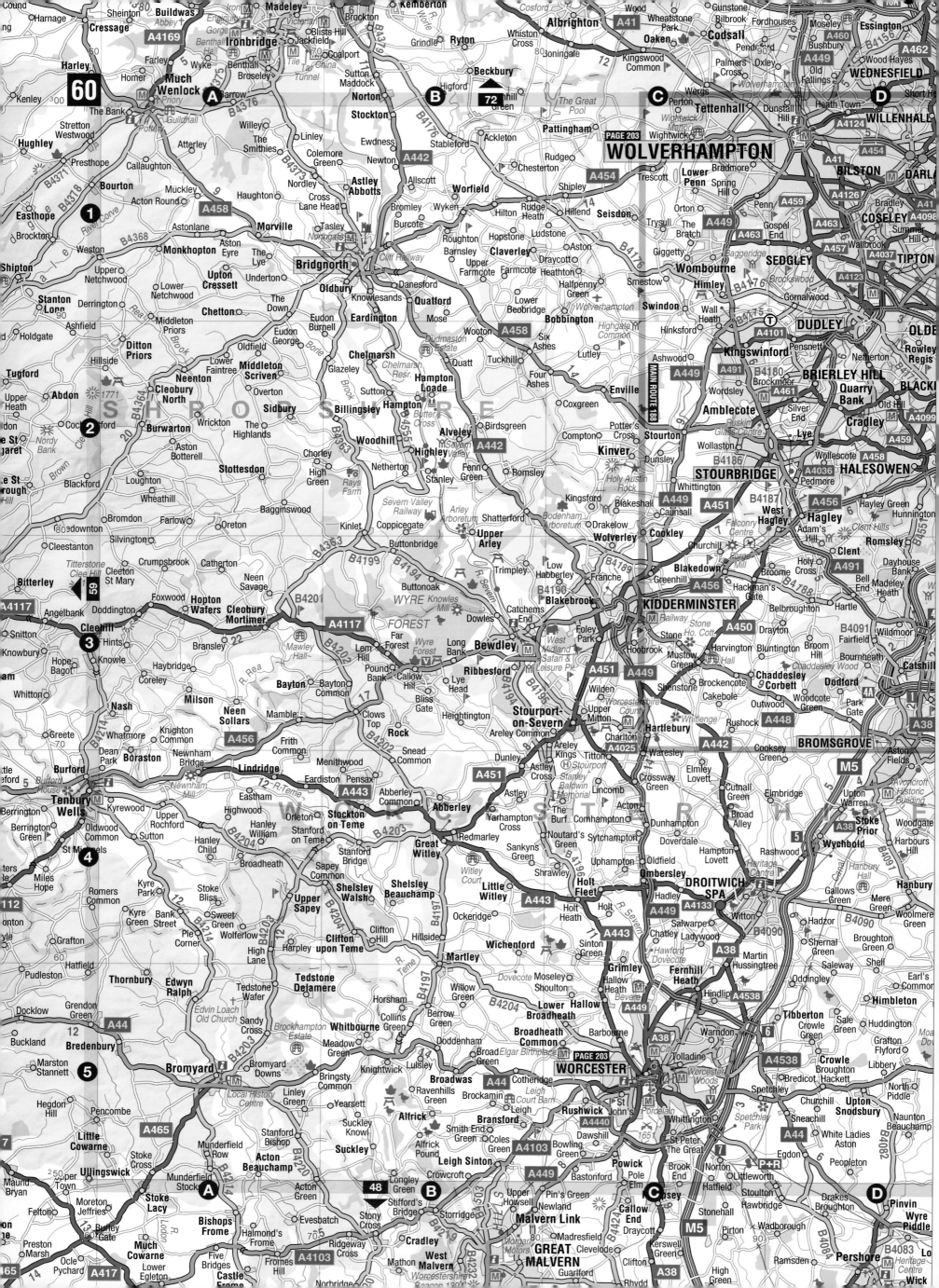

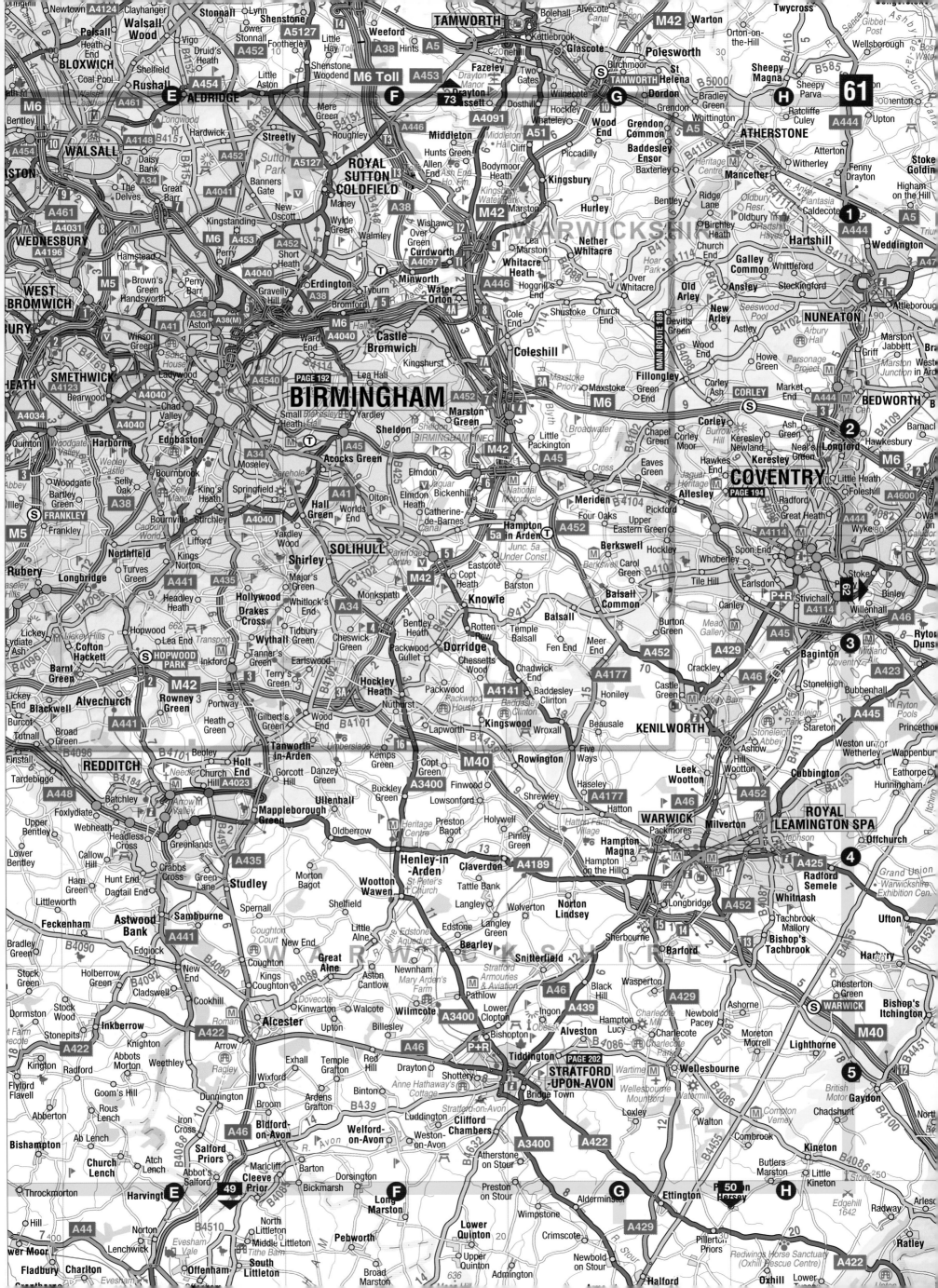

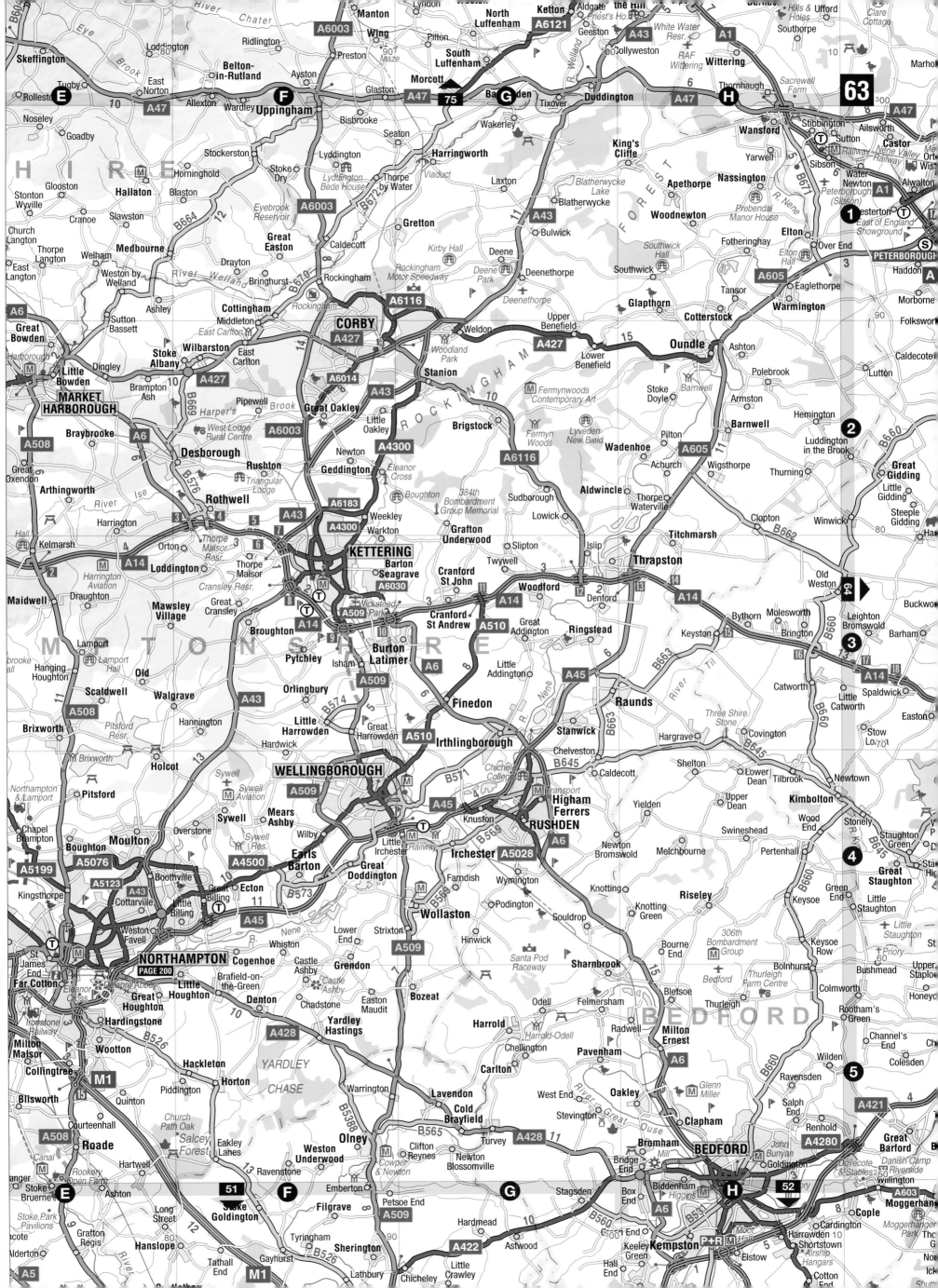

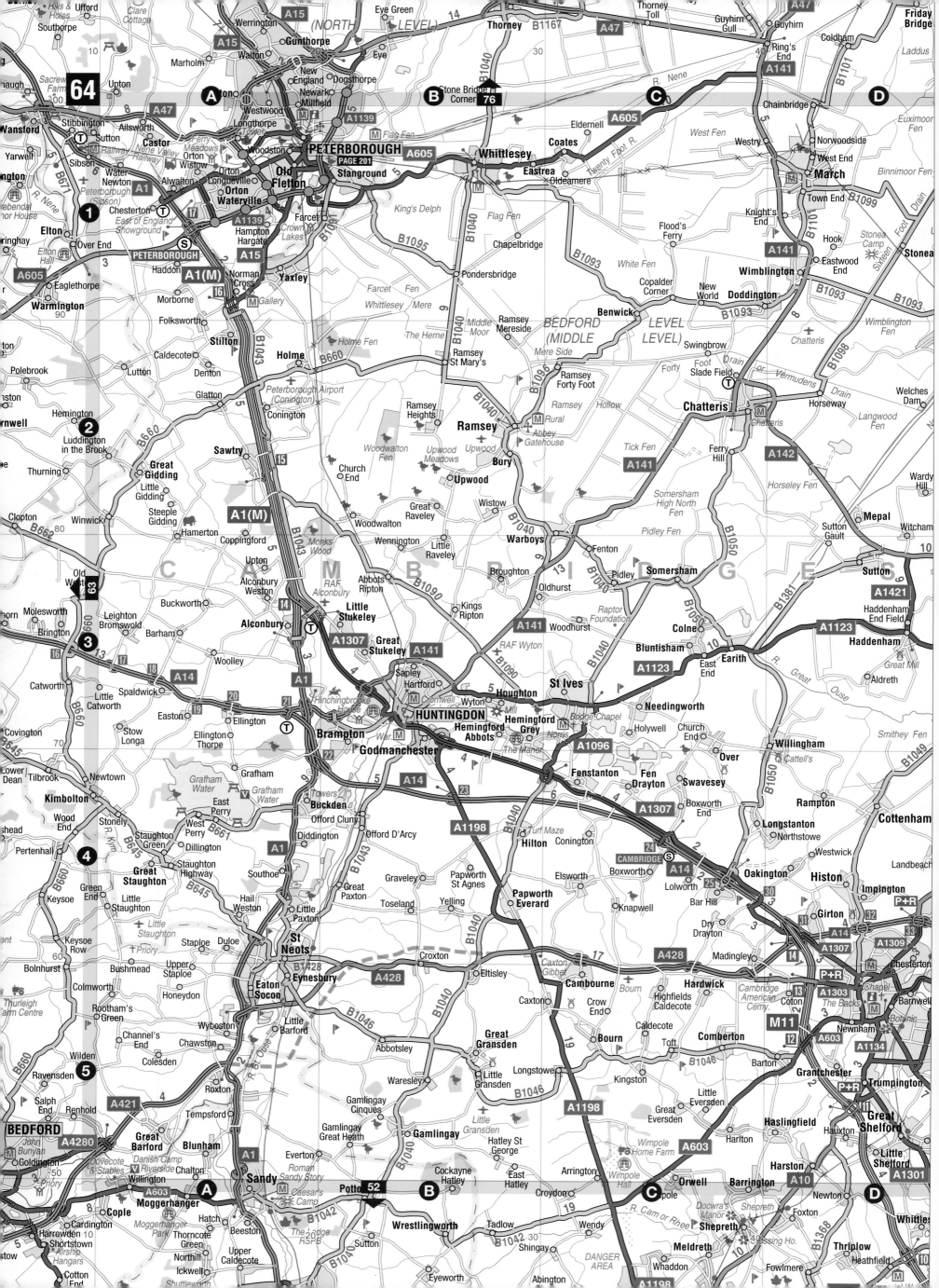

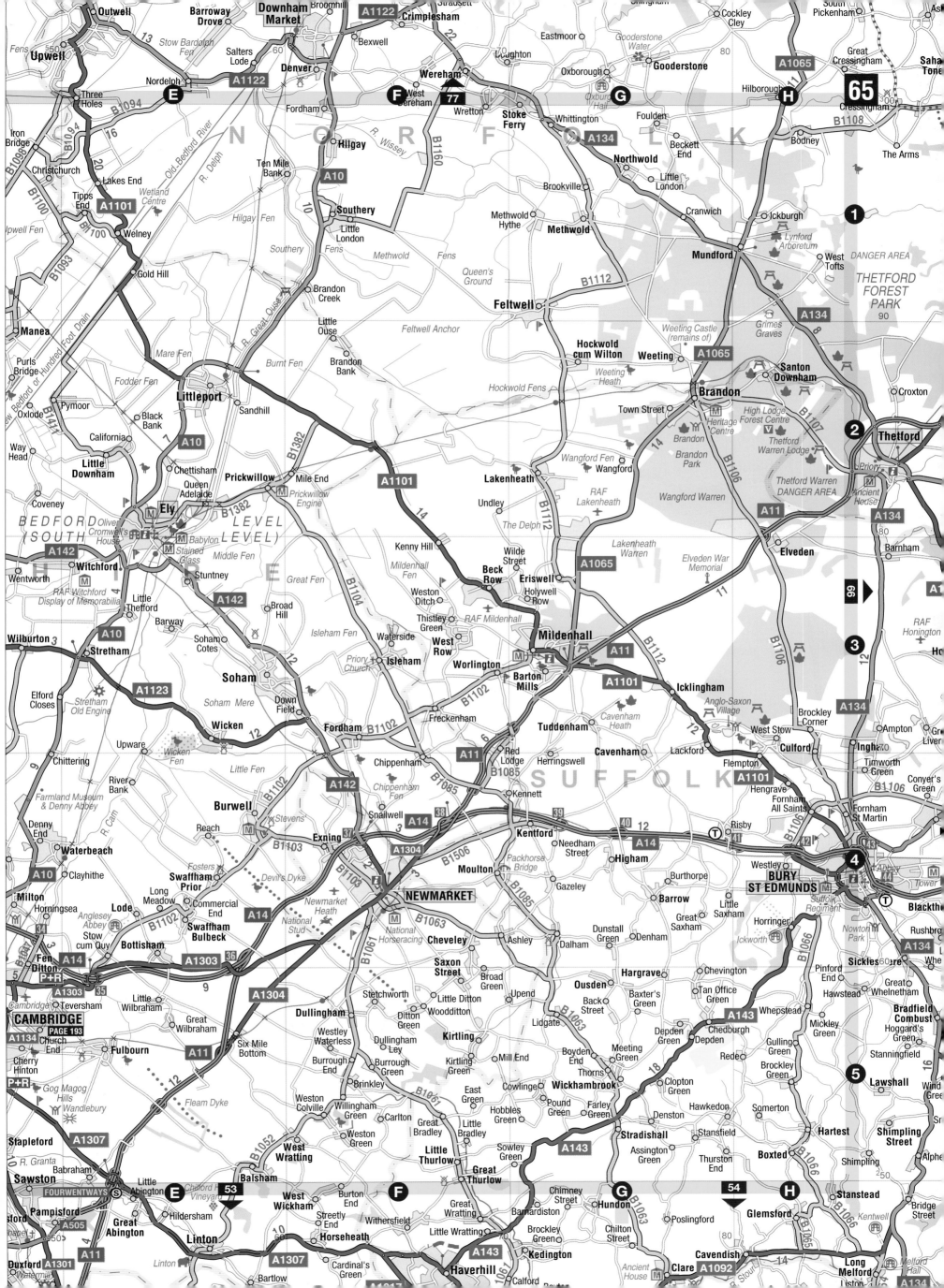

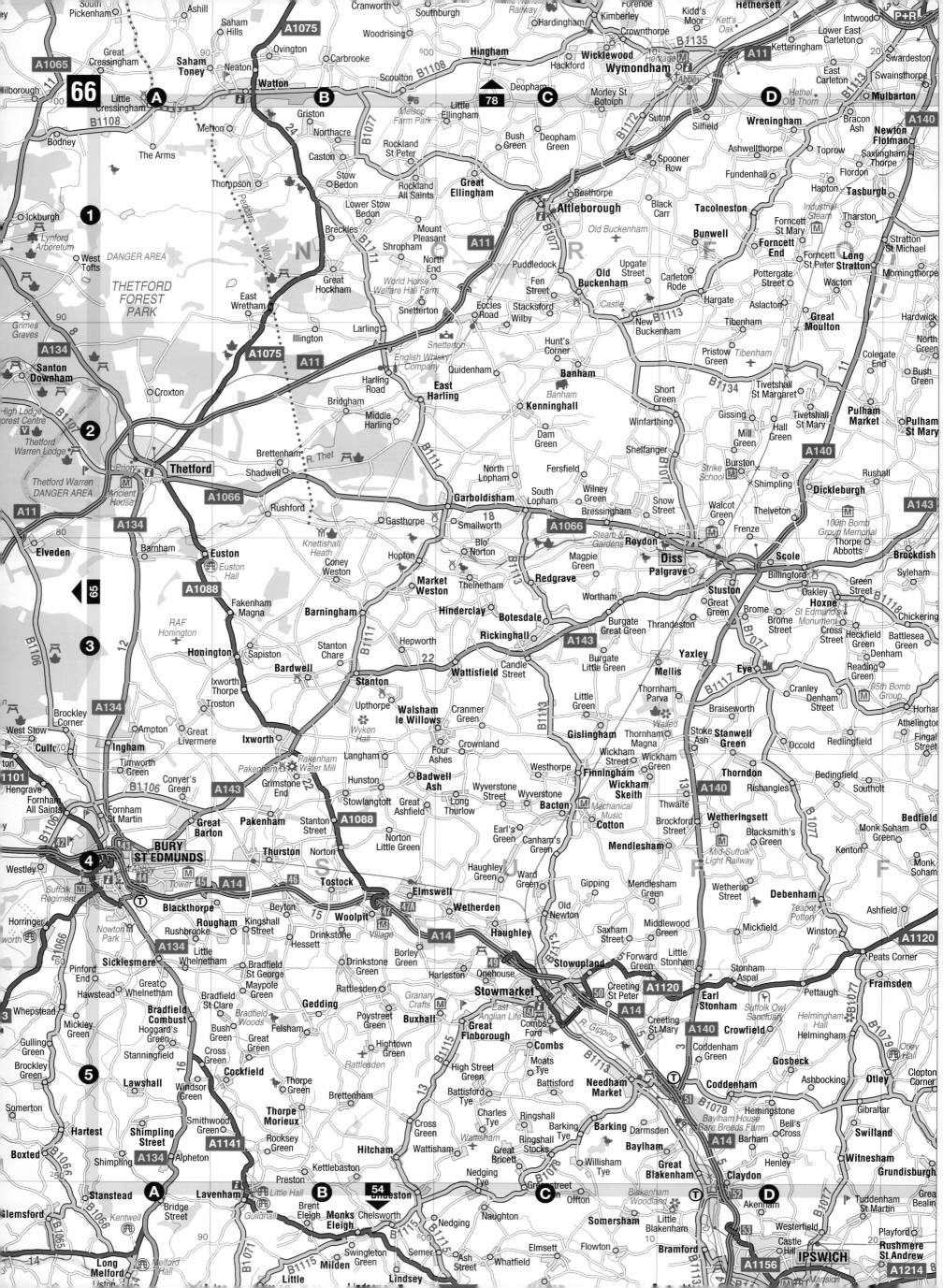

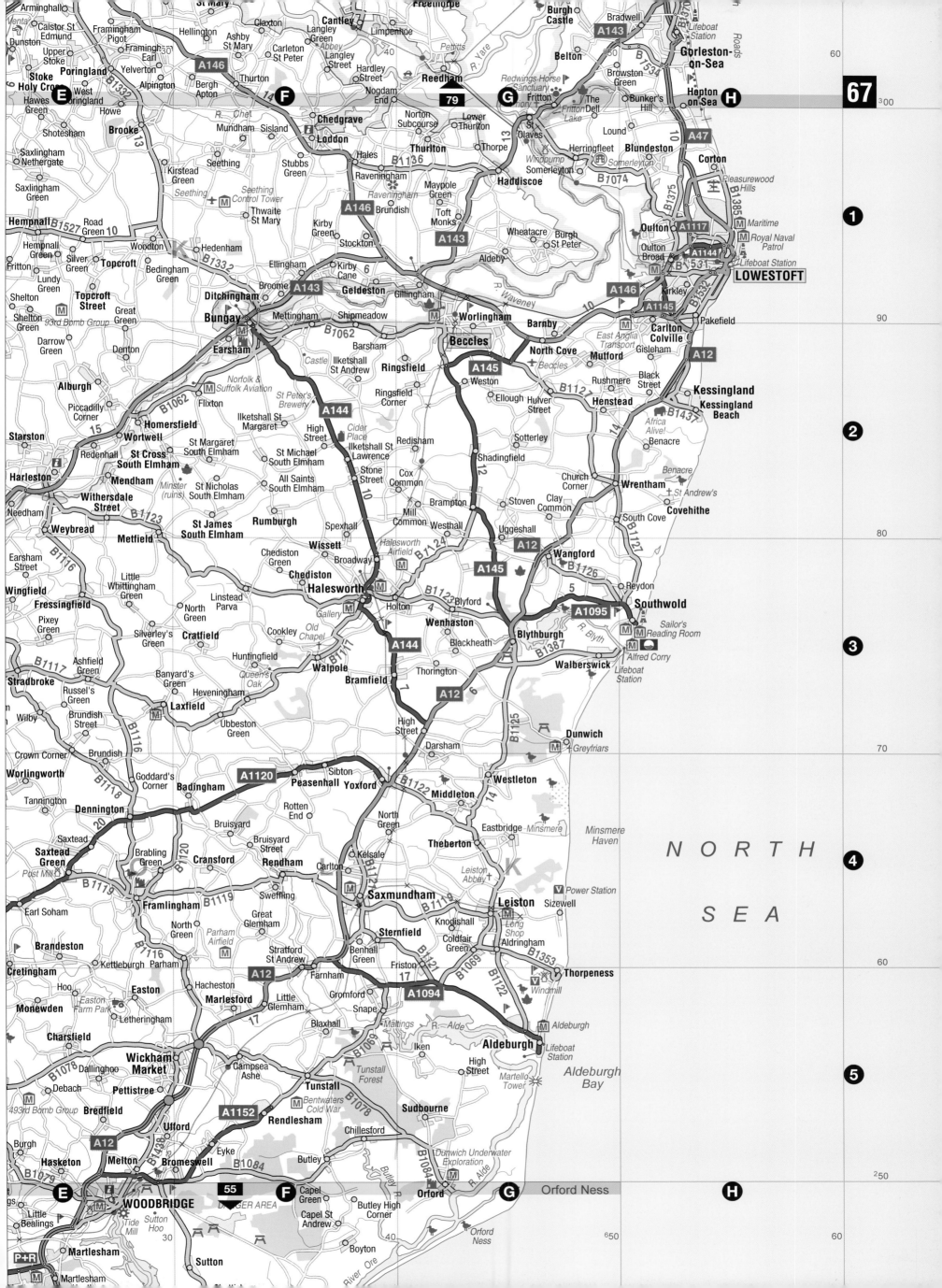

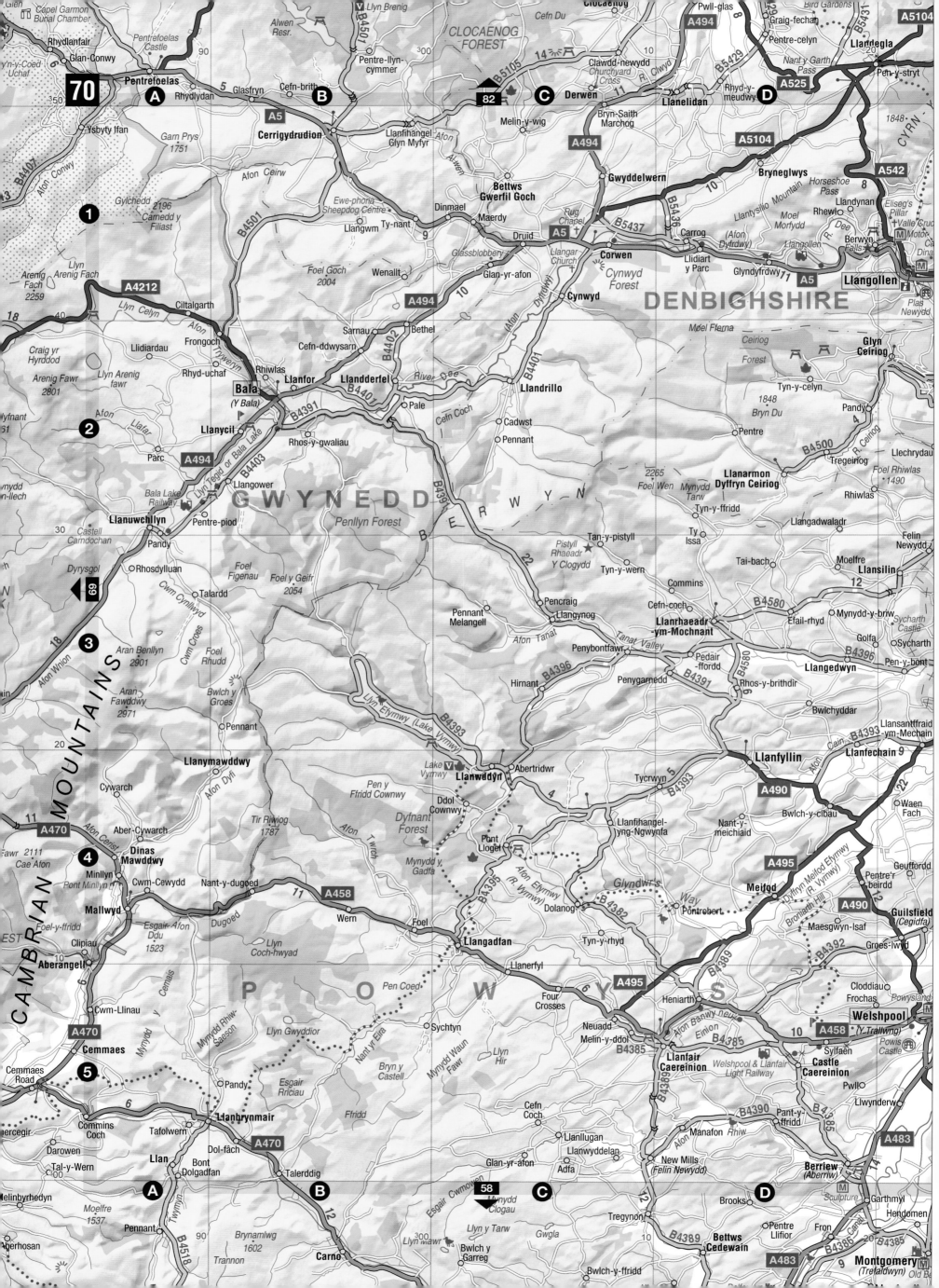

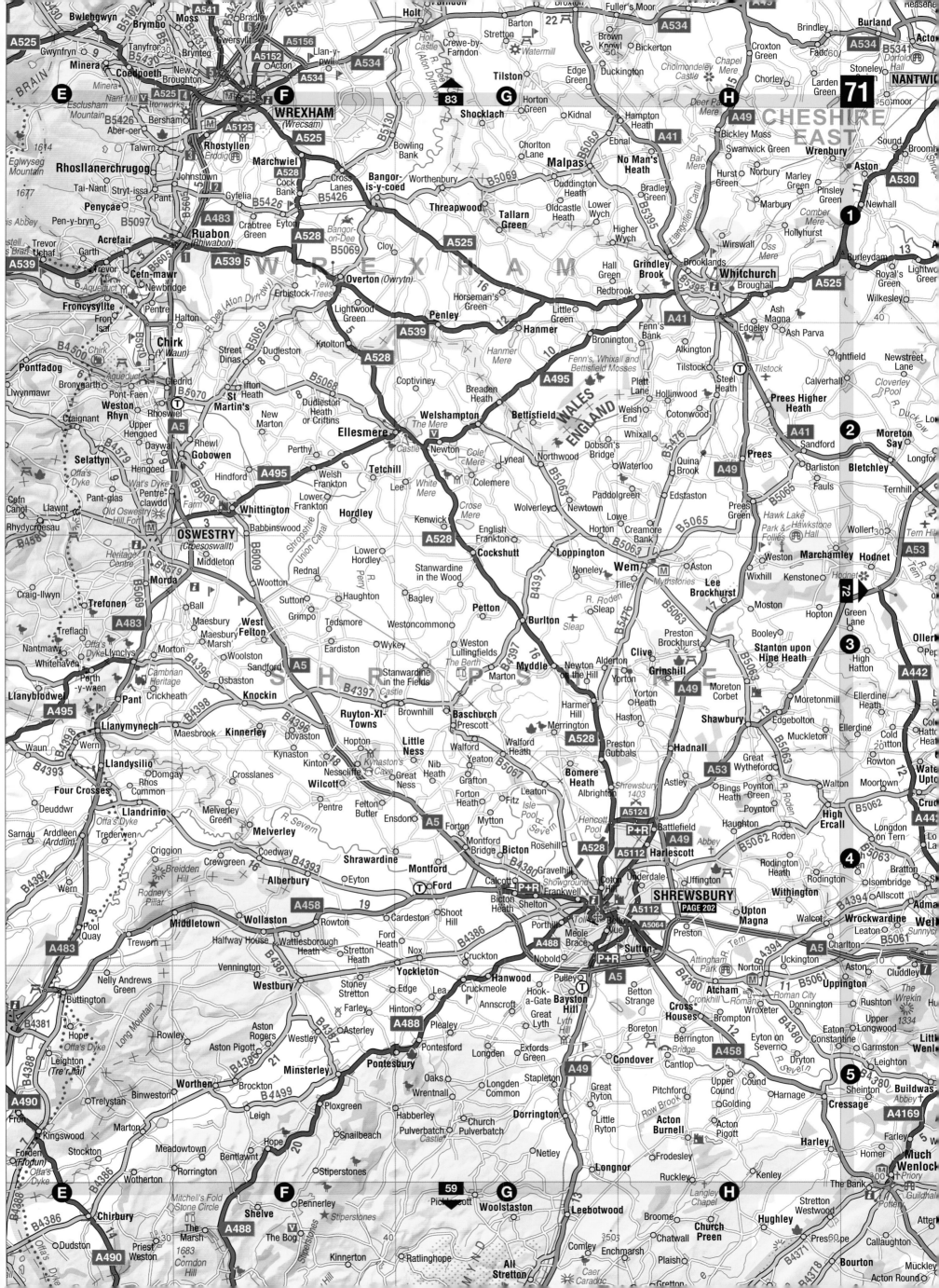

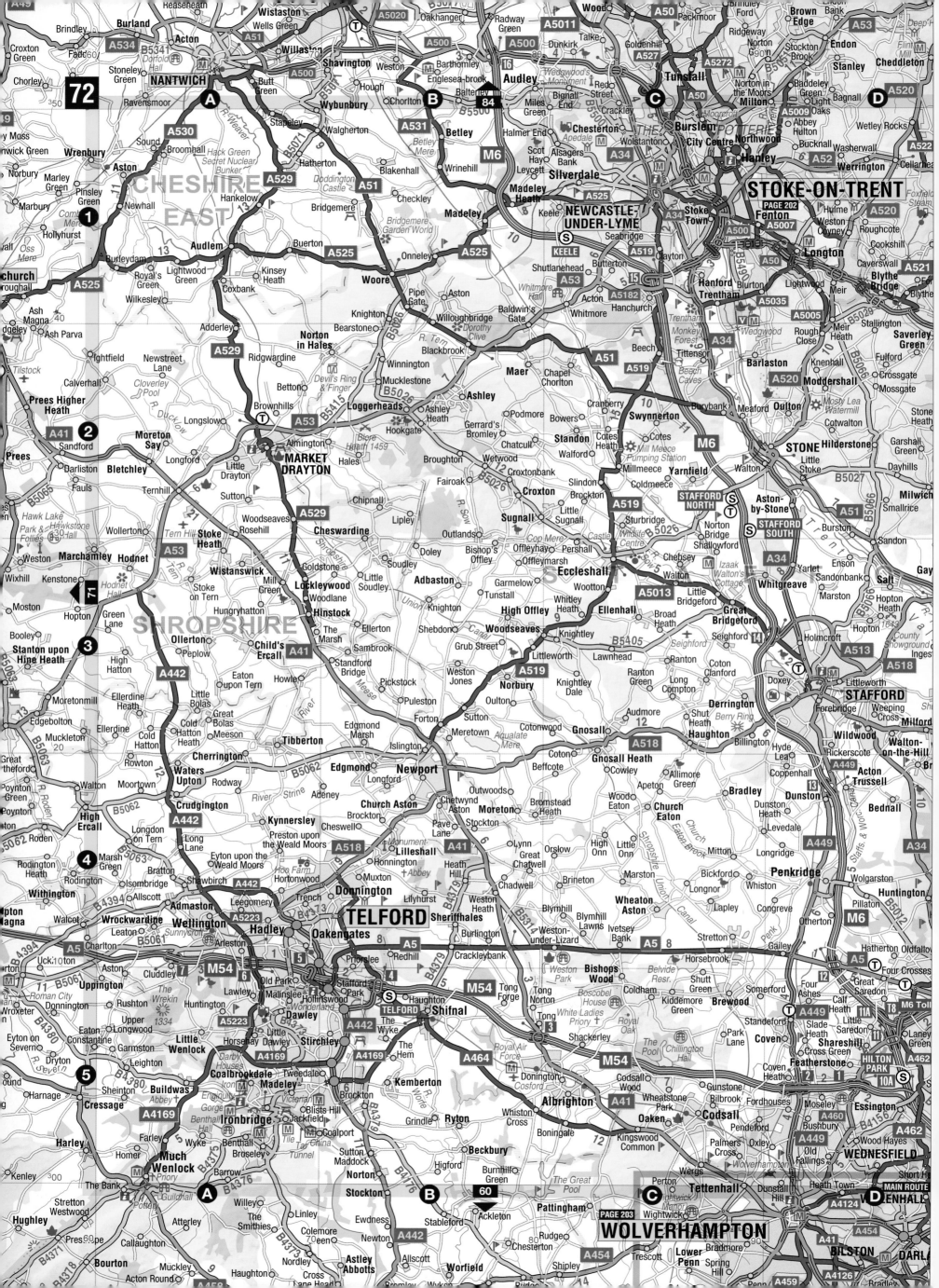

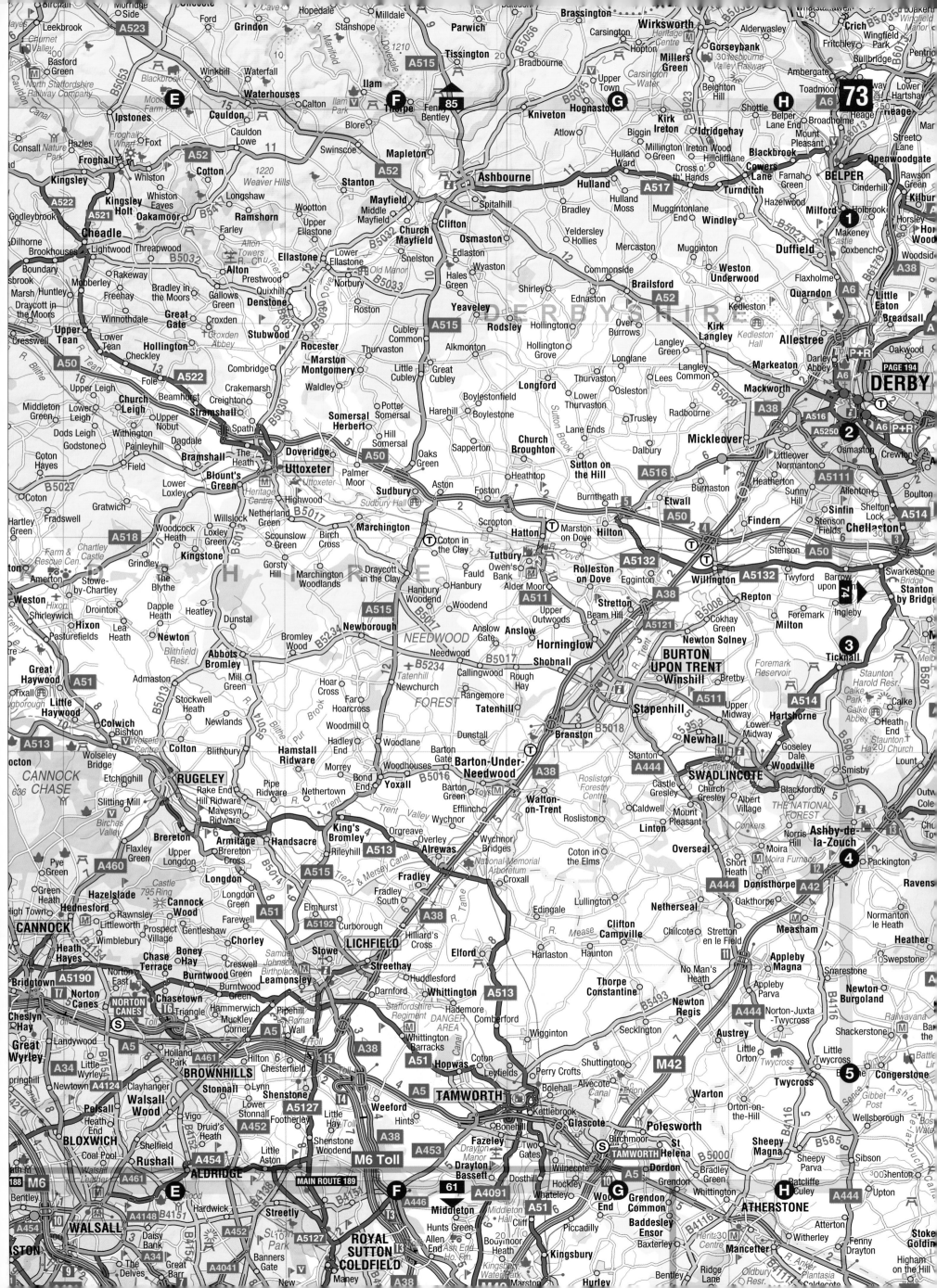

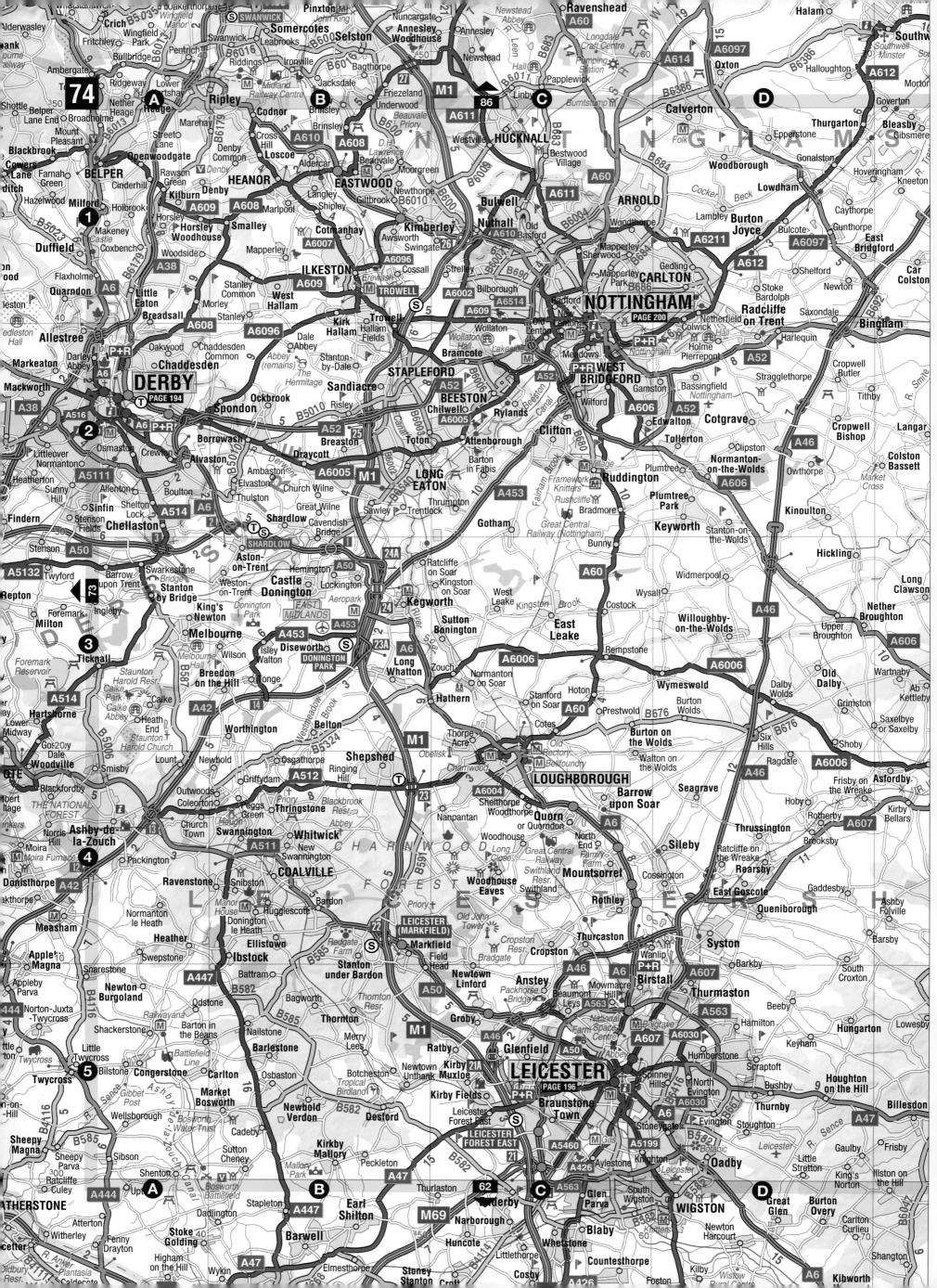

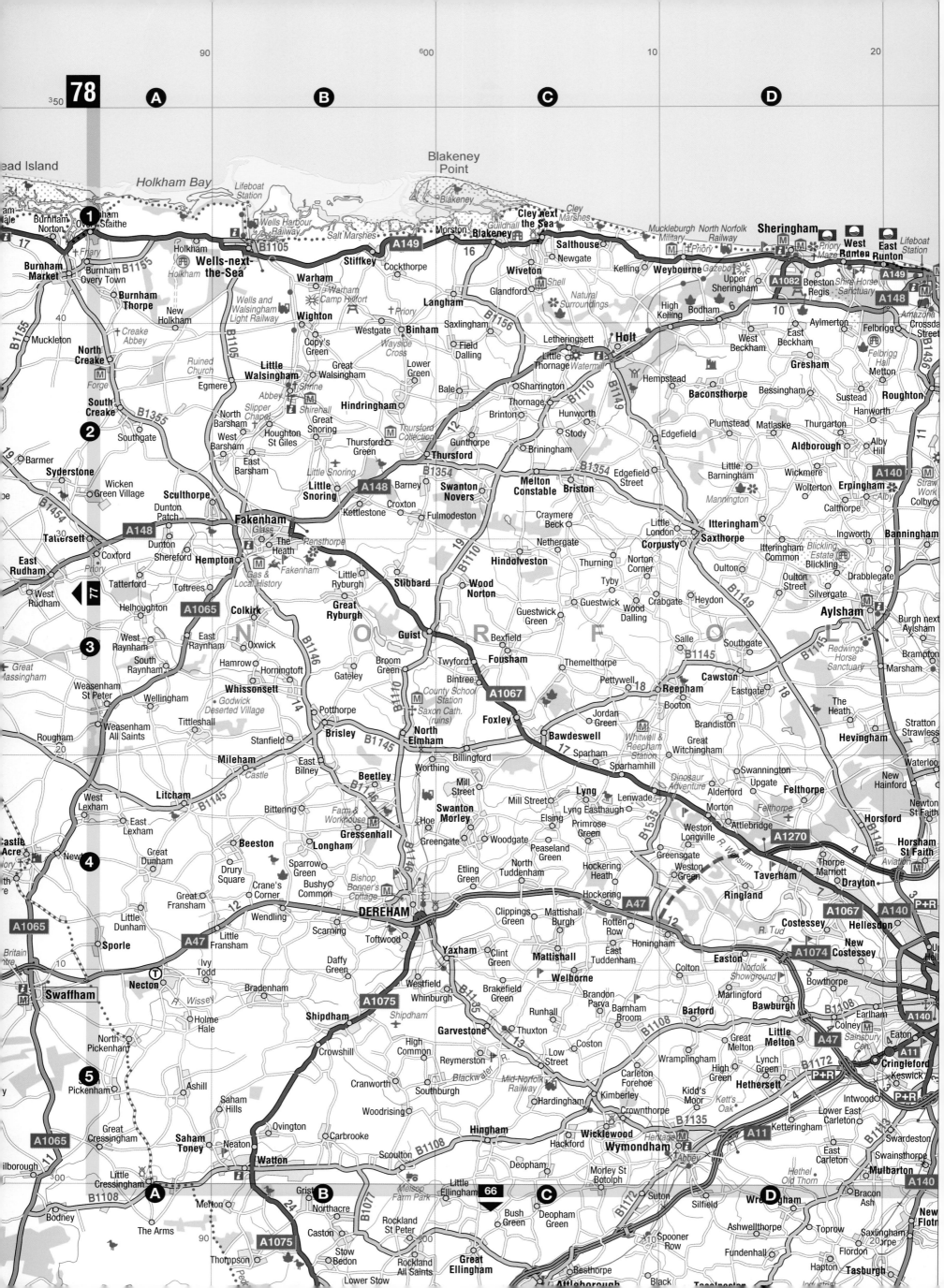

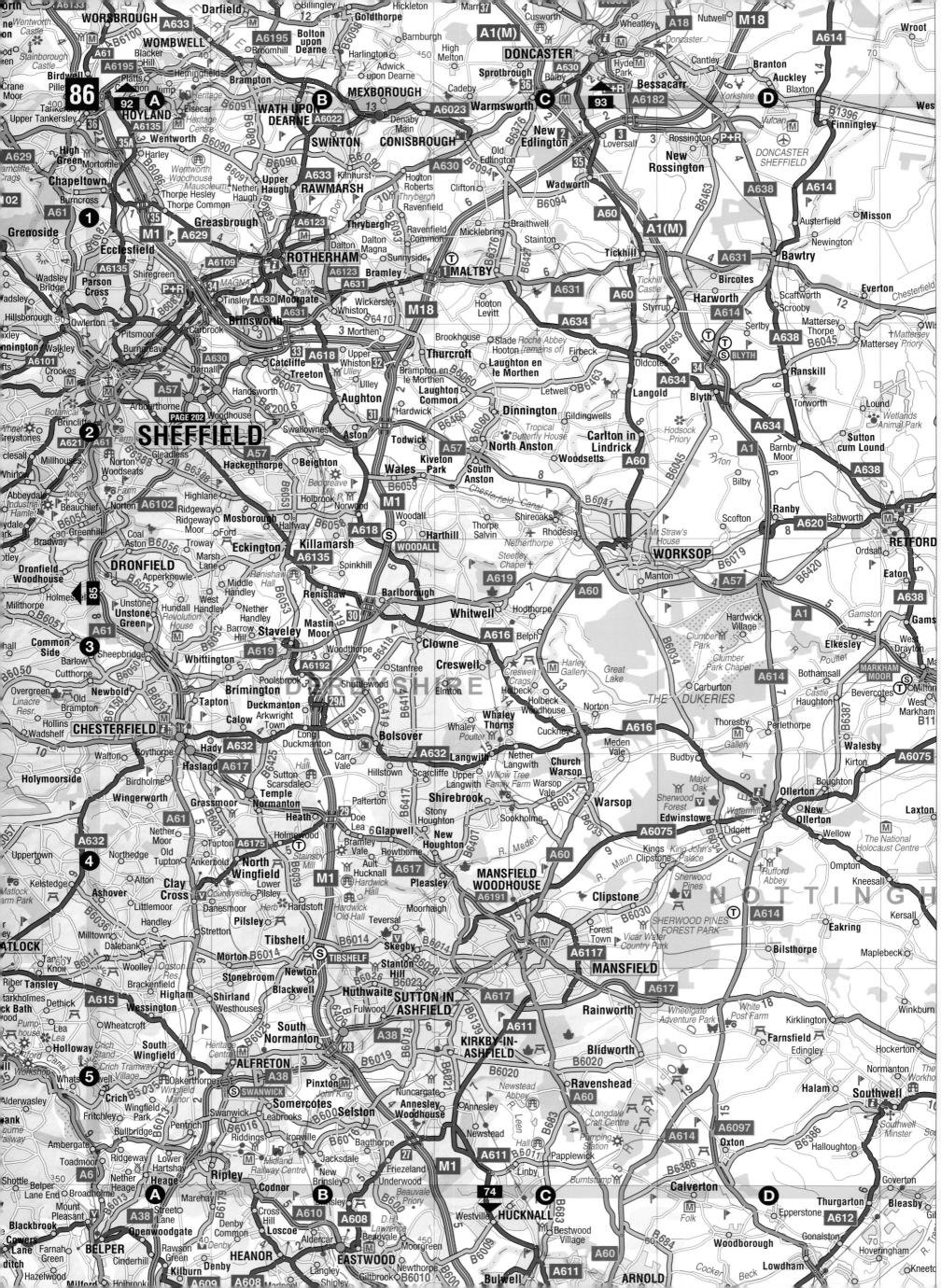

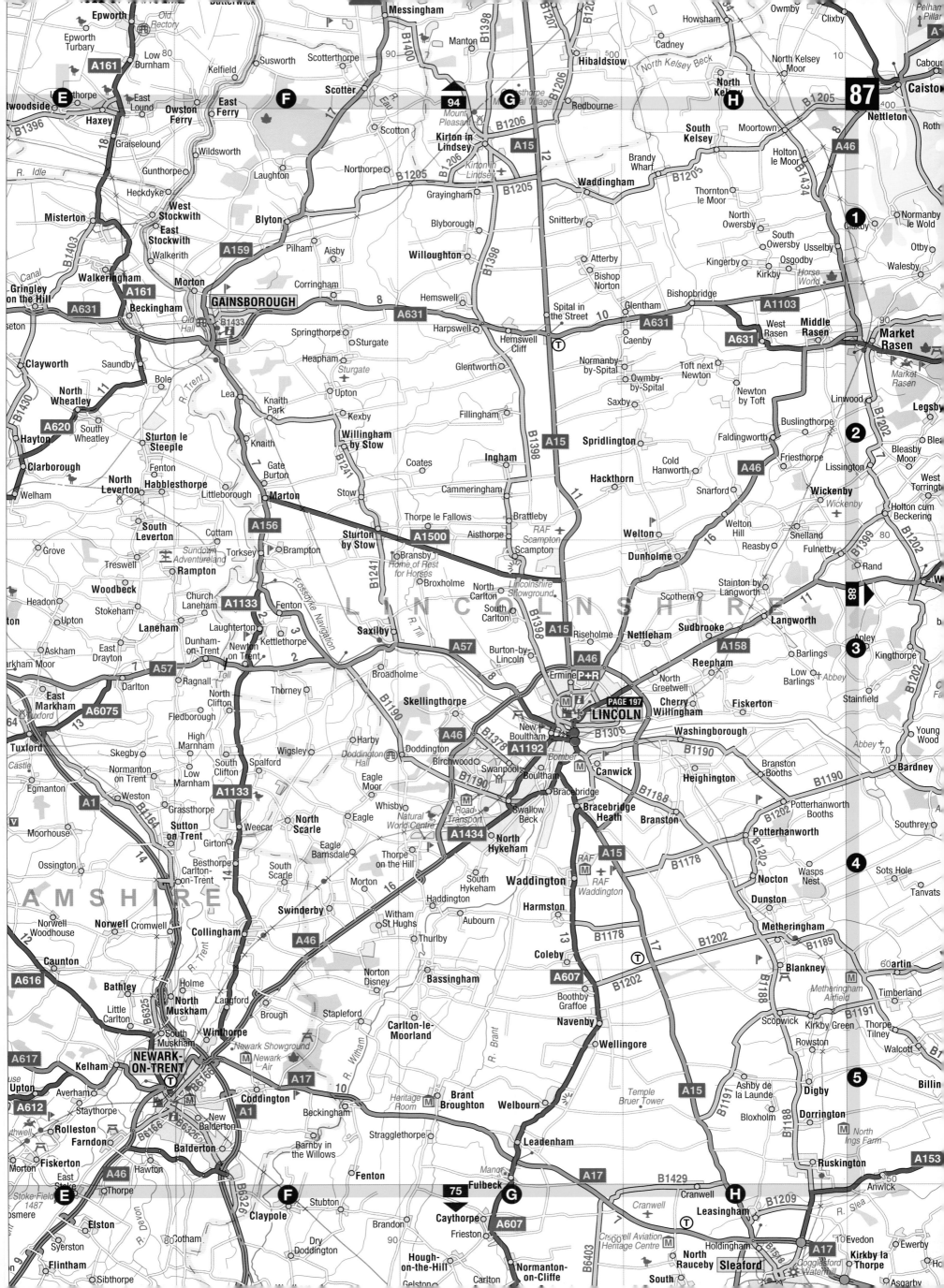

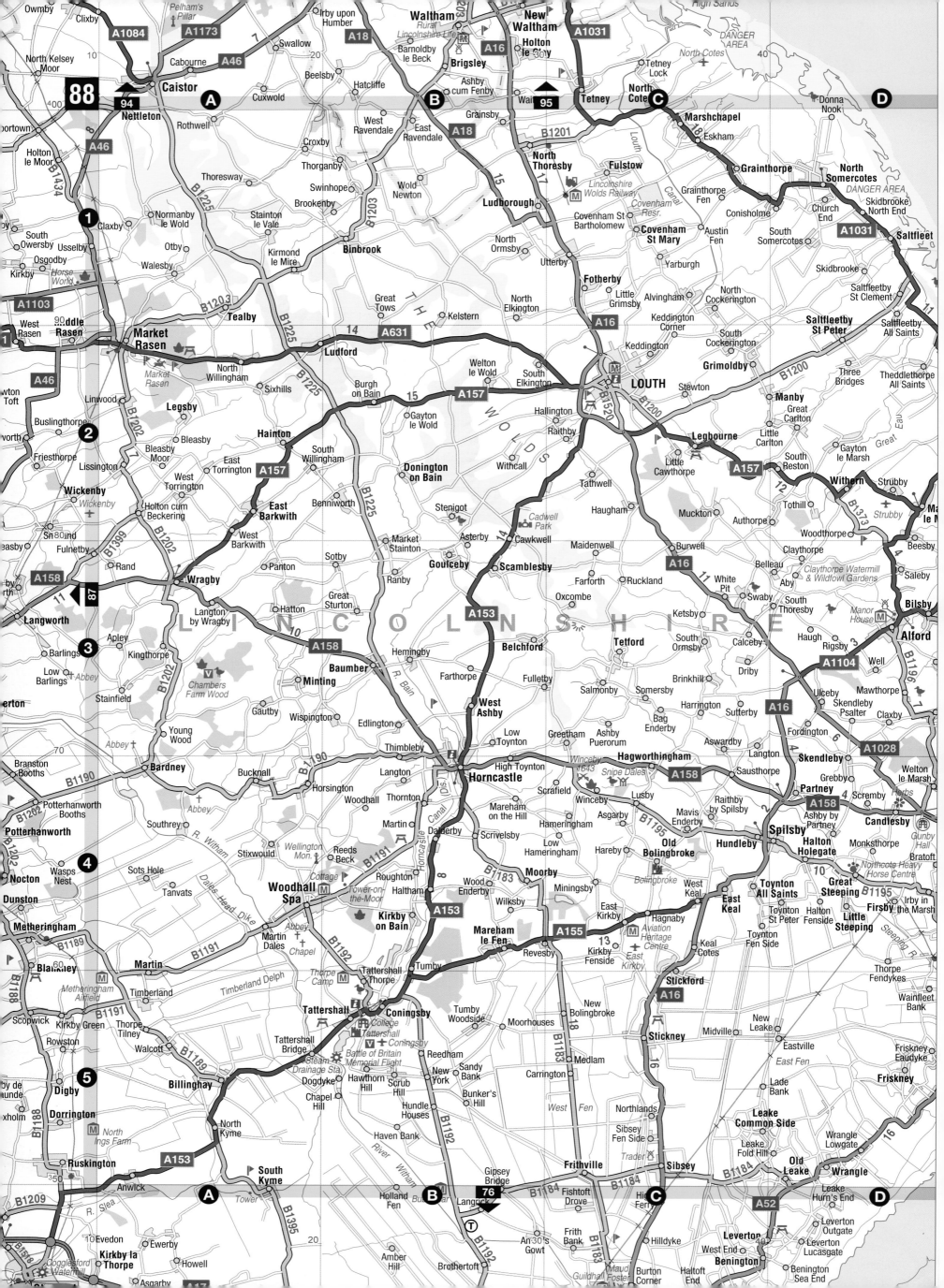

550   60   70   80

❶

N O R T H

S E A

90

Theddlethorpe
St Helen

Seal Sanctuary
& Wildlife Centre

❷

Meers
Bridge

Lifeboat
Station

Mablethorpe

Ye Olde
Curiosity

Trusthorpe

A1104

Thorpe

Sutton on Sea

80

altby
Marsh

Sandilands

A1111

Hannah

A52

Markby

6

15

Thurlby

Huttoft

Anderby
Creek

❸

Anderby

Drainage

B1449

13

Farlesthorpe

Mumby

On Your Marques

Cumberworth

Authorpe
Row

Bonthorpe

Helsey

**Chapel St
Leonards**

Willoughby

Hogsthorpe

Sloothby

A52

Ashley's
Field

Hardys
Animal Farm

70

Hasthorpe

Slackholme
End

Addlethorpe

Ingoldmells

Ingoldmells
Point

Orby

Skegness
(Ingoldmells)

Butlin's

A158

Orby
Marsh

Water
Leisure Park

Seathorne

Winthorpe

Natureland
Seal Sanctuary

❹

**Burgh le
Marsh**

Church
Farm

Bottons
Pleasure Beach

SKEGNESS

Model
Village

Croft

A52

5

Seacroft

Thorpe
St Peter

Croft Marsh

60

Batemans
Brewery

Magdalen

**Wainfleet
All Saints**

Wainfleet
St Mary

Gibraltar

Key's Toft

Gibraltar
Point

❺

DANGER AREA

Deeps

Boston

350

550   60   70   Sc 89 Head Island

Holme
Dunes Brancaster Bay Holkham B

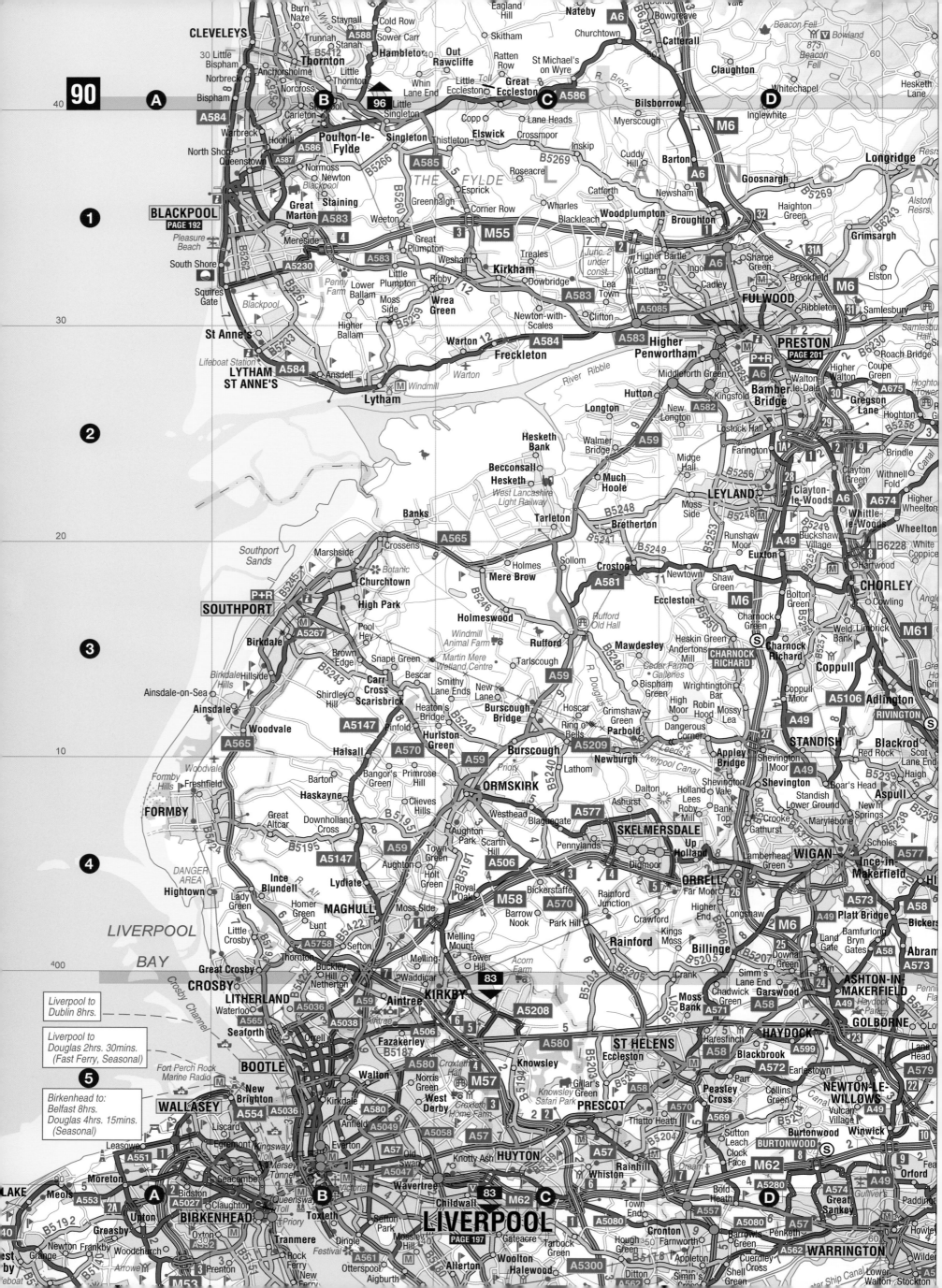

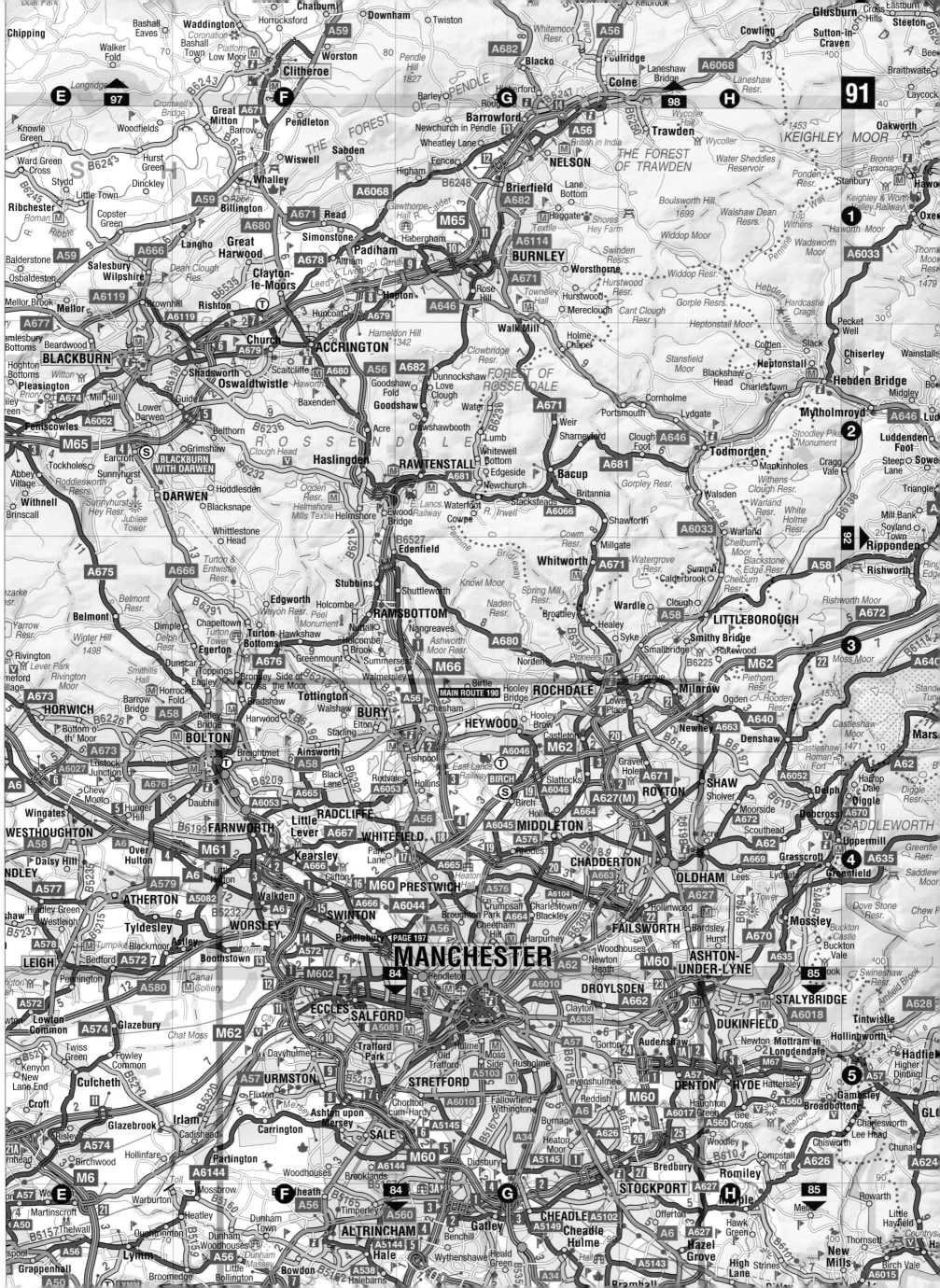

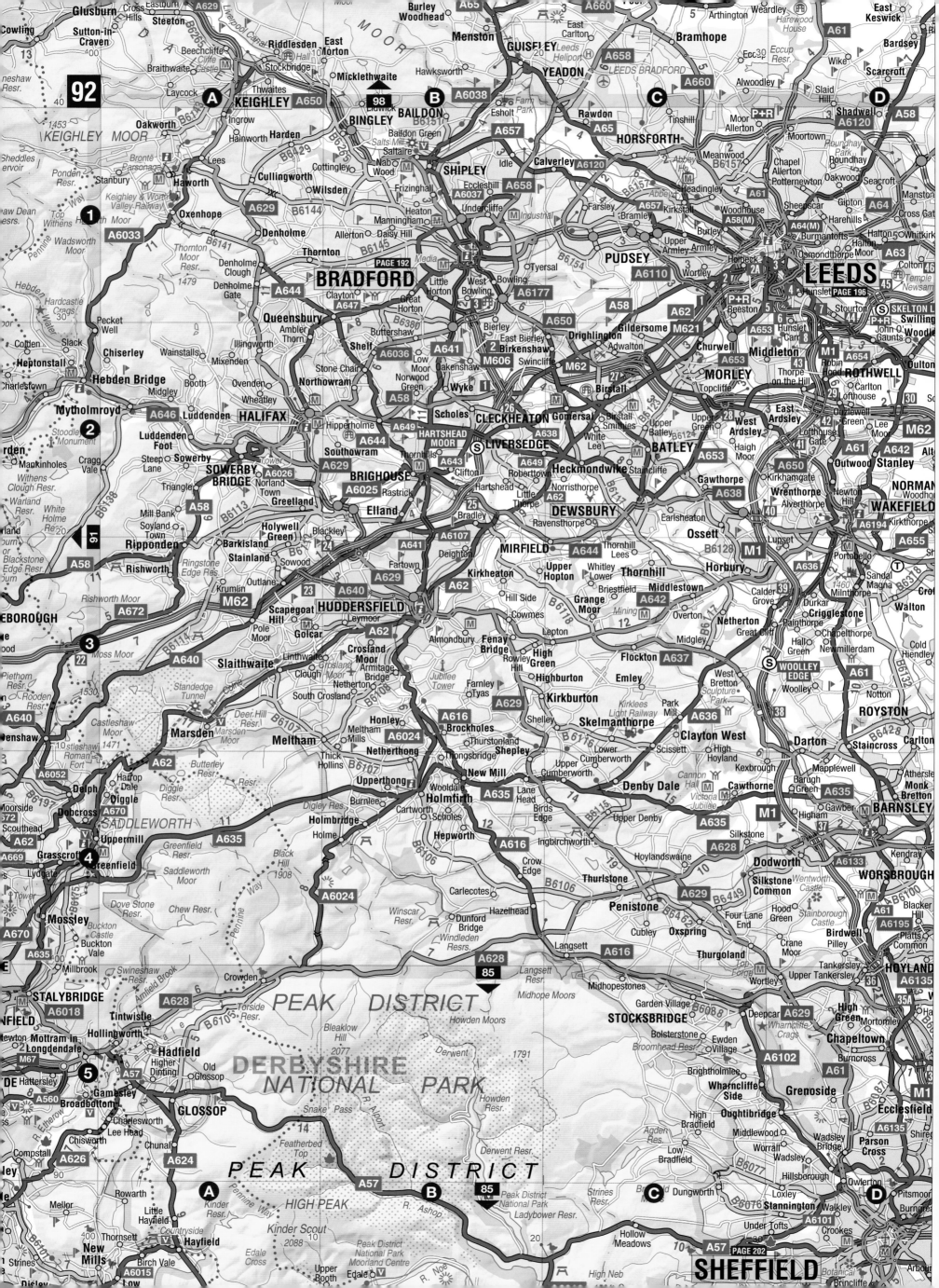

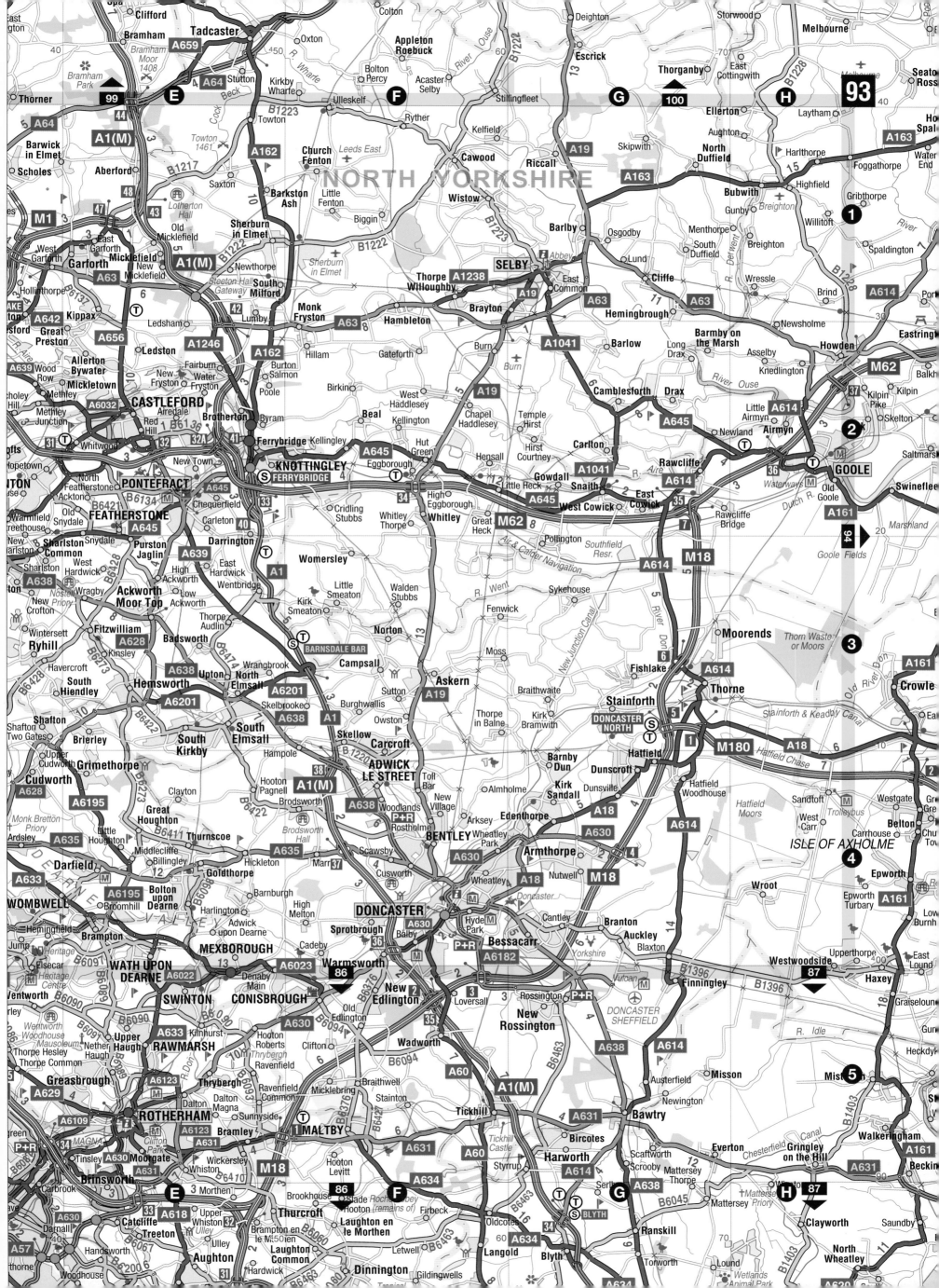

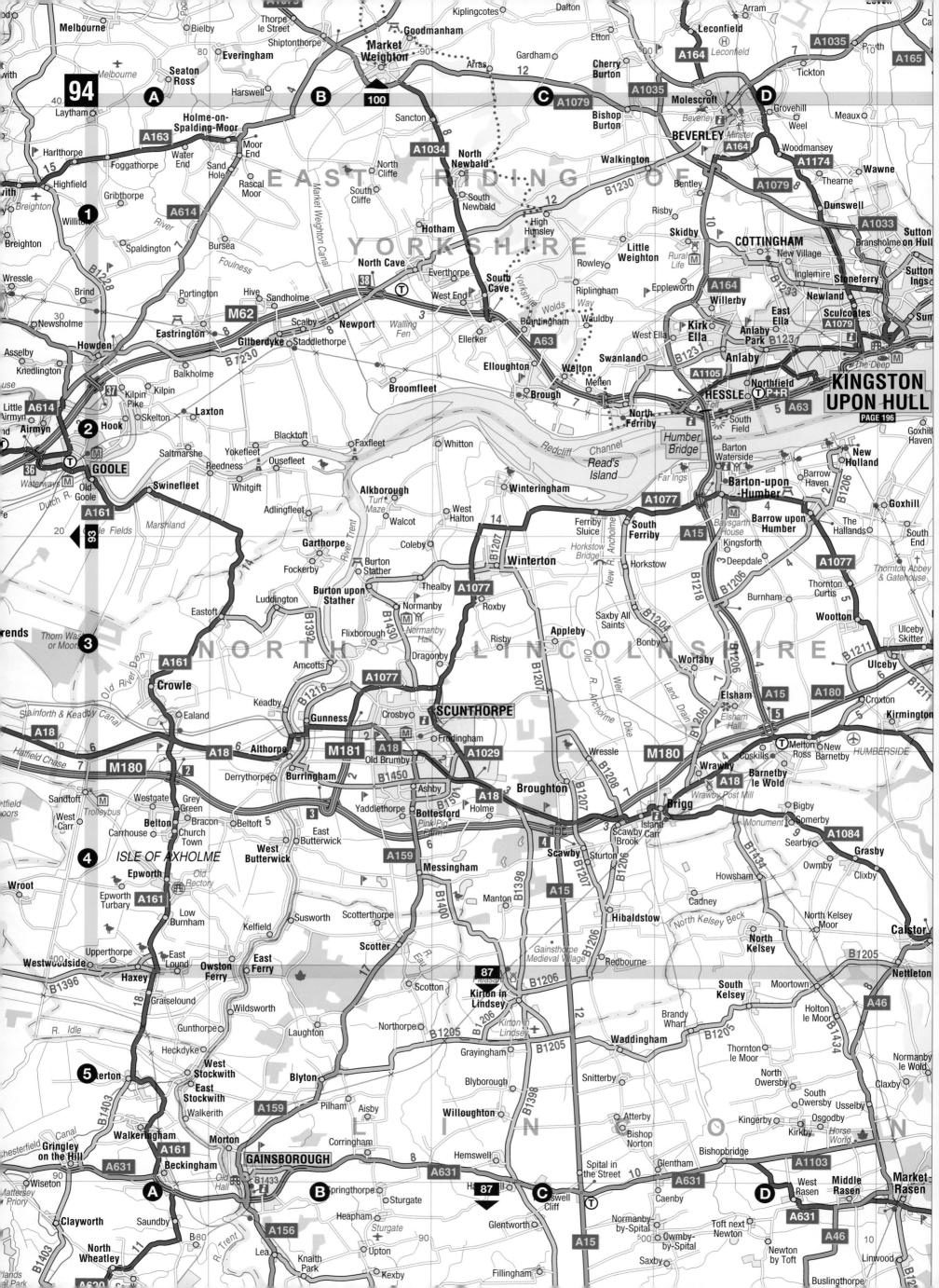

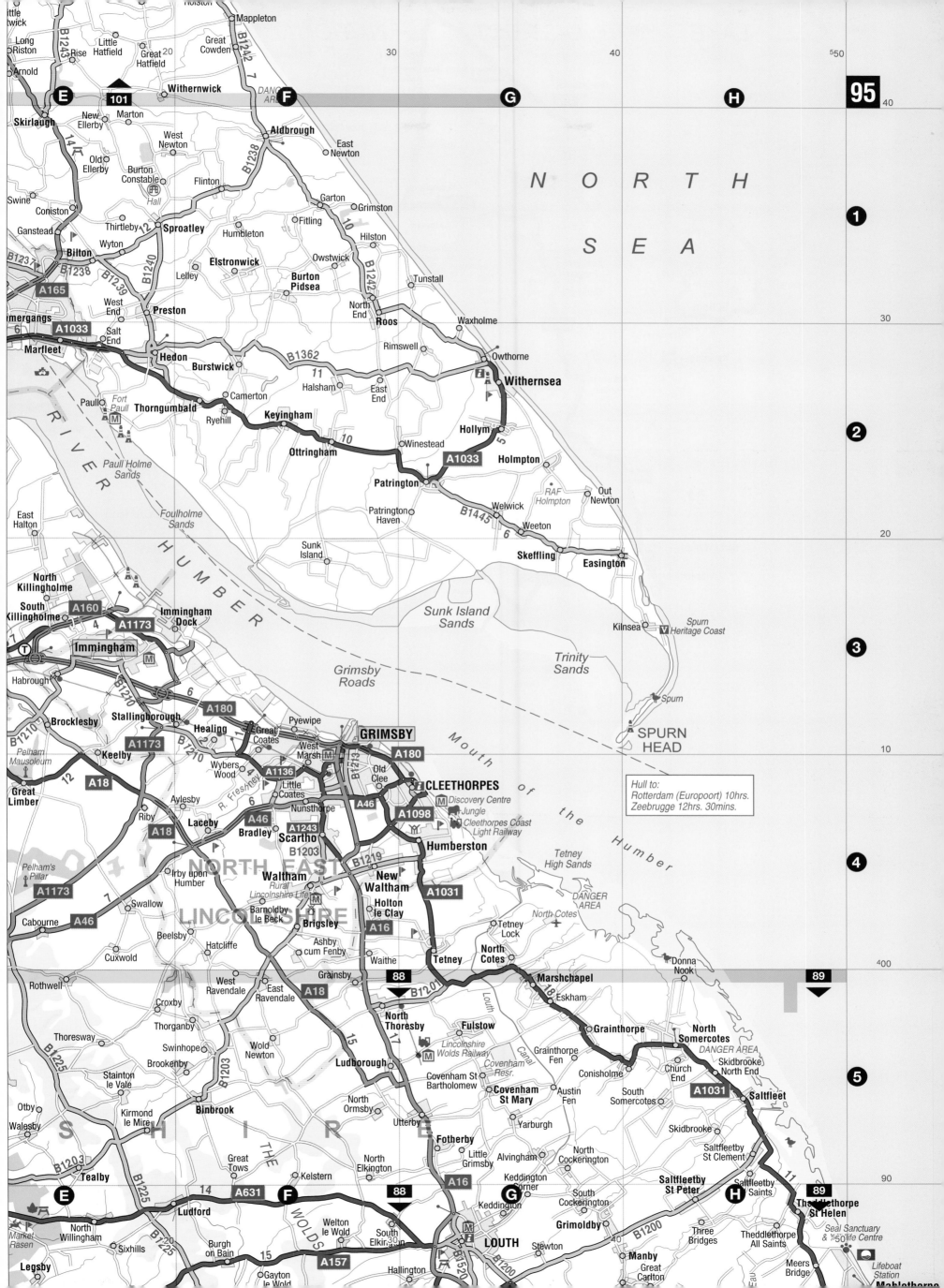

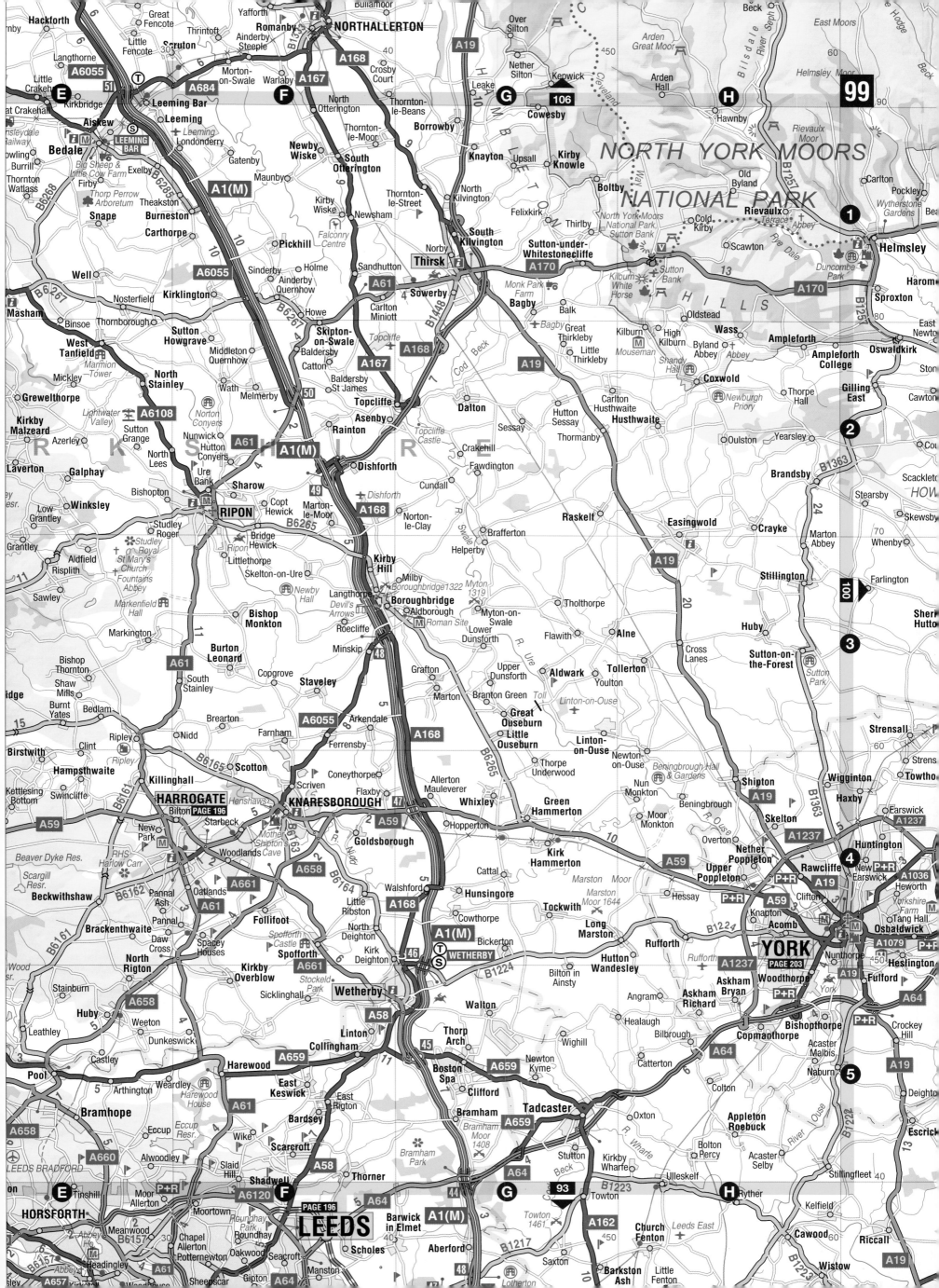

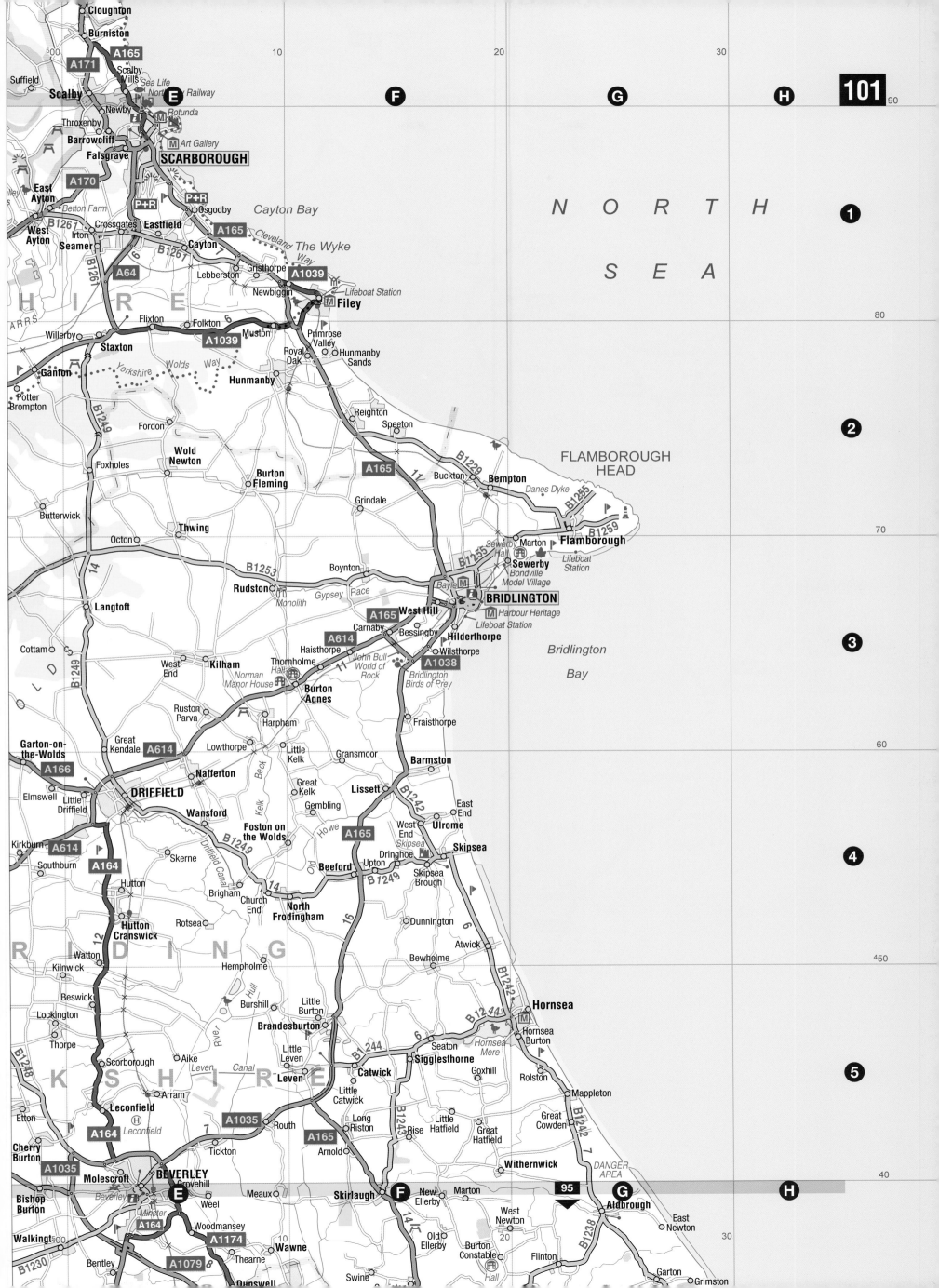

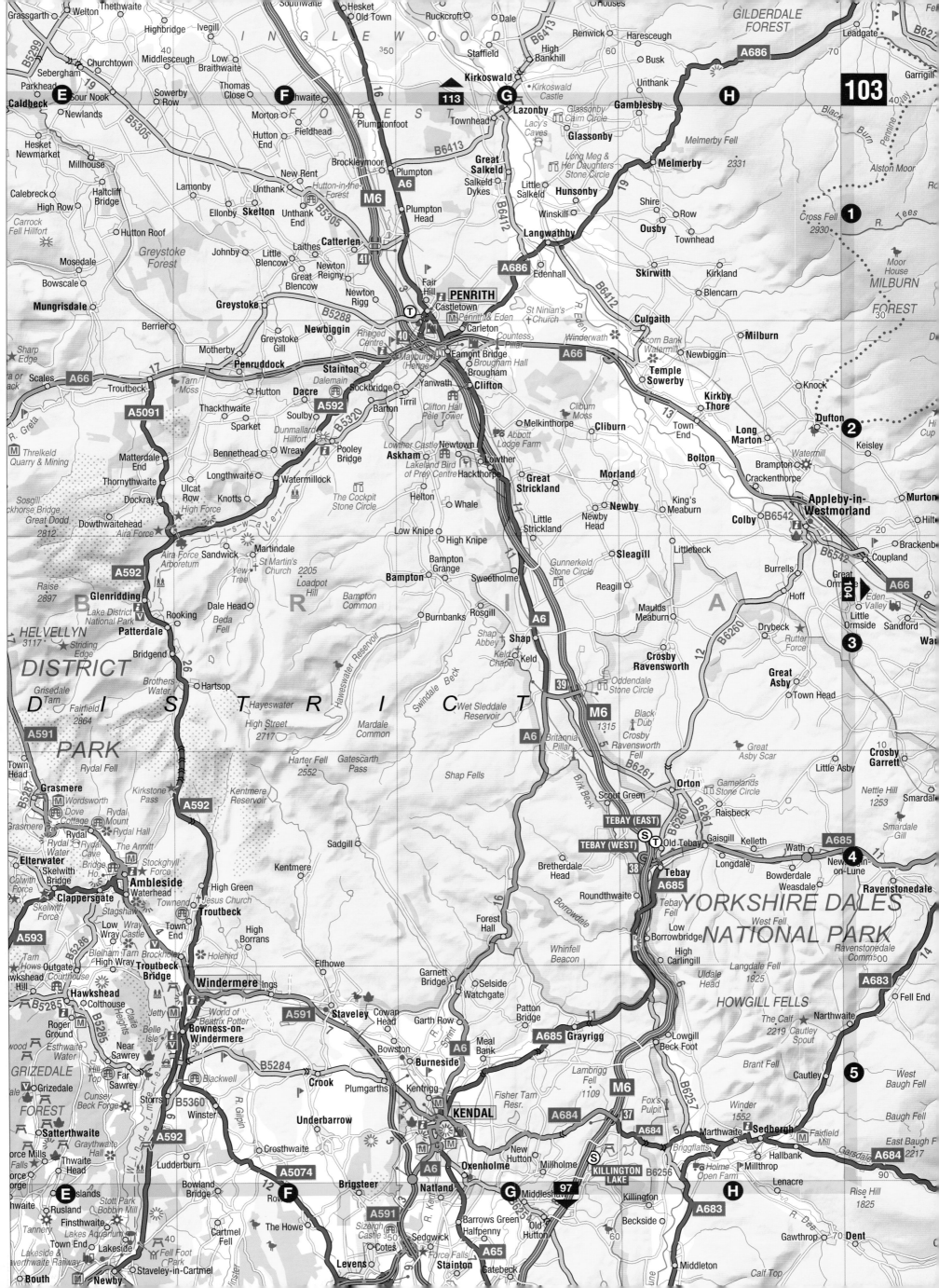

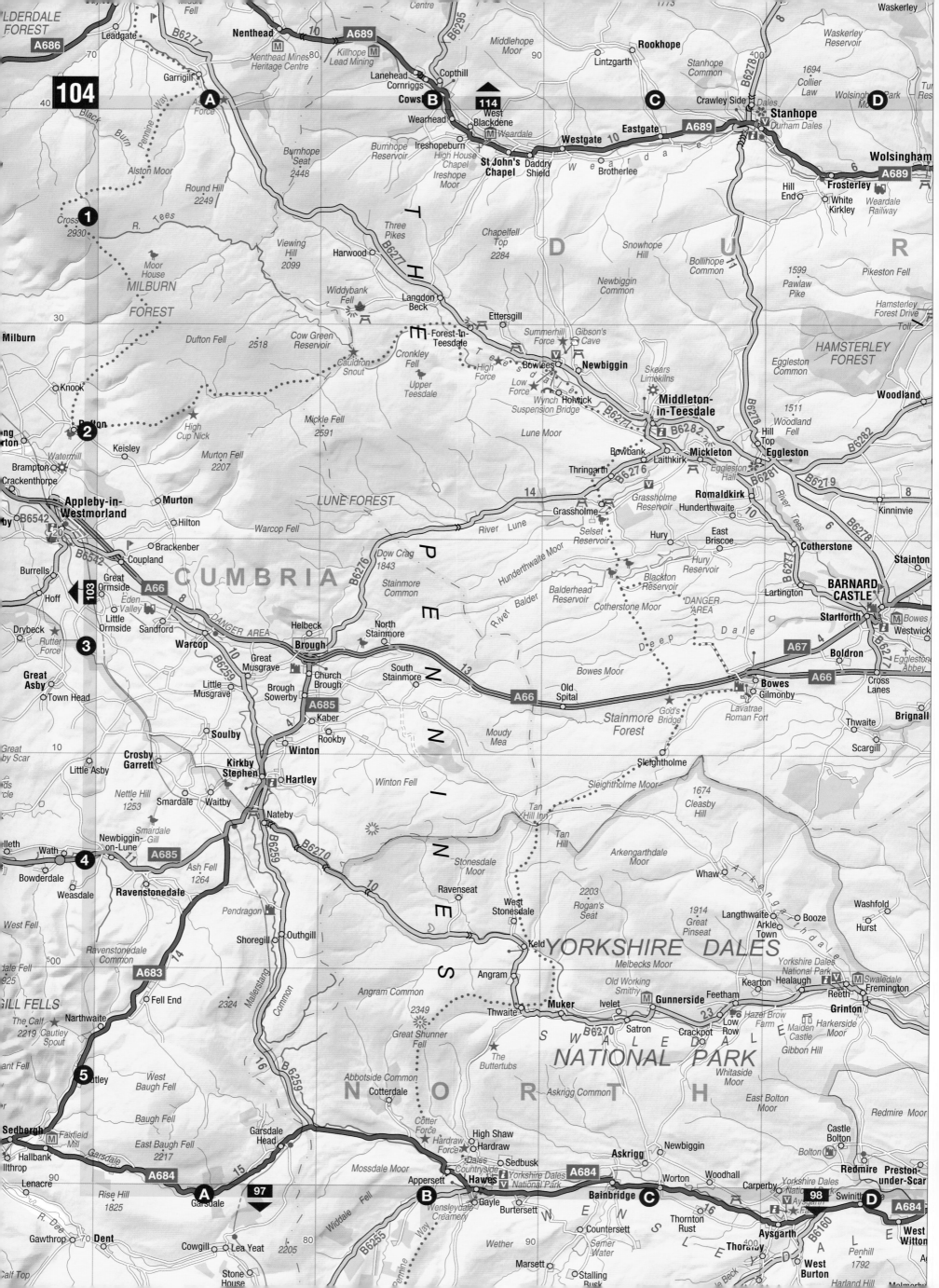

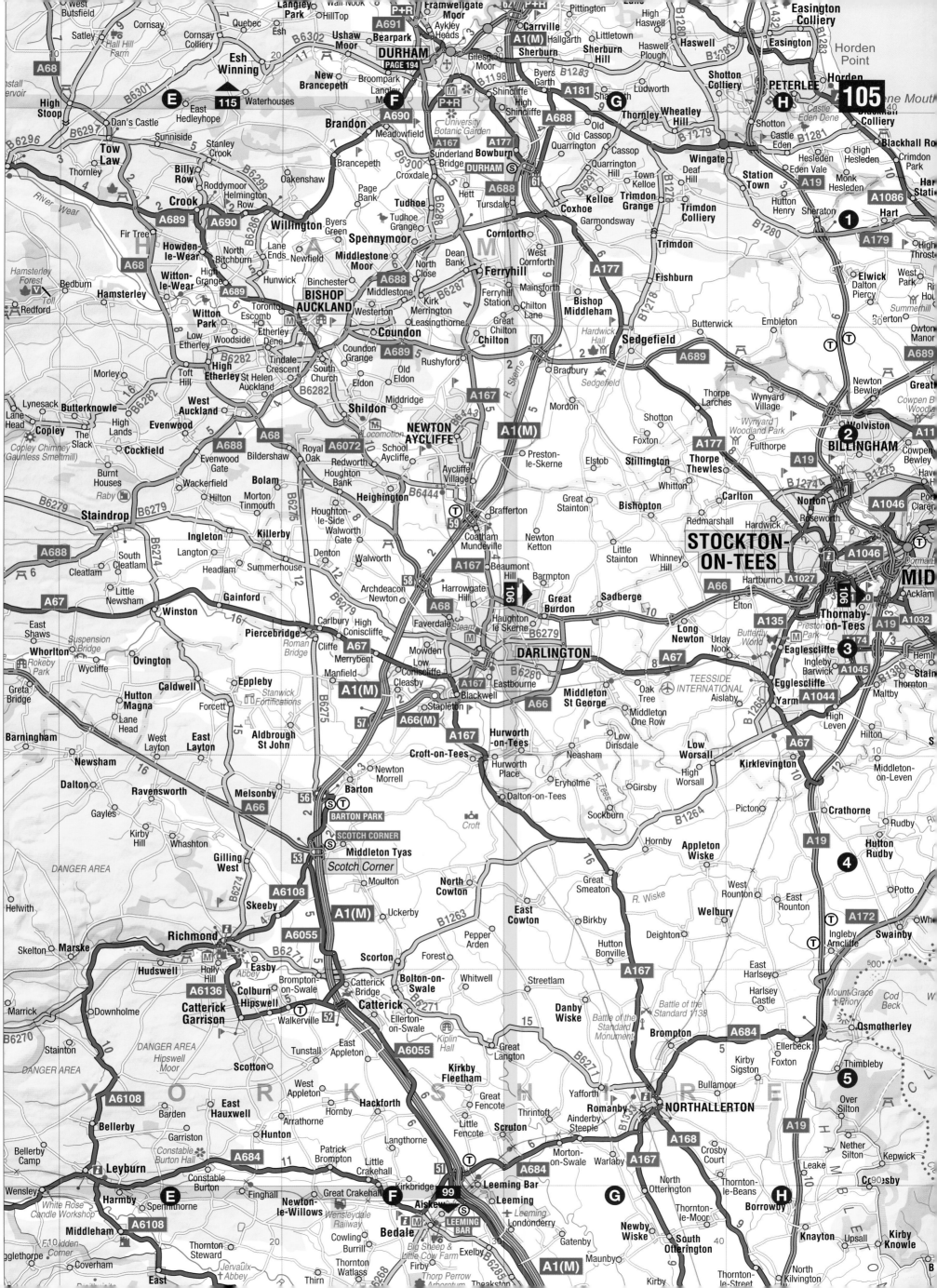

POINT OF AYRE

Rue Point
The Ayres
The Ayres

A16

The Lhen

A10
Cranstal

B6

A10 11
B13
B2
Dhowin
Bride

A10
B3
A19
B4
Crosses
A17
Shellag Point

Jurby Head
Jurby
West
Jurby
East
Andreas
A10

Ballasalla
B5
Sandygate
Civil
B7
War Fort
Regaby
A9
Ramsey
Bay

The Cronk
A13
St
Judes
Dhoor
Grove M
A13
B14
A3
Ramsey
Lhergy
Frissel

Orrisdale
A14
A17
Sulby
B8
Churchtown
Glen
Auldyn
B16
Manx Electric Railway
Port e Vullen

Orrisdale Head
A3
Ballaugh
Ballaleigh
1854
North Barrule
A15
Elfin
Glen
Lewaigue
Maughold
Crosses

Glen
Wyllin
Bishopscourt
Glen
A14
Tholt-y-Will
Glen
Ballajora
Maughold
Head

Kirk
Michael
Ravensdale
SNAEFELL
2036
A18
Corrany
A2
Cornaa
Port Mooar

Glen
Mooar
Ballaleigh
Slieau Dhoo
1601
Clagh Ouyr
Glen Mona
Cashtal
Yn Ard
Port Cornaa

Gob y Deigan
A4
Barregarrow
B10
Sulby
Resr.
21
Snaefell
Mountain
Great
Laxey
Mine
Dhoon
Glen
Bulgham Bay

Knocksharry
A3
Cronk-y-Voddy
B10
Laxey Wheel
Laxey
Dhoon

St Patrick's Isle M
Leece
Ballagyr
Lambfell
Moar
Rhenass
Waterfall
Glen Helen
ISLE
OF
MAN
A18
Laxey
Glen
Minorca
Old Laxey Head

House of
Manannan M
Peel
Glen
Colden
1599
Ballaheannagh
Laxey
B11
Old
Laxey

Contrary Head
Patrick
A20
A1
Ballig
Slieau Ruy
1570
B22
Injebreck
Resr.
B12
Ballacannell

A30
St John's
Greeba
Castle
Baldwin
B21
B20
Laxey Bay

Glen
Maye
Tynwald
Hill
11
A1
Hillberry
B12
Baldrine
Clay Head

Glen Maye
Crosby
Glen
Vine
A2
80

Dalby Point
A27
Lower
Foxdale
A23
Strang
A1
Hillberry
Groudle
Glen Railway
Port Groudle

Niarbyl
Dalby
A3
Eairy
A24
Garth
Union Mills
A22
Willaston
Onchan
Groudle Glen

Niarbyl Bay
A36
Foxdale
B35
B32
A1
A6
A11
Onchan Head

South
Barrule
Spring
Valley
DOUGLAS
A36
Hill 1586
Fort
12
B36
Braaid
A24
Cooil
M
Manx
Douglas Bay

Stroin Vuigh
A27
B3.5
B37
Kewaigue
B80
Douglas Head

Ballamodha
B41
St
Mark's
Newtown
A5
Quine's
Hill
Home for
Old Horses

Fleshwick
Bay
Lingague
Ronague
Grenaby
B30
A25
Keristal
Little Ness

Bradda Head
Bradda
B42
B40
A3
Isle of Man
Steam
Port
Soderick

Bradda Glen
Surby
Ballabeg
A26
B25
Santon Head

Port Erin
Railway
Colby
A7
A5
Rushen
Abbey
A5
Ballasalla

Chambered Cairn
Four Roads
A5
5
ISLE OF MAN
Four Roads
M
The Howe
Port St
Mary
Ballabeg
A12
Derby Fort
St Michael's Island

Cregneash
M
Castletown
Nautical
Scarlett V
M
Rushen
Keys
Derbyhaven

Kitterland
A31
National
Folk
B18

SPANISH HEAD

Calf of Man

Dreswick
Point

Douglas to:
Belfast 2hrs.45mins.
(Fast Ferry, Seasonal)
Birkenhead 4hrs. 15mins.
(Seasonal)
Heysham 3hrs. 30mins.
Dublin 2hrs. 45mins.
(Fast Ferry, Seasonal)
Liverpool 2hrs. 30mins.
(Fast Ferry, Seasonal)

PAGE NOT CONTINUED

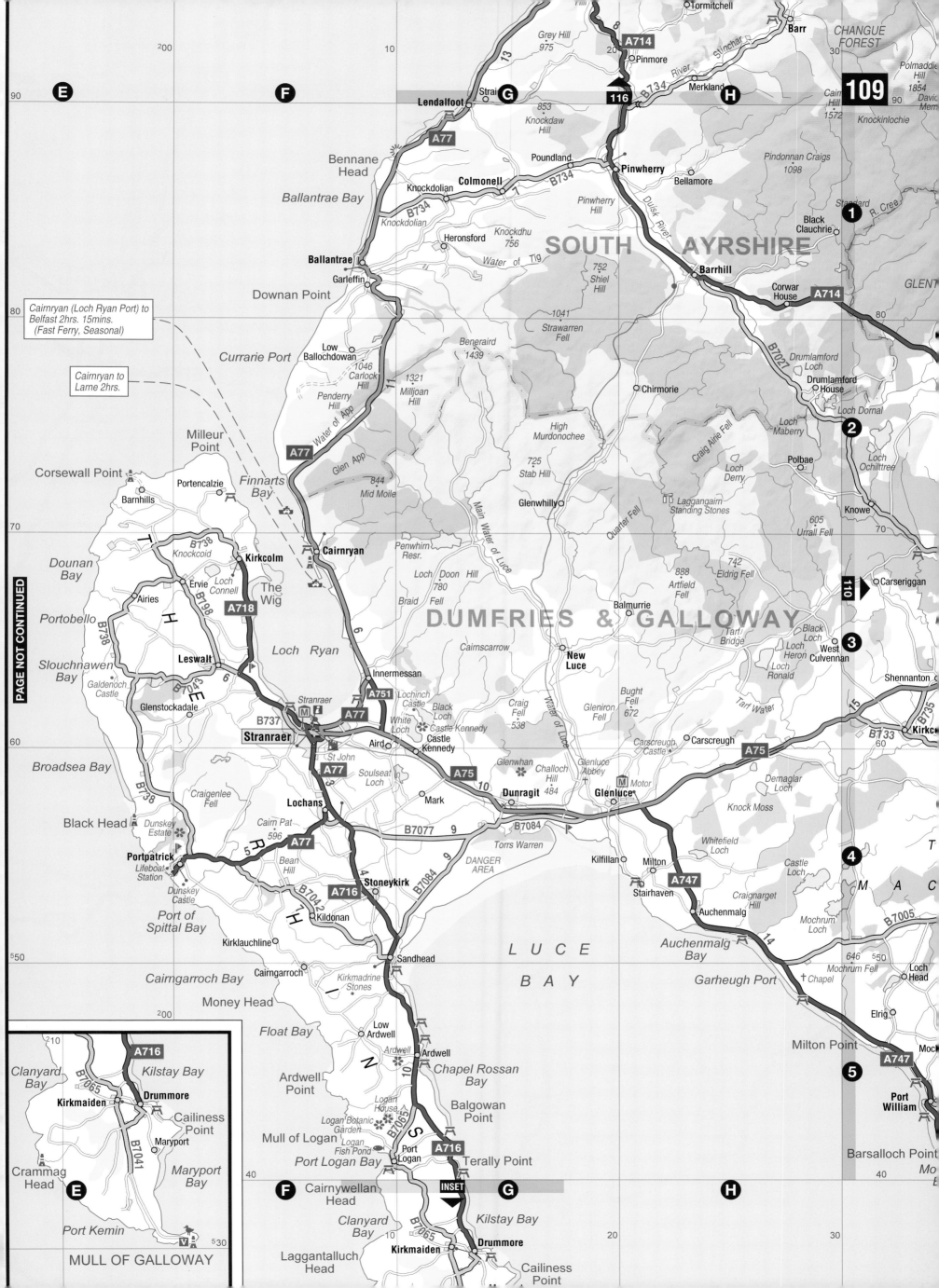

CHANGUE FOREST

Polmaddie
Hill
1854
David Mem

SOUTH AYRSHIRE

DUMFRIES & GALLOWAY

Tormitchell
Barr
Pinmore
A714
Merkland
Cairn Hill
1572

Grey Hill
975
River Stinchar
B734

8
13
20
116

Strai
G
853
Knockdaw
Hill

Lendalfoot
A77

Knockinlochie

Poundland
Pinwherry
B734

Bennane
Head
Colmonell
B734
7

Knockdolian
Pinwherry
Hill
Duisk River

Ballantrae Bay

Standard
R. Cree

Black
Clauchrie
1

Knockdolian

Heronsford
Knockdhu
756
Water of Tig

Pindonnan Craigs
1098

Ballantrae
Garleffin

Downan Point
752
Shiel
Hill

Barrhill
Corwar
House
A714
GLEN

Cairnryan (Loch Ryan Port) to
Belfast 2hrs. 15mins.
(Fast Ferry, Seasonal)

1041

Strawarren
Fell

B7027

Drumlamford
Loch

Cairnryan to
Larne 2hrs.

Currarie Port
Low
Ballochdowan
1046
Carlock
Hill
11

Beneraird
1439

Drumlamford
House

Loch Dornal

Milleur
Point
Penderry
Hill
1321
Milljoan
Hill

Chirmorie
2

Loch
Maberry

Loch Ochiltree

Corsewall Point
Portencalzie

Finnarts
Bay
A77

Glen App
844
Mid Moile

725
Stab Hill

High
Murdonochee

Craig Airie Fell

Loch
Derry

Polbae

Knowe

Barnhills

Glenwhilly

Laggangairn
Standing Stones

Quarter Fell

605
Urrall Fell
70

Dounan
Bay
B738
Knockcoid
Kirkcolm
Cairnryan

Penwhirn
Resr.

888
Artfield
Fell

742
Eldrig Fell

110
Carseriggan

Airies
Ervie
Loch
Connell
B798
The Wig

Loch Doon
780

Braid
Fell

Main Water of Luce

Black
Loch

West
Culvennan
3

Portobello
A718

Loch
Heron
Loch
Ronald

Slouchnawen
Bay
Leswalt
6
Loch Ryan

Cairnscarrow

New
Luce

Tarf
Bridge

Shennanton

Galdenoch
Castle
B7043
E

Innermessan

DUMFRIES & GALLOWAY

Tarf Water

B735
Kirkc

Glenstockadale

Stranraer
B737
A751

Lochinch
Castle
White
Loch
A77

Bught
Fell
672

Gleniron
Fell

15

B733
60

Stranraer
A77
Aird
Castle Kennedy
Castle
Kennedy
Craig
Fell
538

Carscreugh
Castle
Carscreugh
A75

Demaglar
Loch

Broadsea Bay
B738

St John
Soulseat
Loch

Glenwhan
Challoch
Hill 484
Glenluce
Abbey

Motor
Glenluce

Knock Moss

Craigenlee
Fell
Lochans
A77
3

Mark
A75
10
Dunragit

B7084

Whitefield
Loch

Black Head
Dunskey
Estate

Cairn Pat
596
B7077
9

Torrs Warren

Kilfillan

Milton

Castle
Loch
4
M

Portpatrick
Lifeboat
Station
A77
5
R
Bean
Hill

4
Stoneykirk
B7084

9
DANGER
AREA

A747
Stairhaven

Craignarget
Hill

Mochrum
Loch
B7005

Dunskey
Castle
B7042
A716

Kildonan

Auchenmalg

Port of
Spittal Bay
H

Kirklauchline

Sandhead
Auchenmalg
Bay
14

Cairngarroch Bay
Cairngarroch

Kirkmadrine
Stones

LUCE
BAY

Garheugh Port

646
Mochrum Fell
550

Loch
Head

Money Head
200
Float Bay
I
N

Low
Ardwell
Ardwell

Chapel
† Chapel

Elrig

Ardwell
Point
Ardwell

Chapel Rossan
Bay

Milton Point
A747
5

Mo

A716
B7065
Kilstay Bay

Balgowan
Point

Port
William

Clanyard
Bay
Kirkmaiden
Drummore

Logan
House
Logan Botanic
Garden

Barsalloch Point
Mo

Maryport
Cailiness
Point

Mull of Logan
Logan
Fish Pond

Port
Logan
A716
Terally Point

Crammag
Head
E
B7041
Maryport
Bay

Port Logan Bay

F
Cairnywellan
Head
G
H

Port Kemin
530

MULL OF GALLOWAY

Clanyard
Bay
B7065
Kilstay Bay

Kirkmaiden
Drummore

Laggantalluch
Head

Cailiness
Point

PAGE NOT CONTINUED

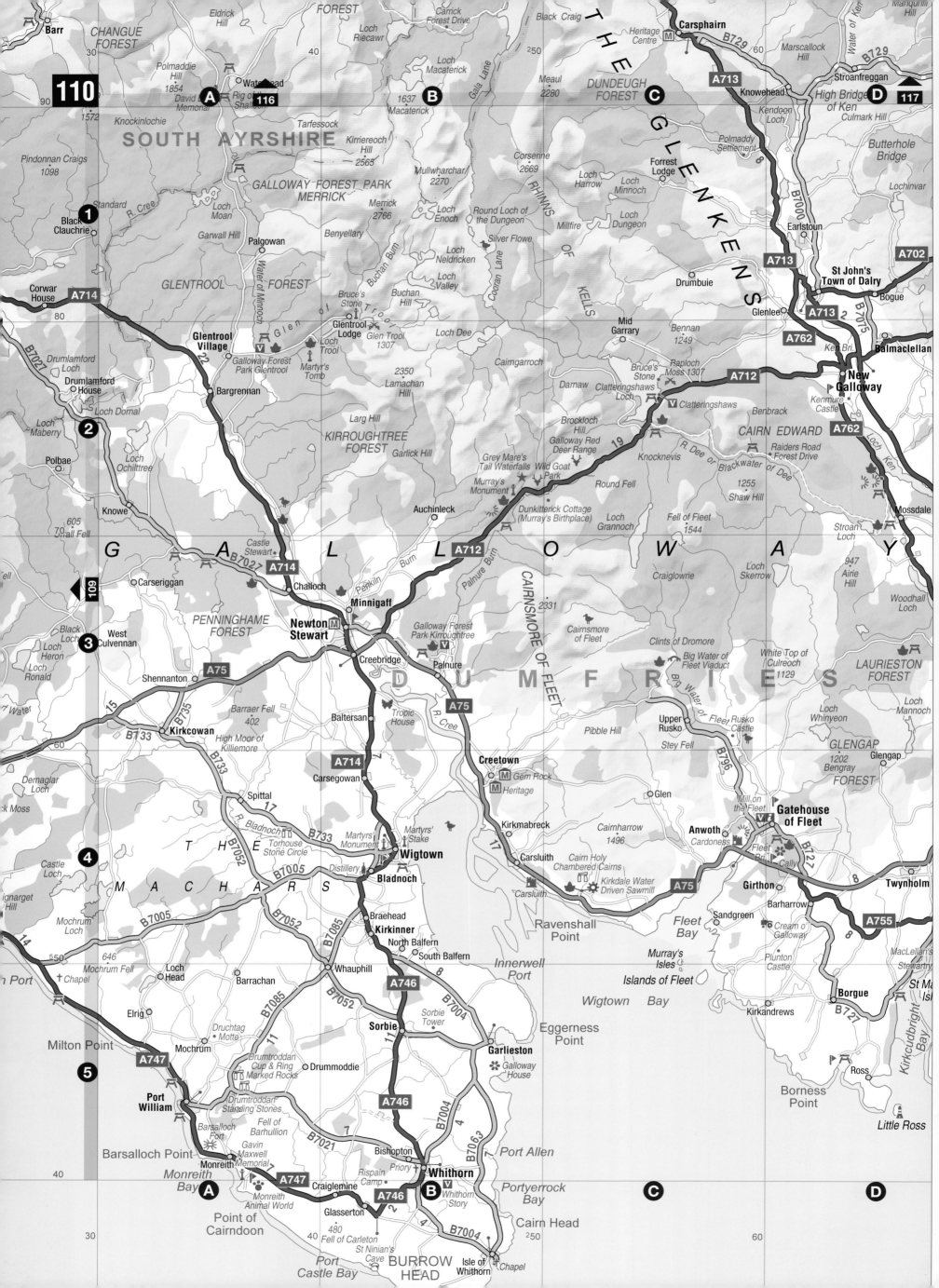

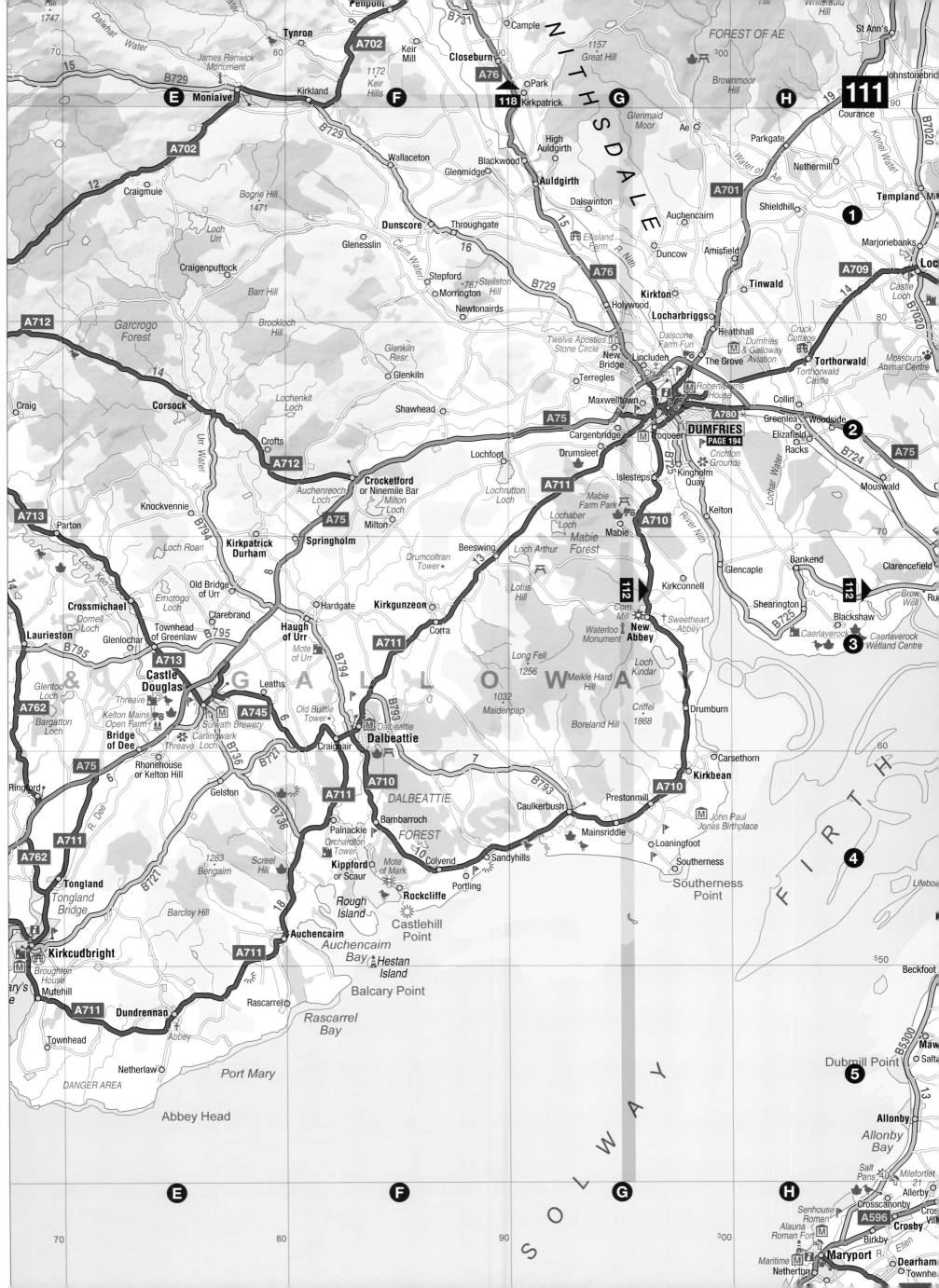

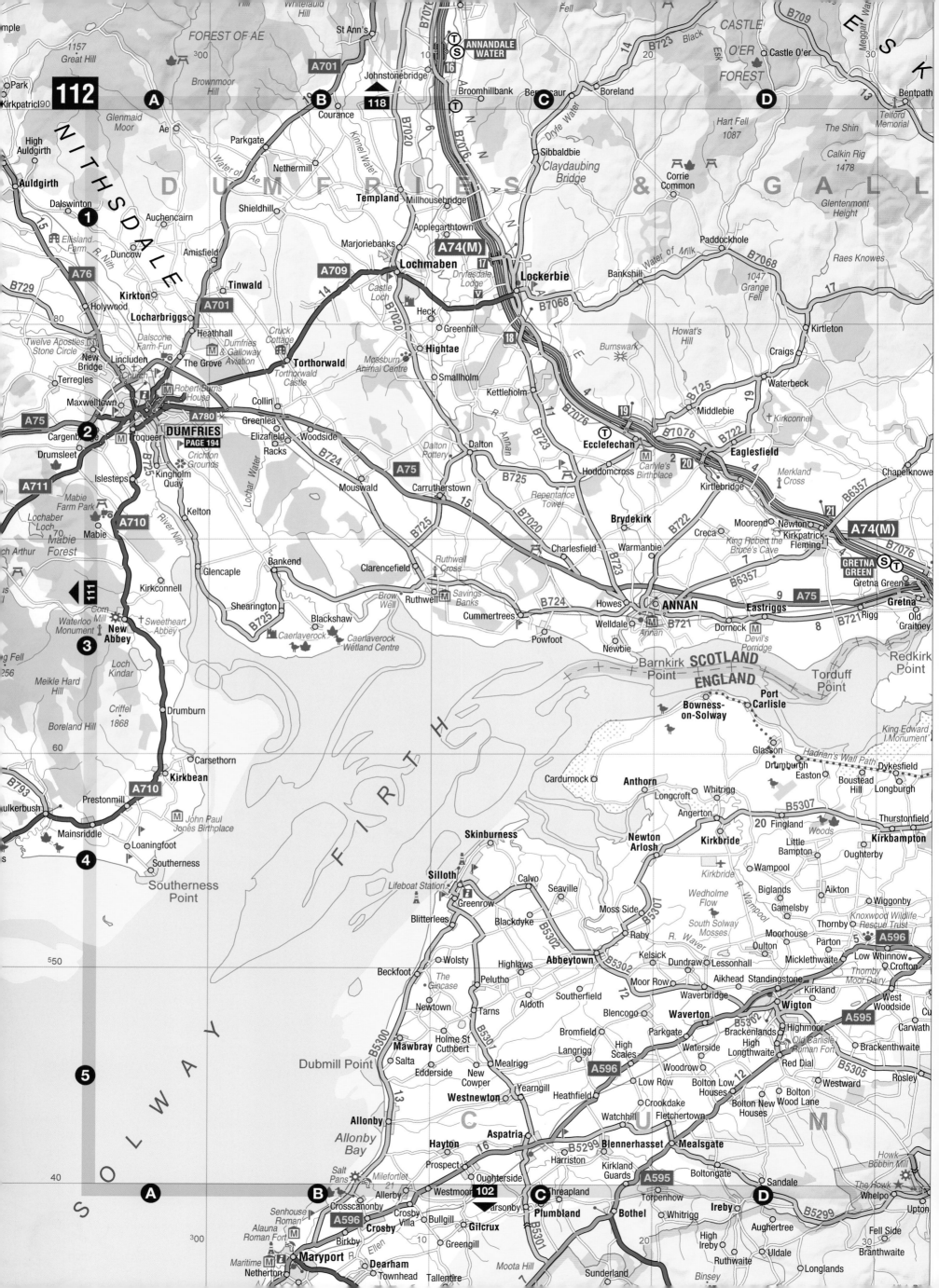

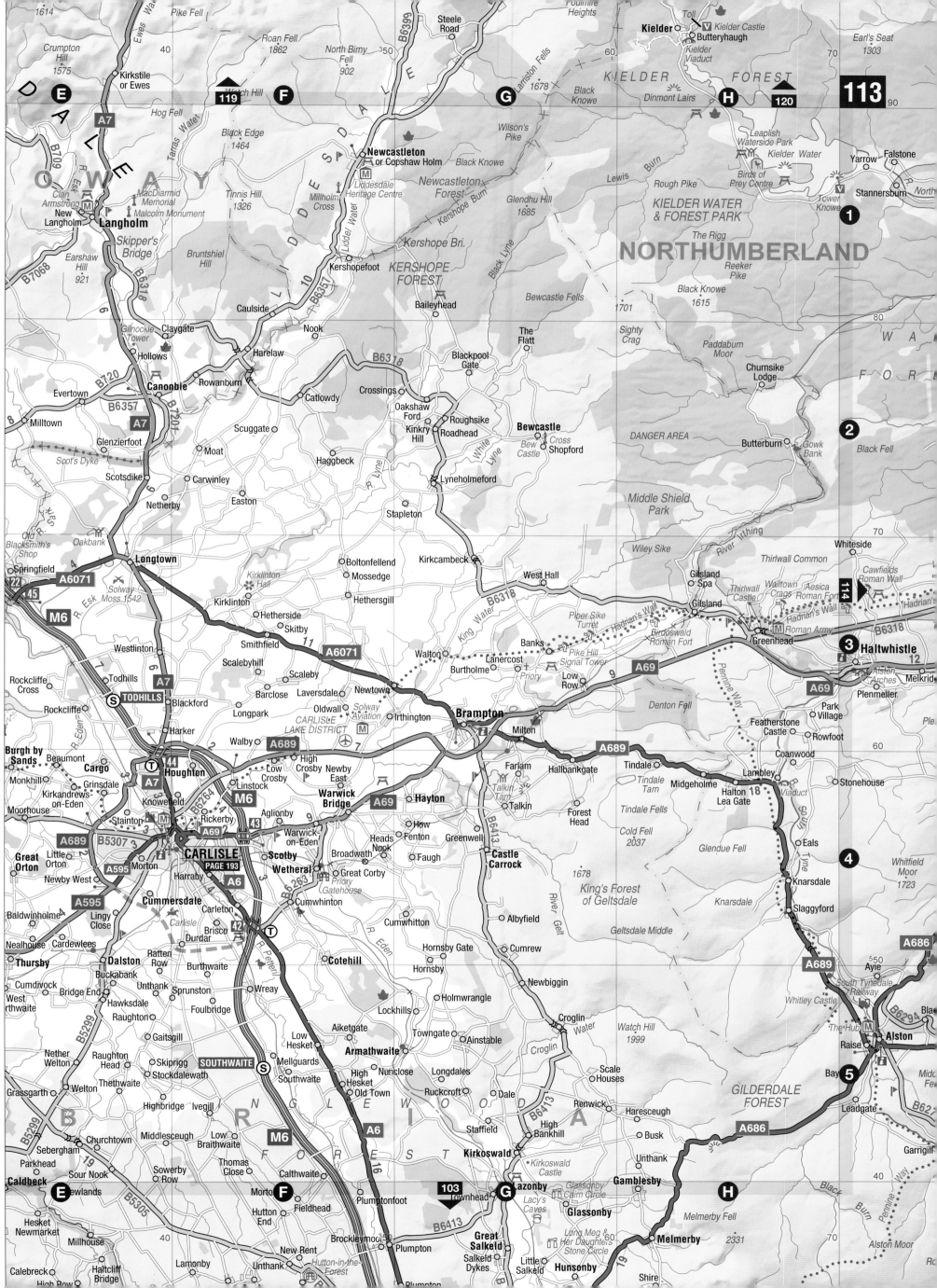

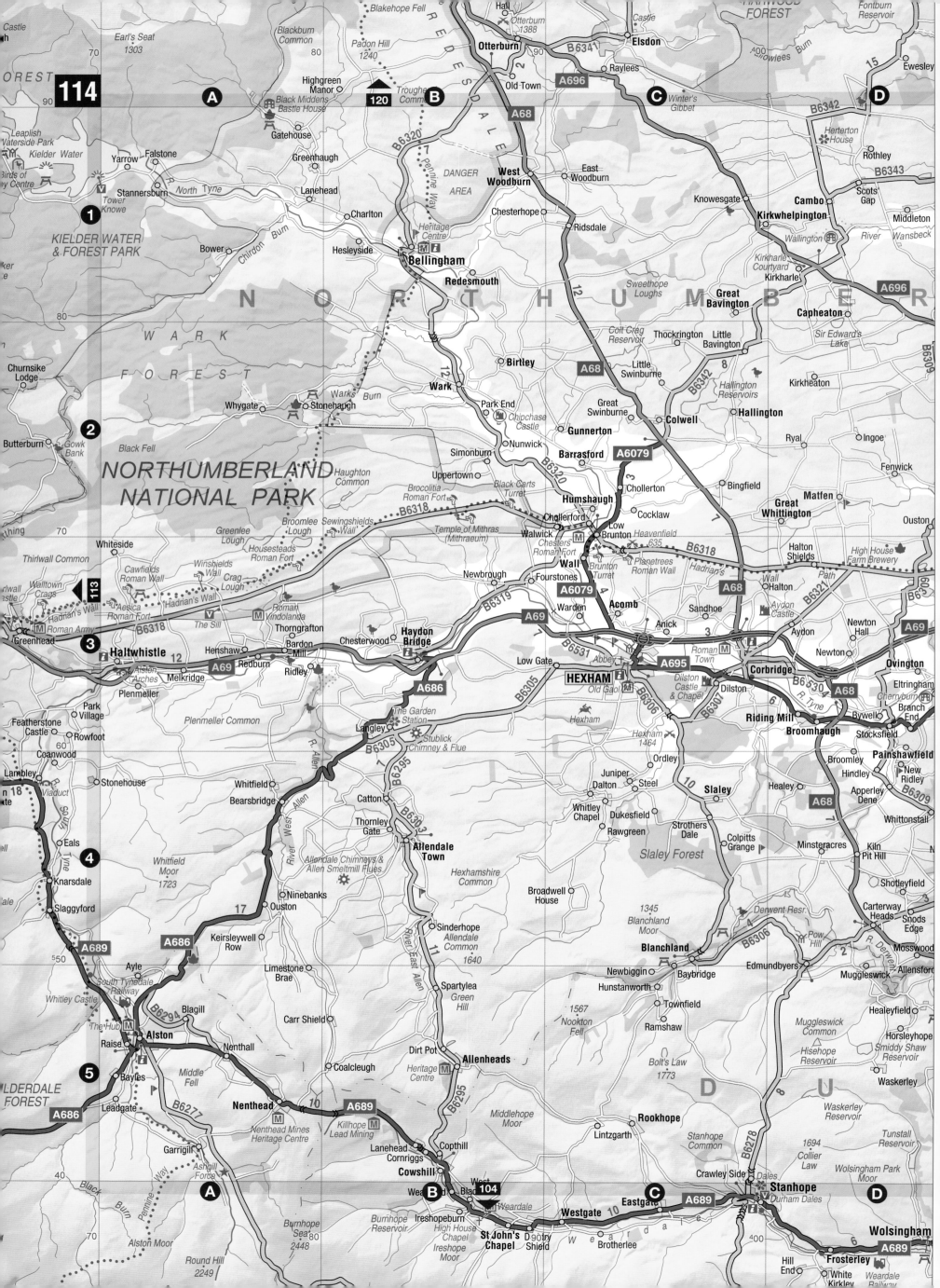

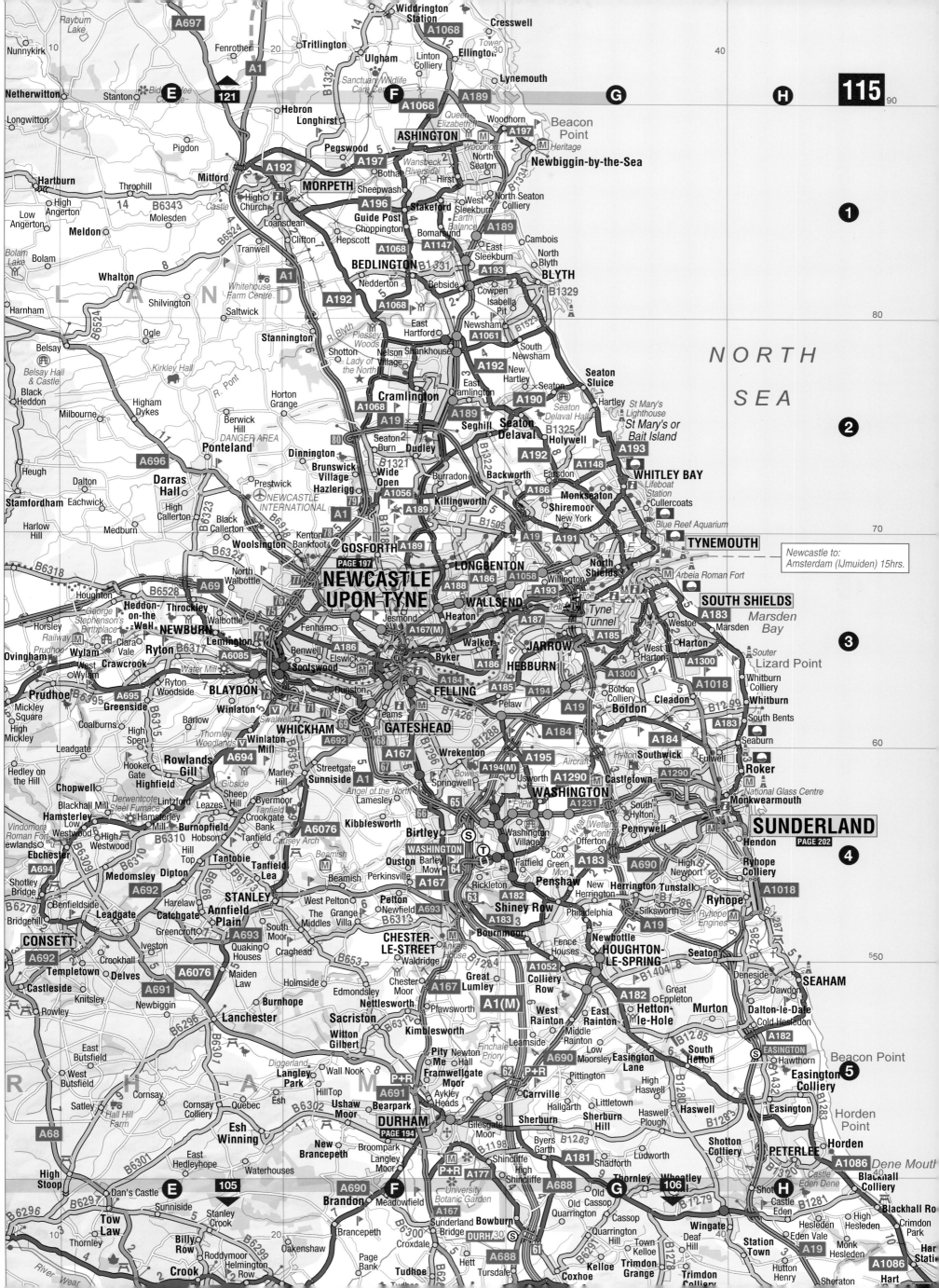

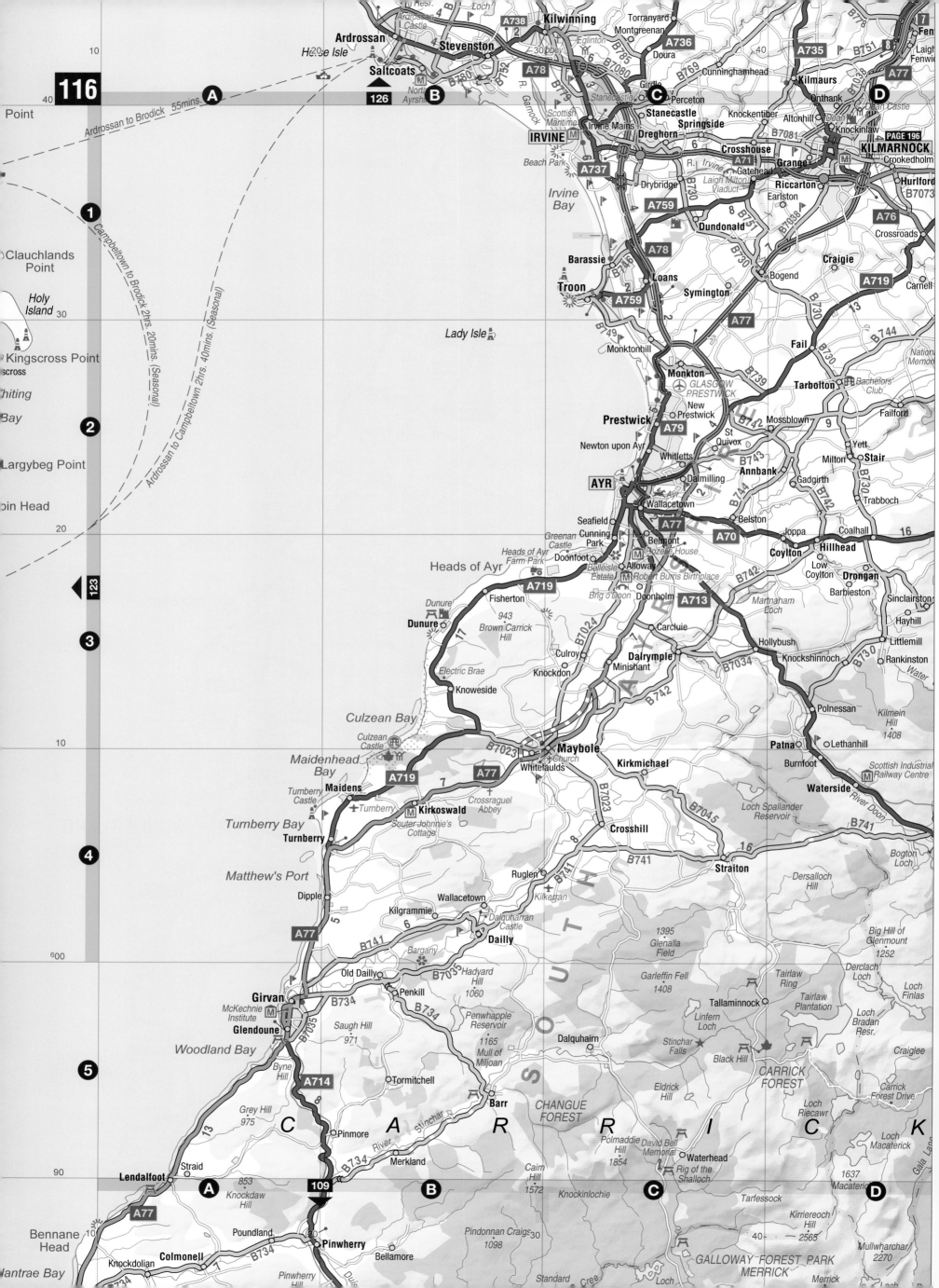

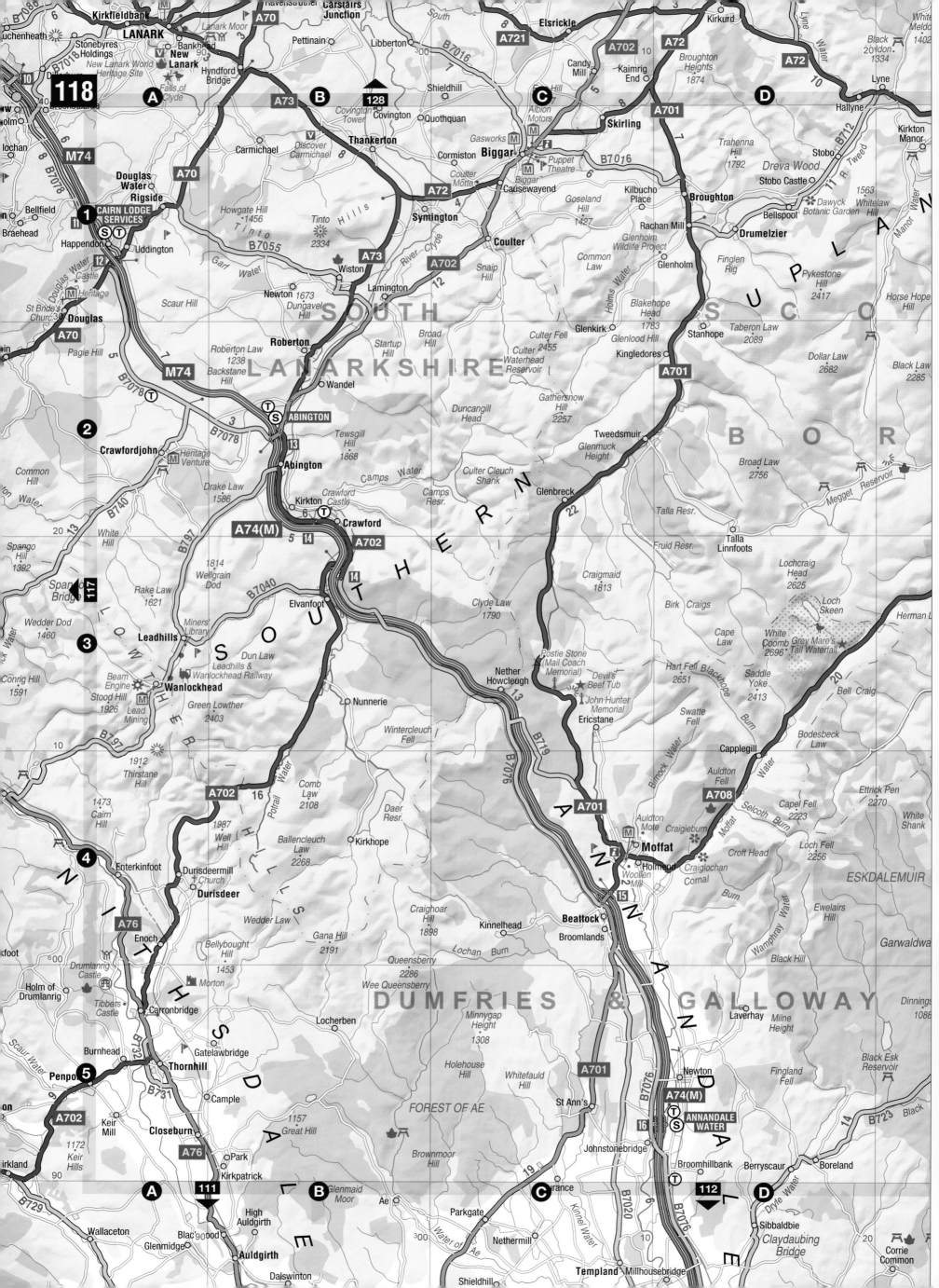

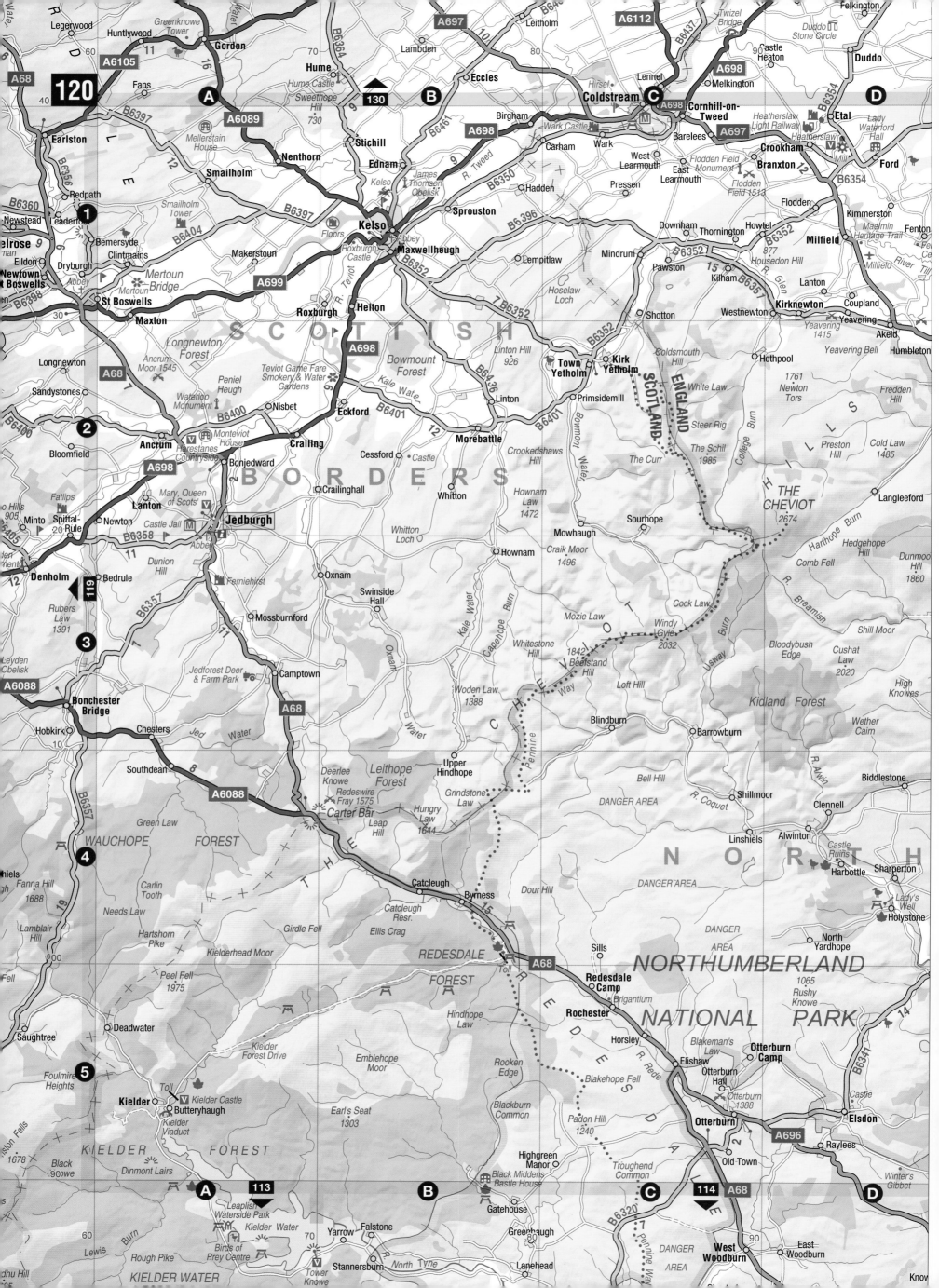

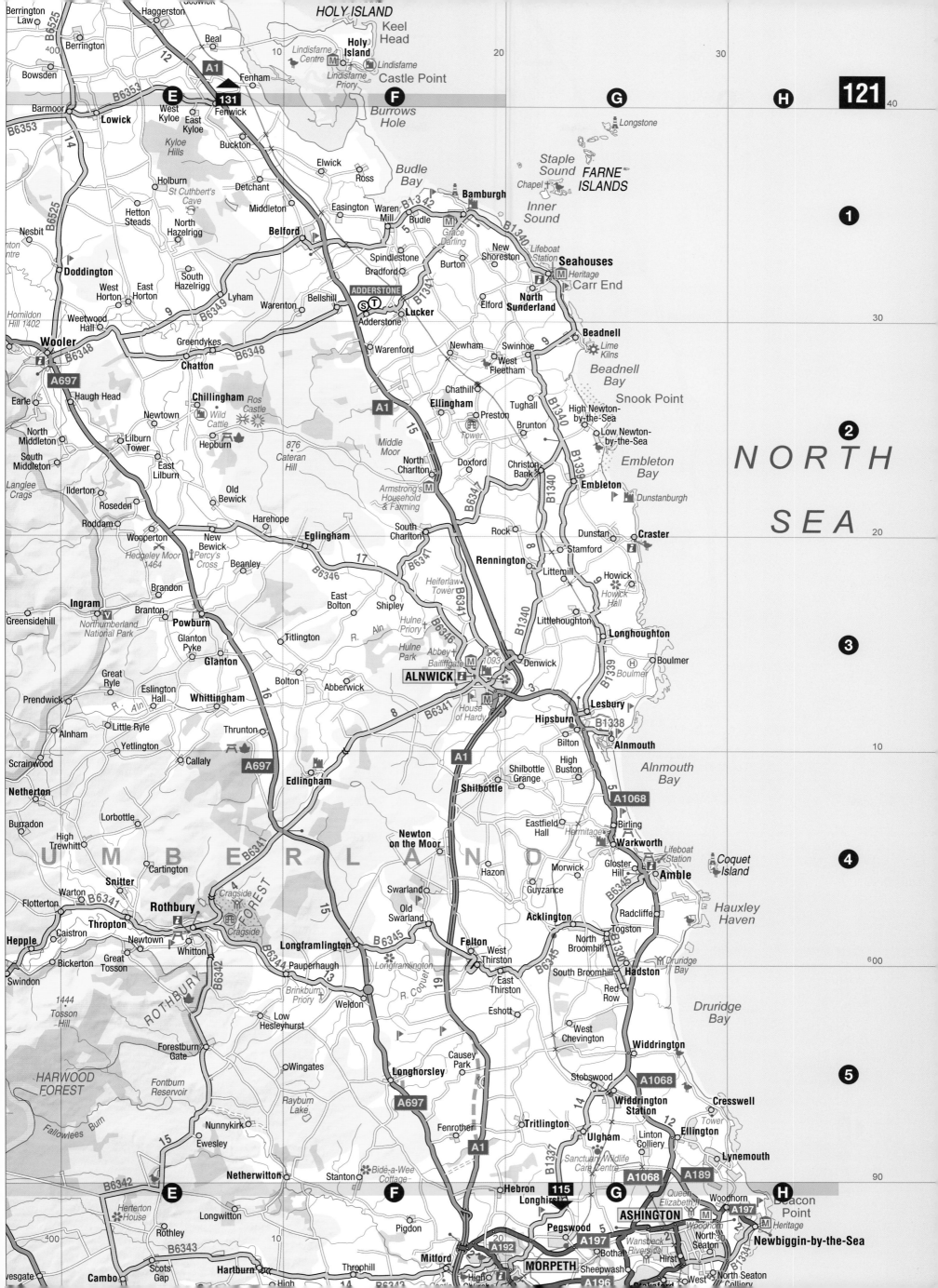

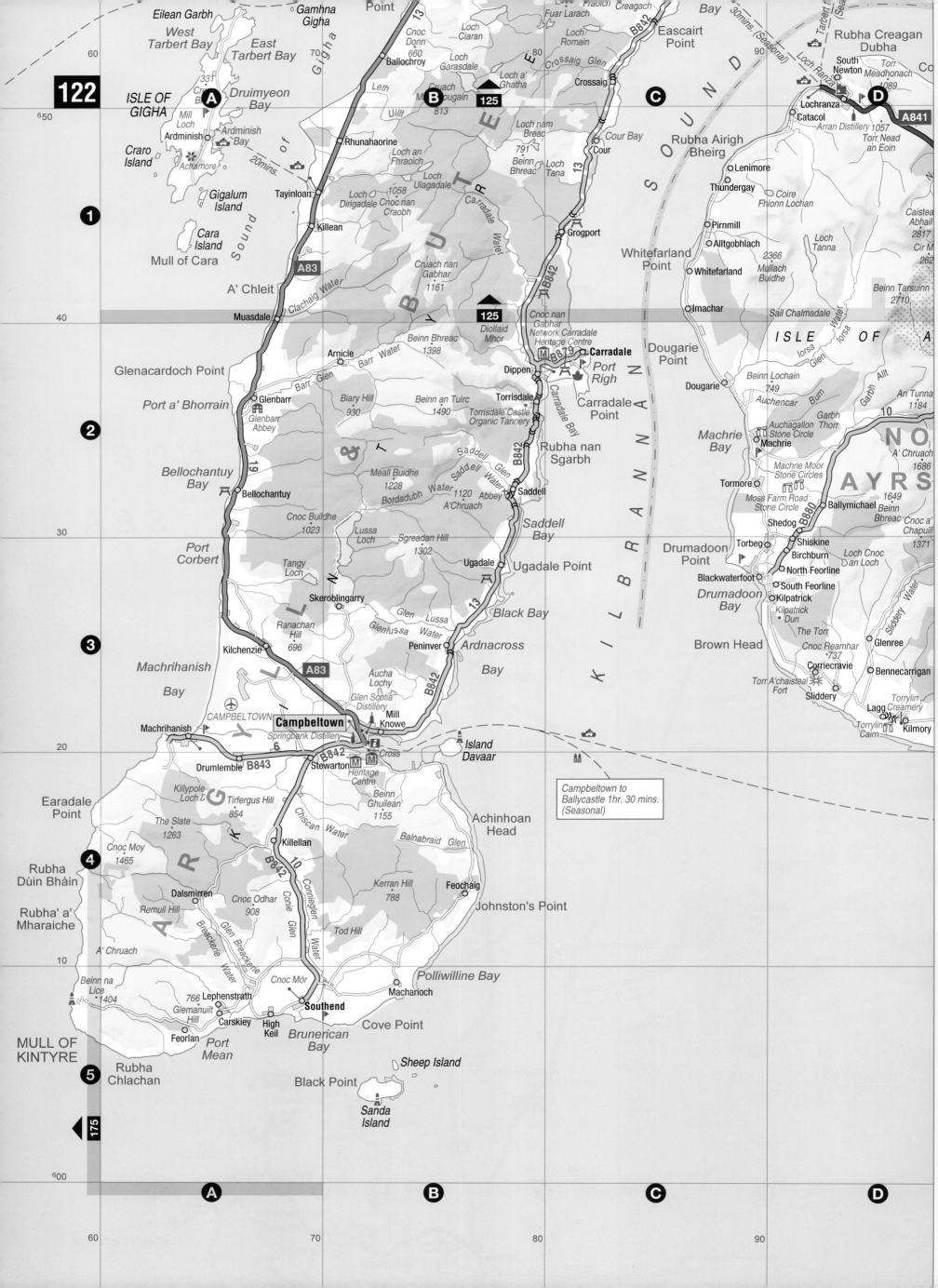

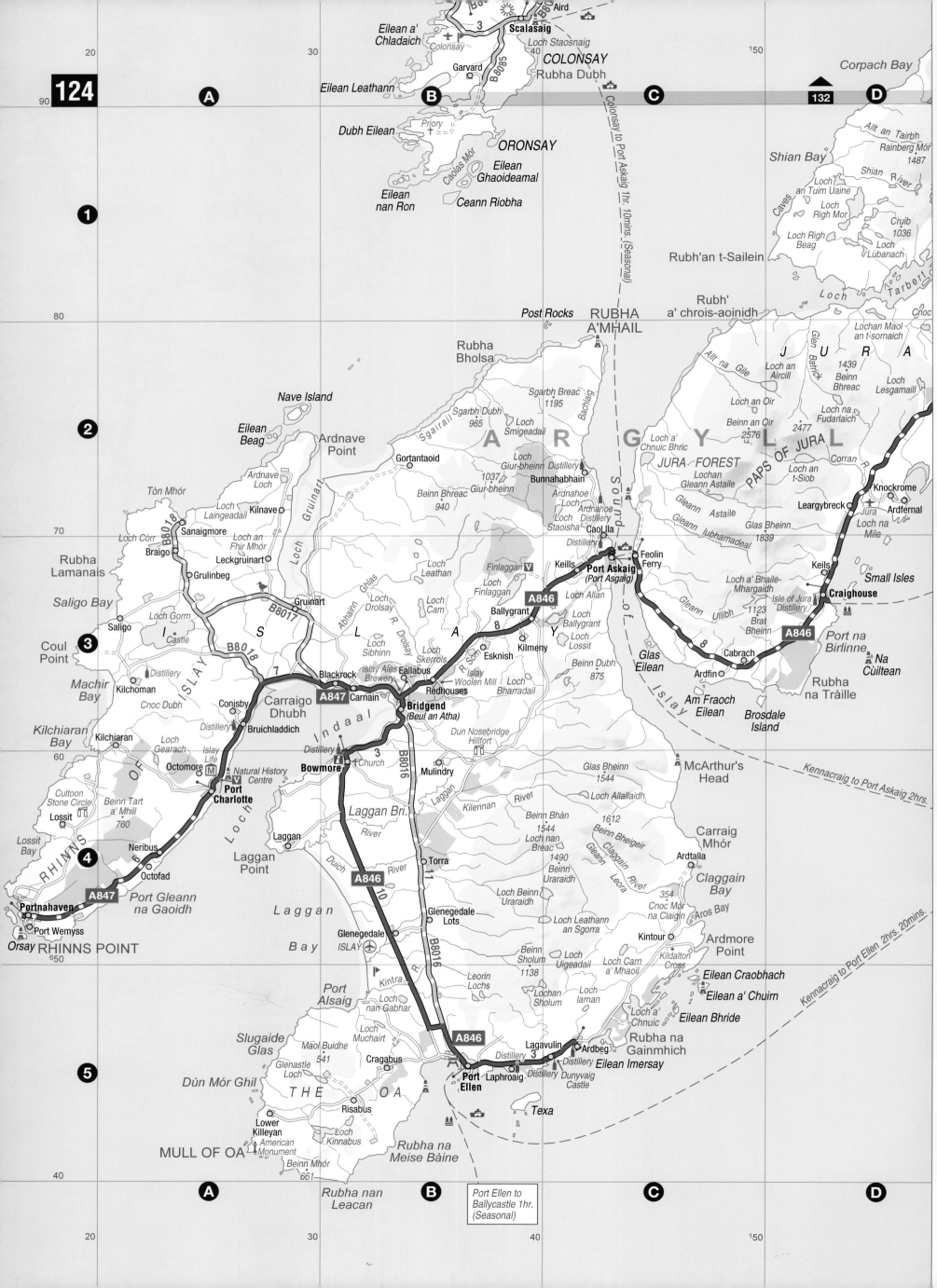

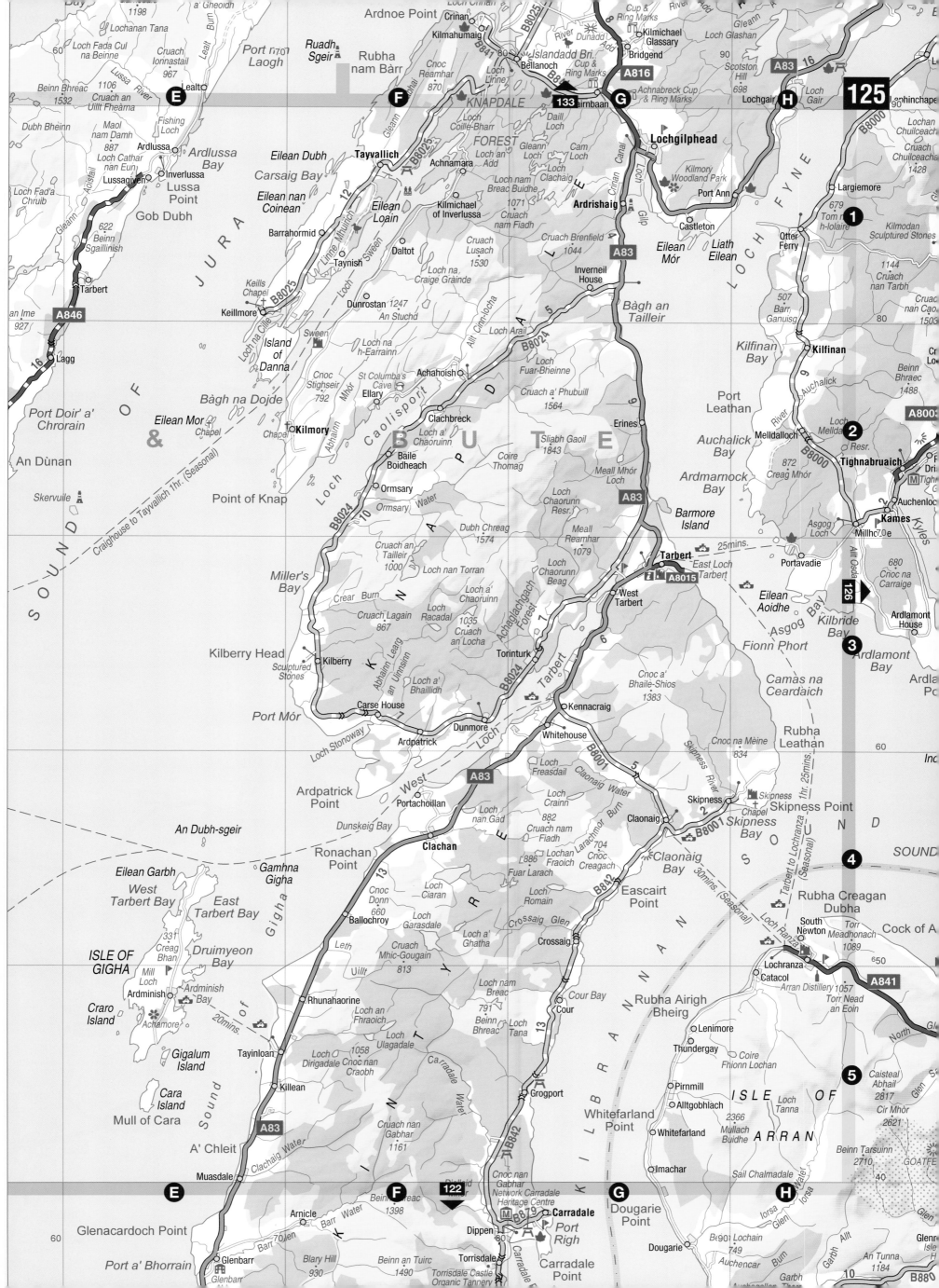

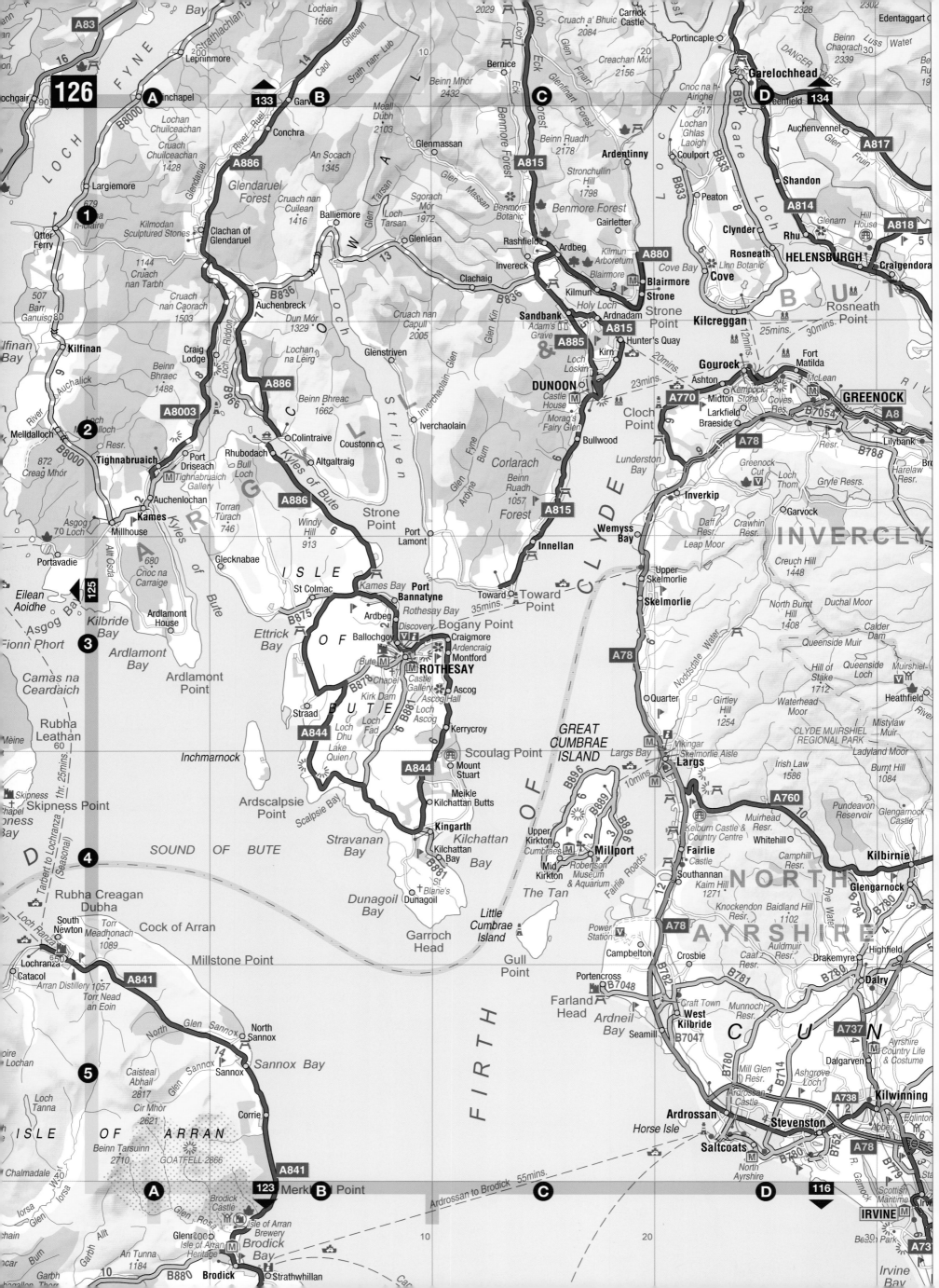

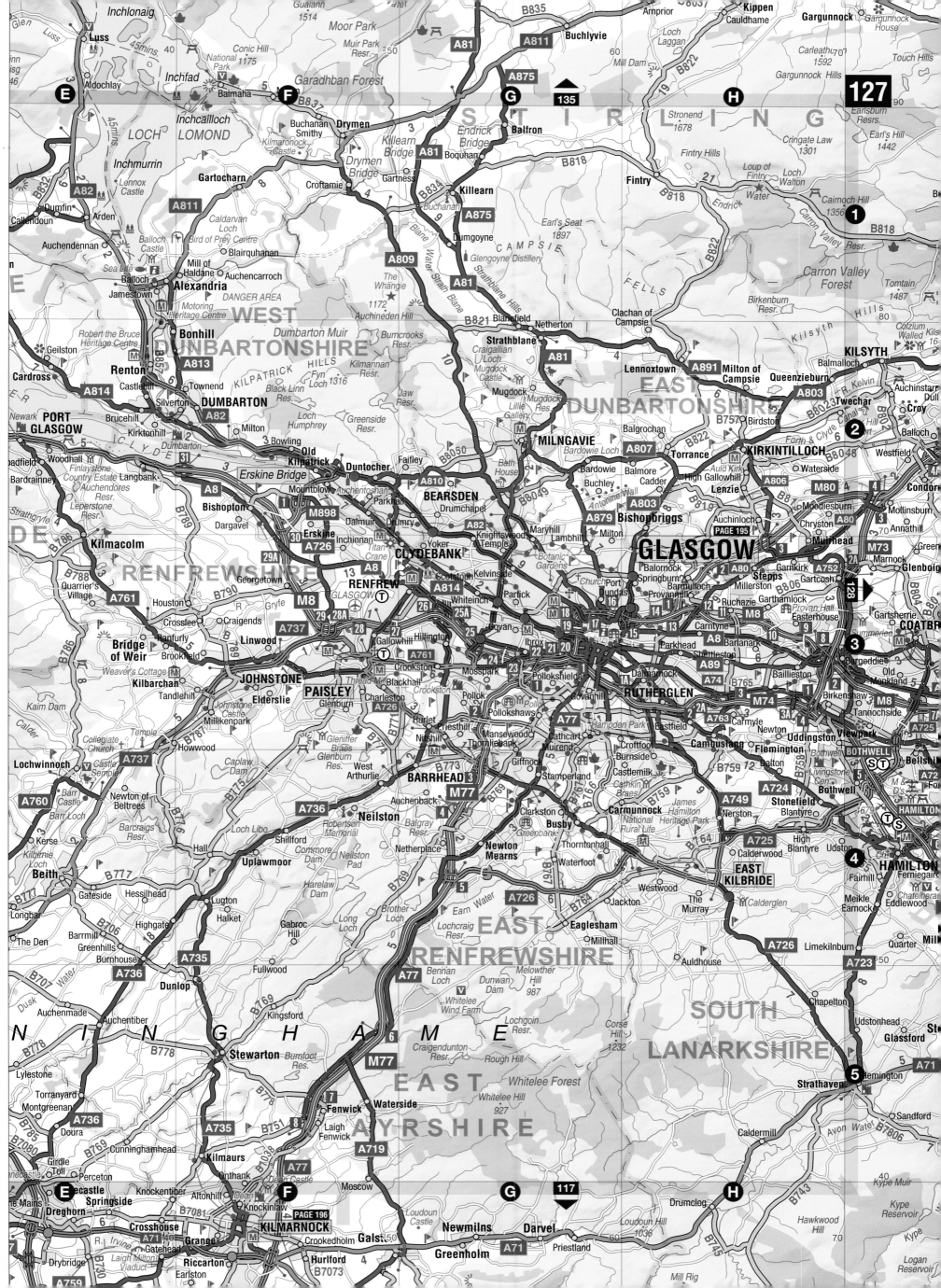

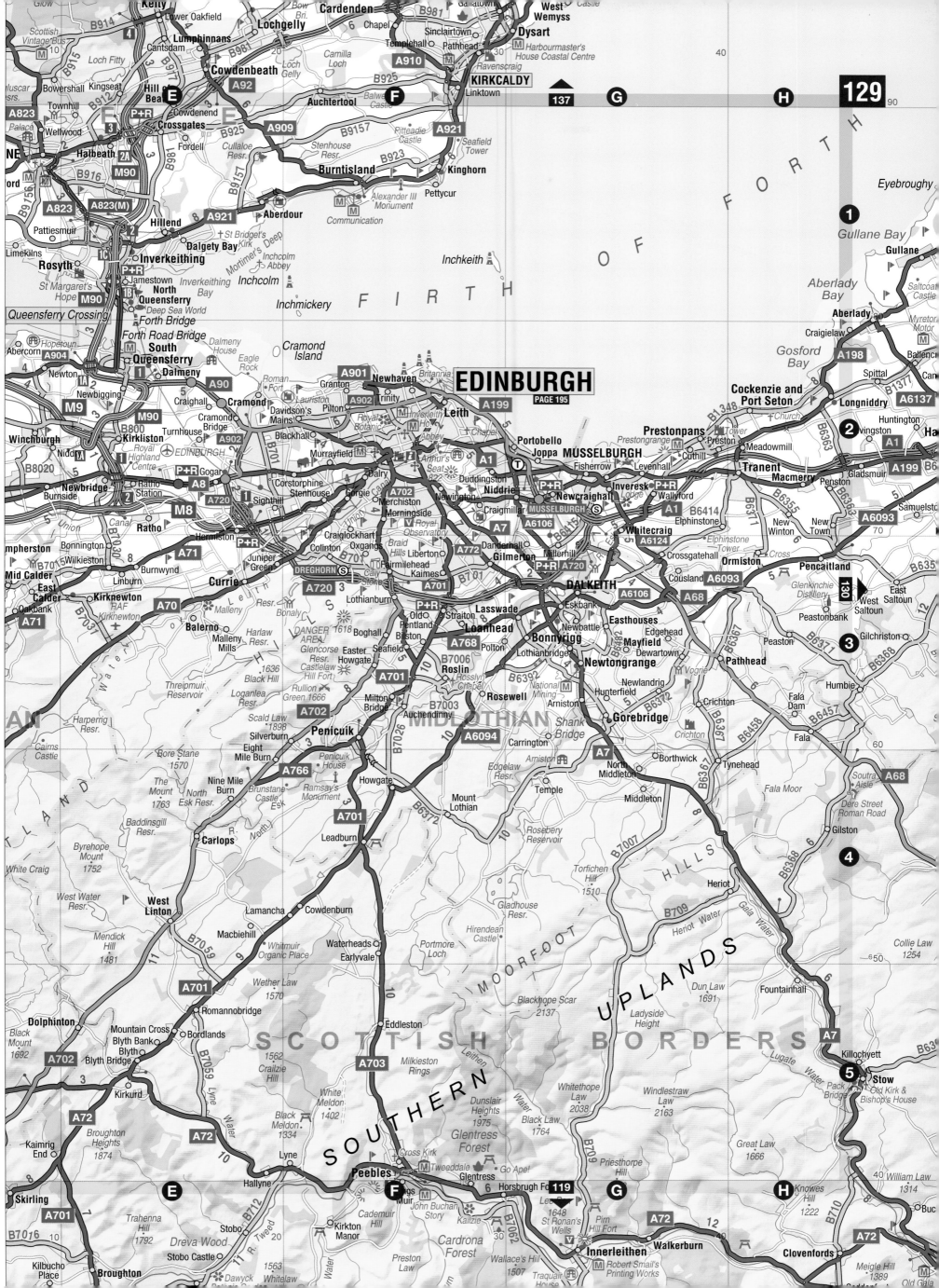

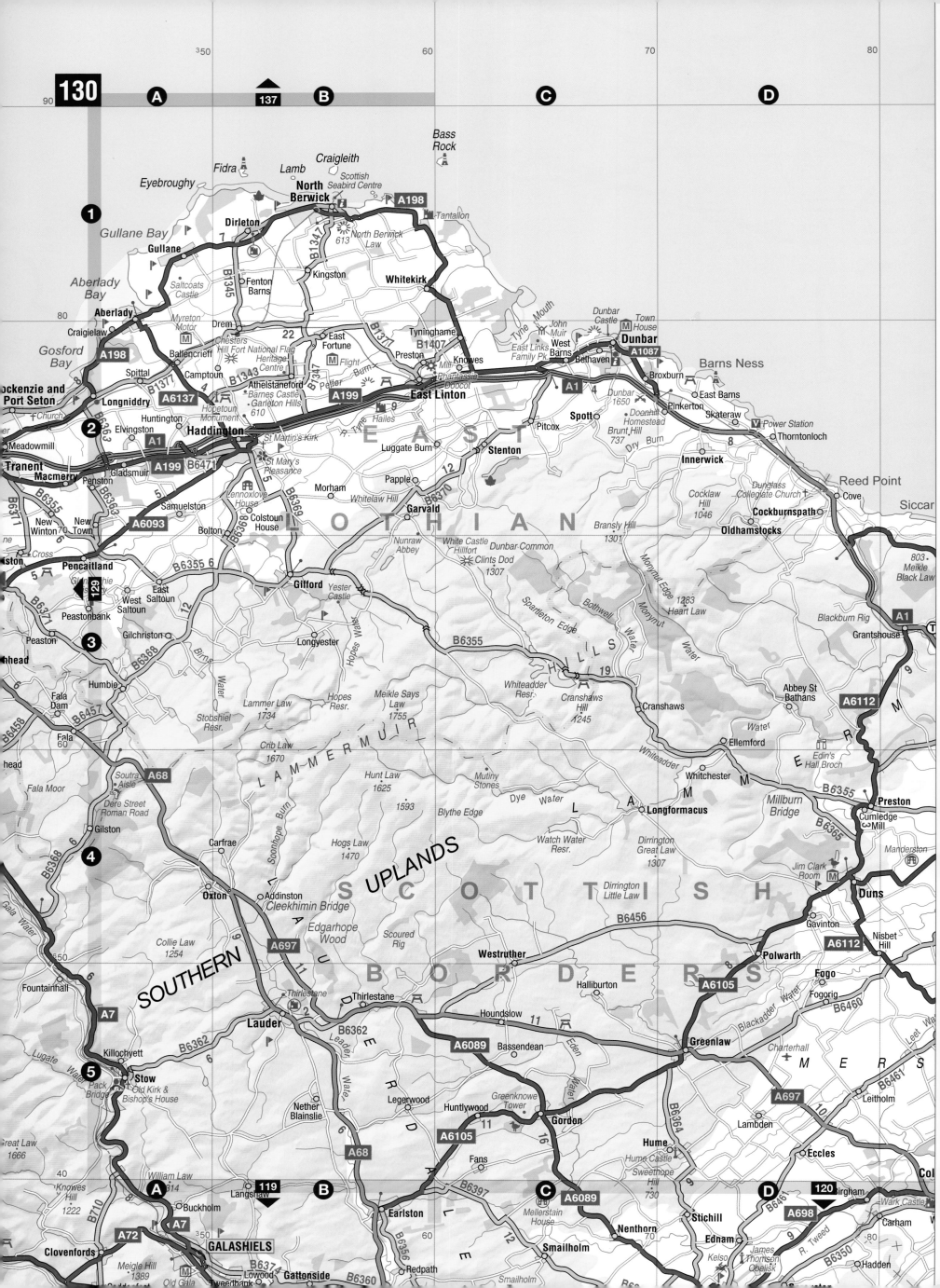

90   400   10   20

90

1

80

N O R T H   S E A

70

2

Point

Fast Castle
Head

*Fast
Castle
Telegraph*
Hill Lumsdaine

ST ABB'S HEAD

Cross Law
744

Coldingham Moor 11

B6438 ○St Abbs

*Lifeboat
Staion* *Coldingham*

Coldingham○↑*Priory* *Bay Lifeboat
Station*

3

A1107

Houndwood

Eye *Water*

M *Gunsgreen
House*

Eyemouth

M

Gunsgreenhill

859
*Horseley
Hill*

B6438

B6355

Reston 18

A1107

Water

Burnmouth ○Ross

Ayton

○Auchencrow

60

B6438

B6437

A1

Lintlaw

B6355

B6355

Chirnside 12

Lamberton○

Marshall
Meadows

Chirnsidebridge

*Tithe
Barn* Clappers○

*Halidon
Hill*

Arch

Edrom

Whiteadder *Water*

Foulden 1333

*Bell
Tower*

4

A6105

A6105

Allanton○

B6437

Hutton

B6460

Paxton

B6461

Castle *Cell Block*

M

BERWICK-UPON-TWEED

B6460

Whitsome○

B6461

Tweed

M
M

Tweedmouth

Fishwick○

*Union
Bridge* Loanend○

Lifeboat Station

Spittal

650

Swinton 12

Horndean○

*Chain Bridge
Honey Farm*

East Ord

A698

*Pot-a-
Doodle-Do* *Redshin
Cove*

A1167

Horncliffe

Murton○

Thornton○

Scremerston○

B6470

Ladykirk

Norham

B6470

West
Allerdean

B6525

○Cheswick

Goswick

LINDISFARNE
HOLY ISLAND

5

Simprim○

Upsettlington○ 12

Shoreswood○ Shoresdean○

Ancroft

Haggerston○

A6112

*Twizel
Bridge* Grindon○

Felkington○

Berrington
Law○

Keel
Head

*Lindisfarne
Centre* M

**Holy
Island** *Lindisfarne
Castle Point*

B6437

*Duddo
Stone Circle*

B6354

Berrington○

Beal○

A1

Fenham○

*Lindisfarne
Priory* *Burrows
Hole*

40

Hirsel

Lennel○

Castle
Heaton○

Duddo

Bowsden○

12

○Melkington

NORTHUMBERLAND

○West
Kyloe

121

E **Cornhill-on-
Tweed**

A698

A697

*Heatherslaw
Light Railway* ○**Etal** **F**

*Waterford
Hall*

Barmoor○

B6353

Lowick

G East
Kyloe

H

Barelees○

○Fenwick

West
Learmouth

Crookham

*Heatherslaw
Mill*

Ford

B6353 14 *Kyloe
Hills*

Buckton

Elwick○

Ross○

*Staple
Sound* FAR
ISLA

East
Learmouth

Cranxton

*Flodden Field
Monument*

B6354 400

10

*Budle
Bay*

Chapel

Pressen○

*Flodden
Field 1513*

Holburn○

*St Cuthbert's
Cave*

Detchant○

Waren○

Middleton

Easington

Bamburgh

20

Inner

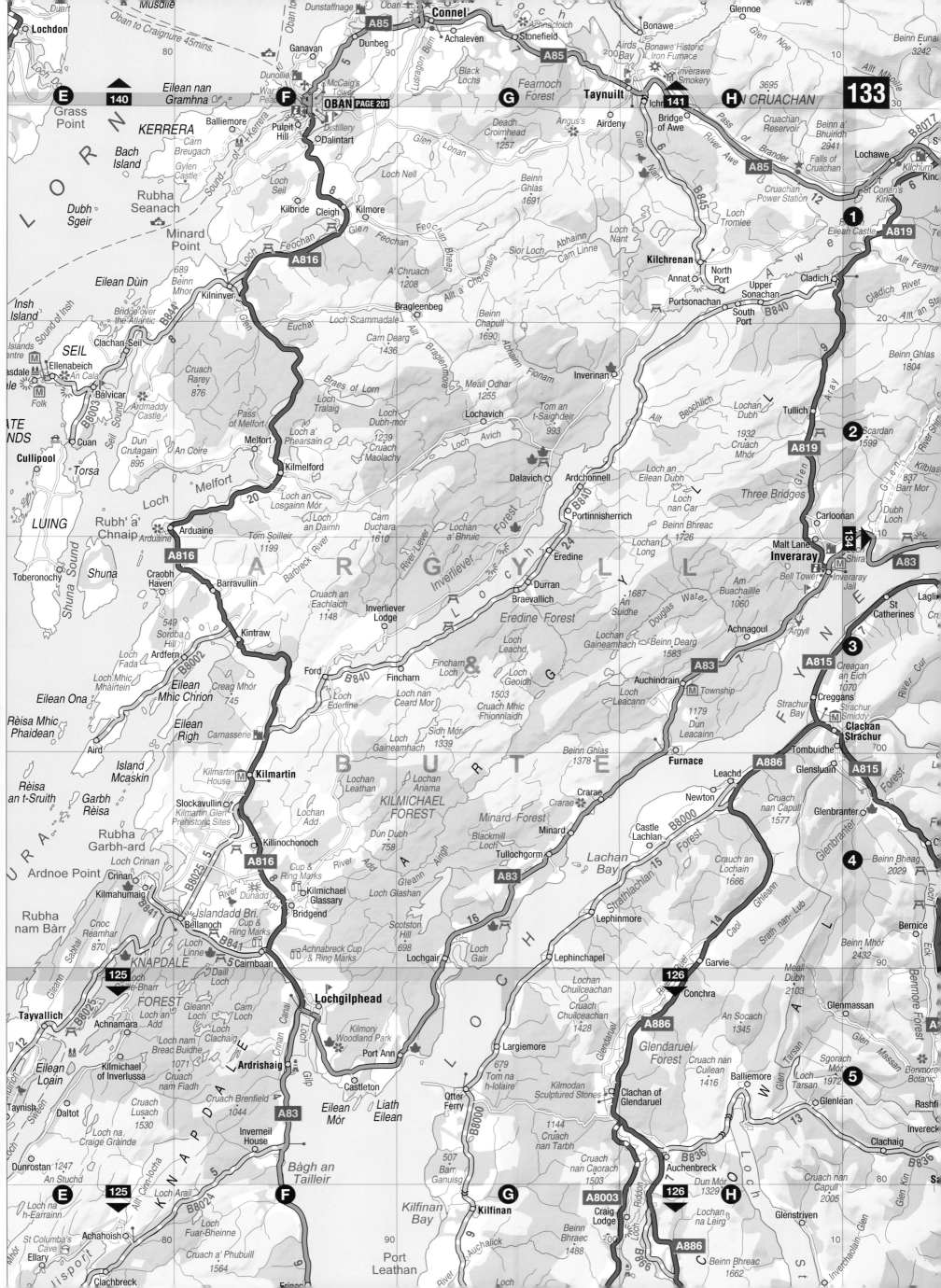

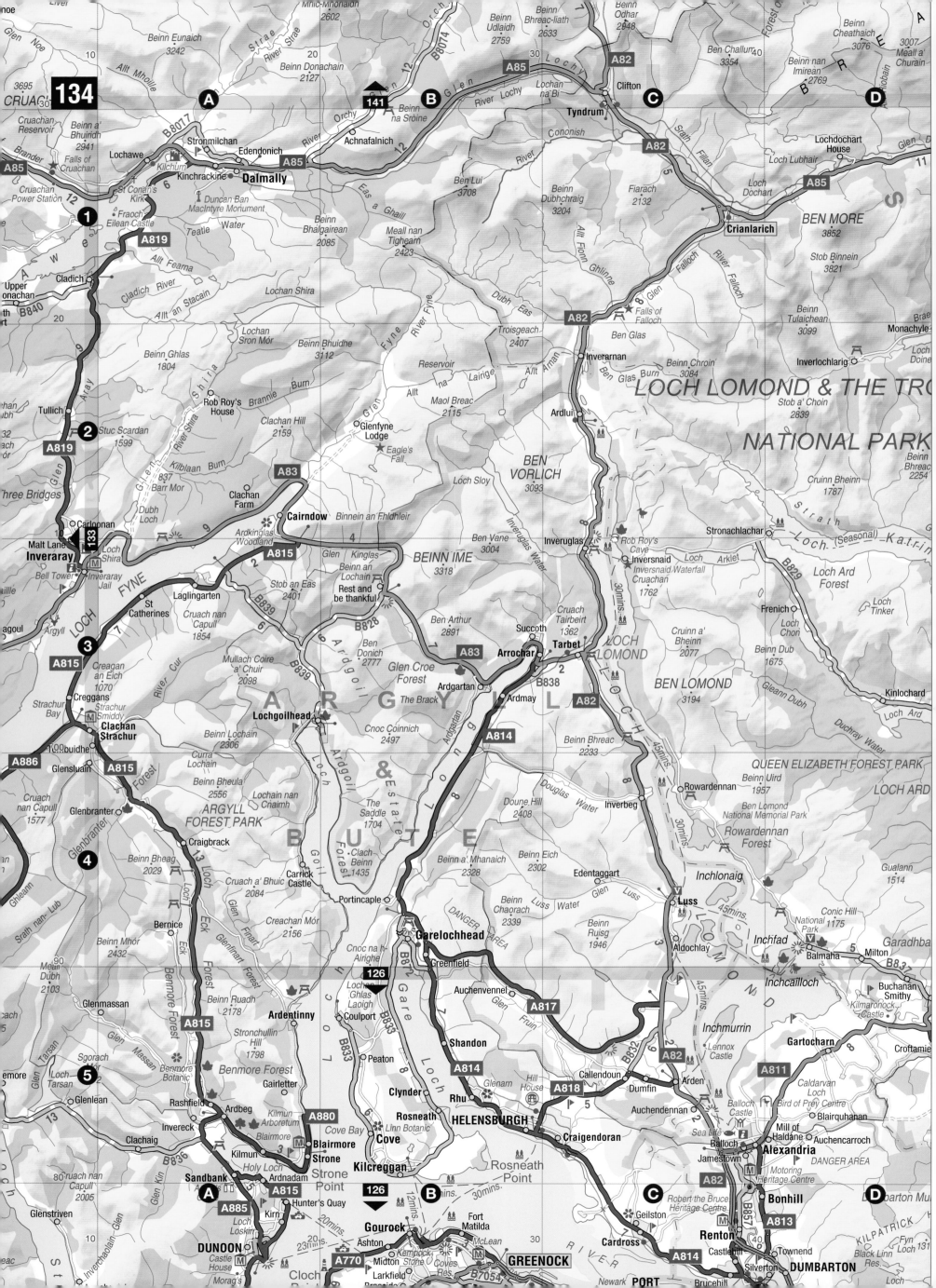

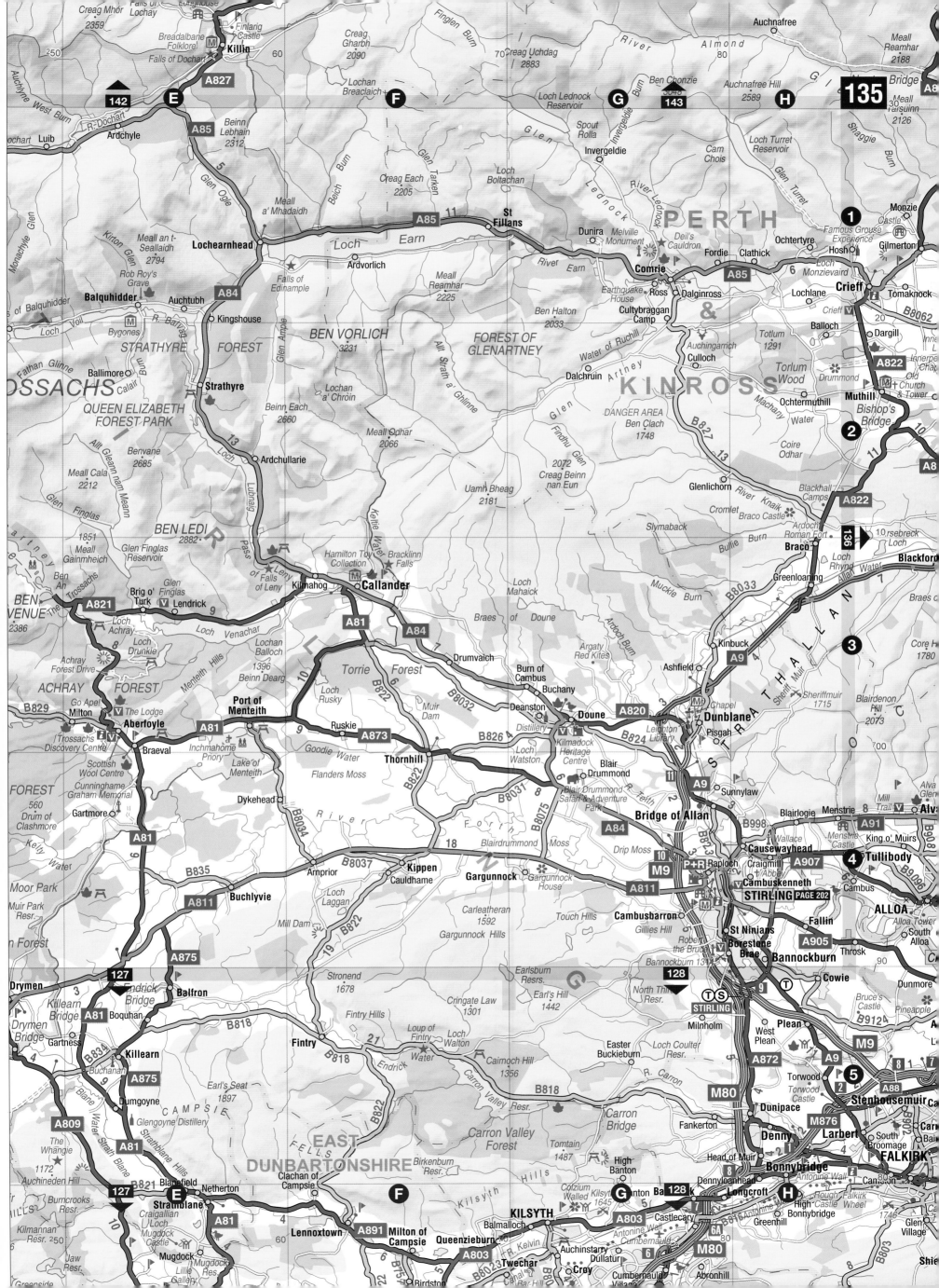

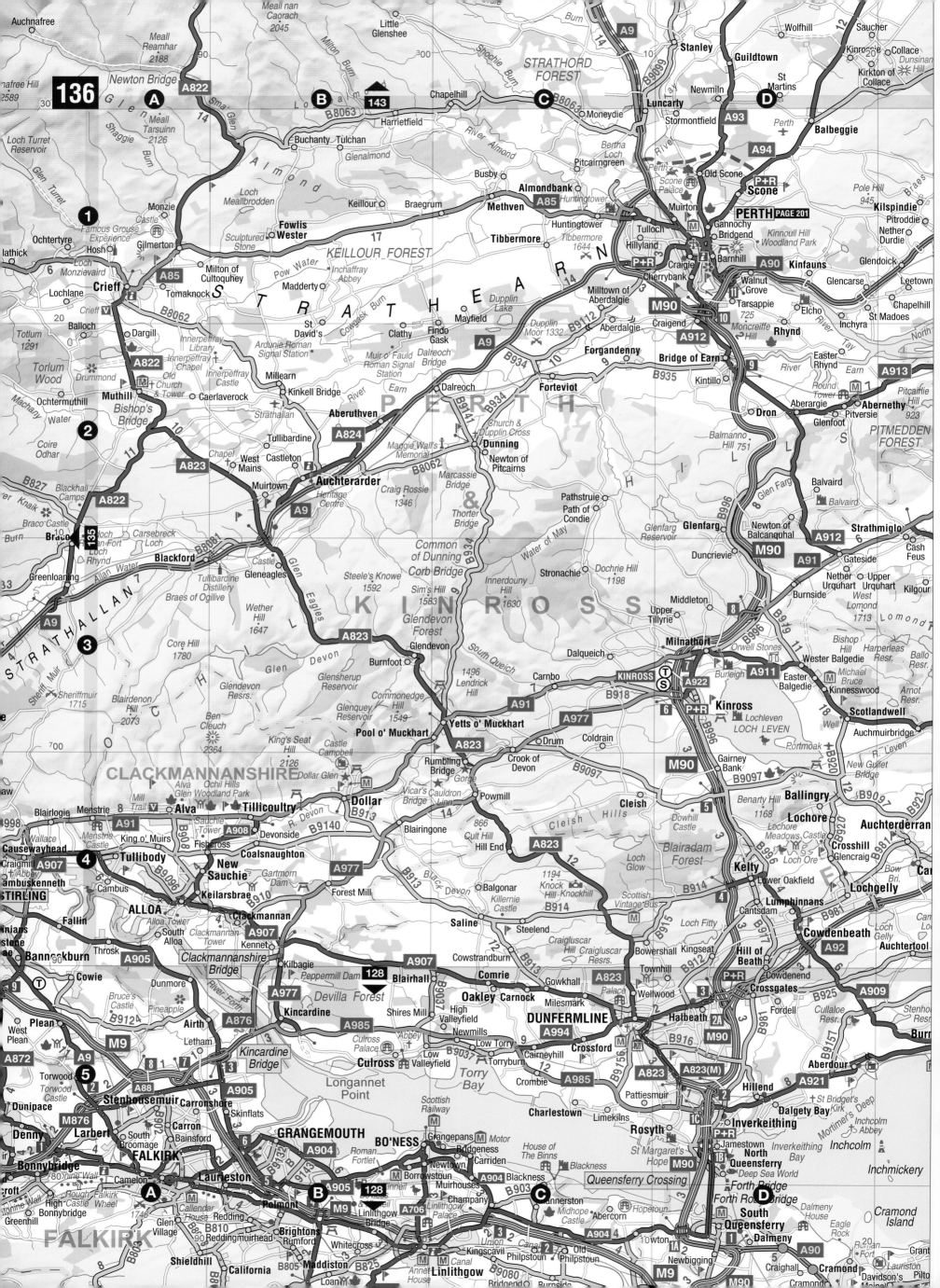

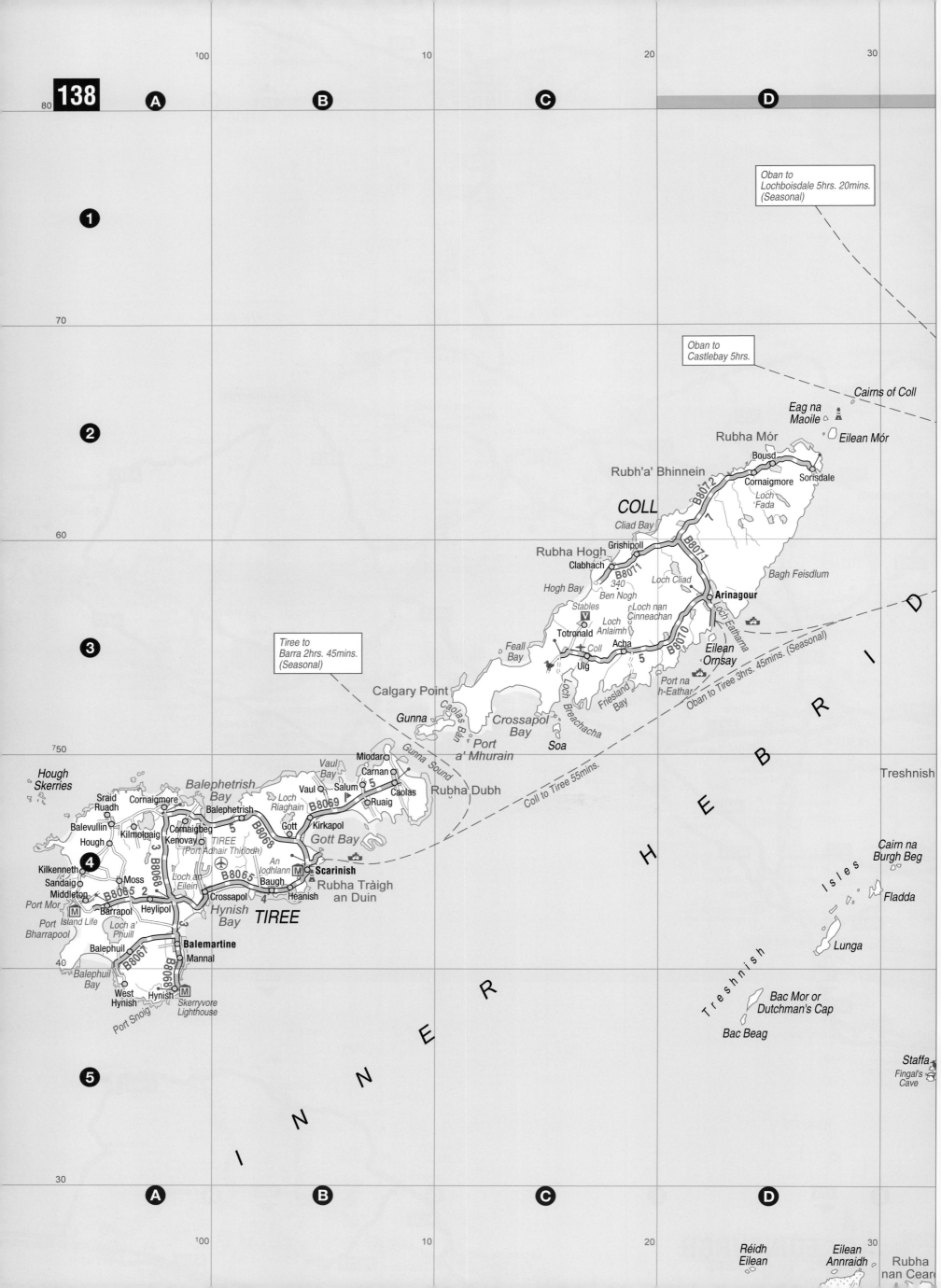

80

100   10   20   30

A   B   C   D

70

Oban to Lochboisdale 5hrs. 20mins. (Seasonal)

1

Oban to Castlebay 5hrs.

Cairns of Coll

2

Eag na Maoile

Eilean Mór

Rubha Mór

Bousd

COLL

Cornaigmore   Sorisdale

Rubh'a' Bhinnein

Loch Fada

60

Cliad Bay

B8072

Rubha Hogh   Grishipoll

Clabhach

B8071

Bagh Feisdlum

Hogh Bay   340   Loch Cliad

Ben Nogh

Arinagour

Stables   Loch nan Cinneachan

Feall Bay   Totronald   Loch Anlaimh   B8010

Coll   Acha   5   Eilean Ornsay

3   Uig   Port na h-Eathar

Tiree to Barra 2hrs. 45mins. (Seasonal)

Calgary Point   Loch Breachacha   Friesland Bay   Oban to Tiree 3hrs. 45mins. (Seasonal)

Gunna   Caolas Bàn   Port a' Mhurain   Crossapol Bay   Soa

H   E   B   R   I   D

750   Gunna Sound   Treshnish

Hough Skerries   Miodar   Coll to Tiree 55mins.

Balephetrish Bay   Vaul Bay   Carnan   Salum   5

Sraid Ruadh   Cornaigmore   Vaul   Caolas   Rubha Dubh

Balevullin   Balephetrish   Loch Riaghain

Hough   Cornaigbeg   B8069   Ruaig

Kilmoluaig   Kenovay   Gott   Kirkapol

5   TIREE   (Port Adhair Thiriodh)   Gott Bay   Cairn na Burgh Beg

Kilkenneth   B8068   An Iodhlann

4   Loch an Eilein   Baugh   Scarinish   Fladda

Sandaig   B8065   Moss   Crossapol   Héanish   Rubha Tràigh an Duin   Treshnish Isles

Middleton   2   Heylipol   4

Port Mor   Barrapol   Hynish Bay   Lunga

Port Bharrapool   Island Life   Loch a' Phuill   TIREE

Balephuil   Balemartine

Balephuil Bay   B8061   Mannal   Bac Mor or Dutchman's Cap

40   B8068

West Hynish   Hynish   Bac Beag

Port Snoig   Skerryvore Lighthouse

I   N   N   E   R   Staffa

Fingal's Cave

5

30

A   B   C   D

100   10   20   30

Réidh Eilean   Eilean Annraidh   Rubha nan Cean

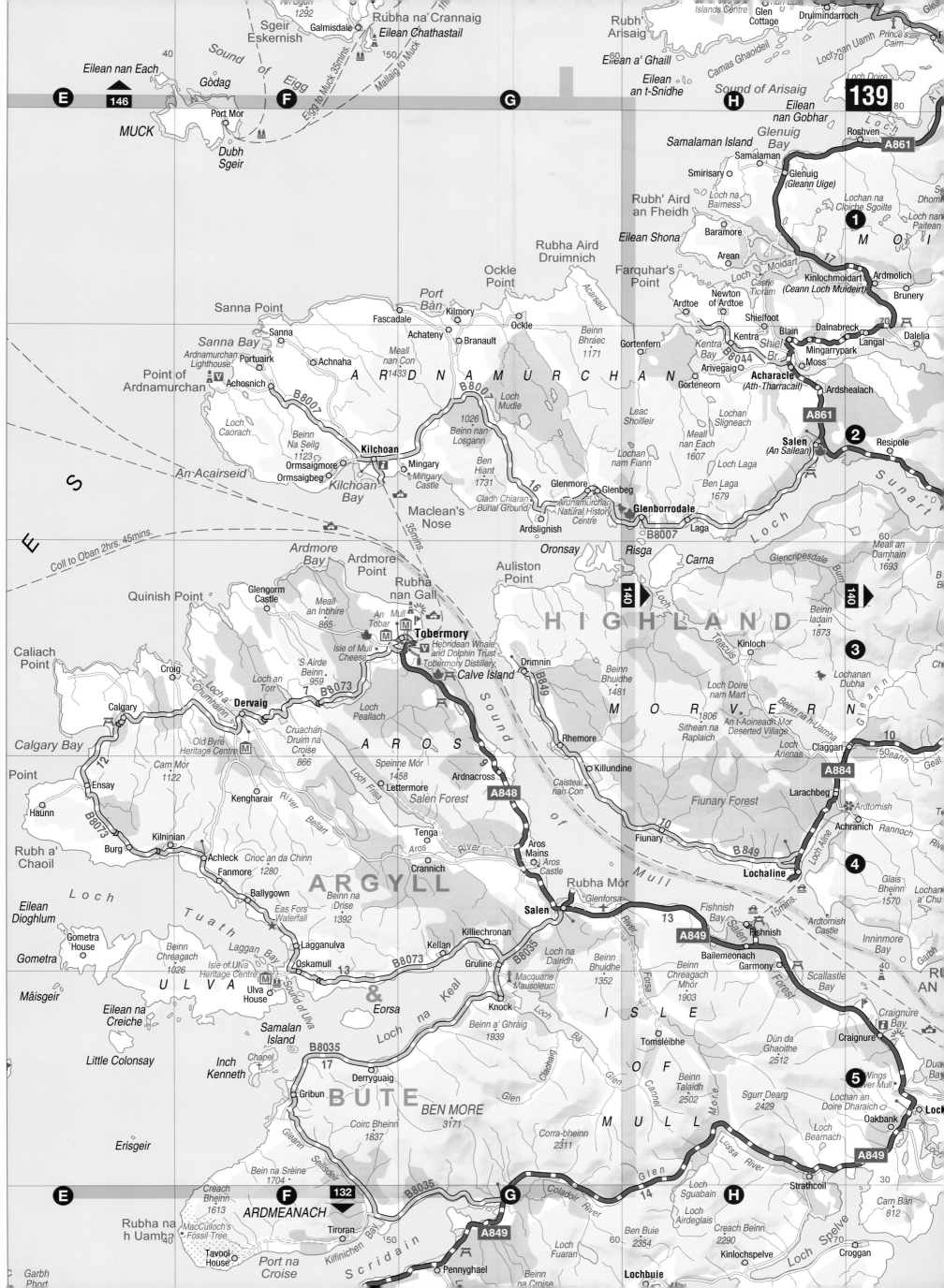

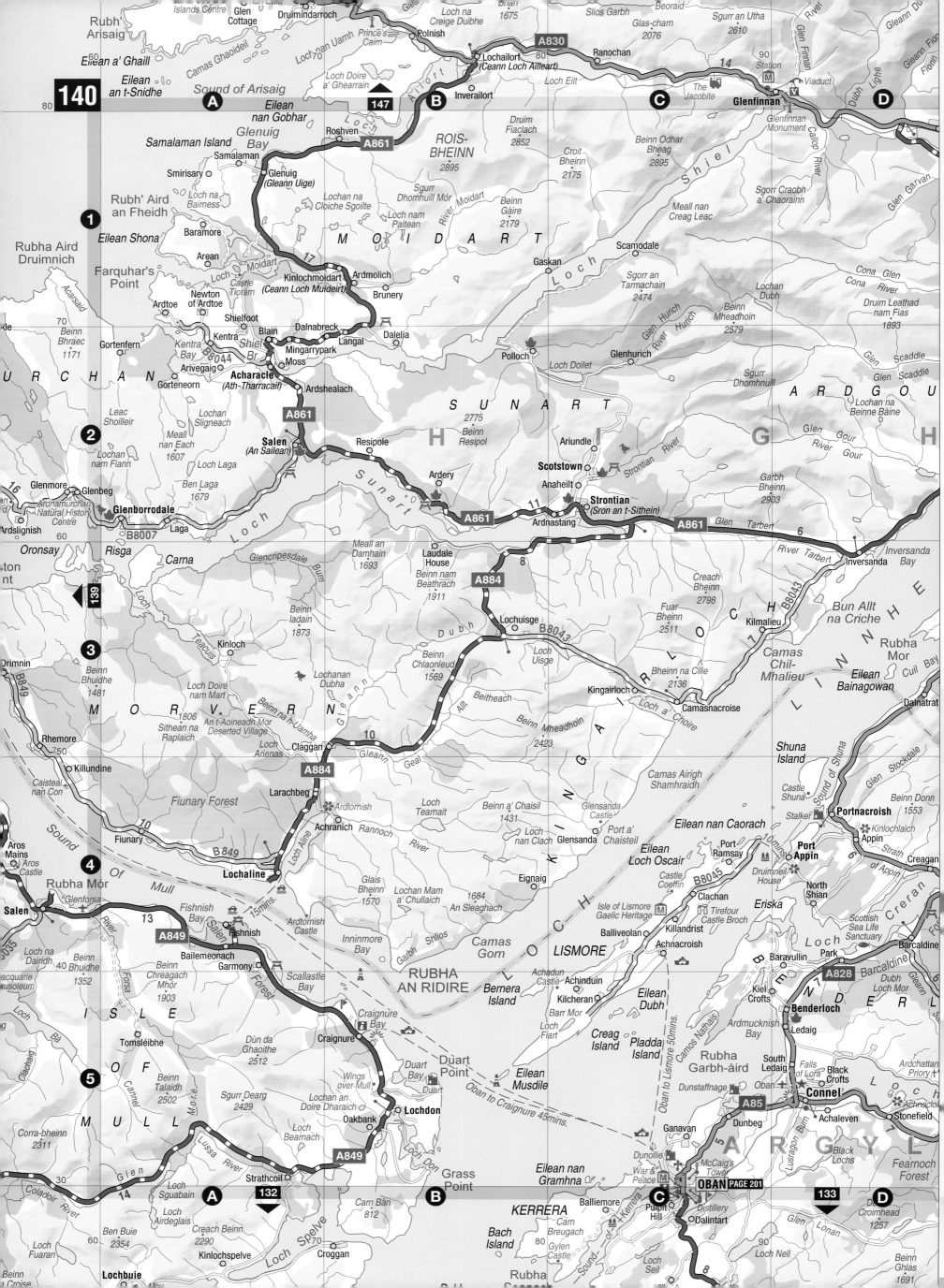

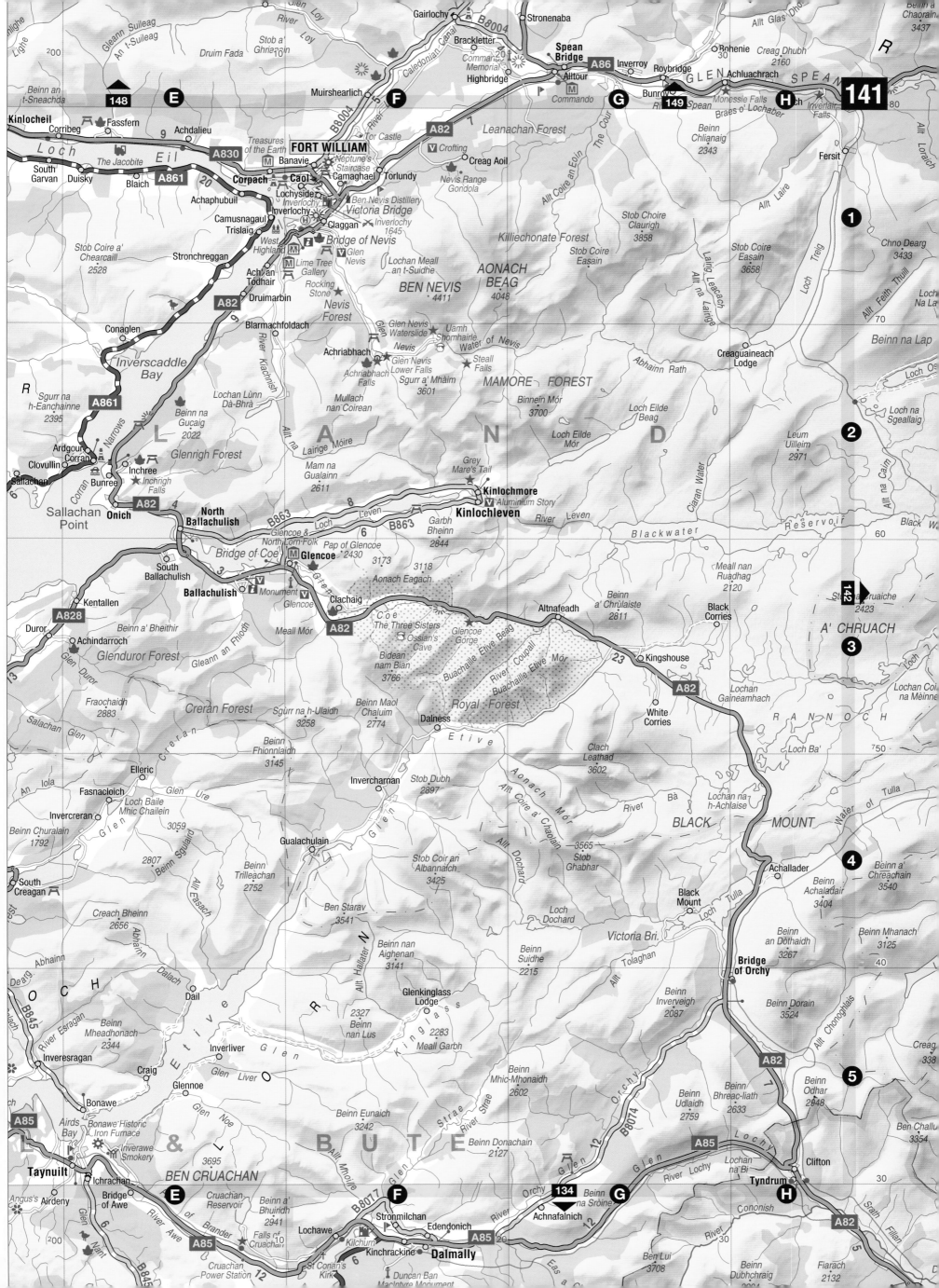

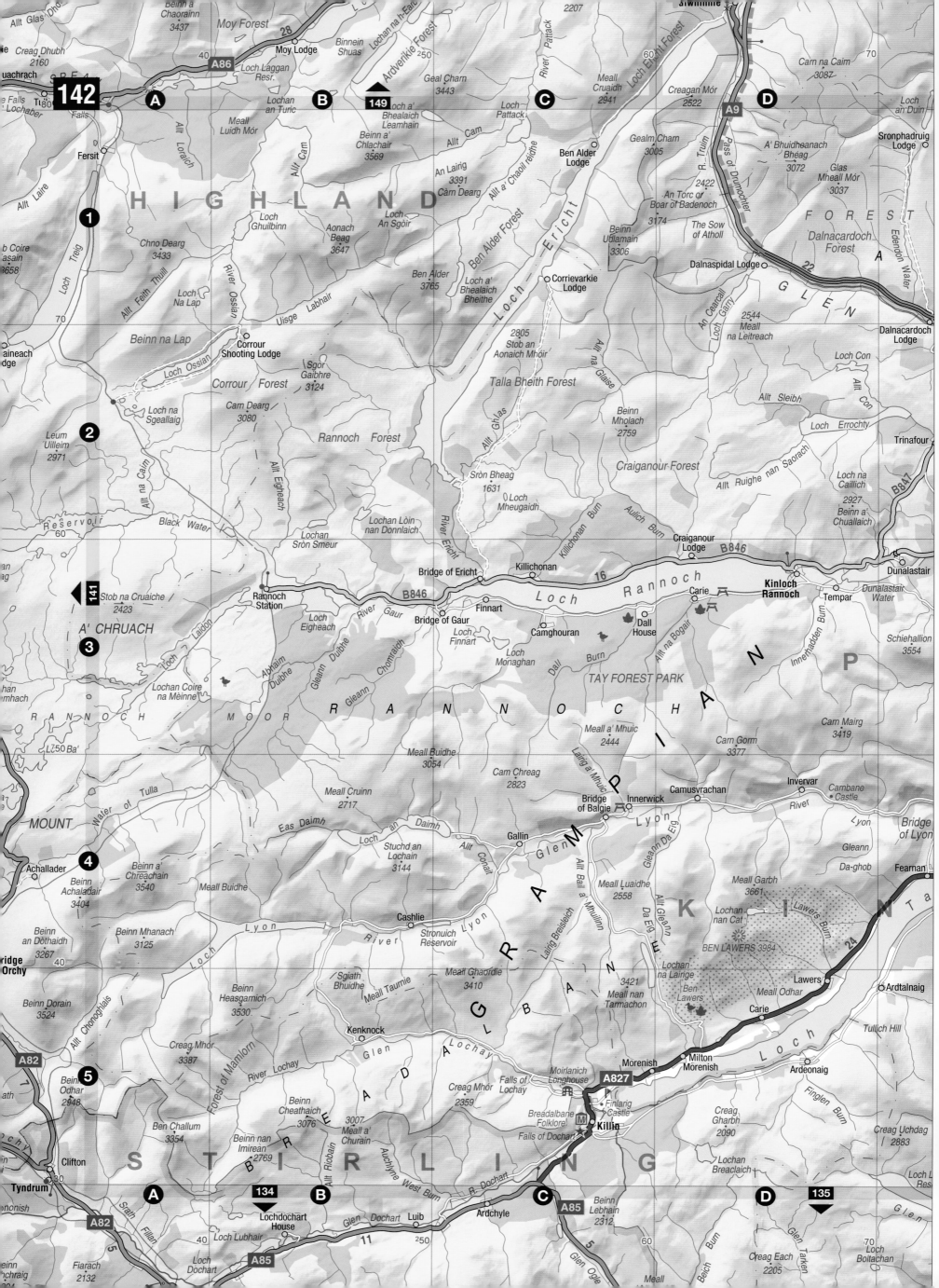

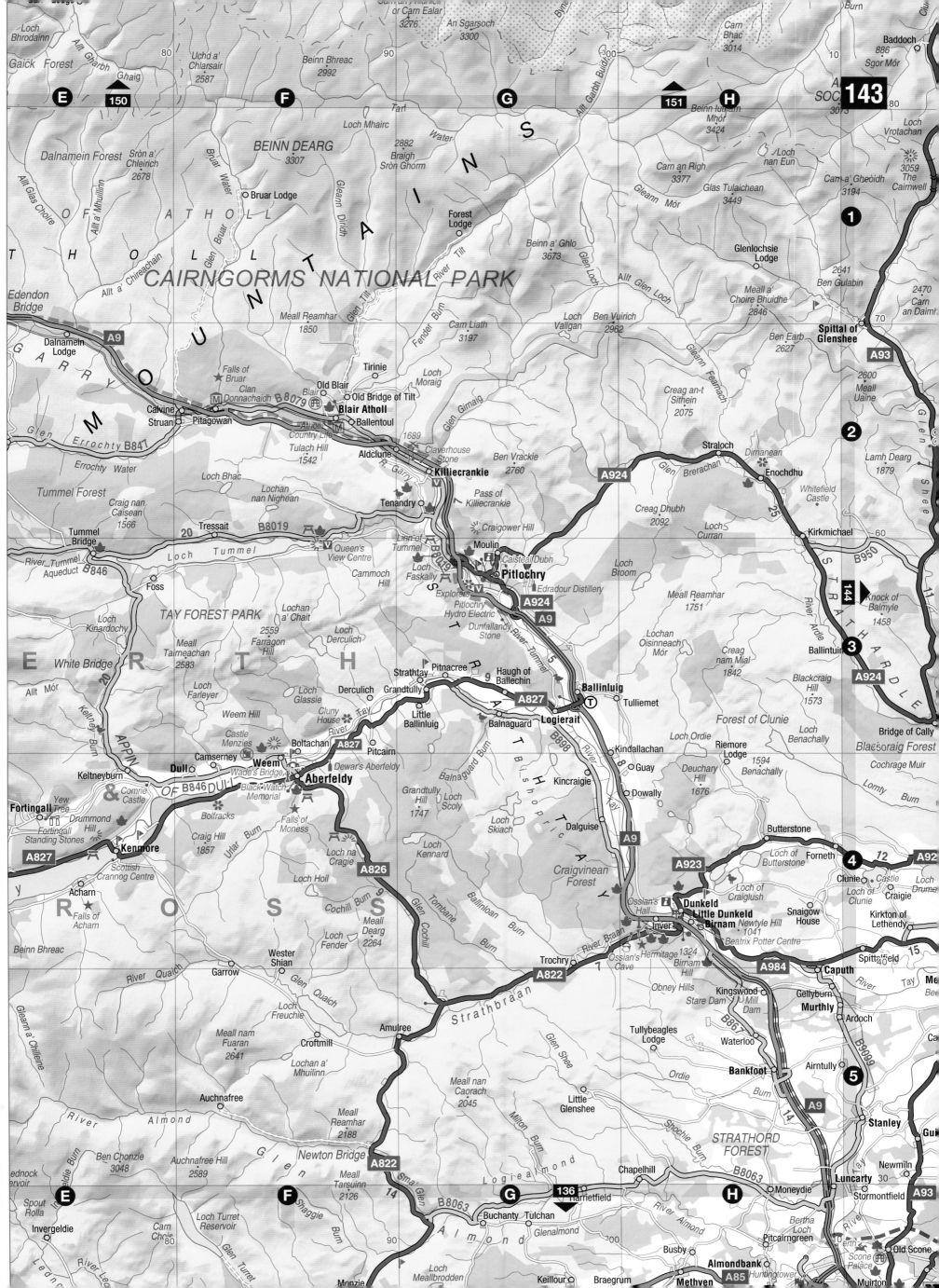

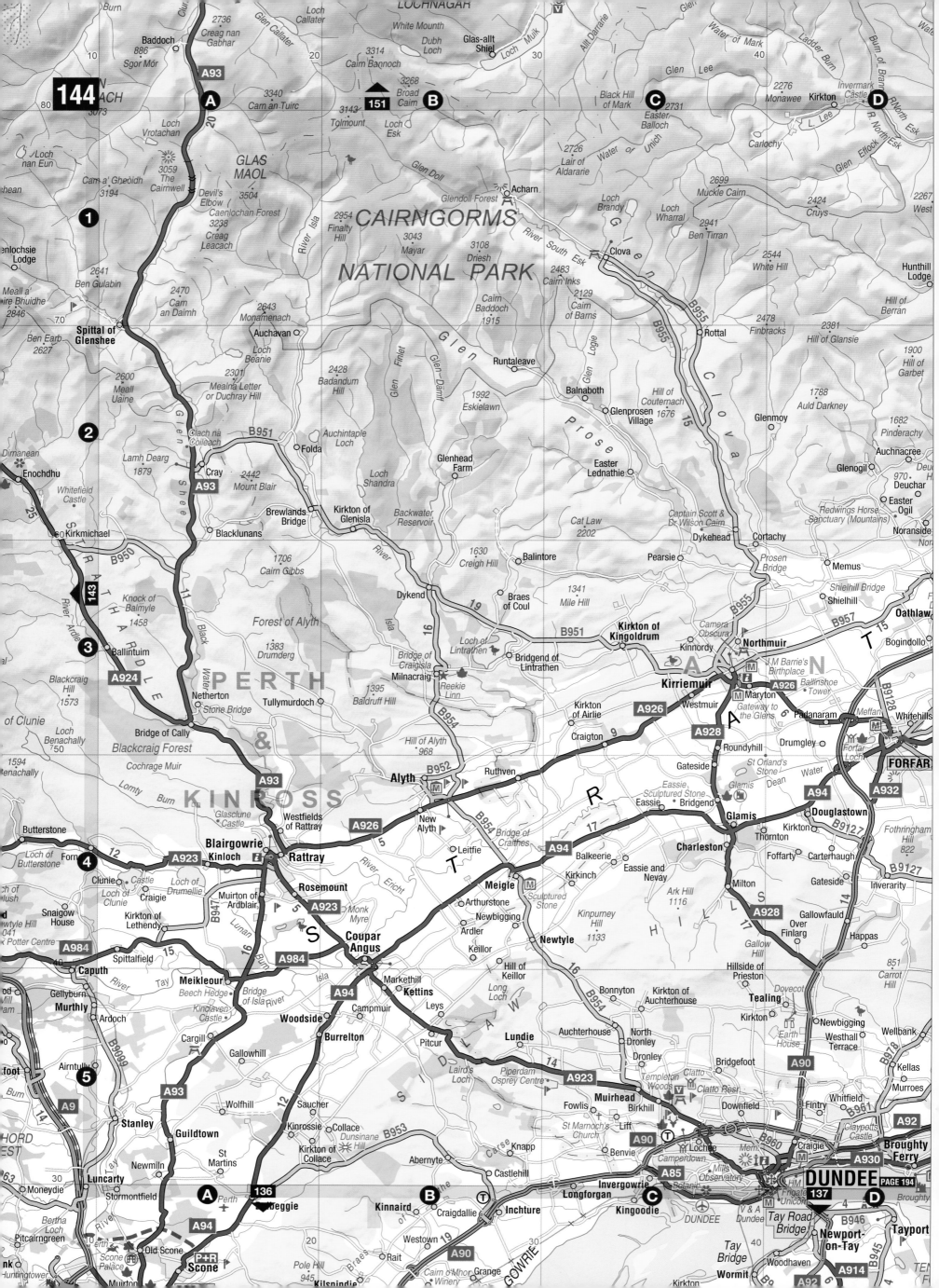

POINT
Bracadale

Ardtreck
B8009
Loch Harport
Fuarain
1442
Balmeanach

1456 Peinchorran
Ben Lee

Sconser to Raasay 25mins
Suisnish
Hill

Fiskavaig
Fernilea
Carbost
Drynoch
40
A863
150
A87
Loch Sligachan
GLAMAIG
2542
Sconser

Rubha nan Clach
30
Dun Ard an t-Sàbhail
Arnaval
1210
Gleann Oraid
Talisker Distillery
Merkadale
River Drynoch
Sligachan

Talisker Bay
154
C
Moll

20
30

Beinn nan Cuithean
Loch Sleadale
Beinn Breac
ISLE OF SKYE
15
Luib

Beinn Bhreac 1468
Eynort
Glen Brittle Forest
MINGINISH
Sgurr nan Gillean 3167
Glen Sligachan
River Sligachan
Marsco 2414
Garbh-bheinn 2649
Glas Bheinn Mhór 1852
Beinn na Cro

1
Loch Eynort
River Brittle
Glen Brittle
Sgurr a' Ghreadaidh 3197
Harta Corrie
CUILLIN HILLS
BLA BHEINN 3046

20
An Dubh-sgeir
Stac an Tuill
Bualintur
Glenbrittle
Loch Brittle
Sgurr Alasdair 3257
3037 Sgurr nan Eag
Loch Coruisk
Sgurr na Stri 1623
Camasunary
Loch na Crèitheach
Kirkibost

10
Ceann na Beinne 736
Rubh' an Dunain Chambered Cairn
Soay Sound
464 Beinn Bhreac
Na Clachan Bhreige Stone Circle
Kilmarie
Ben Meabost 1128
Chocan nan Gobhar
Du Ringill
Chambered Cairn

2
Mol-chlach
SOAY
Loch Scavaig
Elgol
B8083

Prince Charlie's Cave
Dun Grugaig
Glasnakille

Eilean na h-Airde
Rubha na h-Easgainne
Tarskavaig Point

170
THE HEBRIDES
THE HEBRIDES
HIGH

Inver Dalavil

3
CANNA
Carn a' Ghaill 693
Castle
Rùm to Canna 55mins.
Rubha Shamhnan Insir
Mallaig to Canna 2hrs. (Seasonal)
Rubha Charn nan Cearc

Ceann Creag-airighe 426
A' Chill
An Coroghon
Canna Harbour
Kilmory
Camas Pliasgaig
Muck to Canna 1hr. 35mins. (Seasonal)
Geur Rubha

Garrisdale Point
Sanday
Sound of Canna
Guirdil Bay
Kilmory Glen
Mullach Mór 997
Kinloch Castle
Mallaig to Rùm 1hr. 20mins.
Point of Sleat

800
Sgorr Mhór 1273
Kinloch Glen
Loch Scresort
Kinloch

Oigh-sgeir
INNER
Orval 1874
Sgorr Reidh
Long Loch
Loch Gainmhich
Eigg to Rùm 1hr. (Seasonal)

4
SEA OF
Schooner Point
Glen Harris
Loch Fiachanis
Hallival
Askival 2663
RÙM

RÙM
NATIONAL NATURE RESERVE
Ruinsival
Ainshval 2552
Sgurr nan Gillean
Rùm to Muck 1hr. 10mins. (Seasonal)

90
Loch Papadil
Rubha nam Meirleach
SOUND
Cleadale
Rubha nan Tri Chlach

Bay of Laig
Loch Beinn Tighe
OF

5
Rubha an Fhasaidh
EIGG
1hr. 40mins. (Seasonal)

An Sgurr 1292
Sandavore
Kildonnan

Sgeir Eskernish
Galmisdale
Rùbha na Crannaig
Eilean Chathastail

80
Eilean nan Each
Gòdag
Sound of Eigg
Mallaig to Muck
Eigg to Muck 35mins.

138
Port Mor
139

MUCK
Dubh Sgeir

20
30
40
150

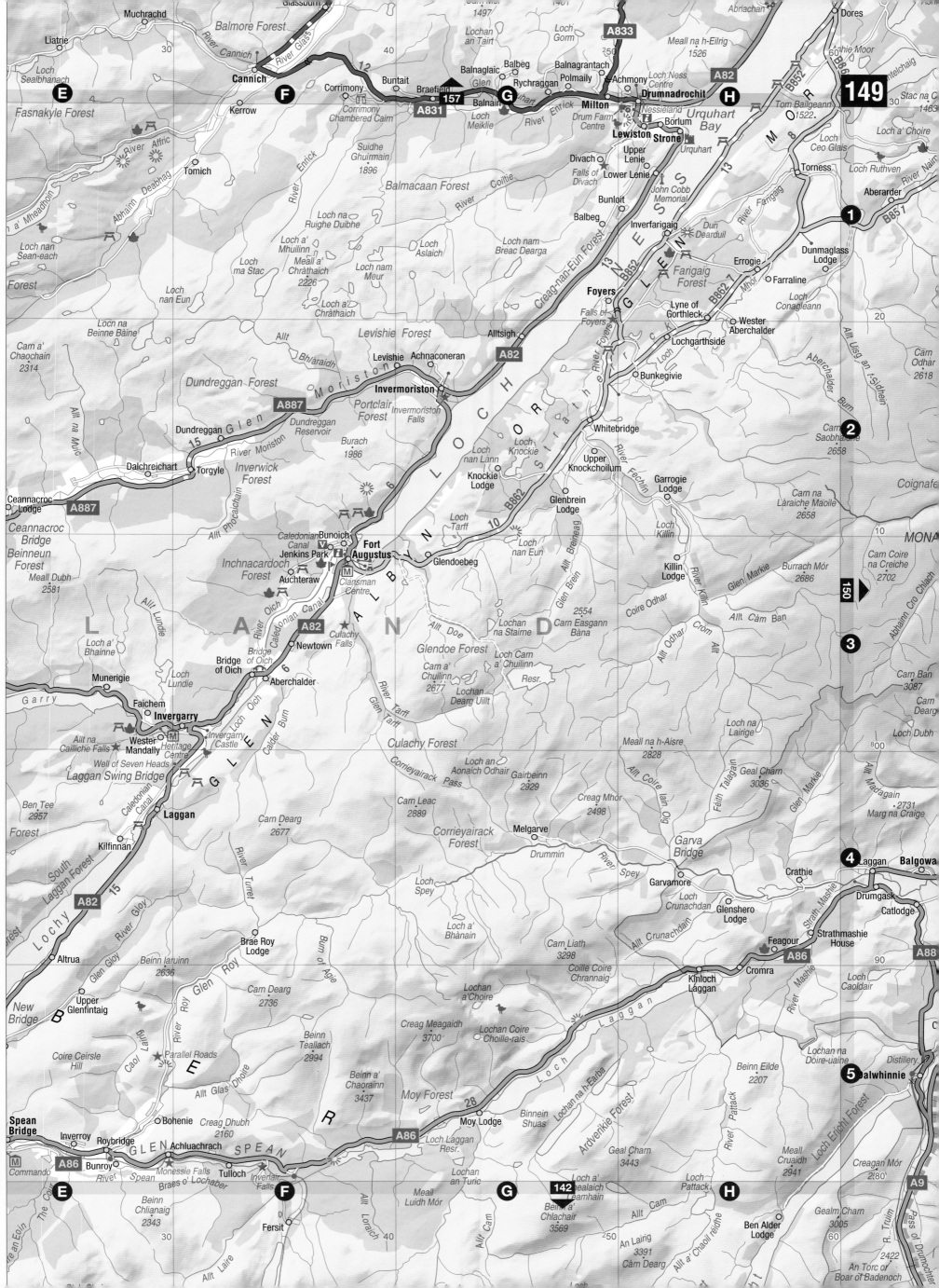

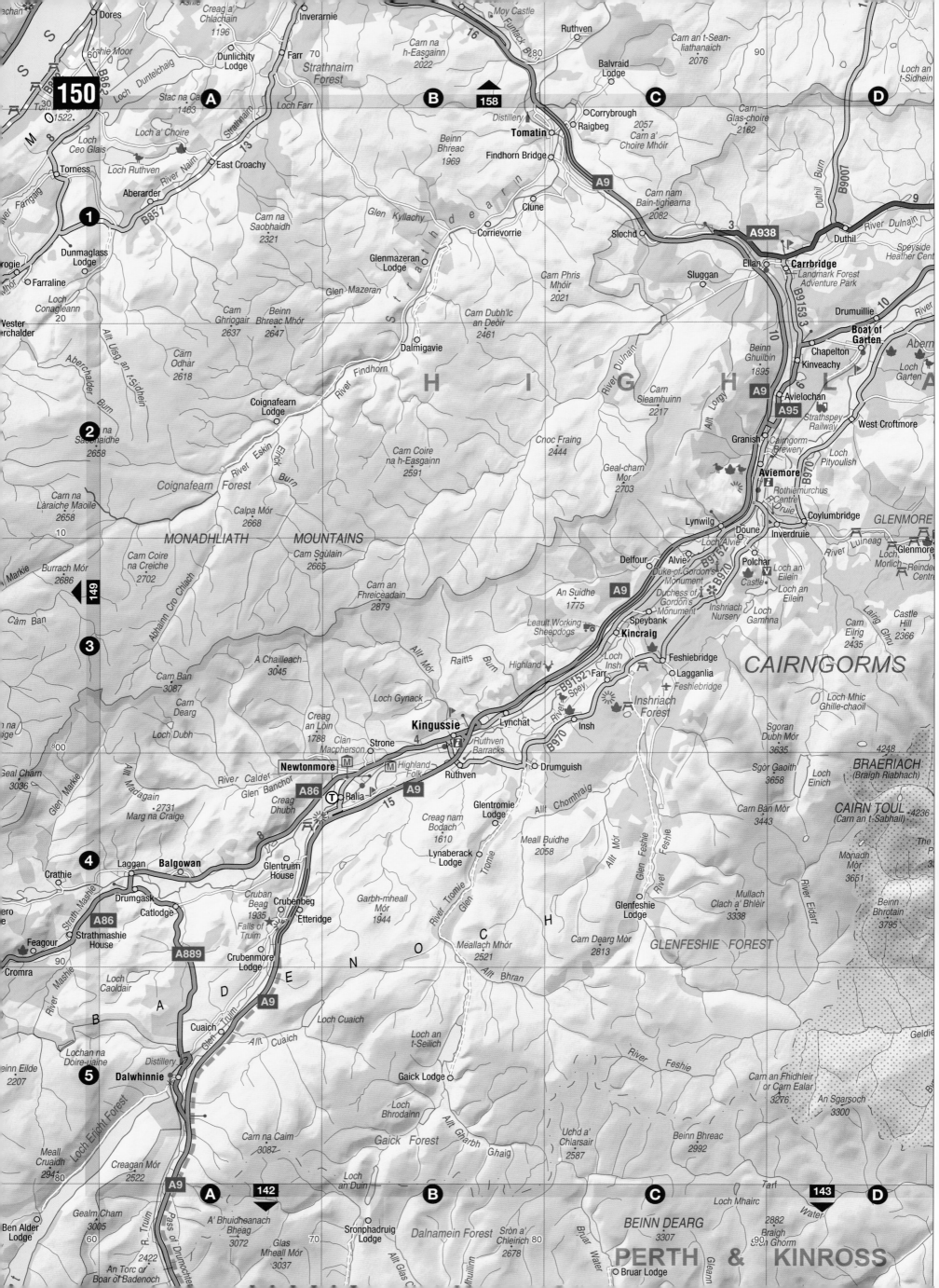

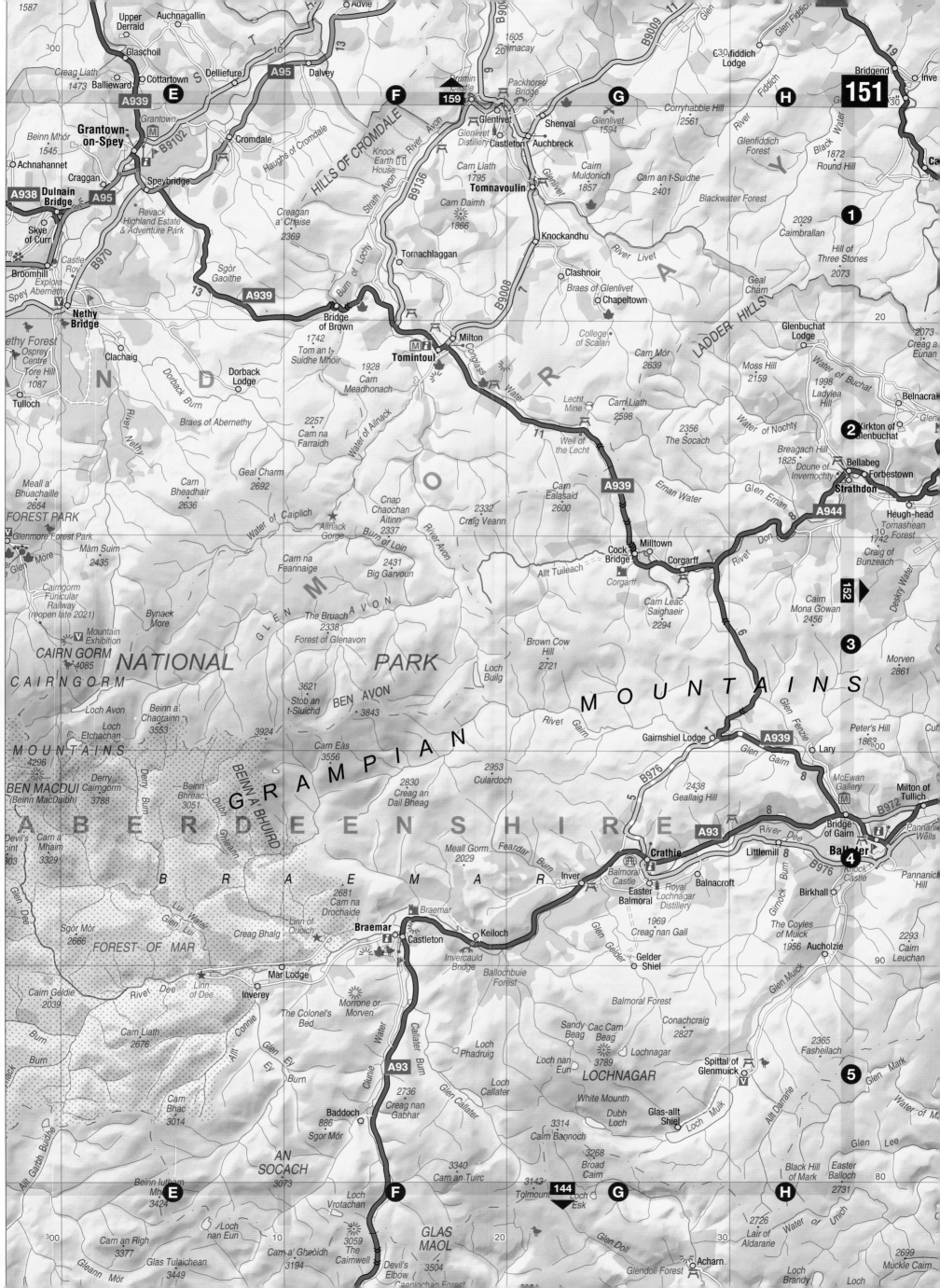

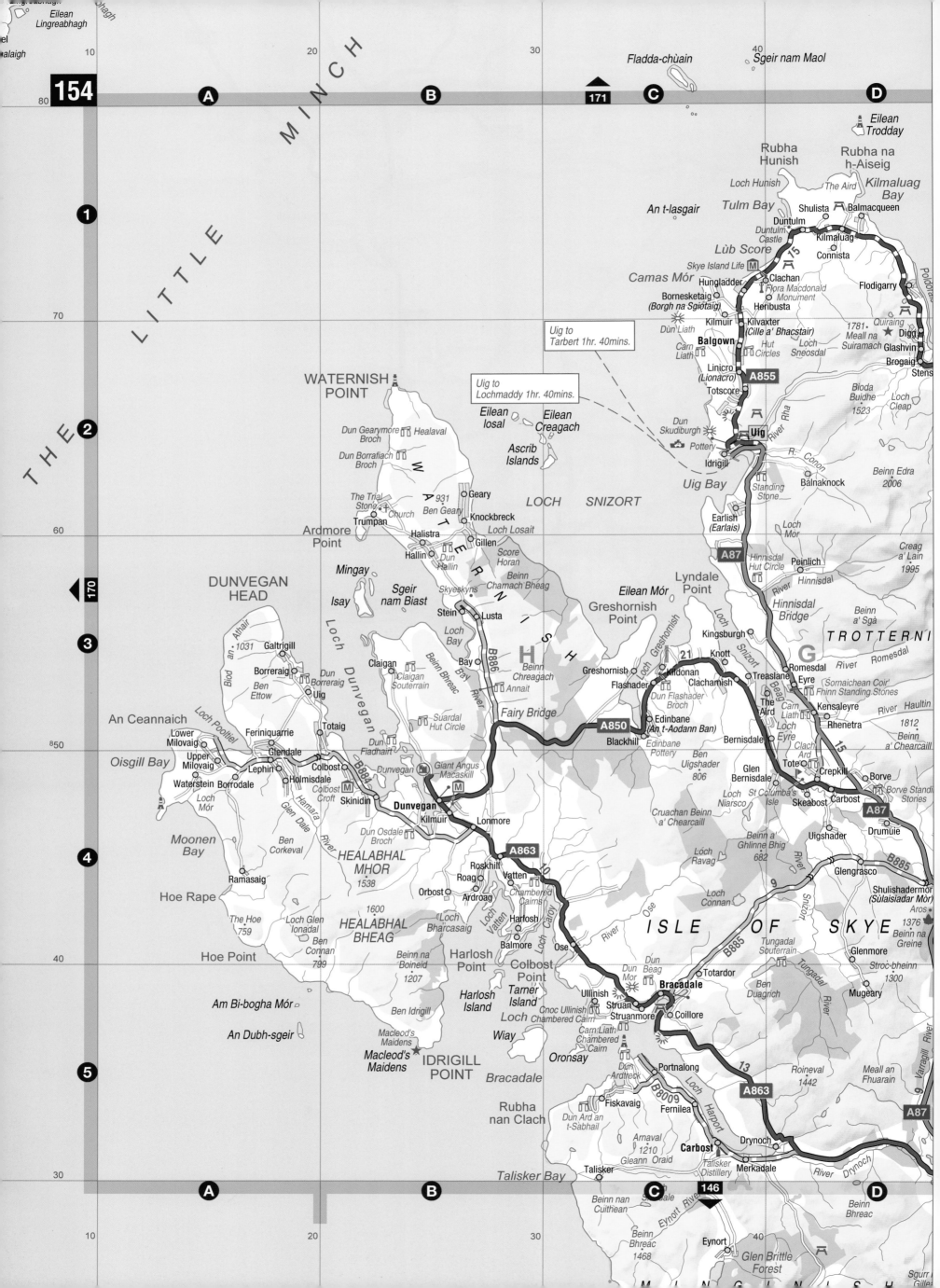

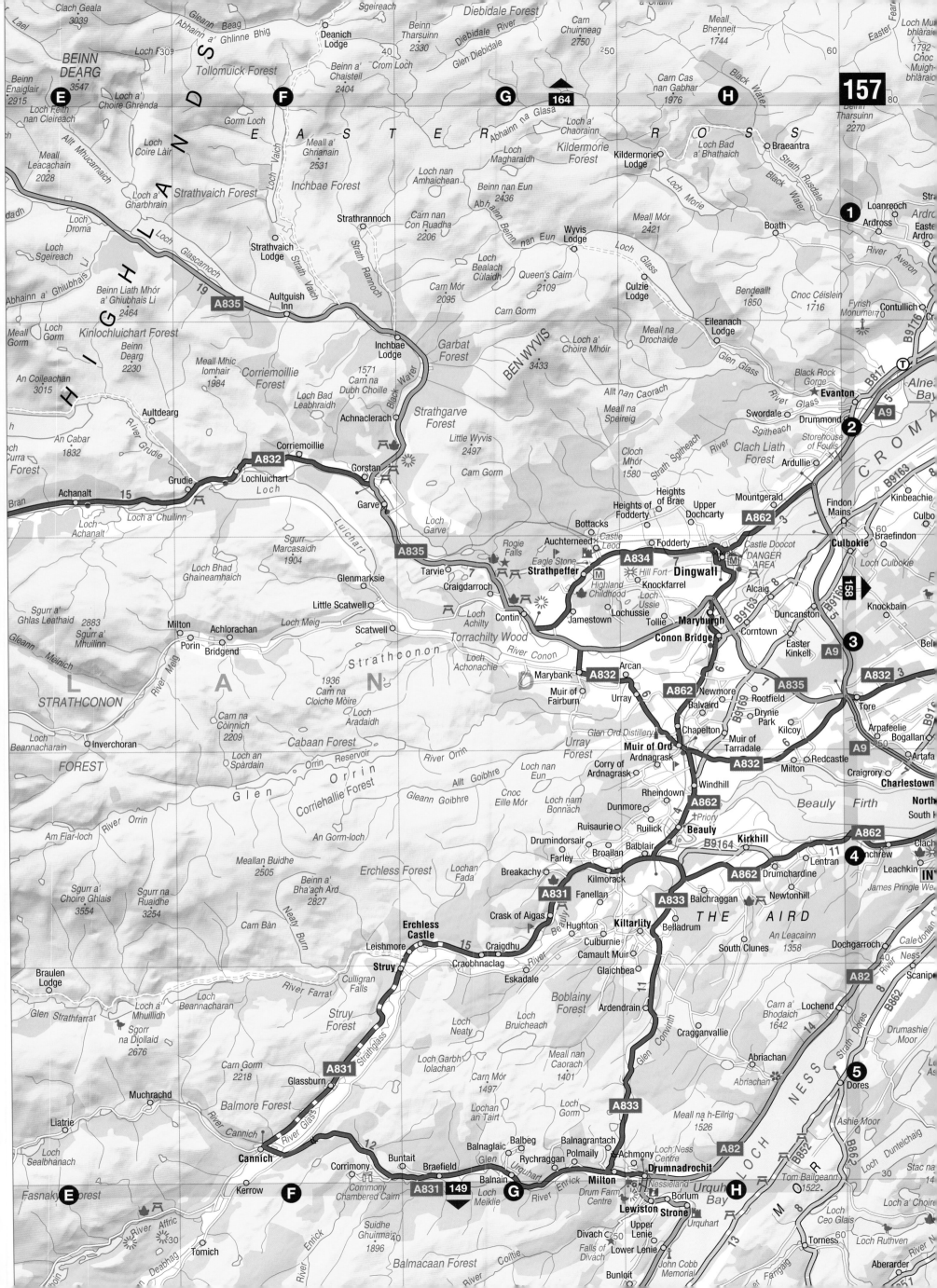

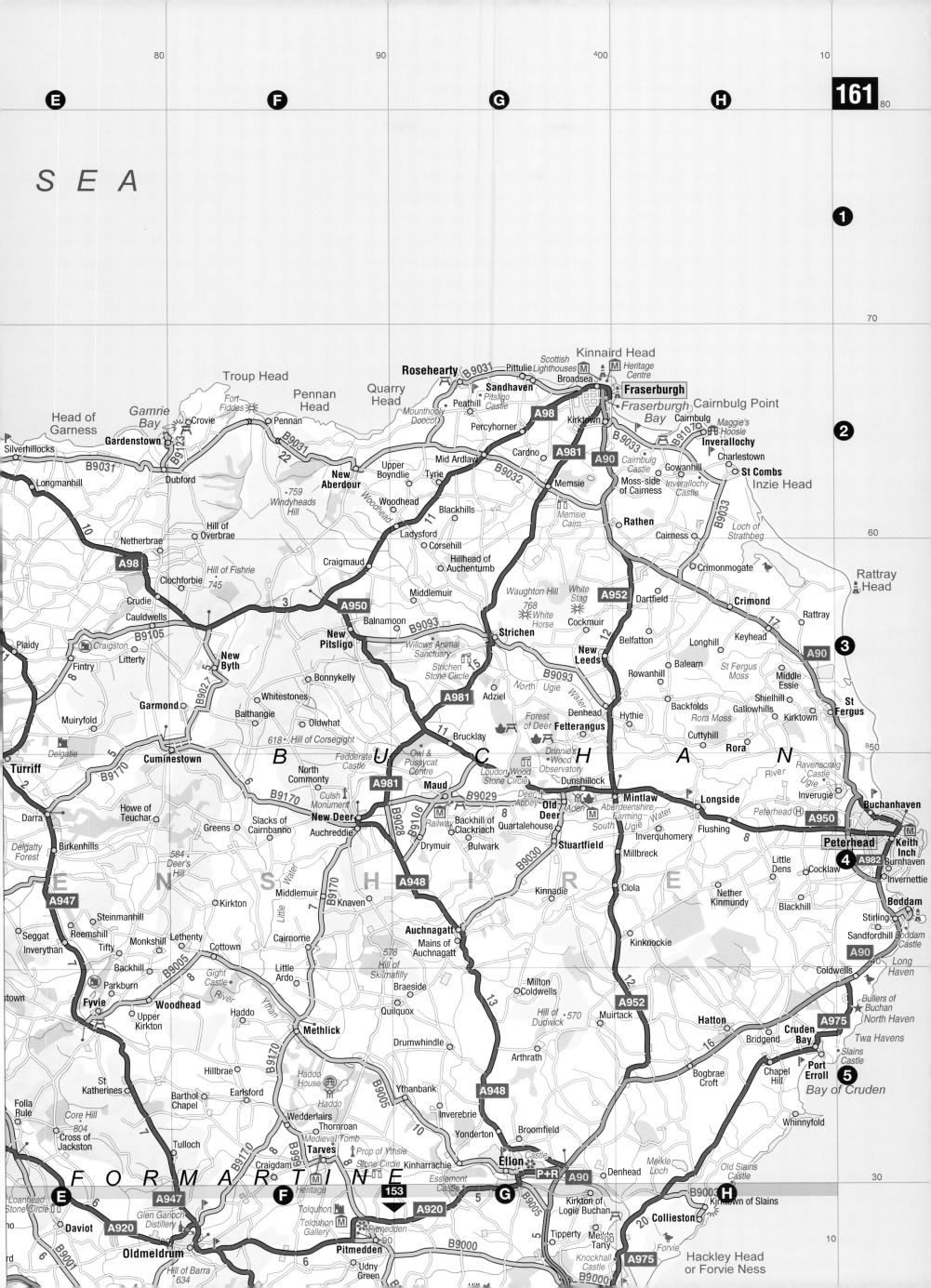

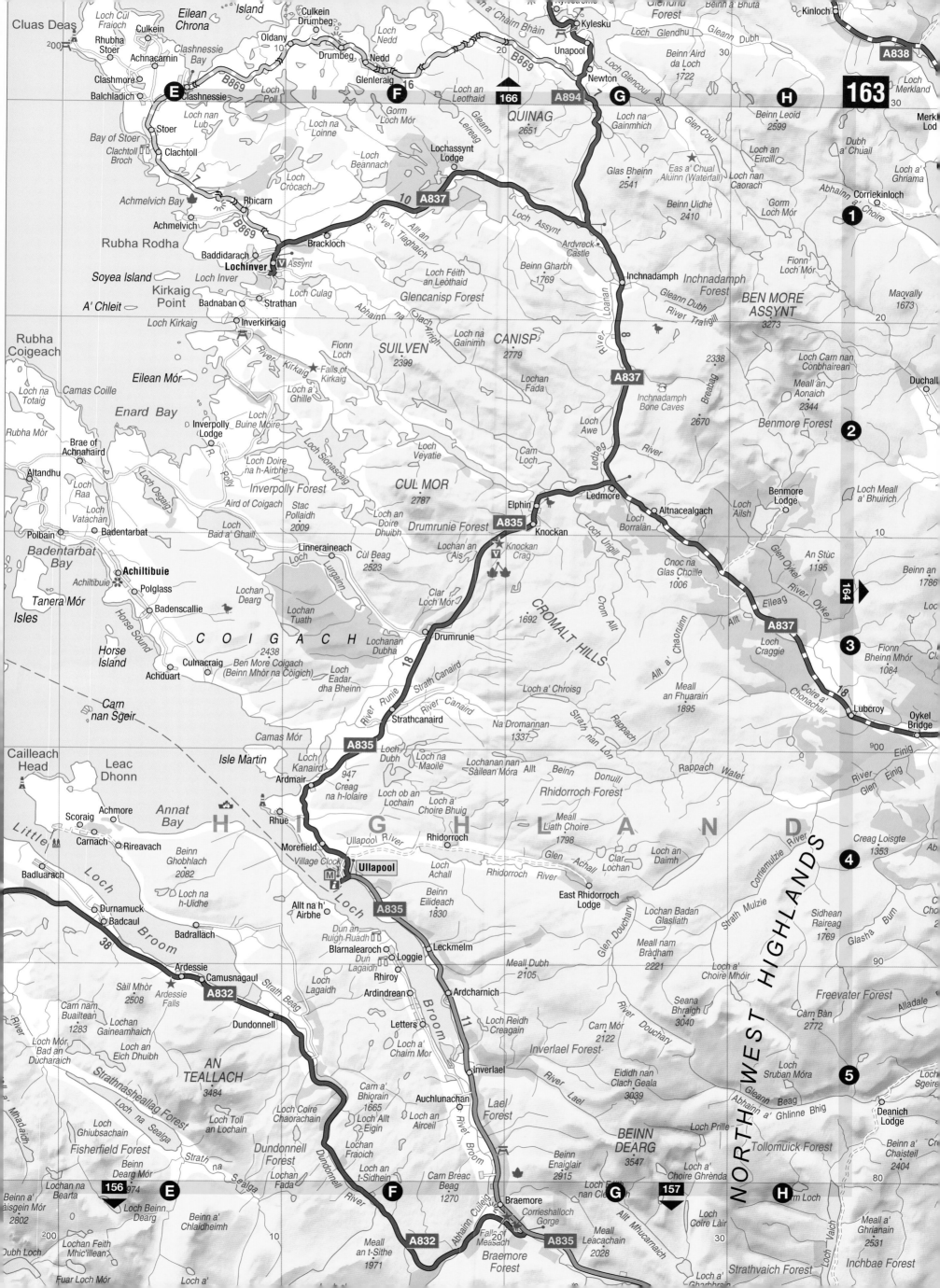

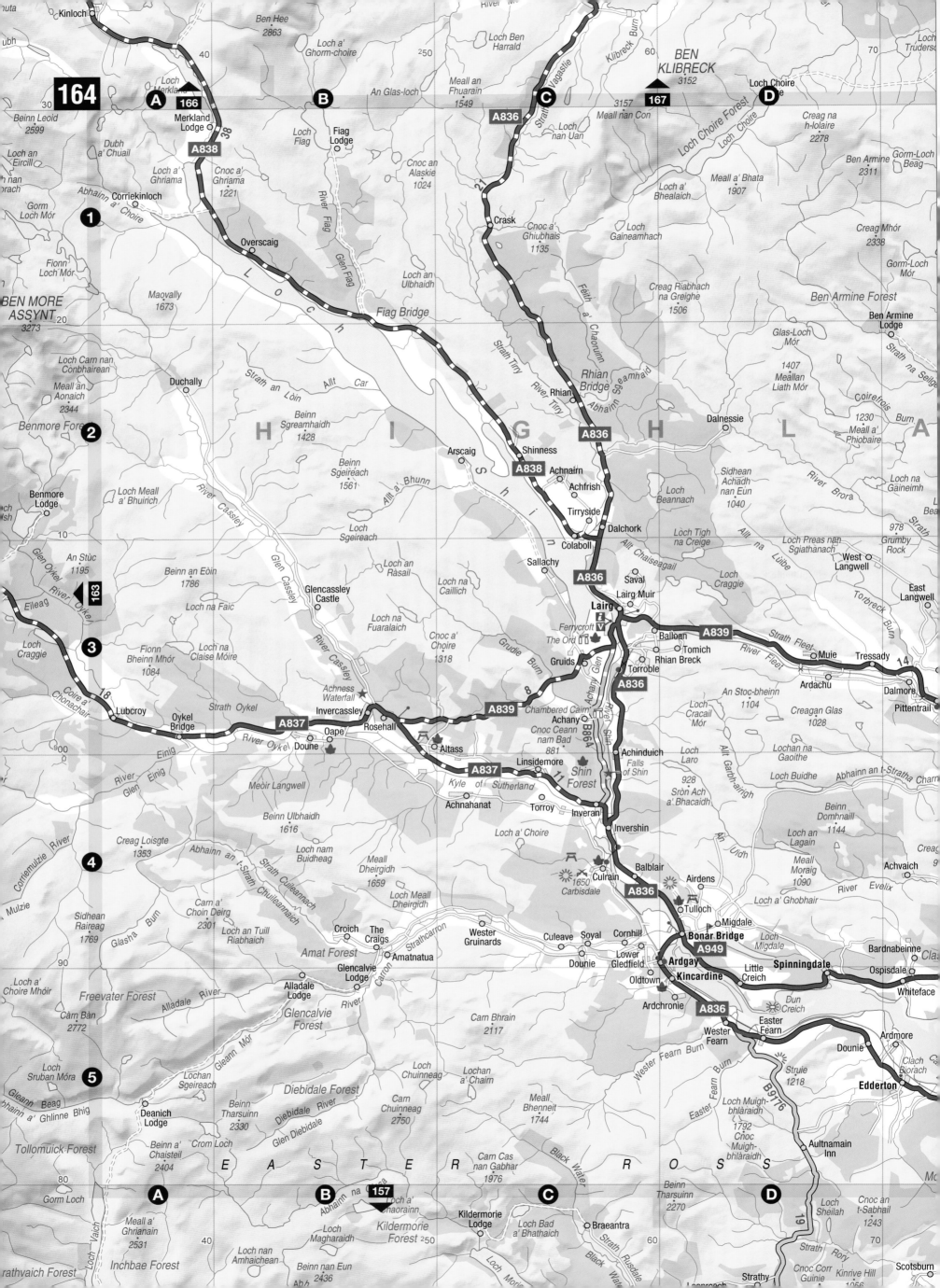

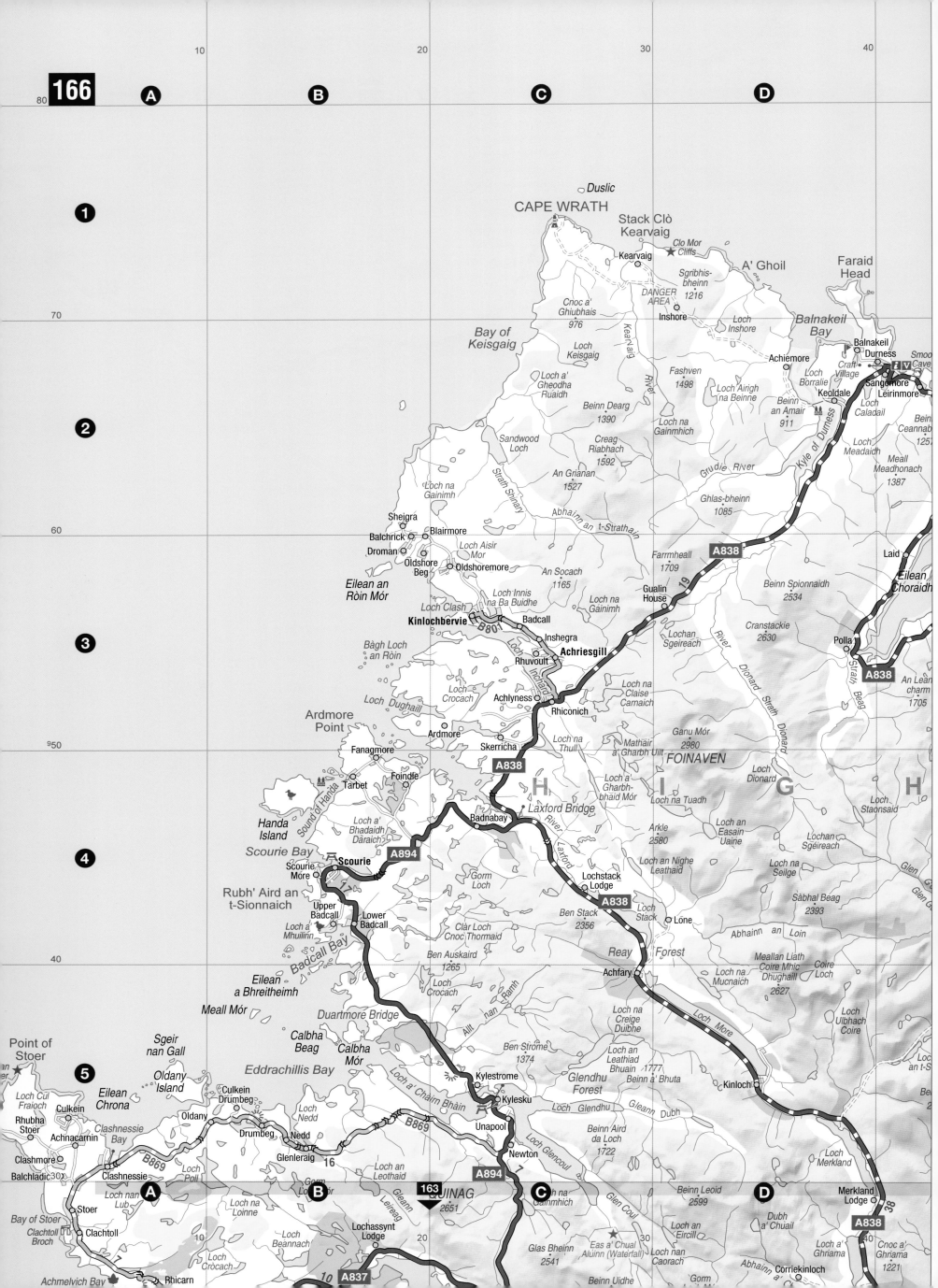

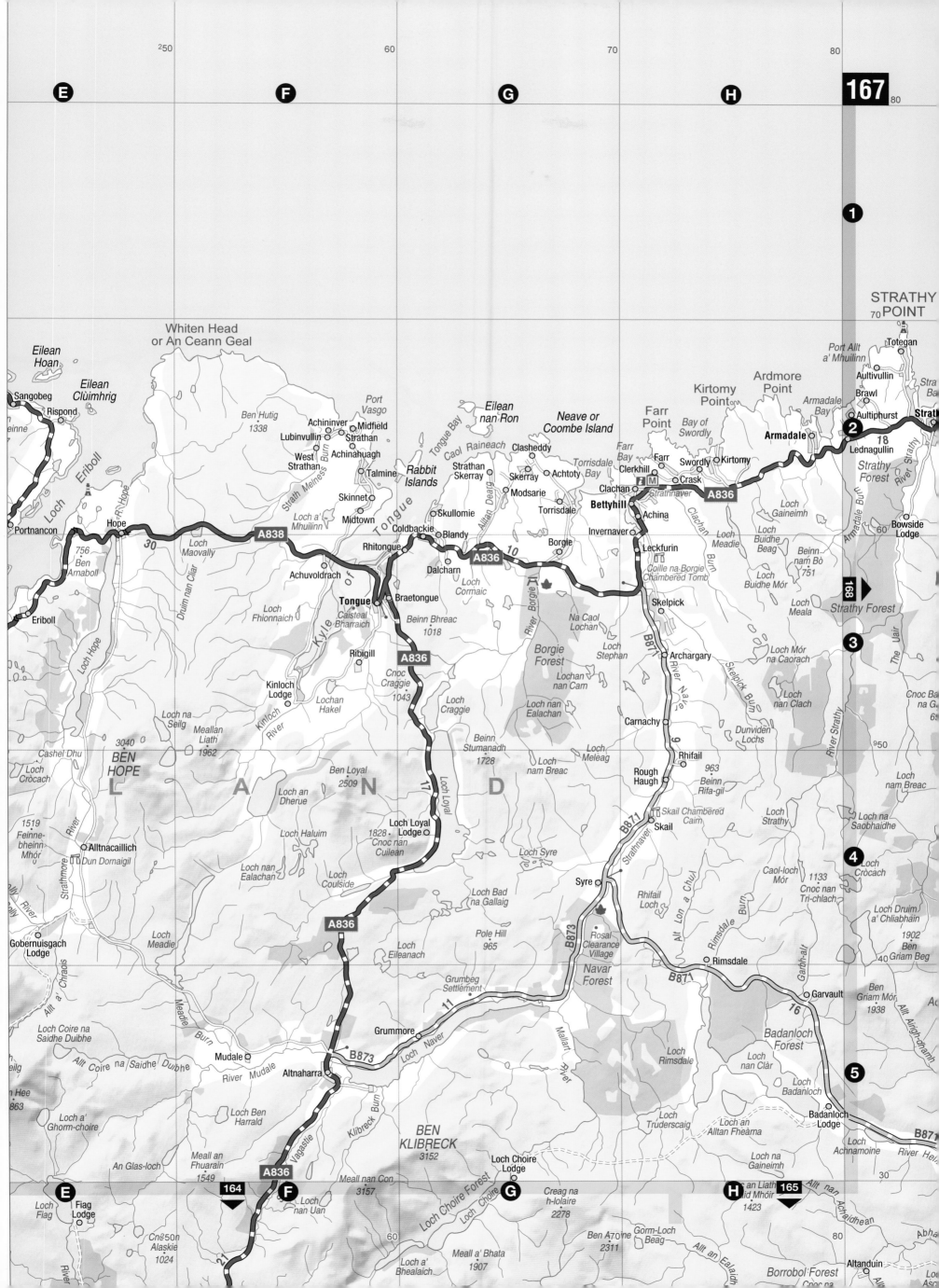

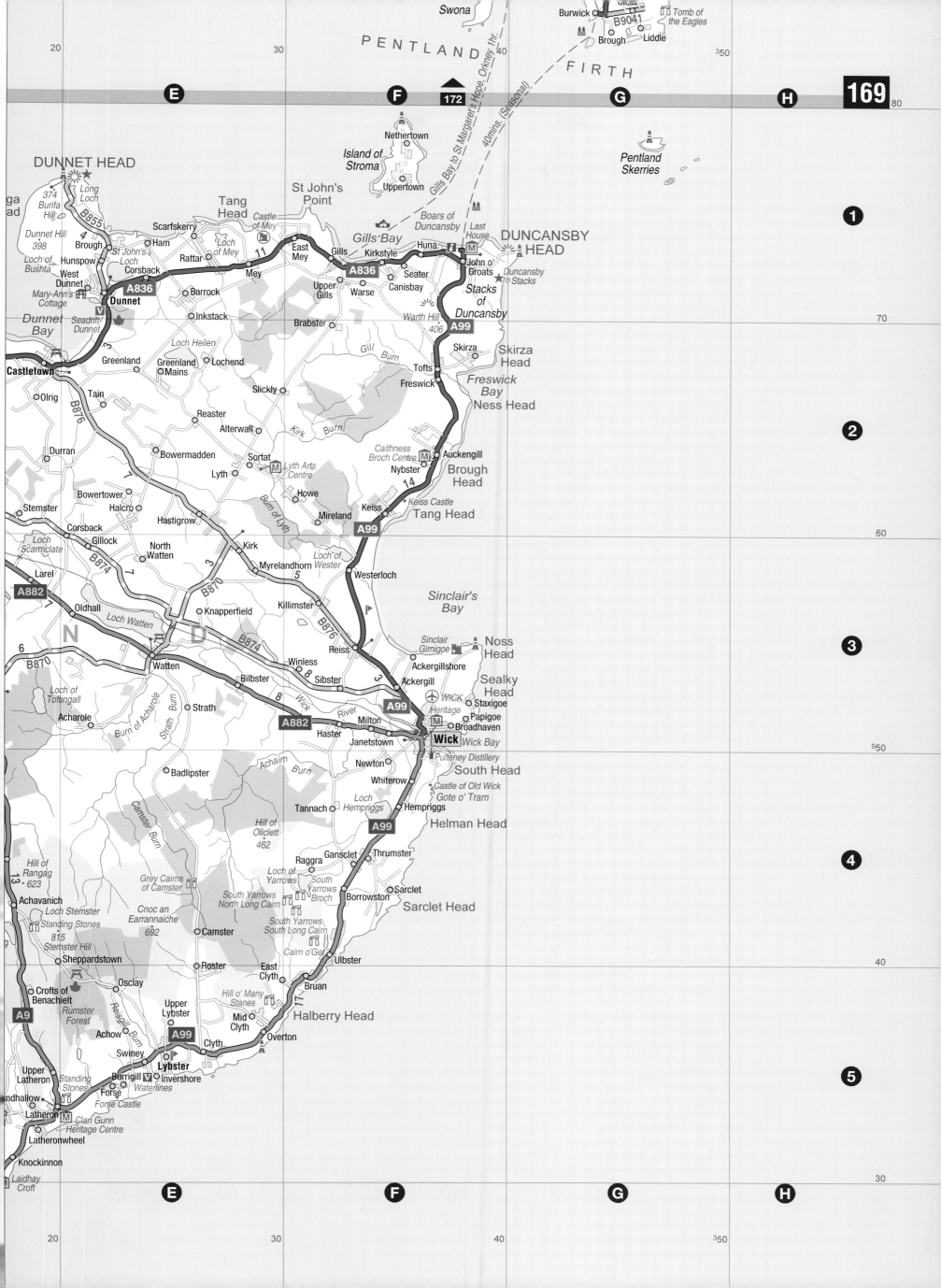

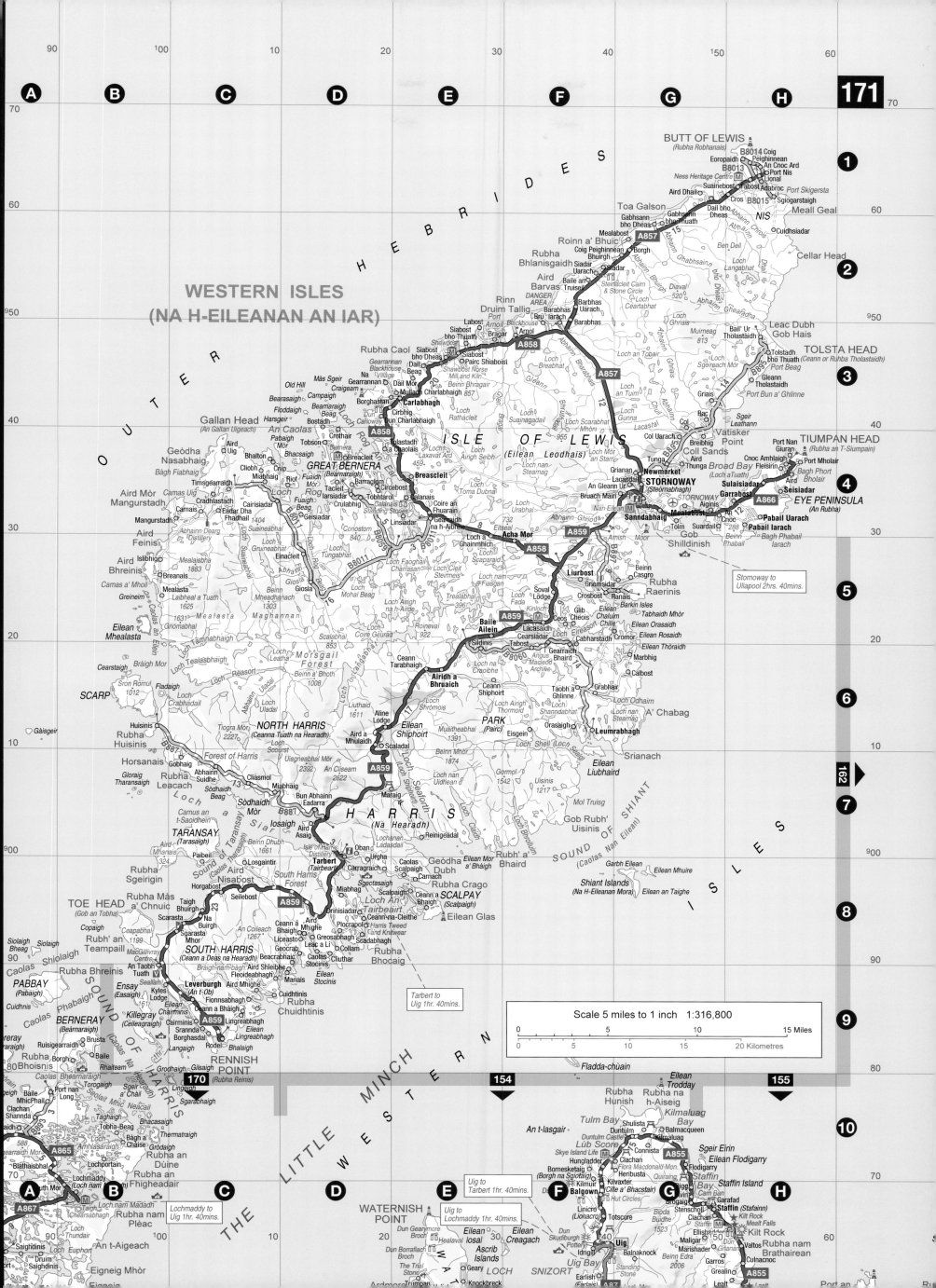

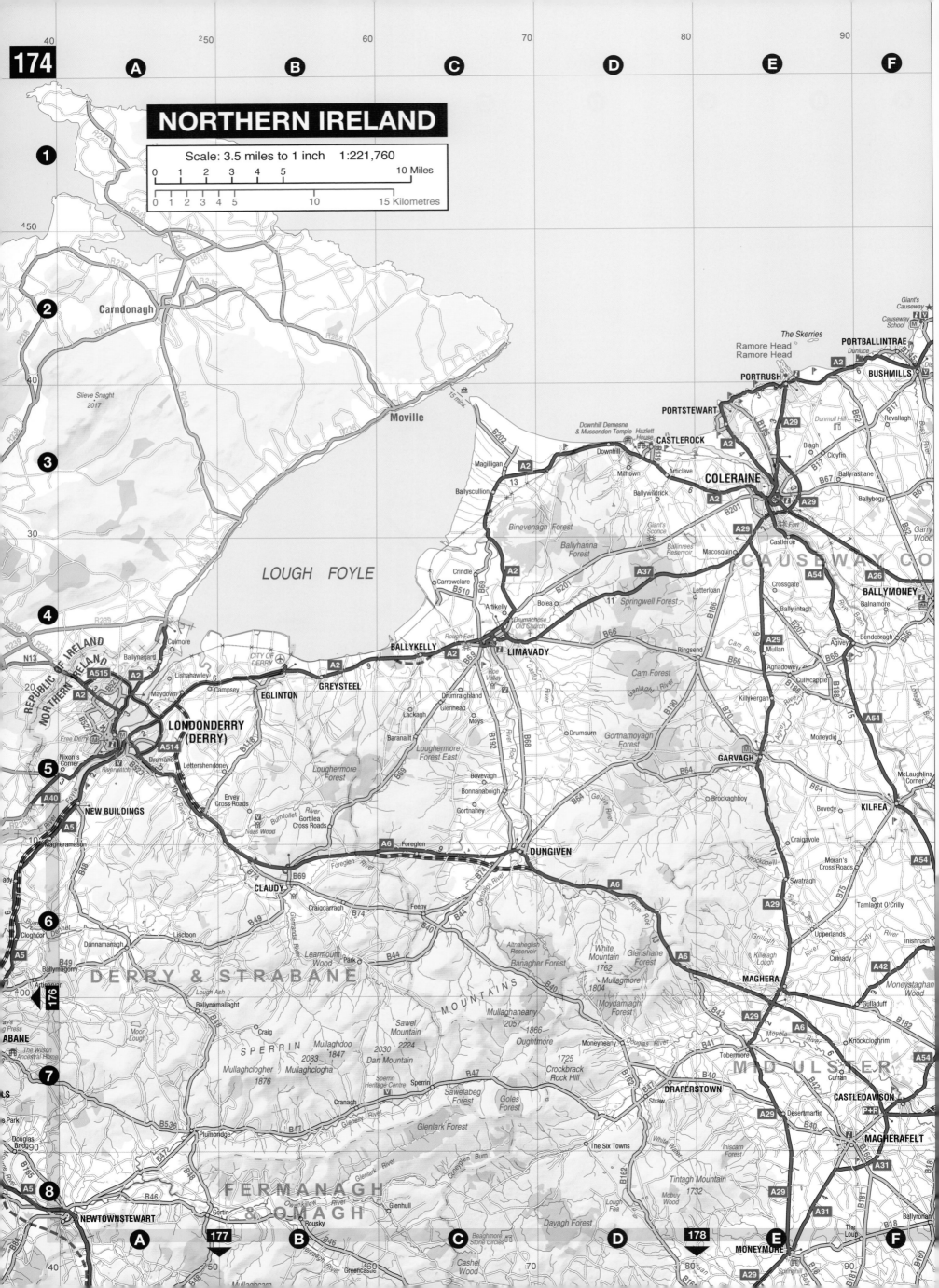

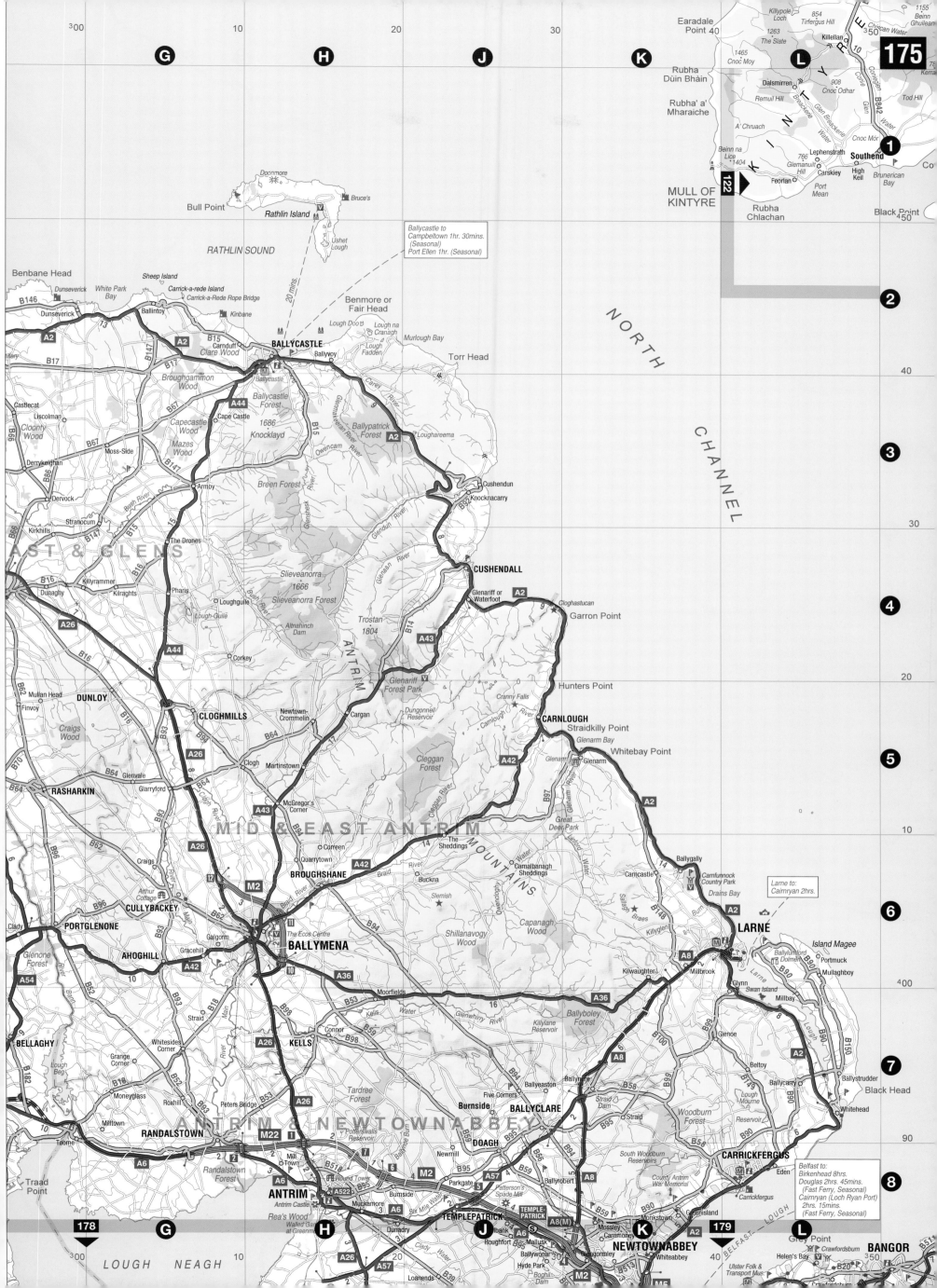

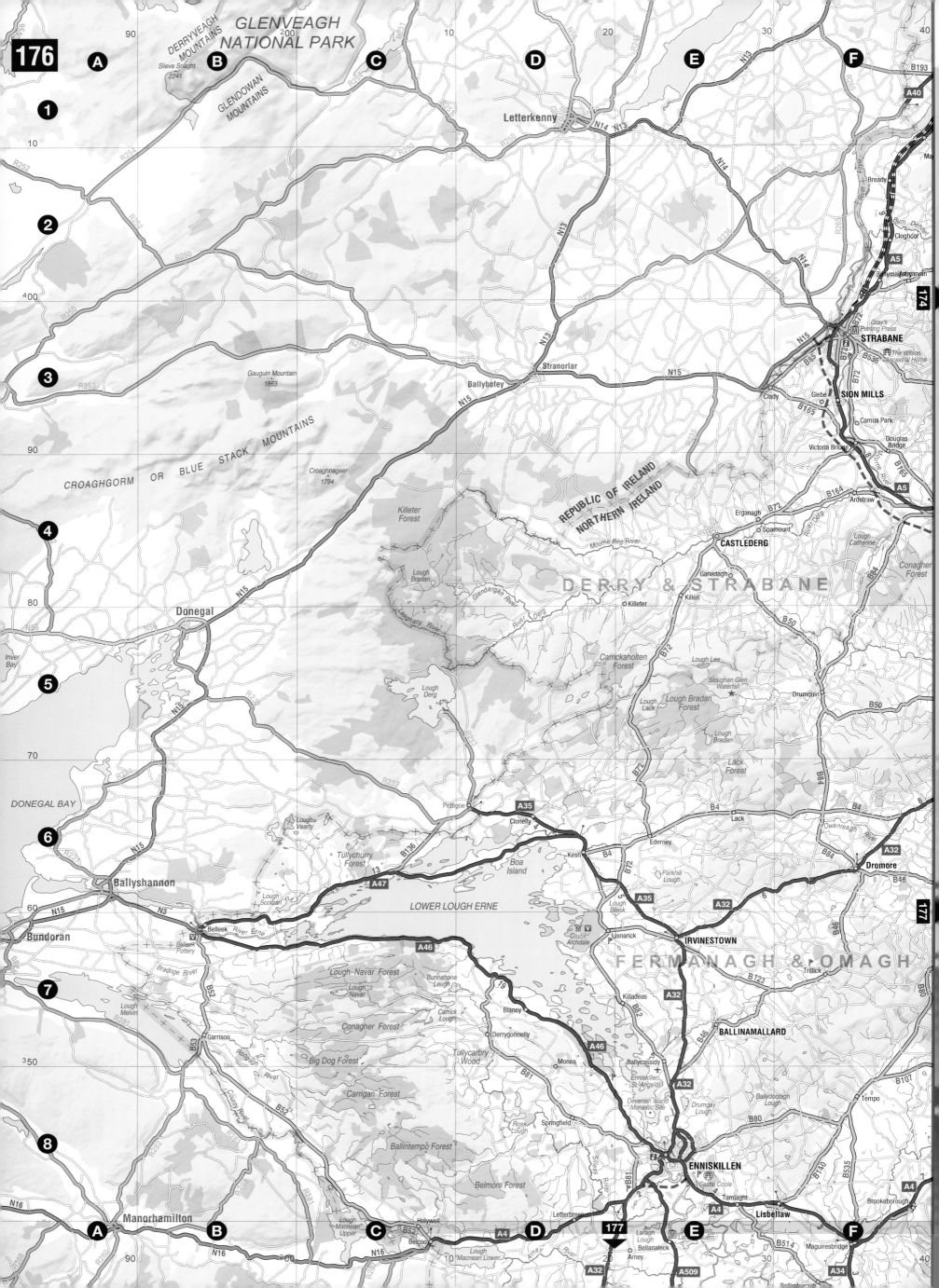

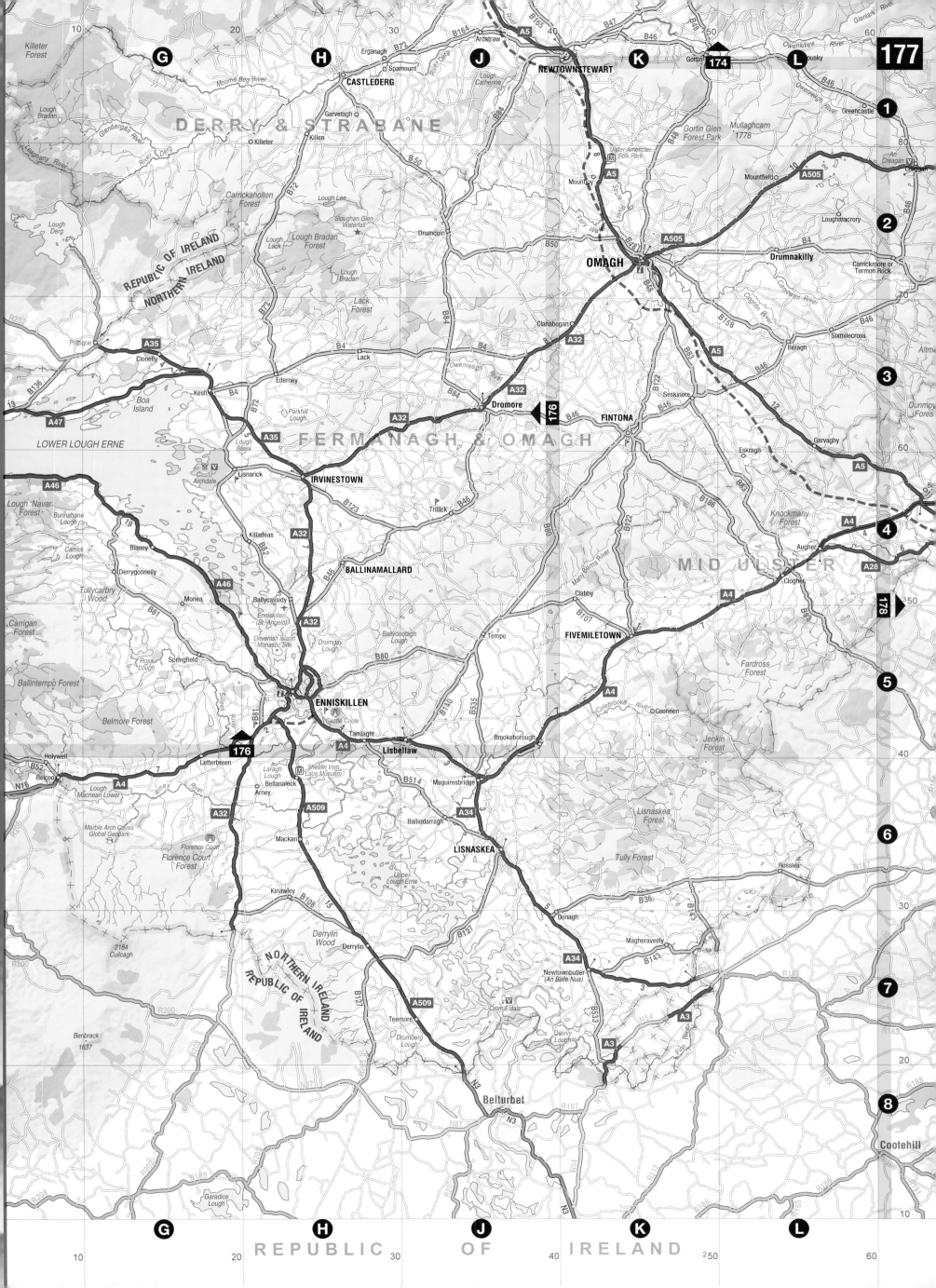

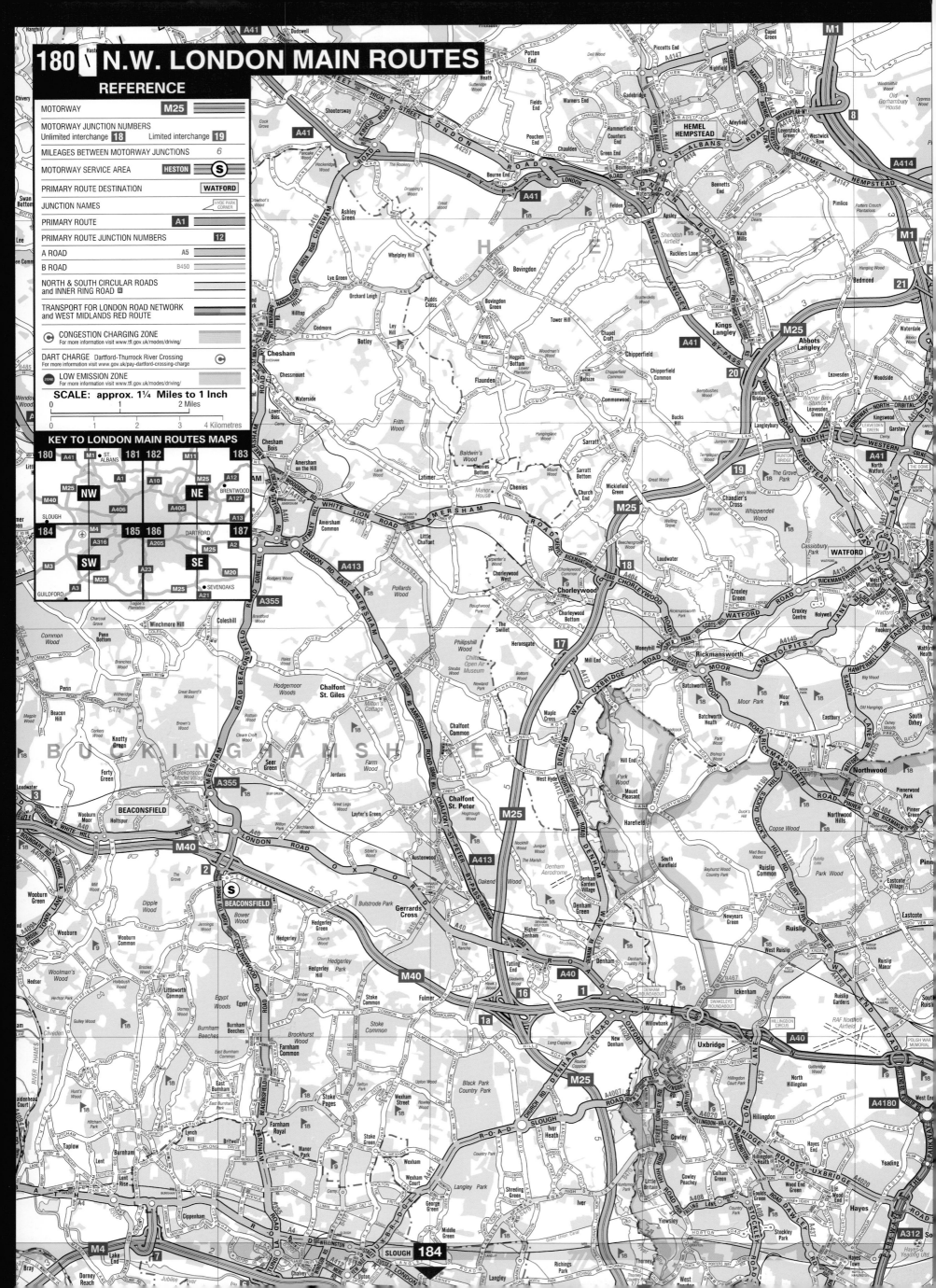

REFERENCE

MOTORWAY	M25
MOTORWAY JUNCTION NUMBERS	
Unlimited interchange 18 Limited interchange 19	
MILEAGES BETWEEN MOTORWAY JUNCTIONS	6
MOTORWAY SERVICE AREA	HESTON (S)
PRIMARY ROUTE DESTINATION	WATFORD
JUNCTION NAMES	HYDE PARK CORNER
PRIMARY ROUTE	A1
PRIMARY ROUTE JUNCTION NUMBERS	12
A ROAD	A5
B ROAD	B450
NORTH & SOUTH CIRCULAR ROADS and INNER RING ROAD	R
TRANSPORT FOR LONDON ROAD NETWORK and WEST MIDLANDS RED ROUTE	
CONGESTION CHARGING ZONE For more information visit www.tfl.gov.uk/modes/driving/	
DART CHARGE Dartford-Thurrock River Crossing For more information visit www.gov.uk/pay-dartford-crossing-charge	(C)
LOW EMISSION ZONE For more information visit www.tfl.gov.uk/modes/driving/	ZONE

SCALE: approx. 1¼ Miles to 1 Inch

0 — 1 — 2 Miles

0 — 1 — 2 — 3 — 4 Kilometres

KEY TO LONDON MAIN ROUTES MAPS

180 NW	181 182 NE	183
184 SW	185 186 SE	187

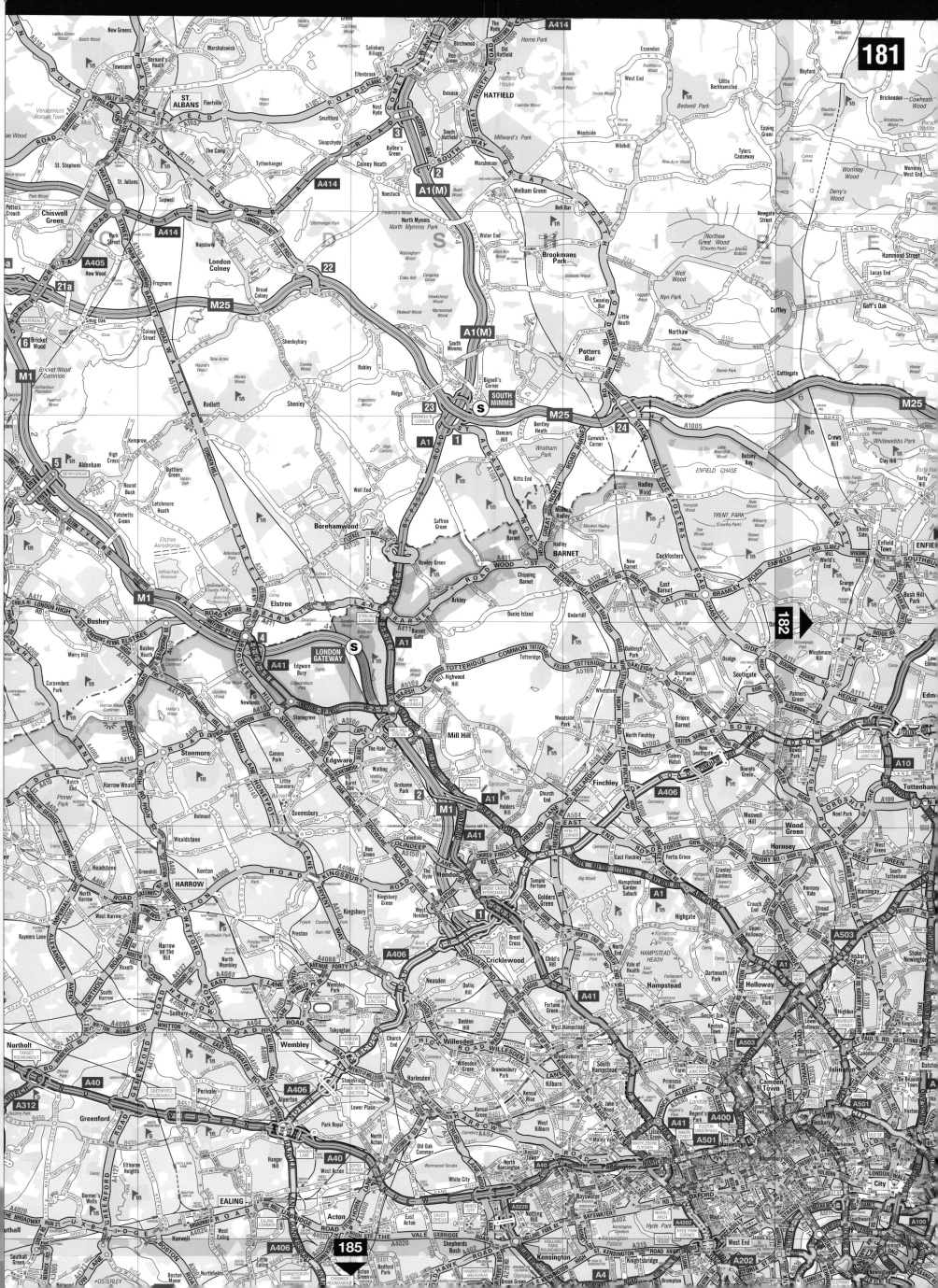

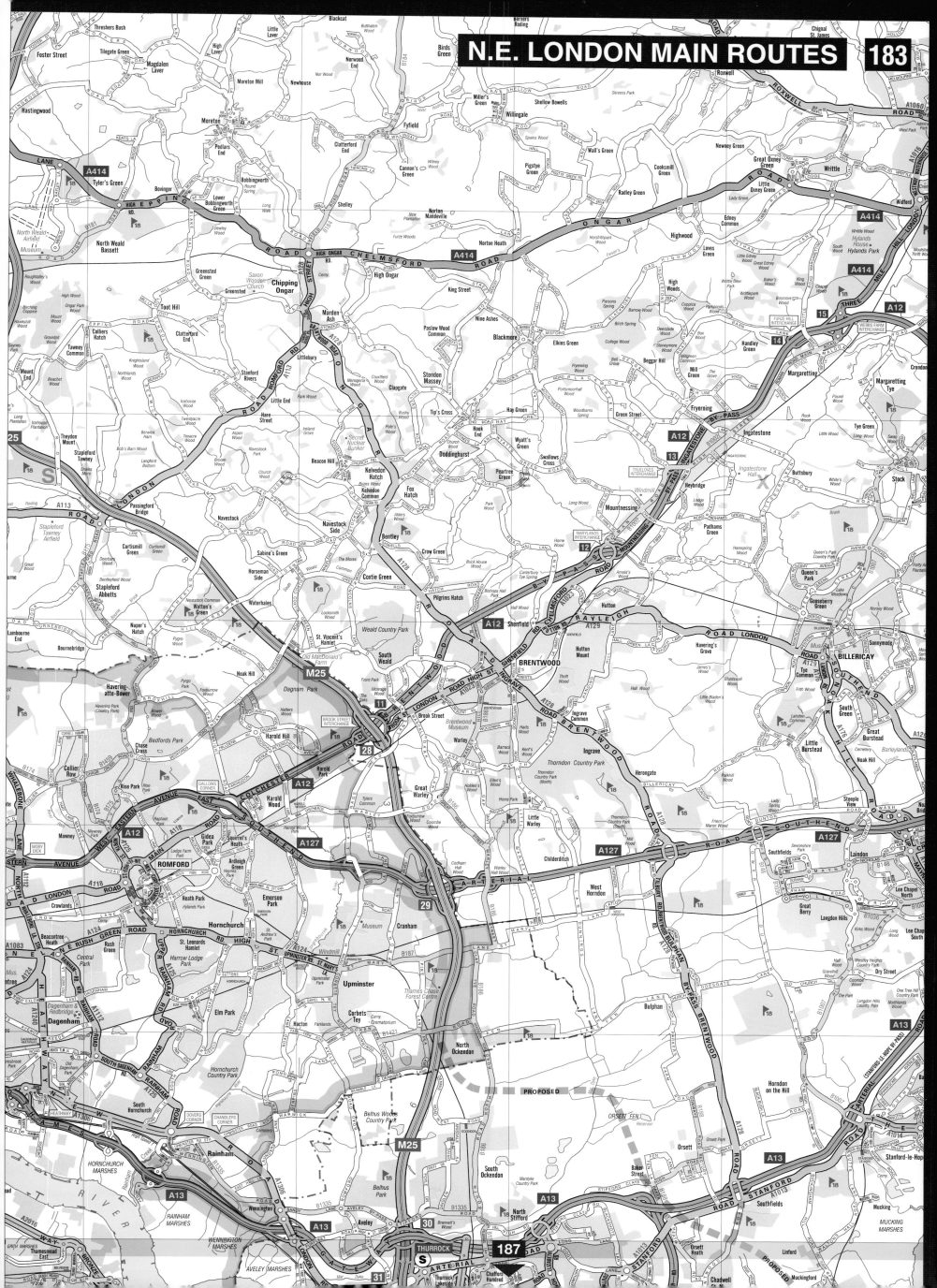

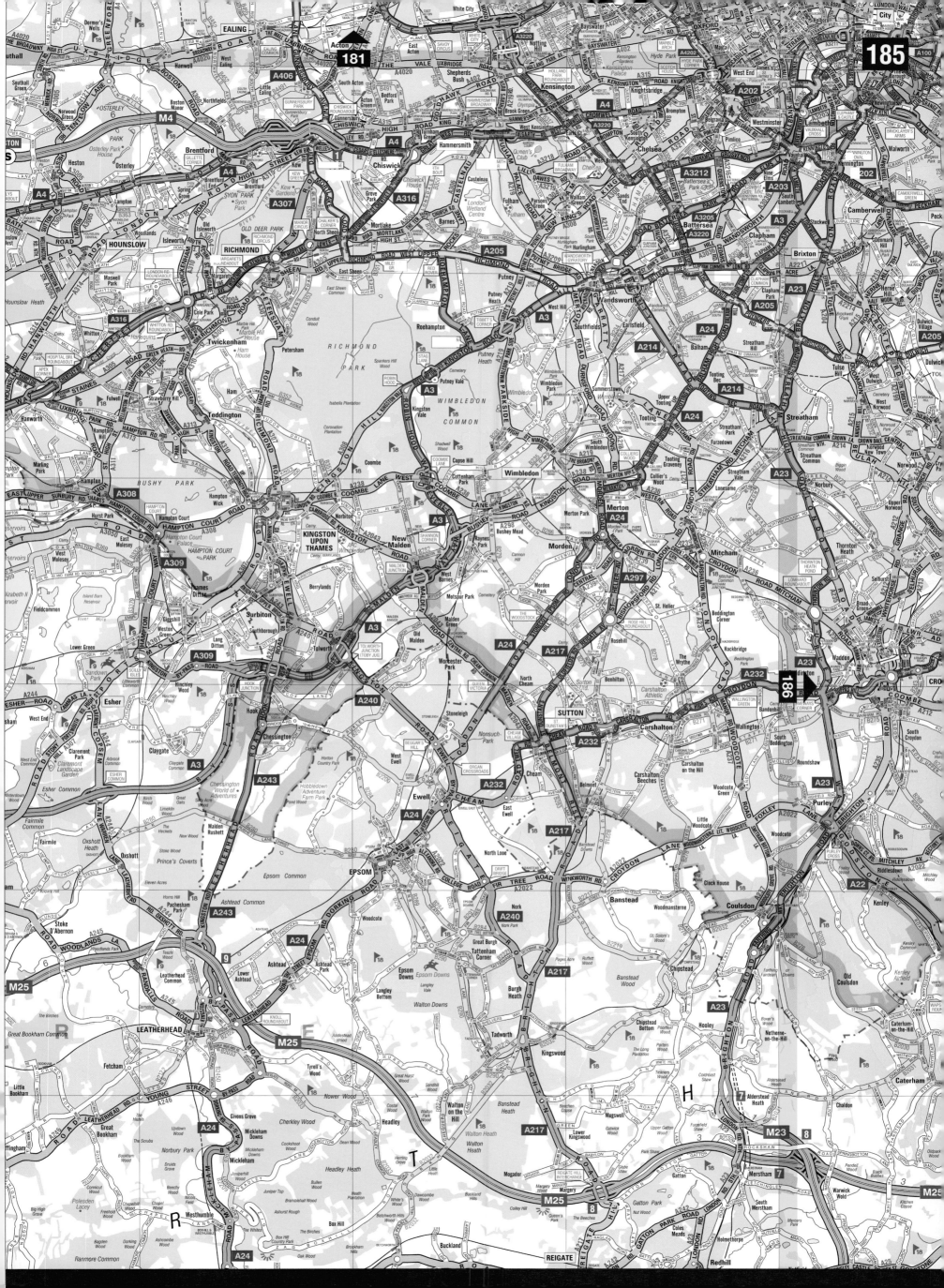

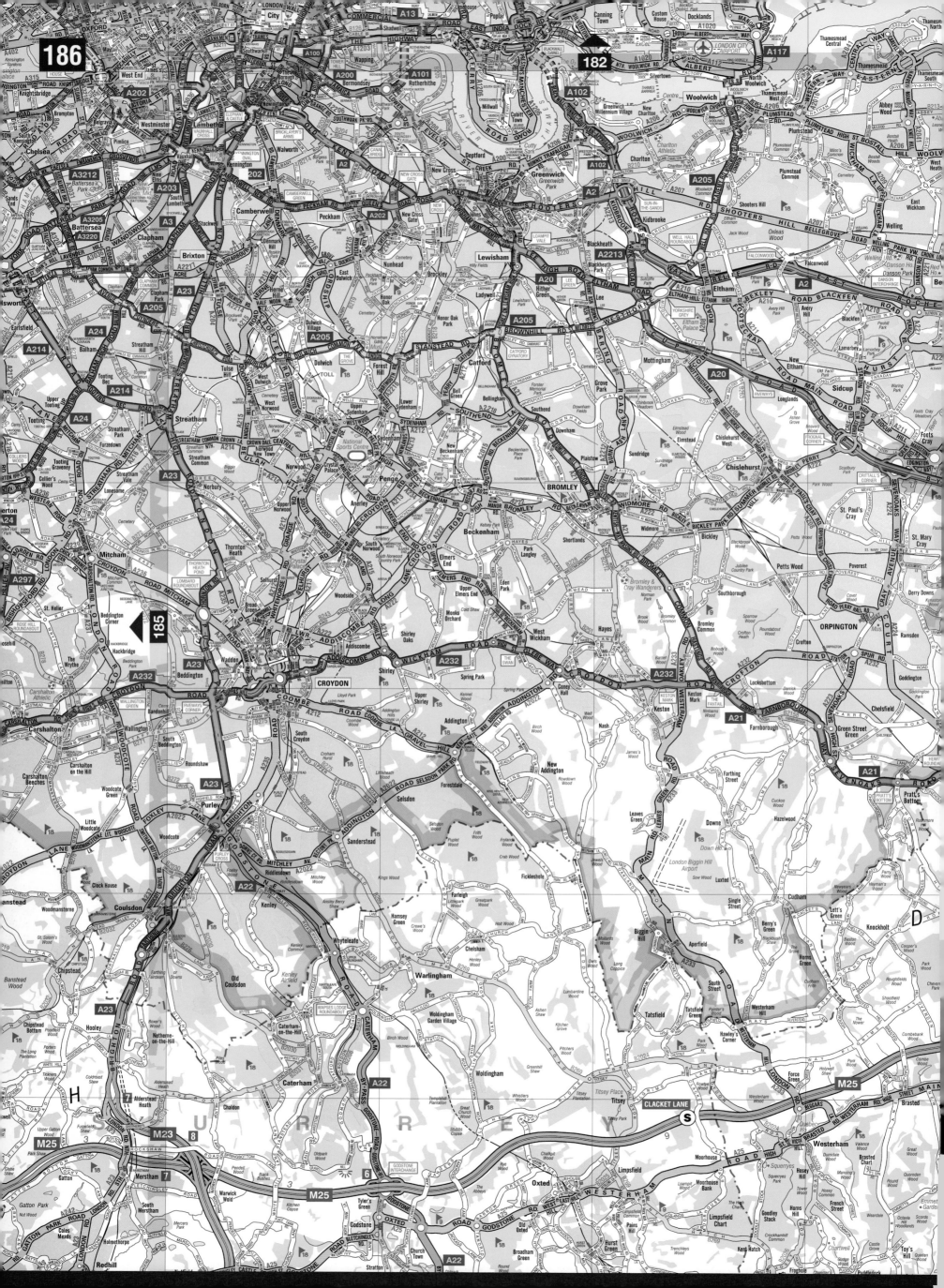

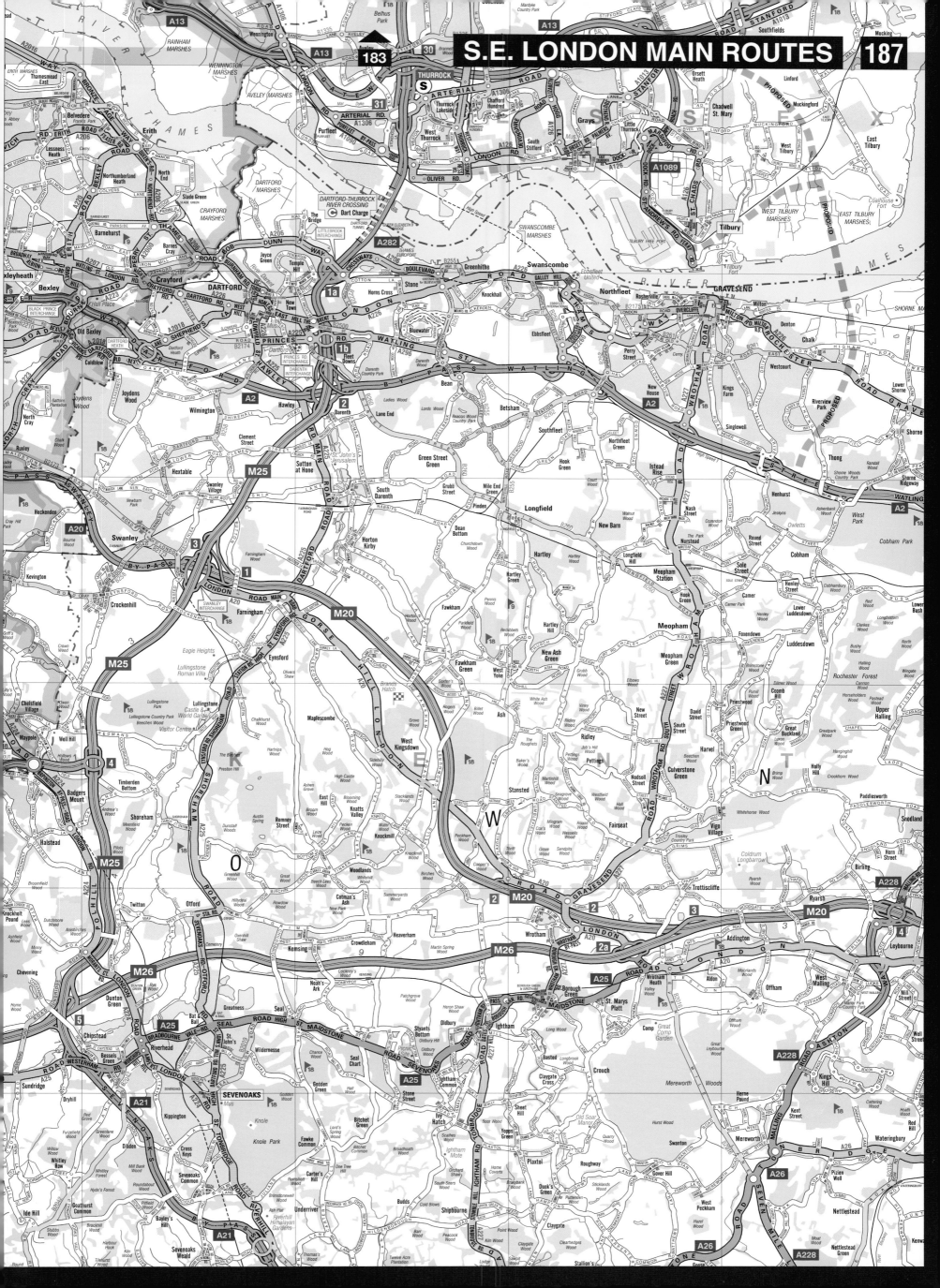

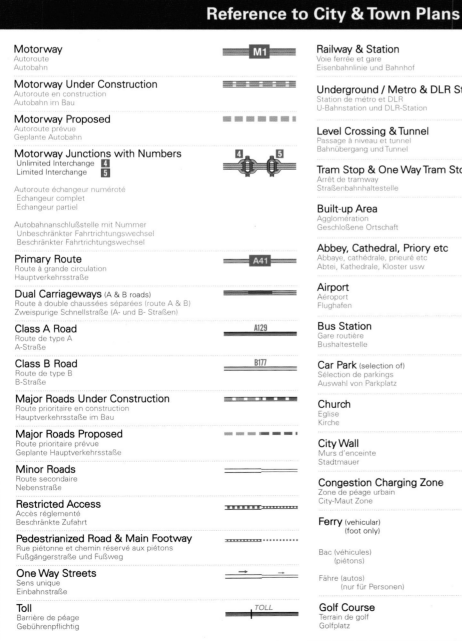

Reference to City & Town Plans   Légende   Zeichenerklärung

Motorway
Autoroute
Autobahn
— M1

Motorway Under Construction
Autoroute en construction
Autobahn im Bau

Motorway Proposed
Autoroute prévue
Geplante Autobahn

Motorway Junctions with Numbers
Unlimited Interchange 4
Limited Interchange 5
Autoroute échangeur numéroté
Échangeur complet
Échangeur partiel
Autobahnanschlußstelle mit Nummer
Unbeschränkter Fahrtrichtungswechsel
Beschränkter Fahrtrichtungswechsel

Primary Route
Route à grande circulation
Hauptverkehrsstraße
A41

Dual Carriageways (A & B roads)
Route à double chaussées séparées (route A & B)
Zweispurige Schnellstraße (A- und B- Straßen)

Class A Road
Route de type A
A-Straße
A129

Class B Road
Route de type B
B-Straße
B177

Major Roads Under Construction
Route prioritaire en construction
Hauptverkehrsstraße im Bau

Major Roads Proposed
Route prioritaire prévue
Geplante Hauptverkehrsstraße

Minor Roads
Route secondaire
Nebenstraße

Restricted Access
Accès réglementé
Beschränkte Zufahrt

Pedestrianized Road & Main Footway
Rue piétonne et chemin réservé aux piétons
Fußgängerstraße und Fußweg

One Way Streets
Sens unique
Einbahnstraße

Toll
Barrière de péage
Gebührenpflichtig
TOLL

Railway & Station
Voie ferrée et gare
Eisenbahnlinie und Bahnhof

Underground / Metro & DLR Station
Station de métro et DLR
U-Bahnstation und DLR-Station

Level Crossing & Tunnel
Passage à niveau et tunnel
Bahnübergang und Tunnel

Tram Stop & One Way Tram Stop
Arrêt de tramway
Straßenbahnhaltestelle

Built-up Area
Agglomération
Geschloßene Ortschaft

Abbey, Cathedral, Priory etc
Abbaye, cathédrale, prieuré etc
Abtei, Kathedrale, Kloster usw

Airport
Aéroport
Flughafen

Bus Station
Gare routière
Bushaltestelle

Car Park (selection of)
Sélection de parkings
Auswahl von Parkplatz

Church
Église
Kirche

City Wall
Murs d'enceinte
Stadtmauer

Congestion Charging Zone
Zone de péage urbain
City-Maut Zone

Ferry (vehicular)
(foot only)
Bac (véhicules)
(piétons)
Fähre (autos)
(nur für Personen)

Golf Course
Terrain de golf
Golfplatz

Heliport
Héliport
Hubschrauberlandeplatz

Hospital
Hôpital
Krankenhaus
H

Lighthouse
Phare
Leuchtturm

Market
Marché
Markt

National Trust Property
(open)
(restricted opening)   NT
(National Trust for Scotland)   NT
National Trust Property   NTS   NTS
(ouvert)
(heures d'ouverture)
(National Trust for Scotland)
National Trust- Eigentum
(geöffnet)
(beschränkte Öffnungszeit)
(National Trust for Scotland)

Park & Ride
Parking relais
Auswahl von Parkplatz

Place of Interest
Curiosité
Sehenswürdigkeit

Police Station
Commissariat de police
Polizeirevier
▲

Post Office
Bureau de poste
Postamt
★

Shopping Area (main street & precinct)
Quartier commerçant (rue et zone principales)
Einkaufsviertel (hauptgeschäftsstraße, fußgängerzone)

Shopmobility
Shopmobility
Shopmobility

Toilet
Toilettes
Toilette
▽

Tourist Information Centre
Syndicat d'initiative
Information

Viewpoint
Vue panoramique
Aussichtspunkt

Visitor Information Centre
Centre d'information touristique
Besucherzentrum
V

ABERDEEN

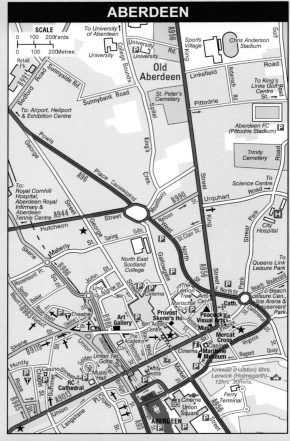

BATH

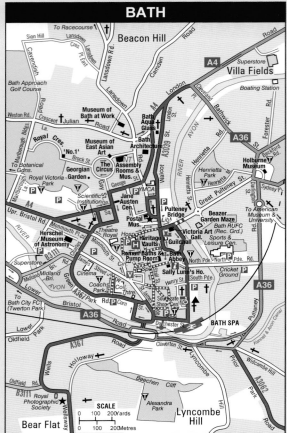

BLACKPOOL

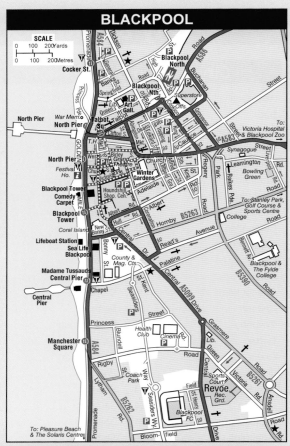

BIRMINGHAM (CITY CENTRE)

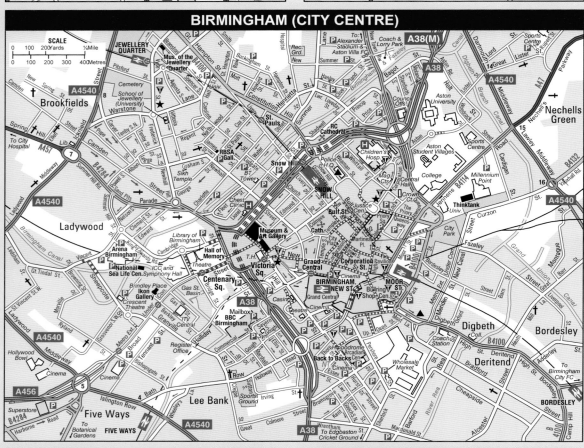

BOURNEMOUTH

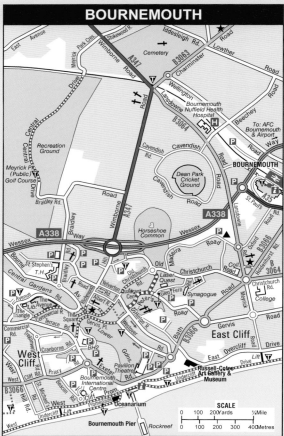

BRADFORD

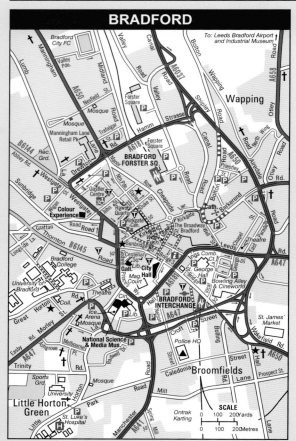

BRIGHTON and HOVE

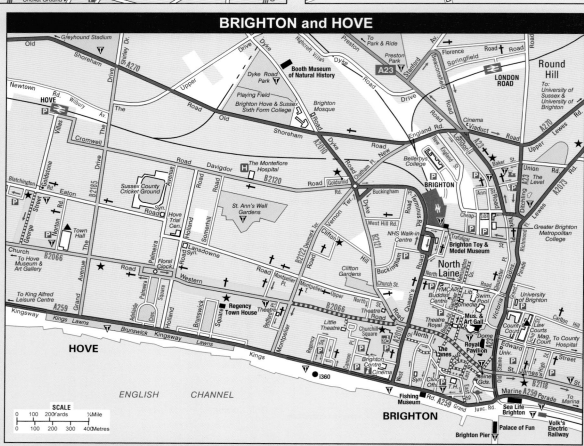

BRISTOL
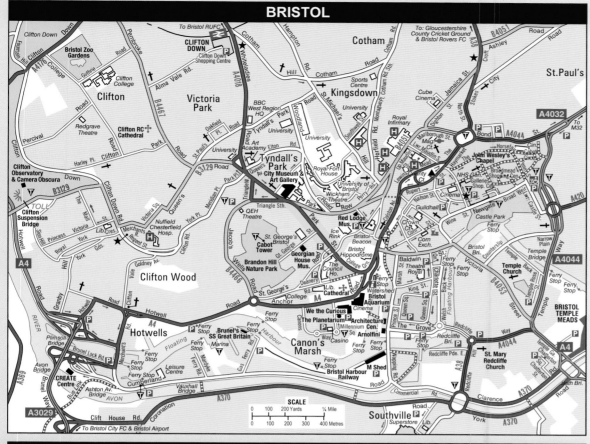

CANTERBURY
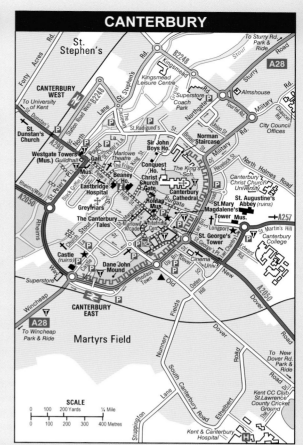

CAMBRIDGE
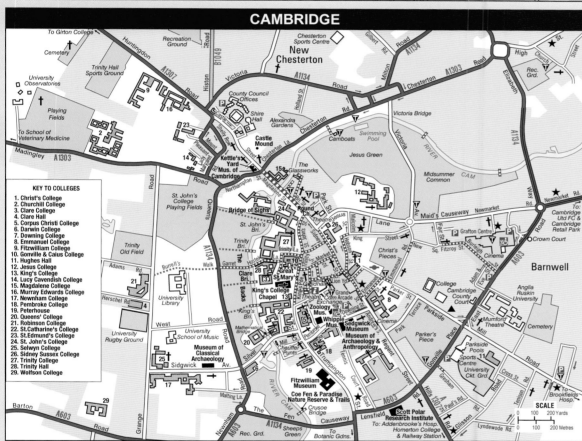

KEY TO COLLEGES
1. Christ's College
2. Churchill College
3. Clare College
4. Clare Hall
5. Corpus Christi College
6. Darwin College
7. Downing College
8. Emmanuel College
9. Fitzwilliam College
10. Gonville & Caius College
11. Hughes Hall
12. Jesus College
13. King's College
14. Lucy Cavendish College
15. Magdalene College
16. Murray Edwards College
17. Newnham College
18. Pembroke College
19. Peterhouse
20. Queens' College
21. Robinson College
22. St.Catharine's College
23. St.Edmund's College
24. St. John's College
25. Selwyn College
26. Sidney Sussex College
27. Trinity College
28. Trinity Hall
29. Wolfson College

CARLISLE
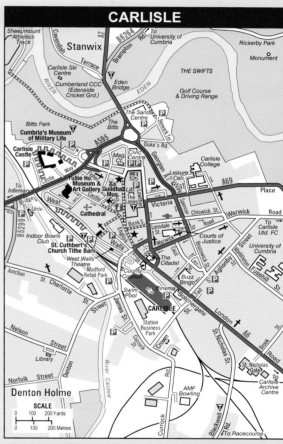

CARDIFF (CAERDYDD)
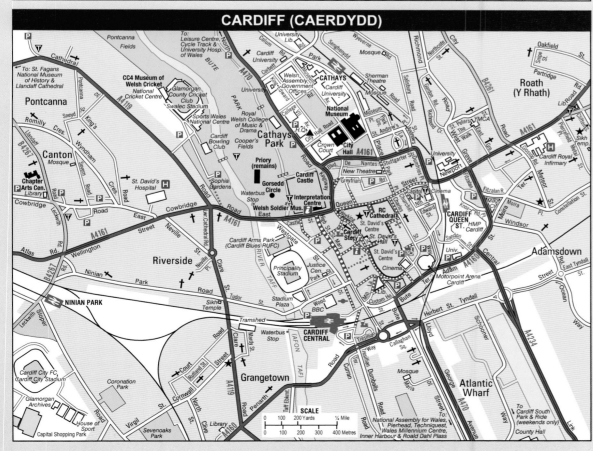

CHELTENHAM
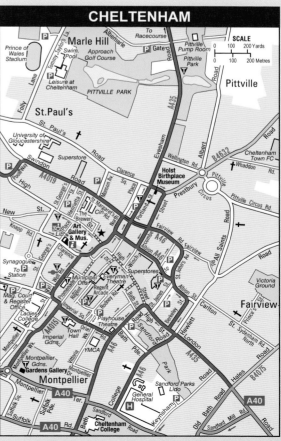

CHESTER

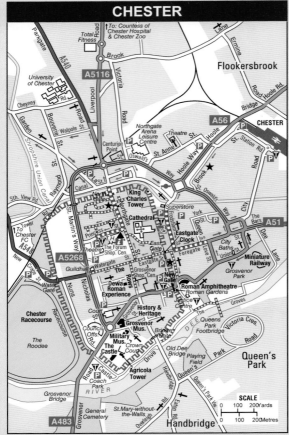

COVENTRY

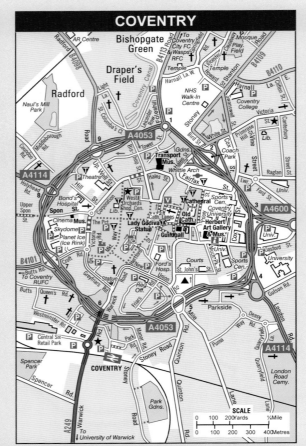

DERBY

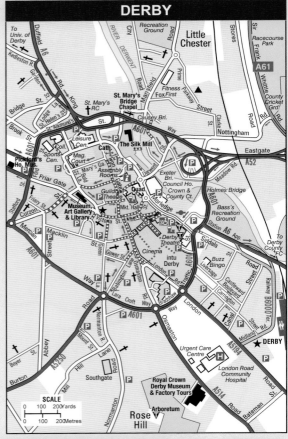

DOVER

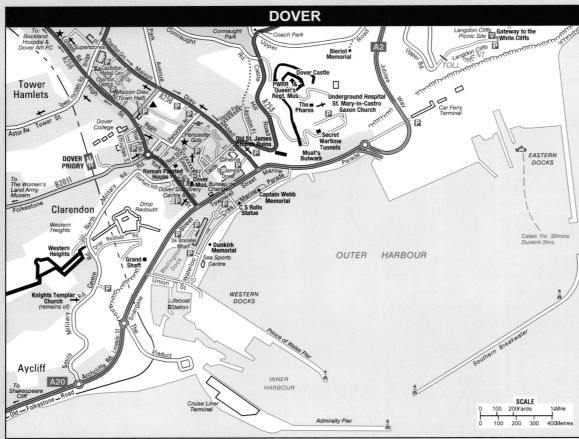

DUMFRIES

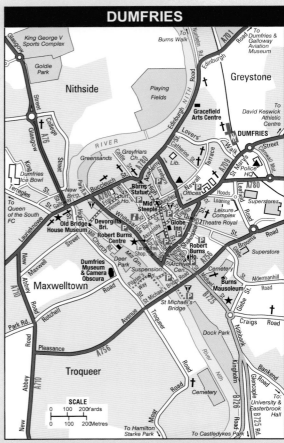

DUNDEE

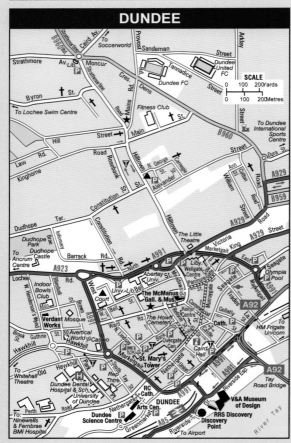

DURHAM

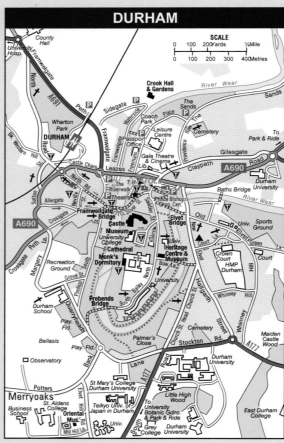

EASTBOURNE

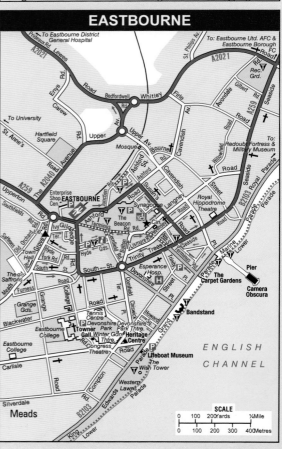

EDINBURGH

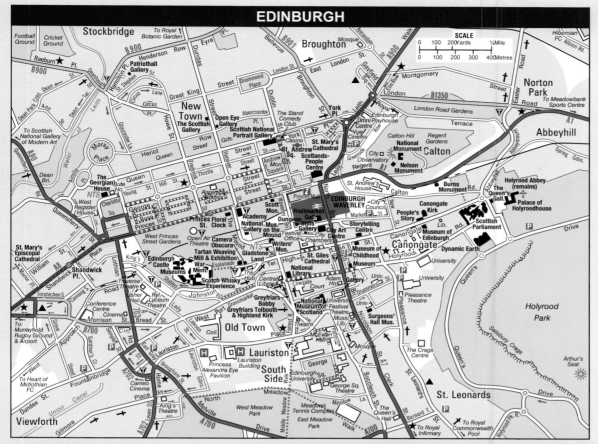

FOLKESTONE

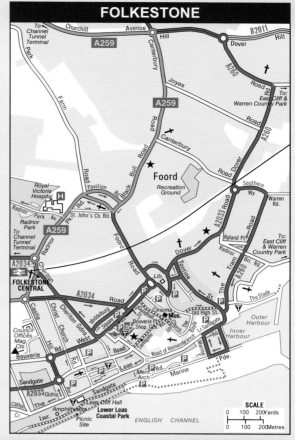

EXETER

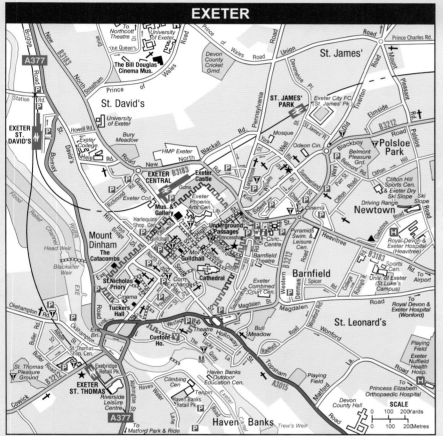

GUILDFORD

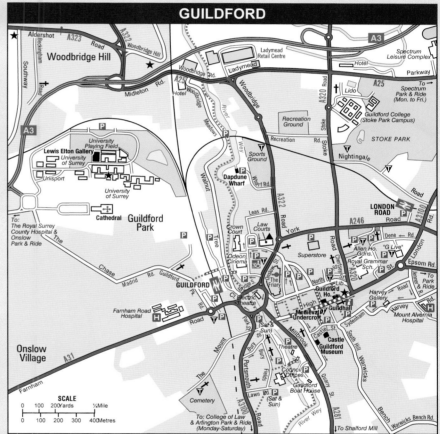

GLASGOW

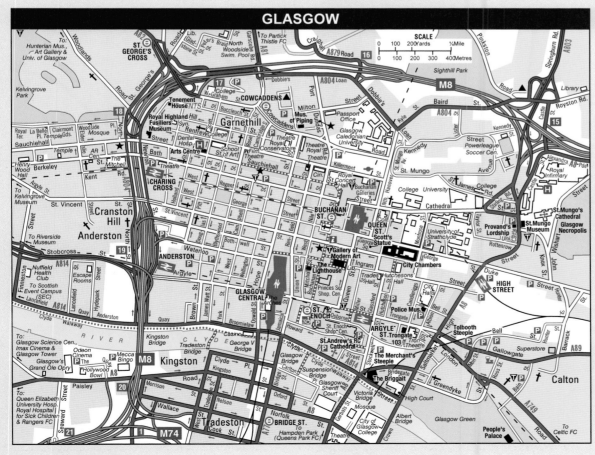

GLOUCESTER

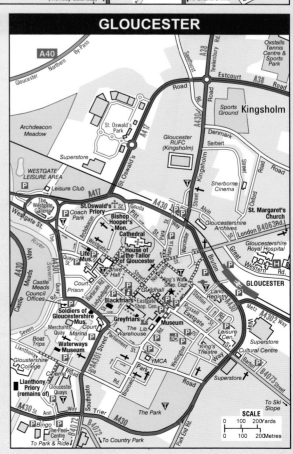

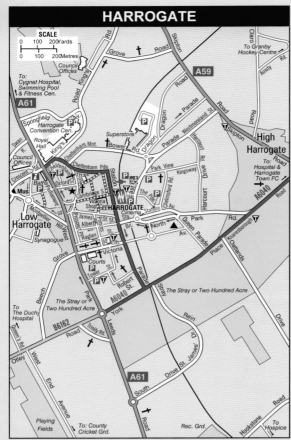

HARROGATE

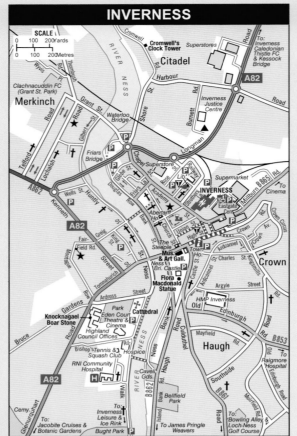

INVERNESS

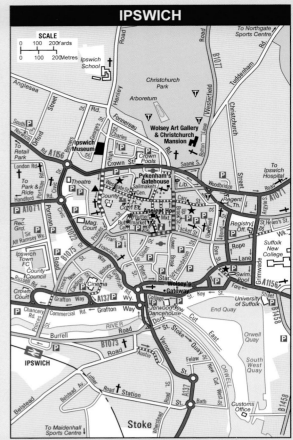

IPSWICH

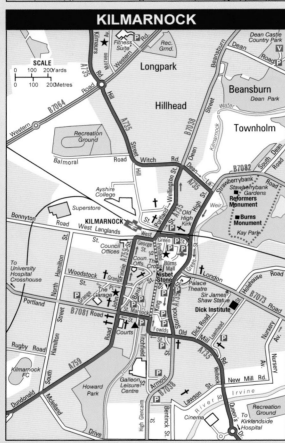

KILMARNOCK

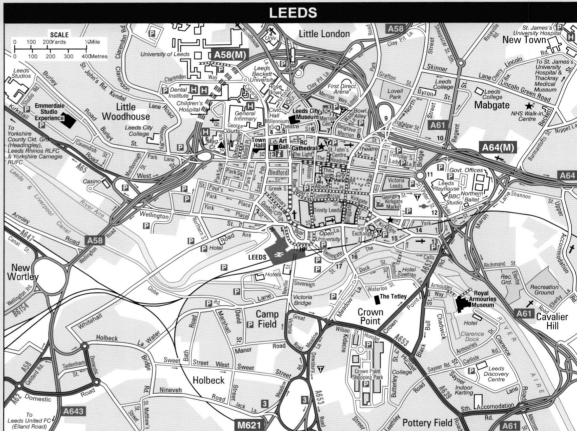

LEEDS

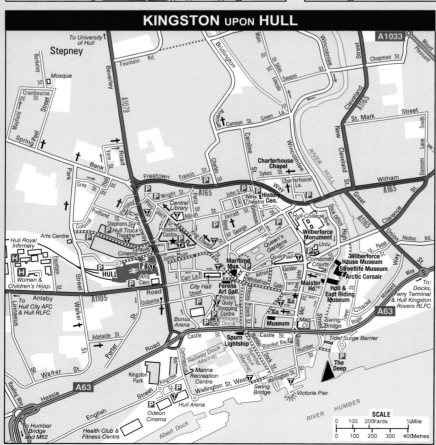

KINGSTON UPON HULL

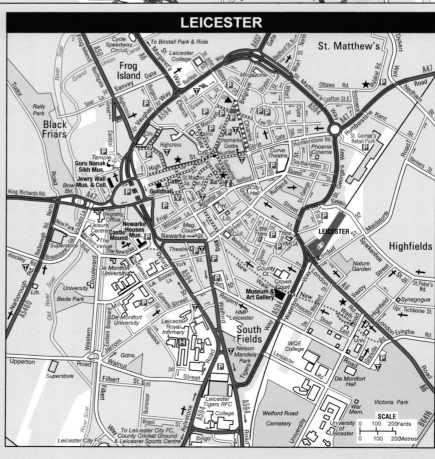

LEICESTER

LINCOLN

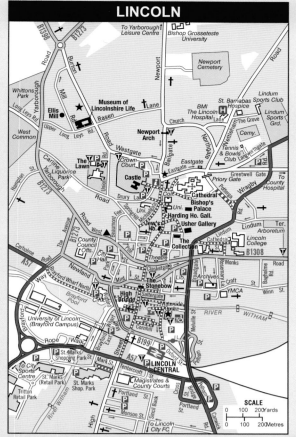

LIVERPOOL

MANCHESTER (CITY CENTRE)

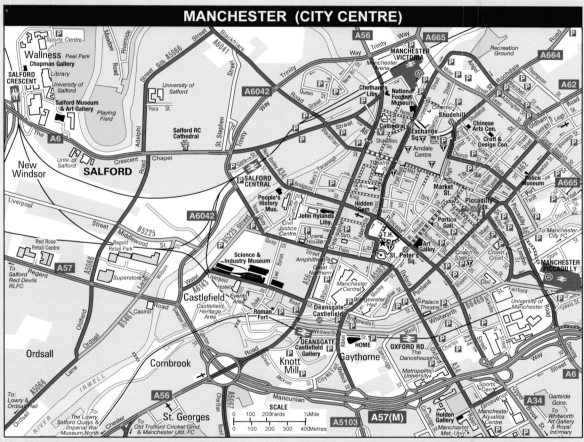

MIDDLESBROUGH

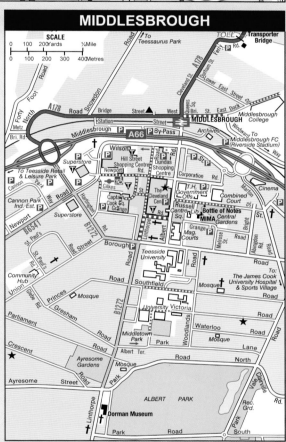

MEDWAY TOWNS

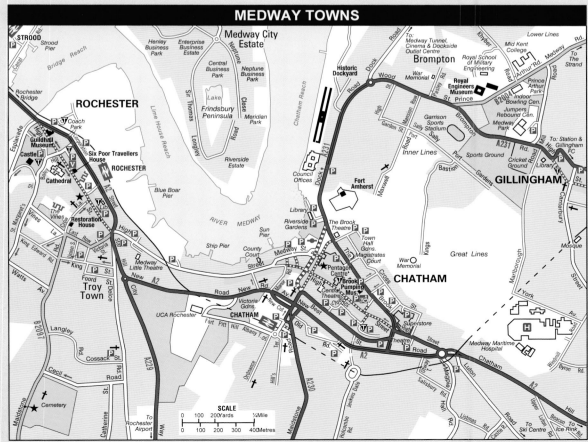

NEWCASTLE UPON TYNE

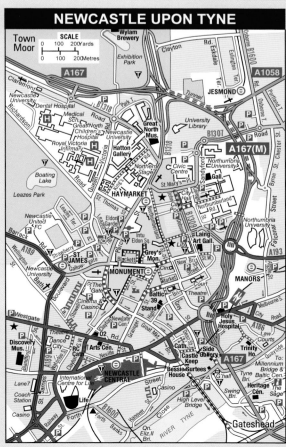

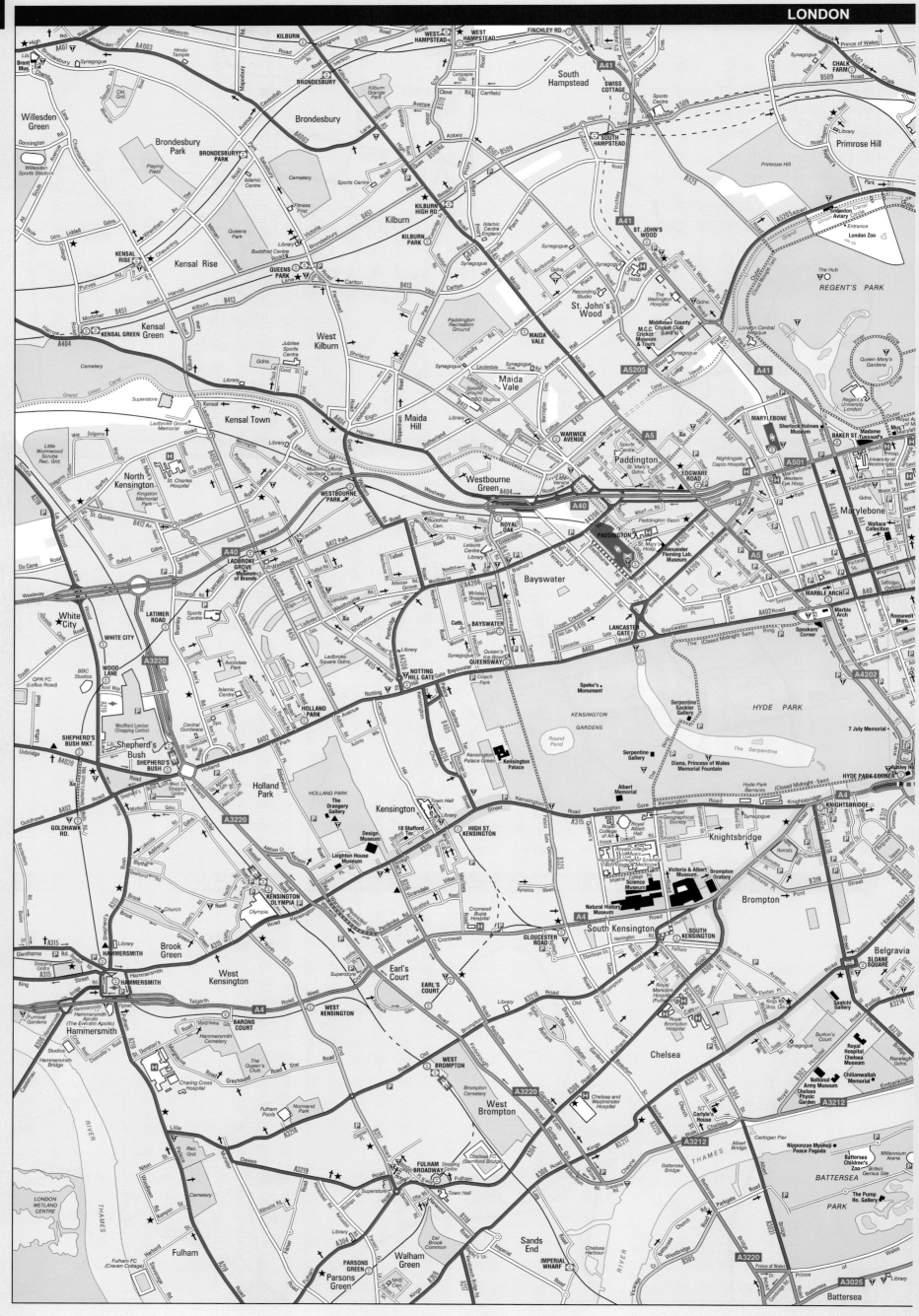

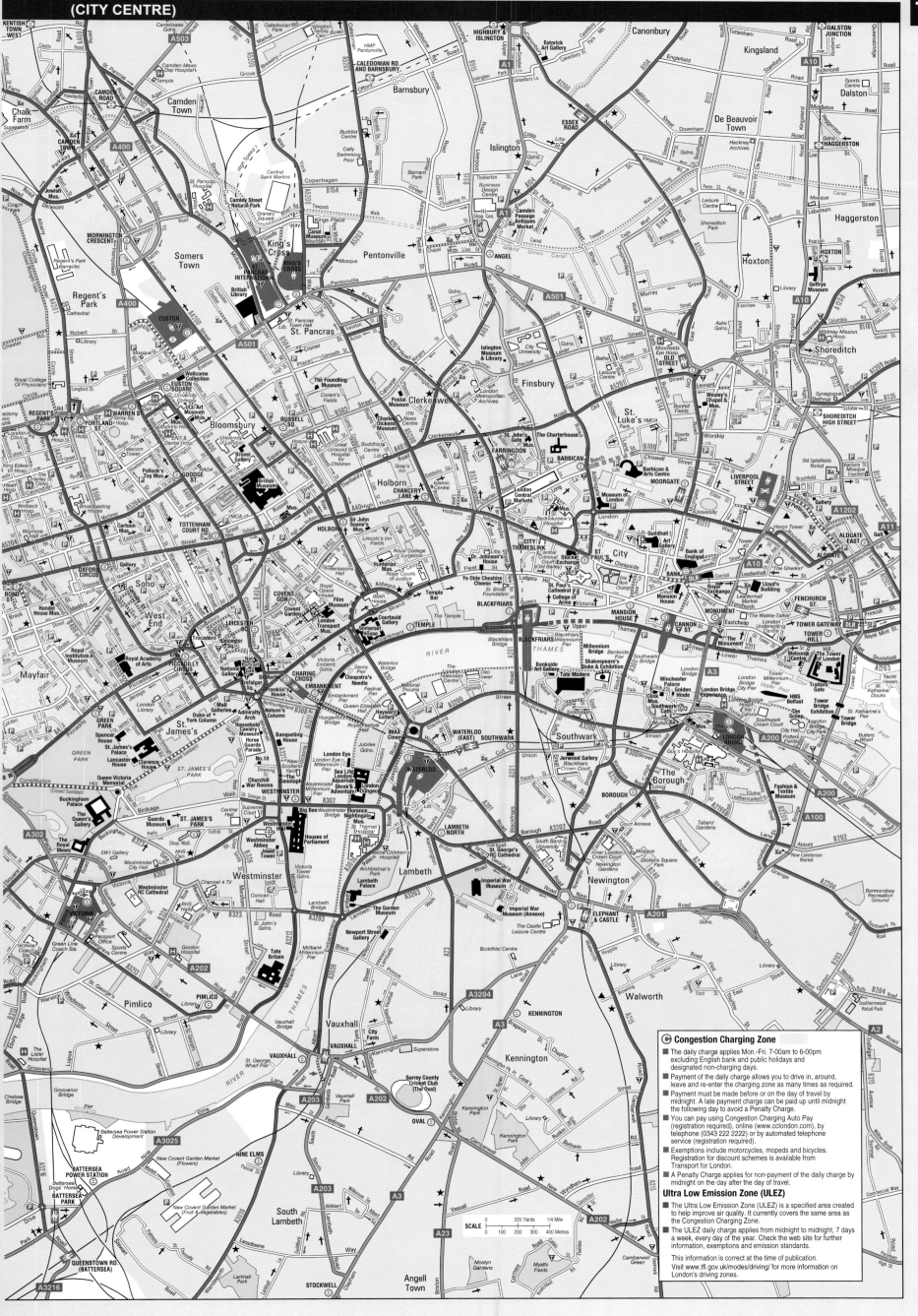

SCALE
0   220 Yards   1/4 Mile
0 100 200 300 400 Metres

MILTON KEYNES

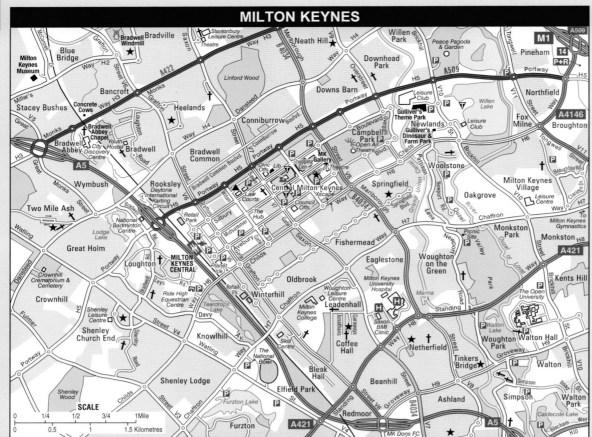

NEWPORT (CASNEWYDD)

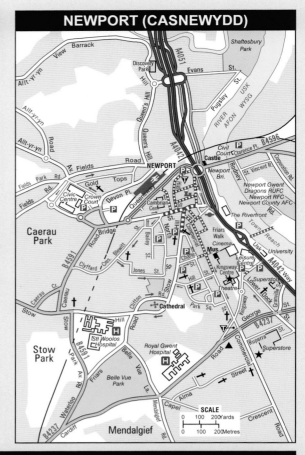

NORWICH

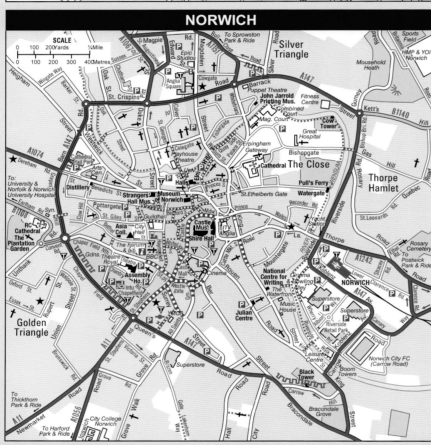

NOTTINGHAM

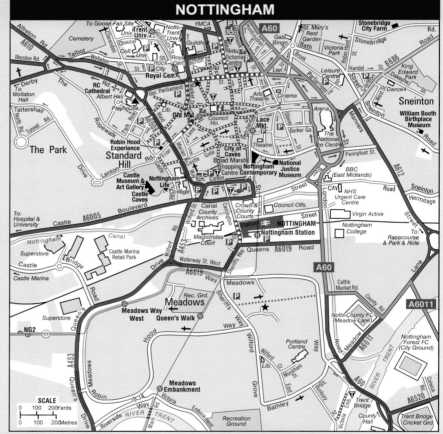

NORTHAMPTON

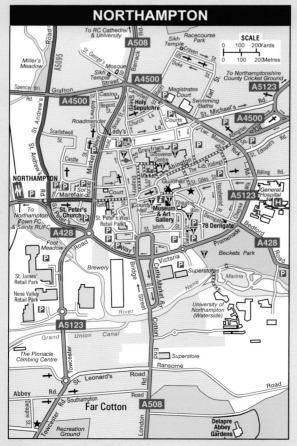

OXFORD

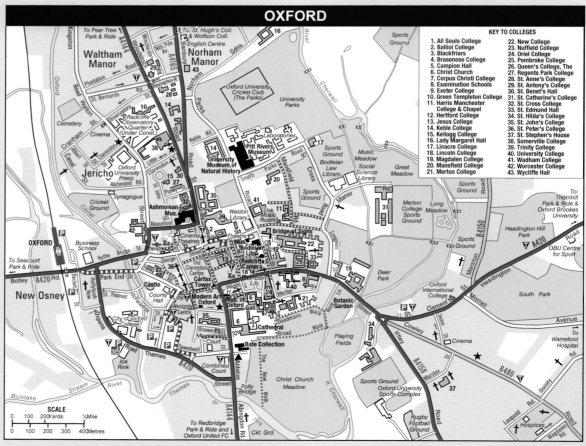

KEY TO COLLEGES

1. All Souls College
2. Balliol College
3. Blackfriars
4. Brasenose College
5. Campion Hall
6. Christ Church
7. Corpus Christi College
8. Examination Schools
9. Exeter College
10. Green Templeton College
11. Harris Manchester College & Chapel
12. Hertford College
13. Jesus College
14. Keble College
15. Kellogg College
16. Lady Margaret Hall
17. Linacre College
18. Lincoln College
19. Magdalen College
20. Mansfield College
21. Merton College
22. New College
23. Nuffield College
24. Oriel College
25. Pembroke College
26. Queen's College, The
27. Regents Park College
28. St. Anne's College
29. St. Antony's College
30. St. Benet's Hall
31. St. Catherine's College
32. St. Cross College
33. St. Edmund Hall
34. St. Hilda's College
35. St. John's College
36. St. Peter's College
37. St. Stephen's House
38. Somerville College
39. Trinity College
40. University College
41. Wadham College
42. Worcester College
43. Wycliffe Hall

OBAN

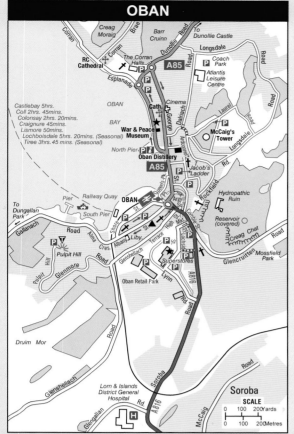

PERTH

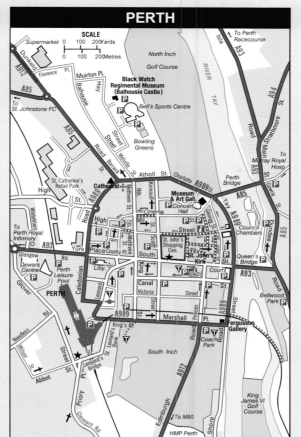

PETERBOROUGH

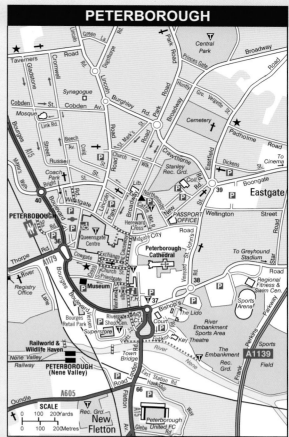

PLYMOUTH

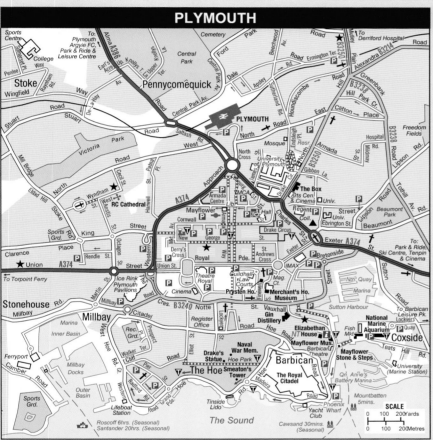

PORTSMOUTH

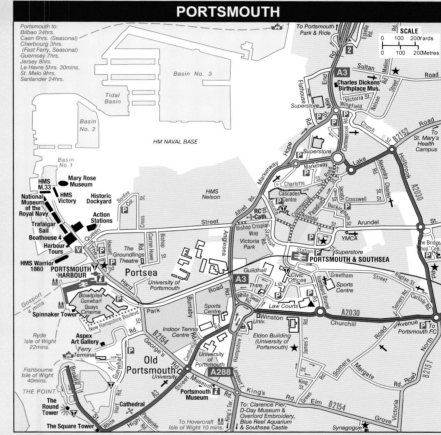

PRESTON

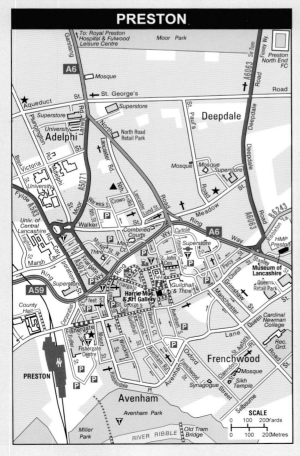

READING

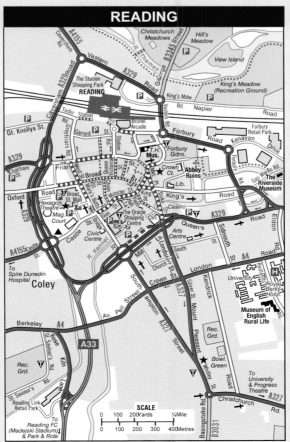

SALISBURY

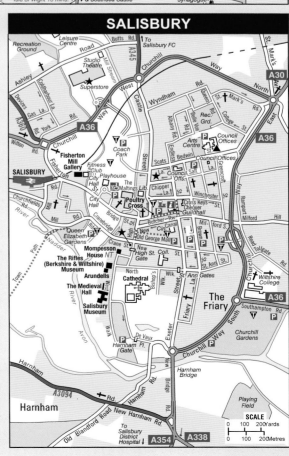

SHEFFIELD

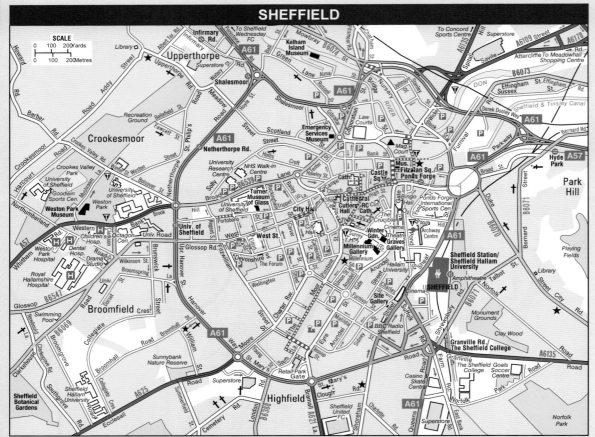

SHREWSBURY

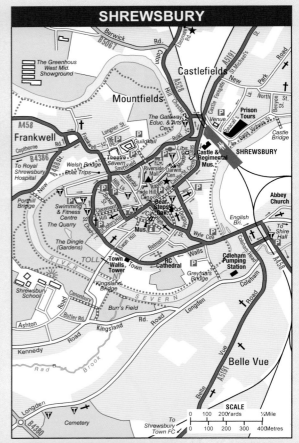

SOUTHAMPTON

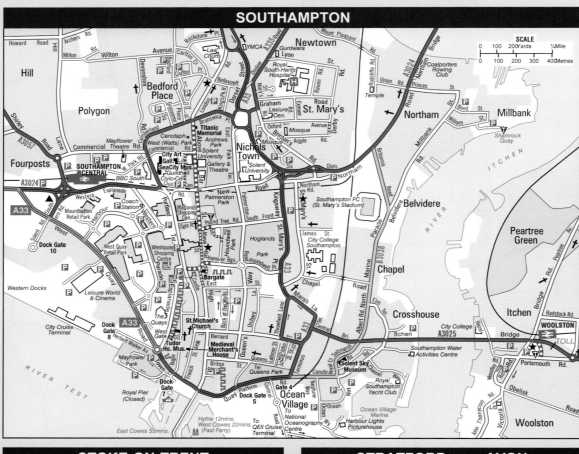

STIRLING

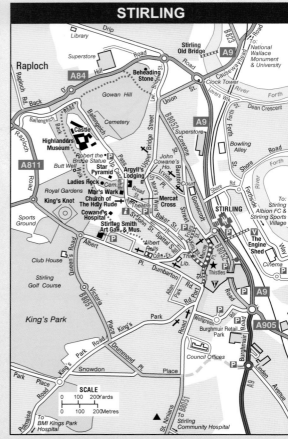

STOKE-ON-TRENT

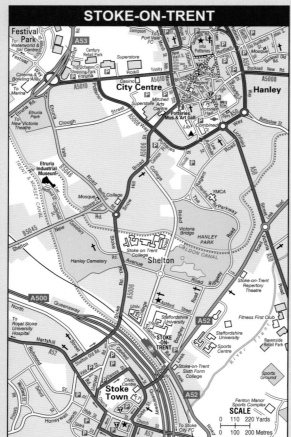

STRATFORD UPON AVON

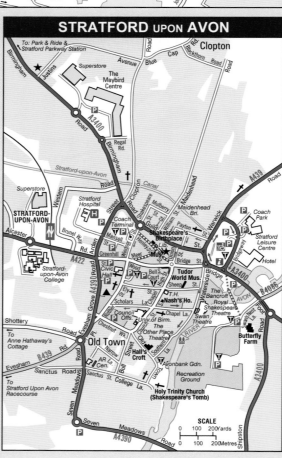

SUNDERLAND

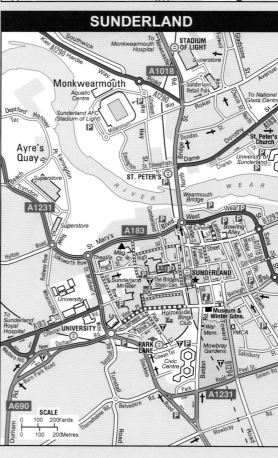

SWANSEA (ABERTAWE)
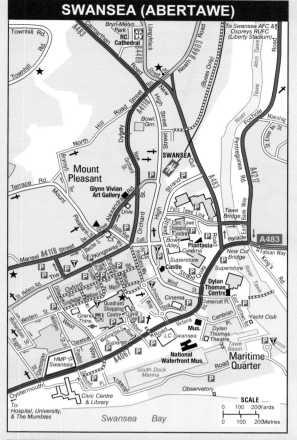

SWINDON
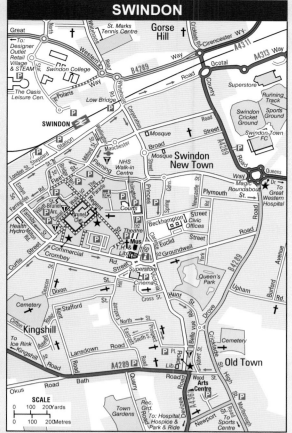

TAUNTON
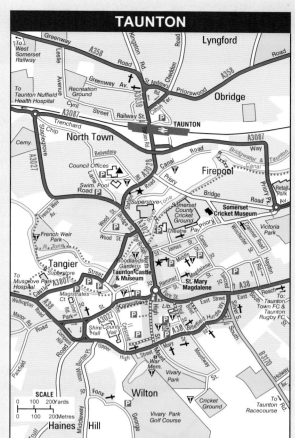

WINCHESTER
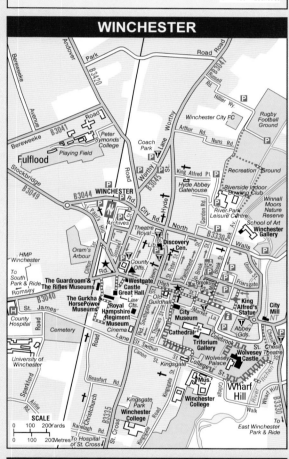

WINDSOR
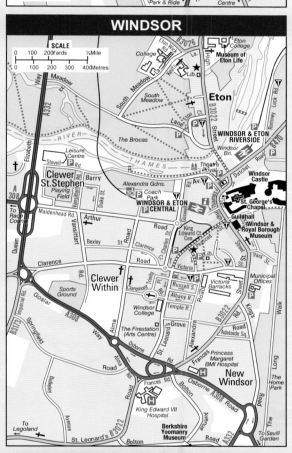

WOLVERHAMPTON
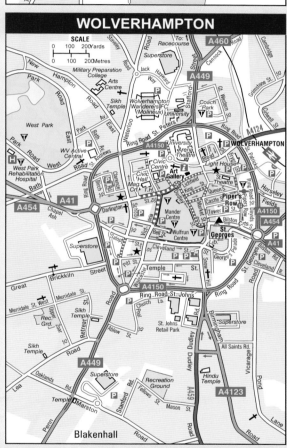

WORCESTER
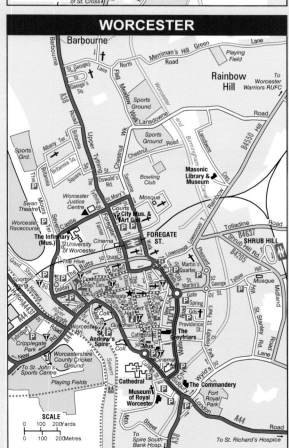

YORK
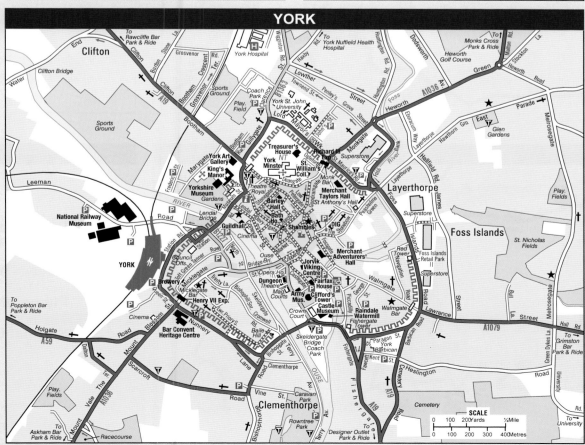

HARWICH

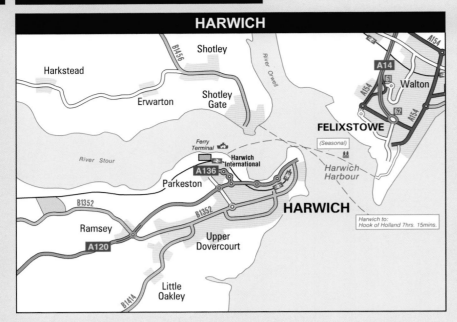

KINGSTON UPON HULL

NEWCASTLE UPON TYNE

NEWHAVEN

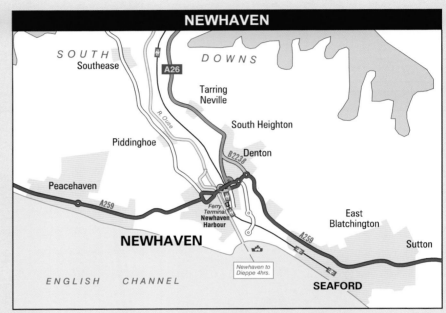

PEMBROKE DOCK (DOC PENFRO)

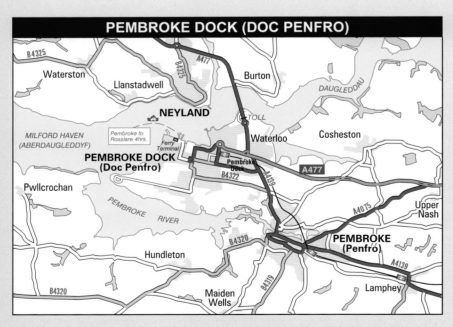

POOLE

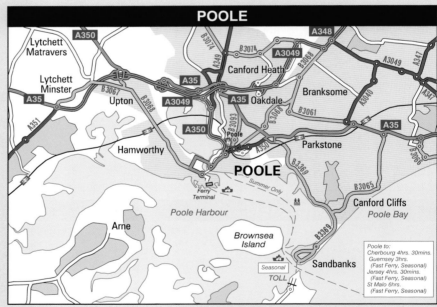

PORTSMOUTH

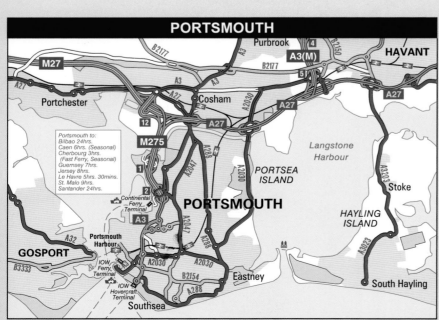

Other Port Plans

Please refer to Town Plans for detailed plans of the following Ports:

Dover - page 194

Plymouth - page 201

Southampton - page 202

BIRMINGHAM

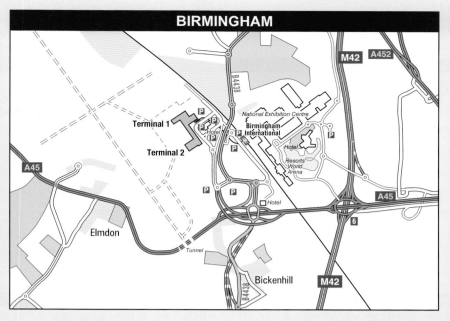

EAST MIDLANDS

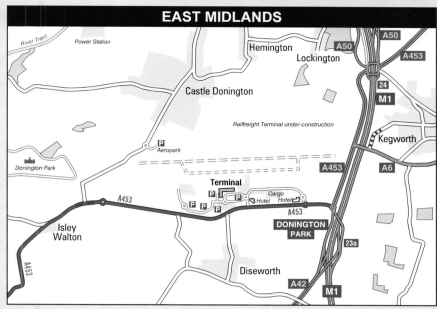

GLASGOW

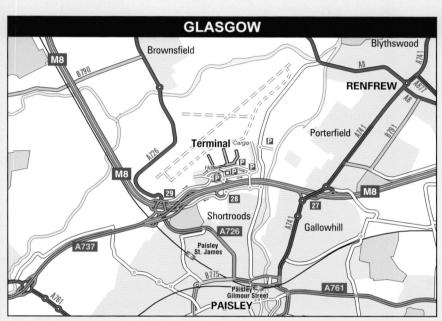

LONDON GATWICK

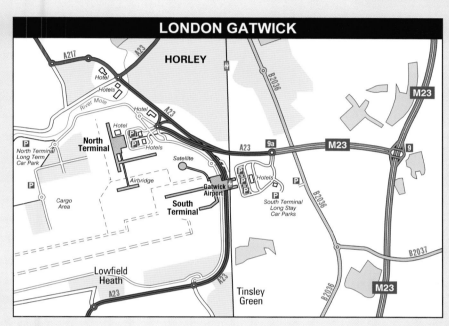

LONDON HEATHROW

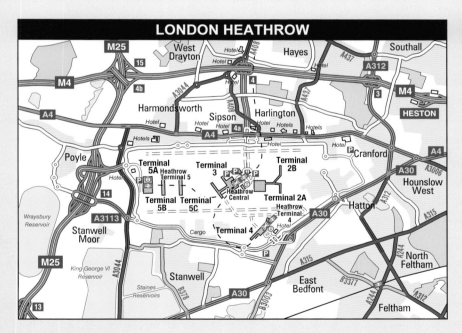

LONDON LUTON

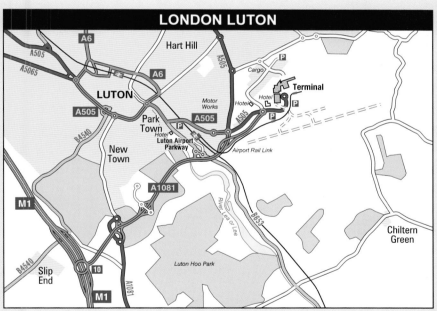

LONDON STANSTED

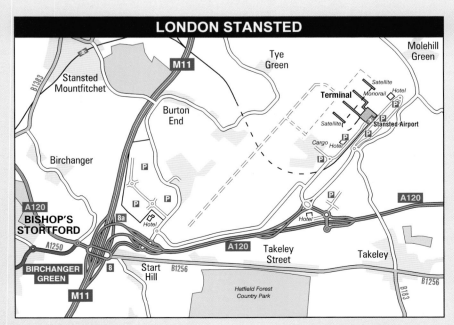

MANCHESTER

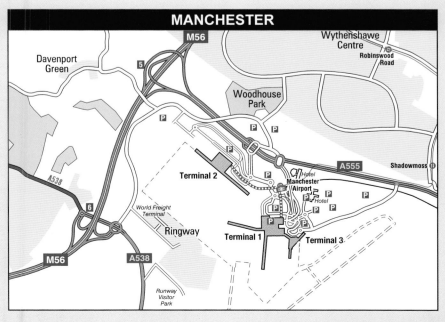

INDEX TO CITIES, TOWNS, VILLAGES, HAMLETS, LOCATIONS, AIRPORTS & PORTS

(1) A strict alphabetical order is used e.g. An Dùnan follows Andreas but precedes Andwell.

(2) The map reference given refers to the actual map square in which the town spot or built-up area is located and not to the place name.

(3) Major towns and destinations are shown in bold, i.e. **Aberdeen.** *Aber* . . . . **192** (3G **153**) Page references for Town Plan entries are shown first.

(4) Where two or more places of the same name occur in the same County or Unitary Authority, the nearest large town is also given; e.g. Achiemore. *High* nr. Durness . . . .2D **166** indicates that Achiemore is located in square 2D on page **166** and is situated near Durness in the Unitary Authority of Highland.

(5) Only one reference is given although due to page overlaps the place may appear on more than one page.

INDEX

[Index entries omitted — dense multi-column gazetteer listing place names with county abbreviations and grid references.]

Annscroft—Bampton

Annscroft. Shrp 5G 71
An Sailean. High 2A 140
Ansdell. Lanc 2B 90
Ansford. Som 3B 22
Ansley. Warw 1G 61
Anslow. Staf 3G 73
Anslow Gate. Staf 3F 73
Ansteadbrook. Surr 2A 26
Anstey. Herts 2E 53
Anstey. Leics 5C 74
Anston. S Lan 5D 128
Anstruther Easter. Fife 3H 137
Anstruther Wester. Fife 3H 137
Ansty. Warw 2A 62
Ansty. W Sus 3D 27
Ansty. Wilts 4E 23
An Taobh Tuath. W Isl 1E 170
An t-Aodann Ban. High 3C 154
An t Ath Leathann. High 1E 147
An Teanga. High 3E 147
Anthill Common. Hants 1E 17
Anthorn. Cumb 4C 112
Antingham. Norf 2E 79
An t-Ob. W Isl 9C 171
Anton's Gowt. Linc 1B 76
Antony. Corn 3A 8
An t-Ord. High 2E 147
Antrim. Ant 8H 175
Antrobus. Ches W 3A 84
Anvil Corner. Devn 2D 10
Anwick. Linc 5A 88
Anwoth. Dum 4C 110
Apethorpe. Nptn 1H 63
Apeton. Staf 4C 72
Apley. Linc 3A 88
Apperknowle. Derbs 3A 86
Apperley. Glos 3D 48
Apperley Dene. Nmbd 4D 114
Appersett. N Yor 5B 104
Appin. Arg 4D 140
Appleby. N Lin 3C 94
Appleby-in-Westmorland.
Cumb 2H 103
Appleby Magna. Leics 5H 73
Appleby Parva. Leics 5H 73
Applecross. High 4G 155
Appledore. Devn
nr. Bideford 3E 19
nr. Tiverton 1D 12
Appledore. Kent 3D 28
Appledore Heath. Kent 2D 28
Appleford. Oxon 2D 36
Applegarthtown. Dum 1C 112
Applemore. Hants 2B 16
Appleshaw. Hants 2B 24
Applethwaite. Cumb 2D 102
Appleton. Hal 2H 83
Appleton. Oxon 5C 50
Appleton-le-Moors.
N Yor 1B 100
Appleton-le-Street.
N Yor 2B 100
Appleton Roebuck. N Yor 5H 99
Appleton Thorn. Warr 2A 84
Appleton Wiske. N Yor 4A 106
Appletree. Nptn 1C 50
Appletreehall. Bord 3H 119
Appletreewick. N Yor 3C 98
Appley. Som 4D 20
Appley Bridge. Lanc 3D 90
Apse Heath. IOW 4D 16
Apsley End. C Beds 2B 52
Apuldram. W Sus 2G 17
Arabella. High 1C 158
Arasaig. High 5E 147
Arbeadie. Abers 4D 152
Arberth. Pemb 3F 43
Arbirlot. Ang 4F 145
Arborfield. Wok 5F 37
Arborfield Cross. Wok 5F 37
Arborfield Garrison. Wok 5F 37
Arbourthorne. S Yor 2A 86
Arbroath. Ang 4F 145
Arbuthnott. Abers 1H 145
Arcan. High 3H 157
Archargary. High 3H 167
Archdeacon Newton. Darl 3F 105
Archiestown. Mor 4G 159
Arclid. Ches E 4B 84
Arclid Green. Ches E 4B 84
Ardachu. High 3D 164
Ardalanish. Arg 2A 132
Ardaneaskan. High 5H 155
Ardarroch. High 5H 155
Ardbeg. Arg
nr. Dunoon 1C 126
on Islay 5C 124
on Isle of Bute 3B 126
Ardboe. M Ulst 2D 178
Ardcharnich. High 5F 163
Ardchiavaig. Arg 2A 132
Ardchonnell. Arg 2G 133
Ardchrishnish. Arg 1B 132
Ardchronie. High 5D 164
Ardchullarie. Stir 2E 135
Ardchyle. Stir 1E 135
Ard-dhubh. High 4G 155
Arddleen. Powy 4E 71
Arddlîn. Powy 4E 71
Ardechive. High 4D 148
Ardeley. Herts 3D 52
Ardelve. High 1A 148
Arden. Arg 1E 127
Ardendrain. High 5H 157
Arden Hall. N Yor 5C 106
Ardens Grafton. Warw 5F 61
Ardentinny. Arg 1C 126
Ardeonaig. Stir 5D 142
Ardersier. High 3B 158
Ardery. High 2B 140
Ardessie. High 5E 163
Ardfern. Arg 3F 133
Ardfernal. Arg 2D 124
Ardfin. Arg 3C 124
Ardgartan. Arg 3B 134
Ardgay. High 4D 164
Ardglass. New M 6K 179
Ardgour. High 2E 141
Ardheslaig. High 3G 155
Ardindrean. High 5F 163
Ardingly. W Sus 3E 27
Ardington. Oxon 3C 36
Ardlamont House. Arg 3A 126
Ardleigh. Essx 3D 54
Ardler. Per 4B 144
Ardley. Oxon 3D 50
Ardlui. Arg 2C 134
Ardlussa. Arg 1E 125
Ardmair. High 4F 163
Ardmay. Arg 3B 134
Ardmillan. Ards 3K 179
Ardminish. Arg 5E 125
Ardmolich. High 1B 140
Ardmore. High
nr. Kinlochbervie 3C 166
nr. Tain 5E 164
Ardnacross. Arg 4G 139
Ardnadam. Arg 1C 126
Ardnagrask. High 4H 157
Ardnamurach. High 4G 147
Ardnarff. High 5A 156
Ardnastang. High 2C 140
Ardoch. Per 5H 143
Ardochy House. High 3E 148
Ardpatrick. Arg 3F 125
Ardrishaig. Arg 1G 125
Ardroag. High 4B 154
Ardross. High 1A 158
Ardrossan. N Ayr 5D 126
Ardshealach. High 2A 140
Ardsley. S Yor 4D 93
Ardslignish. High 2G 139
Ardstraw. Derr 4F 176
Ardtalla. Arg 4C 124
Ardtalnaig. Per 5E 142
Ardtoe. High 1A 140
Arduaine. Arg 2E 133
Ardullie. High 2H 157
Ardvasar. High 3E 147
Ardvorlich. Per 1F 135
Ardwell. Dum 5G 109
Ardwell. Mor 5A 160
Arean. High 1A 140
Areley Common. Worc 3C 60
Areley Kings. Worc 3C 60
Arford. Hants 3G 25
Argoed. Cphy 2E 33
Argoed Mill. Powy 4B 58
Aridhglas. Arg 2B 132
Arinacrinachd. High 3G 155
Arinagour. Arg 3D 138
Arisaig. High 5E 147
Ariundle. High 2C 140
Arivegaig. High 2A 140
Arkendale. N Yor 3F 99
Arkesden. Essx 2E 53
Arkholme. Lanc 2E 97
Arkle Town. N Yor 4D 104
Arkley. G Lon 1D 38
Arksey. S Yor 4F 93
Arkwright Town. Derbs 3B 86
Arlecdon. Cumb 3B 102
Arlescote. Warw 1B 50
Arlesey. C Beds 2B 52
Arleston. Telf 4A 72
Arley. Ches E 2A 84
Arlingham. Glos 4C 48
Arlington. Devn 2G 19
Arlington. E Sus 5G 27
Arlington. Glos 5G 49
Arlington Beccott. Devn 2G 19
Armadail. High 3E 147
Armadale. High
nr. Isleornsay 3E 147
nr. Strathy 2H 167
Armadale. W Lot 3C 128
Armagh. Arm 5C 178
Armathwaite. Cumb 5G 113
Arminghall. Norf 5E 79
Armitage. Staf 4E 73
Armitage Bridge. W Yor 3B 92
Armley. W Yor 1C 92
Armoy. Caus 3G 175
The Arms. Norf 1A 66
Armscote. Warw 1H 49
Armston. Nptn 2H 63
Armthorpe. S Yor 4G 93
Arncliffe. N Yor 2B 98
Arncliffe Cote. N Yor 2B 98
Arncroach. Fife 3H 137
Arne. Dors 4E 15
Arnesby. Leics 1D 62
Arnicle. Arg 2B 122
Arnisdale. High 2G 147
Arnish. High 4E 155
Arniston. Midl 3G 129
Arnol. W Isl 3F 171
Arnold. E Yor 5F 101
Arnold. Notts 1C 74
Arnprior. Stir 4F 135
Arnside. Cumb 2D 96
Aros Mains. Arg 4G 139
Arpafeelie. High 3A 158
Arrad Foot. Cumb 1C 96
Arram. E Yor 5E 101
Arras. E Yor 5D 100
Arrathorne. N Yor 5E 105
Arreton. IOW 4D 16
Arrington. Cambs 5C 64
Arrochar. Arg 3B 134
Arrow. Warw 5E 61
Arscaig. High 2C 164
Artafallie. High 4A 158
Arthington. W Yor 5E 99
Arthingworth. Nptn 2E 63
Arthog. Gwyn 4F 69
Arthrath. Abers 5G 161
Arthurstone. Per 4B 144
Articlave. Caus 3D 174
Artigarvan. Derr 2F 176
Artikelly. Caus 4C 174
Artington. Surr 1A 26
Arundel. W Sus 5B 26
Asby. Cumb 2B 102
Ascog. Arg 3C 126
Ascot. Wind 4A 38
Ascott-under-Wychwood.
Oxon 4B 50
Asenby. N Yor 2F 99
Asfordby. Leics 4E 74
Asfordby Hill. Leics 4E 74
Asgarby. Linc
nr. Horncastle 4C 88
nr. Sleaford 1A 76
Ash. Devn 4E 9
Ash. Dors 1D 14
Ash. Kent
nr. Sandwich 5G 41
nr. Swanley 4H 39
Ash. Som 4H 21
Ash. Surr 1G 25
Ashampstead. W Ber 4D 36
Ashbocking. Suff 5D 66
Ashbourne. Derbs 1F 73
Ashbrittle. Som 4D 20
Ashbrook. Shrp 1G 59
Ashburton. Devn 2D 8
Ashbury. Devn 3F 11
Ashbury. Oxon 3A 36
Ashby. N Lin 4B 94
Ashby by Partney. Linc 4D 88
Ashby cum Fenby. NE Lin 4F 95
Ashby de la Launde. Linc 5H 87
Ashby-de-la-Zouch.
Leics 4A 74
Ashby Folville. Leics 4E 74
Ashby Magna. Leics 1C 62
Ashby Parva. Leics 2C 62
Ashby Puerorum. Linc 3C 88
Ashby St Ledgars. Nptn 4C 62
Ashby St Mary. Norf 5F 79
Ashchurch. Glos 2E 49
Ashcombe. Devn 5C 12
Ashcott. Som 3H 21
Ashdon. Essx 1F 53
Ashe. Hants 2D 24
Asheldham. Essx 5C 54
Ashen. Essx 1H 53
Ashendon. Buck 4F 51
Ashey. IOW 4D 16
Ashfield. Hants 1B 16
Ashfield. Here 3A 48
Ashfield. Shrp 2H 59
Ashfield. Stir 3G 135
Ashfield. Suff 4E 66
Ashfield Green. Suff 3E 67
Ashfold Crossways.
W Sus 3D 26
Ashford. Devn
nr. Barnstaple 3F 19
nr. Kingsbridge 4C 8
Ashford. Hants 1G 15
Ashford. Kent 1E 29
Ashford. Surr 3B 38
Ashford Bowdler. Shrp 3H 59
Ashford Carbonel. Shrp 3H 59
Ashford Hill. Hants 5D 36
Ashford in the Water.
Derbs 4F 85
Ashgill. S Lan 5A 128
Ash Green. Warw 2H 61
Ashgrove. Mor 2G 159
Ashill. Devn 1D 12
Ashill. Norf 5A 78
Ashill. Som 1G 13
Ashingdon. Essx 1C 40
Ashington. Nmbd 1F 115
Ashington. W Sus 4C 26
Ashkirk. Bord 2G 119
Ashleworth. Glos 3D 48
Ashley. Cambs 4F 65
Ashley. Ches E 2B 84
Ashley. Dors 2G 15
Ashley. Glos 2E 35
Ashley. Hants
nr. New Milton 3A 16
nr. Winchester 3B 24
Ashley. Kent 1H 29
Ashley. Nptn 1E 63
Ashley. Staf 2B 72
Ashley. Wilts 5D 34
Ashley Green. Buck 5H 51
Ashley Heath. Dors 2G 15
Ashley Heath. Staf 2B 72
Ashley Moor. Here 4G 59
Ash Magna. Shrp 2H 71
Ashmanhaugh. Norf 3F 79
Ashmansworth. Hants 1C 24
Ashmansworthy. Devn 1D 10
Ashmead Green. Glos 2C 34
Ash Mill. Devn 4A 20
Ashmill. Devn 3D 11
Ashmore. Dors 1E 15
Ashmore Green. W Ber 5D 36
Ashorne. Warw 5H 61
Ashover. Derbs 4A 86
Ashow. Warw 3H 61
Ash Parva. Shrp 2H 71
Ashperton. Here 1B 48
Ashprington. Devn 3E 9
Ash Priors. Som 4E 21
Ashreigney. Devn 1G 11
Ash Street. Suff 1D 54
Ashtead. Surr 5C 38
Ash Thomas. Devn 1D 12
Ashton. Corn 4D 4
Ashton. Here 4H 59
Ashton. Inv 2D 126
Ashton. Nptn
nr. Oundle 2H 63
nr. Roade 1F 51
Ashton. Pet 5A 76
Ashton Common. Wilts 1D 23
Ashton Hayes. Ches W 4H 83
Ashton-in-Makerfield.
G Man 1H 83
Ashton Keynes. Wilts 2F 35
Ashton under Hill. Worc 2E 49
Ashton-under-Lyne.
G Man 1D 84
Ashton upon Mersey.
G Man 1B 84
Ashurst. Hants 1B 16
Ashurst. Kent 2G 27
Ashurst. Lanc 4C 90
Ashurst. W Sus 4C 26
Ashurst Wood. W Sus 2F 27
Ash Vale. Surr 1G 25
Ashwater. Devn 3D 11
Ashwell. Herts 2C 52
Ashwell. Rut 4F 75
Ashwellthorpe. Norf 1D 66
Ashwick. Som 2B 22
Ashwicken. Norf 4G 77
Ashwood. Staf 2C 60
Askam in Furness. Cumb 2B 96
Askern. S Yor 3F 93
Askerswell. Dors 3A 14
Askett. Buck 5G 51
Askham. Cumb 2G 103
Askham. Notts 3E 87
Askham Bryan. York 5H 99
Askham Richard. York 5H 99
Askrigg. N Yor 5C 104
Askwith. N Yor 5D 98
Aslackby. Linc 2H 75
Aslacton. Norf 1D 66
Aslockton. Notts 1E 75
Aspatria. Cumb 5C 112
Aspenden. Herts 3D 52
Asperton. Linc 2B 76
Aspley Guise. C Beds 2H 51
Aspley Heath. C Beds 2H 51
Aspull. G Man 4E 90
Asselby. E Yor 2H 93
Assington. Suff 2C 54
Assington Green. Suff 5G 65
Astbury. Ches E 4C 84
Astcote. Nptn 5D 62
Asterby. Linc 3B 88
Asterley. Shrp 5F 71
Asterton. Shrp 1F 59
Asthall. Oxon 4A 50
Asthall Leigh. Oxon 4B 50
Astle. High 4E 165
Astley. G Man 4F 91
Astley. Shrp 4H 71
Astley. Warw 2H 61
Astley. Worc 4B 60
Astley Abbotts. Shrp 1B 60
Astley Bridge. G Man 3F 91
Astley Cross. Worc 4C 60
Aston. Ches E 1A 72
Aston. Ches W 3H 83
Aston. Derbs
nr. Hope 2F 85
nr. Sudbury 2F 73
Aston. Flin 4F 83
Aston. Here 4G 59
Aston. Herts 3C 52
Aston. Oxon 5B 50
Aston. Shrp
nr. Bridgnorth 1C 60
nr. Wem 3H 71
Aston. S Yor 2B 86
Aston. Staf 1B 72
Aston. Telf 5A 72
Aston. W Mid 1E 61
Aston. Wok 3F 37
Aston Abbotts. Buck 3G 51
Aston Botterell. Shrp 2A 60
Aston-by-Stone. Staf 2D 72
Aston Cantlow. Warw 5F 61
Aston Clinton. Buck 4G 51
Aston Crews. Here 3B 48
Aston Cross. Glos 2E 49
Aston End. Herts 3C 52
Aston Eyre. Shrp 1A 60
Aston Fields. Worc 4D 60
Aston Flamville. Leics 1B 62
Aston Ingham. Here 3B 48
Aston juxta Mondrum.
Ches E 5A 84
Astonlane. Shrp 1A 60
Aston le Walls. Nptn 5B 62
Aston Magna. Glos 2G 49
Aston Munslow. Shrp 2H 59
Aston on Carrant. Glos 2E 49
Aston on Clun. Shrp 2F 59
Aston-on-Trent. Derbs 3B 74
Aston Pigott. Shrp 5F 71
Aston Rogers. Shrp 5F 71
Aston Rowant. Oxon 2F 37
Aston Sandford. Buck 5F 51
Aston Somerville. Worc 2F 49
Aston Subedge. Glos 1G 49
Aston Tirrold. Oxon 3D 36
Aston Upthorpe. Oxon 3D 36
Astrop. Nptn 2D 50
Astwick. C Beds 2C 52
Astwood. Mil 1H 51
Astwood Bank. Worc 4E 61
Aswarby. Linc 2H 75
Aswardby. Linc 3C 88
Atcham. Shrp 5H 71
Atch Lench. Worc 5E 61
Athelhampton. Dors 3C 14
Athelington. Suff 3E 66
Athelney. Som 4G 21
Athelstaneford. E Lot 2B 130
Atherfield Green. IOW 5C 16
Atherington. Devn 4F 19
Atherington. W Sus 5B 26
Athersley. S Yor 4D 92
Atherstone. Warw 1H 61
Atherstone on Stour.
Warw 5G 61
Atherton. G Man 4E 91
Ath-Tharracail. High 2A 140
Atlow. Derbs 1G 73
Attadale. High 5B 156
Attenborough. Notts 2C 74
Atterby. Linc 1G 87
Atterley. Shrp 1A 60
Atterton. Leics 1A 62
Attical. New M 8G 179
Attleborough. Norf 1C 66
Attleborough. Warw 1A 62
Attlebridge. Norf 4D 78
Atwick. E Yor 4F 101
Atworth. Wilts 5D 34
Auberrow. Here 1H 47
Aubourn. Linc 4G 87
Aucharnie. Abers 4D 160
Auchattie. Abers 4D 152
Auchavan. Ang 2A 144
Auchbreck. Mor 1G 151
Auchenback. E Ren 4G 127
Auchenblae. Abers 1G 145
Auchenbrack. Dum 5G 117
Auchenbreck. Arg 1B 126
Auchencairn. Dum
nr. Dalbeattie 4E 111
nr. Dumfries 1A 112
Auchencarroch. W Dun 1F 127
Auchencrow. Bord 3E 131
Auchendennan. Arg 1E 127
Auchendinny. Midl 3F 129
Auchengray. S Lan 4C 128
Auchenhalrig. Mor 2A 160
Auchenheath. S Lan 5B 128
Auchenlochan. Arg 2A 126
Auchenmade. N Ayr 5E 127
Auchenmalg. Dum 4H 109
Auchentiber. N Ayr 5E 127
Auchenvennel. Arg 1D 126
Auchindrain. Arg 3H 133
Auchininna. Abers 4D 160
Auchinleck. Dum 2B 110
Auchinleck. E Ayr 2E 117
Auchinloch. N Lan 2H 127
Auchinstarry. N Lan 2A 128
Auchleven. Abers 1D 152
Auchlochan. S Lan 1H 117
Auchlunachan. High 5F 163
Auchmillan. E Ayr 2E 117
Auchmithie. Ang 4F 145
Auchmuirbridge. Fife 3E 136
Auchmull. Ang 1E 145
Auchnacree. Ang 2D 144
Auchnafree. Per 5F 143
Auchnagallin. High 5E 159
Auchnagatt. Abers 4G 161
Aucholzie. Abers 4H 151
Auchreddie. Abers 4F 161
Auchterarder. Per 2B 136
Auchteraw. High 3F 149
Auchterderran. Fife 4E 136
Auchterhouse. Ang 5C 144
Auchtermuchty. Fife 2E 137
Auchterneed. High 3G 157
Auchtertool. Fife 4E 136
Auchtertyre. High 1G 147
Auchtubh. Stir 1E 135
Auckengill. High 2F 169
Auckley. S Yor 4G 93
Audenshaw. G Man 1D 84
Audlem. Ches E 1A 72
Audley. Staf 5B 84
Audley End. Essx 2F 53
Audmore. Staf 3C 72
Auds. Abers 2D 160
Augher. M Ulst 4L 177
Aughertree. Cumb 1D 102
Aughnacloy. M Ulst 4A 178
Aughton. E Yor 1H 93
Aughton. Lanc
nr. Lancaster 3E 97
nr. Ormskirk 4B 90
Aughton. S Yor 2B 86
Aughton. Wilts 1H 23
Aughton Park. Lanc 4C 90
Auldearn. High 3D 158
Aulden. Here 5G 59
Auldgirth. Dum 1G 111
Auldhouse. S Lan 4H 127
Ault a' chruinn. High 1B 148
Aultbea. High 5C 162
Aultdearg. High 2E 157
Aultgrishan. High 5B 162
Aultguish Inn. High 1F 157
Ault Hucknall. Derbs 4B 86
Aultibea. High 1H 165
Aultiphurst. High 2A 168
Aultivullin. High 2A 168
Aultmore. Mor 3B 160
Aultnamain Inn. High 5D 164
Aunby. Linc 4H 75
Aunsby. Linc 2H 75
Aust. S Glo 3A 34
Austerfield. S Yor 1D 86
Austin Fen. Linc 1C 88
Austrey. Warw 5G 73
Austwick. N Yor 3G 97
Authorpe. Linc 2D 88
Authorpe Row. Linc 3E 89
Avebury. Wilts 5G 35
Avebury Trusloe. Wilts 5F 35
Aveley. Thur 2G 39
Avening. Glos 2D 35
Averham. Notts 5E 87
Aveton Gifford. Devn 4C 8
Avielochan. High 2D 150
Aviemore. High 2C 150
Avington. Hants 3D 24
Avoch. High 3B 158
Avon. Hants 3G 15
Avonbridge. Falk 2C 128
Avon Dassett. Warw 5B 62
Avonmouth. Bris 4A 34
Avonwick. Devn 3D 8
Awbridge. Hants 4B 24
Awliscombe. Devn 2E 13
Awre. Glos 5C 48
Awsworth. Notts 1B 74
Axbridge. Som 1H 21
Axford. Hants 2E 24
Axford. Wilts 5H 35
Axminster. Devn 3G 13
Axmouth. Devn 3F 13
Aycliffe Village. Dur 2F 105
Aydon. Nmbd 3D 114
Aykley Heads. Dur 5F 115
Aylburton. Glos 5B 48
Aylburton Common. Glos 5B 48
Ayle. Nmbd 5A 114
Aylesbeare. Devn 3D 12
Aylesbury. Buck 4G 51
Aylesby. NE Lin 4F 95
Aylescott. Devn 1G 11
Aylesford. Kent 5B 40
Aylesham. Kent 5G 41
Aylestone. Leic 5C 74
Aylmerton. Norf 2D 78
Aylsham. Norf 3D 78
Aylton. Here 2B 48
Aylworth. Glos 3G 49
Aymestrey. Here 4G 59
Aynho. Nptn 2D 50
Ayot Green. Herts 4C 52
Ayot St Lawrence. Herts 4B 52
Ayot St Peter. Herts 4C 52
Ayr. S Ayr 2C 116
Ayres of Selivoe. Shet 7D 173
Ayreville. Torb 2E 9
Aysgarth. N Yor 1C 98
Ayshford. Devn 1D 12
Ayside. Cumb 1C 96
Ayston. Rut 5F 75
Ayton. Bord 3F 131
Aywick. Shet 3G 173
Azerley. N Yor 2E 99

B

Babbacombe. Torb 2F 9
Babbinswood. Shrp 2F 71
Babbs Green. Herts 4D 53
Babcary. Som 4A 22
Babel. Carm 2B 46
Babell. Flin 3D 82
Babingley. Norf 3F 77
Bablock Hythe. Oxon 5C 50
Babraham. Cambs 5E 65
Babworth. Notts 2D 86
Bac. W Isl 3G 171
Bachau. IOA 2D 80
Bacheldre. Powy 1E 59
Bachymbyd Fawr. Den 4C 82
Backaland. Orkn 4E 172
Backaskaill. Orkn 2D 172
Backbarrow. Cumb 1C 96
Backe. Carm 3G 43
Backfolds. Abers 3H 161
Backford. Ches W 3G 83
Backhill. Abers 5E 161
Backhill of Clackriach.
Abers 4G 161
Backies. High 3F 165
Backmuir of New Gilston.
Fife 3G 137
Back of Keppoch. High 5E 147
Back Street. Suff 5G 65
Backwell. N Som 5H 33
Backworth. Tyne 2G 115
Bacon End. Essx 4G 53
Baconsthorpe. Norf 2D 78
Bacton. Here 2G 47
Bacton. Norf 2F 79
Bacton. Suff 4C 66
Bacton Green. Norf 2F 79
Bacup. Lanc 2G 91
Badachonacher. High 1A 158
Badachro. High 1G 155
Badanloch Lodge. High 5H 167
Badavanich. High 3D 156
Badbury. Swin 3G 35
Badby. Nptn 5C 62
Badcall. High 3C 166
Badcaul. High 4E 163
Baddeley Green. Stoke 5D 84
Baddesley Clinton. W Mid 3G 61
Baddesley Ensor. Warw 1G 61
Baddidarach. High 1E 163
Baddoch. Abers 5F 151
Badenscallie. High 3E 163
Badenscoth. Abers 5E 160
Badentarbat. High 2E 163
Badgall. Corn 4C 10
Badgers Mount. Kent 4F 39
Badgeworth. Glos 4E 49
Badgworth. Som 1G 21
Badicaul. High 1F 147
Badingham. Suff 4F 67
Badlesmere. Kent 5E 40
Badlipster. High 4E 169
Badluarach. High 4D 163
Badminton. S Glo 3D 34
Badnaban. High 1E 163
Badnabay. High 4C 166
Badnagie. High 5D 168
Badnellan. High 3F 165
Badninish. High 4E 165
Badrallach. High 4E 163
Badsey. Worc 1F 49
Badshot Lea. Surr 2G 25
Badsworth. W Yor 3E 93
Badwell Ash. Suff 4B 66
Bae Cinmel. Cnwy 2B 82
Bae Colwyn. Cnwy 3A 82
Bae Penrhyn. Cnwy 2H 81
Bagby. N Yor 1G 99
Bag Enderby. Linc 3C 88
Bagendon. Glos 5F 49
Bagginswood. Shrp 2A 60
Bàgh a Chàise. W Isl 1E 170
Bàgh a' Chaisteil. W Isl 9B 170
Bagham. Kent 5E 41
Baghasdal. W Isl 7C 170
Bagh Mor. W Isl 3D 170
Bagh Shiarabhagh. W Isl 8C 170
Bagillt. Flin 3E 82
Baginton. Warw 3H 61
Baglan. Neat 2A 32
Bagley. Shrp 3G 71
Bagley. Som 2H 21
Bagnall. Staf 5D 84
Bagnor. W Ber 5C 36
Bagshot. Surr 4A 38
Bagshot. Wilts 5B 36
Bagstone. S Glo 3B 34
Bagthorpe. Norf 2G 77
Bagthorpe. Notts 5B 86
Bagworth. Leics 5B 74
Bagwy Llydiart. Here 3H 47
Baildon. W Yor 1B 92
Baildon Green. W Yor 1B 92
Baile. W Isl 1E 170
Baile Ailein. W Isl 5E 171
Baile an Truiseil. W Isl 2F 171
Baile Boidheach. Arg 2F 125
Baile Glas. W Isl 3D 170
Bailemeonach. Arg 4A 140
Baile Mhanaich. W Isl 3C 170
Baile Mhartainn. W Isl 1C 170
Baile MhicPhail. W Isl 1D 170
Baile Mor. W Isl 2C 170
Baile Mòr. Arg 2A 132
Baile nan Cailleach. W Isl 3C 170
Baile Raghaill. W Isl 2C 170
Bailey Green. Hants 4E 25
Baileyhead. Cumb 1G 113
Baileysmill. Lis 4H 179
Bailiesward. Abers 5B 160
Bail' Iochdrach. W Isl 3D 170
Baillieston. Glas 3H 127
Bailrigg. Lanc 4D 97
Bail Uachdraich. W Isl 2D 170
Bail' Ur Tholastaidh.
W Isl 3H 171
Bainbridge. N Yor 5C 104
Bainsford. Falk 1B 128
Bainshole. Abers 5D 160
Bainton. E Yor 4D 100
Bainton. Oxon 3D 50
Bainton. Pet 5H 75
Baintown. Fife 3F 137
Baker Street. Thur 2H 39
Bakewell. Derbs 4G 85
Bala. Gwyn 2B 70
Y Bala. Gwyn 2B 70
Balachuirn. High 4E 155
Balbeg. High
nr. Cannich 5G 157
nr. Loch Ness 1G 149
Balbeggie. Per 1D 136
Balblair. High
nr. Bonar Bridge 4C 164
nr. Invergordon 2B 158
nr. Inverness 4H 157
Balby. S Yor 4F 93
Balcathie. Ang 5F 145
Balchladich. High 1E 163
Balchraggan. High 4H 157
Balchrick. High 3B 166
Balcombe. W Sus 2E 27
Balcombe Lane. W Sus 2E 27
Balcurvie. Fife 3F 137
Baldersby. N Yor 2F 99
Baldersby St James. N Yor 2F 99
Balderstone. Lanc 1E 91
Balderton. Ches W 4F 83
Balderton. Notts 5F 87
Baldinnie. Fife 2G 137
Baldock. Herts 2C 52
Baldrine. IOM 3D 108
Baldslow. E Sus 4C 28
Baldwin. IOM 3C 108
Baldwinholme. Cumb 4E 113
Baldwin's Gate. Staf 2B 72
Bale. Norf 2C 78
Balearn. Abers 3H 161
Balemartine. Arg 4A 138
Balephetrish. Arg 4B 138
Balephuil. Arg 4A 138
Balerno. Edin 3E 129
Balevullin. Arg 4A 138
Balfield. Ang 2E 145
Balfour. Orkn 6D 172
Balfron. Stir 1G 127
Balgaveny. Abers 4D 160
Balgonar. Fife 4C 136
Balgowan. High 4A 150
Balgown. High 2C 154
Balgrochan. E Dun 2H 127
Balgy. High 3H 155
Balhalgardy. Abers 1E 153
Baliasta. Shet 1H 173
Baligill. High 2A 168
Balintore. Ang 3B 144
Balintore. High 1C 158
Balintraid. High 1B 158
Balk. N Yor 1G 99
Balkeerie. Ang 4C 144
Balkholme. E Yor 2A 94
Ball. Shrp 3F 71
Ballabeg. IOM 4B 108
Ballacannell. IOM 3D 108
Ballacarnane Beg. IOM 3C 108
Ballachulish. High 3E 141
Ballagyr. IOM 3B 108
Ballajora. IOM 2D 108
Ballaleigh. IOM 3C 108
Ballamodha. IOM 4B 108
Ballantrae. S Ayr 1F 109
Ballards Gore. Essx 1D 40
Ballasalla. IOM
nr. Castletown 4B 108
nr. Kirk Michael 2C 108
Ballater. Abers 4A 152
Ballaugh. IOM 2C 108
Ballencrieff. E Lot 2A 130
Ballencrieff Toll. W Lot 2C 128
Ballentoul. Per 2F 143
Ball Hill. Hants 5C 36
Ballidon. Derbs 5G 85
Balliemore. Arg
nr. Dunoon 1B 126
nr. Oban 1F 133
Ballieward. High 5E 159
Ballig. IOM 3B 108
Ballimore. Stir 2E 135
Ballinamallard. Ferm 7E 176
Ballindarragh. Ferm 6J 177
Ballingdon. Suff 1B 54
Ballinger Common. Buck 5H 51
Ballingham. Here 2A 48
Ballingry. Fife 4D 136
Ballinluig. Per 3G 143
Ballintoy. Caus 2G 175
Ballintuim. Per 3A 144
Balliveolan. Arg 4C 140
Balloan. High 3C 164
Balloch. High 4B 158
Balloch. N Lan 2A 128
Balloch. Per 2H 135
Balloch. W Dun 1E 127
Ballochan. Abers 4C 152
Ballochgoy. Arg 3B 126
Ballochmyle. E Ayr 2E 117
Ballochroy. Arg 4F 125
Balloo. Ards 3J 179
Balls Cross. W Sus 3A 26
Ball's Green. E Sus 2F 27
Ballsmill. New M 8D 178
Ballyalton. New M 5K 179
Ballybogy. Caus 3F 174
Ballycarry. ME Ant 7L 175
Ballycassidy. Ferm 7E 176
Ballycastle. Caus 2H 175
Ballyclare. Ant 7J 175
Ballyeaston. Ant 7J 175
Ballygally. ME Ant 6K 175
Ballygawley. M Ulst 4A 178
Ballygowan. Ards 3J 179
Ballygown. Arg 4F 139
Ballygrant. Arg 3B 124
Ballyhalbert. Ards 3L 179
Ballyholland. New M 7F 178
Ballyhornan. New M 5K 179
Ballykelly. Caus 4C 174
Ballykinler. New M 6J 179
Ballylesson. Lis 3H 179
Ballymagorry. Derr 2F 176
Ballymartin. New M 8H 179
Ballymena. ME Ant 6H 175
Ballymichael. N Ayr 2D 122
Ballymoney. Caus 4F 174
Ballynagard. Derr 4A 174
Ballynahinch. New M 4H 179
Ballynakilly. M Ulst 3C 178
Ballynoe. New M 5J 179
Ballynure. Ant 7K 175
Ballyrashane. Caus 3E 174
Ballyrobert. Ant 8J 175
Ballyronan. M Ulst 8F 174
Ballyroney. Arm 6G 179
Ballyscullion. Caus 3C 174
Ballystrudder. ME Ant 7L 175
Ballyvoy. Caus 2H 175
Ballyward. New M 6G 179
Ballywater. Ards 3L 179
Ballywonard. Ant 1G 179
Balmacara. High 1G 147
Balmaclellan. Dum 2D 110
Balmacqueen. High 1D 154
Balmaha. Stir 4D 134
Balmalcolm. Fife 3F 137
Balmalloch. N Lan 2A 128
Balmeanach. High 5E 155
Balmedie. Abers 2G 153
Balmerino. Fife 1F 137
Balmerlawn. Hants 2B 16
Balmore. E Dun 2H 127
Balmore. High 4B 154
Balmullo. Fife 1G 137
Balmurrie. Dum 3H 109
Balnaboth. Ang 2C 144
Balnabruaich. High 1B 158
Balnabruich. High 5D 168
Balnacoil. High 2F 165
Balnacra. High 4B 156
Balnacroft. Abers 4G 151
Balnageith. Mor 3E 159
Balnaglaic. High 5G 157
Balnagrantach. High 5G 157
Balnaguard. Per 3G 143
Balnahard. Arg 4B 132
Balnain. High 5G 157
Balnakeil. High 2D 166
Balnaknock. High 2D 154
Balnamoon. Abers 3G 161
Balnamoon. Ang 2E 145
Balnamore. Caus 4F 174
Balnapaling. High 2B 158
Balornock. Glas 3H 127
Balquhidder. Stir 1E 135
Balsall. W Mid 3G 61
Balsall Common. W Mid 3G 61
Balscote. Oxon 1B 50
Balsham. Cambs 5E 65
Balstonia. Thur 2A 40
Baltasound. Shet 1H 173
Balterley. Staf 5B 84
Baltersan. Dum 3B 110
Balthangie. Abers 3F 161
Baltonsborough. Som 3A 22
Balvaird. High 3H 157
Balvaird. Per 2D 136
Balvenie. Mor 4H 159
Balvicar. Arg 2E 133
Balvraid. High 2G 147
Balvraid Lodge. High 5C 158
Bamber Bridge. Lanc 2D 90
Bamber's Green. Essx 3F 53
Bamburgh. Nmbd 1F 121
Bamford. Derbs 2G 85
Bamfurlong. G Man 4D 90
Bampton. Cumb 3C 103
Bampton. Devn 4C 20

Bampton—Bishampton

Bampton. Oxon 5B 50
Bampton Grange. Cumb 3G 103
Banavie. High 1F 141
Banbridge. Arm 5F 178
Banbury. Oxon 1C 50
Bancffosfelen. Carm 4E 45
Banchory. Abers 4D 152
Banchory-Devenick. Abers 3G 153
Bancycapel. Carm 4E 45
Bancyfelin. Carm 3H 43
Banc-y-ffordd. Carm 2E 45
Banff. Abers 2D 160
Bangor. Ards 1K 179
Bangor. Gwyn 3E 81
Bangor-is-y-coed. Wrex 1F 71
Bangors. Corn 3C 10
Bangor's Green. Lanc 4B 90
Banham. Norf 2C 66
Bank. Hants 2A 16
The Bank. Ches E 5C 84
The Bank. Shrp 1A 60
Bankend. Dum 3B 112
Bankfoot. Per 5H 143
Bankglen. E Ayr 3F 117
Bankhead. Aber 2F 153
Bankhead. Abers 3D 152
Bankhead. S Lan 5B 128
Bankland. Som 4G 21
Bank Newton. N Yor 4B 98
Banknock. Falk 2A 128
Banks. Cumb 3G 113
Banks. Lanc 2B 90
Bankshill. Dum 1C 112
Bank Street. Worc 4A 60
Bank Top. Lanc 4D 90
Banners Gate. W Mid 1E 61
Banningham. Norf 3E 78
Banniskirk. High 3D 168
Bannister Green. Essx 3G 53
Bannockburn. Stir 4H 135
Banstead. Surr 5D 38
Bantham. Devn 4C 8
Banton. N Lan 2A 128
Banwell. N Som 1G 21
Banyard's Green. Suff 3F 67
Bapchild. Kent 4D 40
Bapton. Wilts 3E 23
Barabhas. W Isl 2F 171
Barabhas Iarach. W Isl 3F 171
Baramore. High 1A 140
Barassie. S Ayr 1C 116
Baravullin. Arg 4D 140
Barbaraville. High 1B 158
Barber Booth. Derbs 2F 85
Barber Green. Cumb 1C 96
Barbhas Uarach. W Isl 2F 171
Barbieston. S Ayr 3D 116
Barbon. Cumb 1F 97
Barbourne. Worc 5C 60
Barbridge. Ches E 5A 84
Barbrook. Devn 2H 19
Barby. Nptn 3C 62
Barby Nortoft. Nptn 3C 62
Barcaldine. Arg 4D 140
Barcheston. Warw 2A 50
Barclose. Cumb 3F 113
Barcombe. E Sus 4F 27
Barcombe Cross. E Sus 4F 27
Barden. N Yor 5E 105
Barden Scale. N Yor 4C 98
Bardfield End Green. Essx 2G 53
Bardfield Saling. Essx 3G 53
Bardister. Shet 4E 173
Bardnabeinne. High 4E 164
Bardney. Linc 4A 88
Bardon. Leics 4B 74
Bardon Mill. Nmbd 3A 114
Bardowie. E Dun 2G 127
Bardrainney. Inv 2E 127
Bardsea. Cumb 2C 96
Bardsey. W Yor 5F 99
Bardsley. G Man 4H 91
Bardwell. Suff 3B 66
Bare. Lanc 3D 96
Barelees. Nmbd 1C 120
Barewood. Here 5F 59
Barford. Hants 3G 25
Barford. Norf 5D 78
Barford. Warw 4G 61
Barford St John. Oxon 2C 50
Barford St Martin. Wilts 3F 23
Barford St Michael. Oxon 2C 50
Barfrestone. Kent 5G 41
Bargeddie. N Lan 3H 127
Bargod. Cphy 2E 33
Bargoed. Cphy 2E 33
Bargrennan. Dum 2A 110
Barham. Cambs 3A 64
Barham. Kent 5G 41
Barham. Suff 5D 66
Barharrow. Dum 4D 110
Bar Hill. Cambs 4C 64
Barholm. Linc 4H 75
Barkby. Leics 5D 74
Barkestone-le-Vale. Leics 2E 75
Barkham. Wok 5F 37
Barking. G Lon 2F 39
Barking. Suff 5C 66
Barkingside. G Lon 2F 39
Barking Tye. Suff 5C 66
Barkisland. W Yor 3A 92
Barkston. Linc 1G 75
Barkston Ash. N Yor 1E 93
Barkway. Herts 2D 53
Barlanark. Glas 3H 127
Barlaston. Staf 2C 72
Barlavington. W Sus 4A 26
Barlborough. Derbs 3B 86
Barlby. N Yor 1G 93
Barlestone. Leics 5B 74
Barley. Herts 2D 53
Barley. Lanc 5H 97
Barley Mow. Tyne 4F 115
Barleythorpe. Rut 5F 75
Barling. Essx 2D 40
Barlings. Linc 3H 87
Barlow. Derbs 3H 85
Barlow. N Yor 2G 93
Barlow. Tyne 3E 115
Barmby Moor. E Yor 5B 100
Barmby on the Marsh. E Yor 2G 93
Barmer. Norf 2H 77
Barming. Kent 5B 40
Barming Heath. Kent 5B 40
Barmoor. Nmbd 1E 121
Barmouth. Gwyn 4F 69
Barmpton. Darl 3A 106
Barmston. E Yor 4F 101
Barmulloch. Glas 3H 127
Barnack. Pet 5H 75
Barnacle. Warw 2A 62
Barnard Castle. Dur 3D 104
Barnard Gate. Oxon 4C 50
Barnardiston. Suff 1H 53
Barnbarroch. Dum 4F 111
Barnburgh. S Yor 4E 93
Barnby. Suff 2G 67
Barnby Dun. S Yor 4G 93
Barnby in the Willows. Notts 5F 87
Barnby Moor. Notts 2D 86
Barnes. G Lon 3D 38
Barnes Street. Kent 1H 27
Barnet. G Lon 1D 38
Barnetby le Wold. N Lin 4D 94
Barney. Norf 2B 78
Barnham. Suff 3A 66
Barnham. W Sus 5A 26
Barnham Broom. Norf 5C 78
Barnhead. Ang 3F 145
Barnhill. D'dee 5D 145
Barnhill. Mor 3F 159
Barnhill. Per 1D 136
Barnhills. Dum 2E 109
Barningham. Dur 3D 105
Barningham. Suff 3B 66
Barnoldby le Beck. NE Lin 4F 95
Barnoldswick. Lanc 5A 98
Barns Green. W Sus 3C 26
Barnsley. Glos 5F 49
Barnsley. Shrp 1B 60
Barnsley. S Yor 4D 92
Barnstaple. Devn 3F 19
Barnston. Essx 4G 53
Barnston. Mers 2E 83
Barnstone. Notts 2E 75
Barnt Green. Worc 3E 61
Barnton. Ches W 3A 84
Barnwell. Cambs 5D 64
Barnwell. Nptn 2H 63
Barnwood. Glos 4D 48
Barons Cross. Here 5G 59
The Barony. Orkn 5B 172
Barr. Dum 4G 117
Barr. S Ayr 5B 116
Barra Airport. W Isl 8B 170
Barrachan. Dum 5A 110
Barraglom. W Isl 4D 171
Barrahormid. Arg 1F 125
Barrapol. Arg 4A 138
Barrasford. Nmbd 2C 114
Barravullin. Arg 3F 133
Barregarrow. IOM 3C 108
Barrhead. E Ren 4G 127
Barrhill. S Ayr 1H 109
Barri. V Glam 5E 32
Barrington. Cambs 1D 53
Barrington. Som 1G 13
Barripper. Corn 3D 4
Barrmill. N Ayr 4E 127
Barrock. High 1E 169
Barrow. Lanc 1F 91
Barrow. Rut 4F 75
Barrow. Shrp 5A 72
Barrow. Som 3C 22
Barrow. Suff 4G 65
Barroway Drove. Norf 5E 77
Barrow Bridge. G Man 3E 91
Barrowburn. Nmbd 3C 120
Barrowby. Linc 2F 75
Barrowcliff. N Yor 1E 101
Barrow Common. N Som 5A 34
Barrowden. Rut 5G 75
Barrowford. Lanc 1G 91
Barrow Gurney. N Som 5A 34
Barrow Haven. N Lin 2D 94
Barrow Hill. Derbs 3B 86
Barrow-in-Furness. Cumb 3B 96
Barrow Nook. Lanc 4C 90
Barrow's Green. Hal 2H 83
Barrows Green. Cumb 1E 97
Barrow Street. Wilts 3D 22
Barrow upon Humber. N Lin 2D 94
Barrow upon Soar. Leics 4C 74
Barrow upon Trent. Derbs 3A 74
Barry. Ang 5E 145
Barry. V Glam 5E 32
Barry Island. V Glam 5E 32
Barsby. Leics 4D 74
Barsham. Suff 2F 67
Barston. W Mid 3G 61
Bartestree. Here 1A 48
Barthol Chapel. Abers 5F 161
Bartholomew Green. Essx 3H 53
Barthomley. Ches E 5B 84
Bartley. Hants 1B 16
Bartley Green. W Mid 2E 61
Bartlow. Cambs 1F 53
Barton. Cambs 5D 64
Barton. Ches W 5G 83
Barton. Cumb 2F 103
Barton. Glos 3G 49
Barton. IOW 4D 16
Barton. Lanc
nr. Ormskirk 4B 90
nr. Preston 1D 90
Barton. N Som 1G 21
Barton. N Yor 4F 105
Barton. Oxon 5D 50
Barton. Torb 2F 9
Barton. Warw 5F 61
Barton Bendish. Norf 5G 77
Barton Gate. Staf 4F 73
Barton Green. Staf 4F 73
Barton Hartsthorn. Buck 2E 51
Barton Hill. N Yor 3B 100
Barton in Fabis. Notts 2C 74
Barton in the Beans. Leics 5A 74
Barton-le-Clay. C Beds 2A 52
Barton-le-Street. N Yor 2B 100
Barton-le-Willows. N Yor 3B 100
Barton Mills. Suff 3G 65
Barton on Sea. Hants 3H 15
Barton-on-the-Heath. Warw 2A 50
Barton St David. Som 3A 22
Barton Seagrave. Nptn 3F 63
Barton Stacey. Hants 2C 24
Barton Town. Devn 2G 19
Barton Turf. Norf 3F 79
Barton-Under-Needwood. Staf 4F 73
Barton-upon-Humber. N Lin 2D 94
Barton Waterside. N Lin 2D 94
Barugh Green. S Yor 4D 92
Barway. Cambs 3E 65
Barwell. Leics 1B 62
Barwick. Herts 4D 53
Barwick. Som 1A 14
Barwick in Elmet. W Yor 1D 93
Baschurch. Shrp 3G 71
Bascote. Warw 4B 62
Basford Green. Staf 5D 85
Bashall Eaves. Lanc 5F 97
Bashall Town. Lanc 5G 97
Bashley. Hants 3H 15
Basildon. Essx 2B 40
Basingstoke. Hants 1E 25
Baslow. Derbs 3G 85
Bason Bridge. Som 2G 21
Bassaleg. Newp 3F 33
Bassendean. Bord 5C 130
Bassenthwaite. Cumb 1D 102
Bassett. Sotn 1C 16
Bassingbourn. Cambs 1D 52
Bassingfield. Notts 2D 74
Bassingham. Linc 4G 87
Bassingthorpe. Linc 3G 75
Bassus Green. Herts 3D 52
Basta. Shet 2G 173
Baston. Linc 4A 76
Bastonford. Worc 5C 60
Bastwick. Norf 4G 79
Batchley. Worc 4E 61
Batchworth. Herts 1B 38
Batcombe. Dors 2B 14
Batcombe. Som 3B 22
Bate Heath. Ches E 3A 84
Bath. Bath 192 (5C 34)
Bathampton. Bath 5C 34
Bathealton. Som 4D 20
Batheaston. Bath 5C 34
Bathford. Bath 5C 34
Bathgate. W Lot 3C 128
Bathley. Notts 5E 87
Bathpool. Corn 5C 10
Bathpool. Som 4F 21
Bathville. W Lot 3C 128
Bathway. Som 1A 22
Batley. W Yor 2C 92
Batsford. Glos 2G 49
Batson. Devn 5D 8
Battersby. N Yor 4C 106
Battersea. G Lon 3D 39
Battisborough Cross. Devn 4C 8
Battisford. Suff 5C 66
Battisford Tye. Suff 5C 66
Battle. E Sus 4B 28
Battle. Powy 2D 46
Battleborough. Som 1G 21
Battledown. Glos 3E 49
Battlefield. Shrp 4H 71
Battlesbridge. Essx 1B 40
Battlesden. C Beds 3H 51
Battlesea Green. Suff 3E 66
Battleton. Som 4C 20
Battram. Leics 5B 74
Battramsley. Hants 3B 16
Batt's Corner. Surr 2G 25
Bauds of Cullen. Mor 2B 160
Baugh. Arg 4B 138
Baughton. Worc 1D 49
Baughurst. Hants 5D 36
Baulking. Oxon 2B 36
Baumber. Linc 3B 88
Baunton. Glos 5F 49
Baverstock. Wilts 3F 23
Bawburgh. Norf 5D 78
Bawdeswell. Norf 3C 78
Bawdrip. Som 3G 21
Bawdsey. Suff 1G 55
Bawsey. Norf 4F 77
Bawtry. S Yor 1D 86
Baxenden. Lanc 2F 91
Baxterley. Warw 1G 61
Baxter's Green. Suff 5G 65
Bay. High 3B 154
Baybridge. Hants 4D 24
Baybridge. Nmbd 4C 114
Baycliff. Cumb 2B 96
Baydon. Wilts 4A 36
Bayford. Herts 5D 52
Bayford. Som 4C 22
Bayles. Cumb 5A 114
Baylham. Suff 5D 66
Baynard's Green. Oxon 3D 50
Bayston Hill. Shrp 5G 71
Baythorne End. Essx 1H 53
Baythorpe. Linc 1B 76
Bayton. Worc 3A 60
Bayton Common. Worc 3B 60
Bayworth. Oxon 5D 50
Beach. S Glo 4C 34
Beachampton. Buck 2F 51
Beachamwell. Norf 5G 77
Beachley. Glos 2A 34
Beacon. Devn 2E 13
Beacon End. Essx 3C 54
Beacon Hill. Surr 3G 25
Beacon's Bottom. Buck 2F 37
Beaconsfield. Buck 1A 38
Beacrabhaic. W Isl 8D 171
Beadlam. N Yor 1A 100
Beadnell. Nmbd 2G 121
Beaford. Devn 1F 11
Beal. Nmbd 5G 131
Beal. N Yor 2F 93
Bealsmill. Corn 5D 10
Beam Hill. Staf 3G 73
Beamhurst. Staf 2E 73
Beaminster. Dors 2H 13
Beamish. Dur 4F 115
Beamond End. Buck 1A 38
Beamsley. N Yor 4C 98
Bean. Kent 3G 39
Beanacre. Wilts 5E 35
Beanley. Nmbd 3E 121
Beaquoy. Orkn 5C 172
Beardwood. Bkbn 2E 91
Beare Green. Surr 1C 26
Bearley. Warw 4F 61
Bearpark. Dur 5F 115
Bearsbridge. Nmbd 4A 114
Bearsden. E Dun 2G 127
Bearsted. Kent 5B 40
Bearstone. Shrp 2B 72
Bearwood. Pool 3F 15
Bearwood. W Mid 2E 61
Beattock. Dum 4C 118
Beauchamp Roding. Essx 4F 53
Beauchief. S Yor 2H 85
Beaufort. Blae 4E 47
Beaulieu. Hants 2B 16
Beauly. High 4H 157
Beaumaris. IOA 3F 81
Beaumont. Cumb 4E 113
Beaumont. Essx 3E 55
Beaumont Hill. Darl 3F 105
Beaumont Leys. Leic 5C 74
Beausale. Warw 3G 61
Beauvale. Notts 1B 74
Beauworth. Hants 4D 24
Beaworthy. Devn 3E 11
Beazley End. Essx 3H 53
Bebington. Mers 2F 83
Bebside. Nmbd 1F 115
Beccles. Suff 2G 67
Becconsall. Lanc 2C 90
Beckbury. Shrp 5B 72
Beckenham. G Lon 4E 39
Beckermet. Cumb 4B 102
Beckett End. Norf 1G 65
Beck Foot. Cumb 5H 103
Beckfoot. Cumb
nr. Broughton in Furness 1A 96
nr. Seascale 4C 102
nr. Silloth 5B 112
Beckford. Worc 2E 49
Beckhampton. Wilts 5F 35
Beck Hole. N Yor 4F 107
Beckingham. Linc 5F 87
Beckingham. Notts 1E 87
Beckington. Som 1D 22
Beckley. E Sus 3C 28
Beckley. Hants 3H 15
Beckley. Oxon 4D 50
Beck Row. Suff 3F 65
Beck Side. Cumb
nr. Cartmel 1C 96
nr. Ulverston 1B 96
Beckside. Cumb 1F 97
Beckton. G Lon 2F 39
Beckwithshaw. N Yor 4E 99
Becontree. G Lon 2F 39
Bedale. N Yor 1E 99
Bedburn. Dur 1E 105
Bedchester. Dors 1D 14
Beddau. Rhon 3D 32
Beddgelert. Gwyn 1E 69
Beddingham. E Sus 5F 27
Beddington. G Lon 4E 39
Bedfield. Suff 4E 66
Bedford. Bed 1A 52
Bedford. G Man 1A 84
Bedham. W Sus 3B 26
Bedhampton. Hants 2F 17
Bedingfield. Suff 4D 66
Bedingham Green. Norf 1E 67
Bedlam. N Yor 3E 99
Bedlar's Green. Essx 3F 53
Bedlington. Nmbd 1F 115
Bedlinog. Mer T 5D 46
Bedminster. Bris 4A 34
Bedmond. Herts 5A 52
Bednall. Staf 4D 72
Bedrule. Bord 3A 120
Bedstone. Shrp 3F 59
Bedwas. Cphy 3E 33
Bedwellty. Cphy 5E 47
Bedworth. Warw 2A 62
Beeby. Leics 5D 74
Beech. Hants 3E 25
Beech. Staf 2C 72
Beechcliffe. W Yor 5C 98
Beech Hill. W Ber 5E 37
Beechingstoke. Wilts 1F 23
Beedon. W Ber 4C 36
Beeford. E Yor 4F 101
Beeley. Derbs 4G 85
Beelsby. NE Lin 4F 95
Beenham. W Ber 5D 36
Beeny. Corn 3B 10
Beer. Devn 4F 13
Beer. Som 3H 21
Beercrocombe. Som 4G 21
Beer Hackett. Dors 1B 14
Beesands. Devn 4E 9
Beesby. Linc 2D 88
Beeson. Devn 4E 9
Beeston. C Beds 1B 52
Beeston. Ches W 5H 83
Beeston. Norf 4B 78
Beeston. Notts 2C 74
Beeston. W Yor 1C 92
Beeston Regis. Norf 1D 78
Beeswing. Dum 3F 111
Beetham. Cumb 2D 97
Beetham. Som 1F 13
Beetley. Norf 4B 78
Beffcote. Staf 4C 72
Began. Card 3F 33
Begbroke. Oxon 4C 50
Begdale. Cambs 5D 76
Begelly. Pemb 4F 43
Beggar Hill. Essx 5G 53
Beggar's Bush. Powy 4E 59
Beggearn Huish. Som 3D 20
Beguildy. Powy 3D 58
Beighton. Norf 5F 79
Beighton. S Yor 2B 86
Beighton Hill. Derbs 5G 85
Beinn Casgro. W Isl 5G 171
Beith. N Ayr 4E 127
Bekesbourne. Kent 5F 41
Belaugh. Norf 4E 79
Belbroughton. Worc 3D 60
Belchalwell. Dors 2C 14
Belchalwell Street. Dors 2C 14
Belchamp Otten. Essx 1B 54
Belchamp St Paul. Essx 1A 54
Belchamp Walter. Essx 1B 54
Belchford. Linc 3B 88
Belcoo. Ferm 6F 177
Belfast. Bel 2H 179
Belfast City George Best Airport. Bel 4H 175
Belfast International Airport. Ant 1F 179
Belfatton. Abers 3H 161
Belford. Nmbd 1F 121
Belgrano. Cnwy 3B 82
Belhaven. E Lot 2C 130
Belhelvie. Abers 2G 153
Belhinnie. Abers 1B 152
Bellabeg. Abers 2A 152
Belladrum. High 4H 157
Bellaghy. M Ulst 7F 175
Bellamore. S Ayr 1H 109
Bellanaleck. Ferm 6H 177
Bellanoch. Arg 4F 133
Bell Busk. N Yor 4B 98
Belleau. Linc 3D 88
Belleek. Ferm 7B 176
Belleek. New M 7D 178
Belleheiglash. Mor 5F 159
Bell End. Worc 3D 60
Bellerby. N Yor 5E 105
Bellerby Camp. N Yor 5D 105
Bellever. Devn 5G 11
Belle Vue. Cumb 1C 102
Belle Vue. Shrp 4G 71
Bellfield. S Lan 1H 117
Belliehill. Ang 2E 145
Bellingdon. Buck 5H 51
Bellingham. Nmbd 1B 114
Bellmount. Norf 3E 77
Bellochantuy. Arg 2A 122
Bellsbank. E Ayr 4D 117
Bell's Cross. Suff 5D 66
Bellshill. N Lan 4A 128
Bellshill. Nmbd 1F 121
Bellside. N Lan 4B 128
Bellspool. Bord 1D 118
Bellsquarry. W Lot 3D 128
Bells Yew Green. E Sus 2H 27
Belmaduthy. High 3A 158
Belmesthorpe. Rut 4H 75
Belmont. Bkbn 3E 91
Belmont. Shet 1G 173
Belmont. S Ayr 2C 116
Belnacraig. Abers 2A 152
Belnie. Linc 2B 76
Belowda. Corn 2D 6
Belper. Derbs 1A 74
Belper Lane End. Derbs 1H 73
Belph. Derbs 3C 86
Belsay. Nmbd 2E 115
Belsford. Devn 3D 9
Belsize. Herts 5A 52
Belstead. Suff 1E 55
Belston. S Ayr 2C 116
Belstone. Devn 3G 11
Belstone Corner. Devn 3G 11
Belthorn. Lanc 2F 91
Beltinge. Kent 4F 41
Beltoft. N Lin 4B 94
Belton. Leics 3B 74
Belton. Linc 2G 75
Belton. Norf 5G 79
Belton. N Lin 4A 94
Belton-in-Rutland. Rut 5F 75
Beltring. Kent 1A 28
Belts of Collonach. Abers 4D 152
Belvedere. G Lon 3F 39
Belvoir. Leics 2F 75
Bembridge. IOW 4E 17
Bemersyde. Bord 1H 119
Bemerton. Wilts 3G 23
Bempton. E Yor 2F 101
Benacre. Suff 2H 67
Ben Alder Lodge. High 1C 142
Ben Armine Lodge. High 2E 164
Benbecula Airport. W Isl 3C 170
Benbuie. Dum 5G 117
Benburb. M Ulst 4C 178
Benchill. G Man 2C 84
Benderloch. Arg 5D 140
Bendish. Herts 3B 52
Bendooragh. Caus 4F 174
Bendronaig Lodge. High 5C 156
Benenden. Kent 2C 28
Benfieldside. Dur 4D 115
Bengate. Norf 3F 79
Bengeworth. Worc 1F 49
Benhall Green. Suff 4F 67
Benholm. Abers 2H 145
Beningbrough. N Yor 4H 99
Benington. Herts 3C 52
Benington. Linc 1C 76
Benington Sea End. Linc 1D 76
Benllech. IOA 2E 81
Benmore Lodge. High 2H 163
Bennacott. Corn 3D 10
Bennah. Devn 4B 12
Bennecarrigan. N Ayr 3D 122
Bennethead. Cumb 2F 103
Benniworth. Linc 2B 88
Benover. Kent 1B 28
Benson. Oxon 2E 36
Benston. Shet 6F 173
Benstonhall. Orkn 4E 172
Bent. Abers 1F 145
Benthall. Shrp 5A 72
Bentham. Glos 4E 49
Benthoul. Aber 3F 153
Bentlawnt. Shrp 5F 71
Bentley. E Yor 1D 94
Bentley. Hants 2F 25
Bentley. S Yor 4F 93
Bentley. Suff 2E 54
Bentley. Warw 1G 61
Bentley. W Mid 1D 61
Bentley Heath. Herts 1D 38
Bentley Heath. W Mid 3F 61
Bentpath. Dum 5F 119
Bents. W Lot 3C 128
Bentworth. Hants 2E 25
Benvie. D'dee 5C 144
Benville. Dors 2A 14
Benwell. Tyne 3F 115
Benwick. Cambs 1C 64
Beoley. Worc 4E 61
Beoraidbeg. High 4E 147
Bepton. W Sus 1G 17
Berden. Essx 3E 53
Beragh. Ferm 3L 177
Bere Alston. Devn 2A 8
Bere Ferrers. Devn 2A 8
Berepper. Corn 4D 4
Bere Regis. Dors 3D 14
Bergh Apton. Norf 5F 79
Berinsfield. Oxon 2D 36
Berkeley. Glos 2B 34
Berkhamsted. Herts 5H 51
Berkley. Som 2D 22
Berkswell. W Mid 3G 61
Bermondsey. G Lon 3E 39
Bernera. High 1G 147
Bernice. Arg 4A 134
Bernisdale. High 3D 154
Berrick Salome. Oxon 2E 36
Berriedale. High 1H 165
Berrier. Cumb 2E 103
Berriew. Powy 5D 70
Berrington. Nmbd 5G 131
Berrington. Shrp 5H 71
Berrington. Worc 4H 59
Berrington Green. Worc 4H 59
Berrington Law. Nmbd 5F 131
Berrow. Som 1G 21
Berrow Green. Worc 5B 60
Berry Cross. Devn 1E 11
Berry Down Cross. Devn 2F 19
Berry Hill. Glos 4A 48
Berry Hill. Pemb 1A 44
Berryhillock. Mor 2C 160
Berrynarbor. Devn 2F 19
Berry Pomeroy. Devn 2E 9
Berryscaur. Dum 5D 118
Berry's Green. G Lon 5F 39
Bersham. Wrex 1F 71
Berthengam. Flin 3D 82
Berwick. E Sus 5G 27
Berwick Bassett. Wilts 4G 35
Berwick Hill. Nmbd 2E 115
Berwick St James. Wilts 3F 23
Berwick St John. Wilts 4E 23
Berwick St Leonard. Wilts 3E 23
Berwick-upon-Tweed. Nmbd 4F 131
Berwyn. Den 1D 70
Bescaby. Leics 3F 75
Bescar. Lanc 3B 90
Besford. Worc 1E 49
Bessacarr. S Yor 4G 93
Bessbrook. New M 7E 178
Bessels Leigh. Oxon 5C 50
Bessingby. E Yor 3F 101
Bessingham. Norf 2D 78
Best Beech Hill. E Sus 2H 27
Besthorpe. Norf 1C 66
Besthorpe. Notts 4F 87
Bestwood Village. Notts 1C 74
Beswick. E Yor 5E 101
Betchworth. Surr 5D 38
Bethania. Cdgn 4E 57
Bethania. Gwyn
nr. Blaenau Ffestiniog 1G 69
nr. Caernarfon 5F 81
Bethel. Gwyn
nr. Bala 2B 70
nr. Caernarfon 4E 81
Bethel. IOA 3C 80
Bethersden. Kent 1D 28
Bethesda. Gwyn 4F 81
Bethesda. Pemb 3E 43
Bethlehem. Carm 3G 45
Bethnal Green. G Lon 2E 39
Betley. Staf 1B 72
Betsham. Kent 3H 39
Betteshanger. Kent 5H 41
Bettiscombe. Dors 3H 13
Bettisfield. Wrex 2G 71
Betton. Shrp 2A 72
Betton Strange. Shrp 5H 71
Bettws. B'end 3C 32
Bettws. Newp 2F 33
Bettws Bledrws. Cdgn 5E 57
Bettws Cedewain. Powy 1D 58
Bettws Gwerfil Goch. Den 1C 70
Bettws Ifan. Cdgn 1D 44
Bettws Newydd. Mon 5G 47
Bettyhill. High 2H 167
Betws. Carm 4G 45
Betws Garmon. Gwyn 5E 81
Betws-y-Coed. Cnwy 5G 81
Betws-yn-Rhos. Cnwy 3B 82
Beulah. Cdgn 1C 44
Beulah. Powy 5B 58
Beul an Atha. Arg 3B 124
Bevendean. Brig 5E 27
Bevercotes. Notts 3E 86
Beverley. E Yor 1D 94
Beverston. Glos 2D 34
Bevington. Glos 2B 34
Bewaldeth. Cumb 1D 102
Bewcastle. Cumb 2G 113
Bewdley. Worc 3B 60
Bewerley. N Yor 3D 98
Bewholme. E Yor 4F 101
Bexfield. Norf 3C 78
Bexhill. E Sus 5B 28
Bexley. G Lon 3F 39
Bexleyheath. G Lon 3F 39
Bexleyhill. W Sus 3A 26
Bexwell. Norf 5F 77
Beyton. Suff 4B 66
Bhalton. W Isl 4C 171
Bhatarsaigh. W Isl 9B 170
Bibbington. Derbs 3E 85
Bibury. Glos 5G 49
Bicester. Oxon 3D 50
Bickenhall. Som 1F 13
Bickenhill. W Mid 2F 61
Bicker. Linc 2B 76
Bicker Bar. Linc 2B 76
Bicker Gauntlet. Linc 2B 76
Bickershaw. G Man 4E 91
Bickerstaffe. Lanc 4C 90
Bickerton. Ches E 5H 83
Bickerton. Nmbd 4D 121
Bickerton. N Yor 4G 99
Bickford. Staf 4C 72
Bickington. Devn
nr. Barnstaple 3F 19
nr. Newton Abbot 5A 12
Bickleigh. Devn
nr. Plymouth 2B 8
nr. Tiverton 2C 12
Bickleton. Devn 3F 19
Bickley. N Yor 5G 107
Bickley Moss. Ches W 1H 71
Bickmarsh. Worc 1G 49
Bicknacre. Essx 5A 54
Bicknoller. Som 3E 20
Bicknor. Kent 5C 40
Bickton. Hants 1G 15
Bicton. Here 4G 59
Bicton. Shrp
nr. Bishop's Castle 2E 59
nr. Shrewsbury 4G 71
Bicton Heath. Shrp 4G 71
Bidborough. Kent 1G 27
Biddenden. Kent 2C 28
Biddenden Green. Kent 1C 28
Biddenham. Bed 1A 52
Biddestone. Wilts 4D 34
Biddisham. Som 1G 21
Biddlesden. Buck 1E 51
Biddlestone. Nmbd 4D 120
Biddulph. Staf 5C 84
Biddulph Moor. Staf 5D 84
Bideford. Devn 4E 19
Bidford-on-Avon. Warw 5E 61
Bidlake. Devn 4F 11
Bidston. Mers 2E 83
Bielby. E Yor 5B 100
Bieldside. Aber 3F 153
Bierley. IOW 5D 16
Bierley. W Yor 1B 92
Bierton. Buck 4G 51
Bigbury. Devn 4C 8
Bigbury-on-Sea. Devn 4C 8
Bigby. Linc 4D 94
Biggar. Cumb 3A 96
Biggar. S Lan 1C 118
Biggin. Derbs
nr. Hartington 5F 85
nr. Hulland 1G 73
Biggin. N Yor 1F 93
Biggings. Shet 5C 173
Biggin Hill. G Lon 5F 39
Biggleswade. C Beds 1B 52
Bighouse. High 2A 168
Bighton. Hants 3E 24
Biglands. Cumb 4D 112
Bignall End. Staf 5C 84
Bignor. W Sus 4A 26
Bigrigg. Cumb 3B 102
Big Sand. High 1G 155
Bigton. Shet 9E 173
Bilberry. Corn 3E 6
Bilborough. Nott 1C 74
Bilbrook. Som 2D 20
Bilbrook. Staf 5C 72
Bilbrough. N Yor 5H 99
Bilbster. High 3E 169
Bilby. Notts 2D 86
Bildershaw. Dur 2F 105
Bildeston. Suff 1C 54
Billericay. Essx 1A 40
Billesdon. Leics 5E 74
Billesley. Warw 5F 61
Billingborough. Linc 2A 76
Billinge. Mers 4D 90
Billingford. Norf
nr. Dereham 3C 78
nr. Diss 3D 66
Billingham. Stoc T 2B 106
Billinghay. Linc 5A 88
Billingley. S Yor 4E 93
Billingshurst. W Sus 3B 26
Billingsley. Shrp 2B 60
Billington. C Beds 3H 51
Billington. Lanc 1F 91
Billington. Staf 3C 72
Billockby. Norf 4G 79
Billy Row. Dur 1E 105
Bilsborrow. Lanc 5E 97
Bilsby. Linc 3D 88
Bilsham. W Sus 5A 26
Bilsington. Kent 2E 29
Bilson Green. Glos 4B 48
Bilsthorpe. Notts 4D 86
Bilston. Midl 3F 129
Bilston. W Mid 1D 60
Bilstone. Leics 5A 74
Bilting. Kent 1E 29
Bilton. E Yor 1E 95
Bilton. Nmbd 3G 121
Bilton. N Yor 4F 99
Bilton. Warw 3B 62
Bilton in Ainsty. N Yor 5G 99
Bimbister. Orkn 6C 172
Binbrook. Linc 1B 88
Binchester. Dur 1F 105
Bincombe. Dors 4B 14
Bindal. High 5G 165
Binegar. Som 2B 22
Bines Green. W Sus 4C 26
Binfield. Brac 4G 37
Binfield Heath. Oxon 4F 37
Bingfield. Nmbd 2C 114
Bingham. Notts 1E 75
Bingham's Melcombe. Dors 2C 14
Bingley. W Yor 1B 92
Bings Heath. Shrp 4H 71
Binham. Norf 2B 78
Binley. Hants 1C 24
Binley. W Mid 3A 62
Binnegar. Dors 4D 15
Binniehill. Falk 2B 128
Binsoe. N Yor 2E 99
Binstead. IOW 3D 16
Binsted. Hants 2F 25
Binsted. W Sus 5A 26
Binton. Warw 5F 61
Bintree. Norf 3C 78
Binweston. Shrp 5F 71
Birch. Essx 4C 54
Birch. G Man 4G 91
Birchall. Staf 5D 85
Bircham Newton. Norf 2G 77
Bircham Tofts. Norf 2G 77
Birchanger. Essx 3F 53
Birchburn. N Ayr 3D 122
Birch Cross. Staf 2F 73
Bircher. Here 4G 59
Birch Green. Essx 4C 54
Birchgrove. Card 3E 33
Birchgrove. Swan 3G 31
Birch Heath. Ches W 4H 83
Birch Hill. Ches W 3H 83
Birchill. Devn 2G 13
Birchington. Kent 4G 41
Birchley Heath. Warw 1G 61
Birchmoor. Warw 5G 73
Birchmoor Green. C Beds 2H 51
Birchover. Derbs 4G 85
Birch Vale. Derbs 2E 85
Birchview. Mor 5F 159
Birchwood. Linc 4G 87
Birchwood. Som 1F 13
Birchwood. Warr 1A 84
Bircotes. Notts 1D 86
Birdbrook. Essx 1H 53
Birdham. W Sus 2G 17
Birdholme. Derbs 4A 86
Birdingbury. Warw 4B 62
Birdlip. Glos 4E 49
Birdsall. N Yor 3C 100
Birds Edge. W Yor 4C 92
Birds Green. Essx 5F 53
Birdsgreen. Shrp 2B 60
Birdsmoorgate. Dors 2G 13
Birdston. E Dun 2H 127
Birdwell. S Yor 4D 92
Birdwood. Glos 4C 48
Birgham. Bord 1B 120
Birichen. High 4E 165
Birkby. Cumb 1B 102
Birkby. N Yor 4A 106
Birkdale. Mers 3B 90
Birkenhead. Mers 2F 83
Birkenhills. Abers 4E 161
Birkenshaw. N Lan 3H 127
Birkenshaw. W Yor 2C 92
Birkhall. Abers 4H 151
Birkhill. Ang 5C 144
Birkholme. Linc 3G 75
Birkin. N Yor 2F 93
Birley. Here 5G 59
Birling. Kent 4A 40
Birling. Nmbd 4G 121
Birling Gap. E Sus 5G 27
Birlingham. Worc 1E 49
Birmingham. W Mid 192 (2E 61)
Birmingham Airport. W Mid 205 (2F 61)
Birnam. Per 4H 143
Birse. Abers 4C 152
Birsemore. Abers 4C 152
Birstall. Leics 5C 74
Birstall. W Yor 2C 92
Birstall Smithies. W Yor 2C 92
Birstwith. N Yor 4E 99
Birthorpe. Linc 2A 76
Birtle. G Man 3G 91
Birtley. Here 4F 59
Birtley. Nmbd 2B 114
Birtley. Tyne 4F 115
Birtsmorton. Worc 2D 48
Birts Street. Worc 2C 48
Bisbrooke. Rut 1F 63
Bisham. Wind 3G 37
Bishampton. Worc 5D 61

Bish Mill—Bray

Bish Mill. Devn 4H 19
Bishop Auckland. Dur 2F 105
Bishopbridge. Linc 1H 87
Bishopbriggs. E Dun 2H 127
Bishop Burton. E Yor 1C 94
Bishopdown. Wilts 3G 23
Bishop Middleham. Dur 1A 106
Bishopmill. Mor 2G 159
Bishop Monkton. N Yor 3F 99
Bishop Norton. Linc 1G 87
Bishopsbourne. Kent 5F 41
Bishops Cannings. Wilts 5F 35
Bishop's Castle. Shrp 2F 59
Bishop's Caundle. Dors 1B 14
Bishop's Cleeve. Glos 3E 49
Bishops Court. New M 5K 179
Bishop's Down. Dors 1B 14
Bishop's Frome. Here 1B 48
Bishop's Green. Essx 4G 53
Bishop's Green. Hants 5D 36
Bishop's Hull. Som 4F 21
Bishop's Itchington. Warw 5A 62
Bishops Lydeard. Som 4E 21
Bishop's Norton. Glos 3D 48
Bishop's Nympton. Devn 4A 20
Bishop's Offley. Staf 3B 72
Bishop's Stortford. Herts 3E 53
Bishop's Sutton. Hants 3E 24
Bishop's Tachbrook.
Warw 4H 61
Bishop's Tawton. Devn 3F 19
Bishopsteignton. Devn 5C 12
Bishopstoke. Hants 1C 16
Bishopston. Swan 4E 31
Bishopstone. Buck 4G 51
Bishopstone. E Sus 5F 27
Bishopstone. Here 1H 47
Bishopstone. Swin 3H 35
Bishopstone. Wilts 4F 23
Bishopstrow. Wilts 2D 23
Bishop Sutton. Bath 1A 22
Bishop's Waltham. Hants 1D 16
Bishops Wood. Staf 5C 72
Bishopswood. Som 1F 13
Bishopsworth. Bris 5A 34
Bishop Thornton. N Yor 3E 99
Bishopthorpe. York 5H 99
Bishopton. Darl 2A 106
Bishopton. Dum 5B 110
Bishopton. N Yor 2E 99
Bishopton. Ren 2F 127
Bishopton. Warw 5F 61
Bishop Wilton. E Yor 4B 100
Bishton. Newp 3G 33
Bishton. Staf 3E 73
Bisley. Glos 5E 49
Bisley. Surr 5A 38
Bispham. Bkpl 5C 96
Bispham Green. Lanc 3C 90
Bissoe. Corn 4B 6
Bisterne. Hants 2G 15
Bisterne Close. Hants 2H 15
Bitchfield. Linc 3G 75
Bittadon. Devn 2F 19
Bittaford. Devn 3C 8
Bittering. Norf 4B 78
Bitterley. Shrp 3H 59
Bitterne. Sotn 1C 16
Bitteswell. Leics 2C 62
Bitton. S Glo 5B 34
Bix. Oxon 3F 37
Bixter. Shet 6E 173
Blaby. Leics 1C 62
Blackawton. Devn 3E 9
Black Bank. Cambs 2E 65
Black Barn. Linc 3D 76
Blackborough. Devn 2D 12
Blackborough. Norf 4F 77
Blackborough End. Norf 4F 77
Black Bourton. Oxon 5A 50
Blackboys. E Sus 3G 27
Blackbrook. Derbs 1H 73
Blackbrook. Mers 1H 83
Blackbrook. Staf 2B 72
Blackbrook. Surr 1C 26
Blackburn. Abers 2F 153
Blackburn. Bkbn 2E 91
Blackburn. W Lot 3C 128
Black Callerton. Tyne 3E 115
Black Carr. Norf 1C 66
Black Clauchrie. S Ayr 1H 109
Black Corries. High 3G 141
Black Crofts. Arg 5D 140
Black Cross. Corn 2D 6
Blackden Heath. Ches E 3B 84
Blackditch. Oxon 5C 50
Black Dog. Devn 2B 12
Blackdog. Abers 2G 153
Blackdown. Dors 2G 13
Blackdyke. Cumb 4C 112
Blacker Hill. S Yor 4D 92
Blackfen. G Lon 3F 39
Blackfield. Hants 2C 16
Blackford. Cumb 3E 113
Blackford. Per 3A 136
Blackford. Shrp 2H 59
Blackford. Som
nr. Burnham-on-Sea 2H 21
nr. Wincanton 4B 22
Blackfordby. Leics 4H 73
Blackgang. IOW 5C 16
Blackhall. Edin 2F 129
Blackhall. Ren 3F 127
Blackhall Colliery. Dur 1B 106
Blackhall Mill. Tyne 4E 115
Blackhall Rocks. Dur 1B 106
Blackham. E Sus 2F 27
Blackheath. Essx 3D 54
Blackheath. G Lon 3E 39
Blackheath. Suff 3G 67
Blackheath. Surr 1B 26
Blackheath. W Mid 2D 61
Black Heddon. Nmbd 2D 115
Black Hill. Warw 5G 61
Blackhill. Abers 4H 161
Blackhill. High 3C 154
Blackhills. Abers 2G 161
Blackhills. High 3D 158
Blackjack. Linc 2B 76
Blackland. Wilts 5F 35
Black Lane. G Man 4F 91
Blackleach. Lanc 1C 90
Blackley. G Man 4G 91
Blackley. W Yor 3B 92
Blacklunans. Per 2A 144
Blackmill. B'end 3C 32
Blackmoor. G Man 4E 91
Blackmoor. Hants 3F 25
Blackmoor Gate. Devn 2G 19
Blackmore. Essx 5G 53
Blackmore End. Essx 2H 53
Blackmore End. Herts 4B 52
Black Mount. Arg 4G 141
Blackness. Falk 2D 128
Blacknest. Hants 2F 25
Blackney. Dors 3H 13
Blacknoll. Dors 4D 14
Black Notley. Essx 3A 54
Blacko. Lanc 5A 98
Black Pill. Swan 3F 31
Blackpool. Bkpl 192 (1B 90)
Blackpool. Devn 4E 9
Blackpool Corner. Dors 3G 13
Blackpool Gate. Cumb 2G 113
Blackridge. W Lot 3B 128
Blackrock. Arg 3B 124
Blackrock. Mon 4F 47
Blackrod. G Man 3E 90
Blackshaw. Dum 3B 112
Blackshaw Head. W Yor 2H 91
Blackshaw Moor. Staf 5E 85
Blackskull. Arm 4F 178
Blacksmith's Green. Suff 4D 66
Blacksnape. Bkbn 2F 91
Blackstone. W Sus 4D 26
Black Street. Suff 2H 67
Black Tar. Pemb 4D 43
Blackthorn. Oxon 4E 50
Blackthorpe. Suff 4B 66
Blacktoft. E Yor 2B 94
Blacktop. Aber 3F 153
Black Torrington. Devn 2E 11
Blacktown. Newp 3F 33
Blackwall Tunnel. G Lon 2E 39
Blackwater. Corn 4B 6
Blackwater. Hants 1G 25
Blackwater. IOW 4D 16
Blackwater. Som 1F 13
Blackwaterfoot. N Ayr 3C 122
Blackwatertown. Arm 4C 178
Blackwell. Darl 3F 105
Blackwell. Derbs
nr. Alfreton 5B 86
nr. Buxton 3F 85
Blackwell. Som 4D 20
Blackwell. Warw 1H 49
Blackwell. Worc 3D 61
Blackwood. Cphy 2E 33
Blackwood. Dum 1G 111
Blackwood. S Lan 5A 128
Blackwood Hill. Staf 5D 84
Blacon. Ches W 4F 83
Bladnoch. Dum 4B 110
Bladon. Oxon 4C 50
Blaenannerch. Cdgn 1C 44
Blaenau Dolwyddelan.
Cnwy 5F 81
Blaenau Ffestiniog. Gwyn 1G 69
Blaenavon. Torf 5F 47
Blaenawey. Mon 4F 47
Blaen Celyn. Cdgn 5C 56
Blaen Clydach. Rhon 2C 32
Blaencwm. Rhon 2C 32
Blaendulais. Neat 5B 46
Blaenffos. Pemb 1F 43
Blaengarw. B'end 2C 32
Blaen-geuffordd. Cdgn 2F 57
Blaengwrach. Neat 5B 46
Blaengwynfi. Neat 2B 32
Blaenllechau. Rhon 2C 32
Blaenpennal. Cdgn 4F 57
Blaenplwyf. Cdgn 3E 57
Blaenporth. Cdgn 1C 44
Blaenrhondda. Rhon 5C 46
Blaenwaun. Carm 2G 43
Blaen-y-coed. Carm 2H 43
Blagdon. N Som 1A 22
Blagdon. Torb 2E 9
Blagdon Hill. Som 1F 13
Blagill. Cumb 5A 114
Blaguegate. Lanc 4C 90
Blaich. High 1E 141
Blain. High 2A 140
Blaina. Blae 5F 47
Blair Atholl. Per 2F 143
Blair Drummond. Stir 4G 135
Blairgowrie. Per 4A 144
Blairhall. Fife 1D 128
Blairingone. Per 4B 136
Blairlogie. Stir 4H 135
Blairmore. Abers 5B 160
Blairmore. Arg 1C 126
Blairmore. High 3B 166
Blairquhanan. W Dun 1F 127
Blaisdon. Glos 4C 48
Blakebrook. Worc 3C 60
Blakedown. Worc 3C 60
Blake End. Essx 3H 53
Blakemere. Here 1G 47
Blakeney. Glos 5B 48
Blakeney. Norf 1C 78
Blakenhall. Ches E 1B 72
Blakenhall. W Mid 1D 60
Blakeshall. Worc 2C 60
Blakesley. Nptn 5D 62
Blanchland. Nmbd 4C 114
Blandford Camp. Dors 2E 15
Blandford Forum. Dors 2D 15
Blandford St Mary. Dors 2D 15
Bland Hill. N Yor 4E 98
Blandy. High 2G 167
Blanefield. Stir 2G 127
Blaney. Ferm 7D 176
Blankney. Linc 4H 87
Blantyre. S Lan 4H 127
Blarmachfoldach. High 2E 141
Blarnalearoch. High 4F 163
Blashford. Hants 2G 15
Blaston. Leics 1F 63
Blatchbridge. Som 2C 22
Blathaisbhal. W Isl 1D 170
Blatherwycke. Nptn 1G 63
Blawith. Cumb 1B 96
Blaxhall. Suff 5F 67
Blaxton. S Yor 4G 93
Blaydon. Tyne 3E 115
Bleadney. Som 2H 21
Bleadon. N Som 1G 21
Blean. Kent 4F 41
Bleary. Arm 4E 178
Bleasby. Linc 2A 88
Bleasby. Notts 1E 74
Bleasby Moor. Linc 2A 88
Blebocraigs. Fife 2G 137
Bleddfa. Powy 4E 58
Bledington. Glos 3H 49
Bledlow. Buck 5F 51
Bledlow Ridge. Buck 2F 37
Blencarn. Cumb 1H 103
Blencogo. Cumb 5C 112
Blendworth. Hants 1F 17
Blennerhasset. Cumb 5C 112
Bletchingdon. Oxon 4D 50
Bletchingley. Surr 5E 39
Bletchley. Mil 2G 51
Bletchley. Shrp 2A 72
Bletherston. Pemb 2E 43
Bletsoe. Bed 5H 63
Blewbury. Oxon 3D 36
Blickling. Norf 3D 78
Blidworth. Notts 5C 86
Blindburn. Nmbd 3C 120
Blindcrake. Cumb 1C 102
Blindley Heath. Surr 1E 27
Blindmoor. Som 1F 13
Blisland. Corn 5B 10
Blissford. Hants 1G 15
Bliss Gate. Worc 3B 60
Blists Hill. Telf 5A 72
Blisworth. Nptn 5E 63
Blithbury. Staf 3E 73
Blitterlees. Cumb 4C 112
Blockley. Glos 2G 49
Blofield. Norf 5F 79
Blofield Heath. Norf 4F 79
Blo' Norton. Norf 3C 66
Bloomfield. Bord 2H 119
Blore. Staf 1F 73
Blount's Green. Staf 2E 73
Bloxham. Oxon 2C 50
Bloxholm. Linc 5H 87
Bloxwich. W Mid 5D 73
Bloxworth. Dors 3D 15
Blubberhouses. N Yor 4D 98
Blue Anchor. Som 2D 20
Blue Anchor. Swan 3E 31
Blue Bell Hill. Kent 4B 40
Blue Row. Essx 4D 54
Bluetown. Kent 5D 40
Blundeston. Suff 1H 67
Blunham. C Beds 5A 64
Blunsdon St Andrew.
Swin 3G 35
Bluntington. Worc 3C 60
Bluntisham. Cambs 3C 64
Blunts. Corn 2H 7
Blurton. Stoke 1C 72
Blyborough. Linc 1G 87
Blyford. Suff 3G 67
Blymhill. Staf 4C 72
Blymhill Lawns. Staf 4C 72
Blyth. Nmbd 1G 115
Blyth. Notts 2D 86
Blyth. Bord 5E 129
Blyth Bank. Bord 5E 129
Blyth Bridge. Bord 5E 129
Blythburgh. Suff 3G 67
The Blythe. Staf 3E 73
Blythe Bridge. Staf 1D 72
Blythe Marsh. Staf 1D 72
Blyton. Linc 1F 87
Boardmills. Lis 4H 179
Boarhills. Fife 2H 137
Boarhunt. Hants 2E 16
Boar's Head. G Man 4D 90
Boarshead. E Sus 2G 27
Boar's Hill. Oxon 5C 50
Boarstall. Buck 4E 51
Boasley Cross. Devn 3E 11
Boath. High 1H 157
Boat of Garten. High 2D 150
Bobbing. Kent 4C 40
Bobbington. Staf 1C 60
Bobbingworth. Essx 5F 53
Bocaddon. Corn 3F 7
Bocking. Essx 3A 54
Bocking Churchstreet.
Essx 3A 54
Boddam. Abers 4H 161
Boddam. Shet 10E 173
Boddington. Glos 3D 49
Bodedern. IOA 2C 80
Bodelwyddan. Den 3C 82
Bodenham. Here 5H 59
Bodenham. Wilts 4G 23
Bodewryd. IOA 1C 80
Bodfari. Den 3C 82
Bodffordd. IOA 3D 80
Bodham. Norf 1D 78
Bodiam. E Sus 3B 28
Bodicote. Oxon 2C 50
Bodieve. Corn 1D 6
Bodinnick. Corn 3F 7
Bodle Street Green. E Sus 4A 28
Bodmin. Corn 2E 7
Bodnant. Cnwy 3H 81
Bodney. Norf 1H 65
Bodorgan. IOA 4C 80
Bodrane. Corn 2G 7
Bodsham. Kent 1F 29
Boduan. Gwyn 2C 68
Bodymoor Heath. Warw 1F 61
The Bog. Shrp 1F 59
Bogallan. High 3A 158
Bogbrae Croft. Abers 5H 161
Bogend. S Ayr 1C 116
Boghall. Midl 3F 129
Boghall. W Lot 3C 128
Boghead. S Lan 5A 128
Bogindollo. Ang 3D 144
Bogmoor. Mor 2A 160
Bogniebrae. Abers 4C 160
Bognor Regis. W Sus 3H 17
Bograxie. Abers 2E 152
Bogside. N Lan 4B 128
Bogton. Abers 3D 160
Bogue. Dum 1D 110
Bohenie. High 5E 149
Bohortha. Corn 5C 6
Boirseam. W Isl 9C 171
Bokiddick. Corn 2E 7
Bolam. Dur 2E 105
Bolam. Nmbd 1D 115
Bolberry. Devn 5C 8
Bold Heath. Mers 2H 83
Boldon. Tyne 3G 115
Boldon Colliery. Tyne 3G 115
Boldre. Hants 3B 16
Boldron. Dur 3D 104
Bole. Notts 2E 87
Bolehall. Staf 5G 73
Bolehill. Derbs 5G 85
Bolenowe. Corn 5A 6
Boleside. Bord 1G 119
Bolham. Devn 1C 12
Bolham Water. Devn 1E 13
Bolingey. Corn 3B 6
Bollington. Ches E 3D 84
Bolney. W Sus 3D 26
Bolnhurst. Bed 5H 63
Bolshan. Ang 3F 145
Bolsover. Derbs 3B 86
Bolsterstone. S Yor 1G 85
Bolstone. Here 2A 48
Boltachan. Per 3F 143
Boltby. N Yor 1G 99
Bolton. Cumb 2H 103
Bolton. E Lot 2B 130
Bolton. E Yor 4B 100
Bolton. G Man 4F 91
Bolton. Nmbd 3F 121
Bolton Abbey. N Yor 4C 98
Bolton-by-Bowland. Lanc 5G 97
Boltonfellend. Cumb 3F 113
Boltongate. Cumb 5D 112
Bolton Green. Lanc 3D 90
Bolton-le-Sands. Lanc 3D 97
Bolton Low Houses.
Cumb 5D 112
Bolton New Houses.
Cumb 5D 112
Bolton-on-Swale. N Yor 5F 105
Bolton Percy. N Yor 5H 99
Bolton Town End. Lanc 3D 97
Bolton upon Dearne.
S Yor 4E 93
Bolton Wood Lane.
Cumb 5D 112
Bolventor. Corn 5B 10
Bomarsund. Nmbd 1F 115
Bomere Heath. Shrp 4G 71
Bonar Bridge. High 4D 164
Bonawe. Arg 5E 141
Bonby. N Lin 3D 94
Boncath. Pemb 1G 43
Bonchester Bridge. Bord 3H 119
Bonchurch. IOW 5D 16
Bond End. Staf 4F 73
Bondleigh. Devn 2G 11
Bonds. Lanc 5D 97
Bonehill. Devn 5H 11
Bonehill. Staf 5F 73
Bo'ness. Falk 1C 128
Boney Hay. Staf 4E 73
Bonham. Wilts 3C 22
Bonhill. W Dun 2E 127
Boningale. Shrp 5C 72
Bonjedward. Bord 2A 120
Bonkle. N Lan 4B 128
Bonnanaboigh. Caus 5C 174
Bonnington. Ang 5E 145
Bonnington. Edin 3E 129
Bonnington. Kent 2E 29
Bonnybank. Fife 3F 137
Bonnybridge. Falk 1B 128
Bonnykelly. Abers 3F 161
Bonnyrigg. Midl 3G 129
Bonnyton. Ang 5C 144
Bonnytown. Fife 2H 137
Bonsall. Derbs 5G 85
Bont. Mon 4G 47
Bontddu. Gwyn 4F 69
Bont Dolgadfan. Powy 5A 70
Y Bont-Faen. V Glam 4C 32
Bontgoch. Cdgn 2F 57
Bonthorpe. Linc 3D 89
Bont Newydd. Gwyn 1G 69
Bont-newydd. Cnwy 3C 82
Bontnewydd. Cdgn 4F 57
Bontnewydd. Gwyn 4D 81
Bontuchel. Den 5C 82
Bonvilston. V Glam 4D 32
Bon-y-maen. Swan 3F 31
Booker. Buck 2G 37
Booley. Shrp 3H 71
Boorley Green. Hants 1D 16
Boosbeck. Red C 3D 106
Boot. Cumb 4C 102
Booth. W Yor 2A 92
Boothby Graffoe. Linc 5G 87
Boothby Pagnell. Linc 2G 75
Booth Green. Ches E 2D 84
Booth of Toft. Shet 4F 173
Boothstown. G Man 4F 91
Boothville. Nptn 4E 63
Bootle. Cumb 1A 96
Bootle. Mers 1F 83
Booton. Norf 3D 78
Booze. N Yor 4D 104
Boquhan. Stir 1G 127
Boraston. Shrp 3A 60
Borden. Kent 4C 40
Borden. W Sus 4G 25
Bordlands. Bord 5E 129
Bordley. N Yor 3B 98
Bordon. Hants 3F 25
Boreham. Essx 5A 54
Boreham. Wilts 2D 23
Boreham Street. E Sus 4A 28
Borehamwood. Herts 1C 38
Boreland. Dum 5D 118
Boreston. Devn 3D 8
Borestone Brae. Stir 4G 135
Boreton. Shrp 5H 71
Borgh. W Isl
on Barra 8B 170
on Benbecula 3C 170
on Berneray 1E 170
on Isle of Lewis 2G 171
Borghasdal. W Isl 9C 171
Borghastan. W Isl 3D 171
Borgh na Sgiotaig. High 1C 154
Borgie. High 3G 167
Borgue. Dum 5D 110
Borgue. High 1H 165
Borley. Essx 1B 54
Borley Green. Essx 1B 54
Borley Green. Suff 4B 66
Borlum. High 1H 149
Bornais. W Isl 6C 170
Bornesketaig. High 1C 154
Boroughbridge. N Yor 3F 99
Borough Green. Kent 5H 39
Borreraig. High 3A 154
Borrobol Lodge. High 1F 165
Borrodale. High 4A 154
Borrowash. Derbs 2B 74
Borrowby. N Yor
nr. Northallerton 1G 99
nr. Whitby 3E 107
Borrowston. High 4F 169
Borrowstonehill. Orkn 7D 172
Borrowstoun. Falk 1C 128
Borstal. Medw 4B 40
Borth. Cdgn 2F 57
Borthwick. Midl 4G 129
Borth-y-Gest. Gwyn 2E 69
Borve. High 4D 154
Borwick. Lanc 2E 97
Bosbury. Here 1B 48
Boscastle. Corn 3A 10
Boscombe. Bour 3G 15
Boscombe. Wilts 3H 23
Boscoppa. Corn 3E 7
Bosham. W Sus 2G 17
Bosherston. Pemb 5D 42
Bosley. Ches E 4D 84
Bossall. N Yor 3B 100
Bossiney. Corn 4A 10
Bossingham. Kent 1F 29
Bossington. Som 2B 20
Bostadh. W Isl 3D 171
Bostock Green. Ches W 4A 84
Boston. Linc 1C 76
Boston Spa. W Yor 5G 99
Boswarthen. Corn 3B 4
Boswinger. Corn 4D 6
Botallack. Corn 3A 4
Botany Bay. G Lon 1D 39
Botcheston. Leics 5B 74
Botesdale. Suff 3C 66
Bothal. Nmbd 1F 115
Bothampstead. W Ber 4D 36
Bothamsall. Notts 3D 86
Bothel. Cumb 1C 102
Bothenhampton. Dors 3H 13
Bothwell. S Lan 4A 128
Botley. Buck 5H 51
Botley. Hants 1D 16
Botley. Oxon 5C 50
Botloe's Green. Glos 3C 48
Botolph Claydon. Buck 3F 51
Botolphs. W Sus 5C 26
Bottacks. High 2G 157
Bottesford. Leics 2F 75
Bottesford. N Lin 4B 94
Bottisham. Cambs 4E 65
Bottlesford. Wilts 1G 23
Bottomcraig. Fife 1F 137
Bottom o' th' Moor. G Man 3E 91
Botton. N Yor 4D 107
Botton Head. Lanc 3F 97
Bottreaux Mill. Devn 4B 20
Botus Fleming. Corn 2A 8
Botwnnog. Gwyn 2B 68
Bough Beech. Kent 1F 27
Boughrood. Powy 2E 47
Boughspring. Glos 2A 34
Boughton. Norf 5F 77
Boughton. Nptn 4E 63
Boughton. Notts 4D 86
Boughton Aluph. Kent 1E 29
Boughton Green. Kent 5B 40
Boughton Lees. Kent 1E 28
Boughton Malherbe. Kent 1C 28
Boughton Monchelsea.
Kent 5B 40
Boughton under Blean.
Kent 5E 41
Boulby. Red C 3E 107
Bouldnor. IOW 4B 16
Bouldon. Shrp 2H 59
Boulmer. Nmbd 3G 121
Boulston. Pemb 3D 42
Boultham. Linc 4G 87
Boulton. Derb 2A 74
Boundary. Staf 1D 73
Bounds. Here 2B 48
Bourn. Cambs 5C 64
Bournbrook. W Mid 2E 61
Bourne. Linc 3H 75
The Bourne. Surr 2G 25
Bourne End. Bed 4H 63
Bourne End. Buck 3G 37
Bourne End. C Beds 1H 51
Bourne End. Herts 5A 52
Bournemouth.
Bour 192 (3F 15)
Bournemouth Airport.
Dors 3G 15
Bournes Green. Glos 5E 49
Bournes Green. S'end 2D 40
Bournheath. Worc 3D 60
Bournmoor. Dur 4G 115
Bournville. W Mid 2E 61
Bourton. Dors 3C 22
Bourton. N Som 5G 33
Bourton. Oxon 3H 35
Bourton. Shrp 1H 59
Bourton. Wilts 5F 35
Bourton on Dunsmore.
Warw 3B 62
Bourton-on-the-Hill. Glos 2G 49
Bourton-on-the-Water.
Glos 3G 49
Bousd. Arg 2D 138
Bousta. Shet 6D 173
Boustead Hill. Cumb 4D 112
Bouth. Cumb 1C 96
Bouthwaite. N Yor 2D 98
Boveney. Buck 3A 38
Boveridge. Dors 1F 15
Boverton. V Glam 5C 32
Bovey Tracey. Devn 5B 12
Bovingdon. Herts 5A 52
Bovingdon Green. Buck 3G 37
Bovinger. Essx 5F 53
Bovington Camp. Dors 4D 14
Bow. Devn 2H 11
Bowbank. Dur 2C 104
Bow Brickhill. Mil 2H 51
Bowbridge. Glos 5D 48
Bowburn. Dur 1A 106
Bowcombe. IOW 4C 16
Bowd. Devn 4E 12
Bowden. Devn 4E 9
Bowden. Bord 1H 119
Bowden Hill. Wilts 5E 35
Bowdens. Som 4H 21
Bowderdale. Cumb 4H 103
Bowdon. G Man 2B 84
Bower. Nmbd 1A 114
Bowerchalke. Wilts 4F 23
Bowerhill. Wilts 5E 35
Bower Hinton. Som 1H 13
Bowermadden. High 2E 169
Bowers. Staf 2C 72
Bowers Gifford. Essx 2B 40
Bowershall. Fife 4C 136
Bowertower. High 2E 169
Bowes. Dur 3C 104
Bowgreave. Lanc 5D 97
Bowhousebog. N Lan 4B 128
Bowithick. Corn 4B 10
Bowland Bridge. Cumb 1D 96
Bowlees. Dur 2C 104
Bowley. Here 5H 59
Bowlhead Green. Surr 2A 26
Bowling. W Dun 2F 127
Bowling. W Yor 1B 92
Bowling Bank. Wrex 1F 71
Bowling Green. Worc 5C 60
Bowlish. Som 2B 22
Bowmanstead. Cumb 5E 102
Bowmore. Arg 4B 124
Bowness-on-Solway.
Cumb 3D 112
Bowness-on-Windermere.
Cumb 5F 103
Bow of Fife. Fife 2F 137
Bowriefauld. Ang 4E 145
Bowscale. Cumb 1E 103
Bowsden. Nmbd 5F 131
Bowside Lodge. High 2A 168
Bowston. Cumb 5F 103
Bow Street. Cdgn 2F 57
Bowthorpe. Norf 5D 78
Box. Glos 5D 48
Box. Wilts 5D 34
Boxbush. Glos 1A 48
Box End. Bed 1A 52
Boxford. Suff 1C 54
Boxford. W Ber 4C 36
Boxgrove. W Sus 5A 26
Box Hill. Wilts 5D 34
Boxley. Kent 5B 40
Boxmoor. Herts 5A 52
Box's Shop. Corn 2C 10
Boxted. Essx 2C 54
Boxted. Suff 5H 65
Boxted Cross. Essx 2D 54
Boxworth. Cambs 4C 64
Boxworth End. Cambs 4C 64
Boyden End. Suff 5G 65
Boyden Gate. Kent 4G 41
Boylestone. Derbs 2F 73
Boylestonfield. Derbs 2F 73
Boyndie. Abers 2D 160
Boynton. E Yor 3F 101
Boys Hill. Dors 1B 14
Boythorpe. Derbs 4A 86
Boyton. Corn 3D 10
Boyton. Suff 1G 55
Boyton. Wilts 3E 23
Boyton Cross. Essx 5G 53
Boyton End. Essx 2G 53
Boyton End. Suff 1H 53
Bozeat. Nptn 5G 63
Braaid. IOM 4C 108
Braal Castle. High 3D 168
Brabling Green. Suff 4E 67
Brabourne. Kent 1F 29
Brabourne Lees. Kent 1E 29
Brabster. High 2F 169
Bracadale. High 5C 154
Bracara. High 4F 147
Braceborough. Linc 4H 75
Bracebridge. Linc 4G 87
Bracebridge Heath. Linc 4G 87
Braceby. Linc 2H 75
Bracewell. Lanc 5A 98
Brackenber. Cumb 3A 104
Brackenfield. Derbs 5A 86
Brackenlands. Cumb 5D 112
Brackenthwaite. Cumb 5D 112
Brackenthwaite. N Yor 4E 99
Brackla. B'end 4C 32
Brackla. High 3C 158
Bracklesham. W Sus 3G 17
Brackletter. High 5D 148
Brackley. Nptn 2D 50
Brackley Hatch. Nptn 1E 51
Brackloch. High 1F 163
Bracknell. Brac 5G 37
Braco. Per 3H 135
Bracobrae. Mor 3C 160
Bracon. N Lin 4A 94
Bracon Ash. Norf 1D 66
Bradbourne. Derbs 5G 85
Bradbury. Dur 2A 106
Bradda. IOM 4A 108
Bradden. Nptn 1E 51
Bradenham. Buck 2G 37
Bradenham. Norf 5B 78
Bradenstoke. Wilts 4F 35
Bradfield. Essx 2E 55
Bradfield. Norf 2E 79
Bradfield. W Ber 4E 36
Bradfield Combust. Suff 5A 66
Bradfield Green. Ches E 5A 84
Bradfield Heath. Essx 3E 55
Bradfield St Clare. Suff 5B 66
Bradfield St George. Suff 4B 66
Bradford. Derbs 4G 85
Bradford. Devn 2E 11
Bradford. Nmbd 1F 121
Bradford. W Yor 192 (1B 92)
Bradford Abbas. Dors 1A 14
Bradford Barton. Devn 1B 12
Bradford Leigh. Wilts 5D 34
Bradford-on-Avon. Wilts 5D 34
Bradford-on-Tone. Som 4E 21
Bradford Peverell. Dors 3B 14
Bradiford. Devn 3F 19
Brading. IOW 4E 16
Bradley. Ches W 3H 83
Bradley. Derbs 1G 73
Bradley. Glos 2C 34
Bradley. Hants 2E 25
Bradley. NE Lin 4F 95
Bradley. N Yor 1C 98
Bradley. Staf 4C 72
Bradley. W Mid 1D 60
Bradley. W Yor 2B 92
Bradley. Wrex 5F 83
Bradley Cross. Som 1H 21
Bradley Green. Ches W 1H 71
Bradley Green. Som 3F 21
Bradley Green. Warw 5G 73
Bradley Green. Worc 4D 61
Bradley in the Moors. Staf 1E 73
Bradley Mount. Ches E 3D 84
Bradley Stoke. S Glo 3B 34
Bradlow. Here 2C 48
Bradmore. Notts 2C 74
Bradmore. W Mid 1C 60
Bradninch. Devn 2D 12
Bradnop. Staf 5E 85
Bradpole. Dors 3H 13
Bradshaw. G Man 3F 91
Bradstone. Devn 4D 11
Bradwall Green. Ches E 4B 84
Bradway. S Yor 2H 85
Bradwell. Derbs 2F 85
Bradwell. Essx 3B 54
Bradwell. Mil 2G 51
Bradwell. Norf 5H 79
Bradwell-on-Sea. Essx 5D 54
Bradwell Waterside. Essx 5C 54
Bradworthy. Devn 1D 10
Brae. High 5C 162
Brae. Shet 5E 173
Braeantra. High 1H 157
Braefield. High 5G 157
Braefindon. High 3A 158
Braegrum. Per 1C 136
Braehead. Ang 3F 145
Braehead. Dum 4B 110
Braehead. Mor 4G 159
Braehead. Orkn 3D 172
Braehead. S Lan
nr. Coalburn 1H 117
nr. Forth 4C 128
Braehoulland. Shet 4D 173
Braemar. Abers 4F 151
Braemore. High
nr. Dunbeath 5C 168
nr. Ullapool 1D 156
Brae of Achnahaird. High 2E 163
Brae Roy Lodge. High 4F 149
Braeside. Abers 5G 161
Braeside. Inv 2D 126
Braes of Coul. Ang 3B 144
Braeswick. Orkn 4F 172
Braetongue. High 3F 167
Braeval. Stir 3E 135
Braevallich. Arg 3G 133
Braewick. Shet 6E 173
Brafferton. Darl 2F 105
Brafferton. N Yor 2G 99
Brafield-on-the-Green.
Nptn 5F 63
Bragar. W Isl 3E 171
Bragbury End. Herts 3C 52
Bragleenbeg. Arg 1G 133
Braichmelyn. Gwyn 4F 81
Braides. Lanc 4D 96
Braidwood. S Lan 5B 128
Braigo. Arg 3A 124
Brailsford. Derbs 1G 73
Braintree. Essx 3A 54
Braiseworth. Suff 3D 66
Braishfield. Hants 4B 24
Braithwaite. Cumb 2D 102
Braithwaite. S Yor 3G 93
Braithwaite. W Yor 5C 98
Braithwell. S Yor 1C 86
Brakefield Green. Norf 5C 78
Bramber. W Sus 4C 26
Brambridge. Hants 4C 24
Bramcote. Notts 2C 74
Bramcote. Warw 2B 62
Bramdean. Hants 4E 24
Bramerton. Norf 5E 79
Bramfield. Herts 4C 52
Bramfield. Suff 3F 67
Bramford. Suff 1E 54
Bramhall. G Man 2C 84
Bramham. W Yor 5G 99
Bramhope. W Yor 5E 99
Bramley. Hants 1E 25
Bramley. S Yor 1B 86
Bramley. Surr 1B 26
Bramley. W Yor 1C 92
Bramley Green. Hants 1E 25
Bramley Head. N Yor 4D 98
Bramley Vale. Derbs 4B 86
Bramling. Kent 5G 41
Brampford Speke. Devn 3C 12
Brampton. Cambs 3B 64
Brampton. Cumb
nr. Appleby-in-Westmorland
2H 103
nr. Carlisle 3G 113
Brampton. Linc 3F 87
Brampton. Norf 3E 78
Brampton. S Yor 4E 93
Brampton. Suff 2G 67
Brampton Abbotts. Here 3B 48
Brampton Ash. Nptn 2E 63
Brampton Bryan. Here 3F 59
Brampton en le Morthen.
S Yor 2B 86
Bramshall. Staf 2E 73
Bramshaw. Hants 1A 16
Bramshill. Hants 5F 37
Bramshott. Hants 3G 25
Branault. High 2G 139
Brancaster. Norf 1G 77
Brancaster Staithe. Norf 1G 77
Brancepeth. Dur 1F 105
Branch End. Nmbd 3D 114
Branchill. Mor 3E 159
Brand End. Linc 1C 76
Branderburgh. Mor 1G 159
Brandesburton. E Yor 5F 101
Brandeston. Suff 4E 67
Brand Green. Glos 3C 48
Brandhill. Shrp 3G 59
Brandis Corner. Devn 2E 11
Brandish Street. Som 2C 20
Brandiston. Norf 3D 78
Brandon. Dur 1F 105
Brandon. Linc 1G 75
Brandon. Nmbd 3E 121
Brandon. Suff 2G 65
Brandon. Warw 3B 62
Brandon Bank. Cambs 2F 65
Brandon Creek. Norf 1F 65
Brandon Parva. Norf 5C 78
Brandsby. N Yor 2H 99
Brandy Wharf. Linc 1H 87
Brane. Corn 4B 4
Bran End. Essx 3G 53
Branksome. Pool 3F 15
Bransbury. Hants 2C 24
Bransby. Linc 3F 87
Branscombe. Devn 4E 13
Bransford. Worc 5B 60
Bransgore. Hants 3G 15
Bransholme. Hull 1E 94
Bransley. Shrp 3A 60
Branston. Leics 3F 75
Branston. Linc 4H 87
Branston. Staf 3G 73
Branston Booths. Linc 4H 87
Branstone. IOW 4D 16
Bransty. Cumb 3A 102
Brant Broughton. Linc 5G 87
Brantham. Suff 2E 54
Branthwaite. Cumb
nr. Caldbeck 1D 102
nr. Workington 2B 102
Brantingham. E Yor 2C 94
Branton. Nmbd 3E 121
Branton. S Yor 4G 93
Branton Green. N Yor 3G 99
Branxholme. Bord 3G 119
Branxton. Nmbd 1C 120
Brassington. Derbs 5G 85
Brasted. Kent 5F 39
Brasted Chart. Kent 5F 39
The Bratch. Staf 1C 60
Brathens. Abers 4D 152
Bratoft. Linc 4D 88
Brattleby. Linc 2G 87
Bratton. Som 2C 20
Bratton. Telf 4A 72
Bratton. Wilts 1E 23
Bratton Clovelly. Devn 3E 11
Bratton Fleming. Devn 3G 19
Bratton Seymour. Som 4B 22
Braughing. Herts 3D 53
Braulen Lodge. High 5E 157
Braunston. Nptn 4C 62
Braunstone Town. Leics 5C 74
Braunston-in-Rutland. Rut 5E 75
Braunton. Devn 3E 19
Brawby. N Yor 2B 100
Brawl. High 2A 168
Brawlbin. High 3C 168
Bray. Wind 3A 38

Braybrooke—Burton

Braybrooke. Nptn 2E 63
Brayford. Devn 3G 19
Bray Shop. Corn 5D 10
Braystones. Cumb 4B 102
Brayton. N Yor 1G 93
Bray Wick. Wind 4G 37
Brazacott. Corn 3C 10
Brea. Corn 4A 6
Breach. W Sus 2F 17
Breachwood Green. Herts 3B 52
Breacleit. W Isl 4D 171
Breaden Heath. Shrp 2G 71
Breadsall. Derbs 1A 74
Breadstone. Glos 5C 48
Breage. Corn 4D 4
Breakachy. High 4G 157
Breakish. High 1E 147
Bream. Glos 5B 48
Breamore. Hants 1G 15
Bream's Meend. Glos 5B 48
Brean. Som 1F 21
Breanais. W Isl 5B 171
Brearton. N Yor 3F 99
Breascleit. W Isl 4E 171
Breaston. Derbs 2B 74
Brecais Àrd. High 1E 147
Brecais Iosal. High 1E 147
Brechfa. Carm 2F 45
Brechin. Ang 3F 145
Breckles. Norf 1B 66
Brecon. Powy 3D 46
Bredbury. G Man 1D 84
Brede. E Sus 4C 28
Bredenbury. Here 5A 60
Bredfield. Suff 5E 67
Bredgar. Kent 4C 40
Bredhurst. Kent 4B 40
Bredicot. Worc 5D 60
Bredon. Worc 2E 49
Bredon's Norton. Worc 2E 49
Bredwardine. Here 1G 47
Breedon on the Hill. Leics 3B 74
Breibhig. W Isl
on Barra 9B 170
on Isle of Lewis 4G 171
Breich. W Lot 3C 128
Breightmet. G Man 4F 91
Breighton. E Yor 1H 93
Breinton. Here 2H 47
Breinton Common. Here 2H 47
Breiwick. Shet 7F 173
Brelston Green. Here 3A 48
Bremhill. Wilts 4E 35
Brenachie. High 1B 158
Brenchley. Kent 1A 28
Brendon. Devn 2A 20
Brent Cross. G Lon 2D 38
Brent Eleigh. Suff 1C 54
Brentford. G Lon 3C 38
Brentingby. Leics 4E 75
Brent Knoll. Som 1G 21
Brent Pelham. Herts 2E 53
Brentwood. Essx 1G 39
Brenzett. Kent 3E 28
Brereton. Staf 4E 73
Brereton Cross. Staf 4E 73
Brereton Green. Ches E 4B 84
Brereton Heath. Ches E 4C 84
Bressingham. Norf 2C 66
Bretby. Derbs 3G 73
Bretford. Warw 3B 62
Bretforton. Worc 1F 49
Bretherdale Head. Cumb 4G 103
Bretherton. Lanc 2C 90
Brettabister. Shet 6F 173
Brettenham. Norf 2B 66
Brettenham. Suff 5B 66
Bretton. Flin 4F 83
Bretton. Pet 5A 76
Brewlands Bridge. Ang 2A 144
Brewood. Staf 5C 72
Briantspuddle. Dors 3D 14
Bricket Wood. Herts 5B 52
Bricklehampton. Worc 1E 49
Bride. IOM 1D 108
Bridekirk. Cumb 1C 102
Bridell. Pemb 1B 44
Bridestowe. Devn 4F 11
Brideswell. Abers 5C 160
Bridford. Devn 4B 12
Bridge. Corn 4A 6
Bridge. Kent 5F 41
Bridge. Som 2G 13
Bridge End. Bed 5H 63
Bridge End. Cumb
nr. Broughton in Furness
. . . . .5D 102
nr. Dalston 5E 113
Bridge End. Linc 2A 76
Bridge End. Shet 8E 173
Bridgefoot. Ang 5C 144
Bridgefoot. Cumb 2B 102
Bridge Green. Essx 2E 53
Bridgehampton. Som 4A 22
Bridge Hewick. N Yor 2F 99
Bridgehill. Dur 4D 115
Bridgemary. Hants 2D 16
Bridgemere. Ches E 1B 72
Bridgemont. Derbs 2E 85
Bridgend. Abers
nr. Huntly 5C 160
nr. Peterhead 5H 161
Bridgend. Ang
nr. Brechin 2E 145
nr. Kirriemuir 4C 144
Bridgend. Arg
nr. Lochgilphead 4F 133
on Islay 3B 124
Bridgend. B'end 3C 32
Bridgend. Cumb 3E 103
Bridgend. Devn 4B 8
Bridgend. Fife 2F 137
Bridgend. High 3F 157
Bridgend. Mor 5A 160
Bridgend. Per 1D 136
Bridgend. W Lot 2D 128
Bridgend of Lintrathen.
Ang 3B 144
Bridgeness. Falk 1D 128
Bridge of Alford. Abers 2C 152
Bridge of Allan. Stir 4G 135
Bridge of Avon. Mor 5F 159
Bridge of Awe. Arg 1H 133
Bridge of Balgie. Per 4C 142
Bridge of Brown. High 1F 151
Bridge of Cally. Per 3A 144
Bridge of Canny. Abers 4D 152
Bridge of Dee. Dum 3E 111
Bridge of Don. Aber 2G 153
Bridge of Dun. Ang 3F 145
Bridge of Dye. Abers 5D 152
Bridge of Earn. Per 2D 136
Bridge of Ericht. Per 3C 142
Bridge of Feugh. Abers 4E 152
Bridge of Gairn. Abers 4A 152
Bridge of Gaur. Per 3C 142
Bridge of Muchalls.
Abers 4F 153
Bridge of Oich. High 3F 149
Bridge of Orchy. Arg 5H 141
Bridge of Walls. Shet 6D 173
Bridge of Weir. Ren 3E 127
Bridge Reeve. Devn 1G 11
Bridgerule. Devn 2C 10
Bridge Sollers. Here 1H 47
Bridge Street. Suff 1B 54
Bridge Town. Warw 5G 61
Bridgetown. Devn 2E 9
Bridgetown. Som 3C 20
Bridge Trafford. Ches W 3G 83
Bridgeyate. S Glo 4B 34
Bridgham. Norf 2B 66
Bridgnorth. Shrp 1B 60
Bridgtown. Staf 5D 73
Bridgwater. Som 3G 21
Bridlington. E Yor 3F 101
Bridport. Dors 3H 13
Bridstow. Here 3A 48
Brierfield. Lanc 1G 91
Brierley. Glos 4B 48
Brierley. Here 5G 59
Brierley. S Yor 3E 93
Brierley Hill. W Mid 2D 60
Brierton. Hart 1B 106
Briestfield. W Yor 3C 92
Brigg. N Lin 4D 94
Briggate. Norf 3F 79
Briggswath. N Yor 4F 107
Brigham. Cumb 1B 102
Brigham. E Yor 4E 101
Brighouse. W Yor 2B 92
Brighstone. IOW 4C 16
Brightgate. Derbs 5G 85
Brighthampton. Oxon 5B 50
Brightholmlee. S Yor 1G 85
Brightley. Devn 3G 11
Brightling. E Sus 3A 28
Brightlingsea. Essx 4D 54
Brighton. Brig 192 (5E 27)
Brighton. Corn 3D 6
Brighton Hill. Hants 2E 24
Brightons. Falk 2C 128
Brightwalton. W Ber 4C 36
Brightwalton Green.
W Ber 4C 36
Brightwell. Suff 1F 55
Brightwell Baldwin. Oxon 2E 37
Brightwell-cum-Sotwell.
Oxon 2D 36
Brignall. Dur 3D 104
Brig o' Turk. Stir 3E 135
Brigsley. NE Lin 4F 95
Brigsteer. Cumb 1D 97
Brigstock. Nptn 2G 63
Brill. Buck 4E 51
Brill. Corn 4E 5
Brilley. Here 1F 47
Brimaston. Pemb 2D 42
Brimfield. Here 4H 59
Brimington. Derbs 3B 86
Brimley. Devn 5B 12
Brimpsfield. Glos 4E 49
Brimpton. W Ber 5D 36
Brims. Orkn 9B 172
Brimscombe. Glos 5D 48
Brimstage. Mers 2F 83
Brincliffe. S Yor 2H 85
Brind. E Yor 1H 93
Brindister. Shet
nr. West Burrafirth 6D 173
nr. West Lerwick 8F 173
Brindle. Lanc 2D 90
Brindley. Ches E 5H 83
Brindley Ford. Stoke 5C 84
Brineton. Staf 4C 72
Bringhurst. Leics 1F 63
Bringsty Common. Here 5A 60
Brington. Cambs 3H 63
Brinian. Orkn 5D 172
Briningham. Norf 2C 78
Brinkhill. Linc 3C 88
Brinkley. Cambs 5F 65
Brinklow. Warw 3B 62
Brinkworth. Wilts 3F 35
Brinscall. Lanc 2E 91
Brinscombe. Som 1H 21
Brinsley. Notts 1B 74
Brinsworth. S Yor 2B 86
Brinton. Norf 2C 78
Brisco. Cumb 4F 113
Brisley. Norf 3B 78
Brislington. Bris 4B 34
Brissenden Green. Kent 2D 28
Bristol. Bris 193 (4A 34)
Bristol Airport. N Som 5A 34
Briston. Norf 2C 78
Britannia. Lanc 2G 91
Britford. Wilts 4G 23
Brithdir. Cphy 5E 47
Brithdir. Cdgn 1D 44
Brithdir. Gwyn 4G 69
Briton Ferry. Neat 3G 31
Britwell Salome. Oxon 2E 37
Brixham. Torb 3F 9
Brixton. Devn 3B 8
Brixton. G Lon 3E 39
Brixton Deverill. Wilts 3D 22
Brixworth. Nptn 3E 63
Brize Norton. Oxon 5B 50
The Broad. Here 4G 59
Broad Alley. Worc 4C 60
Broad Blunsdon. Swin 2G 35
Broadbottom. G Man 1D 85
Broadbridge. W Sus 2G 17
Broadbridge Heath.
W Sus 2C 26
Broad Campden. Glos 2G 49
Broad Chalke. Wilts 4F 23
Broadclyst. Devn 3C 12
Broadfield. Inv 2E 127
Broadfield. Pemb 4F 43
Broadfield. W Sus 2D 26
Broadford. High 1E 147
Broadford Bridge. W Sus 3B 26
Broadgate. Cumb 1A 96
Broad Green. Cambs 5F 65
Broad Green. C Beds 1H 51
Broad Green. Worc
nr. Bromsgrove 3D 61
nr. Worcester 5B 60
Broad Haven. Pemb 3C 42
Broadhaven. High 3F 169
Broad Heath. Staf 3C 72
Broadheath. G Man 2B 84
Broadheath. Worc 4A 60
Broadheath Common.
Worc 5C 60
Broadhembury. Devn 2E 12
Broadhempston. Devn 2E 9
Broad Hill. Cambs 3E 65
Broad Hinton. Wilts 4G 35
Broadholme. Derbs 1A 74
Broadholme. Linc 3F 87
Broadlay. Carm 5D 44
Broad Laying. Hants 5C 36
Broadley. Lanc 3G 91
Broadley. Mor 2A 160
Broadley Common. Essx 5E 53
Broad Marston. Worc 1G 49
Broadmayne. Dors 4C 14
Broadmere. Hants 2E 24
Broadmoor. Pemb 4E 43
Broad Oak. Carm 3F 45
Broad Oak. Cumb 5C 102
Broad Oak. Devn 3D 12
Broad Oak. Dors 1C 14
Broad Oak. E Sus
nr. Hastings 4C 28
nr. Heathfield 3H 27
Broad Oak. Here 3H 47
Broad Oak. Kent 4F 41
Broadoak. Dors 3H 13
Broadoak. Glos 4B 48
Broadoak. Hants 1D 16
Broadrashes. Mor 3B 160
Broadsea. Abers 2G 161
Broad's Green. Essx 4G 53
Broadshard. Som 1H 13
Broadstairs. Kent 4H 41
Broadstone. Pool 3F 15
Broadstone. Shrp 2H 59
Broad Street. E Sus 4C 28
Broad Street. Kent
nr. Ashford 1F 29
nr. Maidstone 5C 40
Broad Street Green. Essx 5B 54
Broad Town. Wilts 4F 35
Broadwas. Worc 5B 60
Broadwath. Cumb 4F 113
Broadway. Carm
nr. Kidwelly 5D 45
nr. Laugharne 4G 43
Broadway. Pemb 3C 42
Broadway. Som 1G 13
Broadway. Suff 3F 67
Broadway. Worc 2F 49
Broadwell. Glos
nr. Cinderford 4A 48
nr. Stow-on-the-Wold . . .3H 49
Broadwell. Oxon 5A 50
Broadwell. Warw 4B 62
Broadwell House. Nmbd 4C 114
Broadwey. Dors 4B 14
Broadwindsor. Dors 2H 13
Broadwoodkelly. Devn 2G 11
Broadwoodwidger. Devn 4E 11
Broallan. High 4G 157
Brobury. Here 1G 47
Brochel. High 4E 155
Brockaghboy. Caus 5E 174
Brockamin. Worc 5B 60
Brockbridge. Hants 1E 16
Brockdish. Norf 3E 66
Brockencote. Worc 3C 60
Brockenhurst. Hants 2A 16
Brocketsbrae. S Lan 1H 117
Brockford Street. Suff 4D 66
Brockhall. Nptn 4D 62
Brockham. Surr 1C 26
Brockhampton. Glos
nr. Bishop's Cleeve 3E 49
nr. Sevenhampton 3F 49
Brockhampton. Here 2A 48
Brockhill. Bord 2F 119
Brockholes. W Yor 3B 92
Brockhurst. Hants 2D 16
Brocklesby. Linc 3E 95
Brockley. N Som 5H 33
Brockley Corner. Suff 3H 65
Brockley Green. Suff
nr. Bury St Edmunds 1H 53
nr. Haverhill 5H 65
Brockleymoor. Cumb 1F 103
Brockmoor. W Mid 2D 60
Brockton. Shrp
nr. Bishop's Castle 2F 59
nr. Madeley 5B 72
nr. Much Wenlock 1H 59
nr. Pontesbury 5F 71
Brockton. Staf 2C 72
Brockton. Telf 4B 72
Brockweir. Glos 5A 48
Brockworth. Glos 4D 49
Brocton. Staf 4D 72
Brodick. N Ayr 2E 123
Brodie. Mor 3D 159
Brodiesord. Abers 3C 160
Brodsworth. S Yor 4F 93
Brogaig. High 2D 154
Brogborough. C Beds 2H 51
Brokenborough. Wilts 3E 35
Broken Cross. Ches E 3C 84
Bromborough. Mers 2F 83
Bromdon. Shrp 2A 60
Brome. Suff 3D 66
Brome Street. Suff 3D 66
Bromeswell. Suff 5F 67
Bromfield. Cumb 5C 112
Bromfield. Shrp 3G 59
Bromford. W Mid 1F 61
Bromham. Bed 5H 63
Bromham. Wilts 5E 35
Bromley. G Lon 4F 39
Bromley. Herts 3E 53
Bromley. Shrp 1B 60
Bromley Cross. G Man 3F 91
Bromley Green. Kent 2D 28
Bromley Wood. Staf 3F 73
Brompton. Medw 4B 40
Brompton. N Yor
nr. Northallerton 5A 106
nr. Scarborough 1D 100
Brompton. Shrp 5H 71
Brompton-on-Swale.
N Yor 5F 105
Brompton Ralph. Som 3D 20
Brompton Regis. Som 3C 20
Bromsash. Here 3B 48
Bromsberrow. Glos 2C 48
Bromsberrow Heath. Glos 2C 48
Bromsgrove. Worc 3D 60
Bromstead Heath. Staf 4B 72
Bromyard. Here 5A 60
Bromyard Downs. Here 5A 60
Bronaber. Gwyn 2G 69
Broncroft. Shrp 2H 59
Brongest. Cdgn 1D 44
Brongwyn. Cdgn 1C 44
Bronington. Wrex 2G 71
Bronllys. Powy 2E 47
Bronnant. Cdgn 4F 57
Bronwydd Arms. Carm 3E 45
Bronydd. Powy 1F 47
Bronygarth. Shrp 2E 71
Brook. Carm 4G 43
Brook. Hants
nr. Cadnam 1A 16
nr. Romsey 4B 24
Brook. IOW 4B 16
Brook. Kent 1E 29
Brook. Surr
nr. Guildford 1B 26
nr. Haslemere 2A 26
Brooke. Norf 1E 67
Brooke. Rut 5F 75
Brookeborough. Ferm 8F 176
Brookenby. Linc 1B 88
Brook End. Worc 1D 48
Brookend. Glos 5B 48
Brookfield. Lanc 1D 90
Brookfield. Ren 3F 127
Brookhouse. Lanc 3E 97
Brookhouse. S Yor 2C 86
Brookhouse Green.
Ches E 4C 84
Brookhouses. Staf 1D 73
Brookhurst. Mers 2F 83
Brookland. Kent 3D 28
Brooklands. G Man 1B 84
Brooklands. Shrp 1H 71
Brookmans Park. Herts 5C 52
Brooks. Powy 1D 58
Brooksby. Leics 4D 74
Brooks Green. W Sus 3C 26
Brook Street. Essx 1G 39
Brook Street. Kent 2D 28
Brook Street. W Sus 3E 27
Brookthorpe. Glos 4D 48
Brookville. Norf 1G 65
Brookwood. Surr 5A 38
Broom. C Beds 1B 52
Broom. Fife 3F 137
Broom. Warw 5E 61
Broome. Norf 1F 67
Broome. Shrp
nr. Cardington 1H 59
nr. Craven Arms 2G 59
Broome. Worc 3D 60
Broomedge. Warr 2B 84
Broomend. Abers 2E 153
Broomer's Corner. W Sus 3C 26
Broomfield. Abers 5G 161
Broomfield. Essx 4H 53
Broomfield. Kent
nr. Herne Bay 4F 41
nr. Maidstone 5C 40
Broomfield. Som 3F 21
Broomfleet. E Yor 2B 94
Broom Green. Norf 3B 78
Broomhall. Ches E 1A 72
Broomhall. Wind 4A 38
Broomhaugh. Nmbd 3D 114
Broom Hill. Dors 2F 15
Broom Hill. Worc 3D 60
Broomhill. High
nr. Grantown-on-Spey
. . . . .1D 151
nr. Invergordon 1B 158
Broomhill. Norf 5F 77
Broomhill. S Yor 4E 93
Broomhillbank. Dum 5D 118
Broomholm. Norf 2F 79
Broomlands. Dum 4C 118
Broomley. Nmbd 3D 114
Broom of Moy. Mor 3E 159
Broompark. Dur 5F 115
Broom's Green. Glos 2C 48
Brora. High 3G 165
Broseley. Shrp 5A 72
Brotherhouse Bar. Linc 4B 76
Brotheridge Green. Worc 1D 48
Brotherlee. Dur 1C 104
Brothertoft. Linc 1B 76
Brotherton. N Yor 2E 93
Brotton. Red C 3D 107
Broubster. High 2C 168
Brough. Cumb 3A 104
Brough. Derbs 2F 85
Brough. E Yor 2C 94
Brough. High 1E 169
Brough. Notts 5F 87
Brough. Orkn
nr. Finstown 6C 172
nr. St Margaret's Hope
. . . . .9D 172
Brough. Shet
nr. Benston 6F 173
nr. Booth of Toft 4F 173
on Bressay 7G 173
on Whalsay 5G 173
Broughall. Shrp 1H 71
Brougham. Cumb 2G 103
Brough Lodge. Shet 2G 173
Broughshane. ME Ant 6H 175
Brough Sowerby. Cumb 3A 104
Broughton. Cambs 3B 64
Broughton. Flin 4F 83
Broughton. Hants 3B 24
Broughton. Lanc 1D 90
Broughton. Mil 2G 51
Broughton. Nptn 3F 63
Broughton. N Lin 4C 94
Broughton. N Yor
nr. Malton 2B 100
nr. Skipton 4B 98
Broughton. Orkn 3D 172
Broughton. Oxon 2C 50
Broughton. Bord 1D 118
Broughton. Staf 2B 72
Broughton. V Glam 4C 32
Broughton Astley. Leics 1C 62
Broughton Beck. Cumb 1B 96
Broughton Cross. Cumb 1B 102
Broughton Gifford. Wilts 5D 35
Broughton Green. Worc 4D 60
Broughton Hackett. Worc 5D 60
Broughton in Furness.
Cumb 1B 96
Broughton Mills. Cumb 5D 102
Broughton Moor. Cumb 1B 102
Broughton Park. G Man 4G 91
Broughton Poggs. Oxon 5H 49
Broughtown. Orkn 3F 172
Broughty Ferry. D'dee 5D 144
Browland. Shet 6D 173
Brownbread Street. E Sus 4A 28
Brown Candover. Hants 3D 24
Brown Edge. Lanc 3B 90
Brown Edge. Staf 5D 84
Brownhill. Bkbn 1E 91
Brownhill. Shrp 3G 71
Brownhills. Shrp 2A 72
Brownhills. W Mid 5E 73
Brown Knowl. Ches W 5G 83
Brownlow. Ches E 4C 84
Brownlow Heath. Ches E 4C 84
Brown's Green. W Mid 1E 61
Brownshill. Glos 5D 49
Brownston. Devn 3C 8
Brownstone. Devn 2A 12
Browston Green. Norf 5G 79
Broxa. N Yor 5G 107
Broxbourne. Herts 5D 52
Broxburn. E Lot 2C 130
Broxburn. W Lot 2D 128
Broxholme. Linc 3G 87
Broxted. Essx 3F 53
Broxton. Ches W 5G 83
Broxwood. Here 5F 59
Broyle Side. E Sus 4F 27
Brù. W Isl 3F 171
Bruach Mairi. W Isl 4G 171
Bruairnis. W Isl 8C 170
Bruan. High 5F 169
Bruar Lodge. Per 1F 143
Brucehill. W Dun 2E 127
Brucklay. Abers 3G 161
Bruera. Ches W 4G 83
Bruern Abbey. Oxon 3A 50
Bruichladdich. Arg 3A 124
Bruisyard. Suff 4F 67
Bruisyard Street. Suff 4F 67
Brund. Staf 4F 85
Brundall. Norf 5F 79
Brundish. Norf 1F 67
Brundish. Suff 4E 67
Brundish Street. Suff 3E 67
Brunery. High 1B 140
Brunswick Village. Tyne 2F 115
Brunthwaite. W Yor 5C 98
Bruntingthorpe. Leics 1D 62
Brunton. Fife 1F 137
Brunton. Nmbd 2G 121
Brunton. Wilts 1H 23
Brushford. Devn 2G 11
Brushford. Som 4C 20
Brusta. W Isl 1E 170
Bruton. Som 3B 22
Bryansford. New M 6H 179
Bryanston. Dors 2D 14
Bryant's Bottom. Buck 2G 37
Brydekirk. Dum 2C 112
Brymbo. Cnwy 3H 81
Brymbo. Wrex 5E 83
Brympton D'Evercy. Som 1A 14
Bryn. Carm 5F 45
Bryn. G Man 4D 90
Bryn. Neat 2B 32
Bryn. Shrp 2E 59
Brynamman. Carm 4H 45
Brynberian. Pemb 1F 43
Brynbryddan. Neat 2A 32
Bryncae. Rhon 3C 32
Bryncethin. B'end 3C 32
Bryncir. Gwyn 1D 69
Bryncoch. Neat 3G 31
Bryncroes. Gwyn 2B 68
Bryncrug. Gwyn 5F 69
Bryn Du. IOA 3C 80
Bryn Eden. Gwyn 3G 69
Bryn Eglwys. Gwyn 4F 81
Bryneglwys. Den 1D 70
Brynford. Flin 3D 82
Bryn Gates. G Man 4D 90
Bryn Golau. Rhon 3D 32
Bryngwran. IOA 3C 80
Bryngwyn. Mon 5G 47
Bryngwyn. Powy 1E 47
Bryn-henllan. Pemb 1E 43
Brynhoffnant. Cdgn 5C 56
Bryn-llwyn. Den 2C 82
Brynllywarch. Powy 2D 58
Bryn-mawr. Gwyn 2B 68
Brynmawr. Blae 4E 47
Brynmenyn. B'end 3C 32
Brynmill. Swan 3F 31
Brynna. Rhon 3C 32
Brynrefail. Gwyn 4E 81
Brynrefail. IOA 2D 81
Brynsadler. Rhon 3D 32
Bryn-Saith Marchog. Den 5C 82
Brynsiencyn. IOA 4D 81
Brynteg. IOA 2D 81
Brynteg. Wrex 5F 83
Brynygwenyn. Mon 4G 47
Bryn-y-maen. Cnwy 3H 81
Buaile nam Bodach.
W Isl 8C 170
Bualintur. High 1C 146
Bubbenhall. Warw 3A 62
Bubwith. E Yor 1H 93
Buccleuch. Bord 3F 119
Buchanan Smithy. Stir 1F 127
Buchanhaven. Abers 4H 161
Buchanty. Per 1B 136
Buchany. Stir 3G 135
Buchley. E Dun 2G 127
Buchlyvie. Stir 4E 135
Buckabank. Cumb 5E 113
Buckden. Cambs 4A 64
Buckden. N Yor 2B 98
Buckenham. Norf 5F 79
Buckerell. Devn 2E 12
Buckfast. Devn 2D 8
Buckfastleigh. Devn 2D 8
Buckhaven. Fife 4F 137
Buckholm. Bord 1G 119
Buckholt. Here 4A 48
Buckhorn Weston. Dors 4C 22
Buckhurst Hill. Essx 1F 39
Buckie. Mor 2B 160
Buckingham. Buck 2E 51
Buckland. Buck 4G 51
Buckland. Glos 2F 49
Buckland. Here 5H 59
Buckland. Herts 2D 52
Buckland. Kent 1H 29
Buckland. Oxon 2B 36
Buckland. Surr 5D 38
Buckland Brewer. Devn 4E 19
Buckland Common. Buck 5H 51
Buckland Dinham. Som 1C 22
Buckland Filleigh. Devn 2E 11
Buckland in the Moor.
Devn 5H 11
Buckland Monachorum.
Devn 2A 8
Buckland Newton. Dors 2B 14
Buckland Ripers. Dors 4B 14
Buckland St Mary. Som 1F 13
Buckland-tout-Saints. Devn 4D 8
Bucklebury. W Ber 4D 36
Bucklegate. Linc 2C 76
Buckleigh. Devn 4E 19
Buckler's Hard. Hants 3C 16
Bucklesham. Suff 1F 55
Buckley. Flin 4E 83
Buckley Green. Warw 4F 61
Buckley Hill. Mers 1F 83
Bucklow Hill. Ches E 2B 84
Buckminster. Leics 3F 75
Bucknall. Linc 4A 88
Bucknall. Stoke 1D 72
Bucknell. Oxon 3D 50
Bucknell. Shrp 3F 59
Buckpool. Mor 2B 160
Bucksburn. Aber 3F 153
Buck's Cross. Devn 4D 18
Bucks Green. W Sus 2B 26
Buckshaw Village. Lanc 2D 90
Bucks Hill. Herts 5A 52
Bucks Horn Oak. Hants 2G 25
Buck's Mills. Devn 4D 18
Buckton. E Yor 2F 101
Buckton. Here 3F 59
Buckton. Nmbd 1E 121
Buckton Vale. G Man 4H 91
Buckworth. Cambs 3A 64
Budby. Notts 4D 86
Bude. Corn 2C 10
Budge's Shop. Corn 3H 7
Budlake. Devn 2C 12
Budle. Nmbd 1F 121
Budleigh Salterton. Devn 4D 12
Budock Water. Corn 5B 6
Buerton. Ches E 1A 72
Buffler's Holt. Buck 2E 51
Bugbrooke. Nptn 5D 62
Buglawton. Ches E 4C 84
Bugle. Corn 3E 6
Bugthorpe. E Yor 4B 100
Buildwas. Shrp 5A 72
Builth Road. Powy 5C 58
Builth Wells. Powy 5C 58
Bulbourne. Herts 4H 51
Bulby. Linc 3H 75
Bulcote. Notts 1D 74
Buldoo. High 2B 168
Bulford. Wilts 2G 23
Bulford Camp. Wilts 2G 23
Bulkeley. Ches E 5H 83
Bulkington. Warw 2A 62
Bulkington. Wilts 1E 23
Bulkworthy. Devn 1D 11
Bullamoor. N Yor 5A 106
Bull Bay. IOA 1D 80
Bullbridge. Derbs 5A 86
Bullgill. Cumb 1B 102
Bull Hill. Hants 3B 16
Bullinghope. Here 2A 48
Bull's Green. Herts 4C 52
Bullwood. Arg 2C 126
Bulmer. Essx 1B 54
Bulmer. N Yor 3A 100
Bulmer Tye. Essx 2B 54
Bulphan. Thur 2H 39
Bulverhythe. E Sus 5B 28
Bulwark. Abers 4G 161
Bulwell. Nott 1C 74
Bulwick. Nptn 1G 63
Bumble's Green. Essx 5E 53
Bun Abhainn Eadarra.
W Isl 7D 171
Bunacaimb. High 5E 147
Bun a' Mhuillinn. W Isl 7C 170
Bunarkaig. High 5D 148
Bunbury. Ches E 5H 83
Bunchrew. High 4A 158
Bundalloch. High 1A 148
Buness. Shet 1H 173
Bunessan. Arg 1A 132
Bungay. Suff 2F 67
Bunkegivie. High 2H 149
Bunker's Hill. Cambs 5D 76
Bunker's Hill. Suff 5H 79
Bunkers Hill. Linc 5B 88
Bunloit. High 1H 149
Bunnahabhain. Arg 2C 124
Bunny. Notts 3C 74
Bunoich. High 3F 149
Bunree. High 2E 141
Bunroy. High 5E 149
Buntait. High 5G 157
Buntingford. Herts 3D 52
Bunting's Green. Essx 2B 54
Bunwell. Norf 1D 66
Burbage. Derbs 3E 85
Burbage. Leics 1B 62
Burbage. Wilts 5H 35
Burcher. Here 4F 59
Burchett's Green. Wind 3G 37
Burcombe. Wilts 3F 23
Burcot. Oxon 2D 36
Burcot. Worc 3D 61
Burcote. Shrp 1B 60
Burcott. Buck 3G 51
Burcott. Som 2A 22
Burdale. N Yor 3C 100
Burdrop. Oxon 2B 50
Bures. Suff 2C 54
The Burf. Worc 4C 60
Burford. Oxon 4A 50
Burford. Shrp 4H 59
Burg. Arg 4E 139
Burgate Great Green. Suff 3C 66
Burgate Little Green. Suff 3C 66
Burgess Hill. W Sus 4E 27
Burgh. Suff 5E 67
Burgh by Sands. Cumb 4E 113
Burgh Castle. Norf 5G 79
Burghclere. Hants 5C 36
Burghead. Mor 2F 159
Burghfield. W Ber 5E 37
Burghfield Common.
W Ber 5E 37
Burghfield Hill. W Ber 5E 37
Burgh Heath. Surr 5D 38
Burghill. Here 1H 47
Burgh le Marsh. Linc 4E 89
Burgh Muir. Abers 2E 153
Burgh next Aylsham. Norf 3E 78
Burgh on Bain. Linc 2B 88
Burgh St Margaret. Norf 4G 79
Burgh St Peter. Norf 1G 67
Burghwallis. S Yor 3F 93
Burham. Kent 4B 40
Buriton. Hants 4F 25
Burland. Ches E 5A 84
Burland. Shet 8E 173
Burlawn. Corn 2D 6
Burleigh. Glos 5D 48
Burleigh. Wind 4G 37
Burlescombe. Devn 1D 12
Burleston. Dors 3C 14
Burlestone. Devn 4E 9
Burley. Hants 2H 15
Burley. Rut 4F 75
Burley. W Yor 1C 92
Burleydam. Ches E 1A 72
Burley Gate. Here 1A 48
Burley in Wharfedale.
W Yor 5D 98
Burley Street. Hants 2H 15
Burley Woodhead. W Yor 5D 98
Burlingjobb. Powy 5E 59
Burlington. Shrp 4B 72
Burlton. Shrp 3G 71
Burmantofts. W Yor 1D 92
Burmarsh. Kent 2F 29
Burmington. Warw 2A 50
Burn. N Yor 2F 93
Burnage. G Man 1C 84
Burnaston. Derbs 2G 73
Burnbanks. Cumb 3G 103
Burnby. E Yor 5C 100
Burncross. S Yor 1H 85
Burneside. Cumb 5G 103
Burness. Orkn 3F 172
Burneston. N Yor 1F 99
Burnett. Bath 5B 34
Burnfoot. E Ayr 4D 116
Burnfoot. Per 3B 136
Burnfoot. Bord
nr. Hawick 3H 119
nr. Roberton 3G 119
Burngreave. S Yor 2A 86
Burnham. Buck 2A 38
Burnham. N Lin 3D 94
Burnham Deepdale. Norf 1H 77
Burnham Green. Herts 4C 52
Burnham Market. Norf 1H 77
Burnham Norton. Norf 1H 77
Burnham-on-Crouch.
Essx 1D 40
Burnham-on-Sea. Som 2G 21
Burnham Overy Staithe.
Norf 1H 77
Burnham Overy Town.
Norf 1H 77
Burnham Thorpe. Norf 1A 78
Burnhaven. Abers 4H 161
Burnhead. Dum 5A 118
Burnhervie. Abers 2E 153
Burnhill Green. Staf 5B 72
Burnhope. Dur 5E 115
Burnhouse. N Ayr 4E 127
Burniston. N Yor 5H 107
Burnlee. W Yor 4B 92
Burnley. Lanc 1G 91
Burnmouth. Bord 3F 131
Burn Naze. Lanc 5C 96
Burn of Cambus. Stir 3G 135
Burnopfield. Dur 4E 115
Burnsall. N Yor 3C 98
Burnside. Ang 3E 145
Burnside. Ant
nr. Antrim 8H 175
nr. Ballyclare 7J 175
Burnside. E Ayr 3E 117
Burnside. Per 3D 136
Burnside. Shet 4D 173
Burnside. S Lan 4H 127
Burnside. W Lot
nr. Broxburn 2D 129
nr. Winchburgh 2D 128
Burntcommon. Surr 5B 38
Burnt Heath. Essx 3D 54
Burntheath. Derbs 2G 73
Burnt Hill. W Ber 4D 36
Burnt Houses. Dur 2E 105
Burntisland. Fife 1F 129
Burnt Oak. G Lon 1D 38
Burnton. E Ayr 4D 117
Burntstalk. Norf 2G 77
Burntwood. Staf 5E 73
Burntwood Green. Staf 5E 73
Burnt Yates. N Yor 3E 99
Burnwynd. Edin 3E 129
Burpham. Surr 5B 38
Burpham. W Sus 5B 26
Burradon. Nmbd 4D 121
Burradon. Tyne 2F 115
Burrafirth. Shet 1H 173
Burragarth. Shet 1G 173
Burras. Corn 5A 6
Burraton. Corn 3A 8
Burravoe. Shet
nr. North Roe 3E 173
on Mainland 5E 173
on Yell 4G 173
Burray Village. Orkn 8D 172
Burrells. Cumb 3H 103
Burrelton. Per 5A 144
Burren. New M 7F 178
Burren Bridge. New M 6H 179
Burridge. Hants 1D 16
Burridge. Som 2G 13
Burrigill. High 5E 169
Burrill. N Yor 1E 99
Burringham. N Lin 4B 94
Burrington. Devn 1G 11
Burrington. Here 3G 59
Burrington. N Som 1H 21
Burrough End. Cambs 5F 65
Burrough Green. Cambs 5F 65
Burrough on the Hill.
Leics 4E 75
Burroughston. Orkn 5E 172
Burrow. Devn 4D 12
Burrow. Som 2C 20
Burrowbridge. Som 4G 21
Burrowhill. Surr 4A 38
Burry. Swan 3D 30
Burry Green. Swan 3D 30
Burry Port. Carm 5E 45
Burscough. Lanc 3C 90
Burscough Bridge. Lanc 3C 90
Bursea. E Yor 1B 94
Burshill. E Yor 5E 101
Bursledon. Hants 2C 16
Burslem. Stoke 1C 72
Burstall. Suff 1D 54
Burstock. Dors 2H 13
Burston. Devn 2H 11
Burston. Norf 2D 66
Burston. Staf 2D 72
Burstow. Surr 1E 27
Burstwick. E Yor 2F 95
Burtersett. N Yor 1A 98
Burtholme. Cumb 3G 113
Burthorpe. Suff 4G 65
Burthwaite. Cumb 5F 113
Burtle. Som 2H 21
Burtoft. Linc 2B 76
Burton. Ches W
nr. Kelsall 4H 83
nr. Neston 3F 83
Burton. Dors
nr. Christchurch 3G 15
nr. Dorchester 3B 14

210 A-Z Great Britain Road Atlas

Burton—Chapelknowe

Burton. Nmbd 1F 121
Burton. Pemb 4D 43
Burton. Som 2E 21
Burton. Wilts
nr. Chippenham 4D 34
nr. Warminster 3D 22
Burton. Wrex 5F 83
Burton Agnes. E Yor 3F 101
Burton Bradstock. Dors 4H 13
Burton-by-Lincoln. Linc 3G 87
Burton Coggles. Linc 3G 75
Burton Constable. E Yor 1E 95
Burton Corner. Linc 1C 76
Burton End. Cambs 1G 53
Burton End. Essx 3F 53
Burton Fleming. E Yor 2E 101
Burton Green. Warw 3G 61
Burton Green. Wrex 5F 83
Burton Hastings. Warw 2B 62
Burton-in-Kendal. Cumb 2E 97
Burton in Lonsdale. N Yor 2F 97
Burton Joyce. Notts 1D 74
Burton Latimer. Nptn 3G 63
Burton Lazars. Leics 4E 75
Burton Leonard. N Yor 3F 99
Burton on the Wolds. Leics 3C 74
Burton Overy. Leics 1D 62
Burton Pedwardine. Linc 1A 76
Burton Pidsea. E Yor 1F 95
Burton Salmon. N Yor 2E 93
Burton's Green. Essx 3B 54
Burton Stather. N Lin 3B 94
Burton upon Stather. N Lin 3B 94
Burton upon Trent. Staf 3G 73
Burton Wolds. Leics 3D 74
Burtonwood. Warr 1H 83
Burwardsley. Ches W 5H 83
Burwarton. Shrp 2A 60
Burwash. E Sus 3A 28
Burwash Common. E Sus 3H 27
Burwash Weald. E Sus 3A 28
Burwell. Cambs 4E 65
Burwell. Linc 3C 88
Burwen. IOA 1D 80
Burwick. Orkn 9D 172
Bury. Cambs 2B 64
Bury. G Man 3G 91
Bury. Som 4C 20
Bury. W Sus 4B 26
Burybank. Staf 2C 72
Bury End. Worc 2F 49
Bury Green. Herts 3E 53
Bury St Edmunds. Suff 4H 65
Burythorpe. N Yor 3B 100
Busbridge. Surr 1A 26
Busby. E Ren 4G 127
Busby. Per 1C 136
Buscot. Oxon 2H 35
Bush. Corn 2C 10
The Bush. M Ulst 3C 178
Bush Bank. Here 5G 59
Bushbury. W Mid 5D 72
Bushby. Leics 5D 74
Bushey. Dors 4E 15
Bushey. Herts 1C 38
Bushey Heath. Herts 1C 38
Bush Green. Norf
nr. Attleborough 1C 66
nr. Harleston 2E 66
Bush Green. Suff 5B 66
Bushley. Worc 2D 49
Bushley Green. Worc 2D 48
Bushmead. Bed 4A 64
Bushmills. Caus 2F 174
Bushmoor. Shrp 2G 59
Bushton. Wilts 4F 35
Bushy Common. Norf 4B 78
Busk. Cumb 5H 113
Buslingthorpe. Linc 2H 87
Bussage. Glos 5D 49
Bussex. Som 3G 21
Busta. Shet 5E 173
Butcher's Cross. E Sus 3G 27
Butcombe. N Som 5A 34
Bute Town. Cphy 5E 46
Butleigh. Som 3A 22
Butleigh Wootton. Som 3A 22
Butlers Marston. Warw 1B 50
Butley. Suff 5F 67
Butley High Corner. Suff 1G 55
Butlocks Heath. Hants 2C 16
Butterburn. Cumb 2H 113
Buttercrambe. N Yor 4B 100
Butterknowle. Dur 2E 105
Butterleigh. Devn 2C 12
Buttermere. Cumb 3C 102
Buttermere. Wilts 5B 36
Buttershaw. W Yor 2B 92
Butterstone. Per 4H 143
Butterton. Staf
nr. Leek 5E 85
nr. Stoke-on-Trent 1C 72
Butterwick. Dur 2A 106
Butterwick. Linc 1C 76
Butterwick. N Yor
nr. Malton 2B 100
nr. Weaverthorpe 2D 101
Butteryhaugh. Nmbd 5A 120
Butt Green. Ches E 5A 84
Buttington. Powy 5E 71
Buttonbridge. Shrp 3B 60
Buttonoak. Shrp 3B 60
Buttsash. Hants 2C 16
Butt's Green. Essx 5A 54
Butt Yeats. Lanc 3E 97
Buxhall. Suff 5C 66
Buxted. E Sus 3F 27
Buxton. Derbs 3E 85
Buxton. Norf 3E 79
Buxworth. Derbs 2E 85
Bwlch. Flin 4E 83
Bwlch. Powy 3E 47
Bwlchderwin. Gwyn 1D 68
Bwlchgwyn. Wrex 5E 83
Bwlch-Llan. Cdgn 5E 57
Bwlchnewydd. Carm 3D 44
Bwlchtocyn. Gwyn 3C 68
Bwlch-y-cibau. Powy 4D 70
Bwlchyddar. Powy 3D 70
Bwlch-y-fadfa. Cdgn 1E 45
Bwlch-y-ffridd. Powy 1C 58
Bwlch y Garreg. Powy 1C 58
Bwlch-y-groes. Pemb 1G 43
Bwlch-y-sarnau. Powy 3C 58
Bybrook. Kent 1E 28
Byermoor. Tyne 4E 115
Byers Garth. Dur 5G 115
Byers Green. Dur 1F 105
Byfield. Nptn 5C 62
Byfleet. Surr 4B 38
Byford. Here 1G 47
Bygrave. Herts 2C 52
Byker. Tyne 3F 115
Byland Abbey. N Yor 2H 99
Bylchau. Cnwy 4B 82
Byley. Ches W 4B 84
Bynea. Carm 3E 31
Byram. N Yor 2E 93
Byrness. Nmbd 4B 120
Bystock. Devn 4D 12
Bythorn. Cambs 3H 63
Byton. Here 4F 59
Bywell. Nmbd 3D 114
Byworth. W Sus 3A 26

C

Cabharstadh. W Isl 6F 171
Cabourne. Linc 4E 95
Cabrach. Arg 3C 124
Cabrach. Mor 1A 152
Cabragh. M Ulst 3B 178
Cabus. Lanc 5D 97
Cadbury. Devn 2C 12
Cadder. E Dun 2H 127
Caddington. C Beds 4A 52
Caddonfoot. Bord 1G 119
Cadeby. Leics 5B 74
Cadeby. S Yor 4F 93
Cadeleigh. Devn 2C 12
Cade Street. E Sus 3H 27
Cadgwith. Corn 5E 5
Cadham. Fife 3E 137
Cadishead. G Man 1B 84
Cadle. Swan 3F 31
Cadley. Lanc 1D 90
Cadley. Wilts
nr. Ludgershall 1H 23
nr. Marlborough 5H 35
Cadmore End. Buck 2F 37
Cadnam. Hants 1A 16
Cadney. N Lin 4D 94
Cadole. Flin 4E 82
Cadoxton-juxta-Neath. Neat 2A 32
Cadwell. Herts 2B 52
Cadwst. Den 2C 70
Caeathro. Gwyn 4E 81
Caehopkin. Powy 4B 46
Caenby. Linc 2H 87
Caerau. B'end 2B 32
Caerau. Card 4E 33
Cae'r-bont. Powy 4B 46
Cae'r-bryn. Carm 4F 45
Caerdeon. Gwyn 4F 69
Caerdydd. Card 193 (4E 33)
Caerfarchell. Pemb 2B 42
Caerffili. Cphy 3E 33
Caerfyrddin. Carm 4E 45
Caergeiliog. IOA 3C 80
Caergwrle. Flin 5F 83
Caergybi. IOA 2B 80
Caerlaverock. Per 2A 136
Caerleon. Newp 2G 33
Caerlleon. Carm 2G 43
Caerllion. Newp 2G 33
Caernarfon. Gwyn 4D 81
Caerphilly. Cphy 3E 33
Caersws. Powy 1C 58
Caerwedros. Cdgn 5C 56
Caerwent. Mon 2H 33
Caerwys. Flin 3D 82
Caim. IOA 2F 81
Caio. Carm 2G 45
Cairinis. W Isl 2D 170
Cairisiadar. W Isl 4C 171
Cairminis. W Isl 9C 171
Cairnbaan. Arg 4F 133
Cairnbulg. Abers 2H 161
Cairncross. Ang 1D 145
Cairndow. Arg 2A 134
Cairness. Abers 2H 161
Cairneyhill. Fife 1D 128
Cairngarroch. Dum 5F 109
Cairnhill. Abers 5D 160
Cairnie. Abers 4B 160
Cairnorrie. Abers 4F 161
Cairnryan. Dum 3F 109
Cairnston. Orkn 6B 172
Caister-on-Sea. Norf 4H 79
Caistor. Linc 4E 94
Caistor St Edmund. Norf 5E 79
Caistron. Nmbd 4D 121
Cakebole. Worc 3C 60
Calais Street. Suff 1C 54
Calanais. W Isl 4E 171
Calbost. W Isl 6G 171
Calbourne. IOW 4C 16
Calceby. Linc 3C 88
Calcot. Glos 4F 49
Calcot Row. W Ber 4E 37
Calcott. Kent 4F 41
Calcott. Shrp 4G 71
Caldback. Shet 1H 173
Caldbeck. Cumb 1E 102
Caldbergh. N Yor 1C 98
Caldecote. Cambs
nr. Cambridge 5C 64
nr. Peterborough 2A 64
Caldecote. Herts 2C 52
Caldecote. Nptn 5D 62
Caldecote. Warw 1A 62
Caldecott. Nptn 4G 63
Caldecott. Oxon 2C 36
Caldecott. Rut 1F 63
Calderbank. N Lan 3A 128
Calder Bridge. Cumb 4B 102
Calderbrook. G Man 3H 91
Caldercruix. N Lan 3B 128
Calder Grove. W Yor 3D 92
Calder Mains. High 3C 168
Caldermill. S Lan 5H 127
Calder Vale. Lanc 5E 97
Calderwood. S Lan 4H 127
Caldicot. Mon 3H 33
Caldwell. Derbs 4G 73
Caldwell. N Yor 3E 105
Caldy. Mers 2E 83
Calebrack. Cumb 1E 103
Caledon. M Ulst 5B 178
Calf Heath. Staf 5D 72
Calford Green. Suff 1G 53
Calfsound. Orkn 4E 172
Calgary. Arg 3E 139
Califer. Mor 3E 159
California. Cambs 2E 65
California. Falk 2C 128
California. Norf 4H 79
California. Suff 1E 55
Calke. Derbs 3A 74
Callakille. High 3F 155
Callaly. Nmbd 4E 121
Callander. Stir 3F 135
Callaughton. Shrp 1A 60
Callendoun. Arg 1E 127
Callestick. Corn 3B 6
Calligarry. High 3E 147
Callington. Corn 2H 7
Callingwood. Staf 3F 73
Callow. Here 2H 47
Callowell. Glos 5D 48
Callow End. Worc 1D 48
Callow Hill. Wilts 3F 35
Callow Hill. Worc
nr. Bewdley 3B 60
nr. Redditch 4E 61
Calmore. Hants 1B 16
Calmsden. Glos 5F 49
Calne. Wilts 4E 35
Calow. Derbs 3B 86
Calshot. Hants 2C 16
Calstock. Corn 2A 8
Calstone Wellington. Wilts 5F 35
Calthorpe. Norf 2D 78
Calthorpe Street. Norf 3G 79
Calthwaite. Cumb 5F 113
Calton. N Yor 4B 98
Calton. Staf 5F 85
Calveley. Ches E 5H 83
Calver. Derbs 3G 85
Calverhall. Shrp 2A 72
Calverleigh. Devn 1C 12
Calverley. W Yor 1C 92
Calvert. Buck 3E 51
Calverton. Mil 2F 51
Calverton. Notts 1D 74
Calvine. Per 2F 143
Calvo. Cumb 4C 112
Cam. Glos 2C 34
Camaghael. High 1F 141
Camas-luinie. High 1B 148
Camasnacroise. High 3C 140
Camastianavaig. High 5E 155
Camasunary. High 2D 146
Camault Muir. High 4H 157
Camb. Shet 2G 173
Camber. E Sus 4D 28
Camberley. Surr 5G 37
Camberwell. G Lon 3E 39
Camblesforth. N Yor 2G 93
Cambo. Nmbd 1D 114
Cambois. Nmbd 1G 115
Camborne. Corn 5A 6
Cambourne. Cambs 5C 64
Cambridge. Cambs 193 (5D 64)
Cambridge. Glos 5C 48
Cambrose. Corn 4A 6
Cambus. Clac 4A 136
Cambusbarron. Stir 4G 135
Cambuskenneth. Stir 4H 135
Cambuslang. S Lan 3H 127
Cambusnethan. N Lan 4B 128
Cambus o' May. Abers 4B 152
Camden Town. G Lon 2D 39
Cameley. Bath 1B 22
Camelford. Corn 4B 10
Camelon. Falk 1B 128
Camelsdale. W Sus 3G 25
Camer's Green. Worc 2C 48
Camerton. Bath 1B 22
Camerton. Cumb 1B 102
Camerton. E Yor 2F 95
Camghouran. Per 3C 142
Camlough. New M 7E 178
Cammachmore. Abers 4G 153
Cammeringham. Linc 2G 87
Camore. High 4E 165
The Camp. Glos 5E 49
Campbelton. N Ayr 4C 126
Campbeltown. Arg 3B 122
Campbeltown Airport. Arg 3A 122
Cample. Dum 5A 118
Campmuir. Per 5B 144
Campsall. S Yor 3F 93
Campsea Ashe. Suff 5F 67
Camps End. Cambs 1G 53
Campsey. Derr 4A 174
Campton. C Beds 2B 52
Camptoun. E Lot 2B 130
Camptown. Bord 3A 120
Camrose. Pemb 2D 42
Camserney. Per 4F 143
Camster. High 4E 169
Camus Croise. High 2E 147
Camuscross. High 2E 147
Camusdarach. High 4E 147
Camusnagaul. High
nr. Fort William 1E 141
nr. Little Loch Broom 5E 163
Camus Park. Derr 3F 176
Camusteel. High 4G 155
Camusterrach. High 4G 155
Camusvrachan. Per 4D 142
Canada. Hants 1A 16
Canadia. E Sus 4B 28
Canaston Bridge. Pemb 3E 43
Candlesby. Linc 4D 88
Candle Street. Suff 3C 66
Candy Mill. S Lan 5D 128
Cane End. Oxon 4E 37
Canewdon. Essx 1D 40
Canford Cliffs. Pool 1F 15
Canford Heath. Pool 3F 15
Canford Magna. Pool 3F 15
Cangate. Norf 4F 79
Canham's Green. Suff 4C 66
Canholes. Derbs 3E 85
Canisbay. High 1F 169
Canley. W Mid 3H 61
Cann. Dors 4D 22
Cann Common. Dors 4D 23
Cannich. High 5F 157
Cannington. Som 3F 21
Cannock. Staf 4D 73
Cannock Wood. Staf 4E 73
Canonbie. Dum 2E 113
Canon Bridge. Here 1H 47
Canon Frome. Here 1B 48
Canon Pyon. Here 1H 47
Canons Ashby. Nptn 5C 62
Canonstown. Corn 3C 4
Canterbury. Kent 193 (5F 41)
Cantley. Norf 5F 79
Cantley. S Yor 4G 93
Cantlop. Shrp 5H 71
Canton. Card 4E 33
Cantray. High 4B 158
Cantraybruich. High 4B 158
Cantraywood. High 4B 158
Cantsdam. Fife 4D 136
Cantsfield. Lanc 2F 97
Canvey Island. Essx 2B 40
Canwick. Linc 4G 87
Canworthy Water. Corn 3C 10
Caol. High 1F 141
Caolas. Arg 4B 138
Caolas. W Isl 9B 170
Caolas Liubharsaigh. W Isl 4D 170
Caolas Scalpaigh. W Isl 8E 171
Caolas Stocinis. W Isl 8D 171
Caol Ila. Arg 2C 124
Caol Loch Ailse. High 1F 147
Caol Reatha. High 1F 147
Capel. Kent 1H 27
Capel. Surr 1C 26
Capel Bangor. Cdgn 2F 57
Capel Betws Lleucu. Cdgn 5F 57
Capel Coch. IOA 2D 80
Capel Curig. Cnwy 5G 81
Capel Cynon. Cdgn 1D 45
Capel Dewi. Carm 3E 45
Capel Dewi. Cdgn
nr. Aberystwyth 2F 57
nr. Llandysul 1E 45
Capel Garmon. Cnwy 5H 81
Capel Green. Suff 1G 55
Capel Gwyn. IOA 3C 80
Capel Gwynfe. Carm 3H 45
Capel Hendre. Carm 4F 45
Capel Isaac. Carm 3F 45
Capel Iwan. Carm 1G 43
Capel-le-Ferne. Kent 2G 29
Capel Llanilltern. Card 4D 32
Capel Mawr. IOA 3D 80
Capel Newydd. Pemb 1G 43
Capel St Andrew. Suff 1G 55
Capel St Mary. Suff 2D 54
Capel Seion. Carm 4F 45
Capel Seion. Cdgn 3F 57
Capel Uchaf. Gwyn 1D 68
Capel-y-ffin. Powy 2F 47
Capenhurst. Ches W 3F 83
Capernwray. Lanc 2E 97
Capheaton. Nmbd 1D 114
Cappagh. M Ulst 3A 178
Cappercleuch. Bord 2E 119
Capplegill. Dum 4D 118
Capton. Devn 3E 9
Capton. Som 3D 20
Caputh. Per 5H 143
Caradon Town. Corn 5C 10
Carbis Bay. Corn 3C 4
Carbost. High
nr. Loch Harport 5C 154
nr. Portree 4D 154
Carbrook. S Yor 2A 86
Carbrooke. Norf 5B 78
Carburton. Notts 3D 86
Carcluie. S Ayr 3C 116
Car Colston. Notts 1E 74
Carcroft. S Yor 4F 93
Cardenden. Fife 4E 136
Cardeston. Shrp 4F 71
Cardewlees. Cumb 4E 113
Cardiff. Card 193 (4E 33)
Cardiff Airport. V Glam 5D 32
Cardigan. Cdgn 1B 44
Cardinal's Green. Cambs 1G 53
Cardington. Bed 1A 52
Cardington. Shrp 1H 59
Cardinham. Corn 2F 7
Cardno. Abers 2G 161
Cardow. Mor 4F 159
Cardross. Arg 2E 127
Cardurnock. Cumb 4C 112
Careby. Linc 4H 75
Careston. Ang 2E 145
Carew. Pemb 4E 43
Carew Cheriton. Pemb 4E 43
Carew Newton. Pemb 4E 43
Carey. Here 2A 48
Carfin. N Lan 4A 128
Carfrae. Bord 4B 130
Cargan. ME Ant 5H 175
Cargate Green. Norf 4F 79
Cargenbridge. Dum 2G 111
Cargill. Per 5A 144
Cargo. Cumb 4E 113
Cargreen. Corn 2A 8
Carham. Nmbd 1C 120
Carhampton. Som 2D 20
Carharrack. Corn 4B 6
Carie. Per
nr. Loch Rannah 3D 142
nr. Loch Tay 5D 142
Carisbrooke. IOW 4C 16
Cark. Cumb 2C 96
Carkeel. Corn 2A 8
Carlabhagh. W Isl 3E 171
Carland Cross. Corn 3C 6
Carlbury. Darl 3F 105
Carlby. Linc 4H 75
Carlecotes. S Yor 4B 92
Carleen. Corn 4D 4
Carlesmoor. N Yor 2D 98
Carleton. Cumb
nr. Carlisle 4F 113
nr. Egremont 4B 102
nr. Penrith 2G 103
Carleton. Lanc 5C 96
Carleton. N Yor 5B 98
Carleton. W Yor 2E 93
Carleton Forehoe. Norf 5C 78
Carleton Rode. Norf 1D 66
Carleton St Peter. Norf 5F 79
Carlidnack. Corn 4E 5
Carlingcott. Bath 1B 22
Carlin How. Red C 3E 107
Carlisle. Cumb 193 (4F 113)
Carloonan. Arg 2H 133
Carlops. Bord 4E 129
Carlton. Bed 5G 63
Carlton. Cambs 5F 65
Carlton. Leics 5A 74
Carlton. N Yor
nr. Helmsley 1A 100
nr. Middleham 1C 98
nr. Selby 2G 93
Carlton. Notts 1D 74
Carlton. S Yor 3D 92
Carlton. Stoc T 2A 106
Carlton. Suff 4F 67
Carlton. W Yor 2D 92
Carlton Colville. Suff 1H 67
Carlton Curlieu. Leics 1D 62
Carlton Husthwaite. N Yor 2G 99
Carlton in Cleveland. N Yor 4C 106
Carlton in Lindrick. Notts 2C 86
Carlton-le-Moorland. Linc 5G 87
Carlton Miniott. N Yor 1F 99
Carlton-on-Trent. Notts 4F 87
Carlton Scroop. Linc 1G 75
Carluke. S Lan 4B 128
Carlyon Bay. Corn 3E 7
Carmarthen. Carm 4E 45
Carmel. Carm 4F 45
Carmel. Flin 3D 82
Carmel. Gwyn 5D 81
Carmel. IOA 2C 80
Carmichael. S Lan 1B 118
Carmunnock. Glas 4H 127
Carmyle. Glas 3H 127
Carmyllie. Ang 4E 145
Carnaby. E Yor 3F 101
Carnach. High
nr. Lochcarron 1C 148
nr. Ullapool 4E 163
Carnach. Mor 4E 159
Carnach. W Isl 8E 171
Carnachy. High 3H 167
Carnain. Arg 3B 124
Carnais. W Isl 4C 171
Carnan. Arg 4B 138
Carnan. W Isl 4C 170
Carnbee. Fife 3H 137
Carnbo. Per 3C 136
Carn Brea Village. Corn 4A 6
Carndu. High 1A 148
Carnduff. Caus 2G 175
Carne. Corn 5D 6
Carnell. S Ayr 1D 116
Carnforth. Lanc 2E 97
Carn-gorm. High 1B 148
Carnhedryn. Pemb 2C 42
Carnhell Green. Corn 3D 4
Carnie. Abers 3F 153
Carnkie. Corn
nr. Falmouth 5B 6
nr. Redruth 5A 6
Carnkief. Corn 3B 6
Carnlough. ME Ant 5J 175
Carnmoney. Ant 1H 179
Carno. Powy 1B 58
Carnock. Fife 1D 128
Carnon Downs. Corn 4B 6
Carnoustie. Ang 5E 145
Carnteel. M Ulst 4A 178
Carntyne. Glas 3H 127
Carnwath. S Lan 5C 128
Carnyorth. Corn 3A 4
Carol Green. W Mid 3G 61
Carpalla. Corn 3D 6
Carperby. N Yor 1C 98
Carradale. Arg 2C 122
Carragraich. W Isl 8D 171
Carrbridge. High 1D 150
Carr Cross. Lanc 3B 90
Carreglefn. IOA 2C 80
Carrhouse. N Lin 4A 94
Carrick Castle. Arg 4A 134
Carrickfergus. ME Ant 8L 175
Carrick Ho. Orkn 4E 172
Carrickmore. Ferm 2A 178
Carriden. Falk 1D 128
Carrington. G Man 1B 84
Carrington. Linc 5C 88
Carrington. Midl 3G 129
Carrog. Cnwy 1G 69
Carrog. Den 1D 70
Carron. Falk 1B 128
Carron. Mor 4G 159
Carronbridge. Dum 5A 118
Carronshore. Falk 1B 128
Carrowclare. Caus 4C 174
Carrowdore. Ards 2K 179
Carrow Hill. Mon 2H 33
Carr Shield. Nmbd 5B 114
Carrutherstown. Dum 2C 112
Carr Vale. Derbs 4B 86
Carrville. Dur 5G 115
Carryduff. Lis 3H 179
Carsaig. Arg 1C 132
Carscreugh. Dum 3H 109
Carsegowan. Dum 4B 110
Carse House. Arg 3F 125
Carseriggan. Dum 3A 110
Carsethorn. Dum 4A 112
Carshalton. G Lon 4D 39
Carsington. Derbs 5G 85
Carskiey. Arg 5A 122
Carsluith. Dum 4B 110
Carson Park. New M 4J 179
Carsphairn. Dum 5E 117
Carstairs. S Lan 5C 128
Carstairs Junction. S Lan 5C 128
Cartbridge. Surr 5B 38
Carterhaugh. Ang 4D 144
Carter's Clay. Hants 4B 24
Carterton. Oxon 5A 50
Carterway Heads. Nmbd 4D 114
Carthew. Corn 3E 6
Carthorpe. N Yor 1F 99
Cartington. Nmbd 4E 121
Cartland. S Lan 5B 128
Cartmel. Cumb 2C 96
Cartmel Fell. Cumb 1D 96
Cartworth. W Yor 4B 92
Carwath. Cumb 5E 112
Carway. Carm 5E 45
Carwinley. Cumb 2F 113
Cascob. Powy 4E 59
Cas-gwent. Mon 2A 34
Cash Feus. Fife 3E 136
Cashlie. Per 4B 142
Cashmoor. Dors 1E 15
Cas-Mael. Pemb 2E 43
Casnewydd. Newp 200 (3G 33)
Cassington. Oxon 4C 50
Cassop. Dur 1A 106
Castell. Cnwy 4G 81
Castell. Den 4D 82
Castell Hendre. Pemb 2E 43
Castell-Nedd. Neat 2A 32
Castell Newydd Emlyn. Carm 1D 44
Castell-y-bwch. Torf 2F 33
Casterton. Cumb 2F 97
Castle. Som 2A 22
Castle Acre. Norf 4H 77
Castle Ashby. Nptn 5F 63
Castlebay. W Isl 9B 170
Castle Bolton. N Yor 5D 104
Castle Bromwich. W Mid 2F 61
Castle Bytham. Linc 4G 75
Castlebythe. Pemb 2E 43
Castle Caereinion. Powy 5D 70
Castle Camps. Cambs 1G 53
Castle Carrock. Cumb 4G 113
Castle Cary. Som 3B 22
Castlecary. N Lan 2A 128
Castlecaulfield. M Ulst 3B 178
Castle Combe. Wilts 4D 34
Castlecraig. High 2C 158
Castledawson. M Ulst 7F 174
Castlederg. Derr 4E 176
Castle Donington. Leics 3B 74
Castle Douglas. Dum 3E 111
Castle Eaton. Swin 2G 35
Castle Eden. Dur 1B 106
Castleford. W Yor 2E 93
Castle Frome. Here 1B 48
Castle Green. Surr 4A 38
Castle Green. Warw 3G 61
Castle Gresley. Derbs 4G 73
Castle Heaton. Nmbd 5F 131
Castle Hedingham. Essx 2A 54
Castle Hill. Kent 1A 28
Castle Hill. Suff 1E 55
Castlehill. Per 5B 144
Castlehill. S Lan 4B 128
Castlehill. W Dun 2E 127
Castle Kennedy. Dum 4G 109
Castle Lachlan. Arg 4H 133
Castlemartin. Pemb 5D 42
Castlemilk. Glas 4H 127
Castlemorris. Pemb 1D 42
Castlemorton. Worc 2C 48
Castle O'er. Dum 5E 119
Castle Park. N Yor 3F 107
Castlerigg. Cumb 2D 102
Castle Rising. Norf 3F 77
Castlerock. Caus 3D 174
Castleroe. Caus 4E 174
Castleside. Dur 5D 115
Castlethorpe. Mil 1F 51
Castleton. Abers 4F 151
Castleton. Arg 1G 125
Castleton. Derbs 2F 85
Castleton. G Man 3G 91
Castleton. Mor 1F 151
Castleton. Newp 3F 33
Castleton. N Yor 4D 107
Castleton. Per 2B 136
Castletown. Cumb 1G 103
Castletown. Dors 5B 14
Castletown. High 2D 169
Castletown. IOM 5B 108
Castletown. Tyne 4G 115
Castlewellan. New M 6H 179
Castley. N Yor 5E 99
Caston. Norf 1B 66
Castor. Pet 1A 64
Caswell. Swan 4E 31
Catacol. N Ayr 5H 125
Catbrook. Mon 5A 48
Catchems End. Worc 3B 60
Catchgate. Dur 4E 115
Catcleugh. Nmbd 4B 120
Catcliffe. S Yor 2B 86
Catcott. Som 3G 21
Caterham. Surr 5E 39
Catfield. Norf 3F 79
Catfield Common. Norf 3F 79
Catfirth. Shet 6F 173
Catford. G Lon 3E 39
Catforth. Lanc 1C 90
Cathcart. Glas 3G 127
Cathedine. Powy 3E 47
Catherine-de-Barnes. W Mid 2F 61
Catherington. Hants 1E 17
Catherston Leweston. Dors 3G 13
Catherton. Shrp 3A 60
Catisfield. Hants 2D 16
Catlodge. High 4A 150
Catlowdy. Cumb 2F 113
Catmore. W Ber 3C 36
Caton. Devn 5A 12
Caton. Lanc 3E 97
Catrine. E Ayr 2E 117
Cat's Ash. Newp 2G 33
Catsfield. E Sus 4B 28
Catsgore. Som 4A 22
Catshill. Worc 3D 60
Cattal. N Yor 4G 99
Cattawade. Suff 2E 54
Catterall. Lanc 5E 97
Catterick. N Yor 5F 105
Catterick Bridge. N Yor 5F 105
Catterick Garrison. N Yor 5E 105
Catterlen. Cumb 1F 103
Catterline. Abers 1H 145
Catterton. N Yor 5H 99
Catteshall. Surr 1A 26
Catthorpe. Leics 3C 62
Cattistock. Dors 3A 14
Catton. Nmbd 4B 114
Catton. N Yor 2F 99
Catwick. E Yor 5F 101
Catworth. Cambs 3H 63
Caudle Green. Glos 4E 49
Caulcott. Oxon 3D 50
Cauldhame. Stir 4F 135
Cauldmill. Bord 3H 119
Cauldon. Staf 1E 73
Cauldon Lowe. Staf 1E 73
Cauldwells. Abers 3E 161
Caulkerbush. Dum 4G 111
Caulside. Dum 1F 113
Caunsall. Worc 2C 60
Caunton. Notts 4E 87
Causewayend. S Lan 1C 118
Causewayhead. Stir 4H 135
Causey Park. Nmbd 5F 121
Caute. Devn 1E 11
Cautley. Cumb 5H 103
Cavendish. Suff 1B 54
Cavendish Bridge. Leics 3B 74
Cavenham. Suff 3G 65
Caversfield. Oxon 3D 50
Caversham. Read 4F 37
Caversham Heights. Read 4E 37
Caverswall. Staf 1D 72
Cawdor. High 3C 158
Cawkwell. Linc 2B 88
Cawood. N Yor 1F 93
Cawsand. Corn 3A 8
Cawston. Norf 3D 78
Cawston. Warw 3B 62
Cawthorne. N Yor 1B 100
Cawthorne. S Yor 4C 92
Cawthorpe. Linc 3H 75
Cawton. N Yor 2A 100
Caxton. Cambs 5C 64
Caynham. Shrp 3H 59
Caythorpe. Linc 1G 75
Caythorpe. Notts 1D 74
Cayton. N Yor 1E 101
Ceallan. W Isl 3D 170
Ceann a Bhaigh. W Isl
on North Uist 2C 170
on Scalpay 8E 171
on South Harris 8D 171
Ceann a Bhàigh. W Isl 9C 171
Ceannacroc Lodge. High 2E 149
Ceann a Deas Loch Baghasdail. W Isl 7C 170
Ceann an Leothaid. High 5E 147
Ceann a Tuath Loch Baghasdail. W Isl 6C 170
Ceann Loch Ailleart. High 5F 147
Ceann Loch Muideirt. High 1B 140
Ceann-na-Cleithe. W Isl 8D 171
Ceann Shiphoirt. W Isl 6E 171
Ceann Tarabhaigh. W Isl 6E 171
Cearsiadar. W Isl 5F 171
Ceathramh Meadhanach. W Isl 1D 170
Cefn Berain. Cnwy 4B 82
Cefn-brith. Cnwy 5B 82
Cefn-bryn-brain. Carm 4H 45
Cefn Bychan. Cphy 2F 33
Cefn-bychan. Flin 4D 82
Cefncaeau. Carm 3E 31
Cefn Canol. Powy 2E 71
Cefn Coch. Powy 5C 70
Cefn-coch. Powy 3D 70
Cefn-coed-y-cymmer. Mer T 5D 46
Cefn Cribwr. B'end 3B 32
Cefn-ddwysarn. Gwyn 2B 70
Cefn Einion. Shrp 2E 59
Cefneithin. Carm 4F 45
Cefn Glas. B'end 3B 32
Cefngorwydd. Powy 1C 46
Cefn Llwyd. Cdgn 2F 57
Cefn-mawr. Wrex 1E 71
Cefn-y-bedd. Flin 5F 83
Cefn-y-coed. Powy 1D 58
Cefn-y-pant. Carm 2F 43
Cegidfa. Powy 4E 70
Ceinewydd. Cdgn 5C 56
Cellan. Cdgn 1G 45
Cellardyke. Fife 3H 137
Cellarhead. Staf 1D 72
Cemaes. IOA 1C 80
Cemmaes. Powy 5H 69
Cemmaes Road. Powy 5H 69
Cenarth. Cdgn 1C 44
Cenin. Gwyn 1D 68
Ceos. W Isl 5F 171
Ceres. Fife 2G 137
Ceri. Powy 2D 58
Cerist. Powy 2B 58
Cerne Abbas. Dors 2B 14
Cerney Wick. Glos 2F 35
Cerrigceinwen. IOA 3D 80
Cerrigydrudion. Cnwy 1B 70
Cess. Norf 4G 79
Cessford. Bord 2B 120
Ceunant. Gwyn 4E 81
Chaceley. Glos 2D 48
Chacewater. Corn 4B 6
Chackmore. Buck 2E 51
Chacombe. Nptn 1C 50
Chadderton. G Man 4H 91
Chaddesden. Derb 2A 74
Chaddesden Common. Derb 2A 74
Chaddesley Corbett. Worc 3C 60
Chaddlehanger. Devn 5E 11
Chaddleworth. W Ber 4C 36
Chadlington. Oxon 3B 50
Chadshunt. Warw 5H 61
Chadstone. Nptn 5F 63
Chad Valley. W Mid 2E 61
Chadwell. Leics 3E 75
Chadwell. Shrp 4B 72
Chadwell Heath. G Lon 2F 39
Chadwell St Mary. Thur 3H 39
Chadwick End. W Mid 3G 61
Chadwick Green. Mers 1H 83
Chaffcombe. Som 1G 13
Chafford Hundred. Thur 3H 39
Chagford. Devn 4H 11
Chailey. E Sus 4E 27
Chain Bridge. Linc 1C 76
Chainbridge. Cambs 5D 76
Chainhurst. Kent 1B 28
Chalbury. Dors 2F 15
Chalbury Common. Dors 2F 15
Chaldon. Surr 5E 39
Chaldon Herring. Dors 4C 14
Chale. IOW 5C 16
Chale Green. IOW 5C 16
Chalfont Common. Buck 1B 38
Chalfont St Giles. Buck 1A 38
Chalfont St Peter. Buck 2B 38
Chalford. Glos 5D 49
Chalgrove. Oxon 2E 37
Chalk. Kent 3A 40
Chalk End. Essx 4G 53
Chalk Hill. Glos 3G 49
Challaborough. Devn 4C 8
Challacombe. Devn 2G 19
Challister. Shet 5G 173
Challoch. Dum 3A 110
Challock. Kent 5E 40
Chalton. C Beds
nr. Bedford 5A 64
nr. Luton 3A 52
Chalton. Hants 1F 17
Chalvington. E Sus 5G 27
Champany. Falk 2D 128
Chance Inn. Fife 2F 137
Chancery. Cdgn 3E 57
Chandler's Cross. Herts 1B 38
Chandler's Cross. Worc 2C 48
Chandler's Ford. Hants 4C 24
Chanlockfoot. Dum 4G 117
Channel's End. Bed 5A 64
Channel Tunnel. Kent 2F 29
Channerwick. Shet 9F 173
Chantry. Som 2C 22
Chantry. Suff 1E 55
Chapel. Cumb 1D 102
Chapel. Fife 4E 137
Chapel Allerton. Som 1H 21
Chapel Allerton. W Yor 1C 92
Chapel Amble. Corn 1D 6
Chapel Brampton. Nptn 4E 63
Chapelbridge. Cambs 1B 64
Chapel Chorlton. Staf 2C 72
Chapel Cleeve. Som 2D 20
Chapel End. C Beds 1A 52
Chapel-en-le-Frith. Derbs 2E 85
Chapelfield. Abers 2G 145
Chapelgate. Linc 3D 76
Chapel Green. Warw
nr. Coventry 2G 61
nr. Southam 4B 62
Chapel Haddlesey. N Yor 2F 93
Chapelhall. N Lan 3A 128
Chapel Hill. Abers 5H 161
Chapel Hill. Linc 5B 88
Chapel Hill. Mon 5A 48
Chapelhill. Per
nr. Glencarse 1E 136
nr. Harrietfield 5H 143
Chapelknowe. Dum 2E 112

Coggeshall Hamlet—Crosby Garrett

Coggeshall Hamlet. Essx 3B 54
Coggins Mill. E Sus 3G 27
Coignafearn Lodge. High 2A 150
Coig Peighinnean. W Isl 1H 171
Coig Peighinnean Bhuirgh. W Isl 2G 171
Coilleag. W Isl 7C 170
Coillemore. High 1A 158
Coillore. High 5C 154
Coire an Fhuarain. W Isl 4E 171
Coity. B'end 3C 32
Cokhay Green. Derbs 3G 73
Col. W Isl 3G 171
Colaboll. High 2C 164
Colan. Corn 2C 6
Colaton Raleigh. Devn 4D 12
Colbost. High 4B 154
Colburn. N Yor 5E 105
Colby. Cumb 2H 103
Colby. IOM 4B 108
Colby. Norf 2E 78
Colchester. Essx 3D 54
Cold Ash. W Ber 5D 36
Cold Ashby. Nptn 3D 62
Cold Ashton. S Glo 4C 34
Cold Aston. Glos 4G 49
Coldbackie. High 3G 167
Cold Blow. Pemb 3F 43
Cold Brayfield. Mil 5G 63
Cold Cotes. N Yor 2G 97
Coldean. Brig 5E 27
Coldeast. Devn 5B 12
Colden. W Yor 2H 91
Colden Common. Hants 4C 24
Coldfair Green. Suff 4G 67
Coldham. Cambs 5D 76
Coldham. Staf 5C 72
Cold Hanworth. Linc 2H 87
Coldharbour. Corn 4B 6
Coldharbour. Dors 3E 15
Coldharbour. Glos 5A 48
Coldharbour. Kent 5G 39
Coldharbour. Surr 1C 26
Cold Hatton. Telf 3A 72
Cold Hatton Heath. Telf 3A 72
Cold Hesledon. Dur 5H 115
Cold Hiendley. W Yor 3D 92
Cold Higham. Nptn 5D 62
Coldingham. Bord 3F 131
Cold Kirby. N Yor 1H 99
Coldmeece. Staf 2C 72
Cold Northcott. Corn 4C 10
Cold Norton. Essx 5B 54
Cold Overton. Leics 4F 75
Coldrain. Per 3C 136
Coldred. Kent 1G 29
Coldridge. Devn 2G 11
Cold Row. Lanc 5C 96
Coldstream. Bord 5E 131
Coldwaltham. W Sus 4B 26
Coldwell. Here 2H 47
Coldwells. Abers 5H 161
Coldwells Croft. Abers 1C 152
Cole. Shet 5E 173
Cole. Som 3B 22
Colebatch. Shrp 2F 59
Colebrook. Devn 2D 12
Colebrooke. Devn 3A 12
Coleburn. Mor 3G 159
Coleby. Linc 4G 87
Coleby. N Lin 3B 94
Cole End. Warw 2G 61
Coleford. Devn 2A 12
Coleford. Glos 4A 48
Coleford. Som 2B 22
Colegate End. Norf 2D 66
Cole Green. Herts 4C 52
Cole Henley. Hants 1C 24
Colehill. Dors 2F 15
Coleman Green. Herts 4B 52
Coleman's Hatch. E Sus 2F 27
Colemere. Shrp 2G 71
Colemore. Hants 3F 25
Colemore Green. Shrp 1B 60
Coleorton. Leics 4B 74
Coleraine. Caus 3E 174
Colerne. Wilts 4D 34
Colesbourne. Glos 4F 49
Colesden. Bed 5A 64
Coles Green. Worc 5B 60
Coleshill. Buck 1A 38
Coleshill. Oxon 2H 35
Coleshill. Warw 2G 61
Colestocks. Devn 2D 12
Colethrop. Glos 4D 48
Coley. Bath 1A 22
Colgate. W Sus 2D 26
Colinsburgh. Fife 3G 137
Colinton. Edin 3F 129
Colintraive. Arg 2B 126
Colkirk. Norf 3B 78
Collace. Per 5B 144
Collam. W Isl 8D 171
Collaton. Devn 5D 8
Collaton St Mary. Torb 2E 9
College of Roseisle. Mor 2F 159
Collessie. Fife 2E 137
Collier Row. G Lon 1F 39
Colliers End. Herts 3D 52
Collier Street. Kent 1B 28
Colliery Row. Tyne 5G 115
Collieston. Abers 1H 153
Collin. Dum 2B 112
Collingbourne Ducis. Wilts 1H 23
Collingbourne Kingston. Wilts 1H 23
Collingham. Notts 4F 87
Collingham. W Yor 5F 99
Collingtree. Nptn 5E 63
Collins Green. Warr 1H 83
Collins Green. Worc 5B 60
Colliston. Ang 4F 145
Colliton. Devn 2D 12
Collydean. Fife 3E 137
Collyweston. Nptn 5G 75
Colmonell. S Ayr 1G 109
Colmworth. Bed 5A 64
Colnbrook. Slo 3B 38
Colne. Cambs 3C 64
Colne. Lanc 5A 98
Colne Engaine. Essx 2B 54
Colney. Norf 5D 78
Colney Heath. Herts 5C 52
Colney Street. Herts 5B 52
Coln Rogers. Glos 5F 49
Coln St Aldwyns. Glos 5G 49
Coln St Dennis. Glos 4F 49
Colpitts Grange. Nmbd 4C 114
Colpy. Abers 5D 160
Colscott. Devn 1D 10
Colsterdale. N Yor 1D 98
Colsterworth. Linc 3G 75
Colston Bassett. Notts 2E 74
Colstoun House. E Lot 2B 130
Coltfield. Mor 2F 159
Colthouse. Cumb 5E 103
Coltishall. Norf 4E 79
Coltness. N Lan 4B 128
Colton. Cumb 1C 96
Colton. Norf 5D 78
Colton. N Yor 5H 99
Colton. Staf 3E 73
Colton. W Yor 1D 92
Colt's Hill. Kent 1H 27
Col Uarach. W Isl 4G 171
Colvend. Dum 4F 111
Colvister. Shet 2G 173
Colwall. Here 1C 48
Colwall Green. Here 1C 48
Colwell. Nmbd 2C 114
Colwich. Staf 3E 73
Colwick. Notts 1D 74
Colwinston. V Glam 4C 32
Colworth. W Sus 5A 26
Colwyn Bay. Cnwy 3A 82
Colyford. Devn 3F 13
Colyton. Devn 3F 13
Combe. Devn 2D 8
Combe. Here 4F 59
Combe. Oxon 4C 50
Combe. W Ber 5B 36
Combe Almer. Dors 3E 15
Combebow. Devn 4E 11
Combe Down. Bath 5C 34
Combe Fishacre. Devn 2E 9
Combe Florey. Som 3E 21
Combe Hay. Bath 5C 34
Combeinteignhead. Devn 5C 12
Combe Martin. Devn 2F 19
Combe Moor. Here 4F 59
Comber. Ards 3J 179
Combe Raleigh. Devn 2E 13
Comberbach. Ches W 3A 84
Comberford. Staf 5F 73
Comberton. Cambs 5C 64
Comberton. Here 4G 59
Combe St Nicholas. Som 1G 13
Combpyne. Devn 3F 13
Combridge. Staf 2E 73
Combrook. Warw 5H 61
Combs. Derbs 3E 85
Combs. Suff 5C 66
Combs Ford. Suff 5C 66
Combwich. Som 2F 21
Comers. Abers 3D 152
Comhampton. Worc 4C 60
Comins Coch. Cdgn 2F 57
Comley. Shrp 1G 59
Commercial End. Cambs 4E 65
Commins. Powy 3D 70
Commins Coch. Powy 5H 69
The Common. Wilts
nr. Salisbury 3H 23
nr. Swindon 3F 35
Commondale. N Yor 3D 106
Common End. Cumb 2B 102
Common Hill. Here 2A 48
Common Moor. Corn 2G 7
Common Side. Derbs 3H 85
Commonside. Ches W 3H 83
Commonside. Derbs 1G 73
Compstall. G Man 1D 84
Compton. Devn 2E 9
Compton. Hants 4C 24
Compton. Staf 2C 60
Compton. Surr 1A 26
Compton. W Ber 4D 36
Compton. W Sus 1F 17
Compton. Wilts 1G 23
Compton Abbas. Dors 1D 15
Compton Abdale. Glos 4F 49
Compton Bassett. Wilts 4F 35
Compton Beauchamp. Oxon 3A 36
Compton Bishop. Som 1G 21
Compton Chamberlayne. Wilts 4F 23
Compton Dando. Bath 5B 34
Compton Dundon. Som 3H 21
Compton Greenfield. S Glo 3A 34
Compton Martin. Bath 1A 22
Compton Pauncefoot. Som 4B 22
Compton Valence. Dors 3A 14
Comrie. Fife 1D 128
Comrie. Per 1G 135
Conaglen. High 2E 141
Conchra. Arg 1B 126
Conchra. High 1A 148
Conder Green. Lanc 4D 96
Conderton. Worc 2E 49
Condicote. Glos 3G 49
Condorrat. N Lan 2A 128
Condover. Shrp 5G 71
Coneyhurst. W Sus 3C 26
Coneyisland. New M 6K 179
Coneysthorpe. N Yor 2B 100
Coneythorpe. N Yor 4F 99
Coney Weston. Suff 3B 66
Conford. Hants 3G 25
Congdon's Shop. Corn 5C 10
Congerstone. Leics 5A 74
Congham. Norf 3G 77
Congleton. Ches E 4C 84
Congl-y-wal. Gwyn 1G 69
Congresbury. N Som 5H 33
Congreve. Staf 4D 72
Conham. S Glo 4B 34
Conicaval. Mor 3D 159
Coningsby. Linc 5B 88
Conington. Cambs
nr. Fenstanton 4C 64
nr. Sawtry 2A 64
Conisbrough. S Yor 1C 86
Conisby. Arg 3A 124
Conisholme. Linc 1D 88
Coniston. Cumb 5E 102
Coniston. E Yor 1E 95
Coniston Cold. N Yor 4B 98
Conistone. N Yor 3B 98
Conlig. Ards 2K 179
Connah's Quay. Flin 3E 83
Connel. Arg 5D 140
Connel Park. E Ayr 3F 117
Connista. High 1D 154
Connor. ME Ant 7H 175
Connor Downs. Corn 3C 4
Conock. Wilts 1F 23
Conon Bridge. High 3H 157
Cononley. N Yor 5B 98
Cononsyth. Ang 4E 145
Conordan. High 5E 155
Consall. Staf 1D 73
Consett. Dur 4E 115
Constable Burton. N Yor 5E 105
Constantine. Corn 4E 5
Constantine Bay. Corn 1C 6
Contin. High 3G 157
Contullich. High 1A 158
Conwy. Cnwy 3G 81
Conyer. Kent 4D 40
Conyer's Green. Suff 4A 66
Cooden. E Sus 5B 28
Cooil. IOM 4C 108
Cookbury. Devn 2E 11
Cookbury Wick. Devn 2D 11
Cookham. Wind 3G 37
Cookham Dean. Wind 3G 37
Cookham Rise. Wind 3G 37
Cookhill. Worc 5E 61
Cookley. Suff 3F 67
Cookley. Worc 2C 60
Cookley Green. Oxon 2E 37
Cookney. Abers 4F 153
Cooksbridge. E Sus 4F 27
Cooksey Green. Worc 4D 60
Cookshill. Staf 1D 72
Cooksmill Green. Essx 5G 53
Cookstown. M Ulst 2C 178
Coolham. W Sus 3C 26
Cooling. Medw 3B 40
Cooling Street. Medw 3B 40
Coombe. Corn
nr. Bude 1C 10
nr. St Austell 3D 6
nr. Truro 4C 6
Coombe. Devn
nr. Sidmouth 3E 12
nr. Teignmouth 5C 12
Coombe. Glos 2C 34
Coombe. Hants 4E 25
Coombe. Wilts 1G 23
Coombe Bissett. Wilts 4G 23
Coombe Hill. Glos 3D 49
Coombe Keynes. Dors 4D 14
Coombes. W Sus 5C 26
Coopersale. Essx 5E 53
Coopersale Street. Essx 5E 53
Cooper's Corner. Kent 1F 27
Cooper Street. Kent 5H 41
Cootham. W Sus 4B 26
Copalder Corner. Cambs 1C 64
Copdock. Suff 1E 54
Copford. Essx 3C 54
Copford Green. Essx 3C 54
Copgrove. N Yor 3F 99
Copister. Shet 4F 173
Cople. Bed 1B 52
Copley. Dur 2D 105
Coplow Dale. Derbs 3F 85
Copmanthorpe. York 5H 99
Copp. Lanc 1C 90
Coppathorne. Corn 2C 10
Coppenhall. Ches E 5B 84
Coppenhall. Staf 4D 72
Coppenhall Moss. Ches E 5B 84
Copperhouse. Corn 3C 4
Coppicegate. Shrp 2B 60
Coppingford. Cambs 2A 64
Copplestone. Devn 2A 12
Coppull. Lanc 3D 90
Coppull Moor. Lanc 3D 90
Copsale. W Sus 3C 26
Copshaw Holm. Bord 1F 113
Copster Green. Lanc 1E 91
Copston Magna. Warw 2B 62
Copt Green. Warw 4F 61
Copthall Green. Essx 5E 53
Copt Heath. W Mid 3F 61
Copt Hewick. N Yor 2F 99
Copthill. Dur 5B 114
Copthorne. W Sus 2E 27
Coptiviney. Shrp 2G 71
Copy's Green. Norf 2B 78
Copythorne. Hants 1B 16
Corbridge. Nmbd 3C 114
Corby. Nptn 2F 63
Corby Glen. Linc 3G 75
Cordon. N Ayr 2E 123
Coreley. Shrp 3A 60
Corfe. Som 1F 13
Corfe Castle. Dors 4E 15
Corfe Mullen. Dors 3E 15
Corfton. Shrp 2G 59
Corgarff. Abers 3G 151
Corhampton. Hants 4E 24
Corkey. Caus 4G 175
Corlae. Dum 5F 117
Corlannau. Neat 2A 32
Corley. Warw 2H 61
Corley Ash. Warw 2G 61
Corley Moor. Warw 2G 61
Cormiston. S Lan 1C 118
Cornaa. IOM 3D 108
Cornaigbeg. Arg 4A 138
Cornaigmore. Arg
on Coll 2D 138
on Tiree 4A 138
Corner Row. Lanc 1C 90
Corney. Cumb 5C 102
Cornforth. Dur 1A 106
Cornhill. Abers 3C 160
Cornhill. High 4C 164
Cornhill-on-Tweed. Nmbd 1C 120
Cornholme. W Yor 2H 91
Cornish Hall End. Essx 2G 53
Cornquoy. Orkn 7E 172
Cornriggs. Dur 5B 114
Cornsay. Dur 5E 115
Cornsay Colliery. Dur 5E 115
Corntown. High 3H 157
Corntown. V Glam 4C 32
Cornwall Airport Newquay. Corn 2C 6
Cornwell. Oxon 3A 50
Cornwood. Devn 3C 8
Cornworthy. Devn 3E 9
Corpach. High 1E 141
Corpusty. Norf 3D 78
Corra. Dum 3F 111
Corran. High
nr. Arnisdale 2E 141
nr. Fort William 3A 148
Corrany. IOM 3D 108
Corribeg. High 1D 141
Corrie. N Ayr 5B 126
Corrie Common. Dum 1D 112
Corriecravie. N Ayr 3D 122
Corriekinloch. High 1A 164
Corriemoillie. High 2F 157
Corrievarkie Lodge. Per 1C 142
Corrievorrie. High 1B 150
Corrigall. Orkn 6C 172
Corrimony. High 5F 157
Corringham. Linc 1F 87
Corringham. Thur 2B 40
Corris. Gwyn 5G 69
Corris Uchaf. Gwyn 5G 69
Corrour Shooting Lodge. High 2B 142
Corry. High 1E 147
Corrybrough. High 1C 150
Corrygills. N Ayr 2E 123
Corry of Ardnagrask. High 4H 157
Corsback. High
nr. Dunnet 1E 169
nr. Halkirk 3E 169
Corscombe. Dors 2A 14
Corse. Abers 4D 160
Corse. Glos 3C 48
Corsehill. Abers 3G 161
Corse Lawn. Worc 2D 48
Corse of Kinnoir. Abers 4C 160
Corsham. Wilts 4D 34
Corsley. Wilts 2D 22
Corsley Heath. Wilts 2D 22
Corsock. Dum 2E 111
Corston. Bath 5B 34
Corston. Wilts 3E 35
Corstorphine. Edin 2F 129
Cortachy. Ang 3C 144
Corton. Suff 1H 67
Corton. Wilts 2E 23
Corton Denham. Som 4B 22
Corwar House. S Ayr 1H 109
Corwen. Den 1C 70
Coryates. Dors 4B 14
Coryton. Devn 4E 11
Coryton. Thur 2B 40
Cosby. Leics 1C 62
Coscote. Oxon 3D 36
Coseley. W Mid 1D 60
Cosgrove. Nptn 1F 51
Cosham. Port 2E 17
Cosheston. Pemb 4E 43
Coskills. N Lin 3D 94
Cosmeston. V Glam 5E 33
Cossall. Notts 1B 74
Cossington. Leics 4D 74
Cossington. Som 2G 21
Costa. Orkn 5C 172
Costessey. Norf 4D 78
Costock. Notts 3C 74
Coston. Leics 3F 75
Coston. Norf 5C 78
Cote. Oxon 5B 50
Cotebrook. Ches W 4H 83
Cotehill. Cumb 4F 113
Cotes. Cumb 1D 97
Cotes. Leics 3C 74
Cotes. Staf 2C 72
Cotesbach. Leics 2C 62
Cotes Heath. Staf 2C 72
Cotford St Luke. Som 4E 21
Cotgrave. Notts 2D 74
Cothal. Abers 2F 153
Cotham. Notts 1E 75
Cothelstone. Som 3E 21
Cotheridge. Worc 5B 60
Cotherstone. Dur 3D 104
Cothill. Oxon 2C 36
Cotland. Mon 5A 48
Cotleigh. Devn 2F 13
Cotmanhay. Derbs 1B 74
Coton. Cambs 5D 64
Coton. Nptn 3D 62
Coton. Staf
nr. Gnosall 3C 72
nr. Stone 2D 73
nr. Tamworth 5F 73
Coton Clanford. Staf 3C 72
Coton Hayes. Staf 2D 73
Coton Hill. Shrp 4G 71
Coton in the Clay. Staf 3F 73
Coton in the Elms. Derbs 4G 73
Cotonwood. Shrp 2H 71
Cotonwood. Staf 3C 72
Cott. Devn 2D 9
Cott. Orkn 5F 172
Cottam. E Yor 3D 101
Cottam. Lanc 1D 90
Cottam. Notts 3F 87
Cottartown. High 5E 159
Cottarville. Nptn 4E 63
Cottenham. Cambs 4D 64
Cotterdale. N Yor 5B 104
Cottered. Herts 3D 52
Cotterstock. Nptn 1H 63
Cottesbrooke. Nptn 3E 62
Cottesmore. Rut 4G 75
Cotteylands. Devn 1C 12
Cottingham. E Yor 1D 94
Cottingham. Nptn 1F 63
Cottingley. W Yor 1B 92
Cottisford. Oxon 2D 50
Cotton. Staf 1E 73
Cotton. Suff 4C 66
Cotton End. Bed 1A 52
Cottown. Abers 4F 161
Cotts. Devn 2A 8
Cotwalton. Staf 2D 72
Couch's Mill. Corn 3F 7
Coughton. Here 3A 48
Coughton. Warw 4E 61
Coulags. High 4B 156
Coulby Newham. Midd 3C 106
Coulderton. Cumb 4A 102
Coulin Lodge. High 3C 156
Coull. Abers 3C 152
Coulport. Arg 1D 126
Coulsdon. G Lon 5D 39
Coulston. Wilts 1E 23
Coulter. S Lan 1C 118
Coultings. Som 2F 21
Coulton. N Yor 2A 100
Cound. Shrp 5H 71
Coundon. Dur 2F 105
Coundon Grange. Dur 2F 105
Countersett. N Yor 1B 98
Countess. Wilts 2G 23
Countess Cross. Essx 2B 54
Countesthorpe. Leics 1C 62
Countisbury. Devn 2H 19
Coupar Angus. Per 4B 144
Coupe Green. Lanc 2D 90
Coupland. Cumb 3A 104
Coupland. Nmbd 1D 120
Cour. Arg 5G 125
Courance. Dum 5C 118
Court-at-Street. Kent 2E 29
Courteachan. High 4E 147
Courteenhall. Nptn 5E 63
Court Henry. Carm 3F 45
Courtsend. Essx 1E 41
Courtway. Som 3F 21
Cousland. Midl 3G 129
Cousley Wood. E Sus 2A 28
Coustonn. Arg 2B 126
Cove. Arg 1D 126
Cove. Devn 1C 12
Cove. Hants 1G 25
Cove. High 4C 162
Cove. Bord 2D 130
Cove Bay. Aber 3G 153
Covehithe. Suff 2H 67
Coven. Staf 5D 72
Coveney. Cambs 2D 65
Covenham St Bartholomew. Linc 1C 88
Covenham St Mary. Linc 1C 88
Coven Heath. Staf 5D 72
Coventry. W Mid 194 (3H 61)
Coverack. Corn 5E 5
Coverham. N Yor 1D 98
Covesea. Mor 1F 159
Covingham. Swin 3G 35
Covington. Cambs 3H 63
Covington. S Lan 1B 118
Cowan Bridge. Lanc 2F 97
Cowan Head. Cumb 5F 103
Cowbar. Red C 3E 107
Cowbeech. E Sus 4H 27
Cowbit. Linc 4B 76
Cowbridge. V Glam 4C 32
Cowden. Kent 1F 27
Cowdenbeath. Fife 4D 136
Cowdenburn. Bord 4F 129
Cowdenend. Fife 4D 136
Cowers Lane. Derbs 1H 73
Cowes. IOW 3C 16
Cowesby. N Yor 1G 99
Cowfold. W Sus 3D 26
Cowfords. Mor 2H 159
Cowgill. Cumb 1G 97
Cowie. Abers 5F 153
Cowie. Stir 1B 128
Cowlam. E Yor 3D 100
Cowley. Devn 3C 12
Cowley. Glos 4E 49
Cowley. G Lon 2B 38
Cowley. Oxon 5D 50
Cowley. Staf 4C 72
Cowleymoor. Devn 1C 12
Cowling. Lanc 3D 90
Cowling. N Yor
nr. Bedale 1E 99
nr. Glusburn 5B 98
Cowlinge. Suff 5G 65
Cowmes. W Yor 3B 92
Cowpe. Lanc 2G 91
Cowpen. Nmbd 1F 115
Cowpen Bewley. Stoc T 2B 106
Cowplain. Hants 1E 17
Cowshill. Dur 5B 114
Cowslip Green. N Som 5H 33
Cowstrandburn. Fife 4C 136
Cowthorpe. N Yor 4G 99
Coxall. Here 3F 59
Coxbank. Ches E 1A 72
Coxbench. Derbs 1A 74
Cox Common. Suff 2G 67
Coxford. Norf 3H 77
Cox Green. Surr 2B 26
Cox Green. Tyne 4G 115
Coxgreen. Staf 2C 60
Coxheath. Kent 5B 40
Coxhoe. Dur 1A 106
Coxley. Som 2A 22
Coxwold. N Yor 2H 99
Coychurch. B'end 3C 32
Coylton. S Ayr 3D 116
Coylumbridge. High 2D 150
Coynach. Abers 3B 152
Coynachie. Abers 5B 160
Coytrahen. B'end 3B 32
Crabbs Cross. Worc 4E 61
Crabgate. Norf 3C 78
Crab Orchard. Dors 2F 15
Crabtree. W Sus 3D 26
Crabtree Green. Wrex 1F 71
Crackaig. High 2G 165
Crackenthorpe. Cumb 2H 103
Crackington Haven. Corn 3B 10
Crackley. Staf 5C 84
Crackley. Warw 3G 61
Crackleybank. Shrp 4B 72
Crackpot. N Yor 5C 104
Cracoe. N Yor 3B 98
Craddock. Devn 1D 12
Cradhlastadh. W Isl 4C 171
Cradley. Here 1C 48
Cradley. W Mid 2D 60
Cradoc. Powy 2D 46
Crafthole. Corn 3H 7
Crafton. Buck 4G 51
Cragabus. Arg 5B 124
Crag Foot. Lanc 2D 97
Craggan. High 1E 151
Cragganmore. Mor 5F 159
Cragganvallie. High 5H 157
Craggie. High 2F 165
Craggiemore. High 5B 158
Cragg Vale. W Yor 2A 92
Craghead. Dur 4F 115
Crai. Powy 3B 46
Craichie. Ang 4E 145
Craig. Arg 5E 141
Craig. Dum 2D 111
Craig. High
nr. Achnashellach 4C 156
nr. Lower Diabaig 2G 155
nr. Stromeferry 5H 155
Craiganour Lodge. Per 3D 142
Craigavon. Arm 4E 178
Craigbrack. Arg 4A 134
Craig-Cefn-Parc. Swan 5G 45
Craigdallie. Per 1E 137
Craigdam. Abers 5F 161
Craigdarragh. Derr 6B 174
Craigdarroch. E Ayr 4F 117
Craigdarroch. High 3G 157
Craigdhu. High 4G 157
Craigearn. Abers 2E 152
Craigellachie. Mor 4G 159
Craigend. Per 1D 136
Craigendoran. Arg 1E 126
Craigends. Ren 3F 127
Craigenputtock. Dum 1E 111
Craigens. E Ayr 3E 117
Craighall. Edin 2E 129
Craighead. Fife 2H 137
Craighouse. Arg 3D 124
Craigie. Abers 2G 153
Craigie. D'dee 5D 144
Craigie. Per
nr. Blairgowrie 4A 144
nr. Perth 1D 136
Craigie. S Ayr 1D 116
Craigielaw. E Lot 2A 130
Craiglemine. Dum 5B 110
Craig-llwyn. Shrp 3E 71
Craiglockhart. Edin 2F 129
Craig Lodge. Arg 2B 126
Craigmalloch. E Ayr 5D 117
Craigmaud. Abers 3F 161
Craigmill. Stir 4H 135
Craigmillar. Edin 2F 129
Craigmore. Arg 3C 126
Craigmuie. Dum 1E 111
Craignair. Dum 3F 111
Craignant. Shrp 2E 71
Craigneuk. N Lan
nr. Airdrie 3A 128
nr. Motherwell 4A 128
Craignure. Arg 5B 140
Craigo. Ang 2F 145
Craigrory. High 4A 158
Craigrothie. Fife 2F 137
Craigs. Dum 2D 112
The Craigs. High 4B 164
Craigshill. W Lot 3D 128
Craigton. Aber 3F 153
Craigton. Abers 3E 152
Craigton. Ang
nr. Carnoustie 5E 145
nr. Kirriemuir 3C 144
Craigton. High 4A 158
Craigtown. High 3A 168
Craig-y-Duke. Neat 5H 45
Craig-y-nos. Powy 4B 46
Craik. Bord 4F 119
Crail. Fife 3H 137
Crailing. Bord 2A 120
Crailinghall. Bord 2A 120
Crakehill. N Yor 2G 99
Crakemarsh. Staf 2E 73
Crambe. N Yor 3B 100
Crambeck. N Yor 3B 100
Cramlington. Nmbd 2F 115
Cramond. Edin 2E 129
Cramond Bridge. Edin 2E 129
Cranage. Ches E 4B 84
Cranagh. Derr 7B 174
Cranberry. Staf 2C 72
Cranborne. Dors 1F 15
Cranbourne. Brac 3A 38
Cranbrook. Devn 3D 12
Cranbrook. Kent 2B 28
Cranbrook Common. Kent 2B 28
Crane Moor. S Yor 4D 92
Crane's Corner. Norf 4B 78
Cranfield. C Beds 1H 51
Cranford. G Lon 3C 38
Cranford St Andrew. Nptn 3G 63
Cranford St John. Nptn 3G 63
Cranham. Glos 4D 49
Cranham. G Lon 2G 39
Crank. Mers 1H 83
Cranleigh. Surr 2B 26
Cranley. Suff 3D 66
Cranloch. Mor 3G 159
Cranmer Green. Suff 3C 66
Cranmore. IOW 3C 16
Cranmore. Linc 5A 76
Crannich. Arg 4G 139
Crannoch. Mor 3B 160
Cranoe. Leics 1E 63
Cransford. Suff 4F 67
Cranshaws. Bord 3C 130
Cranstal. IOM 1D 108
Crantock. Corn 2B 6
Cranwell. Linc 1H 75
Cranwich. Norf 1G 65
Cranworth. Norf 5B 78
Craobh Haven. Arg 3E 133
Craobhnaclag. High 4G 157
Crapstone. Devn 2B 8
Crarae. Arg 4G 133
Crask. High
nr. Bettyhill 2H 167
nr. Lairg 1C 164
Crask of Aigas. High 4G 157
Craster. Nmbd 2G 121
Craswall. Here 2F 47
Cratfield. Suff 3F 67
Crathes. Abers 4E 153
Crathie. Abers 4G 151
Crathie. High 4H 149
Crathorne. N Yor 4B 106
Craven Arms. Shrp 2G 59
Crawcrook. Tyne 3E 115
Crawford. Lanc 4C 90
Crawford. S Lan 2B 118
Crawforddyke. S Lan 4B 128
Crawfordjohn. S Lan 2A 118
Crawfordsburn. Ards 1J 179
Crawick. Dum 3G 117
Crawley. Devn 2F 13
Crawley. Hants 3C 24
Crawley. Oxon 4B 50
Crawley. W Sus 2D 26
Crawley Down. W Sus 2E 27
Crawley End. Essx 1E 53
Crawley Side. Dur 5C 114
Crawshawbooth. Lanc 2G 91
Crawton. Abers 5F 153
Cray. N Yor 2B 98
Cray. Per 2A 144
Crayford. G Lon 3G 39
Crayke. N Yor 2H 99
Craymere Beck. Norf 2C 78
Crays Hill. Essx 1B 40
Cray's Pond. Oxon 3E 37
Crazies Hill. Wok 3F 37
Creacombe. Devn 1B 12
Creagan. Arg 4D 140
Creag Aoil. High 1F 141
Creag Ghoraidh. W Isl 4C 170
Creaguaineach Lodge. High 2H 141
Creamore Bank. Shrp 2H 71
Creaton. Nptn 3E 62
Creca. Dum 2D 112
Credenhill. Here 1H 47
Crediton. Devn 2B 12
Creebridge. Dum 3B 110
Creech. Dors 4E 15
Creech Heathfield. Som 4F 21
Creech St Michael. Som 4F 21
Creed. Corn 4D 6
Creekmoor. Pool 3E 15
Creekmouth. G Lon 2F 39
Creeting St Mary. Suff 5C 66
Creeting St Peter. Suff 5C 66
Creeton. Linc 3H 75
Creetown. Dum 4B 110
Creggan. Ferm 2A 178
Creggan. New M 8D 178
Creggans. Arg 3H 133
Cregneash. IOM 5A 108
Cregrina. Powy 5D 58
Creich. Arg 2B 132
Creich. Fife 1F 137
Creighton. Staf 2E 73
Creigiau. Card 3D 32
Cremyll. Corn 3A 8
Crendell. Dors 1F 15
Crepkill. High 4D 154
Cressage. Shrp 5H 71
Cressbrook. Derbs 3F 85
Cresselly. Pemb 4E 43
Cressing. Essx 3A 54
Cresswell. Nmbd 5G 121
Cresswell. Staf 2D 73
Cresswell Quay. Pemb 4E 43
Creswell. Derbs 3C 86
Creswell Green. Staf 4E 73
Cretingham. Suff 4E 67
Crewe. Ches E 5B 84
Crewe-by-Farndon. Ches W 5G 83
Crewgreen. Powy 4F 71
Crewkerne. Som 2H 13
Crews Hill. G Lon 5D 52
Crewton. Derb 2A 74
Crianlarich. Stir 1C 134
Cribbs Causeway. S Glo 3A 34
Cribyn. Cdgn 5E 57
Criccieth. Gwyn 2D 69
Crich. Derbs 5A 86
Crichton. Midl 3G 129
Crick. Mon 2H 33
Crick. Nptn 3C 62
Crickadarn. Powy 1D 46
Cricket Hill. Hants 5G 37
Cricket Malherbie. Som 1G 13
Cricket St Thomas. Som 2G 13
Crickham. Som 2H 21
Crickheath. Shrp 3E 71
Crickhowell. Powy 4F 47
Cricklade. Wilts 2G 35
Cricklewood. G Lon 2D 38
Cridling Stubbs. N Yor 2F 93
Crieff. Per 1A 136
Criftins. Shrp 2F 71
Criggion. Powy 4E 71
Crigglestone. W Yor 3D 92
Crimchard. Som 2G 13
Crimdon Park. Dur 1B 106
Crimond. Abers 3H 161
Crimonmogate. Abers 3H 161
Crimplesham. Norf 5F 77
Crimscote. Warw 1H 49
Crinan. Arg 4E 133
Cringleford. Norf 5D 78
Crinow. Pemb 3F 43
Cripplesease. Corn 3C 4
Cripplestyle. Dors 1F 15
Cripp's Corner. E Sus 3B 28
Croanford. Corn 5A 10
Crockenhill. Kent 4G 39
Crocker End. Oxon 3F 37
Crockerhill. Hants 2D 16
Crockernwell. Devn 3A 12
Crocker's Ash. Here 4A 48
Crockerton. Wilts 2D 22
Crocketford. Dum 2F 111
Crockey Hill. York 5A 100
Crockham Hill. Kent 5F 39
Crockhurst Street. Kent 1H 27
Crockleford Heath. Essx 3D 54
Croeserw. Neat 2B 32
Croes-Goch. Pemb 1C 42
Croes Hywel. Mon 4G 47
Croes-lan. Cdgn 1D 45
Croesor. Gwyn 1F 69
Croesoswallt. Shrp 3E 71
Croesyceiliog. Carm 4E 45
Croesyceiliog. Torf 2G 33
Croes-y-mwyalch. Torf 2G 33
Croesywaun. Gwyn 5E 81
Croford. Som 4E 20
Croft. Leics 1C 62
Croft. Linc 4E 89
Croft. Warr 1A 84
Croftamie. Stir 1F 127
Croftfoot. Glas 3G 127
Croftmill. Per 5F 143
Crofton. Cumb 4E 112
Crofton. W Yor 3D 93
Crofton. Wilts 5A 36
Croft-on-Tees. N Yor 4F 105
Crofts. Dum 2E 111
Crofts of Benachielt. High 5D 169
Crofts of Dipple. Mor 3H 159
Crofty. Swan 3E 31
Croggan. Arg 1E 132
Croglin. Cumb 5G 113
Croich. High 4B 164
Croick. High 3A 168
Croig. Arg 3E 139
Cromarty. High 2B 158
Crombie. Fife 1D 128
Cromdale. High 1E 151
Cromer. Herts 3C 52
Cromer. Norf 1E 78
Cromford. Derbs 5G 85
Cromhall. S Glo 2B 34
Cromor. W Isl 5G 171
Cromra. High 5H 149
Cromwell. Notts 4E 87
Cronberry. E Ayr 2F 117
Crondall. Hants 2F 25
The Cronk. IOM 2C 108
Cronk-y-Voddy. IOM 3C 108
Cronton. Mers 2G 83
Crook. Cumb 5F 103
Crook. Dur 1E 105
Crookdake. Cumb 5C 112
Crooke. G Man 4D 90
Crookedholm. E Ayr 1D 116
Crooked Soley. Wilts 4B 36
Crookes. S Yor 2H 85
Crookgate Bank. Dur 4E 115
Crookhall. Dur 4E 115
Crookham. Nmbd 1D 120
Crookham. W Ber 5D 36
Crookham Village. Hants 1F 25
Crooklands. Cumb 1E 97
Crook of Devon. Per 3C 136
Crookston. Glas 3G 127
Cropredy. Oxon 1C 50
Cropston. Leics 4C 74
Cropthorne. Worc 1E 49
Cropton. N Yor 1B 100
Cropwell Bishop. Notts 2D 74
Cropwell Butler. Notts 2D 74
Cros. W Isl 1H 171
Crosbie. N Ayr 4D 126
Crosbost. W Isl 5F 171
Crosby. Cumb 1B 102
Crosby. IOM 4C 108
Crosby. Mers 1F 83
Crosby. N Lin 3B 94
Crosby Court. N Yor 5A 106
Crosby Garrett. Cumb 4A 104

Dorstone—Eccleshall

Dorstone. Here 1G 47
Dorton. Buck 4E 51
Dosthill. Staf 5G 73
Dotham. IOA 3C 80
Dottery. Dors 3H 13
Doublebois. Corn 2F 7
Dougarie. N Ayr 2C 122
Doughton. Glos 2D 35
Douglas. IOM 4C 108
Douglas. S Lan 1H 117
Douglas Bridge. Derr 3F 176
Douglastown. Ang 4D 144
Douglas Water. S Lan 1A 118
Doulting. Som 2B 22
Dounby. Orkn 5B 172
Doune. High
nr. Kingussie 2C 150
nr. Lairg 3B 164
Doune. Stir 3G 135
Dounie. High
nr. Bonar Bridge 4C 164
nr. Tain 5D 164
Dounreay, Upper & Lower.
High 2B 168
Doura. N Ayr 5E 127
Dousland. Devn 2B 8
Dovaston. Shrp 3F 71
Dove Holes. Derbs 3E 85
Dovenby. Cumb 1B 102
Dover. Kent 194 (1H 29)
Dovercourt. Essx 2F 55
Doverdale. Worc 4C 60
Doveridge. Derbs 2F 73
Doversgreen. Surr 1D 26
Dowally. Per 4H 143
Dowbridge. Lanc 1C 90
Dowdeswell. Glos 4F 49
Dowlais. Mer T 5D 46
Dowland. Devn 1F 11
Dowlands. Devn 3F 13
Dowles. Worc 3B 60
Dowlesgreen. Wok 5G 37
Dowlish Wake. Som 1G 13
The Down. Shrp 1A 60
Downall Green. Mers 4D 90
Down Ampney. Glos 2G 35
Downderry. Corn
nr. Looe 3H 7
nr. St Austell 3D 6
Downe. G Lon 4F 39
Downend. IOW 4D 16
Downend. S Glo 4B 34
Downend. W Ber 4C 36
Down Field. Cambs 3F 65
Downfield. D'dee 5C 144
Downgate. Corn
nr. Kelly Bray 5D 10
nr. Upton Cross 5C 10
Downham. Essx 1B 40
Downham. Lanc 5G 97
Downham. Nmbd 1C 120
Downham Market. Norf 5F 77
Down Hatherley. Glos 3D 48
Downhead. Som
nr. Frome 2B 22
nr. Yeovil 4A 22
Downhill. Caus 3D 174
Downholland Cross. Lanc 4B 90
Downholme. N Yor 5E 105
Downies. Abers 4G 153
Downley. Buck 2G 37
Downpatrick. New M 5J 179
Down St Mary. Devn 2H 11
Downside. Som
nr. Chilcompton 1B 22
nr. Shepton Mallet 2B 22
Downside. Surr 5C 38
Down Thomas. Devn 3B 8
Downton. Hants 3A 16
Downton. Wilts 4G 23
Downton on the Rock.
Here 3G 59
Dowsby. Linc 3A 76
Dowsdale. Linc 4B 76
Dowthwaitehead. Cumb 2E 103
Doxey. Staf 3D 72
Doxford. Nmbd 2F 121
Doynton. S Glo 4C 34
Drabblegate. Norf 3E 78
Draethen. Cphy 3F 33
Draffan. S Lan 5A 128
Dragonby. N Lin 3C 94
Dragon's Green. W Sus 3C 26
Drakelow. Worc 2C 60
Drakemyre. N Ayr 4D 126
Drakes Broughton. Worc 1E 49
Drakes Cross. Worc 3E 61
Drakewalls. Corn 5E 11
Draperstown. M Ulst 7D 174
Draughton. Nptn 3E 63
Draughton. N Yor 4C 98
Drax. N Yor 2G 93
Draycot. Oxon 5E 51
Draycote. Warw 3B 62
Draycot Foliat. Swin 4G 35
Draycott. Derbs 2B 74
Draycott. Glos 2G 49
Draycott. Shrp 1C 60
Draycott. Som
nr. Cheddar 1H 21
nr. Yeovil 4A 22
Draycott. Worc 1D 48
Draycott in the Clay. Staf 3F 73
Draycott in the Moors.
Staf 1D 73
Drayford. Devn 1A 12
Drayton. Leics 1F 63
Drayton. Linc 2B 76
Drayton. Norf 4D 78
Drayton. Nptn 4C 62
Drayton. Oxon
nr. Abingdon 2C 36
nr. Banbury 1C 50
Drayton. Port 2E 17
Drayton. Som 4H 21
Drayton. Warw 5F 61
Drayton. Worc 3D 60
Drayton Bassett. Staf 5F 73
Drayton Beauchamp.
Buck 4H 51
Drayton Parslow. Buck 3G 51
Drayton St Leonard. Oxon 2D 36
Drebley. N Yor 4C 98
Dreenhill. Pemb 3D 42
Y Drefach. Gwyn 2D 69
Drefach. Carm
nr. Meidrim 4F 45
nr. Newcastle Emlyn 2D 44
nr. Tumble 2G 43
Drefach. Cdgn 1E 45
Dreghorn. N Ayr 1C 116
Drellingore. Kent 1G 29
Drem. E Lot 2B 130
Y Drenewydd. Powy 1D 58
Dreumasdal. W Isl 5C 170
Drewsteignton. Devn 3H 11
Driby. Linc 3C 88
Driffield. E Yor 4E 101
Driffield. Glos 2F 35
Drift. Corn 4B 4
Drigg. Cumb 5B 102
Drighlington. W Yor 2C 92
Drimnin. High 3G 139
Drimpton. Dors 2H 13
Dringhoe. E Yor 4F 101
Drinisiadar. W Isl 8D 171
Drinkstone. Suff 4B 66
Drinkstone Green. Suff 4B 66
Drointon. Staf 3E 73
Droitwich Spa. Worc 4C 60
Droman. High 3B 166
Dromara. Lis 5G 179
Dromore. Arm 4G 179
Dromore. Ferm 6F 176
Dron. Per 2D 136
Dronfield. Derbs 3A 86
Dronfield Woodhouse.
Derbs 3H 85
Drongan. E Ayr 3D 116
Dronley. Ang 5C 144
Droop. Dors 2C 14
Drope. V Glam 4E 32
Droxford. Hants 1E 16
Droylsden. G Man 1C 84
Druggers End. Worc 2C 48
Druid. Den 1C 70
Druid's Heath. W Mid 5E 73
Druidston. Pemb 3C 42
Druim. High 3D 158
Druimarbin. High 1E 141
Druim Fhearna. High 2E 147
Druimindarroch. High 5E 147
Druim Saighdinis. W Isl 2D 170
Drum. Per 3C 136
Drumaness. New M 5H 179
Drumaroad. New M 5H 179
Drumbeg. High 5B 166
Drumblade. Abers 4C 160
Drumbo. Lis 3H 179
Drumbuie. Dum 1C 110
Drumbuie. High 5G 155
Drumburgh. Cumb 4D 112
Drumburn. Dum 3A 112
Drumchapel. Glas 2G 127
Drumchardine. High 4H 157
Drumchork. High 5C 162
Drumclog. S Lan 1F 117
Drumeldrie. Fife 3G 137
Drumelzier. Bord 1D 118
Drumfearn. High 2E 147
Drumgask. High 4A 150
Drumgelloch. N Lan 3A 128
Drumgley. Ang 3D 144
Drumguish. High 4B 150
Drumin. Mor 5F 159
Drumindorsair. High 4G 157
Drumintee. New M 8E 178
Drumlamford House.
S Ayr 2H 109
Drumlasie. Abers 3D 152
Drumlemble. Arg 4A 122
Drumlithie. Abers 5E 153
Drummoddie. Dum 5A 110
Drummond. High 2A 158
Drummore. Dum 5E 109
Drummuir. Mor 4A 160
Drumnacanvy. Arm 4E 178
Drumnadrochit. High 5H 157
Drumnagorrach. Mor 3C 160
Drumnakilly. Ferm 2L 177
Drumoak. Abers 4E 153
Drumquin. Ferm 5F 176
Drumraighland. Caus 4C 174
Drumrunie. High 3F 163
Drumry. W Dun 2G 127
Drums. Abers 1G 153
Drumsleet. Dum 2G 111
Drumsmittal. High 4A 158
Drums of Park. Abers 3C 160
Drumsturdy. Ang 5D 145
Drumsurn. Caus 5D 174
Drumtochty Castle.
Abers 5D 152
Drumuie. High 4D 154
Drumuillie. High 1D 150
Drumvaich. Stir 3F 135
Drumwhindle. Abers 5G 161
Drunkendub. Ang 4F 145
Drury. Flin 4E 83
Drury Square. Norf 4B 78
Drybeck. Cumb 3H 103
Drybridge. Mor 2B 160
Drybridge. N Ayr 1C 116
Drybrook. Glos 4B 48
Drybrook. Here 4A 48
Dryburgh. Bord 1H 119
Dry Doddington. Linc 1F 75
Dry Drayton. Cambs 4C 64
Drym. Corn 3D 4
Drymen. Stir 1F 127
Drymuir. Abers 4G 161
Drynachan Lodge. High 5C 158
Drynie Park. High 3H 157
Drynoch. High 5D 154
Dry Sandford. Oxon 5C 50
Dryslwyn. Carm 3F 45
Dry Street. Essx 2A 40
Dryton. Shrp 5H 71
Dubford. Abers 2E 161
Dubiton. Abers 3D 160
Dubton. Ang 3E 145
Duchally. High 2A 164
Duck End. Essx 3G 53
Duckington. Ches W 5G 83
Ducklington. Oxon 5B 50
Duckmanton. Derbs 3B 86
Duck Street. Hants 2B 24
Dudbridge. Glos 5D 48
Duddenhoe End. Essx 2E 53
Duddingston. Edin 2F 129
Duddington. Nptn 5G 75
Duddleswell. E Sus 3F 27
Duddo. Nmbd 5F 131
Duddon. Ches W 4H 83
Duddon Bridge. Cumb 1A 96
Dudleston. Shrp 2F 71
Dudleston Heath. Shrp 2F 71
Dudley. Tyne 2F 115
Dudley. W Mid 2D 60
Dudston. Shrp 1E 59
Dudwells. Pemb 2D 42
Duffield. Derbs 1H 73
Duffryn. Neat 2B 32
Dufftown. Mor 4H 159
Duffus. Mor 2F 159
Dufton. Cumb 2H 103
Duggleby. N Yor 3C 100
Duirinish. High 5G 155
Duisdalemore. High 2E 147
Duisdeil Mòr. High 2E 147
Duisky. High 1E 141
Dukesfield. Nmbd 4C 114
Dukestown. Blae 5E 47
Dukinfield. G Man 1D 84
Dulas. IOA 2D 81
Dulcote. Som 2A 22
Dulford. Devn 2D 12
Dull. Per 4F 143
Dullatur. N Lan 2A 128
Dullingham. Cambs 5F 65
Dullingham Ley. Cambs 5F 65
Dulnain Bridge. High 1D 151
Duloe. Bed 4A 64
Duloe. Corn 3G 7
Dulverton. Som 4C 20
Dulwich. G Lon 3E 39
Dumbarton. W Dun 2F 127
Dumbleton. Glos 2F 49
Dumfin. Arg 1E 127
Dumfries. Dum 194 (2A 112)
Dumgoyne. Stir 1G 127
Dummer. Hants 2D 24
Dumpford. W Sus 4G 25
Dun. Ang 2F 145
Dunadry. Ant 1F 179
Dunaghy. Caus 4F 175
Dunagoil. Arg 4B 126
Dunalastair. Per 3E 142
Dunan. High 1D 147
Dunball. Som 2G 21
Dunbar. E Lot 2C 130
Dunbeath. High 5D 168
Dunbeg. Arg 5C 140
Dunblane. Stir 3G 135
Dunbog. Fife 2E 137
Dunbridge. Hants 4B 24
Duncanston. Abers 1C 152
Duncanston. High 3H 157
Dun Charlabhaigh. W Isl 3D 171
Dunchideock. Devn 4B 12
Dunchurch. Warw 3B 62
Duncote. Nptn 5D 62
Duncow. Dum 1A 112
Duncrievie. Per 3D 136
Duncton. W Sus 4A 26
Dundee. D'dee 194 (5D 144)
Dundee Airport. D'dee 1F 137
Dundon. Som 3H 21
Dundonald. Lis 2J 179
Dundonald. S Ayr 1C 116
Dundonnell. High 5E 163
Dundraw. Cumb 5D 112
Dundreggan. High 2F 149
Dundrennan. Dum 5E 111
Dundridge. Hants 1D 16
Dundrod. Lis 2G 179
Dundrum. New M 6J 179
Dundry. N Som 5A 34
Dunecht. Abers 3E 153
Dunfermline. Fife 1D 129
Dunford Bridge. S Yor 4B 92
Dungannon. M Ulst 3B 178
Dungate. Kent 5D 40
Dunge. Wilts 1D 23
Dungeness. Kent 4E 29
Dungiven. Caus 6C 174
Dungworth. S Yor 2G 85
Dunham-on-the-Hill.
Ches W 3G 83
Dunham-on-Trent. Notts 3F 87
Dunhampton. Worc 4C 60
Dunham Town. G Man 2B 84
Dunham Woodhouses.
G Man 2B 84
Dunholme. Linc 3H 87
Dunino. Fife 2H 137
Dunipace. Falk 1B 128
Dunira. Per 1G 135
Dunkeld. Per 4H 143
Dunkerton. Bath 1C 22
Dunkeswell. Devn 2E 13
Dunkeswick. N Yor 5F 99
Dunkirk. Kent 5E 41
Dunkirk. S Glo 3C 34
Dunkirk. Staf 5C 84
Dunkirk. Wilts 5E 35
Dunk's Green. Kent 5H 39
Dunlappie. Ang 2E 145
Dunley. Hants 1C 24
Dunley. Worc 4B 60
Dunlichity Lodge. High 5A 158
Dunlop. E Ayr 5F 127
Dunloy. Caus 5G 175
Dunmaglass Lodge.
High 1H 149
Dunmore. Arg 3F 125
Dunmore. Falk 1B 128
Dunmore. High 4H 157
Dunmurry. Bel 3G 179
Dunnamanagh. Derr 6A 174
Dunnaval. New M 8G 179
Dunnet. High 1E 169
Dunnichen. Ang 4E 145
Dunning. Per 2C 136
Dunnington. E Yor 4F 101
Dunnington. Warw 5E 61
Dunnington. York 4A 100
Dunningwell. Cumb 1A 96
Dunnockshaw. Lanc 2G 91
Dunoon. Arg 2C 126
Dunphail. Mor 4E 159
Dunragit. Dum 4G 109
Dunrostan. Arg 1F 125
Duns. Bord 4D 130
Dunsby. Linc 3A 76
Dunscar. G Man 3F 91
Dunscore. Dum 1F 111
Dunscroft. S Yor 4G 93
Dunsdale. Red C 3D 106
Dunsden Green. Oxon 4F 37
Dunsfold. Surr 2B 26
Dunsford. Devn 4B 12
Dunshalt. Fife 2E 137
Dunshillock. Abers 4G 161
Dunsley. N Yor 3F 107
Dunsley. Staf 2C 60
Dunsmore. Buck 5G 51
Dunsop Bridge. Lanc 4F 97
Dunstable. C Beds 3A 52
Dunstal. Staf 3E 73
Dunstall. Staf 3F 73
Dunstall Green. Suff 4G 65
Dunstall Hill. W Mid 5D 72
Dunstan. Nmbd 3G 121
Dunster. Som 2C 20
Duns Tew. Oxon 3C 50
Dunston. Linc 4H 87
Dunston. Norf 5E 79
Dunston. Staf 4D 72
Dunston. Tyne 3F 115
Dunstone. Devn 3B 8
Dunston Heath. Staf 4D 72
Dunsville. S Yor 4G 93
Dunswell. E Yor 1D 94
Dunsyre. S Lan 5D 128
Dunterton. Devn 5D 11
Duntisbourne Abbots.
Glos 5E 49
Duntisbourne Leer. Glos 5E 49
Duntisbourne Rouse. Glos 5E 49
Duntish. Dors 2B 14
Duntocher. W Dun 2F 127
Dunton. Buck 3G 51
Dunton. C Beds 1C 52
Dunton. Norf 2A 78
Dunton Bassett. Leics 1C 62
Dunton Green. Kent 5G 39
Dunton Patch. Norf 2A 78
Duntulm. High 1D 154
Dunure. S Ayr 3B 116
Dunvant. Swan 3E 31
Dunvegan. High 4B 154
Dunwich. Suff 3G 67
Dunwood. Staf 5D 84
Durdar. Cumb 4F 113
Durgates. E Sus 2H 27
Durham. Dur 194 (5F 115)
Durham Tees Valley Airport.
Darl 3A 106
Durisdeer. Dum 4A 118
Durisdeermill. Dum 4A 118
Durkar. W Yor 3D 92
Durleigh. Som 3F 21
Durley. Hants 1D 16
Durley. Wilts 5H 35
Durley Street. Hants 1D 16
Durlow Common. Here 2B 48
Durnamuck. High 4E 163
Durness. High 2E 166
Durno. Abers 1E 152
Durns Town. Hants 3A 16
Duror. High 3D 141
Durran. Arg 3G 133
Durran. High 2D 169
Durrant Green. Kent 2C 28
Durrants. Hants 1F 17
Durrington. W Sus 5C 26
Durrington. Wilts 2G 23
Dursley. Glos 2C 34
Dursley Cross. Glos 4B 48
Durston. Som 4F 21
Durweston. Dors 2D 14
Dury. Shet 6F 173
Duston. Nptn 4E 63
Duthil. High 1D 150
Dutlas. Powy 3E 58
Duton Hill. Essx 3G 53
Dutson. Corn 4D 10
Dutton. Ches W 3H 83
Duxford. Cambs 1E 53
Duxford. Oxon 2B 36
Dwygyfylchi. Cnwy 3G 81
Dwyran. IOA 4D 80
Dyce. Aber 2F 153
Dyffryn. B'end 2B 32
Dyffryn. Carm 2H 43
Dyffryn. Pemb 1D 42
Dyffryn. V Glam 4D 32
Dyffryn Ardudwy. Gwyn 3E 69
Dyffryn Castell. Cdgn 2G 57
Dyffryn Ceidrych. Carm 3H 45
Dyffryn Cellwen. Neat 5B 46
Dyke. Linc 3A 76
Dyke. Mor 3D 159
Dykehead. Ang 2C 144
Dykehead. N Lan 3B 128
Dykehead. Stir 4E 135
Dykend. Ang 3B 144
Dykesfield. Cumb 4E 112
Dylife. Powy 1A 58
Dymchurch. Kent 3F 29
Dymock. Glos 2C 48
Dyrham. S Glo 4C 34
Dysart. Fife 4F 137
Dyserth. Den 3C 82

E

Eachwick. Nmbd 2E 115
Eadar Dha Fhadhail.
W Isl 4C 171
Eagland Hill. Lanc 5D 96
Eagle. Linc 4F 87
Eagle Barnsdale. Linc 4F 87
Eagle Moor. Linc 4F 87
Eaglescliffe. Stoc T 3B 106
Eaglesfield. Cumb 2B 102
Eaglesfield. Dum 2D 112
Eaglesham. E Ren 4G 127
Eaglethorpe. Nptn 1H 63
Eagley. G Man 3F 91
Eairy. IOM 4B 108
Eakley Lanes. Mil 5F 63
Eakring. Notts 4D 86
Ealand. N Lin 3A 94
Ealing. G Lon 2C 38
Eallabus. Arg 3B 124
Eals. Nmbd 4H 113
Eamont Bridge. Cumb 2G 103
Earby. Lanc 5B 98
Earcroft. Bkbn 2E 91
Eardington. Shrp 1B 60
Eardisland. Here 5G 59
Eardisley. Here 1G 47
Eardiston. Shrp 3F 71
Eardiston. Worc 4A 60
Earith. Cambs 3C 64
Earlais. High 2C 154
Earle. Nmbd 2D 121
Earlesfield. Linc 2G 75
Earlestown. Mers 1H 83
Earley. Wok 4F 37
Earlham. Norf 5D 78
Earlish. High 2C 154
Earls Barton. Nptn 4F 63
Earls Colne. Essx 3B 54
Earls Common. Worc 5D 60
Earl's Croome. Worc 1D 48
Earlsdon. W Mid 3H 61
Earlsferry. Fife 3G 137
Earlsford. Abers 5F 161
Earl's Green. Suff 4C 66
Earlsheaton. W Yor 2C 92
Earl Shilton. Leics 1B 62
Earl Soham. Suff 4E 67
Earl Sterndale. Derbs 4E 85
Earlston. E Ayr 1D 116
Earlston. Bord 1H 119
Earl Stonham. Suff 5D 66
Earlstoun. Dum 1D 110
Earlswood. Mon 2H 33
Earlswood. Warw 3F 61
Earlyvale. Bord 4F 129
Earnley. W Sus 3G 17
Earsairidh. W Isl 9C 170
Earsdon. Tyne 2G 115
Earsham. Norf 2F 67
Earsham Street. Suff 3E 67
Earswick. York 4A 100
Eartham. W Sus 5A 26
Earthcott Green. S Glo 3B 34
Easby. N Yor
nr. Great Ayton 4C 106
nr. Richmond 4E 105
Easdale. Arg 2E 133
Easebourne. W Sus 4G 25
Easenhall. Warw 3B 62
Eashing. Surr 1A 26
Easington. Buck 4E 51
Easington. Dur 5H 115
Easington. E Yor 3G 95
Easington. Nmbd 1F 121
Easington. Oxon
nr. Banbury 2C 50
nr. Watlington 2E 37
Easington. Red C 3E 107
Easington Colliery. Dur 5H 115
Easington Lane. Tyne 5G 115
Easingwold. N Yor 2H 99
Eassie. Ang 4C 144
Eassie and Nevay. Ang 4C 144
East Aberthaw. V Glam 5D 32
Eastacombe. Devn 4F 19
Eastacott. Devn 4G 19
East Allington. Devn 4D 8
East Anstey. Devn 4B 20
East Anton. Hants 2B 24
East Appleton. N Yor 5F 105
East Ardsley. W Yor 2D 92
East Ashley. Devn 1G 11
East Ashling. W Sus 2G 17
East Aston. Hants 2C 24
East Ayton. N Yor 1D 101
East Barkwith. Linc 2A 88
East Barnby. N Yor 3F 107
East Barnet. G Lon 1D 39
East Barns. E Lot 2D 130
East Barsham. Norf 2B 78
East Beach. W Sus 3G 17
East Beckham. Norf 2D 78
East Bedfont. G Lon 3B 38
East Bennan. N Ayr 3D 123
East Bergholt. Suff 2D 54
East Bierley. W Yor 2C 92
East Bilney. Norf 4B 78
East Blatchington. E Sus 5F 27
East Bloxworth. Dors 3D 15
East Boldre. Hants 2B 16
East Bolton. Nmbd 3F 121
Eastbourne. E Sus 194 (5H 27)
East Brent. Som 1G 21
East Bridge. Suff 4G 67
East Bridgford. Notts 1D 74
East Briscoe. Dur 3C 104
East Buckland. Devn
nr. Barnstaple 3G 19
nr. Thurlestone 4C 8
East Budleigh. Devn 4D 12
Eastburn. W Yor 5C 98
East Burnham. Buck 2A 38
East Burrafirth. Shet 6E 173
East Burton. Dors 4D 14
Eastbury. Herts 1B 38
Eastbury. W Ber 4B 36
East Butsfield. Dur 5E 115
East Butterleigh. Devn 2C 12
East Butterwick. N Lin 4B 94
Eastby. N Yor 4C 98
East Calder. W Lot 3D 129
East Carleton. Norf 5D 78
East Carlton. Nptn 2F 63
East Carlton. W Yor 5E 98
East Chaldon. Dors 4C 14
East Challow. Oxon 3B 36
East Charleton. Devn 4D 8
East Chelborough. Dors 2A 14
East Chiltington. E Sus 4E 27
East Chinnock. Som 1H 13
East Chisenbury. Wilts 1G 23
Eastchurch. Kent 3D 40
East Clandon. Surr 5B 38
East Claydon. Buck 3F 51
East Clevedon. N Som 4H 33
East Clyne. High 3F 165
East Clyth. High 5E 169
East Coker. Som 1A 14
East Combe. Som 3E 21
Eastcombe. Glos 5D 49
East Common. N Yor 1G 93
East Compton. Som 2B 22
East Cornworthy. Devn 3E 9
Eastcote. G Lon 2C 38
Eastcote. Nptn 5D 62
Eastcote. W Mid 3F 61
Eastcott. Corn 1C 10
Eastcott. Wilts 1F 23
East Cottingwith. E Yor 5B 100
Eastcourt. Wilts
nr. Pewsey 5H 35
nr. Tetbury 2E 35
East Cowes. IOW 3D 16
East Cowick. E Yor 2G 93
East Cowton. N Yor 4A 106
East Cramlington. Nmbd 2F 115
East Cranmore. Som 2B 22
East Creech. Dors 4E 15
East Croachy. High 1A 150
East Dean. E Sus 5G 27
East Dean. Glos 3B 48
East Dean. Hants 4A 24
East Dean. W Sus 4A 26
East Down. Devn 2G 19
East Drayton. Notts 3E 87
East Dundry. N Som 5A 34
East Ella. Hull 2D 94
East End. Cambs 3C 64
East End. Dors 3E 15
East End. E Yor
nr. Ulrome 4F 101
nr. Withernsea 2F 95
East End. Hants
nr. Lymington 3B 16
nr. Newbury 5C 36
East End. Herts 3E 53
East End. Kent
nr. Minster 3D 40
nr. Tenterden 2C 28
East End. N Som 4H 33
East End. Oxon 4B 50
East End. Som 1A 22
East End. Suff 2E 54
Easter Ardross. High 1A 158
Easter Balgedie. Per 3D 136
Easter Balmoral. Abers 4G 151
Easter Brae. High 2A 158
Easter Buckieburn. Stir 1A 128
Easter Compton. S Glo 3A 34
Easter Fearn. High 5D 164
Easter Galcantray. High 4C 158
Eastergate. W Sus 5A 26
Easterhouse. Glas 3H 127
Easter Howgate. Midl 3F 129
Easter Kinkell. High 3H 157
Easter Lednathie. Ang 2C 144
Easter Ogil. Ang 2D 144
Easter Ord. Abers 3F 153
Easter Quarff. Shet 8F 173
Easter Rhynd. Per 2D 136
Easter Skeld. Shet 7E 173
Easter Suddie. High 3A 158
Easterton. Wilts 1F 23
Eastertown. Som 1G 21
Easter Tulloch. Abers 1G 145
East Everleigh. Wilts 1H 23
East Farleigh. Kent 5B 40
East Farndon. Nptn 2E 62
East Ferry. Linc 1F 87
Eastfield. N Lan
nr. Caldercruix 3B 128
nr. Harthill 3C 128
Eastfield. N Yor 1E 101
Eastfield. S Lan 3H 127
Eastfield Hall. Nmbd 4G 121
East Fortune. E Lot 2B 130
East Garforth. W Yor 1E 93
East Garston. W Ber 4B 36
Eastgate. Dur 1C 104
Eastgate. Norf 3D 78
East Ginge. Oxon 3C 36
East Gores. Essx 3B 54
East Goscote. Leics 4D 74
East Grafton. Wilts 5A 36
East Green. Suff 5F 65
East Grimstead. Wilts 4H 23
East Grinstead. W Sus 2E 27
East Guldeford. E Sus 3D 28
East Haddon. Nptn 4D 62
East Hagbourne. Oxon 3D 36
East Halton. N Lin 2E 95
East Ham. G Lon 2F 39
Eastham. Mers 2F 83
Eastham. Worc 4A 60
Eastham Ferry. Mers 2F 83
Easthampstead. Brac 5G 37
Easthampton. Here 4G 59
East Hanney. Oxon 2C 36
East Hanningfield. Essx 5A 54
East Hardwick. W Yor 3E 93
East Harling. Norf 2B 66
East Harlsey. N Yor 5B 106
East Harptree. Bath 1A 22
East Hartford. Nmbd 2F 115
East Harting. W Sus 1G 17
East Hatch. Wilts 4E 23
East Hatley. Cambs 5B 64
Easthaugh. Norf 4C 78
East Hauxwell. N Yor 5E 105
East Haven. Ang 5E 145
Eastheath. Wok 5G 37
East Heckington. Linc 1A 76
East Hedleyhope. Dur 5E 115
East Helmsdale. High 2H 165
East Hendred. Oxon 3C 36
East Heslerton. N Yor 2D 100
East Hoathly. E Sus 4G 27
East Holme. Dors 4D 15
Easthope. Shrp 1H 59
Easthorpe. Essx 3C 54
Easthorpe. Leics 2F 75
East Horrington. Som 2A 22
East Horsley. Surr 5B 38
East Horton. Nmbd 1E 121
Easthouses. Midl 3G 129
East Howe. Bour 3F 15
East Huntspill. Som 2G 21
East Hyde. C Beds 4B 52
East Ilsley. W Ber 3C 36
Eastington. Devn 2H 11
Eastington. Glos
nr. Northleach 4G 49
nr. Stonehouse 5C 48
East Keal. Linc 4C 88
East Kennett. Wilts 5G 35
East Keswick. W Yor 5F 99
East Kilbride. S Lan 4H 127
East Kirkby. Linc 4C 88
East Knapton. N Yor 2C 100
East Knighton. Dors 4D 14
East Knowstone. Devn 4B 20
East Knoyle. Wilts 3D 23
East Kyloe. Nmbd 1E 121
East Lambrook. Som 1H 13
East Langdon. Kent 1H 29
East Langton. Leics 1E 63
East Langwell. High 3E 164
East Lavant. W Sus 2G 17
East Lavington. W Sus 4A 26
East Layton. N Yor 4E 105
Eastleach Martin. Glos 5H 49
Eastleach Turville. Glos 5G 49
East Leake. Notts 3C 74
East Learmouth. Nmbd 1C 120
East Leigh. Devn
nr. Crediton 2G 11
nr. Modbury 3C 8
Eastleigh. Devn 4E 19
Eastleigh. Hants 1C 16
East Lexham. Norf 4A 78
East Lilburn. Nmbd 2E 121
Eastling. Kent 5D 40
East Linton. E Lot 2B 130
East Liss. Hants 4F 25
East Lockinge. Oxon 3C 36
East Looe. Corn 3G 7
East Lound. N Lin 1E 87
East Lulworth. Dors 4D 14
East Lutton. N Yor 3D 100
East Lydford. Som 3A 22
East Lyng. Som 4G 21
East Mains. Abers 4D 152
East Malling. Kent 5B 40
East Marden. W Sus 1G 17
East Markham. Notts 3E 87
East Marton. N Yor 4B 98
East Meon. Hants 4E 25
East Mersea. Essx 4D 54
East Mey. High 1F 169
East Midlands Airport.
Leics 205 (3B 74)
East Molesey. Surr 4C 38
Eastmoor. Norf 5G 77
East Morden. Dors 3E 15
East Morton. W Yor 5D 98
East Ness. N Yor 2A 100
East Newton. E Yor 1F 95
East Newton. N Yor 2A 100
Eastney. Port 3E 17
Eastnor. Here 2C 48
East Norton. Leics 5E 75
East Nynehead. Som 4E 21
East Oakley. Hants 1D 24
Eastoft. N Lin 3B 94
East Ogwell. Devn 5B 12
Easton. Cambs 3A 64
Easton. Cumb
nr. Burgh by Sands 4D 112
nr. Longtown 2F 113
Easton. Devn 4H 11
Easton. Dors 5B 14
Easton. Hants 3D 24
Easton. Linc 3G 75
Easton. Norf 4D 78
Easton. Som 2A 22
Easton. Suff 5E 67
Easton. Wilts 4D 35
Easton Grey. Wilts 3D 35
Easton-in-Gordano.
N Som 4A 34
Easton Maudit. Nptn 5F 63
Easton on the Hill. Nptn 5H 75
Easton Royal. Wilts 5H 35
East Orchard. Dors 1D 14
East Ord. Nmbd 4F 131
East Panson. Devn 3D 10
East Peckham. Kent 1A 28
East Pennard. Som 3A 22
East Perry. Cambs 4A 64
East Pitcorthie. Fife 3H 137
East Portlemouth. Devn 5D 8
East Prawle. Devn 5D 9
East Preston. W Sus 5B 26
East Putford. Devn 1D 10
East Quantoxhead. Som 2E 21
East Rainton. Tyne 5G 115
East Ravendale. NE Lin 1B 88
East Raynham. Norf 3A 78
Eastrea. Cambs 1B 64
East Rhidorroch Lodge.
High 4G 163
Eastriggs. Dum 3D 112
East Rigton. W Yor 5F 99
Eastrington. E Yor 2A 94
East Rounton. N Yor 4B 106
East Row. N Yor 3F 107
East Rudham. Norf 3H 77
East Runton. Norf 1D 78
East Ruston. Norf 3F 79
Eastry. Kent 5H 41
East Saltoun. E Lot 3A 130
East Shaws. Dur 3D 105
East Shefford. W Ber 4B 36
Eastshore. Shet 10E 173
East Sleekburn. Nmbd 1F 115
East Somerton. Norf 4G 79
East Stockwith. Linc 1E 87
East Stoke. Dors 4D 14
East Stoke. Notts 1E 75
East Stoke. Som 1H 13
East Stour. Dors 4D 22
East Stourmouth. Kent 4G 41
East Stowford. Devn 4G 19
East Stratton. Hants 2D 24
East Studdal. Kent 1H 29
East Taphouse. Corn 2F 7
East-the-Water. Devn 4E 19
East Thirston. Nmbd 5F 121
East Tilbury. Thur 3A 40
East Tisted. Hants 3F 25
East Torrington. Linc 2A 88
East Tuddenham. Norf 4C 78
East Tytherley. Hants 4A 24
East Tytherton. Wilts 4E 35
East Village. Devn 2B 12
Eastville. Linc 5D 88
East Wall. Shrp 1H 59
East Walton. Norf 4G 77
East Week. Devn 3G 11
Eastwell. Leics 3E 75
East Wellow. Hants 4B 24
East Wemyss. Fife 4F 137
East Whitburn. W Lot 3C 128
Eastwick. Herts 4E 53
Eastwick. Shet 4E 173
East Williamston. Pemb 4E 43
East Winch. Norf 4F 77
East Winterslow. Wilts 3H 23
East Wittering. W Sus 3F 17
East Witton. N Yor 1D 98
Eastwood. Notts 1B 74
Eastwood. S'end 2C 40
East Woodburn. Nmbd 1C 114
Eastwood End. Cambs 1D 64
East Woodhay. Hants 5C 36
East Woodlands. Som 2C 22
East Worldham. Hants 3F 25
East Worlington. Devn 1A 12
East Wretham. Norf 1B 66
East Youlstone. Devn 1C 10
Eathorpe. Warw 4A 62
Eaton. Ches E 4C 84
Eaton. Ches W 4H 83
Eaton. Leics 3E 75
Eaton. Norf
nr. Heacham 2F 77
nr. Norwich 5E 78
Eaton. Notts 3E 86
Eaton. Oxon 5C 50
Eaton. Shrp
nr. Bishop's Castle 2F 59
nr. Church Stretton 2H 59
Eaton Bishop. Here 2H 47
Eaton Bray. C Beds 3H 51
Eaton Constantine. Shrp 5H 71
Eaton Hastings. Oxon 2A 36
Eaton Socon. Cambs 5A 64
Eaton upon Tern. Shrp 3A 72
Eau Brink. Norf 4E 77
Eaves Green. W Mid 2G 61
Ebberley Hill. Devn 1F 11
Ebberston. N Yor 1C 100
Ebbesbourne Wake. Wilts 4E 23
Ebblake. Dors 2G 15
Ebbsfleet. Kent 3H 39
Ebbw Vale. Blae 5E 47
Ebchester. Dur 4E 115
Ebernoe. W Sus 3A 26
Ebford. Devn 4C 12
Ebley. Glos 5D 48
Ebnal. Ches W 1G 71
Ebrington. Glos 1G 49
Ecchinswell. Hants 1D 24
Ecclefechan. Dum 2C 112
Eccles. G Man 1B 84
Eccles. Kent 4B 40
Eccles. Bord 5D 130
Ecclesall. S Yor 2H 85
Ecclesfield. S Yor 1A 86
Eccles Green. Here 1G 47
Eccleshall. Staf 3C 72

Eccleshill—Fiskerton

Eccleshill. W Yor 1B 92
Ecclesmachan. W Lot 2D 128
Eccles on Sea. Norf 3G 79
Eccles Road. Norf 1C 66
Eccleston. Ches W 4G 83
Eccleston. Lanc 3D 90
Eccleston. Mers 1G 83
Eccup. W Yor 5E 99
Echt. Abers 3E 153
Eckford. Bord 2B 120
Eckington. Derbs 3B 86
Eckington. Worc 1E 49
Ecton. Nptn 4F 63
Edale. Derbs 2F 85
Eday Airport. Orkn 4E 172
Edburton. W Sus 4D 26
Edderside. Cumb 5C 112
Edderton. High 5E 164
Eddington. Kent 4F 41
Eddington. W Ber 5B 36
Eddleston. Bord 5F 129
Eddlewood. S Lan 4A 128
Eden. ME Ant 8L 175
Edenbridge. Kent 1F 27
Edendonich. Arg 1A 134
Edenfield. Lanc 3F 91
Edenhall. Cumb 1G 103
Edenham. Linc 3H 75
Edensor. Derbs 3G 85
Edentaggart. Arg 4C 134
Edenthorpe. S Yor 4G 93
Eden Vale. Dur 1B 106
Edern. Gwyn 2B 68
Ederney. Ferm 6E 176
Edgarley. Som 3A 22
Edgbaston. W Mid 2E 61
Edgcott. Buck 3E 51
Edgcott. Som 3B 20
Edge. Glos 5D 48
Edge. Shrp 5F 71
Edgebolton. Shrp 3H 71
Edge End. Glos 4A 48
Edgefield. Norf 2C 78
Edgefield Street. Norf 2C 78
Edge Green. Ches W 5G 83
Edgehead. Midl 3G 129
Edgeley. Shrp 1H 71
Edgeside. Lanc 2G 91
Edgeworth. Glos 5E 49
Edgiock. Worc 4E 61
Edgmond. Telf 4B 72
Edgmond Marsh. Telf 3B 72
Edgton. Shrp 2F 59
Edgware. G Lon 1C 38
Edgworth. Bkbn 3F 91
Edinbane. High 3C 154
Edinburgh. Edin 195 (2F 129)
Edinburgh Airport. Edin 2E 129
Edingale. Staf 4G 73
Edingley. Notts 5D 86
Edingthorpe. Norf 2F 79
Edington. Som 3G 21
Edington. Wilts 1E 23
Edingworth. Som 1G 21
Edistone. Devn 4C 18
Edithmead. Som 2G 21
Edith Weston. Rut 5G 75
Edlaston. Derbs 1F 73
Edlesborough. Buck 4H 51
Edlingham. Nmbd 4F 121
Edlington. Linc 3B 88
Edmondsham. Dors 1F 15
Edmondsley. Dur 5F 115
Edmondthorpe. Leics 4F 75
Edmonstone. Orkn 5E 172
Edmonton. Corn 1D 6
Edmonton. G Lon 1E 39
Edmundbyers. Dur 4D 114
Ednam. Bord 1B 120
Ednaston. Derbs 1G 73
Edney Common. Essx 5G 53
Edrom. Bord 4E 131
Edstaston. Shrp 2H 71
Edstone. Warw 4F 61
Edwalton. Notts 2C 74
Edwardstone. Suff 1C 54
Edwardsville. Mer T 2D 32
Edwinsford. Carm 2G 45
Edwinstowe. Notts 4D 86
Edworth. C Beds 1C 52
Edwyn Ralph. Here 5A 60
Edzell. Ang 2F 145
Efail-fach. Neat 2A 32
Efail Isaf. Rhon 3D 32
Efailnewydd. Gwyn 2C 68
Efail-rhyd. Powy 3D 70
Efailwen. Carm 2F 43
Efenechtyd. Den 5D 82
Effingham. Surr 5C 38
Effingham Common. Surr 5C 38
Effirth. Shet 6E 173
Efflinch. Staf 4F 73
Efford. Devn 2B 12
Efstigarth. Shet 2F 173
Egbury. Hants 1C 24
Egdon. Worc 5D 60
Egerton. G Man 3F 91
Egerton. Kent 1D 28
Egerton Forstal. Kent 1C 28
Eggborough. N Yor 2F 93
Eggbuckland. Plym 3A 8
Eggesford. Devn 1G 11
Eggington. C Beds 3H 51
Egginton. Derbs 3G 73
Egglescliffe. Stoc T 3B 106
Eggleston. Dur 2C 104
Egham. Surr 3B 38
Egham Hythe. Surr 3B 38
Egleton. Rut 5F 75
Eglingham. Nmbd 3F 121
Eglinton. Derr 1A 174
Eglish. M Ulst 4B 178
Egloshayle. Corn 5A 10
Egloskerry. Corn 4C 10
Eglwysbach. Cnwy 3H 81
Eglwys-Brewis. V Glam 5D 32
Eglwys Fach. Cdgn 1F 57
Eglwyswrw. Pemb 1F 43
Egmanton. Notts 4E 87
Egmere. Norf 2B 78
Egremont. Cumb 3B 102
Egremont. Mers 1F 83
Egton. N Yor 4F 107
Egton Bridge. N Yor 4F 107
Egypt. Buck 2A 38
Egypt. Hants 2C 24
Eight Ash Green. Essx 3C 54
Eight Mile Burn. Midl 4E 129
Eignaig. High 4B 140
Eilanreach. High 2G 147
Eildon. Bord 1H 119
Eileanach Lodge. High 2H 157
Eilean Fhlodaigh. W Isl 3D 170
Eilean Iarmain. High 2F 147
Einacleit. W Isl 5D 171
Eisgein. W Isl 6F 171
Eisingrug. Gwyn 2F 69
Elan Village. Powy 4B 58
Elberton. S Glo 3B 34
Elbridge. W Sus 5A 26
Elburton. Plym 3B 8
Elcho. Per 1D 136
Elcombe. Swin 3G 35
Elcot. W Ber 5B 36
Eldernell. Cambs 1C 64
Eldersfield. Worc 2D 48
Elderslie. Ren 3F 127
Elder Street. Essx 2F 53
Eldon. Dur 2F 105
Eldroth. N Yor 3G 97
Eldwick. W Yor 5D 98
Elfhowe. Cumb 5F 103
Elford. Nmbd 1F 121
Elford. Staf 4F 73
Elford Closes. Cambs 3D 65
Elgin. Mor 2G 159
Elgol. High 2D 146
Elham. Kent 1F 29
Elie. Fife 3G 137
Eling. Hants 1B 16
Eling. W Ber 4D 36
Elishaw. Nmbd 5C 120
Elizafield. Dum 2B 112
Elkesley. Notts 3D 86
Elkington. Nptn 3D 62
Elkins Green. Essx 5G 53
Elkstone. Glos 4E 49
Ellan. High 1C 150
Elland. W Yor 2B 92
Ellary. Arg 2F 125
Ellastone. Staf 1F 73
Ellbridge. Corn 2A 8
Ellel. Lanc 4D 97
Ellemford. Bord 3D 130
Ellenabeich. Arg 2E 133
Ellenborough. Cumb 1B 102
Ellenbrook. Herts 5C 52
Ellenhall. Staf 3C 72
Ellen's Green. Surr 2B 26
Ellerbeck. N Yor 5B 106
Ellerburn. N Yor 1C 100
Ellerby. N Yor 3E 107
Ellerdine. Telf 3A 72
Ellerdine Heath. Telf 3A 72
Ellerhayes. Devn 2C 12
Elleric. Arg 4E 141
Ellerker. E Yor 2C 94
Ellerton. E Yor 1H 93
Ellerton. Shrp 3B 72
Ellerton-on-Swale. N Yor 5F 105
Ellesborough. Buck 5G 51
Ellesmere. Shrp 2F 71
Ellesmere Port. Ches W 3G 83
Ellingham. Hants 2G 15
Ellingham. Norf 1F 67
Ellingham. Nmbd 2F 121
Ellingstring. N Yor 1D 98
Ellington. Cambs 3A 64
Ellington. Nmbd 5G 121
Ellington Thorpe. Cambs 3A 64
Elliot. Ang 5F 145
Ellisfield. Hants 2E 25
Ellishadder. High 2E 155
Ellistown. Leics 4B 74
Ellon. Abers 5G 161
Ellonby. Cumb 1F 103
Ellough. Suff 2G 67
Elloughton. E Yor 2C 94
Ellwood. Glos 5A 48
Elm. Cambs 5D 76
Elmbridge. Glos 4D 48
Elmbridge. Worc 4D 60
Elmdon. Essx 2E 53
Elmdon. W Mid 2F 61
Elmdon Heath. W Mid 2F 61
Elmesthorpe. Leics 1B 62
Elmfield. IOW 3E 16
Elm Hill. Dors 4D 22
Elmhurst. Staf 4F 73
Elmley Castle. Worc 1E 49
Elmley Lovett. Worc 4C 60
Elmore. Glos 4C 48
Elmore Back. Glos 4C 48
Elm Park. G Lon 2G 39
Elmscott. Devn 4C 18
Elmsett. Suff 1D 54
Elmstead. Essx 3D 54
Elmstead Heath. Essx 3D 54
Elmstead Market. Essx 3D 54
Elmsted. Kent 1F 29
Elmstone. Kent 4G 41
Elmstone Hardwicke. Glos 3E 49
Elmswell. E Yor 4D 101
Elmswell. Suff 4B 66
Elmton. Derbs 3C 86
Elphin. High 2G 163
Elphinstone. E Lot 2G 129
Elrick. Abers 3F 153
Elrick. Mor 1B 152
Elrig. Dum 5A 110
Elsdon. Nmbd 5D 120
Elsecar. S Yor 1A 86
Elsenham. Essx 3F 53
Elsfield. Oxon 4D 50
Elsham. N Lin 3D 94
Elsing. Norf 4C 78
Elslack. N Yor 5B 98
Elsrickle. S Lan 5D 128
Elstead. Surr 1A 26
Elsted. W Sus 1G 17
Elsted Marsh. W Sus 4G 25
Elsthorpe. Linc 3H 75
Elstob. Dur 2A 106
Elston. Devn 2A 12
Elston. Lanc 1E 90
Elston. Notts 1E 75
Elston. Wilts 2F 23
Elstone. Devn 1G 11
Elstow. Bed 1A 52
Elstree. Herts 1C 38
Elstronwick. E Yor 1F 95
Elswick. Lanc 1C 90
Elswick. Tyne 3F 115
Elsworth. Cambs 4C 64
Elterwater. Cumb 4E 103
Eltham. G Lon 3F 39
Eltisley. Cambs 5B 64
Elton. Cambs 1H 63
Elton. Ches W 3G 83
Elton. Derbs 4G 85
Elton. Glos 4C 48
Elton. G Man 3F 91
Elton. Here 3G 59
Elton. Notts 2E 75
Elton. Stoc T 3B 106
Elton Green. Ches W 3G 83
Eltringham. Nmbd 3D 115
Elvanfoot. S Lan 3B 118
Elvaston. Derbs 2B 74
Elveden. Suff 3H 65
Elvetham Heath. Hants 1F 25
Elvingston. E Lot 2A 130
Elvington. Kent 5G 41
Elvington. York 5B 100
Elwick. Hart 1B 106
Elwick. Nmbd 1F 121
Elworth. Ches E 4B 84
Elworth. Dors 4A 14
Elworthy. Som 3D 20
Ely. Cambs 2E 65
Ely. Card 4E 33
Emberton. Mil 1G 51
Embleton. Cumb 1C 102
Embleton. Hart 2B 106
Embleton. Nmbd 2G 121
Embo. High 4F 165
Emborough. Som 1B 22
Embo Street. High 4F 165
Embsay. N Yor 4C 98
Emery Down. Hants 2A 16
Emley. W Yor 3C 92
Emmbrook. Wok 5F 37
Emmer Green. Read 4F 37
Emmington. Oxon 5F 51
Emneth. Norf 5D 77
Emneth Hungate. Norf 5E 77
Empingham. Rut 5G 75
Empshott. Hants 3F 25
Emsworth. Hants 2F 17
Enborne. W Ber 5C 36
Enborne Row. W Ber 5C 36
Enchmarsh. Shrp 1H 59
Enderby. Leics 1C 62
Endmoor. Cumb 1E 97
Endon. Staf 5D 84
Endon Bank. Staf 5D 84
Enfield. G Lon 1E 39
Enfield Wash. G Lon 1E 39
Enford. Wilts 1G 23
Engine Common. S Glo 3B 34
Englefield. W Ber 4E 37
Englefield Green. Surr 3A 38
Englesea-brook. Ches E 5B 84
English Bicknor. Glos 4A 48
Englishcombe. Bath 5C 34
English Frankton. Shrp 3G 71
Enham Alamein. Hants 2B 24
Enmore. Som 3F 21
Ennerdale Bridge. Cumb 3B 102
Enniscaven. Corn 3D 6
Enniskillen. Ferm 8E 176
Enoch. Dum 4A 118
Enochdhu. Per 2H 143
Ensay. Arg 4E 139
Ensbury. Bour 3F 15
Ensdon. Shrp 4G 71
Ensis. Devn 4F 19
Enson. Staf 3D 72
Enstone. Oxon 3B 50
Enterkinfoot. Dum 4A 118
Enville. Staf 2C 60
Eolaigearraidh. W Isl 8C 170
Eorabus. Arg 1A 132
Eoropaidh. W Isl 1H 171
Epney. Glos 4C 48
Epperstone. Notts 1D 74
Epping. Essx 5E 53
Epping Green. Essx 5E 53
Epping Green. Herts 5C 52
Epping Upland. Essx 5E 53
Eppleby. N Yor 3E 105
Eppleworth. E Yor 1D 94
Epsom. Surr 4D 38
Epwell. Oxon 1B 50
Epworth. N Lin 4A 94
Epworth Turbary. N Lin 4A 94
Erbistock. Wrex 1F 71
Erbusaig. High 1F 147
Erchless Castle. High 4G 157
Erdington. W Mid 1F 61
Eredine. Arg 3G 133
Erganagh. Derr 4E 176
Eriboll. High 3E 167
Ericstane. Dum 3C 118
Eridge Green. E Sus 2G 27
Erines. Arg 2G 125
Eriswell. Suff 3G 65
Erith. G Lon 3G 39
Erlestoke. Wilts 1E 23
Ermine. Linc 3G 87
Ermington. Devn 3C 8
Ernesettle. Plym 3A 8
Erpingham. Norf 2D 78
Erriott Wood. Kent 5D 40
Errogie. High 1H 149
Errol. Per 1E 137
Errol Station. Per 1E 137
Erskine. Ren 2F 127
Erskine Bridge. Ren 2F 127
Ervie. Dum 3F 109
Erwarton. Suff 2F 55
Erwood. Powy 1D 46
Eryholme. N Yor 4A 106
Eryrys. Den 5E 82
Escalls. Corn 4A 4
Escomb. Dur 1E 105
Escrick. N Yor 5A 100
Esgair. Carm
  nr. Carmarthen 3D 45
  nr. St Clears 3G 43
Esgairgeiliog. Powy 5G 69
Esh. Dur 5E 115
Esher. Surr 4C 38
Esholt. W Yor 5D 98
Eshott. Nmbd 5G 121
Eshton. N Yor 4B 98
Esh Winning. Dur 5E 115
Eskadale. High 5G 157
Eskbank. Midl 3G 129
Eskdale Green. Cumb 4C 102
Eskdalemuir. Dum 5E 119
Eskham. Linc 1C 88
Esknish. Arg 3B 124
Esk Valley. N Yor 4F 107
Eslington Hall. Nmbd 3E 121
Esprick. Lanc 1C 90
Essendine. Rut 4H 75
Essendon. Herts 5C 52
Essich. High 5A 158
Essington. Staf 5D 72
Eston. Red C 3C 106
Estover. Plym 3B 8
Eswick. Shet 6F 173
Etal. Nmbd 1D 120
Etchilhampton. Wilts 5F 35
Etchingham. E Sus 3B 28
Etchinghill. Kent 2F 29
Etchinghill. Staf 4E 73
Etherley Dene. Dur 2E 105
Ethie Haven. Ang 4F 145
Etling Green. Norf 4C 78
Etloe. Glos 5B 48
Eton. Wind 3A 38
Eton Wick. Wind 3A 38
Etteridge. High 4A 150
Ettersgill. Dur 2B 104
Ettiley Heath. Ches E 4B 84
Ettington. Warw 1A 50
Etton. E Yor 5D 101
Etton. Pet 5A 76
Ettrick. Bord 3E 119
Ettrickbridge. Bord 2F 119
Etwall. Derbs 2G 73
Eudon Burnell. Shrp 2B 60
Eudon George. Shrp 2A 60
Euston. Suff 3A 66
Euxton. Lanc 3D 90
Evanstown. B'end 3C 32
Evanton. High 2A 158
Evedon. Linc 1H 75
Evelix. High 4E 165
Evendine. Here 1C 48
Evenjobb. Powy 4E 59
Evenley. Nptn 2D 50
Evenlode. Glos 3H 49
Even Swindon. Swin 3G 35
Evenwood. Dur 2E 105
Evenwood Gate. Dur 2E 105
Everbay. Orkn 5F 172
Evercreech. Som 3B 22
Everdon. Nptn 5C 62
Everingham. E Yor 5C 100
Everleigh. Wilts 1H 23
Everley. N Yor 1D 100
Eversholt. C Beds 2H 51
Evershot. Dors 2A 14
Eversley. Hants 5F 37
Eversley Centre. Hants 5F 37
Eversley Cross. Hants 5F 37
Everthorpe. E Yor 1C 94
Everton. C Beds 5B 64
Everton. Hants 3A 16
Everton. Mers 1F 83
Everton. Notts 1D 86
Evertown. Dum 2E 113
Evesbatch. Here 1B 48
Evesham. Worc 1F 49
Evington. Leic 5D 74
Ewden Village. S Yor 1G 85
Ewdness. Shrp 1B 60
Ewell. Surr 4D 38
Ewell Minnis. Kent 1G 29
Ewelme. Oxon 2E 37
Ewen. Glos 2F 35
Ewenny. V Glam 4C 32
Ewerby. Linc 1A 76
Ewes. Dum 5F 119
Ewesley. Nmbd 5E 121
Ewhurst. Surr 1B 26
Ewhurst Green. E Sus 3B 28
Ewhurst Green. Surr 2B 26
Ewlo. Flin 4E 83
Ewloe. Flin 4E 83
Ewood Bridge. Lanc 2F 91
Eworthy. Devn 3E 11
Ewshot. Hants 1G 25
Ewyas Harold. Here 3G 47
Exbourne. Devn 2G 11
Exbury. Hants 2C 16
Exceat. E Sus 5G 27
Exebridge. Som 4C 20
Exelby. N Yor 1E 99
Exeter. Devn 195 (3C 12)
Exeter Airport. Devn 3D 12
Exford. Som 3B 20
Exfords Green. Shrp 5G 71
Exhall. Warw 5F 61
Exlade Street. Oxon 3E 37
Exminster. Devn 4C 12
Exmouth. Devn 4D 12
Exnaboe. Shet 10E 173
Exning. Suff 4F 65
Exton. Devn 4C 12
Exton. Hants 4E 24
Exton. Rut 4G 75
Exton. Som 3C 20
Exwick. Devn 3C 12
Eyam. Derbs 3G 85
Eydon. Nptn 5C 62
Eye. Here 4G 59
Eye. Pet 5B 76
Eye. Suff 3D 66
Eye Green. Pet 5B 76
Eyemouth. Bord 3F 131
Eyeworth. C Beds 1C 52
Eyhorne Street. Kent 5C 40
Eyke. Suff 5F 67
Eynesbury. Cambs 5A 64
Eynort. High 1B 146
Eynsford. Kent 4G 39
Eynsham. Oxon 5C 50
Eyre. High
  on Isle of Skye 3D 154
  on Raasay 5E 155
Eythorne. Kent 1G 29
Eyton. Here 4G 59
Eyton. Shrp
  nr. Bishop's Castle 2F 59
  nr. Shrewsbury 4F 71
Eyton. Wrex 1F 71
Eyton on Severn. Shrp 5H 71
Eyton upon the Weald Moors. Telf 4A 72

F

Faccombe. Hants 1B 24
Faceby. N Yor 4B 106
Faddiley. Ches E 5H 83
Fadmoor. N Yor 1A 100
Fagwyr. Swan 5G 45
Faichem. High 3E 149
Faifley. W Dun 2G 127
Fail. S Ayr 2D 116
Failand. N Som 4A 34
Failford. S Ayr 2D 116
Failsworth. G Man 4H 91
Fairbourne. Gwyn 4F 69
Fairbourne Heath. Kent 5C 40
Fairburn. N Yor 2E 93
Fairfield. Derbs 3E 85
Fairfield. Kent 3D 28
Fairfield. Worc
  nr. Bromsgrove 3D 60
  nr. Evesham 1F 49
Fairford. Glos 5G 49
Fair Green. Norf 4F 77
Fair Hill. Cumb 1G 103
Fairhill. S Lan 4A 128
Fair Isle Airport. Shet 1B 172
Fairlands. Surr 5A 38
Fairlie. N Ayr 4D 126
Fairlight. E Sus 4C 28
Fairlight Cove. E Sus 4C 28
Fairmile. Devn 3D 12
Fairmile. Surr 4C 38
Fairmilehead. Edin 3F 129
Fair Oak. Devn 1D 12
Fair Oak. Hants
  nr. Eastleigh 1C 16
  nr. Kingsclere 5D 36
Fairoak. Staf 2B 72
Fair Oak Green. Hants 5E 37
Fairseat. Kent 4H 39
Fairstead. Essx 4A 54
Fairstead. Norf 4F 77
Fairwarp. E Sus 3F 27
Fairwater. Card 4E 33
Fairy Cross. Devn 4E 19
Fakenham. Norf 2B 78
Fakenham Magna. Suff 3B 66
Fala. Midl 3H 129
Fala Dam. Midl 3H 129
Falcon. Here 2B 48
Faldingworth. Linc 2H 87
Falfield. S Glo 2B 34
Y Fali. IOA 3B 80
Falkenham. Suff 2F 55
Falkirk. Falk 1B 128
Falkland. Fife 3E 137
Fallin. Stir 4H 135
Fallowfield. G Man 1C 84
Falmer. E Sus 5E 27
Falmouth. Corn 5C 6
Falsgrave. N Yor 1E 101
Falstone. Nmbd 1A 114
Fanagmore. High 4B 166
Fancott. C Beds 3A 52
Fanellan. High 4G 157
Fangdale Beck. N Yor 5C 106
Fangfoss. E Yor 4B 100
Fankerton. Falk 1A 128
Fanmore. Arg 4F 139
Fanner's Green. Essx 4G 53
Fannich Lodge. High 2E 156
Fans. Bord 5C 130
Farcet. Cambs 1B 64
Far Cotton. Nptn 5E 63
Fareham. Hants 2D 16
Farewell. Staf 4E 73
Far Forest. Worc 3B 60
Farforth. Linc 3C 88
Far Green. Glos 5C 48
Far Hoarcross. Staf 3F 73
Faringdon. Oxon 2A 36
Farington. Lanc 2D 90
Farlam. Cumb 4G 113
Farleigh. N Som 5H 33
Farleigh. Surr 4E 39
Farleigh Hungerford. Som 1D 22
Farleigh Wallop. Hants 2E 24
Farleigh Wick. Wilts 5D 34
Farlesthorpe. Linc 3D 88
Farleton. Cumb 1E 97
Farleton. Lanc 3E 97
Farley. High 4G 157
Farley. Shrp
  nr. Shrewsbury 5F 71
  nr. Telford 5A 72
Farley. Staf 1E 73
Farley. Wilts 4H 23
Farley Green. Suff 5G 65
Farley Green. Surr 1B 26
Farley Hill. Wok 5F 37
Farley's End. Glos 4C 48
Farlington. N Yor 3A 100
Farlington. Port 2E 17
Farlow. Shrp 2A 60
Farmborough. Bath 5B 34
Farmcote. Glos 3F 49
Farmcote. Shrp 1B 60
Farmington. Glos 4G 49
Far Moor. G Man 4D 90
Farmoor. Oxon 5C 50
Farmtown. Mor 3C 160
Farnah Green. Derbs 1H 73
Farnborough. G Lon 4F 39
Farnborough. Hants 1G 25
Farnborough. Warw 1C 50
Farnborough. W Ber 3C 36
Farncombe. Surr 1A 26
Farndish. Bed 4G 63
Farndon. Ches W 5G 83
Farndon. Notts 5E 87
Farnell. Ang 3F 145
Farnham. Dors 1E 15
Farnham. Essx 3E 53
Farnham. N Yor 3F 99
Farnham. Suff 4F 67
Farnham. Surr 2G 25
Farnham Common. Buck 2A 38
Farnham Green. Essx 3E 53
Farnham Royal. Buck 2A 38
Farnhill. N Yor 5C 98
Farningham. Kent 4G 39
Farnley. N Yor 5E 98
Farnley Tyas. W Yor 3B 92
Farnsfield. Notts 5D 86
Farnworth. G Man 4F 91
Farnworth. Hal 2H 83
Far Oakridge. Glos 5E 49
Farr. High
  nr. Bettyhill 2H 167
  nr. Inverness 5A 158
  nr. Kingussie 3C 150
Farraline. High 1H 149
Farringdon. Devn 3D 12
Farrington. Dors 1D 14
Farrington Gurney. Bath 1B 22
Far Sawrey. Cumb 5E 103
Farsley. W Yor 1C 92
Farthinghoe. Nptn 2D 50
Farthingstone. Nptn 5D 62
Farthorpe. Linc 3B 88
Fartown. W Yor 3B 92
Farway. Devn 3E 13
Fasag. High 3A 156
Fascadale. High 1G 139
Fasnacloich. Arg 4E 141
Fassfern. High 1E 141
Fatfield. Tyne 4G 115
Faugh. Cumb 4G 113
Fauld. Staf 3F 73
Fauldhouse. W Lot 3C 128
Faulkbourne. Essx 4A 54
Faulkland. Som 1C 22
Fauls. Shrp 2H 71
Faverdale. Darl 3F 105
Faversham. Kent 4E 40
Fawdington. N Yor 2G 99
Fawfieldhead. Staf 4E 85
Fawkham Green. Kent 4G 39
Fawler. Oxon 4B 50
Fawley. Buck 3F 37
Fawley. Hants 2C 16
Fawley. W Ber 3B 36
Fawley Chapel. Here 3A 48
Fawton. Corn 2F 7
Faxfleet. E Yor 2B 94
Faygate. W Sus 2D 26
Fazakerley. Mers 1F 83
Fazeley. Staf 5F 73
Feagour. High 4H 149
Fearann Dhomhnaill. High 3E 147
Fearby. N Yor 1D 98
Fearn. High 1C 158
Fearnan. Per 4E 142
Fearnbeg. High 3G 155
Fearnhead. Warr 1A 84
Fearnmore. High 2G 155
Featherstone. Staf 5D 72
Featherstone. W Yor 2E 93
Featherstone Castle. Nmbd 3H 113
Feckenham. Worc 4E 61
Feering. Essx 3B 54
Feetham. N Yor 5C 104
Feizor. N Yor 3G 97
Felbridge. Surr 2E 27
Felbrigg. Norf 2E 78
Felcourt. Surr 1E 27
Felden. Herts 5A 52
Felhampton. Shrp 2G 59
Felindre. Carm
  nr. Llandeilo 3F 45
  nr. Llandovery 2G 45
  nr. Newcastle Emlyn 2D 44
Felindre. Powy 2D 58
Felindre. Swan 5G 45
Felindre Farchog. Pemb 1F 43
Felinfach. Cdgn 5E 57
Felinfach. Powy 2D 46
Felinfoel. Carm 5F 45
Felingwmisaf. Carm 3F 45
Felingwmuchaf. Carm 3F 45
Y Felinheli. Gwyn 4E 81
Felin Newydd. Powy
  nr. Newtown 5C 70
  nr. Oswestry 3E 70
Felin Wnda. Cdgn 1D 44
Felinwynt. Cdgn 5B 56
Felixkirk. N Yor 1G 99
Felixstowe. Suff 2F 55
Felixstowe Ferry. Suff 2G 55
Felkington. Nmbd 5F 131
Fell End. Cumb 5A 104
Felling. Tyne 3F 115
Fell Side. Cumb 1E 102
Felmersham. Bed 5G 63
Felmingham. Norf 3E 79
Felpham. W Sus 3H 17
Felsham. Suff 5B 66
Felsted. Essx 3G 53
Feltham. G Lon 3C 38
Felthamhill. Surr 3B 38
Felthorpe. Norf 4D 78
Felton. Here 1A 48
Felton. N Som 5A 34
Felton. Nmbd 4F 121
Felton Butler. Shrp 4F 71
Feltwell. Norf 1G 65
Fenay Bridge. W Yor 3B 92
Fence. Lanc 1G 91
Fence Houses. Tyne 4G 115
Fencott. Oxon 4D 50
Fen Ditton. Cambs 4D 65
Fen Drayton. Cambs 4C 64
Fen End. Linc 3B 76
Fen End. W Mid 3G 61
Fenham. Nmbd 5G 131
Fenham. Tyne 3F 115
Fenhouses. Linc 1B 76
Feniscowles. Bkbn 2E 91
Feniton. Devn 3D 12
Fenn Green. Shrp 2B 60
Y Fenni. Mon 4G 47
Fenn's Bank. Wrex 2H 71
Fenn Street. Medw 3B 40
Fenny Bentley. Derbs 5F 85
Fenny Bridges. Devn 3E 12
Fenny Compton. Warw 5B 62
Fenny Drayton. Leics 1H 61
Fenny Stratford. Mil 2G 51
Fenrother. Nmbd 5F 121
Fenstanton. Cambs 4C 64
Fen Street. Norf 1C 66
Fenton. Cambs 3C 64
Fenton. Cumb 4G 113
Fenton. Linc
  nr. Caythorpe 5F 87
  nr. Saxilby 3F 87
Fenton. Nmbd 1D 120
Fenton. Notts 2E 87
Fenton. Stoke 1C 72
Fentonadle. Corn 5A 10
Fenton Barns. E Lot 1B 130
Fenwick. E Ayr 5F 127
Fenwick. Nmbd
  nr. Berwick-upon-Tweed 5G 131
  nr. Hexham 2D 114
Fenwick. S Yor 3F 93
Feochaig. Arg 4B 122
Feock. Corn 5C 6
Feolin Ferry. Arg 3C 124
Feorlan. Arg 5A 122
Ferindonald. High 3E 147
Feriniquarrie. High 3A 154
Fern. Ang 2D 145
Ferndale. Rhon 2C 32
Ferndown. Dors 2F 15
Ferness. High 4D 158
Fernham. Oxon 2A 36
Fernhill. W Sus 1E 27
Fernhill Heath. Worc 5C 60
Fernhurst. W Sus 4G 25
Fernieflatt. Abers 1H 145
Ferniegair. S Lan 4A 128
Fernilea. High 5C 154
Fernilee. Derbs 3E 85
Ferrensby. N Yor 3F 99
Ferriby Sluice. N Lin 2C 94
Ferring. W Sus 5B 26
Ferrybridge. W Yor 2E 93
Ferryden. Ang 3G 145
Ferry Hill. Cambs 2C 64
Ferryhill. Aber 3G 153
Ferryhill. Dur 1F 105
Ferryhill Station. Dur 1A 106
Ferryside. Carm 4D 44
Ferryton. High 2A 158
Fersfield. Norf 2C 66
Fersit. High 1A 142
Y Ferwig. Cdgn 1B 44
Feshiebridge. High 3C 150
Fetcham. Surr 5C 38
Fetterangus. Abers 3G 161
Fettercairn. Abers 1F 145
Fewcott. Oxon 3D 50
Fewston. N Yor 4D 98
Ffairfach. Carm 3G 45
Ffair Rhos. Cdgn 4G 57
Ffaldybrenin. Carm 1G 45
Ffarmers. Carm 1G 45
Ffawyddog. Powy 4F 47
Y Fflint. Flin 3E 83
Ffodun. Powy 5E 71
Ffont-y-gari. V Glam 5D 32
Y Ffor. Gwyn 2C 68
Fforest. Carm 5F 45
Fforest-fach. Swan 3F 31
Fforest Goch. Neat 5H 45
Ffostrasol. Cdgn 1D 44
Ffos-y-ffin. Cdgn 4D 56
Ffrith. Flin 5E 83
Ffwl-y-mwn. V Glam 5D 32
Ffynnon-ddrain. Carm 3E 45
Ffynnongroyw. Flin 2D 82
Ffynnon Gynydd. Powy 1E 47
Ffynnon-oer. Cdgn 5E 57
Fiag Lodge. High 1B 164
Fidden. Arg 2B 132
Fiddington. Glos 2E 49
Fiddington. Som 2F 21
Fiddleford. Dors 1D 14
Fiddlers Hamlet. Essx 5E 53
Field. Staf 2E 73
Field Assarts. Oxon 4B 50
Field Broughton. Cumb 1C 96
Field Dalling. Norf 2C 78
Field Head. Leics 5B 74
Fieldhead. Cumb 1F 103
Fifehead Magdalen. Dors 4C 22
Fifehead Neville. Dors 1C 14
Fifehead St Quintin. Dors 1C 14
Fife Keith. Mor 3B 160
Fifield. Oxon 4H 49
Fifield. Wilts 1G 23
Fifield. Wind 3A 38
Fifield Bavant. Wilts 4F 23
Figheldean. Wilts 2G 23
Filby. Norf 4G 79
Filey. N Yor 1F 101
Filford. Dors 3H 13
Filgrave. Mil 1G 51
Filkins. Oxon 5H 49
Filleigh. Devn
  nr. Crediton 1H 11
  nr. South Molton 4G 19
Fillingham. Linc 2G 87
Fillongley. Warw 2G 61
Filton. S Glo 4B 34
Fimber. E Yor 3C 100
Finavon. Ang 3D 145
Fincham. Norf 5F 77
Finchampstead. Wok 5F 37
Fincharn. Arg 3G 133
Finchdean. Hants 1F 17
Finchingfield. Essx 2G 53
Finchley. G Lon 1D 38
Findern. Derbs 2H 73
Findhorn. Mor 2E 159
Findhorn Bridge. High 1C 150
Findochty. Mor 2B 160
Findo Gask. Per 1C 136
Findon. Abers 4G 153
Findon. W Sus 5C 26
Findon Mains. High 2A 158
Findon Valley. W Sus 5C 26
Finedon. Nptn 3G 63
Fingal Street. Suff 3E 66
Fingest. Buck 2F 37
Finghall. N Yor 1D 98
Fingland. Cumb 4D 112
Fingland. Dum 3G 117
Finglesham. Kent 5H 41
Fingringhoe. Essx 3D 54
Finiskaig. High 4A 148
Finmere. Oxon 2E 51
Finnart. Per 3C 142
Finningham. Suff 4C 66
Finningley. S Yor 1D 86
Finnygaud. Abers 3D 160
Finsbury. G Lon 2E 39
Finstall. Worc 4D 61
Finsthwaite. Cumb 1C 96
Finstock. Oxon 4B 50
Finstown. Orkn 6C 172
Fintona. Ferm 3K 177
Fintry. Abers 3E 161
Fintry. D'dee 5D 144
Fintry. Stir 1H 127
Finvoy. Caus 5F 175
Finwood. Warw 4F 61
Finzean. Abers 4D 152
Fionnphort. Arg 2B 132
Fionnsabhagh. W Isl 9C 171
Firbeck. S Yor 2C 86
Firby. N Yor
  nr. Bedale 1E 99
  nr. Malton 3B 100
Firgrove. G Man 3H 91
Firle. E Sus 5F 27
Firsby. Linc 4D 88
Firsdown. Wilts 3H 23
First Coast. High 4D 162
Firth. Shet 4F 173
Fir Tree. Dur 1E 105
Fishbourne. IOW 3D 16
Fishbourne. W Sus 2G 17
Fishburn. Dur 1A 106
Fishcross. Clac 4A 136
Fisherford. Abers 5D 160
Fisherrow. E Lot 2G 129
Fisher's Pond. Hants 4C 24
Fisher's Row. Lanc 5D 96
Fisherstreet. W Sus 2A 26
Fisherton. High 3B 158
Fisherton. S Ayr 3B 116
Fisherton de la Mere. Wilts 3E 23
Fishguard. Pemb 1D 42
Fishlake. S Yor 3G 93
Fishley. Norf 4G 79
Fishnish. Arg 4A 140
Fishpond Bottom. Dors 3G 13
Fishponds. Bris 4B 34
Fishpool. Glos 3B 48
Fishpool. G Man 3G 91
Fishpools. Powy 4D 58
Fishtoft. Linc 1C 76
Fishtoft Drove. Linc 1C 76
Fishwick. Bord 4F 131
Fiskavaig. High 5C 154
Fiskerton. Linc 3H 87

Fiskerton—Glenancross

Fiskerton. *Notts* 5E 87
Fitch. *Shet* 7E 173
Fitling. *E Yor* 1F 95
Fittleton. *Wilts* 2G 23
Fittleworth. *W Sus* 4B 26
Fitton End. *Cambs* 4D 76
Fitz. *Shrp* 4G 71
Fitzhead. *Som* 4E 20
Fitzwilliam. *W Yor* 3E 93
Fiunary. *High* 4A 140
Five Ash Down. *E Sus* 3F 27
Five Ashes. *E Sus* 3G 27
Five Bells. *Som* 2D 20
Five Bridges. *Here* 1B 48
Fivehead. *Som* 4G 21
Fivelanes. *Corn* 4C 10
Fivemiletown. *M Ulst* 5K 177
Five Oak Green. *Kent* 1H 27
Five Oaks. *W Sus* 3B 26
Five Roads. *Carm* 5E 45
Five Ways. *Warw* 3G 61
Flack's Green. *Essx* 4A 54
Flackwell Heath. *Buck* 3G 37
Fladbury. *Worc* 1E 49
Fladda. *Shet* 3E 173
Fladdabister. *Shet* 8F 173
Flagg. *Derbs* 4F 85
Flamborough. *E Yor* 2G 101
Flamstead. *Herts* 4A 52
Flansham. *W Sus* 5A 26
Flasby. *N Yor* 4B 98
Flash. *Staf* 4E 85
Flashader. *High* 3C 154
The Flatt. *Cumb* 2G 113
Flaunden. *Herts* 5A 52
Flawborough. *Notts* 1E 75
Flawith. *N Yor* 3G 99
Flax Bourton. *N Som* 5A 34
Flaxby. *N Yor* 4F 99
Flaxholme. *Derbs* 1H 73
Flaxley. *Glos* 4B 48
Flaxley Green. *Staf* 4E 73
Flaxpool. *Som* 3E 21
Flaxton. *N Yor* 3A 100
Fleck. *Shet* 10E 173
Fleckney. *Leics* 1D 62
Flecknoe. *Warw* 4C 62
Fledborough. *Notts* 3F 87
Fleet. *Dors* 4B 14
Fleet. *Hants*
nr. Farnborough 1G 25
Fleet. *Hants*
nr. South Hayling 2F 17
Fleet. *Linc* 3C 76
Fleet Hargate. *Linc* 3C 76
Fleetville. *Herts* 5B 52
Fleetwood. *Lanc* 5C 96
Fleggburgh. *Norf* 4G 79
Fleisirin. *W Isl* 4H 171
Flemingston. *V Glam* 5D 32
Flemington. *S Lan*
nr. Glasgow 3H 127
nr. Strathaven 5A 128
Flempton. *Suff* 4H 65
Fleoideabhagh. *W Isl* 9C 171
Fletcher's Green. *Kent* 1G 27
Fletchertown. *Cumb* 5D 112
Fletching. *E Sus* 3F 27
Fleuchary. *High* 4E 165
Flexbury. *Corn* 2C 10
Flexford. *Surr* 1A 26
Flimby. *Cumb* 1B 102
Flimwell. *E Sus* 2B 28
Flint. *Flin* 3E 83
Flintham. *Notts* 1E 75
Flint Mountain. *Flin* 3E 83
Flinton. *E Yor* 1F 95
Flintsham. *Here* 5F 59
Flishinghurst. *Kent* 2B 28
Flitcham. *Norf* 3G 77
Flitton. *C Beds* 2A 52
Flitwick. *C Beds* 2A 52
Flixborough. *N Lin* 3B 94
Flixton. *G Man* 1B 84
Flixton. *N Yor* 2E 101
Flixton. *Suff* 2F 67
Flockton. *W Yor* 3C 92
Flodden. *Nmbd* 1D 120
Flodigarry. *High* 1D 154
Flood's Ferry. *Cambs* 1C 64
Flookburgh. *Cumb* 2C 96
Flordon. *Norf* 1D 66
Flore. *Nptn* 4D 62
Flotterton. *Nmbd* 4D 121
Flowton. *Suff* 1D 54
Flushing. *Abers* 4H 161
Flushing. *Corn* 5C 6
Fluxton. *Devn* 3D 12
Flyford Flavell. *Worc* 5D 61
Fobbing. *Thur* 2B 40
Fochabers. *Mor* 3H 159
Fochriw. *Cphy* 5E 46
Fockerby. *N Lin* 3B 94
Fodderty. *High* 3H 157
Foddington. *Som* 4A 22
Foel. *Powy* 4B 70
Foffarty. *Ang* 4D 144
Foggathorpe. *E Yor* 1A 94
Fogo. *Bord* 5D 130
Fogorig. *Bord* 5D 130
Foindle. *High* 4B 166
Folda. *Ang* 2A 144
Fole. *Staf* 2E 73
Foleshill. *W Mid* 2A 62
Foley Park. *Worc* 3C 60
Folke. *Dors* 1B 14
Folkestone. *Kent* 195 (2G 29)
Folkingham. *Linc* 2H 75
Folkington. *E Sus* 5G 27
Folksworth. *Cambs* 2A 64
Folkton. *N Yor* 2E 101
Folla Rule. *Abers* 5E 161
Follifoot. *N Yor* 4F 99
The Folly. *Herts* 4B 52
Folly Cross. *Devn* 2E 11
Folly Gate. *Devn* 3F 11
Fonmon. *V Glam* 5D 32
Fonthill Bishop. *Wilts* 3E 23
Fonthill Gifford. *Wilts* 3E 23
Fontmell Magna. *Dors* 1D 14
Fontwell. *W Sus* 5A 26
Font-y-gary. *V Glam* 5D 32
Foodieash. *Fife* 2F 137
Foolow. *Derbs* 3F 85
Footdee. *Aber* 3G 153
Footherley. *Staf* 5F 73
Foots Cray. *G Lon* 3F 39
Forbestown. *Abers* 2A 152
Force Forge. *Cumb* 5E 103
Force Mills. *Cumb* 5E 103
Forcett. *N Yor* 3E 105
Ford. *Arg* 3F 133
Ford. *Buck* 5F 51
Ford. *Derbs* 2B 86
Ford. *Devn*
nr. Bideford 4E 19
nr. Holbeton 3C 8
nr. Salcombe 4D 9
Ford. *Glos* 3F 49
Ford. *Nmbd* 1D 120
Ford. *Plym* 3A 8
Ford. *Shrp* 4G 71
Ford. *Som*
nr. Wells 1A 22
nr. Wiveliscombe 4D 20
Ford. *Staf* 5E 85
Ford. *W Sus* 5B 26
Ford. *Wilts*
nr. Chippenham 4D 34
nr. Salisbury 3G 23
Forda. *Devn* 3E 19
Ford Barton. *Devn* 1C 12
Fordcombe. *Kent* 1G 27
Fordell. *Fife* 1E 129
Forden. *Powy* 5E 71
Ford End. *Essx* 4G 53
Forder Green. *Devn* 2D 9
Ford Green. *Lanc* 5D 97
Fordham. *Cambs* 3F 65
Fordham. *Essx* 3C 54
Fordham. *Norf* 1F 65
Fordham Heath. *Essx* 3C 54
Ford Heath. *Shrp* 4G 71
Fordhouses. *W Mid* 5D 72
Fordie. *Per* 1G 135
Fordingbridge. *Hants* 1G 15
Fordington. *Linc* 3D 88
Fordon. *E Yor* 2E 101
Fordoun. *Abers* 1G 145
Ford Street. *Essx* 3C 54
Ford Street. *Som* 1E 13
Fordton. *Devn* 3B 12
Fordwells. *Oxon* 4B 50
Fordwich. *Kent* 5F 41
Fordyce. *Abers* 2C 160
Forebridge. *Staf* 3D 72
Foreglen. *Caus* 6C 174
Foremark. *Derbs* 3H 73
Forest. *N Yor* 4F 105
Forestburn Gate. *Nmbd* 5E 121
Foresterseat. *Mor* 3F 159
Forest Green. *Glos* 2D 34
Forest Green. *Surr* 1C 26
Forest Hall. *Cumb* 4G 103
Forest Head. *Cumb* 4G 113
Forest Hill. *Oxon* 5D 50
Forest-in-Teesdale. *Dur* 2B 104
Forest Lodge. *Per* 1G 143
Forest Mill. *Clac* 4B 136
Forest Row. *E Sus* 2F 27
Forestside. *W Sus* 1F 17
Forest Town. *Notts* 4C 86
Forfar. *Ang* 3D 144
Forgandenny. *Per* 2C 136
Forge. *Powy* 1G 57
The Forge. *Here* 5F 59
Forge Side. *Torf* 5F 47
Forgewood. *N Lan* 4A 128
Forgie. *Mor* 3A 160
Forgue. *Abers* 4D 160
Forkill. *New M* 8E 178
Formby. *Mers* 4B 90
Forncett End. *Norf* 1D 66
Forncett St Mary. *Norf* 1D 66
Forncett St Peter. *Norf* 1D 66
Forneth. *Per* 4H 143
Fornham All Saints. *Suff* 4H 65
Fornham St Martin. *Suff* 4A 66
Forres. *Mor* 3E 159
Forrestfield. *N Lan* 3B 128
Forrest Lodge. *Dum* 1C 110
Forsbrook. *Staf* 1D 72
Forse. *High* 5E 169
Forsinard. *High* 4A 168
Forss. *High* 2C 168
The Forstal. *Kent* 2E 29
Forston. *Dors* 3B 14
Fort Augustus. *High* 3F 149
Forteviot. *Per* 2C 136
Fort George. *High* 3B 158
Forth. *S Lan* 4C 128
Forthampton. *Glos* 2D 48
Forthay. *Glos* 2C 34
Fortingall. *Per* 4E 143
Fort Matilda. *Inv* 2D 126
Forton. *Hants* 2C 24
Forton. *Lanc* 4D 97
Forton. *Shrp* 4G 71
Forton. *Som* 2G 13
Forton. *Staf* 3B 72
Forton Heath. *Shrp* 4G 71
Fortrie. *Abers* 4D 160
Fortrose. *High* 3B 158
Fortuneswell. *Dors* 5B 14
Fort William. *High* 1F 141
Forty Green. *Buck* 1A 38
Forty Hill. *G Lon* 1E 39
Forward Green. *Suff* 5C 66
Fosbury. *Wilts* 1B 24
Foscot. *Oxon* 3H 49
Fosdyke. *Linc* 2C 76
Foss. *Per* 3E 143
Fossebridge. *Glos* 4F 49
Foster Street. *Essx* 5E 53
Foston. *Derbs* 2F 73
Foston. *Leics* 1D 62
Foston. *Linc* 1F 75
Foston. *N Yor* 3A 100
Foston on the Wolds.
E Yor 4F 101
Fotherby. *Linc* 1C 88
Fothergill. *Cumb* 1B 102
Fotheringhay. *Nptn* 1H 63
Foubister. *Orkn* 7E 172
Foula Airport. *Shet* 8A 173
Foul Anchor. *Cambs* 4D 76
Foulbridge. *Cumb* 5F 113
Foulden. *Norf* 1G 65
Foulden. *Bord* 4F 131
Foul Mile. *E Sus* 4H 27
Foulridge. *Lanc* 5A 98
Foulsham. *Norf* 3C 78
Fountainhall. *Bord* 5H 129
The Four Alls. *Shrp* 2A 72
Four Ashes. *Staf*
nr. Cannock 5D 72
nr. Kinver 2C 60
Four Ashes. *Suff* 3C 66
Four Crosses. *Powy*
nr. Llanerfyl 5C 70
nr. Llanymynech 4E 71
Four Crosses. *Staf* 5D 72
Four Elms. *Kent* 1F 27
Four Forks. *Som* 3F 21
Four Gotes. *Cambs* 4D 76
Four Lane End. *S Yor* 4C 92
Four Lane Ends. *Lanc* 4E 97
Four Lanes. *Corn* 5A 6
Fourlanes End. *Ches E* 5C 84
Four Marks. *Hants* 3E 25
Four Mile Bridge. *IOA* 3B 80
Four Oaks. *E Sus* 3C 28
Four Oaks. *Glos* 3B 48
Four Oaks. *W Mid* 2G 61
Four Roads. *Carm* 5E 45
Four Roads. *IOM* 5B 108
Fourstones. *Nmbd* 3B 114
Four Throws. *Kent* 3B 28
Fovant. *Wilts* 4F 23
Foveran. *Abers* 1G 153
Fowey. *Corn* 3F 7
Fowlershill. *Aber* 2G 153
Fowley Common. *Warr* 1A 84
Fowlis. *Ang* 5C 144
Fowlis Wester. *Per* 1B 136
Fowlmere. *Cambs* 1E 53
Fownhope. *Here* 2A 48
Fox Corner. *Surr* 5A 38
Foxcote. *Glos* 4F 49
Foxcote. *Som* 1C 22
Foxdale. *IOM* 4B 108
Foxearth. *Essx* 1B 54
Foxfield. *Cumb* 1B 96
Foxham. *Wilts* 4E 35
Fox Hatch. *Essx* 1G 39
Foxhole. *Corn* 3D 6
Foxholes. *N Yor* 2E 101
Foxhunt Green. *E Sus* 4G 27
Fox Lane. *Hants* 1G 25
Foxley. *Norf* 3C 78
Foxley. *Nptn* 5D 62
Foxley. *Wilts* 3D 35
Foxlydiate. *Worc* 4E 61
Fox Street. *Essx* 3D 54
Foxt. *Staf* 1E 73
Foxton. *Cambs* 1E 53
Foxton. *Dur* 2A 106
Foxton. *Leics* 2D 62
Foxton. *N Yor* 5B 106
Foxup. *N Yor* 2A 98
Foxwist Green. *Ches W* 4A 84
Foxwood. *Shrp* 3A 60
Foy. *Here* 3A 48
Foyers. *High* 1G 149
Foynesfield. *High* 3C 158
Fraddam. *Corn* 3C 4
Fraddon. *Corn* 3D 6
Fradley. *Staf* 4F 73
Fradley South. *Staf* 4F 73
Fradswell. *Staf* 2D 73
Fraisthorpe. *E Yor* 3F 101
Framfield. *E Sus* 3F 27
Framingham Earl. *Norf* 5E 79
Framingham Pigot. *Norf* 5E 79
Framlingham. *Suff* 4E 67
Frampton. *Dors* 3B 14
Frampton. *Linc* 2C 76
Frampton Cotterell. *S Glo* 3B 34
Frampton Mansell. *Glos* 5E 49
Frampton on Severn. *Glos* 5C 48
Frampton West End. *Linc* 1B 76
Framsden. *Suff* 5D 66
Framwellgate Moor. *Dur* 5F 115
Franche. *Worc* 3C 60
Frandley. *Ches W* 3A 84
Frankby. *Mers* 2E 83
Frankfort. *Norf* 3F 79
Frankley. *Worc* 2D 61
Frank's Bridge. *Powy* 5D 58
Frankton. *Warw* 3B 62
Frankwell. *Shrp* 4G 71
Frant. *E Sus* 2G 27
Fraserburgh. *Abers* 2G 161
Frating Green. *Essx* 3D 54
Fratton. *Port* 2E 17
Freathy. *Corn* 3A 8
Freckenham. *Suff* 3F 65
Freckleton. *Lanc* 2C 90
Freeby. *Leics* 3F 75
Freefolk Priors. *Hants* 2C 24
Freehay. *Staf* 1E 73
Freeland. *Oxon* 4C 50
Freester. *Shet* 6F 173
Freethorpe. *Norf* 5G 79
Freiston. *Linc* 1C 76
Freiston Shore. *Linc* 1C 76
Fremington. *Devn* 3F 19
Fremington. *N Yor* 5D 104
Frenchay. *S Glo* 4B 34
Frenchbeer. *Devn* 4G 11
Frenich. *Stir* 3D 134
Frensham. *Surr* 2G 25
Frenze. *Norf* 2D 66
Fresgoe. *High* 2B 168
Freshfield. *Mers* 4A 90
Freshford. *Bath* 5C 34
Freshwater. *IOW* 4B 16
Freshwater Bay. *IOW* 4B 16
Freshwater East. *Pemb* 5E 43
Fressingfield. *Suff* 3E 67
Freston. *Suff* 2E 55
Freswick. *High* 2F 169
Fretherne. *Glos* 5C 48
Frettenham. *Norf* 4E 79
Freuchie. *Fife* 3E 137
Freystrop. *Pemb* 3D 42
Friar's Gate. *E Sus* 2F 27
Friar Waddon. *Dors* 4B 14
Friday Bridge. *Cambs* 5D 76
Friday Street. *E Sus* 5H 27
Friday Street. *Surr* 1C 26
Fridaythorpe. *E Yor* 4C 100
Friden. *Derbs* 4F 85
Friern Barnet. *G Lon* 1D 39
Friesthorpe. *Linc* 2H 87
Frieston. *Linc* 1G 75
Frieth. *Buck* 2F 37
Friezeland. *Notts* 5B 86
Frilford. *Oxon* 2C 36
Frilsham. *W Ber* 4D 36
Frimley. *Surr* 1G 25
Frimley Green. *Surr* 1G 25
Frindsbury. *Medw* 4B 40
Fring. *Norf* 2G 77
Fringford. *Oxon* 3E 50
Frinsted. *Kent* 5C 40
Frinton-on-Sea. *Essx* 4F 55
Friockheim. *Ang* 4E 145
Friog. *Gwyn* 4F 69
Frisby. *Leics* 5E 74
Frisby on the Wreake.
Leics 4D 74
Friskney. *Linc* 5D 88
Friskney Eaudyke. *Linc* 5D 88
Friston. *E Sus* 5G 27
Friston. *Suff* 4G 67
Fritchley. *Derbs* 5A 86
Fritham. *Hants* 1H 15
Frith Bank. *Linc* 1C 76
Frith Common. *Worc* 4A 60
Frithelstock. *Devn* 1E 11
Frithelstock Stone. *Devn* 1E 11
Frithsden. *Herts* 5A 52
Frithville. *Linc* 5C 88
Frittenden. *Kent* 1C 28
Frittiscombe. *Devn* 4E 9
Fritton. *Norf*
nr. Great Yarmouth 5G 79
nr. Long Stratton 1E 67
Fritwell. *Oxon* 3D 50
Frizinghall. *W Yor* 1B 92
Frizington. *Cumb* 3B 102
Frobost. *W Isl* 6C 170
Frocester. *Glos* 5C 48
Frochas. *Powy* 5D 70
Frodesley. *Shrp* 5H 71
Frodingham. *N Lin* 3C 94
Frodsham. *Ches W* 3H 83
Froggatt. *Derbs* 3G 85
Froghall. *Staf* 1E 73
Frogham. *Hants* 1G 15
Frogham. *Kent* 5G 41
Frogmore. *Devn* 4D 8
Frogmore. *Hants* 5G 37
Frogmore. *Herts* 5B 52
Frognall. *Linc* 4A 76
Frogshall. *Norf* 2E 79
Frogwell. *Corn* 2H 7
Frolesworth. *Leics* 1C 62
Frome. *Som* 2C 22
Fromefield. *Som* 2C 22
Frome St Quintin. *Dors* 2A 14
Fromes Hill. *Here* 1B 48
Fron. *Gwyn* 2C 68
Fron. *Powy*
nr. Llandrindod Wells 4C 58
nr. Newtown 1D 58
nr. Welshpool 5E 71
Y Fron. *Gwyn* 5E 81
Froncysyllte. *Wrex* 1E 71
Frongoch. *Gwyn* 2B 70
Fron Isaf. *Wrex* 1E 71
Froneleu. *Gwyn* 2G 69
Frosterley. *Dur* 1D 104
Frotoft. *Orkn* 5D 172
Froxfield. *C Beds* 2H 51
Froxfield. *Wilts* 5A 36
Froxfield Green. *Hants* 4F 25
Fryern Hill. *Hants* 4C 24
Fryerning. *Essx* 5G 53
Fryton. *N Yor* 2A 100
Fugglestone St Peter.
Wilts 3G 23
Fulbeck. *Linc* 5G 87
Fulbourn. *Cambs* 5E 65
Fulbrook. *Oxon* 4A 50
Fulflood. *Hants* 3C 24
Fulford. *Som* 4F 21
Fulford. *Staf* 2D 72
Fulford. *York* 5A 100
Fulham. *G Lon* 3D 38
Fulking. *W Sus* 4D 26
Fuller's Moor. *Ches W* 5G 83
Fuller Street. *Essx* 4H 53
Fullerton. *Hants* 3B 24
Fulletby. *Linc* 3B 88
Full Sutton. *E Yor* 4B 100
Fullwood. *E Ayr* 4F 127
Fulmer. *Buck* 2A 38
Fulmodestone. *Norf* 2B 78
Fulnetby. *Linc* 3H 87
Fulney. *Linc* 3B 76
Fulstow. *Linc* 1C 88
Fulthorpe. *Stoc T* 2B 106
Fulwell. *Tyne* 4G 115
Fulwood. *Lanc* 1D 90
Fulwood. *Notts* 5B 86
Fulwood. *Som* 1F 13
Fulwood. *S Yor* 2G 85
Fundenhall. *Norf* 1D 66
Funtington. *W Sus* 2G 17
Funtley. *Hants* 2D 16
Funzie. *Shet* 2H 173
Furley. *Devn* 2F 13
Furnace. *Arg* 3H 133
Furnace. *Carm* 5F 45
Furnace. *Cdgn* 1F 57
Furner's Green. *E Sus* 3F 27
Furness Vale. *Derbs* 2E 85
Furneux Pelham. *Herts* 3E 53
Furzebrook. *Dors* 4E 15
Furzehill. *Devn* 2H 19
Furzehill. *Dors* 2F 15
Furzeley Corner. *Hants* 1E 17
Furzey Lodge. *Hants* 2B 16
Furzley. *Hants* 1A 16
Fyfield. *Essx* 5F 53
Fyfield. *Glos* 5H 49
Fyfield. *Hants* 2A 24
Fyfield. *Oxon* 2C 36
Fyfield. *Wilts* 5G 35
The Fylde. *Lanc* 1B 90
Fylingthorpe. *N Yor* 4G 107
Fyning. *W Sus* 4G 25
Fyvie. *Abers* 5E 161

G

Gabhsann bho Dheas.
W Isl 2G 171
Gabhsann bho Thuath.
W Isl 2G 171
Gabroc Hill. *E Ayr* 4F 127
Gadbrook. *Surr* 1D 26
Gaddesby. *Leics* 4D 74
Gadfa. *IOA* 2D 80
Gadgirth. *S Ayr* 2D 116
Gaer. *Powy* 3E 47
Gaerwen. *IOA* 3D 81
Gagingwell. *Oxon* 3C 50
Gaick Lodge. *High* 5B 150
Gailey. *Staf* 4D 72
Gainford. *Dur* 3E 105
Gainsborough. *Linc* 1F 87
Gainsborough. *Suff* 1E 55
Gainsford End. *Essx* 2H 53
Gairletter. *Arg* 1C 126
Gairloch. *Abers* 3E 153
Gairloch. *High* 1H 155
Gairlochy. *High* 5D 148
Gairney Bank. *Per* 4D 136
Gairnshiel Lodge. *Abers* 3G 151
Gaisgill. *Cumb* 4H 103
Gaitsgill. *Cumb* 5E 113
Galashiels. *Bord* 1G 119
Galgate. *Lanc* 4D 97
Galhampton. *Som* 4B 22
Gallatown. *Fife* 4E 137
Galley Common. *Warw* 1H 61
Galleyend. *Essx* 5H 53
Galleywood. *Essx* 5H 53
Gallin. *Per* 4C 142
Gallowfauld. *Ang* 4D 144
Gallowhill. *Per* 5A 144
Gallowhill. *Ren* 3F 127
Gallowhills. *Abers* 3H 161
Gallows Green. *Staf* 1E 73
Gallows Green. *Worc* 4D 60
Gallowstree Common.
Oxon 3E 37
Galltair. *High* 1G 147
Gallt Melyd. *Den* 2C 82
Galmington. *Som* 4F 21
Galmisdale. *High* 5C 146
Galmpton. *Devn* 4C 8
Galmpton. *Torb* 3E 9
Galmpton Warborough.
Torb 3E 9
Galphay. *N Yor* 2E 99
Galston. *E Ayr* 1D 117
Galton. *Dors* 4C 14
Galtrigill. *High* 3A 154
Gamblesby. *Cumb* 1H 103
Gamblestown. *Arm* 4F 178
Gamelsby. *Cumb* 4D 112
Gamesley. *Derbs* 1E 85
Gamlingay. *Cambs* 5B 64
Gamlingay Cinques.
Cambs 5B 64
Gamlingay Great Heath.
Cambs 5B 64
Gammaton. *Devn* 4E 19
Gammersgill. *N Yor* 1C 98
Gamston. *Notts*
nr. Nottingham 2D 74
nr. Retford 3E 86
Ganarew. *Here* 4A 48
Ganavan. *Arg* 5C 140
Ganborough. *Glos* 3G 49
Gang. *Corn* 2H 7
Ganllwyd. *Gwyn* 3G 69
Gannochy. *Ang* 1E 145
Gannochy. *Per* 1D 136
Gansclet. *High* 4F 169
Ganstead. *E Yor* 1E 95
Ganthorpe. *N Yor* 2A 100
Ganton. *N Yor* 2D 101
Gants Hill. *G Lon* 2F 39
Gappah. *Devn* 5B 12
Garafad. *High* 2D 155
Garboldisham. *Norf* 2C 66
Garden City. *Flin* 4F 83
Gardeners Green. *Wok* 5G 37
Gardenstown. *Abers* 2F 161
Garden Village. *S Yor* 1G 85
Garden Village. *Swan* 3E 31
Garderhouse. *Shet* 7E 173
Gardham. *E Yor* 5D 100
Gardie. *Shet*
on Papa Stour 5C 173
on Unst 1H 173
Gardie Ho. *Shet* 7F 173
Gare Hill. *Wilts* 2C 22
Garelochhead. *Arg* 4B 134
Garford. *Oxon* 2C 36
Garforth. *W Yor* 1E 93
Gargrave. *N Yor* 4B 98
Gargunnock. *Stir* 4G 135
Garleffin. *S Ayr* 1F 109
Garlieston. *Dum* 5B 110
Garlinge Green. *Kent* 5F 41
Garlogie. *Abers* 3E 153
Garmelow. *Staf* 3B 72
Garmond. *Abers* 3F 161
Garmondsway. *Dur* 1A 106
Garmony. *Arg* 4A 140
Garmouth. *Mor* 2H 159
Garmston. *Shrp* 5A 72
Garnant. *Carm* 4G 45
Garndiffaith. *Torf* 5F 47
Garndolbenmaen. *Gwyn* 1D 69
Garnett Bridge. *Cumb* 5G 103
Garnfadryn. *Gwyn* 2B 68
Garnkirk. *N Lan* 3H 127
Garnlydan. *Blae* 4E 47
Garnsgate. *Linc* 3D 76
Garnswllt. *Swan* 5G 45
Garn yr Erw. *Torf* 4F 47
Garrabost. *W Isl* 4H 171
Garrallan. *E Ayr* 3E 117
Garras. *Corn* 4E 5
Garreg. *Gwyn* 1F 69
Garrigill. *Cumb* 5A 114
Garrison. *Ferm* 7B 176
Garriston. *N Yor* 5E 105
Garrogie Lodge. *High* 2H 149
Garros. *High* 2D 155
Garrow. *Per* 4F 143
Garsdale. *Cumb* 1G 97
Garsdale Head. *Cumb* 5A 104
Garsdon. *Wilts* 3E 35
Garshall Green. *Staf* 2D 72
Garsington. *Oxon* 5D 50
Garstang. *Lanc* 5D 97
Garston. *Mers* 2G 83
Garswood. *Mers* 1H 83
Gartcosh. *N Lan* 3H 127
Garth. *B'end* 2B 32
Garth. *Cdgn* 2F 57
Garth. *Gwyn* 2E 69
Garth. *IOM* 4C 108
Garth. *Powy*
nr. Builth Wells 1C 46
nr. Knighton 3E 59
Garth. *Shet*
nr. Sandness 6D 173
nr. Skellister 6F 173
Garth. *Wrex* 1E 71
Garthamlock. *Glas* 3H 127
Garthbrengy. *Powy* 2D 46
Gartheli. *Cdgn* 5E 57
Garthmyl. *Powy* 1D 58
Garthorpe. *Leics* 3F 75
Garthorpe. *N Lin* 3B 94
Garth Owen. *Powy* 1D 58
Garth Place. *Cphy* 3E 33
Garth Row. *Cumb* 5G 103
Gartly. *Abers* 5C 160
Gartmore. *Stir* 4E 135
Gartness. *N Lan* 3A 128
Gartness. *Stir* 1G 127
Gartocharn. *W Dun* 1F 127
Garton. *E Yor* 1F 95
Garton-on-the-Wolds.
E Yor 4D 101
Gartsherrie. *N Lan* 3A 128
Gartymore. *High* 2H 165
Garvagh. *Caus* 5F 174
Garvaghy. *Ferm* 3L 177
Garvald. *E Lot* 2B 130
Garvamore. *High* 4H 149
Garvard. *Arg* 4A 132
Garvault. *High* 5H 167
Garve. *High* 2F 157
Garvestone. *Norf* 5C 78
Garvetagh. *Derr* 4E 176
Garvie. *Arg* 4H 133
Garvock. *Abers* 1G 145
Garvock. *Inv* 2D 126
Garway. *Here* 3H 47
Garway Common. *Here* 3H 47
Garway Hill. *Here* 3H 47
Garwick. *Linc* 1A 76
Gaskan. *High* 1C 140
Gasper. *Wilts* 3C 22
Gastard. *Wilts* 5D 35
Gasthorpe. *Norf* 2B 66
Gatcombe. *IOW* 4C 16
Gateacre. *Mers* 2G 83
Gatebeck. *Cumb* 1E 97
Gate Burton. *Linc* 2F 87
Gateforth. *N Yor* 2F 93
Gatehead. *E Ayr* 1C 116
Gate Helmsley. *N Yor* 4A 100
Gatehouse. *Nmbd* 1A 114
Gatehouse of Fleet. *Dum* 4D 110
Gatelawbridge. *Dum* 5B 118
Gateley. *Norf* 3B 78
Gatenby. *N Yor* 1F 99
Gatesgarth. *Cumb* 3C 102
Gateshead. *Tyne* 3F 115
Gatesheath. *Ches W* 4G 83
Gateside. *Ang*
nr. Forfar 4D 144
nr. Kirriemuir 4C 144
Gateside. *Fife* 3D 136
Gateside. *N Ayr* 4E 127
Gathurst. *G Man* 4D 90
Gatley. *G Man* 2C 84
Gatton. *Surr* 5D 39
Gattonside. *Bord* 1H 119
Gatwick Airport.
W Sus 205 (1D 26)
Gaufron. *Powy* 4B 58
Gaulby. *Leics* 5D 74
Gauldry. *Fife* 1F 137
Gaultree. *Norf* 5D 77
Gaunt's Common. *Dors* 2F 15
Gaunt's Earthcott. *S Glo* 3B 34
Gautby. *Linc* 3A 88
Gavinton. *Bord* 4D 130
Gawber. *S Yor* 4D 92
Gawcott. *Buck* 2E 51
Gawsworth. *Ches E* 4C 84
Gawthorpe. *W Yor* 2C 92
Gawthrop. *Cumb* 1F 97
Gawthwaite. *Cumb* 1B 96
Gay Bowers. *Essx* 5A 54
Gaydon. *Warw* 5A 62
Gayfield. *Orkn* 2D 172
Gayhurst. *Mil* 1G 51
Gayle. *N Yor* 1A 98
Gayles. *N Yor* 4E 105
Gay Street. *W Sus* 3B 26
Gayton. *Mers* 2E 83
Gayton. *Norf* 4G 77
Gayton. *Nptn* 5E 62
Gayton. *Staf* 3D 73
Gayton le Marsh. *Linc* 2D 88
Gayton le Wold. *Linc* 2B 88
Gayton Thorpe. *Norf* 4G 77
Gaywood. *Norf* 3F 77
Gazeley. *Suff* 4G 65
Geanies. *High* 1C 158
Gearraidh Bhailteas.
W Isl 6C 170
Gearraidh Bhaird. *W Isl* 6F 171
Gearraidh ma Monadh.
W Isl 7C 170
Gearraidh na h-Aibhne.
W Isl 4E 171
Geary. *High* 2B 154
Geddes. *High* 3C 158
Gedding. *Suff* 5B 66
Geddington. *Nptn* 2F 63
Gedintailor. *High* 5E 155
Gedling. *Notts* 1D 74
Gedney. *Linc* 3D 76
Gedney Broadgate. *Linc* 3D 76
Gedney Drove End. *Linc* 3D 76
Gedney Dyke. *Linc* 3D 76
Gedney Hill. *Linc* 4C 76
Gee Cross. *G Man* 1D 84
Geeston. *Rut* 5G 75
Geilston. *Arg* 2E 127
Geirinis. *W Isl* 4C 170
Geise. *High* 2D 168
Geisiadar. *W Isl* 4D 171
Gelder Shiel. *Abers* 5G 151
Geldeston. *Norf* 1F 67
Gell. *Cnwy* 4A 82
Gelli. *Pemb* 3E 43
Gelli. *Rhon* 2C 32
Gellifor. *Den* 4D 82
Gelligaer. *Cphy* 2E 33
Y Gelli Gandryll. *Powy* 1F 47
Gellilydan. *Gwyn* 2F 69
Gellinudd. *Neat* 5H 45
Gellyburn. *Per* 5H 143
Gellywen. *Carm* 2G 43
Gelston. *Dum* 4E 111
Gelston. *Linc* 1G 75
Gembling. *E Yor* 4F 101
Geneva. *Cdgn* 5D 56
Gentleshaw. *Staf* 4E 73
Geocrab. *W Isl* 8D 171
George Best Belfast City Airport.
Bel 2H 179
George Green. *Buck* 2A 38
Georgeham. *Devn* 3E 19
George Nympton. *Devn* 4H 19
Georgetown. *Blae* 5E 47
Georgetown. *Ren* 3F 127
Georth. *Orkn* 5C 172
Gerlan. *Gwyn* 4F 81
Germansweek. *Devn* 3E 11
Germoe. *Corn* 4C 4
Gerrans. *Corn* 5C 6
Gerrard's Bromley. *Staf* 2B 72
Gerrards Cross. *Buck* 2A 38
Gerston. *High* 3D 168
Gestingthorpe. *Essx* 2B 54
Gethsemane. *Pemb* 1A 44
Geuffordd. *Powy* 4E 70
Gibraltar. *Buck* 4F 51
Gibraltar. *Linc* 5E 89
Gibraltar. *Suff* 5D 66
Gibsmere. *Notts* 1E 74
Giddeahall. *Wilts* 4D 34
Gidea Park. *G Lon* 2G 39
Gidleigh. *Devn* 4G 11
Giffnock. *E Ren* 4G 127
Gifford. *E Lot* 3B 130
Giffordtown. *Fife* 2E 137
Giggetty. *Staf* 1C 60
Giggleswick. *N Yor* 3H 97
Gignog. *Pemb* 2C 42
Gilberdyke. *E Yor* 2B 94
Gilbert's End. *Worc* 1D 48
Gilbert's Green. *Warw* 3F 61
Gilchriston. *E Lot* 3A 130
Gilcrux. *Cumb* 1C 102
Gildersome. *W Yor* 2C 92
Gildingwells. *S Yor* 2C 86
Gilesgate Moor. *Dur* 5F 115
Gileston. *V Glam* 5D 32
Gilfach. *Cphy* 2E 33
Gilfach Goch. *Rhon* 3C 32
Gilfachreda. *Cdgn* 5D 56
Gilford. *Arm* 5E 178
Gilgarran. *Cumb* 2B 102
Gillamoor. *N Yor* 5D 107
Gillan. *Corn* 4E 5
Gillar's Green. *Mers* 1G 83
Gillen. *High* 3B 154
Gilling East. *N Yor* 2A 100
Gillingham. *Dors* 4D 22
Gillingham. *Medw*
. . . **Medway Towns 197 (4B 40)**
Gillingham. *Norf* 1G 67
Gilling West. *N Yor* 4E 105
Gillock. *High* 3E 169
Gillow Heath. *Staf* 5C 84
Gills. *High* 1F 169
Gill's Green. *Kent* 2B 28
Gilmanscleuch. *Bord* 2F 119
Gilmerton. *Edin* 3F 129
Gilmerton. *Per* 1A 136
Gilmonby. *Dur* 3C 104
Gilmorton. *Leics* 2C 62
Gilsland. *Nmbd* 3H 113
Gilsland Spa. *Cumb* 3H 113
Gilston. *Bord* 4H 129
Giltbrook. *Notts* 1B 74
Gilwern. *Mon* 4F 47
Gimingham. *Norf* 2E 79
Giosla. *W Isl* 5D 171
Gipping. *Suff* 4C 66
Gipsey Bridge. *Linc* 1B 76
Gipton. *W Yor* 1D 92
Girdle Toll. *N Ayr* 5E 127
Girlsta. *Shet* 6F 173
Girsby. *N Yor* 4A 106
Girthon. *Dum* 4D 110
Girton. *Cambs* 4D 64
Girton. *Notts* 4F 87
Girvan. *S Ayr* 5A 116
Gisburn. *Lanc* 5H 97
Gisleham. *Suff* 2H 67
Gislingham. *Suff* 3C 66
Gissing. *Norf* 2D 66
Gittisham. *Devn* 3E 13
Gladestry. *Powy* 5E 59
Gladsmuir. *E Lot* 2A 130
Glaichbea. *High* 5H 157
Glais. *Swan* 5H 45
Glaisdale. *N Yor* 4E 107
Glame. *High* 4E 155
Glamis. *Ang* 4C 144
Glanaman. *Carm* 4G 45
Glan-Conwy. *Cnwy* 5H 81
Glandford. *Norf* 1C 78
Glan Duar. *Carm* 1F 45
Glandwr. *Blae* 5F 47
Glandwr. *Pemb* 2F 43
Glan-Dwyfach. *Gwyn* 1D 69
Glandy Cross. *Carm* 2F 43
Glandyfi. *Cdgn* 1F 57
Glangrwyney. *Powy* 4F 47
Glanmule. *Powy* 1D 58
Glan-rhyd. *Pemb* 1F 43
Glan-rhyd. *Powy* 5A 46
Glanrhyd. *Gwyn* 2B 68
Glanrhyd. *Pemb* 1B 44
Glanton. *Nmbd* 3E 121
Glanton Pyke. *Nmbd* 3E 121
Glanvilles Wootton. *Dors* 2B 14
Glan-y-don. *Flin* 3D 82
Glan-y-nant. *Powy* 2B 58
Glan-yr-afon. *Gwyn* 1C 70
Glan-yr-afon. *IOA* 2F 81
Glan-yr-afon. *Powy* 5C 70
Glan-y-wern. *Gwyn* 2F 69
Glapthorn. *Nptn* 1H 63
Glapwell. *Derbs* 4B 86
Glarryford. *ME Ant* 5G 175
Glas Aird. *Arg* 4A 132
Glas-allt Shiel. *Abers* 5G 151
Glasbury. *Powy* 2E 47
Glaschoil. *High* 5E 159
Glascoed. *Den* 3B 82
Glascoed. *Mon* 5G 47
Glascote. *Staf* 5G 73
Glascwm. *Powy* 5D 58
Glasfryn. *Cnwy* 5B 82
Glasgow. *Glas* 195 (3G 127)
Glasgow Airport.
Ren 205 (3F 127)
Glasgow Prestwick Airport.
S Ayr 2C 116
Glashvin. *High* 2D 154
Glasinfryn. *Gwyn* 4E 81
Glas na Cardaich. *High* 4E 147
Glasnacardoch. *High* 4E 147
Glasnakille. *High* 2D 146
Glaspwll. *Cdgn* 1G 57
Glassburn. *High* 5F 157
Glassenbury. *Kent* 2B 28
Glasserton. *Dum* 5B 110
Glassford. *S Lan* 5A 128
Glassgreen. *Mor* 2G 159
Glasshouse. *Glos* 3C 48
Glasshouses. *N Yor* 3D 98
Glasson. *Cumb* 3D 112
Glasson. *Lanc* 4D 96
Glassonby. *Cumb* 1G 103
Glasswater. *New M* 4J 179
Glasterlaw. *Ang* 3E 145
Glaston. *Rut* 5F 75
Glastonbury. *Som* 3H 21
Glatton. *Cambs* 2A 64
Glazebrook. *Warr* 1A 84
Glazebury. *Warr* 1A 84
Glazeley. *Shrp* 2B 60
Gleadless. *S Yor* 2A 86
Gleadsmoss. *Ches E* 4C 84
Gleann Dail bho Dheas.
W Isl 7C 170
Gleann Tholastaidh.
W Isl 3H 171
Gleann Uige. *High* 1A 140
Gleaston. *Cumb* 2B 96
Glebe. *Derr* 3F 176
Glecknabae. *Arg* 3B 126
Gledrid. *Shrp* 2E 71
Gleniant. *Powy* 1B 58
Glemsford. *Suff* 1B 54
Glen. *Dum* 4C 110
Glenancross. *High* 4E 147

H

Hackness—Heol-y-Cyw

Hackness. *N Yor* 5G 107
Hackness. *Orkn* 8C 172
Hackney. *G Lon* 2E 39
Hackthorn. *Linc* 2G 87
Hackthorpe. *Cumb* 2G 103
Haclait. *W Isl* 4D 170
Haconby. *Linc* 3A 76
Hadden. *Bord* 1B 120
Haddenham. *Buck* 5F 51
Haddenham. *Cambs* 3D 64
Haddenham End Field.
Cambs 3D 64
Haddington. *E Lot* 2B 130
Haddington. *Linc* 4G 87
Haddiscoe. *Norf* 1G 67
Haddo. *Abers* 5F 161
Haddon. *Cambs* 1A 64
Hademore. *Staf* 5F 73
Hadfield. *Derbs* 1E 85
Hadham Cross. *Herts* 4E 53
Hadham Ford. *Herts* 3E 53
Hadleigh. *Essx* 2C 40
Hadleigh. *Suff* 1D 54
Hadleigh Heath. *Suff* 1C 54
Hadley. *Telf* 4A 72
Hadley. *Worc* 4C 60
Hadley End. *Staf* 3F 73
Hadley Wood. *G Lon* 1D 38
Hadlow. *Kent* 1H 27
Hadlow Down. *E Sus* 3G 27
Hadnall. *Shrp* 3H 71
Hadstock. *Essx* 1F 53
Hadston. *Nmbd* 4G 121
Hady. *Derbs* 3A 86
Hadzor. *Worc* 4D 60
Haffenden Quarter. *Kent* 1C 28
Haggate. *Lanc* 1G 91
Haggbeck. *Cumb* 2F 113
Haggersta. *Shet* 7E 173
Haggerston. *Nmbd* 5G 131
Haggrister. *Shet* 4E 173
Hagley. *Here* 1A 48
Hagley. *Worc* 2D 60
Hagnaby. *Linc* 4C 88
Hagworthingham. *Linc* 4C 88
Haigh. *G Man* 4E 90
Haigh Moor. *W Yor* 2C 92
Haighton Green. *Lanc* 1D 90
Haile. *Cumb* 4B 102
Hailes. *Glos* 2F 49
Hailey. *Herts* 4D 52
Hailey. *Oxon* 4B 50
Hailsham. *E Sus* 5G 27
Hail Weston. *Cambs* 4A 64
Hainault. *G Lon* 1F 39
Hainford. *Norf* 4E 78
Hainton. *Linc* 2A 88
Hainworth. *W Yor* 1A 92
Haisthorpe. *E Yor* 3F 101
Hakin. *Pemb* 4C 42
Halam. *Notts* 5D 86
Halbeath. *Fife* 1E 129
Halberton. *Devn* 1D 12
Halcro. *High* 2E 169
Hale. *Cumb* 2E 97
Hale. *G Man* 2B 84
Hale. *Hal* 2G 83
Hale. *Hants* 1G 15
Hale. *Surr* 2G 25
Hale Bank. *Hal* 2G 83
Halebarns. *G Man* 2B 84
Hales. *Norf* 1F 67
Hales. *Staf* 2B 72
Halesgate. *Linc* 3C 76
Hales Green. *Derbs* 1F 73
Halesowen. *W Mid* 2D 60
Hale Street. *Kent* 1A 28
Halesworth. *Suff* 3F 67
Halewood. *Mers* 2G 83
Halford. *Shrp* 2G 59
Halford. *Warw* 1A 50
Halfpenny. *Cumb* 1E 97
Halfpenny Furze. *Carm* 3G 43
Halfpenny Green. *Staf* 1C 60
Halfway. *Carm*
nr. Llandeilo 2G 45
nr. Llandovery 2B 46
Halfway. *S Yor* 2B 86
Halfway. *W Ber* 5C 36
Halfway House. *Shrp* 4F 71
Halfway Houses. *Kent* 3D 40
Halgabron. *Corn* 4A 10
Halifax. *W Yor* 2A 92
Halistra. *High* 3B 154
Halket. *E Ayr* 4F 127
Halkirk. *High* 3D 168
Halkyn. *Flin* 3E 82
Hall. *E Ren* 4F 127
Hallam Fields. *Derbs* 1B 74
Halland. *E Sus* 4G 27
The Hallands. *N Lin* 2D 94
Hallaton. *Leics* 1E 63
Hallatrow. *Bath* 1B 22
Hallbank. *Cumb* 5H 103
Hallbankgate. *Cumb* 4G 113
Hall Dunnerdale. *Cumb* 5D 102
Hallen. *S Glo* 3A 34
Hall End. *Bed* 1A 52
Hallgarth. *Dur* 5G 115
Hall Green. *Ches E* 5C 84
Hall Green. *Norf* 2D 66
Hall Green. *W Mid* 2F 61
Hall Green. *W Yor* 3D 92
Hall Green. *Wrex* 1G 71
Halliburton. *Bord* 5C 130
Hallin. *High* 3B 154
Halling. *Medw* 4B 40
Hallington. *Linc* 2C 88
Hallington. *Nmbd* 2C 114
Halloughton. *Notts* 5D 86
Hallow. *Worc* 5C 60
Hallow Heath. *Worc* 5C 60
Hallowsgate. *Ches W* 4H 83
Hallsands. *Devn* 5E 9
Hall's Green. *Herts* 3C 52
Hallspill. *Devn* 4E 19
Hallthwaites. *Cumb* 1A 96
Hall Waberthwaite.
Cumb 5C 102
Hallwood Green. *Glos* 2B 48
Hallworthy. *Corn* 4B 10
Hallyne. *Bord* 5E 129
Halmer End. *Staf* 1C 72
Halmond's Frome. *Here* 1B 48
Halmore. *Glos* 5B 48
Halnaker. *W Sus* 5A 26
Halsall. *Lanc* 3B 90
Halse. *Nptn* 1D 50
Halse. *Som* 4E 21
Halsetown. *Corn* 3C 4
Halsham. *E Yor* 2F 95
Halsinger. *Devn* 3F 19
Halstead. *Essx* 2B 54
Halstead. *Kent* 4F 39
Halstead. *Leics* 5E 75
Halstock. *Dors* 2A 14
Halsway. *Som* 3E 21
Haltcliff Bridge. *Cumb* 1E 103
Haltham. *Linc* 4B 88
Haltoft End. *Linc* 1C 76
Halton. *Buck* 5G 51
Halton. *Hal* 2H 83
Halton. *Lanc* 3E 97
Halton. *Nmbd* 3C 114
Halton. *W Yor* 1D 92
Halton. *Wrex* 2F 71
Halton East. *N Yor* 4C 98
Halton Fenside. *Linc* 4D 88
Halton Gill. *N Yor* 2A 98
Halton Holegate. *Linc* 4D 88
Halton Lea Gate. *Nmbd* 4H 113
Halton Moor. *W Yor* 1D 92
Halton Shields. *Nmbd* 3D 114
Halton West. *N Yor* 4H 97
Haltwhistle. *Nmbd* 3A 114
Halvergate. *Norf* 5G 79
Halwell. *Devn* 3D 9
Halwill. *Devn* 3E 11
Halwill Junction. *Devn* 3E 11
Ham. *Devn* 2F 13
Ham. *Glos* 2B 34
Ham. *G Lon* 3C 38
Ham. *High* 1E 169
Ham. *Kent* 5H 41
Ham. *Plym* 3A 8
Ham. *Shet* 8A 173
Ham. *Som*
nr. Ilminster 1F 13
nr. Taunton 4F 21
nr. Wellington 4E 21
Ham. *Wilts* 5B 36
Hambleden. *Buck* 3F 37
Hambledon. *Hants* 1E 17
Hambledon. *Surr* 2A 26
Hamble-le-Rice. *Hants* 2C 16
Hambleton. *Lanc* 5C 96
Hambleton. *N Yor* 1F 93
Hambridge. *Som* 4G 21
Hambrook. *S Glo* 4B 34
Hambrook. *W Sus* 2F 17
Ham Common. *Dors* 4D 22
Hameringham. *Linc* 4C 88
Hamerton. *Cambs* 3A 64
Ham Green. *Here* 1C 48
Ham Green. *Kent* 4C 40
Ham Green. *N Som* 4A 34
Ham Green. *Worc* 4E 61
Ham Hill. *Kent* 4A 40
Hamilton. *Leic* 5D 74
Hamilton. *S Lan* 4A 128
Hamiltonsbawn. *Arm* 5D 178
Hamister. *Shet* 5G 173
Hammer. *W Sus* 3G 25
Hammersmith. *G Lon* 3D 38
Hammerwich. *Staf* 5E 73
Hammerwood. *E Sus* 2F 27
Hammill. *Kent* 5G 41
Hammond Street. *Herts* 5D 52
Hammoon. *Dors* 1D 14
Hamnavoe. *Shet*
nr. Braehoulland 3D 173
nr. Burland 8E 173
nr. Lunna 4F 173
on Yell 3F 173
Hamp. *Som* 3G 21
Hampden Park. *E Sus* 5G 27
Hampen. *Glos* 4F 49
Hamperden End. *Essx* 2F 53
Hamperley. *Shrp* 2G 59
Hampnett. *Glos* 4F 49
Hampole. *S Yor* 3F 93
Hampreston. *Dors* 3F 15
Hampstead. *G Lon* 2D 38
Hampstead Norreys.
W Ber 4D 36
Hampsthwaite. *N Yor* 4E 99
Hampton. *Devn* 3F 13
Hampton. *G Lon* 3C 38
Hampton. *Kent* 4F 41
Hampton. *Shrp* 2B 60
Hampton. *Swin* 2G 35
Hampton. *Worc* 1F 49
Hampton Bishop. *Here* 2A 48
Hampton Fields. *Glos* 2D 35
Hampton Hargate. *Pet* 1A 64
Hampton Heath. *Ches W* 1H 71
Hampton in Arden. *W Mid* 2G 61
Hampton Loade. *Shrp* 2B 60
Hampton Lovett. *Worc* 4C 60
Hampton Lucy. *Warw* 5G 61
Hampton Magna. *Warw* 4G 61
Hampton on the Hill.
Warw 4G 61
Hampton Poyle. *Oxon* 4D 50
Hampton Wick. *G Lon* 4C 38
Hamptworth. *Wilts* 1H 15
Hamrow. *Norf* 3B 78
Hamsey. *E Sus* 4F 27
Hamsey Green. *Surr* 5E 39
Hamstall Ridware. *Staf* 4F 73
Hamstead. *IOW* 3C 16
Hamstead. *W Mid* 1E 61
Hamstead Marshall.
W Ber 5C 36
Hamsterley. *Dur*
nr. Consett 4E 115
nr. Wolsingham 1E 105
Hamsterley Mill. *Dur* 4E 115
Ham Street. *Som* 3A 22
Hamstreet. *Kent* 2E 28
Hamworthy. *Pool* 3E 15
Hanbury. *Staf* 3F 73
Hanbury. *Worc* 4D 60
Hanbury Woodend. *Staf* 3F 73
Hanby. *Linc* 2H 75
Hanchurch. *Staf* 1C 72
Hand and Pen. *Devn* 3D 12
Handbridge. *Ches W* 4G 83
Handcross. *W Sus* 2D 26
Handforth. *Ches E* 2C 84
Handley. *Ches W* 5G 83
Handley. *Derbs* 4A 86
Handsacre. *Staf* 4E 73
Handsworth. *S Yor* 2B 86
Handsworth. *W Mid* 1E 61
Handy Cross. *Buck* 2G 37
Hanford. *Dors* 1D 14
Hanford. *Stoke* 1C 72
Hangersley. *Hants* 2G 15
Hanging Houghton. *Nptn* 3E 63
Hanging Langford. *Wilts* 3F 23
Hangleton. *Brig* 5D 26
Hangleton. *W Sus* 5B 26
Hanham. *S Glo* 4B 34
Hanham Green. *S Glo* 4B 34
Hankelow. *Ches E* 1A 72
Hankerton. *Wilts* 2E 35
Hankham. *E Sus* 5H 27
Hanley.
Stoke **Stoke 202** (1C 72)
Hanley Castle. *Worc* 1D 48
Hanley Childe. *Worc* 4A 60
Hanley Swan. *Worc* 1D 48
Hanley William. *Worc* 4A 60
Hanlith. *N Yor* 3B 98
Hanmer. *Wrex* 2G 71
Hannaborough. *Devn* 2F 11
Hannaford. *Devn* 4G 19
Hannah. *Linc* 3E 89
Hannington. *Hants* 1D 24
Hannington. *Nptn* 3F 63
Hannington. *Swin* 2G 35
Hannington Wick. *Swin* 2G 35
Hanscombe End. *C Beds* 2B 52
Hanslope. *Mil* 1G 51
Hanthorpe. *Linc* 3H 75
Hanwell. *G Lon* 2C 38
Hanwell. *Oxon* 1C 50
Hanwood. *Shrp* 5G 71
Hanworth. *G Lon* 3C 38
Hanworth. *Norf* 2D 78
Happas. *Ang* 4D 144
Happendon. *S Lan* 1A 118
Happisburgh. *Norf* 2F 79
Happisburgh Common.
Norf 3F 79
Hapsford. *Ches W* 3G 83
Hapton. *Lanc* 1F 91
Hapton. *Norf* 1D 66
Harberton. *Devn* 3D 9
Harbertonford. *Devn* 3D 9
Harbledown. *Kent* 5F 41
Harborne. *W Mid* 2E 61
Harborough Magna.
Warw 3B 62
Harbottle. *Nmbd* 4D 120
Harbourneford. *Devn* 2D 8
Harbours Hill. *Worc* 4D 60
Harbridge. *Hants* 1G 15
Harbury. *Warw* 4A 62
Harby. *Leics* 2E 75
Harby. *Notts* 3F 87
Harcombe. *Devn* 3E 13
Harcombe Bottom. *Devn* 3G 13
Harcourt. *Corn* 5C 6
Harden. *W Yor* 1A 92
Hardenhuish. *Wilts* 4E 35
Hardgate. *Abers* 3E 153
Hardgate. *Dum* 3F 111
Hardham. *W Sus* 4B 26
Hardingham. *Norf* 5C 78
Hardingstone. *Nptn* 5E 63
Hardings Wood. *Staf* 5C 84
Hardington. *Som* 1C 22
Hardington Mandeville.
Som 1A 14
Hardington Marsh. *Som* 2A 14
Hardington Moor. *Som* 1A 14
Hardley. *Hants* 2C 16
Hardley Street. *Norf* 5F 79
Hardmead. *Mil* 1H 51
Hardraw. *N Yor* 5B 104
Hardstoft. *Derbs* 4B 86
Hardway. *Hants* 2E 16
Hardway. *Som* 3C 22
Hardwick. *Buck* 4G 51
Hardwick. *Cambs* 5C 64
Hardwick. *Norf* 2E 66
Hardwick. *Nptn* 4F 63
Hardwick. *Oxon*
nr. Bicester 3D 50
nr. Witney 5B 50
Hardwick. *Shrp* 1F 59
Hardwick. *S Yor* 2B 86
Hardwick. *Stoc T* 2B 106
Hardwick. *W Mid* 1E 61
Hardwicke. *Glos*
nr. Cheltenham 3E 49
nr. Gloucester 4C 48
Hardwicke. *Here* 1F 47
Hardwick Village. *Notts* 3D 86
Hardy's Green. *Essx* 3C 54
Hare. *Som* 1F 13
Hareby. *Linc* 4C 88
Hareden. *Lanc* 4F 97
Harefield. *G Lon* 1B 38
Hare Green. *Essx* 3D 54
Hare Hatch. *Wok* 4G 37
Harehill. *Derbs* 2F 73
Harehills. *W Yor* 1D 92
Harehope. *Nmbd* 2E 121
Harelaw. *Dum* 2F 113
Harelaw. *Dur* 4E 115
Hareplain. *Kent* 2C 28
Haresceugh. *Cumb* 5H 113
Harescombe. *Glos* 4D 48
Haresfield. *Glos* 4D 48
Haresfinch. *Mers* 1H 83
Hareshaw. *N Lan* 3B 128
Hare Street. *Essx* 5E 53
Hare Street. *Herts* 3D 53
Harewood. *W Yor* 5F 99
Harewood End. *Here* 3A 48
Harford. *Devn* 3C 8
Hargate. *Norf* 1D 66
Hargatewall. *Derbs* 3F 85
Hargrave. *Ches W* 4G 83
Hargrave. *Nptn* 3H 63
Hargrave. *Suff* 5G 65
Harker. *Cumb* 3E 113
Harkland. *Shet* 3F 173
Harkstead. *Suff* 2E 55
Harlaston. *Staf* 4G 73
Harlaxton. *Linc* 2F 75
Harlech. *Gwyn* 2E 69
Harlequin. *Notts* 2D 74
Harlescott. *Shrp* 4H 71
Harleston. *Devn* 4D 9
Harleston. *Norf* 2E 67
Harleston. *Suff* 4C 66
Harlestone. *Nptn* 4E 62
Harley. *Shrp* 5H 71
Harley. *S Yor* 1A 86
Harling Road. *Norf* 2B 66
Harlington. *C Beds* 2A 52
Harlington. *G Lon* 3B 38
Harlington. *S Yor* 4E 93
Harlosh. *High* 4B 154
Harlow. *Essx* 4E 53
Harlow Hill. *Nmbd* 3D 115
Harlsey Castle. *N Yor* 5B 106
Harlthorpe. *E Yor* 1H 93
Harlton. *Cambs* 5C 64
Harlyn Bay. *Corn* 1C 6
Harman's Cross. *Dors* 4E 15
Harmby. *N Yor* 1D 98
Harmer Green. *Herts* 4C 52
Harmer Hill. *Shrp* 3G 71
Harmondsworth. *G Lon* 3B 38
Harmston. *Linc* 4G 87
Harnage. *Shrp* 5H 71
Harnham. *Nmbd* 1D 115
Harnham. *Wilts* 4G 23
Harnhill. *Glos* 5F 49
Harold Hill. *G Lon* 1G 39
Haroldston West. *Pemb* 3C 42
Haroldswick. *Shet* 1H 173
Harold Wood. *G Lon* 1G 39
Harome. *N Yor* 1A 100
Harpenden. *Herts* 4B 52
Harpford. *Devn* 3D 12
Harpham. *E Yor* 3E 101
Harpley. *Norf* 3G 77
Harpley. *Worc* 4A 60
Harpole. *Nptn* 4D 62
Harpsdale. *High* 3D 168
Harpsden. *Oxon* 3F 37
Harpswell. *Linc* 2G 87
Harpurhey. *G Man* 4G 91
Harpur Hill. *Derbs* 3E 85
Harraby. *Cumb* 4F 113
Harracott. *Devn* 4F 19
Harrapool. *High* 1E 147
Harrapul. *High* 1E 147
Harrietfield. *Per* 1B 136
Harrietsham. *Kent* 5C 40
Harrington. *Cumb* 2A 102
Harrington. *Linc* 3C 88
Harrington. *Nptn* 2E 63
Harringworth. *Nptn* 1G 63
Harriseahead. *Staf* 5C 84
Harriston. *Cumb* 5C 112
Harrogate. *N Yor* **196** (4F 99)
Harrold. *Bed* 5G 63
Harrop Dale. *G Man* 4A 92
Harrow. *G Lon* 2C 38
Harrowbarrow. *Corn* 2H 7
Harrowden. *Bed* 1A 52
Harrowgate Hill. *Darl* 3F 105
Harrow on the Hill. *G Lon* 2C 38
Harrow Weald. *G Lon* 1C 38
Harry Stoke. *S Glo* 4B 34
Harston. *Cambs* 5D 64
Harston. *Leics* 2F 75
Harswell. *E Yor* 5C 100
Hart. *Hart* 1B 106
Hartburn. *Nmbd* 1D 115
Hartburn. *Stoc T* 3B 106
Hartest. *Suff* 5H 65
Hartfield. *E Sus* 2F 27
Hartford. *Cambs* 3B 64
Hartford. *Ches W* 3A 84
Hartford. *Som* 4C 20
Hartford Bridge. *Hants* 1F 25
Hartford End. *Essx* 4G 53
Harthill. *Ches W* 5H 83
Harthill. *N Lan* 3C 128
Harthill. *S Yor* 2B 86
Hartington. *Derbs* 4F 85
Hartland. *Devn* 4C 18
Hartland Quay. *Devn* 4C 18
Hartle. *Worc* 3D 60
Hartlebury. *Worc* 3C 60
Hartlepool. *Hart* 1C 106
Hartley. *Cumb* 4A 104
Hartley. *Kent*
nr. Cranbrook 2B 28
nr. Dartford 4H 39
Hartley. *Nmbd* 2G 115
Hartley Green. *Staf* 3D 73
Hartley Mauditt. *Hants* 3F 25
Hartley Wespall. *Hants* 1E 25
Hartley Wintney. *Hants* 1F 25
Hartlip. *Kent* 4C 40
Hartmount Holdings.
High 1B 158
Hartoft End. *N Yor* 5E 107
Harton. *N Yor* 3B 100
Harton. *Shrp* 2G 59
Harton. *Tyne* 3G 115
Hartpury. *Glos* 3D 48
Hartshead. *W Yor* 2B 92
Hartshill. *Warw* 1H 61
Hartshorne. *Derbs* 3H 73
Hartsop. *Cumb* 3F 103
Hart Station. *Hart* 1B 106
Hartswell. *Som* 4D 20
Hartwell. *Nptn* 5E 63
Hartwood. *Lanc* 3D 90
Hartwood. *N Lan* 4B 128
Harvel. *Kent* 4A 40
Harvington. *Worc*
nr. Evesham 1F 49
nr. Kidderminster 3C 60
Harwell. *Oxon* 3C 36
Harwich. *Essx* **204** (2F 55)
Harwood. *Dur* 1B 104
Harwood. *G Man* 3F 91
Harwood Dale. *N Yor* 5G 107
Harworth. *Notts* 1D 86
Hascombe. *Surr* 2A 26
Haselbech. *Nptn* 3E 62
Haselbury Plucknett.
Som 1H 13
Haseley. *Warw* 4G 61
Hasfield. *Glos* 3D 48
Hasguard. *Pemb* 4C 42
Haskayne. *Lanc* 4B 90
Hasketon. *Suff* 5E 67
Hasland. *Derbs* 4A 86
Haslemere. *Surr* 2A 26
Haslingden. *Lanc* 2F 91
Haslingfield. *Cambs* 5D 64
Haslington. *Ches E* 5B 84
Hassall. *Ches E* 5B 84
Hassall Green. *Ches E* 5B 84
Hassell Street. *Kent* 1E 29
Hassendean. *Bord* 2H 119
Hassingham. *Norf* 5F 79
Hassness. *Cumb* 3C 102
Hassocks. *W Sus* 4E 27
Hassop. *Derbs* 3G 85
Haster. *High* 3F 169
Hasthorpe. *Linc* 4D 89
Hastigrow. *High* 2E 169
Hastingleigh. *Kent* 1E 29
Hastings. *E Sus* 5C 28
Hastingwood. *Essx* 5E 53
Hastoe. *Herts* 5H 51
Haston. *Shrp* 3H 71
Haswell. *Dur* 5G 115
Haswell Plough. *Dur* 5G 115
Hatch. *C Beds* 1B 52
Hatch Beauchamp. *Som* 4G 21
Hatch End. *G Lon* 1C 38
Hatch Green. *Som* 1G 13
Hatching Green. *Herts* 4B 52
Hatchmere. *Ches W* 3H 83
Hatch Warren. *Hants* 2E 24
Hatcliffe. *NE Lin* 4F 95
Hatfield. *Here* 5H 59
Hatfield. *Herts* 5C 52
Hatfield. *S Yor* 4G 93
Hatfield. *Worc* 5C 60
Hatfield Broad Oak. *Essx* 4F 53
Hatfield Garden Village.
Herts 5C 52
Hatfield Heath. *Essx* 4F 53
Hatfield Hyde. *Herts* 4C 52
Hatfield Peverel. *Essx* 4A 54
Hatfield Woodhouse.
S Yor 4G 93
Hatford. *Oxon* 2B 36
Hatherden. *Hants* 1B 24
Hatherleigh. *Devn* 2F 11
Hathern. *Leics* 3B 74
Hatherop. *Glos* 5G 49
Hathersage. *Derbs* 2G 85
Hathersage Booths. *Derbs* 2G 85
Hatherton. *Ches E* 1A 72
Hatherton. *Staf* 4D 72
Hatley St George. *Cambs* 5B 64
Hatt. *Corn* 2H 7
Hattersley. *G Man* 1D 85
Hattingley. *Hants* 3E 25
Hatton. *Abers* 5H 161
Hatton. *Derbs* 2G 73
Hatton. *G Lon* 3B 38
Hatton. *Linc* 3A 88
Hatton. *Shrp* 1G 59
Hatton. *Warr* 2A 84
Hatton. *Warw* 4G 61
Hattoncrook. *Abers* 1F 153
Hatton Heath. *Ches W* 4G 83
Hatton of Fintray. *Abers* 2F 153
Haugh. *E Ayr* 2D 117
Haugh. *Linc* 3D 88
Haugham. *Linc* 2C 88
Haugh Head. *Nmbd* 2E 121
Haughley. *Suff* 4C 66
Haughley Green. *Suff* 4C 66
Haugh of Ballechin. *Per* 3G 143
Haugh of Glass. *Mor* 5B 160
Haugh of Urr. *Dum* 3F 111
Haughton. *Ches E* 5H 83
Haughton. *Notts* 3D 86
Haughton. *Shrp*
nr. Bridgnorth 1A 60
nr. Oswestry 3F 71
nr. Shifnal 5B 72
nr. Shrewsbury 4H 71
Haughton. *Staf* 3C 72
Haughton Green. *G Man* 1D 84
Haughton le Skerne. *Darl* 3A 106
Haultwick. *Herts* 3D 52
Haunn. *Arg* 4E 139
Haunn. *W Isl* 7C 170
Haunton. *Staf* 4G 73
Hauxton. *Cambs* 5D 64
Havannah. *Ches E* 4C 84
Havant. *Hants* 2F 17
Haven. *Here* 5G 59
The Haven. *W Sus* 2B 26
Haven Bank. *Linc* 5B 88
Havenstreet. *IOW* 3D 16
Havercroft. *W Yor* 3D 93
Haverfordwest. *Pemb* 3D 42
Haverhill. *Suff* 1G 53
Haverigg. *Cumb* 2A 96
Havering-Atte-Bower.
G Lon 1G 39
Havering's Grove. *Essx* 1A 40
Haversham. *Mil* 1G 51
Haverthwaite. *Cumb* 1C 96
Haverton Hill. *Stoc T* 2B 106
Havyatt. *Som* 3A 22
Hawarden. *Flin* 4F 83
Hawbridge. *Worc* 1E 49
Hawcoat. *Cumb* 2B 96
Hawcross. *Glos* 2C 48
Hawen. *Cdgn* 1D 44
Hawes. *N Yor* 1A 98
Hawes Green. *Norf* 1E 67
Hawick. *Bord* 3H 119
Hawkchurch. *Devn* 2G 13
Hawkedon. *Suff* 5G 65
Hawkenbury. *Kent* 1C 28
Hawkeridge. *Wilts* 1D 22
Hawkerland. *Devn* 4D 12
Hawkesbury. *S Glo* 3C 34
Hawkesbury. *Warw* 2A 62
Hawkesbury Upton. *S Glo* 3C 34
Hawkes End. *W Mid* 2G 61
Hawk Green. *G Man* 2D 84
Hawkhurst. *Kent* 2B 28
Hawkhurst Common.
E Sus 4G 27
Hawkinge. *Kent* 1G 29
Hawkley. *Hants* 4F 25
Hawkridge. *Som* 3B 20
Hawksdale. *Cumb* 5E 113
Hawkshaw. *G Man* 3F 91
Hawkshead. *Cumb* 5E 103
Hawkshead Hill. *Cumb* 5E 103
Hawkswick. *N Yor* 2B 98
Hawksworth. *Notts* 1E 75
Hawksworth. *W Yor* 5D 98
Hawkwell. *Essx* 1C 40
Hawley. *Hants* 1G 25
Hawley. *Kent* 3G 39
Hawling. *Glos* 3F 49
Hawnby. *N Yor* 1H 99
Haworth. *W Yor* 1A 92
Hawstead. *Suff* 5A 66
Hawthorn. *Dur* 5H 115
Hawthorn Hill. *Brac* 4G 37
Hawthorn Hill. *Linc* 5B 88
Hawthorpe. *Linc* 3H 75
Hawton. *Notts* 5E 87
Haxby. *York* 4A 100
Haxey. *N Lin* 1E 87
Haybridge. *Shrp* 3A 60
Haybridge. *Som* 2A 22
Haydock. *Mers* 1H 83
Haydon. *Bath* 1B 22
Haydon. *Dors* 1B 14
Haydon. *Som* 4F 21
Haydon Bridge. *Nmbd* 3B 114
Haydon Wick. *Swin* 3G 35
Haye. *Corn* 2H 7
Hayes. *G Lon*
nr. Bromley 4F 39
Hayes. *G Lon*
nr. Uxbridge 2B 38
Hayfield. *Derbs* 2E 85
Hay Green. *Norf* 4E 77
Hayhill. *E Ayr* 3D 116
Haylands. *IOW* 3D 16
Hayle. *Corn* 3C 4
Hayley Green. *W Mid* 2D 60
Hayling Island. *Hants* 3F 17
Hayne. *Devn* 2B 12
Haynes. *C Beds* 1A 52
Haynes West End. *C Beds* 1A 52
Hay-on-Wye. *Powy* 1F 47
Hayscastle. *Pemb* 2C 42
Hayscastle Cross. *Pemb* 2D 42
Hayshead. *Ang* 4F 145
Hay Street. *Herts* 3D 53
Hayton. *Aber* 3G 153
Hayton. *Cumb*
nr. Aspatria 5C 112
nr. Brampton 4G 113
Hayton. *E Yor* 5C 100
Hayton. *Notts* 2E 87
Hayton's Bent. *Shrp* 2H 59
Haytor Vale. *Devn* 5A 12
Haytown. *Devn* 1D 11
Haywards Heath. *W Sus* 3E 27
Haywood. *S Lan* 4C 128
Hazelbank. *S Lan* 5B 128
Hazelbury Bryan. *Dors* 2C 14
Hazeleigh. *Essx* 5B 54
Hazeley. *Hants* 1F 25
Hazel Grove. *G Man* 2D 84
Hazelhead. *S Yor* 4B 92
Hazelslade. *Staf* 4E 73
Hazel Street. *Kent* 2A 28
Hazelton Walls. *Fife* 1F 137
Hazelwood. *Derbs* 1H 73
Hazlemere. *Buck* 2G 37
Hazler. *Shrp* 1G 59
Hazlerigg. *Tyne* 2F 115
Hazles. *Staf* 1E 73
Hazleton. *Glos* 4F 49
Hazon. *Nmbd* 4F 121
Heacham. *Norf* 2F 77
Headbourne Worthy.
Hants 3C 24
Headcorn. *Kent* 1C 28
Headingley. *W Yor* 1C 92
Headington. *Oxon* 5D 50
Headlam. *Dur* 3E 105
Headless Cross. *Worc* 4E 61
Headley. *Hants*
nr. Haslemere 3G 25
nr. Kingsclere 5D 36
Headley. *Surr* 5D 38
Headley Down. *Hants* 3G 25
Headley Heath. *Worc* 3E 61
Headley Park. *Bris* 5A 34
Head of Muir. *Falk* 1B 128
Headon. *Notts* 3E 87
Heads Nook. *Cumb* 4F 113
Heage. *Derbs* 5A 86
Healaugh. *N Yor*
nr. Grinton 5D 104
nr. York 5H 99
Heald Green. *G Man* 2C 84
Heale. *Devn* 2G 19
Healey. *G Man* 3G 91
Healey. *Nmbd* 4D 114
Healey. *N Yor* 1D 98
Healeyfield. *Dur* 5D 114
Healing. *NE Lin* 3F 95
Heamoor. *Corn* 3B 4
Heanish. *Arg* 4B 138
Heanor. *Derbs* 1B 74
Heanton Punchardon.
Devn 3F 19
Heapham. *Linc* 2F 87
Heartsease. *Powy* 4D 58
Heasley Mill. *Devn* 3H 19
Heaste. *High* 2E 147
Heath. *Derbs* 4B 86
The Heath. *Norf*
nr. Buxton 3E 79
nr. Fakenham 3B 78
nr. Hevingham 3D 78
The Heath. *Staf* 2E 73
The Heath. *Suff* 2E 55
Heath and Reach. *C Beds* 3H 51
Heath Common. *W Sus* 4C 26
Heathcote. *Derbs* 4F 85
Heath Cross. *Devn* 3H 11
Heathencote. *Nptn* 1F 51
Heath End. *Hants* 5D 36
Heath End. *Leics* 3A 74
Heath End. *W Mid* 5E 73
Heather. *Leics* 4A 74
Heatherfield. *High* 4D 155
Heatherton. *Derb* 2H 73
Heathfield. *Cambs* 1E 53
Heathfield. *Cumb* 5C 112
Heathfield. *Devn* 5B 12
Heathfield. *E Sus* 3G 27
Heathfield. *Ren* 3E 126
Heathfield. *Som*
nr. Lydeard St Lawrence
3E 21
nr. Norton Fitzwarren 4E 21
Heath Green. *Worc* 3E 61
Heathhall. *Dum* 2A 112
Heath Hayes. *Staf* 4E 73
Heath Hill. *Shrp* 4B 72
Heath House. *Som* 2H 21
Heathrow Airport.
G Lon **205** (3B 38)
Heathstock. *Devn* 2F 13
Heathton. *Shrp* 1C 60
Heathtop. *Derbs* 2G 73
Heath Town. *W Mid* 1D 60
Heatley. *Staf* 3E 73
Heatley. *Warr* 2B 84
Heaton. *Lanc* 3D 96
Heaton. *Staf* 4D 84
Heaton. *Tyne* 3F 115
Heaton. *W Yor* 1B 92
Heaton Moor. *G Man* 1C 84
Heaton's Bridge. *Lanc* 3C 90
Heaverham. *Kent* 5G 39
Heavitree. *Devn* 3C 12
Hebburn. *Tyne* 3G 115
Hebden. *N Yor* 3C 98
Hebden Bridge. *W Yor* 2H 91
Hebden Green. *Ches W* 4A 84
Hebing End. *Herts* 3D 52
Hebron. *Carm* 2F 43
Hebron. *Nmbd* 1E 115
Heck. *Dum* 1B 112
Heckdyke. *Notts* 1E 87
Heckfield. *Hants* 5F 37
Heckfield Green. *Suff* 3D 66
Heckfordbridge. *Essx* 3C 54
Heckington. *Linc* 1A 76
Heckmondwike. *W Yor* 2C 92
Heddington. *Wilts* 5E 35
Heddle. *Orkn* 6C 172
Heddon. *Devn* 4G 19
Heddon-on-the-Wall.
Nmbd 3E 115
Hedenham. *Norf* 1F 67
Hedge End. *Hants* 1C 16
Hedgerley. *Buck* 2A 38
Hedging. *Som* 4G 21
Hedley on the Hill. *Nmbd* 4D 115
Hednesford. *Staf* 4E 73
Hedon. *E Yor* 2E 95
Hegdon Hill. *Here* 5H 59
Heglibister. *Shet* 6E 173
Heighington. *Darl* 2F 105
Heighington. *Linc* 4H 87
Heightington. *Worc* 3B 60
Heights of Brae. *High* 2H 157
Heights of Fodderty.
High 2H 157
Heights of Kinlochewe.
High 2C 156
Heiton. *Bord* 1B 120
Hele. *Devn*
nr. Exeter 2C 12
nr. Holsworthy 3D 10
nr. Ilfracombe 2F 19
Hele. *Torb* 2F 9
Helen's Bay. *Ards* 1J 179
Helensburgh. *Arg* 1D 126
Helford. *Corn* 4E 5
Helhoughton. *Norf* 3A 78
Helions Bumpstead. *Essx* 1G 53
Helland. *Corn* 5A 10
Helland. *Som* 4G 21
Hellandbridge. *Corn* 5A 10
Hellesdon. *Norf* 4E 78
Hellesveor. *Corn* 2C 4
Hellidon. *Nptn* 5C 62
Hellifield. *N Yor* 4A 98
Hellingly. *E Sus* 4G 27
Hellington. *Norf* 5F 79
Hellister. *Shet* 7E 173
Helmdon. *Nptn* 1D 50
Helmingham. *Suff* 5D 66
Helmington Row. *Dur* 1E 105
Helmsdale. *High* 2H 165
Helmshore. *Lanc* 2F 91
Helmsley. *N Yor* 1A 100
Helperby. *N Yor* 3G 99
Helperthorpe. *N Yor* 2D 100
Helpringham. *Linc* 1A 76
Helpston. *Pet* 5A 76
Helsby. *Ches W* 3G 83
Helsey. *Linc* 3E 89
Helston. *Corn* 4D 4
Helstone. *Corn* 4A 10
Helton. *Cumb* 2G 103
Helwith. *N Yor* 4D 105
Helwith Bridge. *N Yor* 3H 97
Helygain. *Flin* 3E 82
The Hem. *Shrp* 5B 72
Hemblington. *Norf* 4F 79
Hemel Hempstead. *Herts* 5A 52
Hemerdon. *Devn* 3B 8
Hemingbrough. *N Yor* 1G 93
Hemingby. *Linc* 3B 88
Hemingfield. *S Yor* 4D 93
Hemingford Abbots.
Cambs 3B 64
Hemingford Grey. *Cambs* 3B 64
Hemingstone. *Suff* 5D 66
Hemington. *Leics* 3B 74
Hemington. *Nptn* 2H 63
Hemington. *Som* 1C 22
Hemley. *Suff* 1F 55
Hemlington. *Midd* 3B 106
Hempholme. *E Yor* 4E 101
Hempnall. *Norf* 1E 67
Hempnall Green. *Norf* 1E 67
Hempriggs. *High* 4F 169
Hemp's Green. *Essx* 3C 54
Hempstead. *Essx* 2G 53
Hempstead. *Medw* 4B 40
Hempstead. *Norf*
nr. Holt 2D 78
nr. Stalham 3G 79
Hempsted. *Glos* 4D 48
Hempton. *Norf* 3B 78
Hempton. *Oxon* 2C 50
Hemsby. *Norf* 4G 79
Hemswell. *Linc* 1G 87
Hemswell Cliff. *Linc* 2G 87
Hemsworth. *Dors* 2E 15
Hemsworth. *W Yor* 3E 93
Hemyock. *Devn* 1E 13
Henallt. *Carm* 3E 45
Henbury. *Bris* 4A 34
Henbury. *Ches E* 3C 84
Hendomen. *Powy* 1E 58
Hendon. *G Lon* 2D 38
Hendon. *Tyne* 4H 115
Hendra. *Corn* 3D 6
Hendre. *B'end* 3C 32
Hendreforgan. *Rhon* 3C 32
Hendy. *Carm* 5F 45
Heneglwys. *IOA* 3D 80
Henfeddau Fawr. *Pemb* 1G 43
Henfield. *S Glo* 4B 34
Henfield. *W Sus* 4D 26
Henford. *Devn* 3D 10
Hengoed. *Cphy* 2E 33
Hengoed. *Shrp* 2E 71
Hengrave. *Suff* 4H 65
Henham. *Essx* 3F 53
Heniarth. *Powy* 5D 70
Henlade. *Som* 4F 21
Henley. *Dors* 2B 14
Henley. *Shrp*
nr. Church Stretton 2G 59
nr. Ludlow 3H 59
Henley. *Som* 3H 21
Henley. *Suff* 5D 66
Henley. *W Sus* 4G 25
Henley Down. *E Sus* 4B 28
Henley-in-Arden. *Warw* 4F 61
Henley-on-Thames.
Oxon 3F 37
Henley Street. *Kent* 4A 40
Henllan. *Cdgn* 1D 44
Henllan. *Den* 4C 82
Henllan. *Mon* 3F 47
Henllan Amgoed. *Carm* 3F 43
Henllys. *Torf* 2F 33
Henlow. *C Beds* 2B 52
Hennock. *Devn* 4B 12
Henny Street. *Essx* 2B 54
Henryd. *Cnwy* 3G 81
Henry's Moat. *Pemb* 2E 43
Hensall. *N Yor* 2F 93
Henshaw. *Nmbd* 3A 114
Hensingham. *Cumb* 3A 102
Henstead. *Suff* 2G 67
Hensting. *Hants* 4C 24
Henstridge. *Som* 1C 14
Henstridge Ash. *Som* 4C 22
Henstridge Bowden. *Som* 4B 22
Henstridge Marsh. *Som* 4C 22
Henton. *Oxon* 5F 51
Henton. *Som* 2H 21
Henwood. *Corn* 5C 10
Heogan. *Shet* 7F 173
Heolgerrig. *Mer T* 5D 46
Heol Senni. *Powy* 3C 46
Heol-y-Cyw. *B'end* 3C 32

Hepburn—Howell

Hepburn. Nmbd 2E 121
Hepple. Nmbd 4D 121
Hepscott. Nmbd 1F 115
Heptonstall. W Yor 2H 91
Hepworth. Suff 3B 66
Hepworth. W Yor 4B 92
Herbrandston. Pemb 4C 42
Hereford. Here 2A 48
Heribusta. High 1D 154
Heriot. Bord 4H 129
Hermiston. Edin 2E 129
Hermitage. Dors 2B 14
Hermitage. Bord 5H 119
Hermitage. W Ber 4D 36
Hermitage. W Sus 2F 17
Hermon. Carm
nr. Llandeilo 3G 45
nr. Newcastle Emlyn 2D 44
Hermon. IOA 4C 80
Hermon. Pemb 1G 43
Herne. Kent 4F 41
Herne Bay. Kent 4F 41
Herne Common. Kent 4F 41
Herne Pound. Kent 5A 40
Herner. Devn 4F 19
Hernhill. Kent 4E 41
Herodsfoot. Corn 2G 7
Heronden. Kent 5G 41
Herongate. Essx 1H 39
Heronsford. S Ayr 1G 109
Heronsgate. Herts 1B 38
Heron's Ghyll. E Sus 3F 27
Herra. Shet 2H 173
Herriard. Hants 2E 25
Herringfleet. Suff 1G 67
Herringswell. Suff 4G 65
Herrington. Tyne 4G 115
Hersden. Kent 4G 41
Hersham. Corn 2C 10
Hersham. Surr 4C 38
Herstmonceux. E Sus 4H 27
Herston. Dors 5F 15
Herston. Orkn 8D 172
Hertford. Herts 4D 52
Hertford Heath. Herts 4D 52
Hertingfordbury. Herts 4D 52
Hesketh. Lanc 2C 90
Hesketh Bank. Lanc 2C 90
Hesketh Lane. Lanc 5F 97
Hesket Newmarket.
Cumb 1E 103
Heskin Green. Lanc 3D 90
Hesleden. Dur 1B 106
Hesleyside. Nmbd 1B 114
Heslington. York 4A 100
Hessay. York 4H 99
Hessenford. Corn 3H 7
Hessett. Suff 4B 66
Hessilhead. N Ayr 4E 127
Hessle. E Yor 2D 94
Hestaford. Shet 6D 173
Hest Bank. Lanc 3D 96
Hester's Way. Glos 3E 49
Hestinsetter. Shet 7D 173
Heston. G Lon 3C 38
Hestwall. Orkn 6B 172
Heswall. Mers 2E 83
Hethe. Oxon 3D 50
Hethelpit Cross. Glos 3C 48
Hethersett. Norf 5D 78
Hethersgill. Cumb 3F 113
Hetherside. Cumb 3F 113
Hethpool. Nmbd 2C 120
Hett. Dur 1F 105
Hetton. N Yor 4B 98
Hetton-le-Hole. Tyne 5G 115
Hetton Steads. Nmbd 1E 121
Heugh. Nmbd 2D 115
Heugh-head. Abers 2A 152
Heveningham. Suff 3F 67
Hever. Kent 1F 27
Heversham. Cumb 1D 97
Hevingham. Norf 3D 78
Hewas Water. Corn 4D 6
Hewelsfield. Glos 5A 48
Hewish. N Som 5H 33
Hewish. Som 2H 13
Hewood. Dors 2G 13
Heworth. York 4A 100
Hexham. Nmbd 3C 114
Hextable. Kent 3G 39
Hexton. Herts 2B 52
Hexworthy. Devn 5G 11
Heybridge. Essx
nr. Brentwood 1H 39
nr. Maldon 5B 54
Heybridge Basin. Essx 5B 54
Heybrook Bay. Devn 4A 8
Heydon. Cambs 1E 53
Heydon. Norf 3D 78
Heydour. Linc 2H 75
Heylipol. Arg 4A 138
Heyop. Powy 3E 59
Heysham. Lanc 3D 96
Heyshott. W Sus 1G 17
Heytesbury. Wilts 2E 23
Heythrop. Oxon 3B 50
Heywood. G Man 3G 91
Heywood. Wilts 1D 22
Hibaldstow. N Lin 4C 94
Hickleton. S Yor 4E 93
Hickling. Norf 3G 79
Hickling. Notts 3D 74
Hickling Green. Norf 3G 79
Hickling Heath. Norf 3G 79
Hickstead. W Sus 3D 26
Hidcote Bartrim. Glos 1G 49
Hidcote Boyce. Glos 1G 49
Higford. Shrp 5B 72
High Ackworth. W Yor 3E 93
Higham. Derbs 5A 86
Higham. Kent 3B 40
Higham. Lanc 1G 91
Higham. S Yor 4D 92
Higham. Suff
nr. Ipswich 2D 54
nr. Newmarket 4G 65
Higham Dykes. Nmbd 2E 115
Higham Ferrers. Nptn 4G 63
Higham Gobion. C Beds 2B 52
Higham on the Hill. Leics 1A 62
Highampton. Devn 2E 11
Higham Wood. Kent 1H 27
High Angerton. Nmbd 1D 115
High Auldgirth. Dum 1G 111
High Bankhill. Cumb 5G 113
High Banton. N Lan 1A 128
High Barnet. G Lon 1D 38
High Beech. Essx 1F 39
High Bentham. N Yor 3F 97
High Bickington. Devn 4G 19
High Biggins. Cumb 2F 97
High Birkwith. N Yor 2G 97
High Blantyre. S Lan 4H 127
High Bonnybridge. Falk 2B 128
High Borrans. Cumb 4F 103
High Bradfield. S Yor 1G 85
High Bray. Devn 3G 19
Highbridge. Cumb 5E 113
Highbridge. High 5E 148
Highbridge. Som 2G 21
Highbrook. W Sus 2E 27
High Brooms. Kent 1G 27
High Bullen. Devn 4F 19
Highburton. W Yor 3B 92
Highbury. Som 2B 22
High Buston. Nmbd 4G 121
High Callerton. Nmbd 2E 115
High Carlingill. Cumb 4H 103
High Catton. E Yor 4B 100
High Church. Nmbd 1E 115
Highclere. Hants 5C 36
Highcliffe. Dors 3H 15
High Cogges. Oxon 5B 50
High Common. Norf 5B 78
High Coniscliffe. Darl 3F 105
High Crosby. Cumb 4F 113
High Cross. Hants 4F 25
High Cross. Herts 4D 52
High Easter. Essx 4G 53
High Eggborough. N Yor 2F 93
High Ellington. N Yor 1D 98
Higher Alham. Som 2B 22
Higher Ansty. Dors 2C 14
Higher Ashton. Devn 4B 12
Higher Ballam. Lanc 1B 90
Higher Bartle. Lanc 1D 90
Higher Bockhampton.
Dors 3C 14
Higher Bojewyan. Corn 3A 4
High Ercall. Telf 4H 71
Higher Cheriton. Devn 2E 12
Higher Clovelly. Devn 4D 18
Higher Compton. Plym 3A 8
Higher Dean. Devn 2D 8
Higher Dinting. Derbs 1E 85
Higher Dunstone. Devn 5H 11
Higher End. G Man 4D 90
Higherford. Lanc 5A 98
Higher Gabwell. Devn 2F 9
Higher Halstock Leigh.
Dors 2A 14
Higher Heysham. Lanc 3D 96
Higher Hurdsfield. Ches E 3D 84
Higher Kingcombe. Dors 3A 14
Higher Kinnerton. Flin 4F 83
Higher Melcombe. Dors 2C 14
Higher Penwortham. Lanc 2D 90
Higher Porthpean. Corn 3E 7
Higher Poynton. Ches E 2D 84
Higher Shotton. Flin 4F 83
Higher Shurlach. Ches W 3A 84
Higher Slade. Devn 2F 19
Higher Tale. Devn 2D 12
Higher Town. IOS 1B 4
Higher Town. Som 2C 20
Highertown. Corn 4C 6
Higher Vexford. Som 3E 20
Higher Walton. Lanc 2D 90
Higher Walton. Warr 2H 83
Higher Whatcombe. Dors 2D 14
Higher Wheelton. Lanc 2E 90
Higher Whiteleigh. Corn 3C 10
Higher Whitley. Ches W 2A 84
Higher Wincham. Ches W 3A 84
Higher Wraxall. Dors 2A 14
Higher Wych. Ches W 1G 71
Higher Yalberton. Torb 3E 9
High Etherley. Dur 2E 105
High Ferry. Linc 1C 76
Highfield. E Yor 1H 93
Highfield. N Ayr 4E 126
Highfield. Tyne 4E 115
Highfields Caldecote.
Cambs 5C 64
High Gallowhill. E Dun 2H 127
High Garrett. Essx 3A 54
Highgate. G Lon 2D 39
Highgate. N Ayr 4E 127
Highgate. Powy 1D 58
High Grange. Dur 1E 105
High Green. Cumb 4F 103
High Green. Norf 5D 78
High Green. Shrp 2B 60
High Green. S Yor 1H 85
High Green. W Yor 3B 92
High Green. Worc 1D 49
Highgreen Manor. Nmbd 5C 120
High Halden. Kent 2C 28
High Halstow. Medw 3B 40
High Ham. Som 3H 21
High Harrington. Cumb 2B 102
High Haswell. Dur 5G 115
High Hatton. Shrp 3A 72
High Hawsker. N Yor 4G 107
High Hesket. Cumb 5F 113
High Hesleden. Dur 1B 106
High Hoyland. S Yor 3C 92
High Hunsley. E Yor 1C 94
High Hurstwood. E Sus 3F 27
High Hutton. N Yor 3B 100
High Ireby. Cumb 1D 102
High Keil. Arg 5A 122
High Kelling. Norf 2D 78
High Kilburn. N Yor 2H 99
High Knipe. Cumb 3G 103
High Lands. Dur 2E 105
The Highlands. Shrp 2A 60
High Lane. G Man 2D 84
High Lane. Worc 4A 60
Highlane. Ches E 4C 84
Highlane. Derbs 2B 86
High Laver. Essx 5F 53
Highlaws. Cumb 5C 112
Highleadon. Glos 3C 48
High Legh. Ches E 2B 84
Highleigh. W Sus 3G 17
High Leven. Stoc T 3B 106
Highley. Shrp 2B 60
High Littleton. Bath 1B 22
High Longthwaite. Cumb 5D 112
High Lorton. Cumb 2C 102
High Marishes. N Yor 2C 100
High Marnham. Notts 3F 87
High Melton. S Yor 4F 93
High Mickley. Nmbd 3D 115
High Moor. Lanc 3D 90
Highmoor. Cumb 5D 112
Highmoor. Oxon 3F 37
Highmoor Cross. Oxon 3F 37
Highmoor Hill. Mon 3H 33
Highnam. Glos 4C 48
High Newport. Tyne 4G 115
High Newton. Cumb 1D 96
High Newton-by-the-Sea.
Nmbd 2G 121
High Nibthwaite. Cumb 1B 96
High Offley. Staf 3B 72
High Ongar. Essx 5F 53
High Onn. Staf 4C 72
High Orchard. Glos 4D 48
High Park. Mers 3B 90
High Roding. Essx 4G 53
High Row. Cumb 1E 103
High Salvington. W Sus 5C 26
High Scales. Cumb 5C 112
High Shaw. N Yor 5B 104
High Shincliffe. Dur 5F 115
High Side. Cumb 1D 102
High Spen. Tyne 3E 115
Highsted. Kent 5D 40
High Stoop. Dur 5E 115
High Street. Corn 3D 6
High Street. Suff
nr. Aldeburgh 5G 67
nr. Bungay 2F 67
nr. Yoxford 3G 67
High Street Green. Suff 5C 66
Highstreet Green. Essx 2A 54
Highstreet Green. Surr 2A 26
Hightae. Dum 2B 112
High Throston. Hart 1B 106
High Town. Staf 4D 73
Hightown. Ches E 4C 84
Hightown. Mers 4A 90
Hightown Green. Suff 5B 66
High Toynton. Linc 4B 88
High Trewhitt. Nmbd 4E 121
High Valleyfield. Fife 1D 128
Highway. Here 1H 47
Highweek. Devn 5B 12
High Westwood. Dur 4E 115
Highwood. Staf 2E 73
Highwood. Worc 4A 60
High Worsall. N Yor 4A 106
Highworth. Swin 2H 35
High Wray. Cumb 5E 103
High Wych. Herts 4E 53
High Wycombe. Buck 2G 37
Hilborough. Norf 5H 77
Hilcott. Wilts 1G 23
Hildenborough. Kent 1G 27
Hildersham. Cambs 1F 53
Hilderstone. Staf 2D 72
Hilderthorpe. E Yor 3F 101
Hilfield. Dors 2B 14
Hilgay. Norf 1F 65
Hill. S Glo 2B 34
Hill. Warw 4B 62
Hill. Worc 1E 49
The Hill. Cumb 1A 96
Hillam. N Yor 2F 93
Hillbeck. Cumb 3A 104
Hillberry. IOM 4C 108
Hillborough. Kent 4G 41
Hillbourne. Pool 3F 15
Hillbrae. Abers
nr. Aberchirder 4D 160
nr. Inverurie 1E 153
nr. Methlick 5F 161
Hill Brow. Hants 4F 25
Hillbutts. Dors 2E 15
Hillclifflane. Derbs 1G 73
Hillcommon. Som 4E 21
Hill Deverill. Wilts 2D 22
Hilldyke. Linc 1C 76
Hill End. Dur 1D 104
Hill End. Fife 4C 136
Hill End. N Yor 4C 98
Hillend. Fife 1E 129
Hillend. N Lan 3B 128
Hillend. Shrp 1C 60
Hillend. Swan 3D 30
Hillersland. Glos 4A 48
Hillerton. Devn 3H 11
Hillesden. Buck 3E 51
Hillesley. Glos 3C 34
Hillfarrance. Som 4E 21
Hill Gate. Here 3H 47
Hill Green. Essx 2E 53
Hill Green. W Ber 4C 36
Hillhall. Lis 3G 179
Hill Head. Hants 2D 16
Hillhead. Abers 5C 160
Hillhead. Devn 3F 9
Hillhead. S Ayr 3D 116
Hillhead of Auchentumb.
Abers 3G 161
Hilliard's Cross. Staf 4F 73
Hilliclay. High 2D 168
Hillingdon. G Lon 2B 38
Hillington. Glas 3G 127
Hillington. Norf 3G 77
Hillmorton. Warw 3C 62
Hill of Beath. Fife 4D 136
Hill of Fearn. High 1C 158
Hill of Fiddes. Abers 1G 153
Hill of Keillor. Ang 4B 144
Hill of Overbrae. Abers 2F 161
Hill Ridware. Staf 4E 73
Hillsborough. Lis 4G 179
Hillsborough. S Yor 1H 85
Hill Side. W Yor 3B 92
Hillside. Abers 4G 153
Hillside. Ang 2G 145
Hillside. Devn 2D 8
Hillside. Mers 3B 90
Hillside. Orkn 5C 172
Hillside. Shet 5F 173
Hillside. Shrp 2A 60
Hillside. Worc 4B 60
Hillside of Prieston. Ang 5C 144
Hill Somersal. Derbs 2F 73
Hillstown. Derbs 4B 86
Hillstreet. Hants 1B 16
Hillswick. Shet 4D 173
Hill Top. Dur
nr. Barnard Castle 2C 104
nr. Durham 5F 115
nr. Stanley 4E 115
Hilltown. New M 7G 179
Hill View. Dors 3E 15
Hillwell. Shet 10E 173
Hill Wootton. Warw 4H 61
Hillyland. Per 1C 136
Hilmarton. Wilts 4F 35
Hilperton. Wilts 1D 22
Hilperton Marsh. Wilts 1D 22
Hilsea. Port 2E 17
Hilston. E Yor 1F 95
Hiltingbury. Hants 4C 24
Hilton. Cambs 4B 64
Hilton. Cumb 2A 104
Hilton. Derbs 2G 73
Hilton. Dors 2C 14
Hilton. Dur 2E 105
Hilton. High 5E 165
Hilton. Shrp 1B 60
Hilton. Staf 5E 73
Hilton. Stoc T 3B 106
Hilton of Cadboll. High 1C 158
Himbleton. Worc 5D 60
Himley. Staf 1C 60
Hincaster. Cumb 1E 97
Hinchwick. Glos 3G 49
Hinckley. Leics 1B 62
Hinderclay. Suff 3C 66
Hinderwell. N Yor 3E 107
Hindford. Shrp 2F 71
Hindhead. Surr 3G 25
Hindley. G Man 4E 90
Hindley. Nmbd 4D 114
Hindley Green. G Man 4E 91
Hindlip. Worc 5C 60
Hindolveston. Norf 3C 78
Hindon. Wilts 3E 23
Hindringham. Norf 2B 78
Hingham. Norf 5C 78
Hinksford. Staf 2C 60
Hinstock. Shrp 3A 72
Hintlesham. Suff 1D 54
Hinton. Hants 3H 15
Hinton. Here 2G 47
Hinton. Nptn 5C 62
Hinton. Shrp 5G 71
Hinton. S Glo 4C 34
Hinton Ampner. Hants 4D 24
Hinton Blewett. Bath 1A 22
Hinton Charterhouse.
Bath 1C 22
Hinton-in-the-Hedges.
Nptn 2D 50
Hinton Martell. Dors 2F 15
Hinton on the Green. Worc 1F 49
Hinton Parva. Swin 3H 35
Hinton St George. Som 1H 13
Hinton St Mary. Dors 1C 14
Hinton Waldrist. Oxon 2B 36
Hints. Shrp 3A 60
Hints. Staf 5F 73
Hinwick. Bed 4G 63
Hinxhill. Kent 1E 29
Hinxton. Cambs 1E 53
Hinxworth. Herts 1C 52
Hipley. Hants 1E 16
Hipperholme. W Yor 2B 92
Hipsburn. Nmbd 3G 121
Hipswell. N Yor 5E 105
Hiraeth. Carm 2F 43
Hirn. Abers 3E 153
Hirnant. Powy 3C 70
Hirst. N Lan 3B 128
Hirst. Nmbd 1F 115
Hirst Courtney. N Yor 2G 93
Hirwaen. Den 4D 82
Hirwaun. Rhon 5C 46
Hiscott. Devn 4F 19
Histon. Cambs 4D 64
Hitcham. Suff 5B 66
Hitchin. Herts 3B 52
Hittisleigh. Devn 3H 11
Hittisleigh Barton. Devn 3H 11
Hive. E Yor 1B 94
Hixon. Staf 3E 73
Hoaden. Kent 5G 41
Hoar Cross. Staf 3F 73
Hoarwithy. Here 3A 48
Hoath. Kent 4G 41
Yr Hôb. Flin 5F 83
Hobarris. Shrp 3F 59
Hobbister. Orkn 7C 172
Hobbles Green. Suff 5G 65
Hobbs Cross. Essx 1F 39
Hobkirk. Bord 3H 119
Hobson. Dur 4E 115
Hoby. Leics 4D 74
Hockering. Norf 4C 78
Hockering Heath. Norf 4C 78
Hockerton. Notts 5E 86
Hockley. Essx 1C 40
Hockley. Staf 5G 73
Hockley. W Mid 3G 61
Hockley Heath. W Mid 3F 61
Hockliffe. C Beds 3H 51
Hockwold cum Wilton.
Norf 2G 65
Hockworthy. Devn 1D 12
Hoddesdon. Herts 5D 52
Hoddlesden. Bkbn 2F 91
Hoddomcross. Dum 2C 112
Hodgeston. Pemb 5E 43
Hodley. Powy 1D 58
Hodnet. Shrp 3A 72
Hodsoll Street. Kent 4H 39
Hodson. Swin 3G 35
Hodthorpe. Derbs 3C 86
Hoe. Norf 4B 78
The Hoe. Plym 3A 8
Hoe Gate. Hants 1E 17
Hoff. Cumb 3H 103
Hoffleet Stow. Linc 2B 76
Hogaland. Shet 4E 173
Hogben's Hill. Kent 5E 41
Hoggard's Green. Suff 5A 66
Hoggeston. Buck 3G 51
Hoggrill's End. Warw 1G 61
Hogha Gearraidh. W Isl 1C 170
Hoghton. Lanc 2E 90
Hoghton Bottoms. Lanc 2E 91
Hognaston. Derbs 5G 85
Hogsthorpe. Linc 3E 89
Hogstock. Dors 2E 15
Holbeach. Linc 3C 76
Holbeach Bank. Linc 3C 76
Holbeach Clough. Linc 3C 76
Holbeach Drove. Linc 4C 76
Holbeach Hurn. Linc 3C 76
Holbeach St Johns. Linc 4C 76
Holbeach St Marks. Linc 2C 76
Holbeach St Matthew.
Linc 2D 76
Holbeck. Notts 3C 86
Holbeck. W Yor 1C 92
Holbeck Woodhouse.
Notts 3C 86
Holberrow Green. Worc 5E 61
Holbeton. Devn 3C 8
Holborn. G Lon 2E 39
Holbrook. Derbs 1A 74
Holbrook. S Yor 2B 86
Holbrook. Suff 2E 55
Holburn. Nmbd 1E 121
Holbury. Hants 2C 16
Holcombe. Devn 5C 12
Holcombe. G Man 3F 91
Holcombe. Som 2B 22
Holcombe Brook. G Man 3F 91
Holcombe Rogus. Devn 1D 12
Holcot. Nptn 4E 63
Holden. Lanc 5G 97
Holdenby. Nptn 4D 62
Holder's Green. Essx 3G 53
Holdgate. Shrp 2H 59
Holdingham. Linc 1H 75
Holditch. Dors 2G 13
Holemoor. Devn 2E 11
Hole Street. W Sus 4C 26
Holford. Som 2E 21
Holker. Cumb 2C 96
Holkham. Norf 1A 78
Hollacombe. Devn 2D 11
Holland. Orkn
on Papa Westray 2D 172
on Stronsay 5F 172
Holland Fen. Linc 1B 76
Holland Lees. Lanc 4D 90
Holland-on-Sea. Essx 4F 55
Holland Park. W Mid 5E 73
Hollandstoun. Orkn 2G 172
Hollesley. Suff 1G 55
Hollinfare. Warr 1A 84
Hollingbourne. Kent 5C 40
Hollingbury. Brig 5E 27
Hollingdon. Buck 3G 51
Hollingrove. E Sus 3A 28
Hollington. Derbs 2G 73
Hollington. E Sus 4B 28
Hollington. Staf 2E 73
Hollington Grove. Derbs 2G 73
Hollingworth. G Man 1E 85
Hollins. Derbs 3H 85
Hollins. G Man
nr. Bury 4G 91
nr. Middleton 4G 91
Hollinsclough. Staf 4E 85
Hollinswood. Telf 5B 72
Hollinthorpe. W Yor 1D 93
Hollinwood. G Man 4H 91
Hollinwood. Shrp 2H 71
Hollocombe. Devn 1G 11
Holloway. Derbs 5H 85
Hollowell. Nptn 3D 62
Hollow Meadows. S Yor 2G 85
Hollows. Dum 2E 113
Hollybush. Cphy 5E 47
Hollybush. E Ayr 3C 116
Hollybush. Worc 2C 48
Holly End. Norf 5D 77
Holly Hill. N Yor 4E 105
Hollyhurst. Shrp 1H 71
Hollym. E Yor 2G 95
Hollywood. Worc 3E 61
Holmacott. Devn 4F 19
Holmbridge. W Yor 4B 92
Holmbury St Mary. Surr 1C 26
Holmbush. Corn 3E 7
Holmcroft. Staf 3D 72
Holme. Cambs 2A 64
Holme. Cumb 2E 97
Holme. N Lin 4C 94
Holme. N Yor 1F 99
Holme. Notts 5F 87
Holme. W Yor 4B 92
Holmebridge. Dors 4D 15
Holme Chapel. Lanc 2G 91
Holme Hale. Norf 5A 78
Holme Lacy. Here 2A 48
Holme Marsh. Here 5F 59
Holmend. Dum 4C 118
Holme next the Sea. Norf 1G 77
Holme-on-Spalding-Moor.
E Yor 1B 94
Holme on the Wolds.
E Yor 5D 100
Holme Pierrepont. Notts 2D 74
Holmer. Here 1A 48
Holmer Green. Buck 1A 38
Holmes. Lanc 3C 90
Holme St Cuthbert. Cumb 5C 112
Holmes Chapel. Ches E 4B 84
Holmesfield. Derbs 3H 85
Holmeswood. Lanc 3C 90
Holmewood. Derbs 4B 86
Holmfirth. W Yor 4B 92
Holmhead. E Ayr 2E 117
Holmisdale. High 4A 154
Holm of Drumlanrig.
Dum 5H 117
Holmpton. E Yor 2G 95
Holmrook. Cumb 5B 102
Holmsgarth. Shet 7F 173
Holmside. Dur 5F 115
Holmwrangle. Cumb 5G 113
Holne. Devn 2D 8
Holsworthy. Devn 2D 10
Holsworthy Beacon. Devn 2D 10
Holt. Dors 2F 15
Holt. Norf 2C 78
Holt. Wilts 5D 34
Holt. Worc 4C 60
Holt. Wrex 5G 83
Holtby. York 4A 100
Holt End. Hants 3E 25
Holt End. Worc 4E 61
Holt Fleet. Worc 4C 60
Holt Green. Lanc 4B 90
Holt Heath. Dors 2F 15
Holt Heath. Worc 4C 60
Holton. Oxon 5D 50
Holton. Som 4B 22
Holton. Suff 3F 67
Holton cum Beckering.
Linc 2A 88
Holton Heath. Dors 3E 15
Holton le Clay. Linc 4F 95
Holton le Moor. Linc 1H 87
Holton St Mary. Suff 2D 54
Holt Pound. Hants 2G 25
Holtsmere End. Herts 4A 52
Holtye. E Sus 2F 27
Holwell. Dors 1C 14
Holwell. Herts 2B 52
Holwell. Leics 3E 75
Holwell. Oxon 5H 49
Holwell. Som 2C 22
Holwick. Dur 2C 104
Holworth. Dors 4C 14
Holybourne. Hants 2F 25
Holy City. Devn 2G 13
Holy Cross. Worc 3D 60
Holyfield. Essx 5D 53
Holyhead. IOA 2B 80
Holy Island. Nmbd 5H 131
Holymoorside. Derbs 4H 85
Holyport. Wind 4G 37
Holystone. Nmbd 4D 120
Holytown. N Lan 3A 128
Holywell. Cambs 3C 64
Holywell. Corn 3B 6
Holywell. Dors 2A 14
Holywell. Flin 3D 82
Holywell. Glos 2C 34
Holywell. Nmbd 2G 115
Holywell. Warw 4F 61
Holywell Green. W Yor 3A 92
Holywell Lake. Som 4E 20
Holywell Row. Suff 3G 65
Holywood. Ards 2J 179
Holywood. Dum 1G 111
Homer. Shrp 5A 72
Homer Green. Mers 4B 90
Homersfield. Suff 2E 67
Hom Green. Here 3A 48
Homington. Wilts 4G 23
Honeyborough. Pemb 4D 42
Honeybourne. Worc 1G 49
Honeychurch. Devn 2G 11
Honeydon. Bed 5A 64
Honey Hill. Kent 4F 41
Honey Street. Wilts 5G 35
Honey Tye. Suff 2C 54
Honeywick. C Beds 3H 51
Honiley. Warw 3G 61
Honing. Norf 3F 79
Honingham. Norf 4D 78
Honington. Linc 1G 75
Honington. Suff 3B 66
Honington. Warw 1A 50
Honiton. Devn 2E 13
Honley. W Yor 3B 92
Honnington. Telf 4B 72
Hoo. Suff 5E 67
Hoobrook. Worc 3C 60
Hood Green. S Yor 4D 92
Hooe. E Sus 5A 28
Hooe. Plym 3B 8
Hooe Common. E Sus 4A 28
Hoo Green. Ches E 2B 84
Hoohill. Bkpl 1B 90
Hook. Cambs 1D 64
Hook. E Yor 2A 94
Hook. G Lon 4C 38
Hook. Hants
nr. Basingstoke 1F 25
nr. Fareham 2D 16
Hook. Pemb 3D 43
Hook. Wilts 3F 35
Hook-a-Gate. Shrp 5G 71
Hook Bank. Worc 1D 48
Hooke. Dors 2A 14
Hooker Gate. Tyne 4E 115
Hookgate. Staf 2B 72
Hook Green. Kent
nr. Lamberhurst 2A 28
nr. Meopham 4H 39
nr. Southfleet 3H 39
Hook Norton. Oxon 2B 50
Hook's Cross. Herts 3C 52
Hook Street. Glos 2B 34
Hookway. Devn 3B 12
Hookwood. Surr 1D 26
Hoole. Ches W 4G 83
Hooley. Surr 5D 39
Hooley Bridge. G Man 3G 91
Hooley Brow. G Man 3G 91
Hoo St Werburgh. Medw 3B 40
Hooton. Ches W 3F 83
Hooton Levitt. S Yor 1C 86
Hooton Pagnell. S Yor 4E 93
Hooton Roberts. S Yor 1B 86
Hoove. Shet 7E 173
Hope. Derbs 2F 85
Hope. Flin 5F 83
Hope. High 2E 167
Hope. Powy 5E 71
Hope. Shrp 5F 71
Hope. Staf 5F 85
Hope Bagot. Shrp 3H 59
Hope Bowdler. Shrp 1G 59
Hopedale. Staf 5F 85
Hope Green. Ches E 2D 84
Hopeman. Mor 2F 159
Hope Mansell. Here 4B 48
Hopesay. Shrp 2F 59
Hope's Green. Essx 2B 40
Hopetown. W Yor 2D 93
Hope under Dinmore.
Here 5H 59
Hopley's Green. Here 5F 59
Hopperton. N Yor 4G 99
Hop Pole. Linc 4A 76
Hopstone. Shrp 1B 60
Hopton. Derbs 5G 85
Hopton. Powy 1E 59
Hopton. Shrp
nr. Oswestry 3F 71
nr. Wem 3H 71
Hopton. Staf 3D 72
Hopton. Suff 3B 66
Hopton Cangeford. Shrp 2H 59
Hopton Castle. Shrp 3F 59
Hopton Heath. Staf 3D 72
Hoptonheath. Shrp 3F 59
Hopton on Sea. Norf 5H 79
Hopton Wafers. Shrp 3A 60
Hopwas. Staf 5F 73
Hopwood. Worc 3E 61
Horam. E Sus 4G 27
Horbling. Linc 2A 76
Horbury. W Yor 3C 92
Horcott. Glos 5G 49
Horden. Dur 5H 115
Horderley. Shrp 2G 59
Hordle. Hants 3A 16
Hordley. Shrp 2F 71
Horeb. Carm
nr. Brechfa 3F 45
nr. Llanelli 5E 45
Horeb. Cdgn 1D 45
Horfield. Bris 4A 34
Horgabost. W Isl 8C 171
Horham. Suff 3E 66
Horkstow. N Lin 3C 94
Horley. Oxon 1C 50
Horley. Surr 1D 27
Horn Ash. Dors 2G 13
Hornblotton Green. Som 3A 22
Hornby. Lanc 3E 97
Hornby. N Yor
nr. Appleton Wiske 4A 106
nr. Catterick Garrison 5F 105
Horncastle. Linc 4B 88
Hornchurch. G Lon 2G 39
Horncliffe. Nmbd 5F 131
Horndean. Hants 1F 17
Horndean. Bord 5E 131
Horndon. Devn 4F 11
Horndon on the Hill. Thur 2A 40
Horne. Surr 1E 27
Horner. Som 2C 20
Horning. Norf 4F 79
Horninghold. Leics 1F 63
Horninglow. Staf 3G 73
Horningsea. Cambs 4D 65
Horningsham. Wilts 2D 22
Horningtoft. Norf 3B 78
Hornsbury. Som 1G 13
Hornsby. Cumb 4G 113
Hornsbygate. Cumb 4G 113
Horns Corner. Kent 3B 28
Horns Cross. Devn 4D 19
Hornsea. E Yor 5G 101
Hornsea Burton. E Yor 5G 101
Hornsey. G Lon 2E 39
Hornton. Oxon 1B 50
Horpit. Swin 3H 35
Horrabridge. Devn 2B 8
Horringer. Suff 4H 65
Horringford. IOW 4D 16
Horrocks Fold. G Man 3F 91
Horrocksford. Lanc 5G 97
Horsbrugh Ford. Bord 1E 119
Horsebridge. Devn 5E 11
Horsebridge. Hants 3B 24
Horsebrook. Staf 4C 72
Horsecastle. N Som 5H 33
Horsehay. Telf 5A 72
Horseheath. Cambs 1G 53
Horsehouse. N Yor 1C 98
Horsell. Surr 5A 38
Horseman's Green. Wrex 1G 71
Horsenden. Buck 5F 51
Horseway. Cambs 2D 64
Horsey. Norf 3G 79
Horsey. Som 3G 21
Horsford. Norf 4D 78
Horsforth. W Yor 1C 92
Horsham. W Sus 2C 26
Horsham. Worc 5B 60
Horsham St Faith. Norf 4E 78
Horsington. Linc 4A 88
Horsington. Som 4C 22
Horsley. Derbs 1A 74
Horsley. Glos 2D 34
Horsley. Nmbd
nr. Prudhoe 3D 115
nr. Rochester 5C 120
Horsley Cross. Essx 3E 54
Horsleycross Street. Essx 3E 54
Horsleyhill. Bord 3H 119
Horsleyhope. Dur 5D 114
Horsley Woodhouse.
Derbs 1A 74
Horsmonden. Kent 1A 28
Horspath. Oxon 5D 50
Horstead. Norf 4E 79
Horsted Keynes. W Sus 3E 27
Horton. Buck 4H 51
Horton. Dors 2F 15
Horton. Lanc 4A 98
Horton. Nptn 5F 63
Horton. Shrp 2G 71
Horton. Som 1G 13
Horton. S Glo 3C 34
Horton. Staf 5D 84
Horton. Swan 4D 30
Horton. Wilts 5F 35
Horton. Wind 3B 38
Horton Cross. Som 1G 13
Horton-cum-Studley.
Oxon 4D 50
Horton Grange. Nmbd 2F 115
Horton Green. Ches W 1G 71
Horton Heath. Hants 1C 16
Horton in Ribblesdale.
N Yor 2H 97
Horton Kirby. Kent 4G 39
Hortonwood. Telf 4A 72
Horwich. G Man 3E 91
Horwich End. Derbs 2E 85
Horwood. Devn 4F 19
Hoscar. Lanc 3C 90
Hose. Leics 3E 75
Hosh. Per 1A 136
Hosta. W Isl 1C 170
Hoswick. Shet 9F 173
Hotham. E Yor 1B 94
Hothfield. Kent 1D 28
Hoton. Leics 3C 74
Houbie. Shet 2H 173
Hough. Arg 4A 138
Hough. Ches E
nr. Crewe 5B 84
nr. Wilmslow 3C 84
Hougham. Linc 1F 75
Hough Green. Hal 2G 83
Hough-on-the-Hill. Linc 1G 75
Houghton. Cambs 3B 64
Houghton. Cumb 4F 113
Houghton. Hants 3B 24
Houghton. Nmbd 3E 115
Houghton. Pemb 4D 43
Houghton. W Sus 4B 26
Houghton Bank. Darl 2F 105
Houghton Conquest.
C Beds 1A 52
Houghton Green. E Sus 3D 28
Houghton-le-Side. Darl 2F 105
Houghton-le-Spring.
Tyne 4G 115
Houghton on the Hill.
Leics 5D 74
Houghton Regis. C Beds 3A 52
Houghton St Giles. Norf 2B 78
Houlland. Shet
on Mainland 6E 173
on Yell 4G 173
Houlsyke. N Yor 4E 107
Houlton. Warw 3C 62
Hound. Hants 2C 16
Hound Green. Hants 1F 25
Houndslow. Bord 5C 130
Houndsmoor. Som 4E 21
Houndwood. Bord 3E 131
Hounsdown. Hants 1B 16
Hounslow. G Lon 3C 38
Housabister. Shet 6F 173
Housay. Shet 4H 173
Househill. High 3C 158
Housetter. Shet 3E 173
Houss. Shet 8E 173
Houston. Ren 3F 127
Housty. High 5D 168
Houton. Orkn 7C 172
Hove. Brig 192 (5D 27)
Hoveringham. Notts 1D 74
Hoveton. Norf 4F 79
Hovingham. N Yor 2A 100
How. Cumb 4G 113
How Caple. Here 2B 48
Howden. E Yor 2H 93
Howden-le-Wear. Dur 1E 105
Howe. High 2F 169
Howe. Norf 5E 79
Howe. N Yor 1F 99
The Howe. Cumb 1D 96
The Howe. IOM 5A 108
Howe Green. Essx 5H 53
Howe Green. Warw 2H 61
Howegreen. Essx 5B 54
Howell. Linc 1A 76

How End—Kilmore

How End. C Beds 1A 52
Howe of Teuchar. Abers 4E 161
Howes. Dum 3C 112
Howe Street. Essx
nr. Chelmsford 4G 53
nr. Finchingfield 2G 53
Howey. Powy 5C 58
Howgate. Midl 4F 129
Howgill. Lanc 5H 97
Howgill. N Yor 4C 98
How Green. Kent 1F 27
How Hill. Norf 4F 79
Howick. Nmbd 3G 121
Howle. Telf 3A 72
Howle Hill. Here 3B 48
Howleigh. Som 1F 13
Howlett End. Essx 2F 53
Howley. Som 2F 13
Howley. Warr 2A 84
Hownam. Bord 3B 120
Howsham. N Lin 4D 94
Howsham. N Yor 3B 100
Howtel. Nmbd 1C 120
Howt Green. Kent 4C 40
Howton. Here 3H 47
Howwood. Ren 3E 127
Hoxne. Suff 3D 66
Hoylake. Mers 2E 82
Hoyland. S Yor 4D 92
Hoylandswaine. S Yor 4C 92
Hoyle. W Sus 4A 26
Hubberholme. N Yor 2B 98
Hubberston. Pemb 4C 42
Hubbert's Bridge. Linc 1B 76
Huby. N Yor
nr. Harrogate 5E 99
nr. York 3H 99
Hucclecote. Glos 4D 48
Hucking. Kent 5C 40
Hucknall. Notts 1C 74
Huddersfield. W Yor 3B 92
Huddington. Worc 5D 60
Huddlesford. Staf 5F 73
Hudswell. N Yor 4E 105
Huggate. E Yor 4C 100
Hugglescote. Leics 4B 74
Hughenden Valley. Buck 2G 37
Hughley. Shrp 1H 59
Hughton. High 4G 157
Hugh Town. IOS 1B 4
Hugus. Corn 4B 6
Huish. Devn 1F 11
Huish. Wilts 5G 35
Huish Champflower. Som 4D 20
Huish Episcopi. Som 4H 21
Huisinis. W Isl 6B 171
Hulcote. Nptn 1F 51
Hulcott. Buck 4G 51
Hulham. Devn 4D 12
Hull. Hull 196 (2E 94)
Hulland. Derbs 1G 73
Hulland Moss. Derbs 1G 73
Hulland Ward. Derbs 1G 73
Hullavington. Wilts 3D 35
Hullbridge. Essx 1C 40
Hulme. G Man 1C 84
Hulme. Staf 1D 72
Hulme End. Staf 5F 85
Hulme Walfield. Ches E 4C 84
Hulverstone. IOW 4B 16
Hulver Street. Suff 2G 67
Humber. Devn 5C 12
Humber. Here 5H 59
Humber Bridge. N Lin 2D 94
Humberside Airport. N Lin 3D 94
Humberston. NE Lin 4G 95
Humberstone. Leic 5D 74
Humbie. E Lot 3A 130
Humbleton. E Yor 1F 95
Humbleton. Nmbd 2D 121
Humby. Linc 2H 75
Hume. Bord 5D 130
Humshaugh. Nmbd 2C 114
Huna. High 1F 169
Huncoat. Lanc 1F 91
Huncote. Leics 1C 62
Hundall. Derbs 3A 86
Hunderthwaite. Dur 2C 104
Hundleby. Linc 4C 88
Hundle Houses. Linc 5B 88
Hundleton. Pemb 4D 42
Hundon. Suff 1H 53
The Hundred. Here 4H 59
Hundred Acres. Hants 1D 16
Hundred House. Powy 5D 58
Hungarton. Leics 5D 74
Hungerford. Hants 1G 15
Hungerford. Shrp 2H 59
Hungerford. Som 2D 20
Hungerford. W Ber 5B 36
Hungerford Newtown. W Ber 4B 36
Hunger Hill. G Man 4E 91
Hungerton. Linc 2F 75
Hungladder. High 1C 154
Hungryhatton. Shrp 3A 72
Hunmanby. N Yor 2E 101
Hunmanby Sands. N Yor 2F 101
Hunningham. Warw 4A 62
Hunnington. Worc 2D 60
Hunny Hill. IOW 4C 16
Hunsdon. Herts 4E 53
Hunsdonbury. Herts 4E 53
Hunsingore. N Yor 4G 99
Hunslet. W Yor 1D 92
Hunslet Carr. W Yor 1D 92
Hunsonby. Cumb 1G 103
Hunspow. High 1E 169
Hunstanton. Norf 1F 77
Hunstanworth. Dur 5C 114
Hunston. Suff 4B 66
Hunston. W Sus 2G 17
Hunstrete. Bath 5B 34
Hunt End. Worc 4E 61
Hunterfield. Midl 3G 129
Hunters Forstal. Kent 4F 41
Hunter's Quay. Arg 2C 126
Huntham. Som 4G 21
Hunthill Lodge. Ang 1D 144
Huntingdon. Cambs 3B 64
Huntingfield. Suff 3F 67
Huntingford. Wilts 4D 22
Huntington. Ches W 4G 83
Huntington. E Lot 2A 130
Huntington. Here 5E 59
Huntington. Staf 4D 72
Huntington. Telf 5A 72
Huntington. York 4A 100
Huntingtower. Per 1C 136
Huntley. Glos 4C 48
Huntley. Staf 1E 73
Huntly. Abers 5C 160
Huntlywood. Bord 5C 130
Hunton. Hants 3C 24
Hunton. Kent 1B 28
Hunton. N Yor 5E 105
Hunton Bridge. Herts 1B 38
Hunt's Corner. Norf 2C 66
Huntscott. Som 2C 20
Hunt's Cross. Mers 2G 83
Hunts Green. Warw 1F 61
Huntsham. Devn 4D 20
Huntshaw. Devn 4F 19
Huntspill. Som 2G 21
Huntstile. Som 3F 21
Huntworth. Som 3G 21
Hunwick. Dur 1E 105
Hunworth. Norf 2C 78
Hurcott. Som
nr. Ilminster 1G 13
nr. Somerton 4A 22
Hurdcott. Wilts 3G 23
Hurdley. Powy 1E 59
Hurdsfield. Ches E 3D 84
Hurlet. Glas 3G 127
Hurley. Warw 1G 61
Hurley. Wind 3G 37
Hurlford. E Ayr 1D 116
Hurliness. Orkn 9B 172
Hurlston Green. Lanc 3C 90
Hurn. Dors 3G 15
Hursey. Dors 2H 13
Hursley. Hants 4C 24
Hurst. G Man 4H 91
Hurst. N Yor 4D 104
Hurst. Som 1H 13
Hurst. Wok 4F 37
Hurstbourne Priors. Hants 2C 24
Hurstbourne Tarrant. Hants 1B 24
Hurst Green. Ches E 1H 71
Hurst Green. E Sus 3B 28
Hurst Green. Essx 4D 54
Hurst Green. Lanc 1E 91
Hurst Green. Surr 5E 39
Hurstley. Here 1G 47
Hurstpierpoint. W Sus 4D 27
Hurstway Common. Here 1G 47
Hurst Wickham. W Sus 4D 27
Hurstwood. Lanc 1G 91
Hurtmore. Surr 1A 26
Hurworth-on-Tees. Darl 3A 106
Hurworth Place. Darl 4F 105
Hury. Dur 3C 104
Husbands Bosworth. Leics 2D 62
Husborne Crawley. C Beds 2H 51
Husthwaite. N Yor 2H 99
Hutcherleigh. Devn 3D 9
Hut Green. N Yor 2F 93
Huthwaite. Notts 5B 86
Huttoft. Linc 3E 89
Hutton. Cumb 2F 103
Hutton. E Yor 4E 101
Hutton. Essx 1H 39
Hutton. Lanc 2C 90
Hutton. N Som 1G 21
Hutton. Bord 4F 131
Hutton Bonville. N Yor 4A 106
Hutton Buscel. N Yor 1D 100
Hutton Conyers. N Yor 2F 99
Hutton Cranswick. E Yor 4E 101
Hutton End. Cumb 1F 103
Hutton Gate. Red C 3C 106
Hutton Henry. Dur 1B 106
Hutton-le-Hole. N Yor 1B 100
Hutton Magna. Dur 3E 105
Hutton Mulgrave. N Yor 4F 107
Hutton Roof. Cumb
nr. Kirkby Lonsdale 2E 97
nr. Penrith 1E 103
Hutton Rudby. N Yor 4B 106
Huttons Ambo. N Yor 3B 100
Hutton Sessay. N Yor 2G 99
Hutton Village. Red C 3D 106
Hutton Wandesley. N Yor 4H 99
Huxham. Devn 3C 12
Huxham Green. Som 3A 22
Huxley. Ches W 4H 83
Huxter. Shet
on Mainland 6C 173
on Whalsay 5G 173
Huyton. Mers 1G 83
Hwlffordd. Pemb 3D 42
Hycemoor. Cumb 1A 96
Hyde. Glos
nr. Stroud 5D 49
nr. Winchcombe 3F 49
Hyde. G Man 1D 84
Hyde Heath. Buck 5H 51
Hyde Lea. Staf 4D 72
Hyde Park. S Yor 4F 93
Hydestile. Surr 1A 26
Hyndford Bridge. S Lan 5C 128
Hynish. Arg 5A 138
Hyssington. Powy 1F 59
Hythe. Hants 2C 16
Hythe. Kent 2F 29
Hythe End. Wind 3B 38
Hythie. Abers 3H 161
Hyton. Cumb 1A 96

I

Ianstown. Mor 2B 160
Iarsiadar. W Isl 4D 171
Ibberton. Dors 2C 14
Ible. Derbs 5G 85
Ibrox. Glas 3G 127
Ibsley. Hants 2G 15
Ibstock. Leics 4B 74
Ibstone. Buck 2F 37
Ibthorpe. Hants 1B 24
Iburndale. N Yor 4F 107
Ibworth. Hants 1D 24
Icelton. N Som 5G 33
Ichrachan. Arg 5E 141
Ickburgh. Norf 1H 65
Ickenham. G Lon 2B 38
Ickenthwaite. Cumb 1C 96
Ickford. Buck 5E 51
Ickham. Kent 5G 41
Ickleford. Herts 2B 52
Icklesham. E Sus 4C 28
Ickleton. Cambs 1E 53
Icklingham. Suff 3G 65
Ickwell. C Beds 1B 52
Icomb. Glos 3H 49
Idbury. Oxon 4H 49
Iddesleigh. Devn 2F 11
Ide. Devn 3B 12
Ideford. Devn 5B 12
Ide Hill. Kent 5F 39
Iden. E Sus 3D 28
Iden Green. Kent
nr. Benenden 2C 28
nr. Goudhurst 2B 28
Idle. W Yor 1B 92
Idless. Corn 4C 6
Idlicote. Warw 1A 50
Idmiston. Wilts 3G 23
Idole. Carm 4E 45
Idridgehay. Derbs 1G 73
Idrigill. High 2C 154
Idstone. Oxon 3A 36
Iffley. Oxon 5D 50
Ifield. W Sus 2D 26
Ifieldwood. W Sus 2D 26
Ifold. W Sus 2B 26
Iford. E Sus 5F 27
Ifton Heath. Shrp 2F 71
Ightfield. Shrp 2H 71
Ightham. Kent 5G 39
Iken. Suff 5G 67
Ilam. Staf 5F 85
Ilchester. Som 4A 22
Ilderton. Nmbd 2E 121
Ilford. G Lon 2F 39
Ilford. Som 1G 13
Ilfracombe. Devn 2F 19
Ilkeston. Derbs 1B 74
Ilketshall St Andrew. Suff 2F 67
Ilketshall St Lawrence. Suff 2F 67
Ilketshall St Margaret. Suff 2F 67
Ilkley. W Yor 5D 98
Illand. Corn 5C 10
Illey. W Mid 2D 61
Illidge Green. Ches E 4B 84
Illington. Norf 2B 66
Illingworth. W Yor 2A 92
Illogan. Corn 4A 6
Illogan Highway. Corn 4A 6
Illston on the Hill. Leics 1E 62
Ilmer. Buck 5F 51
Ilmington. Warw 1H 49
Ilminster. Som 1G 13
Ilsington. Devn 5A 12
Ilsington. Dors 3C 14
Ilston. Swan 3E 31
Ilton. N Yor 2D 98
Ilton. Som 1G 13
Imachar. N Ayr 5G 125
Imber. Wilts 2E 23
Immingham. NE Lin 3E 95
Immingham Dock. NE Lin 3F 95
Impington. Cambs 4D 64
Ince. Ches W 3G 83
Ince Blundell. Mers 4B 90
Ince-in-Makerfield. G Man 4D 90
Inchbae Lodge. High 2G 157
Inchbare. Ang 2F 145
Inchberry. Mor 3H 159
Inchbraoch. Ang 3G 145
Inchbrook. Glos 5D 48
Incheril. High 2C 156
Inchinnan. Ren 3F 127
Inchlaggan. High 3D 148
Inchmichael. Per 1E 137
Inchnadamph. High 1G 163
Inchree. High 2E 141
Inchture. Per 1E 137
Inchyra. Per 1D 136
Indian Queens. Corn 3D 6
Ingatestone. Essx 1H 39
Ingbirchworth. S Yor 4C 92
Ingestre. Staf 3D 73
Ingham. Linc 2G 87
Ingham. Norf 3F 79
Ingham. Suff 3A 66
Ingham Corner. Norf 3F 79
Ingleborough. Norf 4D 76
Ingleby. Derbs 3H 73
Ingleby Arncliffe. N Yor 4B 106
Ingleby Barwick. Stoc T 3B 106
Ingleby Greenhow. N Yor 4C 106
Ingleigh Green. Devn 2G 11
Inglemire. Hull 1D 94
Inglesbatch. Bath 5C 34
Ingleton. Dur 2E 105
Ingleton. N Yor 2F 97
Inglewhite. Lanc 5E 97
Ingoe. Nmbd 2D 114
Ingol. Lanc 1D 90
Ingoldisthorpe. Norf 2F 77
Ingoldmells. Linc 4E 89
Ingoldsby. Linc 2H 75
Ingon. Warw 5G 61
Ingram. Nmbd 3E 121
Ingrave. Essx 1H 39
Ingrow. W Yor 1A 92
Ings. Cumb 5F 103
Ingst. S Glo 3A 34
Ingthorpe. Rut 5G 75
Ingworth. Norf 3D 78
Inishrush. M Ulst 6F 174
Inkberrow. Worc 5E 61
Inkford. Worc 3E 61
Inkpen. W Ber 5B 36
Inkstack. High 1E 169
Innellan. Arg 3C 126
Inner Hope. Devn 5C 8
Innerleith. Fife 2E 137
Innerleithen. Bord 1F 119
Innerleven. Fife 3F 137
Innermessan. Dum 3F 109
Innerwick. E Lot 2D 130
Innerwick. Per 4C 142
Innsworth. Glos 3D 48
Insch. Abers 1D 152
Insh. High 3C 150
Inshegra. High 3C 166
Inshore. High 1D 166
Inskip. Lanc 1C 90
Instow. Devn 3E 19
Intwood. Norf 5D 78
Inver. Abers 4G 151
Inver. High 5F 165
Inver. Per 4H 143
Inverailort. High 5F 147
Inveralligin. High 3H 155
Inverallochy. Abers 2H 161
Inveramsay. Abers 1E 153
Inveran. High 4C 164
Inveraray. Arg 3H 133
Inverarish. High 5E 155
Inverarity. Ang 4D 144
Inverarnan. Stir 2C 134
Inverarnie. High 5A 158
Inverbeg. Arg 4C 134
Inverbervie. Abers 1H 145
Inverboyndie. Abers 2D 160
Invercassley. High 3B 164
Invercharnan. High 4F 141
Inverchoran. High 3E 157
Invercreran. Arg 4E 141
Inverdruie. High 2D 150
Inverebrie. Abers 5G 161
Invereck. Arg 1C 126
Inveresk. E Lot 2G 129
Inveresragan. Arg 5D 141
Inverey. Abers 5E 151
Inverfarigaig. High 1H 149
Invergarry. High 3F 149
Invergeldie. Per 1G 135
Invergordon. High 2B 158
Invergowrie. Per 5C 144
Inverguseran. High 3F 147
Inverharroch. Mor 5A 160
Inverie. High 3F 147
Inverinan. Arg 2G 133
Inverinate. High 1B 148
Inverkeilor. Ang 4F 145
Inverkeithing. Fife 1E 129
Inverkeithny. Abers 4D 160
Inverkip. Inv 2D 126
Inverkirkaig. High 2E 163
Inverlael. High 5F 163
Inverliever Lodge. Arg 3F 133
Inverliver. Arg 5E 141
Inverlochlarig. Stir 2D 134
Inverlochy. High 1F 141
Inverlussa. Arg 1E 125
Inver Mallie. High 5D 148
Invermarkie. Abers 5B 160
Invermoriston. High 2G 149
Invernaver. High 2H 167
Inverneil House. Arg 1G 125
Inverness. High 196 (4A 158)
Inverness Airport. High 3B 158
Invernettie. Abers 4H 161
Inverpolly Lodge. High 2E 163
Inverquhomery. Abers 4H 161
Inverroy. High 5E 149
Inversanda. High 3D 140
Invershiel. High 2B 148
Invershin. High 4C 164
Invershore. High 5E 169
Inversnaid. Stir 3C 134
Inverugie. Abers 4H 161
Inveruglas. Arg 3C 134
Inverurie. Abers 1E 153
Invervar. Per 4D 142
Inverythan. Abers 4E 161
Inwardleigh. Devn 3F 11
Inworth. Essx 4B 54
Iochdar. W Isl 4C 170
Iping. W Sus 4G 25
Ipplepen. Devn 2E 9
Ipsden. Oxon 3E 37
Ipstones. Staf 1E 73
Ipswich. Suff 196 (1E 55)
Irby. Mers 2E 83
Irby in the Marsh. Linc 4D 88
Irby upon Humber. NE Lin 4E 95
Irchester. Nptn 4G 63
Ireby. Cumb 1D 102
Ireby. Lanc 2F 97
Ireland. Shet 9E 173
Ireleth. Cumb 2B 96
Ireshopeburn. Dur 1B 104
Ireton Wood. Derbs 1G 73
Irlam. G Man 1B 84
Irnham. Linc 3H 75
Iron Acton. S Glo 3B 34
Iron Bridge. Cambs 1D 65
Ironbridge. Telf 5A 72
Iron Cross. Warw 5E 61
Ironville. Derbs 5B 86
Irstead. Norf 3F 79
Irthington. Cumb 3F 113
Irthlingborough. Nptn 3G 63
Irton. N Yor 1E 101
Irvine. N Ayr 1C 116
Irvine Mains. N Ayr 1C 116
Irvinestown. Ferm 7E 176
Isabella Pit. Nmbd 1G 115
Isauld. High 2B 168
Isbister. Orkn 6C 172
Isbister. Shet
on Mainland 2E 173
on Whalsay 5G 173
Isfield. E Sus 4F 27
Isham. Nptn 3F 63
Island Carr. N Lin 4C 94
Islay Airport. Arg 4B 124
Isle Abbotts. Som 4G 21
Isle Brewers. Som 4G 21
Isleham. Cambs 3F 65
Isle of Man Airport. IOM 5B 108
Isle of Thanet. Kent 4H 41
Isle of Whithorn. Dum 5B 110
Isle of Wight. IOW 4C 16
Isleornsay. High 2F 147
Islesburgh. Shet 5E 173
Isles of Scilly Airport. IOS 1B 4
Islesteps. Dum 2A 112
Isleworth. G Lon 3C 38
Isley Walton. Leics 3B 74
Islibhig. W Isl 5B 171
Islington. G Lon 2E 39
Islington. Telf 3B 72
Islip. Nptn 3G 63
Islip. Oxon 4D 50
Isombridge. Telf 4A 72
Istead Rise. Kent 4H 39
Itchen. Sotn 1C 16
Itchen Abbas. Hants 3D 24
Itchenor. W Sus 2F 17
Itchen Stoke. Hants 3D 24
Itchingfield. W Sus 3C 26
Itchington. S Glo 3B 34
Itlaw. Abers 3D 160
Itteringham. Norf 2D 78
Itteringham Common. Norf 3D 78
Itton. Devn 3G 11
Itton Common. Mon 2H 33
Ivegill. Cumb 5F 113
Ivelet. N Yor 5C 104
Iverchaolain. Arg 2B 126
Iver Heath. Buck 2B 38
Iveston. Dur 4E 115
Ivetsey Bank. Staf 4C 72
Ivinghoe. Buck 4H 51
Ivinghoe Aston. Buck 4H 51
Ivington. Here 5G 59
Ivington Green. Here 5G 59
Ivybridge. Devn 3C 8
Ivychurch. Kent 3E 29
Ivy Hatch. Kent 5G 39
Ivy Todd. Norf 5A 78
Iwade. Kent 4D 40
Iwerne Courtney. Dors 1D 14
Iwerne Minster. Dors 1D 14
Ixworth. Suff 3B 66
Ixworth Thorpe. Suff 3B 66

J

Jackfield. Shrp 5A 72
Jack Hill. N Yor 4D 98
Jacksdale. Notts 5B 86
Jackton. S Lan 4G 127
Jacobstow. Corn 3B 10
Jacobstowe. Devn 2F 11
Jacobs Well. Surr 5A 38
Jameston. Pemb 5E 43
Jamestown. Dum 5F 119
Jamestown. Fife 1E 129
Jamestown. High 3G 157
Jamestown. W Dun 1E 127
Janetstown. High
nr. Thurso 2C 168
nr. Wick 3F 169
Jarrow. Tyne 3G 115
Jarvis Brook. E Sus 3G 27
Jasper's Green. Essx 3H 53
Jaywick. Essx 4E 55
Jedburgh. Bord 2A 120
Jeffreyston. Pemb 4E 43
Jemimaville. High 2B 158
Jenkins Park. High 3F 149
Jersey Marine. Neat 3G 31
Jesmond. Tyne 3F 115
Jevington. E Sus 5G 27
Jingle Street. Mon 4H 47
Jockey End. Herts 4A 52
Jodrell Bank. Ches E 3B 84
Johnby. Cumb 1F 103
John O'Gaunts. W Yor 2D 92
John o' Groats. High 1F 169
John's Cross. E Sus 3B 28
Johnshaven. Abers 2G 145
Johnson Street. Norf 4F 79
Johnston. Pemb 3D 42
Johnstone. Ren 3F 127
Johnstonebridge. Dum 5C 118
Johnstown. Carm 4E 45
Johnstown. Wrex 1F 71
Jonesborough. New M 8E 178
Joppa. Edin 2G 129
Joppa. S Ayr 3D 116
Jordan Green. Norf 3C 78
Jordans. Buck 1A 38
Jordanston. Pemb 1D 42
Jump. S Yor 4D 93
Jumpers Common. Dors 3G 15
Juniper. Nmbd 4C 114
Juniper Green. Edin 3E 129
Jurby East. IOM 2C 108
Jurby West. IOM 2C 108
Jury's Gap. E Sus 4D 28

K

Kaber. Cumb 3A 104
Kaimend. S Lan 5C 128
Kaimes. Edin 3F 129
Kaimrig End. Bord 5D 129
Kames. Arg 2A 126
Kames. E Ayr 2F 117
Katesbridge. Arm 5G 179
Kea. Corn 4C 6
Keadby. N Lin 3B 94
Keady. Arm 6C 178
Keal Cotes. Linc 4C 88
Kearsley. G Man 4F 91
Kearsney. Kent 1G 29
Kearstwick. Cumb 1F 97
Kearton. N Yor 5C 104
Kearvaig. High 1C 166
Keasden. N Yor 3G 97
Keason. Corn 2H 7
Keckwick. Hal 2H 83
Keddington. Linc 2C 88
Keddington Corner. Linc 2C 88
Kedington. Suff 1H 53
Kedleston. Derbs 1H 73
Kedlock Feus. Fife 2F 137
Keekle. Cumb 3B 102
Keelby. Linc 3E 95
Keele. Staf 1C 72
Keeley Green. Bed 1A 52
Keeston. Pemb 3D 42
Keevil. Wilts 1E 23
Kegworth. Leics 3B 74
Kehelland. Corn 2D 4
Keig. Abers 2D 152
Keighley. W Yor 5C 98
Keilarsbrae. Clac 4A 136
Keillmore. Arg 1E 125
Keillor. Per 4B 144
Keillour. Per 1B 136
Keills. Arg 3C 124
Keiloch. Abers 4F 151
Keils. Arg 3D 124
Keinton Mandeville. Som 3A 22
Keir Mill. Dum 5A 118
Keirsleywell Row. Nmbd 4A 114
Keisby. Linc 3H 75
Keisley. Cumb 2A 104
Keiss. High 2F 169
Keith. Mor 3B 160
Keith Inch. Abers 4H 161
Kelbrook. Lanc 5B 98
Kelby. Linc 1H 75
Keld. Cumb 3G 103
Keld. N Yor 4B 104
Keldholme. N Yor 1B 100
Kelfield. N Lin 4B 94
Kelfield. N Yor 1F 93
Kelham. Notts 5E 87
Kellacott. Devn 4E 11
Kellan. Arg 4G 139
Kellas. Ang 5D 144
Kellas. Mor 3F 159
Kellaton. Devn 5E 9
Kelleth. Cumb 4H 103
Kelling. Norf 1C 78
Kellingley. N Yor 2F 93
Kellington. N Yor 2F 93
Kelloe. Dur 1A 106
Kelloholm. Dum 3G 117
Kells. Cumb 3A 102
Kells. ME Ant 7H 175
Kelly. Devn 4D 11
Kelly Bray. Corn 5D 10
Kelmarsh. Nptn 3E 63
Kelmscott. Oxon 2H 35
Kelsale. Suff 4F 67
Kelsall. Ches W 4H 83
Kelshall. Herts 2D 52
Kelsick. Cumb 4C 112
Kelso. Bord 1B 120
Kelstedge. Derbs 4H 85
Kelstern. Linc 1B 88
Kelsterton. Flin 3E 83
Kelston. Bath 5C 34
Keltneyburn. Per 4E 143
Kelton. Dum 2A 112
Kelton Hill. Dum 4E 111
Kelty. Fife 4D 136
Kelvedon. Essx 4B 54
Kelvedon Hatch. Essx 1G 39
Kelvinside. Glas 3G 127
Kelynack. Corn 3A 4
Kemback. Fife 2G 137
Kemberton. Shrp 5B 72
Kemble. Glos 2E 35
Kemerton. Worc 2E 49
Kemeys Commander. Mon 5G 47
Kemnay. Abers 2E 153
Kempe's Corner. Kent 1E 29
Kempley. Glos 3B 48
Kempley Green. Glos 3B 48
Kempsey. Worc 1D 48
Kempsford. Glos 2G 35
Kemps Green. Warw 3F 61
Kempshott. Hants 2E 24
Kempston. Bed 1A 52
Kempston Hardwick. Bed 1A 52
Kempton. Shrp 2F 59
Kemp Town. Brig 5E 27
Kemsing. Kent 5G 39
Kemsley. Kent 4D 40
Kenardington. Kent 2D 28
Kenchester. Here 1H 47
Kencot. Oxon 5A 50
Kendal. Cumb 5G 103
Kendleshire. S Glo 4B 34
Kendray. S Yor 4D 92
Kenfig. B'end 3B 32
Kenfig Hill. B'end 3B 32
Kengharair. Arg 4F 139
Kenilworth. Warw 3G 61
Kenknock. Stir 5B 142
Kenley. G Lon 5E 39
Kenley. Shrp 5H 71
Kenmore. High 3G 155
Kenmore. Per 4E 143
Kenn. Devn 4C 12
Kenn. N Som 5H 33
Kennacraig. Arg 3G 125
Kenneggy Downs. Corn 4C 4
Kennerleigh. Devn 2B 12
Kennet. Clac 4B 136
Kennethmont. Abers 1C 152
Kennett. Cambs 4G 65
Kennford. Devn 4C 12
Kenninghall. Norf 2C 66
Kennington. Kent 1E 28
Kennington. Oxon 5D 50
Kennoway. Fife 3F 137
Kennyhill. Suff 3F 65
Kennythorpe. N Yor 3B 100
Kenovay. Arg 4A 138
Kensaleyre. High 3D 154
Kensington. G Lon 3D 38
Kenstone. Shrp 3H 71
Kensworth. C Beds 4A 52
Kensworth Common. C Beds 4A 52
Kentallen. High 3E 141
Kentchurch. Here 3H 47
Kentford. Suff 4G 65
Kentisbeare. Devn 2D 12
Kentisbury. Devn 2G 19
Kentisbury Ford. Devn 2G 19
Kentmere. Cumb 4F 103
Kenton. Devn 4C 12
Kenton. G Lon 2C 38
Kenton. Suff 4D 66
Kenton Bankfoot. Tyne 3F 115
Kentra. High 2A 140
Kentrigg. Cumb 5G 103
Kents Bank. Cumb 2C 96
Kent's Green. Glos 3C 48
Kent's Oak. Hants 4B 24
Kent Street. E Sus 4B 28
Kent Street. Kent 5A 40
Kent Street. W Sus 3D 26
Kenwick. Shrp 2G 71
Kenwyn. Corn 4C 6
Kenyon. Warr 1A 84
Keoldale. High 2D 166
Keppoch. High 1B 148
Kepwick. N Yor 5B 106
Keresley. W Mid 2H 61
Keresley Newland. Warw 2H 61
Keristal. IOM 4C 108
Kerne Bridge. Here 4A 48
Kerridge. Ches E 3D 84
Kerris. Corn 4B 4
Kerrow. High 5F 157
Kerry. Powy 1D 58
Kerrycroy. Arg 3C 126
Kerry's Gate. Here 2G 47
Kersall. Notts 4E 86
Kersbrook. Devn 4D 12
Kerse. Ren 4E 127
Kersey. Suff 1D 54
Kershopefoot. Cumb 1F 113
Kersoe. Worc 1E 49
Kerswell. Devn 2D 12
Kerswell Green. Worc 1D 48
Kesgrave. Suff 1F 55
Kesh. Ferm 6D 176
Kessingland. Suff 2H 67
Kessingland Beach. Suff 2H 67
Kestle. Corn 4D 6
Kestle Mill. Corn 3C 6
Keston. G Lon 4F 39
Keswick. Cumb 2D 102
Keswick. Norf
nr. North Walsham 2F 79
nr. Norwich 5E 78
Ketsby. Linc 3C 88
Kettering. Nptn 3F 63
Ketteringham. Norf 5D 78
Kettins. Per 5B 144
Kettlebaston. Suff 5B 66
Kettlebridge. Fife 3F 137
Kettlebrook. Staf 5G 73
Kettleburgh. Suff 4E 67
Kettleholm. Dum 2C 112
Kettleness. N Yor 3F 107
Kettleshulme. Ches E 3D 85
Kettlesing. N Yor 4E 98
Kettlesing Bottom. N Yor 4E 99
Kettlestone. Norf 2B 78
Kettlethorpe. Linc 3F 87
Kettletoft. Orkn 4F 172
Kettlewell. N Yor 2B 98
Ketton. Rut 5G 75
Kew. G Lon 3C 38
Kewaigue. IOM 4C 108
Kewstoke. N Som 5G 33
Kexbrough. S Yor 4C 92
Kexby. Linc 2F 87
Kexby. York 4B 100
Keyford. Som 2C 22
Key Green. Ches E 4C 84
Key Green. N Yor 4F 107
Keyham. Leics 5D 74
Keyhaven. Hants 3B 16
Keyhead. Abers 3H 161
Keyingham. E Yor 2F 95
Keymer. W Sus 4E 27
Keynsham. Bath 5B 34
Keysoe. Bed 4H 63
Keysoe Row. Bed 4H 63
Key's Toft. Linc 5D 89
Keyston. Cambs 3H 63
Key Street. Kent 4C 40
Keyworth. Notts 2D 74
Kibblesworth. Tyne 4F 115
Kibworth Beauchamp. Leics 1D 62
Kibworth Harcourt. Leics 1D 62
Kidbrooke. G Lon 3F 39
Kidburngill. Cumb 2B 102
Kiddemore Green. Staf 5C 72
Kidderminster. Worc 3C 60
Kiddington. Oxon 3C 50
Kidd's Moor. Norf 5D 78
Kidlington. Oxon 4C 50
Kidmore End. Oxon 4E 37
Kidnal. Ches W 1G 71
Kidsgrove. Staf 5C 84
Kidstones. N Yor 1B 98
Kidwelly. Carm 5E 45
Kiel Crofts. Arg 5D 140
Kielder. Nmbd 5A 120
Kilbagie. Fife 4B 136
Kilbarchan. Ren 3F 127
Kilbeg. High 3E 147
Kilberry. Arg 3F 125
Kilbirnie. N Ayr 4E 126
Kilbride. Arg 1F 133
Kilbride. High 1D 147
Kilbucho Place. Bord 1C 118
Kilburn. Derbs 1A 74
Kilburn. G Lon 2D 38
Kilburn. N Yor 2H 99
Kilby. Leics 1D 62
Kilchattan. Arg 4A 132
Kilchattan Bay. Arg 4C 126
Kilchenzie. Arg 3A 122
Kilcheran. Arg 5C 140
Kilchiaran. Arg 3A 124
Kilchoan. High
nr. Inverie 4F 147
nr. Tobermory 2F 139
Kilchoman. Arg 3A 124
Kilchrenan. Arg 1H 133
Kilclief. New M 5K 179
Kilconquhar. Fife 3G 137
Kilcoo. New M 6G 179
Kilcot. Glos 3B 48
Kilcoy. High 3H 157
Kilcreggan. Arg 1D 126
Kildale. N Yor 4D 106
Kildary. High 1B 158
Kildermorie Lodge. High 1H 157
Kildonan. Dum 4F 109
Kildonan. High
nr. Helmsdale 1G 165
on Isle of Skye 3C 154
Kildonan. N Ayr 3E 123
Kildonnan. High 5C 146
Kildrummy. Abers 2B 152
Kildwick. N Yor 5C 98
Kilfillan. Dum 4H 109
Kilfinan. Arg 2H 125
Kilfinnan. High 4E 149
Kilgetty. Pemb 4F 43
Kilgour. Fife 3E 136
Kilgrammie. S Ayr 4B 116
Kilham. E Yor 3E 101
Kilham. Nmbd 1C 120
Kilkeel. New M 8H 179
Kilkenneth. Arg 4A 138
Kilkhampton. Corn 1C 10
Killadeas. Ferm 7E 176
Killamarsh. Derbs 2B 86
Killandrist. Arg 4C 140
Killay. Swan 3F 31
Killean. Arg 5E 125
Killearn. Stir 1G 127
Killeen. M Ulst 3C 178
Killellan. Arg 4A 122
Killen. Derr 4E 176
Killen. High 3A 158
Killerby. Darl 3E 105
Killeter. Derr 4E 176
Killichonan. Per 3C 142
Killiechronan. Arg 4G 139
Killiecrankie. Per 2G 143
Killilan. High 5B 156
Killimster. High 3F 169
Killin. Stir 5C 142
Killinchy. Ards 3K 179
Killinghall. N Yor 4E 99
Killington. Cumb 1F 97
Killingworth. Tyne 2F 115
Killin Lodge. High 3H 149
Killinochonoch. Arg 4F 133
Killochyett. Bord 5A 130
Killough. New M 6K 179
Killowen. New M 8F 179
Killundine. High 4G 139
Killylea. Arm 5B 178
Killyleagh. New M 4K 179
Killyrammer. Caus 4F 175
Kilmacolm. Inv 3E 127
Kilmahog. Stir 3F 135
Kilmahumaig. Arg 4E 133
Kilmalieu. High 3C 140
Kilmaluag. High 1D 154
Kilmany. Fife 1F 137
Kilmarie. High 2D 146
Kilmarnock. E Ayr 196 (1D 116)
Kilmaron. Fife 2F 137
Kilmartin. Arg 4F 133
Kilmaurs. E Ayr 5F 127
Kilmelford. Arg 2F 133
Kilmeny. Arg 3B 124
Kilmersdon. Som 1B 22
Kilmeston. Hants 4D 24
Kilmichael Glassary. Arg 4F 133
Kilmichael of Inverlussa. Arg 1F 125
Kilmington. Devn 3F 13
Kilmington. Wilts 3C 22
Kilmoluaig. Arg 4A 138
Kilmorack. High 4G 157
Kilmore. Arg 1F 133

Lea—Llanfihangel-y-Creuddyn

Lea. Shrp
nr. Bishop's Castle 2F 59
nr. Shrewsbury 5G 71
Lea. Wilts 3E 35
Leabrooks. Derbs 5B 86
Leac a Li. W Isl 8D 171
Leachd. Arg 4H 133
Leachkin. High 4A 158
Leachpool. Pemb 3D 42
Leadburn. Midl 4F 129
Leadenham. Linc 5G 87
Leaden Roding. Essx 4F 53
Leaderfoot. Bord 1H 119
Leadgate. Cumb 5A 114
Leadgate. Dur 4E 115
Leadgate. Nmbd 4E 115
Leadhills. S Lan 3A 118
Leadingcross Green. Kent 5C 40
Lea End. Worc 3E 61
Leafield. Oxon 4B 50
Leagrave. Lutn 3A 52
Lea Hall. W Mid 2F 61
Lea Heath. Staf 3E 73
Leake. N Yor 5B 106
Leake Common Side. Linc 5C 88
Leake Fold Hill. Linc 5D 88
Leake Hurn's End. Linc 1D 76
Lealholm. N Yor 4E 107
Lealt. Arg 4D 132
Lealt. High 2E 155
Leam. Derbs 3G 85
Lea Marston. Warw 1G 61
Leamington Hastings.
Warw 4B 62
Leamington Spa, Royal.
Warw 4H 61
Leamonsley. Staf 5F 73
Leamside. Dur 5G 115
Leargybreck. Arg 2D 124
Lease Rigg. N Yor 4F 107
Leasgill. Cumb 1D 97
Leasingham. Linc 1H 75
Leasingthorne. Dur 1F 105
Leasowe. Mers 1E 83
Leatherhead. Surr 5C 38
Leathley. N Yor 5E 99
Leaths. Dum 3E 111
Leaton. Shrp 4G 71
Leaton. Telf 4A 72
Lea Town. Lanc 1C 90
Leaveland. Kent 5E 40
Leavenheath. Suff 2C 54
Leavening. N Yor 3B 100
Leaves Green. G Lon 4F 39
Lea Yeat. Cumb 1G 97
Leazes. Dur 4E 115
Lebberston. N Yor 1E 101
Lechlade on Thames.
Glos 2H 35
Leck. Lanc 2F 97
Leckford. Hants 3B 24
Leckfurin. High 3H 167
Leckgruinart. Arg 3A 124
Leckhampstead. Buck 2F 51
Leckhampstead. W Ber 4C 36
Leckhampton. Glos 4E 49
Leckmelm. High 4F 163
Leckwith. V Glam 4E 33
Leconfield. E Yor 5E 101
Ledaig. Arg 5D 140
Ledburn. Buck 3H 51
Ledbury. Here 2C 48
Ledgemoor. Here 5G 59
Ledgowan. High 3D 156
Ledicot. Here 4G 59
Ledmore. High 2G 163
Lednabirichen. High 4E 165
Lednagullin. High 2A 168
Ledsham. Ches W 3F 83
Ledsham. W Yor 2E 93
Ledston. W Yor 2E 93
Ledstone. Devn 4D 8
Ledwell. Oxon 3C 50
Lee. Devn
nr. Ilfracombe 2E 19
nr. South Molton 4B 20
Lee. G Lon 3E 39
Lee. Hants 1B 16
Lee. Lanc 4E 97
Lee. Shrp 2G 71
The Lee. Buck 5H 51
Leeans. Shet 7E 173
Leebotten. Shet 9F 173
Leebotwood. Shrp 1G 59
Lee Brockhurst. Shrp 3H 71
Leece. Cumb 3B 96
Leechpool. Mon 3A 34
Lee Clump. Buck 5H 51
Leeds. Kent 5C 40
Leeds. W Yor 196 (1C 92)
Leeds Bradford Airport.
W Yor 5E 99
Leedstown. Corn 3D 4
Leegomery. Telf 4A 72
Lee Head. Derbs 1E 85
Leek. Staf 5D 85
Leekbrook. Staf 5D 85
Leek Wootton. Warw 4G 61
Lee Mill. Devn 3B 8
Leeming. N Yor 1E 99
Leeming Bar. N Yor 5F 105
Lee Moor. Devn 2B 8
Lee Moor. W Yor 2D 92
Lee-on-the-Solent. Hants 2D 16
Lees. Derbs 2G 73
Lees. G Man 4H 91
Lees. W Yor 1A 92
The Lees. Kent 5E 40
Leeswood. Flin 4E 83
Leetown. Per 1E 136
Leftwich. Ches W 3A 84
Legbourne. Linc 2C 88
Legburthwaite. Cumb 3E 102
Legerwood. Bord 5B 130
Legsby. Linc 2A 88
Leicester. Leic 196 (5C 74)
Leicester Forest East.
Leics 5C 74
Leigh. Dors 2B 14
Leigh. G Man 4E 91
Leigh. Kent 1G 27
Leigh. Shrp 5F 71
Leigh. Surr 1D 26
Leigh. Wilts 2F 35
Leigh. Worc 5B 60
The Leigh. Glos 3D 48
Leigham. Plym 3B 8
Leigh Beck. Essx 2C 40
Leigh Common. Som 4C 22
Leigh Delamere. Wilts 4D 35
Leigh Green. Kent 2D 28
Leighland Chapel. Som 3D 20
Leigh-on-Sea. S'end 2C 40
Leigh Park. Hants 2F 17
Leigh Sinton. Worc 5B 60
Leighterton. Glos 2D 34
Leighton. N Yor 2D 98
Leighton. Powy 5E 71
Leighton. Shrp 5A 72
Leighton. Som 2C 22
Leighton Bromswold.
Cambs 3A 64
Leighton Buzzard. C Beds 3H 51
Leigh-upon-Mendip. Som 2B 22
Leinthall Earls. Here 4G 59
Leinthall Starkes. Here 4G 59
Leintwardine. Here 3G 59
Leire. Leics 1C 62
Leirinmore. High 2E 166
Leishmore. High 4G 157
Leiston. Suff 4G 67
Leitfie. Per 4B 144
Leith. Edin 2F 129
Leitholm. Bord 5D 130
Leitrim. New M 6H 179
Lelant. Corn 3C 4
Lelant Downs. Corn 3C 4
Lelley. E Yor 1F 95
Lem Hill. Shrp 3B 60
Lemington. Tyne 3E 115
Lempitlaw. Bord 1B 120
Lemsford. Herts 4C 52
Lenacre. Cumb 1F 97
Lenchie. Abers 5C 160
Lenchwick. Worc 1F 49
Lendalfoot. S Ayr 1G 109
Lendrick. Stir 3E 135
Lenham. Kent 5C 40
Lenham Heath. Kent 1D 28
Lenimore. N Ayr 5G 125
Lennel. Bord 5E 131
Lennoxtown. E Dun 2H 127
Lenton. Linc 2H 75
Lentran. High 4H 157
Lenwade. Norf 4C 78
Lenzie. E Dun 2H 127
Leochel Cushnie. Abers 2C 152
Leogh. Shet 1B 172
Leominster. Here 5G 59
Leonard Stanley. Glos 5D 48
Lepe. Hants 3C 16
Lephenstrath. Arg 5A 122
Lephin. High 4A 154
Lephinchapel. Arg 4G 133
Lephinmore. Arg 4G 133
Leppington. N Yor 3B 100
Lepton. W Yor 3C 92
Lerryn. Corn 3F 7
Lerwick. Shet 7F 173
Lerwick (Tingwall) Airport.
Shet 7F 173
Lesbury. Nmbd 3G 121
Leslie. Abers 1C 152
Leslie. Fife 3E 137
Lesmahagow. S Lan 1H 117
Lesnewth. Corn 3B 10
Lessingham. Norf 3F 79
Lessonhall. Cumb 4D 112
Leswalt. Dum 3F 109
Letchmore Heath. Herts 1C 38
Letchworth Garden City.
Herts 2C 52
Letcombe Bassett. Oxon 3B 36
Letcombe Regis. Oxon 3B 36
Letham. Ang 4E 145
Letham. Falk 1B 128
Letham. Fife 2F 137
Lethanhill. E Ayr 3D 116
Lethenty. Abers 4F 161
Letheringham. Suff 5E 67
Letheringsett. Norf 2C 78
Lettaford. Devn 4H 11
Lettan. Orkn 3G 172
Letter. Abers 2E 153
Letterewe. High 1B 156
Letterfearn. High 1A 148
Lettermore. Arg 4F 139
Letters. High 5F 163
Lettershendoney. Derr 5B 174
Letterston. Pemb 2D 42
Letton. Here
nr. Kington 1G 47
nr. Leintwardine 3F 59
Letty Green. Herts 4C 52
Letwell. S Yor 2C 86
Leuchars. Fife 1G 137
Leumrabhagh. W Isl 6F 171
Leusdon. Devn 5H 11
Levaneap. Shet 5F 173
Levedale. Staf 4C 72
Leven. E Yor 5F 101
Leven. Fife 3F 137
Levencorroch. N Ayr 3E 123
Levenhall. E Lot 2G 129
Levens. Cumb 1D 97
Levens Green. Herts 3D 52
Levenshulme. G Man 1C 84
Levenwick. Shet 9F 173
Leverburgh. W Isl 9C 171
Leverington. Cambs 4D 76
Leverton. Linc 1C 76
Leverton. W Ber 4B 36
Leverton Lucasgate. Linc 1D 76
Leverton Outgate. Linc 1D 76
Levington. Suff 2F 55
Levisham. N Yor 5F 107
Levishie. High 2G 149
Lew. Oxon 5B 50
Lewaigue. IOM 2D 108
Lewannick. Corn 4C 10
Lewdown. Devn 4E 11
Lewes. E Sus 4F 27
Leweston. Pemb 2D 42
Lewisham. G Lon 3E 39
Lewiston. High 1H 149
Lewistown. B'end 3C 32
Lewknor. Oxon 2F 37
Leworthy. Devn
nr. Barnstaple 3G 19
nr. Holsworthy 2D 10
Lewson Street. Kent 4D 40
Lewthorn Cross. Devn 5A 12
Lewtrenchard. Devn 4E 11
Ley. Corn 2F 7
Leybourne. Kent 5A 40
Leyburn. N Yor 5E 105
Leycett. Staf 1B 72
Leyfields. Staf 5G 73
Ley Green. Herts 3B 52
Ley Hill. Buck 5H 51
Leyland. Lanc 2D 90
Leylodge. Abers 2E 153
Leymoor. W Yor 3B 92
Leys. Per 5B 144
Leysdown-on-Sea. Kent 3E 41
Leysmill. Ang 4F 145
Leyton. G Lon 2E 39
Leytonstone. G Lon 2E 39
Lezant. Corn 5D 10
Leziate. Norf 4F 77
Lhanbryde. Mor 2G 159
The Lhen. IOM 1C 108
Liatrie. High 5E 157
Libanus. Powy 3C 46
Libberton. S Lan 5C 128
Libbery. Worc 5D 60
Liberton. Edin 3F 129
Liceasto. W Isl 8D 171
Lichfield. Staf 5F 73
Lickey. Worc 3D 61
Lickey End. Worc 3D 60
Lickfold. W Sus 3A 26
Liddaton. Devn 4E 11
Liddington. Swin 3H 35
Liddle. Orkn 9D 172
Lidgate. Suff 5G 65
Lidgett. Notts 4D 86
Lidham Hill. E Sus 4C 28
Lidlington. C Beds 2H 51
Lidsey. W Sus 5A 26
Lidstone. Oxon 3B 50
Lienassie. High 1B 148
Liff. Ang 5C 144
Lifford. W Mid 2E 61
Lifton. Devn 4D 11
Liftondown. Devn 4D 10
Lighthorne. Warw 5H 61
Light Oaks. Stoke 5D 84
Lightwater. Surr 4A 38
Lightwood. Staf 1E 73
Lightwood. Stoke 1D 72
Lightwood Green. Ches E 1A 72
Lightwood Green. Wrex 1F 71
Lilbourne. Nptn 3C 62
Lilburn Tower. Nmbd 2E 121
Lillesdon. Som 4G 21
Lilleshall. Telf 4B 72
Lilley. Herts 3B 52
Lilliesleaf. Bord 2H 119
Lillingstone Dayrell. Buck 2F 51
Lillingstone Lovell. Buck 1F 51
Lillington. Dors 1B 14
Lilstock. Som 2E 21
Lilybank. Inv 2E 126
Lilyhurst. Shrp 4B 72
Limavady. Caus 4C 174
Limbrick. Lanc 3E 90
Limbury. Lutn 3A 52
Limekilnburn. S Lan 4A 128
Limekilns. Fife 1D 129
Limerigg. Falk 2B 128
Limestone Brae. Nmbd 5A 114
Lime Street. Worc 2D 48
Limington. Som 4A 22
Limpenhoe. Norf 5F 79
Limpley Stoke. Wilts 5C 34
Limpsfield. Surr 5F 39
Limpsfield Chart. Surr 5F 39
Linburn. W Lot 3E 129
Linby. Notts 5C 86
Linchmere. W Sus 3G 25
Lincluden. Dum 2A 112
Lincoln. Linc 197 (3G 87)
Lincomb. Worc 4C 60
Lindale. Cumb 1D 96
Lindal in Furness. Cumb 2B 96
Lindean. Bord 1G 119
Linden. Glos 4D 48
Lindfield. W Sus 3E 27
Lindford. Hants 3G 25
Lindores. Fife 2E 137
Lindridge. Worc 4A 60
Lindsell. Essx 3G 53
Lindsey. Suff 1C 54
Lindsey Tye. Suff 1C 54
Linford. Hants 2G 15
Linford. Thur 3A 40
Lingague. IOM 4B 108
Lingdale. Red C 3D 106
Lingen. Here 4F 59
Lingfield. Surr 1E 27
Lingreabhagh. W Isl 9C 171
Lingwood. Norf 5F 79
Lingy Close. Cumb 4E 113
Linicro. High 2C 154
Linkend. Worc 2D 48
Linkenholt. Hants 1B 24
Linkinhorne. Corn 5D 10
Linklater. Orkn 9D 172
Linksness. Orkn 6E 172
Linktown. Fife 4E 137
Linkwood. Mor 2G 159
Linley. Shrp
nr. Bishop's Castle 1F 59
nr. Bridgnorth 1A 60
Linley Green. Here 5A 60
Linlithgow. W Lot 2C 128
Linlithgow Bridge. Falk 2C 128
Linneraineach. High 3F 163
Linshiels. Nmbd 4C 120
Linsiadar. W Isl 4E 171
Linsidemore. High 4C 164
Linslade. C Beds 3H 51
Linstead Parva. Suff 3F 67
Linstock. Cumb 4F 113
Linthwaite. W Yor 3B 92
Lintlaw. Bord 4E 131
Lintmill. Mor 2C 160
Linton. Cambs 1F 53
Linton. Derbs 4G 73
Linton. Here 3B 48
Linton. Kent 1B 28
Linton. N Yor 3B 98
Linton. Bord 2B 120
Linton. W Yor 5F 99
Linton Colliery. Nmbd 5G 121
Linton Hill. Here 3B 48
Linton-on-Ouse. N Yor 3G 99
Lintzford. Dur 4E 115
Lintzgarth. Dur 5C 114
Linwood. Hants 2G 15
Linwood. Linc 2A 88
Linwood. Ren 3F 127
Lionacleit. W Isl 4C 170
Lionacro. High 2C 154
Lionacuidhe. W Isl 4C 170
Lional. W Isl 1H 171
Liphook. Hants 3G 25
Lipley. Shrp 2B 72
Lipyeate. Som 1B 22
Liquo. N Lan 4B 128
Lisbane. Ards 3J 179
Lisbellaw. Ferm 8F 176
Lisburn. Lis 3G 179
Liscard. Mers 1F 83
Liscolman. Caus 3F 175
Liscombe. Som 3B 20
Lishahawley. Derr 4A 174
Liskeard. Corn 2G 7
Lislea. New M 7E 178
Lisle Court. Hants 3B 16
Lisnarick. Ferm 7D 176
Lisnaskea. Ferm 6J 177
Liss. Hants 4F 25
Liss Forest. Hants 4F 25
Lissett. E Yor 4F 101
Lissington. Linc 2A 88
Liston. Essx 1B 54
Listooder. New M 4J 179
Lisvane. Card 3E 33
Liswerry. Newp 3G 33
Litcham. Norf 4A 78
Litchard. B'end 3C 32
Litchborough. Nptn 5D 62
Litchfield. Hants 1C 24
Litherland. Mers 1F 83
Litlington. Cambs 1D 52
Litlington. E Sus 5G 27
Littemill. Nmbd 3G 121
Litterty. Abers 3E 161
Little Abington. Cambs 1F 53
Little Addington. Nptn 3G 63
Little Airmyn. N Yor 2H 93
Little Alne. Warw 4F 61
Little Ardo. Abers 5F 161
Little Asby. Cumb 4H 103
Little Aston. Staf 5E 73
Little Atherfield. IOW 4C 16
Little Ayton. N Yor 3C 106
Little Baddow. Essx 5A 54
Little Badminton. S Glo 3D 34
Little Ballinluig. Per 3G 143
Little Bampton. Cumb 4D 112
Little Bardfield. Essx 2G 53
Little Barford. Bed 5A 64
Little Barningham. Norf 2D 78
Little Barrington. Glos 4H 49
Little Barrow. Ches W 4G 83
Little Barugh. N Yor 2B 100
Little Bavington. Nmbd 2C 114
Little Bealings. Suff 1F 55
Littlebeck. Cumb 3H 103
Little Bedwyn. Wilts 5A 36
Little Bentley. Essx 3E 54
Little Berkhamsted. Herts 5C 52
Little Billing. Nptn 4F 63
Little Billington. C Beds 3H 51
Little Birch. Here 2A 48
Little Bispham. Bkpl 5C 96
Little Blakenham. Suff 1E 54
Little Blencow. Cumb 1F 103
Little Bognor. W Sus 3B 26
Little Bolas. Shrp 3A 72
Little Bollington. Ches E 2B 84
Little Bookham. Surr 5C 38
Littleborough. Devn 1B 12
Littleborough. G Man 3H 91
Littleborough. Notts 2F 87
Littlebourne. Kent 5G 41
Little Bourton. Oxon 1C 50
Little Bowden. Leics 2E 63
Little Bradley. Suff 5F 65
Little Brampton. Shrp 2F 59
Little Brechin. Ang 2E 145
Littlebredy. Dors 4A 14
Little Brickhill. Mil 2H 51
Little Bridgeford. Staf 3C 72
Little Brington. Nptn 4D 62
Little Bromley. Essx 3D 54
Little Broughton. Cumb 1B 102
Little Budworth. Ches W 4H 83
Little Burstead. Essx 1A 40
Little Burton. E Yor 5F 101
Littlebury. Essx 2F 53
Littlebury Green. Essx 2E 53
Little Bytham. Linc 4H 75
Little Canfield. Essx 3F 53
Little Canford. Dors 3F 15
Little Carlton. Linc 2C 88
Little Carlton. Notts 5E 87
Little Casterton. Rut 5H 75
Little Catwick. E Yor 5F 101
Little Catworth. Cambs 3A 64
Little Cawthorpe. Linc 2C 88
Little Chalfont. Buck 1A 38
Little Chart. Kent 1D 28
Little Chesterford. Essx 1F 53
Little Cheverell. Wilts 1E 23
Little Chishill. Cambs 2E 53
Little Clacton. Essx 4E 55
Little Clanfield. Oxon 5A 50
Little Clifton. Cumb 2B 102
Little Coates. NE Lin 4F 95
Little Comberton. Worc 1E 49
Little Common. E Sus 5B 28
Little Compton. Warw 2A 50
Little Cornard. Suff 2B 54
Littlecote. Buck 3G 51
Littlecott. Wilts 1G 23
Little Cowarne. Here 5A 60
Little Coxwell. Oxon 2A 36
Little Crakehall. N Yor 5F 105
Little Crawley. Mil 1H 51
Little Creich. High 5D 164
Little Cressingham. Norf 5A 78
Little Crosby. Mers 4B 90
Little Crosthwaite. Cumb 2D 102
Little Cubley. Derbs 2F 73
Little Dalby. Leics 4E 75
Little Dawley. Telf 5A 72
Littledean. Glos 4B 48
Little Dens. Abers 4H 161
Little Dewchurch. Here 2A 48
Little Ditton. Cambs 5F 65
Little Down. Hants 1B 24
Little Downham. Cambs 2E 65
Little Drayton. Shrp 2A 72
Little Driffield. E Yor 4E 101
Little Dunham. Norf 4A 78
Little Dunkeld. Per 4H 143
Little Dunmow. Essx 3G 53
Little Easton. Essx 3G 53
Little Eaton. Derbs 1A 74
Little Eccleston. Lanc 5D 96
Little Ellingham. Norf 1C 66
Little Elm. Som 2C 22
Little End. Essx 5F 53
Little Everdon. Nptn 5C 62
Little Eversden. Cambs 5C 64
Little Faringdon. Oxon 5H 49
Little Fencote. N Yor 5F 105
Little Fenton. N Yor 1F 93
Littleferry. High 4F 165
Little Fransham. Norf 4B 78
Little Gaddesden. Herts 4H 51
Little Garway. Here 3H 47
Little Gidding. Cambs 2A 64
Little Glemham. Suff 5F 67
Little Glenshee. Per 5G 143
Little Gransden. Cambs 5B 64
Little Green. Suff 3C 66
Little Green. Wrex 1G 71
Little Grimsby. Linc 1C 88
Little Habton. N Yor 2B 100
Little Hadham. Herts 3E 53
Little Hale. Linc 1A 76
Little Hallingbury. Essx 4E 53
Littleham. Devn
nr. Bideford 4E 19
nr. Exmouth 4D 12
Little Hampden. Buck 5G 51
Littlehampton. W Sus 5B 26
Little Haresfield. Glos 5D 48
Little Harrowden. Nptn 3F 63
Little Haseley. Oxon 5E 51
Little Hatfield. E Yor 5F 101
Little Hautbois. Norf 3E 79
Little Haven. Pemb 3C 42
Little Hay. Staf 5F 73
Little Hayfield. Derbs 2E 85
Little Haywood. Staf 3E 73
Little Heath. W Mid 2H 61
Little Heck. N Yor 2F 93
Littlehempston. Devn 2E 9
Little Herbert's. Glos 4E 49
Little Hereford. Here 4H 59
Little Horkesley. Essx 2C 54
Little Hormead. Herts 3D 53
Little Horsted. E Sus 4F 27
Little Horton. W Yor 1B 92
Little Horwood. Buck 2F 51
Little Houghton. Nptn 5F 63
Little Houghton. S Yor 4E 93
Littlehoughton. Nmbd 3G 121
Little Hucklow. Derbs 3F 85
Little Hulton. G Man 4F 91
Little Irchester. Nptn 4G 63
Little Kelk. E Yor 3E 101
Little Kimble. Buck 5G 51
Little Kineton. Warw 5H 61
Little Kingshill. Buck 2G 37
Little Langdale. Cumb 4E 102
Little Langford. Wilts 3F 23
Little Laver. Essx 5F 53
Little Lawford. Warw 3B 62
Little Leigh. Ches W 3A 84
Little Leighs. Essx 4H 53
Little Leven. E Yor 5E 101
Little Lever. G Man 4F 91
Little Linford. Mil 1G 51
Little London. Buck 4E 51
Little London. E Sus 4G 27
Little London. Hants
nr. Andover 2B 24
nr. Basingstoke 1E 24
Little London. Linc
nr. Long Sutton 3D 76
nr. Spalding 3B 76
Little London. Norf
nr. North Walsham 2E 79
nr. Northwold 1G 65
nr. Saxthorpe 2D 78
nr. Southery 1F 65
Little London. Powy 2C 58
Little Longstone. Derbs 3F 85
Little Malvern. Worc 1C 48
Little Maplestead. Essx 2B 54
Little Marcle. Here 2B 48
Little Marlow. Buck 3G 37
Little Massingham. Norf 3G 77
Little Melton. Norf 5D 78
Little Mill. Mon 5G 47
Littlemill. Abers 4H 151
Littlemill. E Ayr 3D 116
Littlemill. High 4D 158
Little Milton. Oxon 5E 50
Little Missenden. Buck 1A 38
Littlemoor. Derbs 4A 86
Littlemoor. Dors 4B 14
Littlemore. Oxon 5D 50
Little Mountain. Flin 4E 83
Little Musgrave. Cumb 3A 104
Little Ness. Shrp 4G 71
Little Neston. Ches W 3E 83
Little Newcastle. Pemb 2D 43
Little Newsham. Dur 3E 105
Little Oakley. Essx 3F 55
Little Oakley. Nptn 2F 63
Little Onn. Staf 4C 72
Little Ormside. Cumb 3A 104
Little Orton. Cumb 4E 113
Little Orton. Leics 5H 73
Little Ouse. Cambs 2F 65
Little Ouseburn. N Yor 3G 99
Littleover. Derb 2H 73
Little Packington. Warw 2G 61
Little Paxton. Cambs 4A 64
Little Petherick. Corn 1D 6
Little Plumpton. Lanc 1B 90
Little Plumstead. Norf 4F 79
Little Ponton. Linc 2G 75
Littleport. Cambs 2E 65
Little Posbrook. Hants 2D 16
Little Potheridge. Devn 1F 11
Little Preston. Nptn 5C 62
Little Raveley. Cambs 3B 64
Little Reynoldston. Swan 4D 31
Little Ribston. N Yor 4F 99
Little Rissington. Glos 4G 49
Little Rogart. High 3E 165
Little Rollright. Oxon 2A 50
Little Ryburgh. Norf 3B 78
Little Ryle. Nmbd 3E 121
Little Ryton. Shrp 5G 71
Little Salkeld. Cumb 1G 103
Little Sampford. Essx 2G 53
Little Sandhurst. Brac 5G 37
Little Saredon. Staf 5D 72
Little Saxham. Suff 4G 65
Little Scatwell. High 3F 157
Little Shelford. Cambs 5D 64
Little Shoddesden. Hants 2A 24
Little Singleton. Lanc 1B 90
Little Smeaton. N Yor 3F 93
Little Snoring. Norf 2B 78
Little Sodbury. S Glo 3C 34
Little Somborne. Hants 3B 24
Little Somerford. Wilts 3E 35
Little Soudley. Shrp 3B 72
Little Stainforth. N Yor 3H 97
Little Stainton. Darl 3A 106
Little Stanney. Ches W 3G 83
Little Staughton. Bed 4A 64
Little Steeping. Linc 4D 88
Littlester. Shet 3G 173
Little Stoke. Staf 2D 72
Littlestone-on-Sea. Kent 3E 29
Little Stonham. Suff 4D 66
Little Stretton. Leics 5D 74
Little Stretton. Shrp 1G 59
Little Strickland. Cumb 3G 103
Little Stukeley. Cambs 3B 64
Little Sugnall. Staf 2C 72
Little Sutton. Ches W 3F 83
Little Sutton. Linc 3D 76
Little Swinburne. Nmbd 2C 114
Little Tew. Oxon 3B 50
Little Tey. Essx 3B 54
Little Thetford. Cambs 3E 65
Little Thirkleby. N Yor 2G 99
Little Thornage. Norf 2C 78
Little Thornton. Lanc 5C 96
Little Thorpe. W Yor 2B 92
Littlethorpe. Leics 1C 62
Littlethorpe. N Yor 3F 99
Little Thurlow. Suff 5F 65
Little Thurrock. Thur 3H 39
Littleton. Ches W 4G 83
Littleton. Hants 3C 24
Littleton. Som 3H 21
Littleton. Surr
nr. Guildford 1A 26
nr. Staines 4B 38
Littleton Drew. Wilts 3D 34
Littleton Pannell. Wilts 1F 23
Littleton-upon-Severn.
S Glo 3A 34
Little Torboll. High 4E 165
Little Torrington. Devn 1E 11
Little Totham. Essx 4B 54
Little Town. Cumb 3D 102
Little Town. Lanc 1E 91
Littletown. Dur 5G 115
Littletown. High 5E 165
Little Twycross. Leics 5H 73
Little Urswick. Cumb 2B 96
Little Wakering. Essx 2D 40
Little Walden. Essx 1F 53
Little Waldingfield. Suff 1C 54
Little Walsingham. Norf 2B 78
Little Waltham. Essx 4H 53
Little Warley. Essx 1H 39
Little Weighton. E Yor 1C 94
Little Wenham. Suff 2D 54
Little Wenlock. Telf 5A 72
Little Whelnetham. Suff 4A 66
Little Whittingham Green.
Suff 3E 67
Littlewick Green. Wind 4G 37
Little Wilbraham. Cambs 5E 65
Littlewindsor. Dors 2H 13
Little Wisbeach. Linc 2A 76
Little Witcombe. Glos 4E 49
Little Witley. Worc 4B 60
Little Wittenham. Oxon 2D 36
Little Wolford. Warw 2A 50
Littleworth. Bed 1A 52
Littleworth. Glos 2G 49
Littleworth. Oxon 2B 36
Littleworth. Staf
nr. Cannock 4E 73
nr. Eccleshall 3B 72
nr. Stafford 3D 72
Littleworth. W Sus 3C 26
Littleworth. Worc
nr. Redditch 4D 61
nr. Worcester 5C 60
Little Wratting. Suff 1G 53
Little Wymondley. Herts 3C 52
Little Wyrley. Staf 5E 73
Little Yeldham. Essx 2A 54
Littley Green. Essx 4G 53
Litton. Derbs 3F 85
Litton. N Yor 2B 98
Litton. Som 1A 22
Litton Cheney. Dors 3A 14
Liurbost. W Isl 5F 171
Liverpool. Mers 197 (1F 83)
Liverpool John Lennon Airport.
Mers 2G 83
Liversedge. W Yor 2B 92
Liverton. Devn 5B 12
Liverton. Red C 3E 107
Liverton Mines. Red C 3E 107
Livingston. W Lot 3D 128
Livingston Village. W Lot 3D 128
Lixwm. Flin 3D 82
Lizard. Corn 5E 5
Llaingoch. IOA 2B 80
Llaithddu. Powy 2C 58
Llampha. V Glam 4C 32
Llan. Powy 5A 70
Llanaber. Gwyn 4F 69
Llanaelhaearn. Gwyn 1C 68
Llanaeron. Cdgn 4D 57
Llanafan. Cdgn 3F 57
Llanafan-fawr. Powy 5B 58
Llanafan-fechan. Powy 5B 58
Llanallgo. IOA 2D 81
Llanandras. Powy 4F 59
Llananno. Powy 3C 58
Llanarmon. Gwyn 2D 68
Llanarmon Dyffryn Ceiriog.
Wrex 2D 70
Llanarmon-yn-Ial. Den 5D 82
Llanarth. Cdgn 5D 56
Llanarth. Mon 4G 47
Llanarthne. Carm 3F 45
Llanasa. Flin 2D 82
Llanbabo. IOA 2C 80
Llanbadarn Fawr. Cdgn 2F 57
Llanbadarn Fynydd. Powy 3D 58
Llanbadarn-y-garreg.
Powy 1E 46
Llanbadoc. Mon 5G 47
Llanbadrig. IOA 1C 80
Llanbeder. Newp 2G 33
Llanbedr. Gwyn 3E 69
Llanbedr. Powy
nr. Crickhowell 3F 47
nr. Hay-on-Wye 1E 47
Llanbedr-Dyffryn-Clwyd.
Den 5D 82
Llanbedrgoch. IOA 2E 81
Llanbedrog. Gwyn 2C 68
Llanbedr Pont Steffan.
Cdgn 1F 45
Llanbedr-y-cennin. Cnwy 4G 81
Llanberis. Gwyn 4E 81
Llanbethery. V Glam 5D 32
Llanbister. Powy 3D 58
Llanblethian. V Glam 4C 32
Llanboidy. Carm 2G 43
Llanbradach. Cphy 2E 33
Llanbrynmair. Powy 5A 70
Llanbydderi. V Glam 5D 32
Llancadle. V Glam 5D 32
Llancarfan. V Glam 4D 32
Llancatal. V Glam 5D 32
Llancayo. Mon 5G 47
Llancloudy. Here 3H 47
Llancoch. Powy 3E 58
Llancynfelyn. Cdgn 1F 57
Llandaff. Card 4E 33
Llandanwg. Gwyn 3E 69
Llandarcy. Neat 3G 31
Llandawke. Carm 3G 43
Llanddaniel Fab. IOA 3D 81
Llanddarog. Carm 4F 45
Llanddeiniol. Cdgn 3E 57
Llanddeiniolen. Gwyn 4E 81
Llandderfel. Gwyn 2B 70
Llanddeusant. Carm 3A 46
Llanddeusant. IOA 2C 80
Llanddew. Powy 2D 46
Llanddewi. Swan 4D 30
Llanddewi Brefi. Cdgn 5F 57
Llanddewi'r Cwm. Powy 1D 46
Llanddewi Rhydderch.
Mon 4G 47
Llanddewi Velfrey. Pemb 3F 43
Llanddewi Ystradenni.
Powy 4D 58
Llanddoged. Cnwy 4H 81
Llanddona. IOA 3E 81
Llanddowror. Carm 3G 43
Llanddulas. Cnwy 3B 82
Llanddwywe. Gwyn 3E 69
Llanddyfnan. IOA 3E 81
Llandecwyn. Gwyn 2F 69
Llandefaelog Fach. Powy 2D 46
Llandefaelog-tre'r-graig.
Powy 2E 47
Llandefalle. Powy 2E 46
Llandegfan. IOA 3E 81
Llandegla. Den 5D 82
Llandegley. Powy 4D 58
Llandegveth. Mon 2G 33
Llandeilo. Carm 3G 45
Llandeilo Graban. Powy 1D 46
Llandeilo'r Fan. Powy 2B 46
Llandeloy. Pemb 2C 42
Llandenny. Mon 5H 47
Llandevaud. Newp 2H 33
Llandevenny. Mon 3H 33
Llandilo. Pemb 2F 43
Llandinabo. Here 3A 48
Llandinam. Powy 2C 58
Llandissilio. Pemb 2F 43
Llandogo. Mon 5A 48
Llandough. V Glam
nr. Cowbridge 4C 32
nr. Penarth 4E 33
Llandovery. Carm 2A 46
Llandow. V Glam 4C 32
Llandre. Cdgn 2F 57
Llandrillo. Den 2C 70
Llandrillo-yn-Rhos. Cnwy 2H 81
Llandrindod. Powy 4C 58
Llandrindod Wells. Powy 4C 58
Llandrinio. Powy 4E 71
Llandudno. Cnwy 2G 81
Llandudno Junction.
Cnwy 3G 81
Llandudoch. Pemb 1B 44
Llandw. V Glam 4C 32
Llandwrog. Gwyn 5D 80
Llandybie. Carm 4G 45
Llandyfaelog. Carm 4E 45
Llandyfan. Carm 4G 45
Llandyfriog. Cdgn 1D 44
Llandyfrydog. IOA 2D 80
Llandygai. Gwyn 3F 81
Llandygwydd. Cdgn 1C 44
Llandynan. Den 1D 70
Llandyrnog. Den 4D 82
Llandysilio. Powy 4E 71
Llandyssil. Powy 1D 58
Llandysul. Cdgn 1E 45
Llanedeyrn. Card 3F 33
Llaneglwys. Powy 2D 46
Llanegryn. Gwyn 5F 69
Llanegwad. Carm 3F 45
Llaneilian. IOA 1D 80
Llanelian-yn-Rhos. Cnwy 3A 82
Llanelidan. Den 5D 82
Llanelieu. Powy 2E 47
Llanellen. Mon 4G 47
Llanelli. Carm 3E 31
Llanelltyd. Gwyn 4G 69
Llanelly. Mon 4F 47
Llanelly Hill. Mon 4F 47
Llanelwedd. Powy 5C 58
Llan-Elwy. Den 3C 82
Llanenddwyn. Gwyn 3E 69
Llanengan. Gwyn 3B 68
Llanerch. Powy 1F 59
Llanerchymedd. IOA 2D 80
Llanerfyl. Powy 5C 70
Llaneuddog. IOA 2D 80
Llanfachraeth. IOA 2C 80
Llanfachreth. Gwyn 3G 69
Llanfaelog. IOA 3C 80
Llanfaelrhys. Gwyn 3B 68
Llanfaenor. Mon 4H 47
Llanfaes. IOA 3F 81
Llanfaes. Powy 3D 46
Llanfaethlu. IOA 2C 80
Llanfaglan. Gwyn 4D 80
Llanfair. Gwyn 3E 69
Llanfair. Here 1F 47
Llanfair Caereinion. Powy 5D 70
Llanfair Clydogau. Cdgn 5F 57
Llanfair Dyffryn Clwyd.
Den 5D 82
Llanfairfechan. Cnwy 3F 81
Llanfair-Nant-Gwyn. Pemb 1F 43
Llanfair Pwllgwyngyll. IOA 3E 81
Llanfair Talhaiarn. Cnwy 3B 82
Llanfair Waterdine. Shrp 3E 59
Llanfair-ym-Muallt. Powy 5C 58
Llanfairyneubwll. IOA 3C 80
Llanfairynghornwy. IOA 1C 80
Llanfallteg. Carm 3F 43
Llanfallteg West. Carm 3F 43
Llanfaredd. Powy 5C 58
Llanfarian. Cdgn 3E 57
Llanfechain. Powy 3D 70
Llanfechell. IOA 1C 80
Llanfendigaid. Gwyn 5E 69
Llanferres. Den 4D 82
Llan Ffestiniog. Gwyn 1G 69
Llanfflewyn. IOA 2C 80
Llanfihangel-ar-Arth.
Carm 2E 45
Llanfihangel Glyn Myfyr.
Cnwy 1B 70
Llanfihangel Nant Bran.
Powy 2C 46
Llanfihangel-Nant-Melan.
Powy 5D 58
Llanfihangel near Rogiet.
Mon 3H 33
Llanfihangel Rhydithon.
Powy 4D 58
Llanfihangel Tal-y-llyn.
Powy 3E 46
Llanfihangel-uwch-Gwili.
Carm 3E 45
Llanfihangel-y-Creuddyn.
Cdgn 3F 57

Millgate—New Bewick

Millgate. Lanc 3G 91
Mill Green. Essx 5G 53
Mill Green. Norf 2D 66
Mill Green. Shrp 3A 72
Mill Green. Staf 3E 73
Mill Green. Suff 1C 54
Millhalf. Here 1F 47
Millhall. E Ren 4G 127
Millhayes. Devn
nr. Honiton 2F 13
nr. Wellington 1E 13
Millhead. Lanc 2D 97
Millheugh. S Lan 4A 128
Mill Hill. Bkbn 2E 91
Mill Hill. G Lon 1D 38
Millholme. Cumb 5G 103
Millhouse. Arg 2A 126
Millhouse. Cumb 1E 103
Millhousebridge. Dum 1C 112
Millhouses. S Yor 2H 85
Millikenpark. Ren 3F 127
Millington. E Yor 4C 100
Millington Green. Derbs 1G 73
Millisle. Ards 2K 179
Mill Knowe. Arg 3B 122
Mill Lane. Hants 1F 25
Millmeece. Staf 2C 72
Mill of Craigievar. Abers 2C 152
Mill of Fintray. Abers 2F 153
Mill of Haldane. W Dun 1F 127
Millom. Cumb 1A 96
Millow. C Beds 1C 52
Millpool. Corn 5B 10
Millport. N Ayr 4C 126
Mill Side. Cumb 1D 96
Mill Street. Norf
nr. Lyng 4C 78
nr. Swanton Morley 4C 78
Millthorpe. Derbs 3H 85
Millthorpe. Linc 2A 76
Millthrop. Cumb 5H 103
Milltimber. Aber 3F 153
Mill Town. Ant 8H 175
Milltown. Abers
nr. Corgarff 3G 151
nr. Lumsden 2B 152
Milltown. Ant 7G 175
Milltown. Arm
nr. Banbridge 5F 178
nr. Coalisland 3D 178
nr. Richhill 5D 178
Milltown. Corn 3F 7
Milltown. Derbs 4A 86
Milltown. Devn 3F 19
Milltown. Dum 2E 113
Milltown of Aberdalgie.
Per 1C 136
Milltown of Auchindoun.
Mor 4A 160
Milltown of Campfield.
Abers 3D 152
Milltown of Edinvillie.
Mor 4G 159
Milltown of Rothiemay.
Mor 4C 160
Milltown of Towie. Abers 2B 152
Milnacraig. Ang 3B 144
Milnathort. Per 3D 136
Milngavie. E Dun 2G 127
Milnholm. Stir 1A 128
Milnrow. G Man 3H 91
Milnthorpe. Cumb 1D 97
Milnthorpe. W Yor 3D 92
Milson. Shrp 3A 60
Milstead. Kent 5D 40
Milston. Wilts 2G 23
Milthorpe. Nptn 1D 50
Milton. Ang 4C 144
Milton. Cambs 4D 65
Milton. Cumb
nr. Brampton 3G 113
nr. Crooklands 1E 97
Milton. Derbs 3H 73
Milton. Dum
nr. Crocketford 2F 111
nr. Glenluce 4H 109
Milton. Glas 3G 127
Milton. High
nr. Achnasheen 3F 157
nr. Applecross 4G 155
nr. Drumnadrochit 5G 157
nr. Invergordon 1B 158
nr. Inverness 4H 157
nr. Wick 3F 169
Milton. Mor
nr. Cullen 2C 160
nr. Tomintoul 2F 151
Milton. N Som 5G 33
Milton. Notts 3E 86
Milton. Oxon
nr. Bloxham 2C 50
nr. Didcot 2C 36
Milton. Pemb 4E 43
Milton. Port 3E 17
Milton. Som 4H 21
Milton. S Ayr 2D 116
Milton. Stir
nr. Aberfoyle 3E 135
nr. Drymen 4D 134
Milton. Stoke 5D 84
Milton. W Dun 2F 127
Milton Abbas. Dors 2D 14
Milton Abbot. Devn 5E 11
Milton Auchlossan.
Abers 3C 152
Milton Bridge. Midl 3F 129
Milton Bryan. C Beds 2H 51
Milton Clevedon. Som 3B 22
Milton Coldwells. Abers 5G 161
Milton Combe. Devn 2A 8
Milton Common. Oxon 5E 51
Milton Damerel. Devn 1D 11
Miltonduff. Mor 2F 159
Milton End. Glos 5G 49
Milton Ernest. Bed 5H 63
Milton Green. Ches W 5G 83
Milton Hill. Devn 5C 12
Milton Hill. Oxon 2C 36
Milton Keynes. Mil 200 (2G 51)
Milton Keynes Village. Mil 2G 51
Milton Lilbourne. Wilts 5G 35
Milton Malsor. Nptn 5E 63
Milton Morenish. Per 5D 142
Milton of Auchinhove.
Abers 3C 152
Milton of Balgonie. Fife 3F 137
Milton of Barras. Abers 1H 145
Milton of Campsie.
E Dun 2H 127
Milton of Cultoquhey.
Per 1A 136
Milton of Cushnie. Abers 2C 152
Milton of Finavon. Ang 3D 145
Milton of Gollanfield.
High 3B 158
Milton of Lesmore.
Abers 1B 152
Milton of Leys. High 4A 158
Milton of Tullich. Abers 4A 152
Milton on Stour. Dors 4C 22
Milton Regis. Kent 4C 40
Milton Street. E Sus 5G 27
Milton-under-Wychwood.
Oxon 4A 50
Milverton. Som 4E 20
Milverton. Warw 4H 61
Milwich. Staf 2D 72
Mimbridge. Surr 4A 38
Minard. Arg 4G 133
Minchington. Dors 1E 15
Minchinhampton. Glos 5D 48
Mindrum. Nmbd 1C 120
Minehead. Som 2C 20
Minera. Wrex 5E 83
Minerstown. New M 6J 179
Minety. Wilts 2F 35
Minffordd. Gwyn 2E 69
Mingarrypark. High 2A 140
Mingary. High 2G 139
Mingearraidh. W Isl 6C 170
Miningsby. Linc 4C 88
Minions. Corn 5C 10
Minishant. S Ayr 3C 116
Minllyn. Gwyn 4A 70
Minnigaff. Dum 3B 110
Minorca. IOM 3D 108
Minskip. N Yor 3F 99
Minstead. Hants 1A 16
Minsted. W Sus 4G 25
Minster. Kent
nr. Ramsgate 4H 41
Minster. Kent
nr. Sheerness 3D 40
Minsteracres. Nmbd 4D 114
Minsterley. Shrp 5F 71
Minster Lovell. Oxon 4B 50
Minsterworth. Glos 4C 48
Minterne Magna. Dors 2B 14
Minterne Parva. Dors 2B 14
Minting. Linc 3A 88
Mintlaw. Abers 4H 161
Minto. Bord 2H 119
Minton. Shrp 1G 59
Minwear. Pemb 3E 43
Minworth. W Mid 1F 61
Miodar. Arg 4B 138
Mirbister. Orkn 5C 172
Mirehouse. Cumb 3A 102
Mireland. High 2F 169
Mirfield. W Yor 3C 92
Miserden. Glos 5E 49
Miskin. Rhon 3D 32
Misson. Notts 1D 86
Misterton. Leics 2C 62
Misterton. Notts 1E 87
Misterton. Som 2H 13
Mistley. Essx 2E 54
Mistley Heath. Essx 2E 55
Mitcham. G Lon 4D 39
Mitcheldean. Glos 4B 48
Mitchell. Corn 3C 6
Mitchel Troy. Mon 4H 47
Mitcheltroy Common.
Mon 5H 47
Mitford. Nmbd 1E 115
Mithian. Corn 3B 6
Mitton. Staf 4C 72
Mixbury. Oxon 2E 50
Mixenden. W Yor 2A 92
Mixon. Staf 5E 85
Moaness. Orkn 7B 172
Moarfield. Shet 1G 173
Moat. Cumb 2F 113
Moats Tye. Suff 5C 66
Mobberley. Ches E 3B 84
Mobberley. Staf 1E 73
Moccas. Here 1G 47
Mochdre. Cnwy 3H 81
Mochdre. Powy 2C 58
Mochrum. Dum 5A 110
Mockbeggar. Hants 2G 15
Mockerkin. Cumb 2B 102
Modbury. Devn 3C 8
Moddershall. Staf 2D 72
Modsarie. High 2G 167
Moelfre. Cnwy 3B 82
Moelfre. IOA 2E 81
Moelfre. Powy 3D 70
Moffat. Dum 4C 118
Moggerhanger. C Beds 1B 52
Mogworthy. Devn 1B 12
Moira. Leics 4H 73
Moira. Lis 3F 178
Molash. Kent 5E 41
Mol-chlach. High 2C 146
Mold. Flin 4E 83
Molehill Green. Essx 3F 53
Molescroft. E Yor 5E 101
Molesden. Nmbd 1E 115
Molesworth. Cambs 3H 63
Moll. High 1D 146
Molland. Devn 4B 20
Mollington. Ches W 3F 83
Mollington. Oxon 1C 50
Mollinsburn. N Lan 2A 128
Monachty. Cdgn 4E 57
Monachyle. Stir 2D 135
Monar Lodge. High 4E 156
Monaughty. Powy 4E 59
Monea. Ferm 7D 176
Monewden. Suff 5E 67
Moneydie. Per 1C 136
Moneyglass. Ant 7G 175
Moneymore. M Ulst 1C 178
Moneyneany. M Ulst 7D 174
Moneyreagh. Lis 3J 179
Moneyrow Green. Wind 4G 37
Moneyslane. Arm 6G 179
Moniaive. Dum 5G 117
Monifieth. Ang 5E 145
Monikie. Ang 5E 145
Monimail. Fife 2E 137
Monington. Pemb 1B 44
Monk Bretton. S Yor 4D 92
Monken Hadley. G Lon 1D 38
Monk Fryston. N Yor 2F 93
Monk Hesleden. Dur 1B 106
Monkhide. Here 1B 48
Monkhill. Cumb 4E 113
Monkhopton. Shrp 1A 60
Monkland. Here 5G 59
Monkleigh. Devn 4E 19
Monknash. V Glam 4C 32
Monkokehampton. Devn 2F 11
Monkseaton. Tyne 2G 115
Monks Eleigh. Suff 1C 54
Monk's Gate. W Sus 3D 26
Monk's Heath. Ches E 3C 84
Monk Sherborne. Hants 1E 24
Monkshill. Abers 4E 161
Monksilver. Som 3D 20
Monks Kirby. Warw 2B 62
Monk Soham. Suff 4E 66
Monk Soham Green. Suff 4E 66
Monkspath. W Mid 3F 61
Monks Risborough. Buck 5G 51
Monksthorpe. Linc 4D 88
Monkstown. Ant 1H 179
Monk Street. Essx 3G 53
Monkswood. Mon 5G 47
Monkton. Devn 2E 13
Monkton. Kent 4G 41
Monkton. Pemb 4D 42
Monkton. S Ayr 2C 116
Monkton Combe. Bath 5C 34
Monkton Deverill. Wilts 3D 22
Monkton Farleigh. Wilts 5D 34
Monkton Heathfield. Som 4F 21
Monktonhill. S Ayr 2C 116
Monkton Up Wimborne.
Dors 1F 15
Monkton Wyld. Dors 3G 13
Monkwearmouth. Tyne 4G 115
Monkwood. Dors 3H 13
Monkwood. Hants 3E 25
Monmarsh. Here 1A 48
Monmouth. Mon 4A 48
Monnington on Wye.
Here 1G 47
Monreith. Dum 5A 110
Montacute. Som 1H 13
Monteith. Arm 5F 179
Montford. Arg 3C 126
Montford. Shrp 4G 71
Montford Bridge. Shrp 4G 71
Montgarrie. Abers 2C 152
Montgarswood. E Ayr 2E 117
Montgomery. Powy 1E 58
Montgreenan. N Ayr 5E 127
Montrave. Fife 3F 137
Montrose. Ang 3G 145
Monxton. Hants 2B 24
Monyash. Derbs 4F 85
Monymusk. Abers 2D 152
Monzie. Per 1A 136
Moodiesburn. N Lan 2H 127
Moon's Green. Kent 3C 28
Moonzie. Fife 2F 137
Moor. Som 1H 13
The Moor. Kent 3B 28
Moor Allerton. W Yor 1C 92
Moorbath. Dors 3H 13
Moorbrae. Shet 3F 173
Moorby. Linc 4B 88
Moorcot. Here 5F 59
Moor Crichel. Dors 2E 15
Moor Cross. Devn 3C 8
Moordown. Bour 3F 15
Moore. Hal 2H 83
Moor End. E Yor 1B 94
Moorend. Dum 2D 112
Moorend. Glos
nr. Dursley 5C 48
nr. Gloucester 4D 48
Moorends. S Yor 3G 93
Moorfields. ME Ant 7H 175
Moorgate. S Yor 1B 86
Moor Green. Wilts 5D 34
Moorgreen. Hants 1C 16
Moorgreen. Notts 1B 74
Moorhaigh. Notts 4C 86
Moorhall. Derbs 3H 85
Moorhampton. Here 1G 47
Moorhouse. Cumb
nr. Carlisle 4E 113
nr. Wigton 4D 112
Moorhouse. Notts 4E 87
Moorhouse. Surr 5F 39
Moorhouses. Linc 5B 88
Moorland. Som 3G 21
Moorlinch. Som 3H 21
Moor Monkton. N Yor 4H 99
Moor of Granary. Mor 3E 159
Moor Row. Cumb
nr. Whitehaven 3B 102
nr. Wigton 5D 112
Moorsholm. Red C 3D 107
Moorside. Dors 1C 14
Moorside. G Man 4H 91
Moortown. Devn 3D 10
Moortown. Hants 2G 15
Moortown. IOW 4C 16
Moortown. Linc 1H 87
Moortown. M Ulst 2D 178
Moortown. Telf 4A 72
Moortown. W Yor 1D 92
Morangie. High 5E 165
Morar. High 4E 147
Morborne. Cambs 1A 64
Morchard Bishop. Devn 2A 12
Morcombelake. Dors 3H 13
Morcott. Rut 5G 75
Morda. Shrp 3E 71
Morden. G Lon 4D 38
Mordiford. Here 2A 48
Mordon. Dur 2A 106
More. Shrp 1F 59
Morebath. Devn 4C 20
Morebattle. Bord 2B 120
Morecambe. Lanc 3D 96
Morefield. High 4F 163
Moreleigh. Devn 3D 8
Morenish. Per 5C 142
Moresby Parks. Cumb 3A 102
Morestead. Hants 4D 24
Moreton. Dors 4D 14
Moreton. Essx 5F 53
Moreton. Here 4H 59
Moreton. Mers 1E 83
Moreton. Oxon 5E 51
Moreton. Staf 4B 72
Moreton Corbet. Shrp 3H 71
Moretonhampstead.
Devn 4A 12
Moreton-in-Marsh. Glos 2H 49
Moreton Jeffries. Here 1B 48
Moreton Morrell. Warw 5H 61
Moreton on Lugg. Here 1A 48
Moreton Pinkney. Nptn 1D 50
Moreton Say. Shrp 2A 72
Moreton Valence. Glos 5C 48
Morfa. Cdgn 5C 56
Morfa Bach. Carm 4D 44
Morfa Bychan. Gwyn 2E 69
Morfa Glas. Neat 5B 46
Morfa Nefyn. Gwyn 1B 68
Morganstown. Card 3E 33
Morgan's Vale. Wilts 4G 23
Morham. E Lot 2B 130
Moriah. Cdgn 3F 57
Morland. Cumb 2G 103
Morley. Ches E 2C 84
Morley. Derbs 1A 74
Morley. Dur 2E 105
Morley. W Yor 2C 92
Morley St Botolph. Norf 1C 66
Morningside. Edin 2F 129
Morningside. N Lan 4B 128
Morningthorpe. Norf 1E 67
Morpeth. Nmbd 1F 115
Morrey. Staf 4F 73
Morridge Side. Staf 5E 85
Morridge Top. Staf 4E 85
Morrington. Dum 1F 111
Morris Green. Essx 2H 53
Morriston. Swan 3F 31
Morston. Norf 1C 78
Mortehoe. Devn 2E 19
Morthen. S Yor 2B 86
Mortimer. W Ber 5E 37
Mortimer's Cross. Here 4G 59
Mortimer West End.
Hants 5E 37
Mortomley. S Yor 1H 85
Morton. Cumb
nr. Calthwaite 1F 103
nr. Carlisle 4E 113
Morton. Derbs 4B 86
Morton. Linc
nr. Bourne 3H 75
nr. Gainsborough 1F 87
nr. Lincoln 4F 87
Morton. Norf 4D 78
Morton. Notts 5E 87
Morton. Shrp 3E 71
Morton. S Glo 2B 34
Morton Bagot. Warw 4F 61
Morton Mill. Shrp 3H 71
Morton-on-Swale. N Yor 5A 106
Morton Tinmouth. Dur 2E 105
Morvah. Corn 3B 4
Morval. Corn 3G 7
Morvich. High
nr. Golspie 3E 165
nr. Shiel Bridge 1B 148
Morvil. Pemb 1E 43
Morville. Shrp 1A 60
Morwenstow. Corn 1C 10
Morwick. Nmbd 4G 121
Mosborough. S Yor 2B 86
Moscow. E Ayr 5F 127
Mose. Shrp 1B 60
Mosedale. Cumb 1E 103
Moseley. W Mid
nr. Birmingham 2E 61
nr. Wolverhampton 5D 72
Moseley. Worc 5C 60
Moss. Arg 4A 138
Moss. High 2A 140
Moss. S Yor 3F 93
Moss. Wrex 5F 83
Mossatt. Abers 2B 152
Moss Bank. Mers 1H 83
Mossbank. Shet 4F 173
Mossblown. S Ayr 2D 116
Mossbrow. G Man 2B 84
Mossburnford. Bord 3A 120
Mossdale. Dum 2D 110
Mossedge. Cumb 3F 113
Mossend. N Lan 3A 128
Mossgate. Staf 2D 72
Moss Lane. Ches E 3D 84
Mossley. Ant 1H 179
Mossley. Ches E 4C 84
Mossley. G Man 4H 91
Mossley Hill. Mers 2F 83
Moss of Barmuckity.
Mor 2G 159
Mosspark. Glas 3G 127
Mosspaul. Bord 5G 119
Moss Side. Cumb 4C 112
Moss Side. G Man 1C 84
Moss Side. Lanc
nr. Blackpool 1B 90
nr. Preston 2D 90
Moss Side. Mers 4B 90
Moss-Side. Caus 3G 175
Moss-side. High 3C 158
Moss-side of Cairness.
Abers 2H 161
Mosstodloch. Mor 2H 159
Mosswood. Nmbd 4D 114
Mossy Lea. Lanc 3D 90
Mosterton. Dors 2H 13
Moston. Shrp 3H 71
Moston Green. Ches E 4B 84
Mostyn. Flin 2D 82
Mostyn Quay. Flin 2D 82
Motcombe. Dors 4D 22
Mothecombe. Devn 4C 8
Motherby. Cumb 2F 103
Motherwell. N Lan 4A 128
Mottingham. G Lon 3F 39
Mottisfont. Hants 4B 24
Mottistone. IOW 4C 16
Mottram in Longdendale.
G Man 1D 85
Mottram St Andrew.
Ches E 3C 84
Mott's Mill. E Sus 2G 27
Mouldsworth. Ches W 3H 83
Moulin. Per 3G 143
Moulsecoomb. Brig 5E 27
Moulsford. Oxon 3D 36
Moulsoe. Mil 1H 51
Moulton. Ches W 4A 84
Moulton. Linc 3C 76
Moulton. Nptn 4E 63
Moulton. N Yor 4F 105
Moulton. Suff 4F 65
Moulton. V Glam 4D 32
Moulton Chapel. Linc 4B 76
Moulton Eaugate. Linc 4C 76
Moulton St Mary. Norf 5F 79
Moulton Seas End. Linc 3C 76
Mount. Corn
nr. Bodmin 2F 7
nr. Newquay 3B 6
Mountain Ash. Rhon 2D 32
Mountain Cross. Bord 5E 129
Mountain Street. Kent 5E 41
Mountain Water. Pemb 2D 42
Mount Ambrose. Corn 4B 6
Mountbenger. Bord 2F 119
Mountblow. W Dun 2F 127
Mount Bures. Essx 2C 54
Mountfield. E Sus 3B 28
Mountfield. Ferm 2L 177
Mountgerald. High 2H 157
Mount Hawke. Corn 4B 6
Mount High. High 2A 158
Mountjoy. Corn 2C 6
Mountjoy. Ferm 2K 177
Mount Lothian. Midl 4F 129
Mountnessing. Essx 1H 39
Mountnorris. Arm 6D 178
Mounton. Mon 2A 34
Mount Pleasant. Buck 2E 51
Mount Pleasant. Ches E 5C 84
Mount Pleasant. Derbs
nr. Derby 1H 73
nr. Swadlincote 4G 73
Mount Pleasant. E Sus 4F 27
Mount Pleasant. Hants 3A 16
Mount Pleasant. Norf 1B 66
Mount Skippett. Oxon 4B 50
Mountsorrel. Leics 4C 74
Mount Stuart. Arg 4C 126
Mousehole. Corn 4B 4
Mouswald. Dum 2B 112
Mow Cop. Ches E 5C 84
Mowden. Darl 3F 105
Mowhaugh. Bord 2C 120
Mowmacre Hill. Leic 5C 74
Mowsley. Leics 2D 62
Moy. High 5B 158
Moy. M Ulst 4C 178
Moygashel. M Ulst 3C 178
Moylgrove. Pemb 1B 44
Moy Lodge. High 5G 149
Muasdale. Arg 5E 125
Muchalls. Abers 4G 153
Much Birch. Here 2A 48
Much Cowarne. Here 1B 48
Much Dewchurch. Here 2H 47
Muchelney. Som 4H 21
Muchelney Ham. Som 4H 21
Much Hadham. Herts 4E 53
Much Hoole. Lanc 2C 90
Muchlarnick. Corn 3G 7
Much Marcle. Here 2B 48
Muchrachd. High 5E 157
Much Wenlock. Shrp 5A 72
Mucking. Thur 2A 40
Muckle Breck. Shet 5G 173
Muckleford. Dors 3B 14
Mucklestone. Staf 2B 72
Muckleton. Norf 2H 77
Muckleton. Shrp 3H 71
Muckley. Shrp 1A 60
Muckley Corner. Staf 5E 73
Muckton. Linc 2C 88
Mudale. High 5F 167
Muddiford. Devn 3F 19
Mudeford. Dors 3G 15
Mudford. Som 1A 14
Mudgley. Som 2H 21
Mugdock. Stir 2G 127
Mugeary. High 5D 154
Muggington. Derbs 1G 73
Mugingtonlane End.
Derbs 1G 73
Muggleswick. Dur 4D 114
Mugswell. Surr 5D 38
Muie. High 3D 164
Muirden. Abers 3E 160
Muirdrum. Ang 5E 145
Muiredge. Per 1E 137
Muirend. Glas 3G 127
Muirhead. Ang 5C 144
Muirhead. Fife 3E 137
Muirhead. N Lan 3H 127
Muirhouses. Falk 1D 128
Muirkirk. E Ayr 2F 117
Muir of Alford. Abers 2C 152
Muir of Fairburn. High 3G 157
Muir of Fowlis. Abers 2C 152
Muir of Miltonduff. Mor 3F 159
Muir of Ord. High 3H 157
Muir of Tarradale. High 3H 157
Muirshearlich. High 5D 148
Muirtack. Abers 5G 161
Muirton. High 2B 158
Muirton. Per 1D 136
Muirton of Ardblair. Per 4A 144
Muirtown. Per 2B 136
Muiryfold. Abers 3E 161
Muker. N Yor 5C 104
Mulbarton. Norf 5D 78
Mulben. Mor 3A 160
Mulindry. Arg 4B 124
Mulla. Shet 5F 173
Mullach Charlabhaigh.
W Isl 3E 171
Mullacott. Devn 2F 19
Mullaghbane. New M 8D 178
Mullaghboy. ME Ant 6L 175
Mullaghglass. New M 7E 178
Mullion. Corn 5D 5
Mullion Cove. Corn 5D 4
Mumbles. Swan 4F 31
Mumby. Linc 3E 89
Munderfield Row. Here 5A 60
Munderfield Stocks. Here 5A 60
Mundesley. Norf 2F 79
Mundford. Norf 1H 65
Mundham. Norf 1F 67
Mundon. Essx 5B 54
Munerigie. High 3E 149
Muness. Shet 1H 173
Mungasdale. High 4D 162
Mungrisdale. Cumb 1E 103
Munlochy. High 3A 158
Munsley. Here 1B 48
Munslow. Shrp 2H 59
Murchington. Devn 4G 11
Murcot. Worc 1F 49
Murcott. Oxon 4D 50
Murdishaw. Hal 2H 83
Murieston. W Lot 3D 128
Murkle. High 2D 168
Murlaggan. High 4C 148
Murra. Orkn 7B 172
The Murray. S Lan 4H 127
Murrayfield. Edin 2F 129
Murrell Green. Hants 1F 25
Murroes. Ang 5D 144
Murrow. Cambs 5C 76
Mursley. Buck 3G 51
Murthly. Per 5H 143
Murton. Cumb 2A 104
Murton. Dur 5G 115
Murton. Nmbd 5F 131
Murton. Swan 4E 31
Murton. York 4A 100
Musbury. Devn 3F 13
Muscoates. N Yor 1A 100
Muscott. Nptn 4D 62
Musselburgh. E Lot 2G 129
Muston. Leics 2F 75
Muston. N Yor 2E 101
Mustow Green. Worc 3C 60
Muswell Hill. G Lon 2D 39
Mutehill. Dum 5D 111
Mutford. Suff 2G 67
Muthill. Per 2A 136
Mutterton. Devn 2D 12
Muxton. Telf 4B 72
Mwmbwls. Swan 4F 31
Mybster. High 3D 168
Myddfai. Carm 2A 46
Myddle. Shrp 3G 71
Mydroilyn. Cdgn 5D 56
Myerscough. Lanc 1C 90
Mylor Bridge. Corn 5C 6
Mylor Churchtown. Corn 5C 6
Mynachlog-ddu. Pemb 1F 43
Mynydd-bach. Mon 2H 33
Mynydd Isa. Flin 4E 83
Mynyddislwyn. Cphy 2E 33
Mynydd Llandegai. Gwyn 4F 81
Mynydd Mechell. IOA 1C 80
Mynydd-y-briw. Powy 3D 70
Mynyddygarreg. Carm 5E 45
Mynytho. Gwyn 2C 68
Myrebird. Abers 4E 153
Myrelandhorn. High 3E 169
Mytchett. Surr 1G 25
The Mythe. Glos 2D 49
Mytholmroyd. W Yor 2A 92
Myton-on-Swale. N Yor 3G 99
Mytton. Shrp 4G 71

N

Naast. High 5C 162
Na Buirgh. W Isl 8C 171
Naburn. York 5H 99
Nab Wood. W Yor 1B 92
Nackington. Kent 5F 41
Nacton. Suff 1F 55
Nafferton. E Yor 4E 101
Na Gearrannan. W Isl 3D 171
Nailbridge. Glos 4B 48
Nailsbourne. Som 4F 21
Nailsea. N Som 4H 33
Nailstone. Leics 5B 74
Nailsworth. Glos 2D 34
Nairn. High 3C 158
Nalderswood. Surr 1D 26
Nancegollan. Corn 3D 4
Nancledra. Corn 3B 4
Nangreaves. G Man 3G 91
Nanhyfer. Pemb 1E 43
Nannerch. Flin 4D 82
Nanpantan. Leics 4C 74
Nanpean. Corn 3D 6
Nanstallon. Corn 2E 7
Nant-ddu. Powy 4D 46
Nanternis. Cdgn 5C 56
Nantgaredig. Carm 3E 45
Nantgarw. Rhon 3E 33
Nant Glas. Powy 4B 58
Nantglyn. Den 4C 82
Nantgwyn. Powy 3B 58
Nantlle. Gwyn 5E 81
Nantmawr. Shrp 3E 71
Nantmel. Powy 4C 58
Nantmor. Gwyn 1F 69
Nant Peris. Gwyn 5F 81
Nantwich. Ches E 5A 84
Nant-y-bai. Carm 1A 46
Nant-y-bwch. Blae 4E 47
Nant-y-Derry. Mon 5G 47
Nant-y-dugoed. Powy 4B 70
Nant-y-felin. Cnwy 3F 81
Nantyffyllon. B'end 2B 32
Nantyglo. Blae 4E 47
Nant-y-meichiaid. Powy 4D 70
Nant-y-moel. B'end 2C 32
Nant-y-pandy. Cnwy 3F 81
Naphill. Buck 2G 37
Nappa. N Yor 4A 98
Napton on the Hill. Warw 4B 62
Narberth. Pemb 3F 43
Narberth Bridge. Pemb 3F 43
Narborough. Leics 1C 62
Narborough. Norf 4G 77
Narkurs. Corn 3H 7
The Narth. Mon 5A 48
Narthwaite. Cumb 5A 104
Nasareth. Gwyn 5D 80
Naseby. Nptn 3D 62
Nash. Buck 2F 51
Nash. Here 4F 59
Nash. Kent 5G 41
Nash. Newp 3G 33
Nash. Shrp 3A 60
Nash Lee. Buck 5G 51
Nassington. Nptn 1H 63
Nasty. Herts 3D 52
Natcott. Devn 4C 18
Nateby. Cumb 4A 104
Nateby. Lanc 5D 96
Nately Scures. Hants 1F 25
Natland. Cumb 1E 97
Naughton. Suff 1D 54
Naunton. Glos 3G 49
Naunton. Worc 2D 49
Naunton Beauchamp.
Worc 5D 60
Navenby. Linc 5G 87
Navestock. Essx 1G 39
Navestock Side. Essx 1G 39
Navidale. High 2H 165
Nawton. N Yor 1A 100
Nayland. Suff 2C 54
Nazeing. Essx 5E 53
Neacroft. Hants 3G 15
Nealhouse. Cumb 4E 113
Neal's Green. Warw 2H 61
Near Sawrey. Cumb 5E 103
Neasden. G Lon 2D 38
Neasham. Darl 3A 106
Neath. Neat 2A 32
Neath Abbey. Neat 3G 31
Neatishead. Norf 3F 79
Neaton. Norf 5B 78
Nebo. Cdgn 4E 57
Nebo. Cnwy 5H 81
Nebo. Gwyn 5D 81
Nebo. IOA 1D 80
Necton. Norf 5A 78
Nedd. High 5B 166
Nedderton. Nmbd 1F 115
Nedging. Suff 1D 54
Nedging Tye. Suff 1D 54
Needham. Norf 2E 67
Needham Market. Suff 5C 66
Needham Street. Suff 4G 65
Needingworth. Cambs 3C 64
Needwood. Staf 3F 73
Neen Savage. Shrp 3A 60
Neen Sollars. Shrp 3A 60
Neenton. Shrp 2A 60
Nefyn. Gwyn 1C 68
Neilston. E Ren 4F 127
Neithrop. Oxon 1C 50
Nelly Andrews Green.
Powy 5E 71
Nelson. Cphy 2E 32
Nelson. Lanc 1G 91
Nelson Village. Nmbd 2F 115
Nemphlar. S Lan 5B 128
Nempnett Thrubwell.
Bath 5A 34
Nene Terrace. Linc 5B 76
Nenthall. Cumb 5A 114
Nenthead. Cumb 5A 114
Nenthorn. Bord 1A 120
Nercwys. Flin 4E 83
Neribus. Arg 4A 124
Nerston. S Lan 4H 127
Nesbit. Nmbd 1D 121
Nesfield. N Yor 5C 98
Ness. Ches W 3F 83
Nesscliffe. Shrp 4F 71
Ness of Tenston. Orkn 6B 172
Neston. Ches W 3E 83
Neston. Wilts 5D 34
Nethanfoot. S Lan 5B 128
Nether Alderley. Ches E 3C 84
Netheravon. Wilts 2G 23
Nether Blainslie. Bord 5B 130
Netherbrae. Abers 3E 161
Netherbrough. Orkn 6C 172
Nether Broughton. Leics 3D 74
Netherburn. S Lan 5B 128
Nether Burrow. Lanc 2F 97
Netherbury. Dors 3H 13
Netherby. Cumb 2E 113
Nether Careston. Ang 3E 145
Nether Cerne. Dors 3B 14
Nether Compton. Dors 1A 14
Nethercote. Glos 3G 49
Nethercote. Warw 4C 62
Nethercott. Devn 3E 19
Nethercott. Oxon 3C 50
Nether Dallachy. Mor 2A 160
Nether Durdie. Per 1E 136
Nether End. Derbs 3G 85
Netherend. Glos 5A 48
Nether Exe. Devn 2C 12
Netherfield. E Sus 4B 28
Netherfield. Notts 1D 74
Nethergate. Norf 3C 78
Netherhampton. Wilts 4G 23
Nether Handley. Derbs 3B 86
Nether Haugh. S Yor 1B 86
Nether Heage. Derbs 5A 86
Nether Heyford. Nptn 5D 62
Nether Howcleugh.
S Lan 3C 118
Nether Kellet. Lanc 3E 97
Nether Kinmundy. Abers 4H 161
Netherland Green. Staf 2F 73
Nether Langwith. Notts 3C 86
Netherlaw. Dum 5E 111
Netherley. Abers 4F 153
Nethermill. Dum 1B 112
Nethermills. Mor 3C 160
Nether Moor. Derbs 4A 86
Nether Padley. Derbs 3G 85
Netherplace. E Ren 4G 127
Nether Poppleton. York 4H 99
Netherseal. Derbs 4G 73
Nether Silton. N Yor 5B 106
Nether Stowey. Som 3E 21
Nether Street. Essx 4F 53
Netherstreet. Wilts 5E 35
Netherthird. E Ayr 3E 117
Netherthong. W Yor 4B 92
Netherton. Ang 3E 145
Netherton. Cumb 1B 102
Netherton. Devn 5B 12
Netherton. Hants 1B 24
Netherton. Here 3A 48
Netherton. Mers 1F 83
Netherton. N Lan 4A 128
Netherton. Nmbd 4D 121
Netherton. Per 3A 144
Netherton. Shrp 2B 60
Netherton. Stir 2G 127
Netherton. W Mid 2D 60
Netherton. W Yor
nr. Armitage Bridge 3B 92
nr. Horbury 3C 92
Netherton. Worc 1E 49
Nethertown. Cumb 4A 102
Nethertown. High 1F 169
Nethertown. Staf 4F 73
Nether Urquhart. Fife 3D 136
Nether Wallop. Hants 3B 24
Nether Wasdale. Cumb 4C 102
Nether Welton. Cumb 5E 113
Nether Westcote. Glos 3H 49
Nether Whitacre. Warw 1G 61
Nether Winchendon. Buck 4F 51
Netherwitton. Nmbd 5F 121
Nether Worton. Oxon 2C 50
Nethy Bridge. High 1E 151
Netley. Shrp 5G 71
Netley Abbey. Hants 2C 16
Netley Marsh. Hants 1B 16
Nettlebed. Oxon 3F 37
Nettlebridge. Som 2B 22
Nettlecombe. Dors 3A 14
Nettlecombe. IOW 5D 16
Nettleden. Herts 4A 52
Nettleham. Linc 3H 87
Nettlestead. Kent 5A 40
Nettlestead Green. Kent 5A 40
Nettlestone. IOW 3E 16
Nettlesworth. Dur 5F 115
Nettleton. Linc 4E 94
Nettleton. Wilts 4D 34
Netton. Devn 4B 8
Netton. Wilts 3G 23
Neuadd. Powy 5C 70
The Neuk. Abers 4E 153
Nevendon. Essx 1B 40
Nevern. Pemb 1E 43
New Abbey. Dum 3A 112
New Aberdour. Abers 2F 161
New Addington. G Lon 4E 39
Newall. W Yor 5E 98
New Alresford. Hants 3D 24
New Alyth. Per 4B 144
Newark. Orkn 3G 172
Newark. Pet 5B 76
Newark-on-Trent. Notts 5E 87
New Arley. Warw 2G 61
Newarthill. N Lan 4A 128
New Ash Green. Kent 4H 39
New Balderton. Notts 5F 87
New Barn. Kent 4H 39
New Barnetby. N Lin 3D 94
Newbattle. Midl 3G 129
New Bewick. Nmbd 2E 121

Newbie—Oake

Newbie. Dum 3C 112
Newbiggin. Cumb
nr. Appleby 2H 103
nr. Barrow-in-Furness 3B 96
nr. Cumrew 5G 113
nr. Penrith 2F 103
nr. Seascale 5B 102
Newbiggin. Dur
nr. Consett 5E 115
nr. Holwick 2C 104
Newbiggin. Nmbd 5C 114
Newbiggin. N Yor
nr. Askrigg 5C 104
nr. Filey 1F 101
nr. Thoralby 1B 98
Newbiggin-by-the-Sea. Nmbd 1G 115
Newbigging. Ang
nr. Monikie 5D 145
nr. Newtyle 4B 144
nr. Tealing 5D 144
Newbigging. Edin 2E 129
Newbigging. S Lan 5D 128
Newbiggin-on-Lune. Cumb 4A 104
Newbold. Derbs 3A 86
Newbold. Leics 4B 74
Newbold on Avon. Warw 3B 62
Newbold on Stour. Warw 1H 49
Newbold Pacey. Warw 5G 61
Newbold Verdon. Leics 5B 74
New Bolingbroke. Linc 5C 88
Newborough. IOA 4D 80
Newborough. Pet 5B 76
Newborough. Staf 3F 73
Newbottle. Nptn 2D 50
Newbottle. Tyne 4G 115
New Boultham. Linc 3G 87
Newbourne. Suff 1F 55
New Brancepeth. Dur 5F 115
New Bridge. Dum 2G 111
Newbridge. Cphy 2F 33
Newbridge. Cdgn 5E 57
Newbridge. Corn 3B 4
Newbridge. Edin 2E 129
Newbridge. Hants 1A 16
Newbridge. IOW 4C 16
Newbridge. N Yor 1C 100
Newbridge. Pemb 1D 42
Newbridge. Wrex 1E 71
Newbridge Green. Worc 2D 48
Newbridge-on-Usk. Mon 2G 33
Newbridge on Wye. Powy 5C 58
New Brighton. Flin 4E 83
New Brighton. Hants 2F 17
New Brighton. Mers 1F 83
New Brinsley. Notts 5B 86
Newbrough. Nmbd 3B 114
New Broughton. Wrex 5F 83
New Buckenham. Norf 1C 66
New Buildings. Derr 5A 174
Newbuildings. Devn 2A 12
Newburgh. Abers 1G 153
Newburgh. Fife 2E 137
Newburgh. Lanc 3C 90
Newburn. Tyne 3E 115
Newbury. W Ber 5C 36
Newbury. Wilts 2D 22
Newby. Cumb 2G 103
Newby. N Yor
nr. Ingleton 2G 97
nr. Scarborough 1E 101
nr. Stokesley 3C 106
Newby Bridge. Cumb 1C 96
Newby Cote. N Yor 2G 97
Newby East. Cumb 4F 113
Newby Head. Cumb 2G 103
New Byth. Abers 3F 161
Newby West. Cumb 4E 113
Newby Wiske. N Yor 1F 99
Newcastle. Ards 4L 179
Newcastle. B'end 3B 32
Newcastle. Mon 4H 47
Newcastle. New M 6H 179
Newcastle. Shrp 2E 59
Newcastle Emlyn. Carm 1D 44
Newcastle International Airport. Tyne 2E 115
Newcastleton. Bord 1F 113
Newcastle-under-Lyme. Staf 1C 72
Newcastle upon Tyne. Tyne **197** (3F 115)
Newchapel. Pemb 1G 43
Newchapel. Powy 2B 58
Newchapel. Staf 5C 84
Newchapel. Surr 1E 27
New Cheriton. Hants 4D 24
Newchurch. Carm 3D 45
Newchurch. Here 5F 59
Newchurch. IOW 4D 16
Newchurch. Kent 2E 29
Newchurch. Lanc 2G 91
Newchurch. Mon 2H 33
Newchurch. Powy 5E 58
Newchurch. Staf 3F 73
Newchurch in Pendle. Lanc 1G 91
New Costessey. Norf 4D 78
Newcott. Devn 2F 13
New Cowper. Cumb 5C 112
Newcraighall. Edin 2G 129
New Crofton. W Yor 3D 93
New Cross. Cdgn 3F 57
New Cross. Som 1H 13
New Cumnock. E Ayr 3F 117
New Deer. Abers 4F 161
New Denham. Buck 2B 38
Newdigate. Surr 1C 26
New Duston. Nptn 4E 62
New Earswick. York 4A 100
New Edlington. S Yor 1C 86
New Elgin. Mor 2G 159
New Ellerby. E Yor 1E 95
Newell Green. Brac 4G 37
New Eltham. G Lon 3F 39
New End. Warw 4F 61
New End. Worc 5E 61
Newenden. Kent 3C 28
New England. Essx 1H 53
New England. Pet 5A 76
Newent. Glos 3C 48
New Ferry. Mers 2F 83
Newfield. Dur
nr. Chester-le-Street 4F 115
nr. Willington 1F 105
Newfound. Hants 1D 24
New Fryston. W Yor 2E 93
Newgale. Pemb 2C 42
New Galloway. Dum 2D 110
Newgate. Norf 1C 78
Newgate Street. Herts 5D 52
New Greens. Herts 5B 52
New Grimsby. IOS 1A 4
New Hainford. Norf 4E 78
Newhall. Ches E 1A 72
Newhall. Derbs 3G 73
Newham. Nmbd 2F 121
New Hartley. Nmbd 2G 115
Newhaven. Derbs 4F 85
Newhaven. E Sus **204** (5F 27)
Newhaven. Edin 2F 129
New Haw. Surr 4B 38
New Hedges. Pemb 4F 43
New Herrington. Tyne 4G 115
Newhey. G Man 3H 91
New Holkham. Norf 2A 78
New Holland. N Lin 2D 94
Newholm. N Yor 3F 107
New Houghton. Derbs 4C 86
New Houghton. Norf 3G 77
Newhouse. N Lan 3A 128
New Houses. N Yor 2H 97
New Hutton. Cumb 5G 103
New Hythe. Kent 5B 40
Newick. E Sus 3F 27
Newingreen. Kent 2F 29
Newington. Edin 2F 129
Newington. Kent
nr. Folkestone 2F 29
nr. Sittingbourne 4C 40
Newington. Notts 1D 86
Newington. Oxon 2E 36
Newington Bagpath. Glos 2D 34
New Inn. Carm 2E 45
New Inn. Mon 5H 47
New Inn. N Yor 2H 97
New Inn. Torf 2G 33
New Invention. Shrp 3E 59
New Kelso. High 4B 156
New Lanark. S Lan 5B 128
Newland. Glos 5A 48
Newland. Hull 1D 94
Newland. N Yor 2G 93
Newland. Som 3B 20
Newland. Worc 1C 48
Newlandrig. Midl 3G 129
Newlands. Cumb 1E 103
Newlands. High 4B 158
Newlands. Nmbd 4D 115
Newlands. Staf 3E 73
Newlands of Geise. High 2C 168
Newlands of Tynet. Mor 2A 160
Newlands Park. IOA 2B 80
New Lane. Lanc 3C 90
New Lane End. Warr 1A 84
New Langholm. Dum 1E 113
New Leake. Linc 5D 88
New Leeds. Abers 3G 161
New Lenton. Nott 2C 74
New Longton. Lanc 2D 90
Newlot. Orkn 6E 172
New Luce. Dum 3G 109
Newlyn. Corn 4B 4
Newmachar. Abers 2F 153
Newmains. N Lan 4B 128
New Mains of Ury. Abers 5F 153
New Malden. G Lon 4D 38
Newman's Green. Suff 1B 54
Newmarket. Suff 4F 65
Newmarket. W Isl 4G 171
New Marske. Red C 2D 106
New Marton. Shrp 2F 71
New Micklefield. W Yor 1E 93
New Mill. Abers 4E 160
New Mill. Corn 3B 4
New Mill. Herts 4H 51
New Mill. W Yor 4B 92
New Mill. Wilts 5G 35
Newmill. Ant 8J 175
Newmill. Mor 3B 160
Newmill. Bord 3G 119
Newmillerdam. W Yor 3D 92
New Mills. Corn 3C 6
New Mills. Derbs 2E 85
New Mills. Mon 5A 48
New Mills. Powy 5C 70
Newmills. Arm 4E 178
Newmills. Fife 1D 128
Newmills. High 2A 158
Newmills. M Ulst 3C 178
Newmiln. Per 5A 144
Newmilns. E Ayr 1E 117
New Milton. Hants 3H 15
New Mistley. Essx 2E 54
New Moat. Pemb 2E 43
Newmore. High
nr. Dingwall 3H 157
nr. Invergordon 1A 158
Newnham. Cambs 5D 64
Newnham. Glos 4B 48
Newnham. Hants 1F 25
Newnham. Herts 2C 52
Newnham. Kent 5D 40
Newnham. Nptn 5C 62
Newnham. Warw 4F 61
Newnham Bridge. Worc 4A 60
New Ollerton. Notts 4D 86
New Oscott. W Mid 1E 61
Newpark. Fife 2G 137
New Pitsligo. Abers 3F 161
New Polzeath. Corn 1D 6
Newport. Corn 4D 10
Newport. Devn 3F 19
Newport. E Yor 1B 94
Newport. Essx 2F 53
Newport. Glos 2B 34
Newport. High 1H 165
Newport. IOW 4D 16
Newport. Newp **200** (3G 33)
Newport. Norf 4H 79
Newport. Pemb 1E 43
Newport. Som 4G 21
Newport. Telf 4B 72
Newport-on-Tay. Fife 1G 137
Newport Pagnell. Mil 1G 51
Newpound Common. W Sus 3B 26
New Prestwick. S Ayr 2C 116
New Quay. Cdgn 5C 56
Newquay. Corn 2C 6
Newquay Cornwall Airport. Corn 2C 6
New Rackheath. Norf 4E 79
New Radnor. Powy 4E 58
New Rent. Cumb 1F 103
New Ridley. Nmbd 4D 114
New Romney. Kent 3E 29
New Rossington. S Yor 1D 86
New Row. Cdgn 3G 57
Newry. New M 7E 178
New Sauchie. Clac 4A 136
Newsbank. Ches E 4C 84
Newseat. Abers 5E 160
Newsham. Lanc 1D 90
Newsham. Nmbd 2G 115
Newsham. N Yor
nr. Richmond 3E 105
nr. Thirsk 1F 99
New Sharlston. W Yor 2D 93
Newsholme. E Yor 2H 93
Newsholme. Lanc 4H 97
New Shoreston. Nmbd 1F 121
New Springs. G Man 4D 90
Newstead. Notts 5C 86
Newstead. Bord 1H 119
New Stevenston. N Lan 4A 128
New Street. Here 5F 59
Newstreet Lane. Shrp 2A 72
New Swanage. Dors 4F 15
New Swannington. Leics 4B 74
Newthorpe. N Yor 1E 93
Newthorpe. Notts 1B 74
Newton. Arg 4H 133
Newton. B'end 4B 32
Newton. Cambs
nr. Cambridge 1E 53
nr. Wisbech 4D 76
Newton. Ches W
nr. Chester 4G 83
nr. Tattenhall 5H 83
Newton. Cumb 2B 96
Newton. Derbs 5B 86
Newton. Dors 1C 14
Newton. Dum
nr. Annan 2D 112
nr. Moffat 5D 118
Newton. G Man 1D 84
Newton. Here
nr. Ewyas Harold 2G 47
nr. Leominster 5H 59
Newton. High
nr. Cromarty 2B 158
nr. Inverness 4B 158
nr. Kylestrome 5C 166
nr. Wick 4F 169
Newton. Lanc
nr. Blackpool 1B 90
nr. Carnforth 2E 97
nr. Clitheroe 4F 97
Newton. Linc 2H 75
Newton. Mers 2E 83
Newton. Mor 2F 159
Newton. Norf 4H 77
Newton. Nptn 2F 63
Newton. Nmbd 3D 114
Newton. Notts 1D 74
Newton. Bord 2A 120
Newton. Shet 8E 173
Newton. Shrp
nr. Bridgnorth 1B 60
nr. Wem 2G 71
Newton. Som 3E 20
Newton. S Lan
nr. Glasgow 3H 127
nr. Lanark 1B 118
Newton. Staf 3E 73
Newton. Suff 1C 54
Newton. Swan 4F 31
Newton. Warw 3C 62
Newton. W Lot 2D 129
Newton. Wilts 4H 23
Newton Abbot. Devn 5B 12
Newtonairds. Dum 1F 111
Newton Arlosh. Cumb 4D 112
Newton Aycliffe. Dur 2F 105
Newton Bewley. Hart 2B 106
Newton Blossomville. Mil 5G 63
Newton Bromswold. Nptn 4G 63
Newton Burgoland. Leics 5A 74
Newton by Toft. Linc 2H 87
Newton Ferrers. Devn 4B 8
Newton Flotman. Norf 1E 66
Newtongrange. Midl 3G 129
Newton Green. Mon 2A 34
Newton Hall. Dur 5F 115
Newton Hall. Nmbd 3D 114
Newton Harcourt. Leics 1D 62
Newton Heath. G Man 4G 91
Newton Hill. W Yor 2D 92
Newtonhill. Abers 4G 153
Newtonhill. High 4H 157
Newton Ketton. Darl 2A 106
Newton Kyme. N Yor 5G 99
Newton-le-Willows. Mers 1H 83
Newton-le-Willows. N Yor 1E 98
Newton Longville. Buck 2G 51
Newton Mearns. E Ren 4G 127
Newtonmore. High 4B 150
Newton Morrell. N Yor 4F 105
Newton Mulgrave. N Yor 3E 107
Newton of Ardtoe. High 1A 140
Newton of Balcanquhal. Per 2D 136
Newton of Beltrees. Ren 4E 127
Newton of Falkland. Fife 3E 137
Newton of Mountblairy. Abers 3D 160
Newton of Pitcairns. Per 2C 136
Newton-on-Ouse. N Yor 4H 99
Newton-on-Rawcliffe. N Yor 5F 107
Newton on the Hill. Shrp 3G 71
Newton-on-the-Moor. Nmbd 4F 121
Newton on Trent. Linc 3F 87
Newton Poppleford. Devn 4D 12
Newton Purcell. Oxon 2E 51
Newton Regis. Warw 5G 73
Newton Reigny. Cumb 1F 103
Newton Rigg. Cumb 1F 103
Newton St Cyres. Devn 3B 12
Newton St Faith. Norf 4E 78
Newton St Loe. Bath 5C 34
Newton St Petrock. Devn 1E 11
Newton Solney. Derbs 3G 73
Newton Stacey. Hants 2C 24
Newton Stewart. Dum 3B 110
Newton Toney. Wilts 2H 23
Newton Tony. Wilts 2H 23
Newton Tracey. Devn 4F 19
Newton under Roseberry. Red C 3C 106
Newton upon Ayr. S Ayr 2C 116
Newton upon Derwent. E Yor 5B 100
Newton Valence. Hants 3F 25
Newton-with-Scales. Lanc 1C 90
New Town. Dors 1E 15
New Town. E Lot 2H 129
New Town. Lutn 3A 52
New Town. W Yor 2E 93
Newtown. Abers 2E 160
Newtown. Cambs 4H 63
Newtown. Corn 5C 10
Newtown. Cumb
nr. Aspatria 5B 112
nr. Brampton 3G 113
nr. Penrith 2G 103
Newtown. Derbs 2D 85
Newtown. Devn 4A 20
Newtown. Dors 2H 13
Newtown. Falk 1C 128
Newtown. Glos
nr. Lydney 5B 48
nr. Tewkesbury 2E 49
Newtown. Hants
nr. Bishop's Waltham 1D 16
nr. Liphook 3G 25
nr. Lyndhurst 1A 16
nr. Newbury 5C 36
nr. Romsey 4B 24
nr. Warsash 2C 16
nr. Wickham 1E 16
Newtown. Here
nr. Little Dewchurch 2A 48
nr. Stretton Grandison 1B 48
Newtown. High 3F 149
Newtown. IOM 4C 108
Newtown. IOW 3C 16
Newtown. Lanc 3D 90
Newtown. Nmbd
nr. Rothbury 4E 121
nr. Wooler 2E 121
Newtown. Pool 3F 15
Newtown. Powy 1D 58
Newtown. Rhon 2D 32
Newtown. Shet 3F 173
Newtown. Shrp 2G 71
Newtown. Som 1F 13
Newtown. Staf
nr. Biddulph 4D 84
nr. Cannock 5D 73
nr. Longnor 4E 85
Newtown. Wilts 4E 23
Newtownabbey. Ant 1H 179
Newtownards. Ards 2J 179
Newtownbutler. Ferm 7K 177
Newtown-Crommelin. ME Ant 5H 175
Newtownhamilton. New M 7D 178
Newtown-in-St Martin. Corn 4E 5
Newtown Linford. Leics 5C 74
Newtown St Boswells. Bord 1H 119
Newtownstewart. Derr 8A 174
Newtown Unthank. Leics 5B 74
New Tredegar. Cphy 5E 47
Newtyle. Ang 4B 144
New Village. E Yor 1D 94
New Village. S Yor 4F 93
New Walsoken. Cambs 5D 76
New Waltham. NE Lin 4F 95
New Winton. E Lot 2H 129
New World. Cambs 1C 64
New Yatt. Oxon 4B 50
Newyears Green. G Lon 2B 38
New York. Linc 5B 88
New York. Tyne 2G 115
Nextend. Here 5F 59
Neyland. Pemb 4D 42
Nib Heath. Shrp 4G 71
Nicholashayne. Devn 1E 12
Nicholaston. Swan 4E 31
Nidd. N Yor 3F 99
Niddrie. Edin 2G 129
Niddry. W Lot 2D 129
Nigg. Aber 3G 153
Nigg. High 1C 158
Nigg Ferry. High 2B 158
Nightcott. Som 4B 20
Nimmer. Som 1G 13
Nine Ashes. Essx 5F 53
Ninebanks. Nmbd 4A 114
Nine Elms. Swin 3G 35
Ninemile Bar. Dum 2F 111
Nine Mile Burn. Midl 4E 129
Ninfield. E Sus 4B 28
Ningwood. IOW 4C 16
Nisbet. Bord 2A 120
Nisbet Hill. Bord 4D 130
Niton. IOW 5D 16
Nitshill. Glas 3G 127
Niwbwrch. IOA 4D 80
Nixon's Corner. Derr 5A 174
Noak Hill. G Lon 1G 39
Nobold. Shrp 4G 71
Nobottle. Nptn 4D 62
Nocton. Linc 4H 87
Nogdam End. Norf 5F 79
Noke. Oxon 4D 50
Nolton. Pemb 3C 42
Nolton Haven. Pemb 3C 42
No Man's Heath. Ches W 1H 71
No Man's Heath. Warw 5G 73
Nomansland. Devn 1B 12
Nomansland. Wilts 1A 16
Noneley. Shrp 3G 71
Noness. Shet 9F 173
Nonikiln. High 1A 158
Nonington. Kent 5G 41
Nook. Cumb
nr. Longtown 2F 113
nr. Milnthorpe 1E 97
Noranside. Ang 2D 144
Norbreck. Bkpl 5C 96
Norbridge. Here 1C 48
Norbury. Ches E 1H 71
Norbury. Derbs 1F 73
Norbury. Shrp 1F 59
Norbury. Staf 3B 72
Norby. N Yor 1G 99
Norby. Shet 6C 173
Norcross. Lanc 5C 96
Nordelph. Norf 5E 77
Norden. G Man 3G 91
Nordley. Shrp 1A 60
Norham. Nmbd 5F 131
Norland Town. W Yor 2A 92
Norley. Ches W 3H 83
Norleywood. Hants 3B 16
Normanby. N Lin 3B 94
Normanby. N Yor 1B 100
Normanby. Red C 3C 106
Normanby-by-Spital. Linc 2H 87
Normanby le Wold. Linc 1A 88
Norman Cross. Cambs 1A 64
Normandy. Surr 5A 38
Norman's Bay. E Sus 5A 28
Norman's Green. Devn 2D 12
Normanton. Derb 2H 73
Normanton. Leics 1F 75
Normanton. Notts 5E 86
Normanton. W Yor 2D 93
Normanton le Heath. Leics 4A 74
Normanton-on-Cliffe. Linc 1G 75
Normanton on Soar. Notts 3C 74
Normanton-on-the-Wolds. Notts 2D 74
Normanton on Trent. Notts 4E 87
Normoss. Lanc 1B 90
Norrington Common. Wilts 5D 35
Norris Green. Mers 1F 83
Norris Hill. Leics 4H 73
Norristhorpe. W Yor 2C 92
Northacre. Norf 1B 66
Northall. Buck 3H 51
Northallerton. N Yor 5A 106
Northam. Devn 4E 19
Northam. Sotn 1C 16
Northampton. Nptn **200** (4E 63)
North Anston. S Yor 2C 86
North Ascot. Brac 4A 38
North Aston. Oxon 3C 50
Northaw. Herts 5C 52
Northay. Som 1F 13
North Baddesley. Hants 4B 24
North Balfern. Dum 4B 110
North Ballachulish. High 2E 141
North Barrow. Som 4B 22
North Barsham. Norf 2B 78
Northbeck. Linc 1H 75
North Benfleet. Essx 2B 40
North Bersted. W Sus 5A 26
North Berwick. E Lot 1B 130
North Bitchburn. Dur 1E 105
North Blyth. Nmbd 1G 115
North Boarhunt. Hants 1E 16
North Bockhampton. Dors 3G 15
Northborough. Pet 5A 76
Northbourne. Kent 5H 41
Northbourne. Oxon 3D 36
North Bovey. Devn 4H 11
North Bowood. Dors 3H 13
North Bradley. Wilts 1D 22
North Brentor. Devn 4E 11
North Brewham. Som 3C 22
Northbrook. Oxon 3C 50
North Brook End. Cambs 1C 52
North Broomhill. Nmbd 4G 121
North Buckland. Devn 2E 19
North Burlingham. Norf 4F 79
North Cadbury. Som 4B 22
North Carlton. Linc 3G 87
North Cave. E Yor 1B 94
North Cerney. Glos 5F 49
North Chailey. E Sus 3E 27
Northchapel. W Sus 3A 26
North Charford. Hants 1G 15
North Charlton. Nmbd 2F 121
North Cheriton. Som 4B 22
North Chideock. Dors 3H 13
Northchurch. Herts 5H 51
North Cliffe. E Yor 1B 94
North Clifton. Notts 3F 87
North Close. Dur 1F 105
North Cockerington. Linc 1C 88
North Coker. Som 1A 14
North Collafirth. Shet 3E 173
North Common. E Sus 3E 27
North Commonty. Abers 4F 161
North Coombe. Devn 1B 12
North Cornelly. B'end 3B 32
North Cotes. Linc 4G 95
Northcott. Devn
nr. Boyton 3D 10
nr. Culmstock 1D 12
Northcourt. Oxon 2D 36
North Cove. Suff 2G 67
North Cowton. N Yor 4F 105
North Craigo. Ang 2F 145
North Crawley. Mil 1H 51
North Cray. G Lon 3F 39
North Creake. Norf 2A 78
North Curry. Som 4G 21
North Dalton. E Yor 4D 100
North Deighton. N Yor 4F 99
North Dronley. Ang 5C 144
North Duffield. N Yor 1G 93
Northdyke. Orkn 5B 172
Northedge. Derbs 4A 86
North Elkington. Linc 1B 88
North Elmham. Norf 3B 78
North Elmsall. W Yor 3E 93
North End. E Yor 1F 95
North End. Essx
nr. Great Dunmow 4G 53
nr. Great Yeldham 2A 54
North End. Hants 5C 36
North End. Leics 4C 74
North End. Linc 1B 76
North End. Norf 1B 66
North End. N Som 5H 33
North End. Port 2E 17
North End. W Sus 5C 26
North End. Wilts 2F 35
Northend. Buck 2F 37
Northend. Warw 5A 62
North Erradale. High 5B 162
North Evington. Leic 5D 74
North Fambridge. Essx 1C 40
North Fearns. High 5E 155
North Featherstone. W Yor 2E 93
North Feorline. N Ayr 3D 122
North Ferriby. E Yor 2C 94
Northfield. Aber 3F 153
Northfield. E Yor 2D 94
Northfield. Som 3F 21
Northfield. W Mid 3E 61
Northfleet. Kent 3H 39
North Frodingham. E Yor 4F 101
Northgate. Linc 3A 76
North Gluss. Shet 4E 173
North Gorley. Hants 1G 15
North Green. Norf 2E 66
North Green. Suff
nr. Framlingham 4F 67
nr. Halesworth 3F 67
nr. Saxmundham 4F 67
North Greetwell. Linc 3H 87
North Grimston. N Yor 3C 100
North Halling. Medw 4B 40
North Hayling. Hants 2F 17
North Hazelrigg. Nmbd 1E 121
North Heasley. Devn 3H 19
North Heath. W Sus 3B 26
North Hill. Corn 5C 10
North Holmwood. Surr 1C 26
North Huish. Devn 3D 8
North Hykeham. Linc 4G 87
Northiam. E Sus 3C 28
Northill. C Beds 1B 52
Northington. Hants 3D 24
North Kelsey. Linc 4D 94
North Kelsey Moor. Linc 4D 94
North Kessock. High 4A 158
North Killingholme. N Lin 3E 95
North Kilvington. N Yor 1G 99
North Kilworth. Leics 2D 62
North Kyme. Linc 5A 88
North Lancing. W Sus 5C 26
Northlands. Linc 5C 88
Northleach. Glos 4G 49
North Lee. Buck 5G 51
North Lees. N Yor 2E 99
North Leigh. Kent 1F 29
North Leigh. Oxon 4B 50
Northleigh. Devn
nr. Barnstaple 3G 19
nr. Honiton 3E 13
North Leverton. Notts 2E 87
Northlew. Devn 3F 11
North Littleton. Worc 1F 49
North Lopham. Norf 2C 66
North Luffenham. Rut 5G 75
North Marden. W Sus 1G 17
North Marston. Buck 3F 51
North Middleton. Midl 4G 129
North Middleton. Nmbd 2E 121
North Molton. Devn 4H 19
North Moor. N Yor 1D 100
Northmoor. Oxon 5C 50
Northmoor Green. Som 3G 21
North Moreton. Oxon 3D 36
Northmuir. Ang 3C 144
North Mundham. W Sus 2G 17
North Murie. Per 1E 137
North Muskham. Notts 5E 87
North Ness. Orkn 8C 172
North Newbald. E Yor 1C 94
North Newington. Oxon 2C 50
North Newnton. Wilts 1G 23
North Newton. Som 3F 21
Northney. Hants 2F 17
North Nibley. Glos 2C 34
North Oakley. Hants 1D 24
North Ockendon. G Lon 2G 39
Northolt. G Lon 2C 38
Northop. Flin 4E 83
Northop Hall. Flin 4E 83
North Ormesby. Midd 3C 106
North Ormsby. Linc 1B 88
Northorpe. Linc
nr. Bourne 4H 75
nr. Donington 2B 76
nr. Gainsborough 1F 87
North Otterington. N Yor 1F 99
Northover. Som
nr. Glastonbury 3H 21
nr. Yeovil 4A 22
North Owersby. Linc 1H 87
Northowram. W Yor 2B 92
North Perrott. Som 2H 13
North Petherton. Som 3F 21
North Petherwin. Corn 4C 10
North Pickenham. Norf 5A 78
North Piddle. Worc 5D 60
North Poorton. Dors 3A 14
North Port. Arg 1H 133
Northport. Dors 4E 15
North Queensferry. Fife 1E 129
North Radworthy. Devn 3A 20
North Rauceby. Linc 1H 75
Northrepps. Norf 2E 79
North Rigton. N Yor 5E 99
North Rode. Ches E 4C 84
North Roe. Shet 3E 173
North Ronaldsay Airport. Orkn 2G 172
North Row. Cumb 1D 102
North Runcton. Norf 4F 77
North Sannox. N Ayr 5B 126
North Scale. Cumb 2A 96
North Scarle. Linc 4F 87
North Seaton. Nmbd 1F 115
North Seaton Colliery. Nmbd 1F 115
North Sheen. G Lon 3C 38
North Shian. Arg 4D 140
North Shields. Tyne 3G 115
North Shoebury. S'end 2D 40
North Shore. Bkpl 1B 90
North Side. Cumb 2B 102
North Skelton. Red C 3D 106
North Somercotes. Linc 1D 88
North Stainley. N Yor 2E 99
North Stainmore. Cumb 3B 104
North Stifford. Thur 2H 39
North Stoke. Bath 5C 34
North Stoke. Oxon 3E 36
North Stoke. W Sus 4B 26
Northstowe. Cambs 4D 64
North Street. Hants 3E 25
North Street. Kent 5E 40
North Street. Medw 3C 40
North Street. W Ber 4E 37
North Sunderland. Nmbd 1G 121
North Tamerton. Corn 3D 10
North Tawton. Devn 2G 11
North Thoresby. Linc 1B 88
North Tidworth. Wilts 2H 23
North Town. Devn 2F 11
North Town. Shet 10E 173
Northtown. Orkn 8D 172
North Tuddenham. Norf 4C 78
North Walbottle. Tyne 3E 115
Northwall. Orkn 3G 172
North Walney. Cumb 3A 96
North Walsham. Norf 2E 79
North Waltham. Hants 2D 24
North Warnborough. Hants 1F 25
North Water Bridge. Ang 2F 145
North Watten. High 3E 169
Northway. Glos 2E 49
Northway. Swan 4E 31
North Weald Bassett. Essx 5F 53
North Weston. N Som 4H 33
North Weston. Oxon 5E 51
North Wheatley. Notts 2E 87
North Whilborough. Devn 2E 9
Northwich. Ches W 3A 84
North Wick. Bath 5A 34
Northwick. Som 2G 21
Northwick. S Glo 3A 34
North Widcombe. Bath 1A 22
North Willingham. Linc 2A 88
North Wingfield. Derbs 4B 86
North Witham. Linc 3G 75
Northwold. Norf 1G 65
Northwood. Derbs 4G 85
Northwood. G Lon 1B 38
Northwood. IOW 3C 16
Northwood. Kent 4H 41
Northwood. Shrp 2G 71
Northwood. Stoke 1C 72
Northwood Green. Glos 4C 48
North Wootton. Dors 1B 14
North Wootton. Norf 3F 77
North Wootton. Som 2A 22
North Wraxall. Wilts 4D 34
North Wroughton. Swin 3G 35
North Yardhope. Nmbd 4D 120
Norton. Devn 3E 9
Norton. Glos 3D 48
Norton. Hal 2H 83
Norton. Herts 2C 52
Norton. IOW 4B 16
Norton. Mon 3H 47
Norton. Nptn 4D 62
Norton. Notts 3C 86
Norton. Powy 4F 59
Norton. Shrp
nr. Ludlow 2G 59
nr. Madeley 5B 72
nr. Shrewsbury 5H 71
Norton. S Yor
nr. Askern 3F 93
nr. Sheffield 2A 86
Norton. Stoc T 2B 106
Norton. Suff 4B 66
Norton. Swan 4F 31
Norton. W Sus
nr. Selsey 3G 17
nr. Westergate 5A 26
Norton. Wilts 3D 35
Norton. Worc
nr. Evesham 1F 49
nr. Worcester 5C 60
Norton Bavant. Wilts 2E 23
Norton Bridge. Staf 2C 72
Norton Canes. Staf 5E 73
Norton Canon. Here 1G 47
Norton Corner. Norf 3C 78
Norton Disney. Linc 5F 87
Norton East. Staf 5E 73
Norton Ferris. Wilts 3C 22
Norton Fitzwarren. Som 4F 21
Norton Green. IOW 4B 16
Norton Green. Stoke 5D 84
Norton Hawkfield. Bath 5A 34
Norton Heath. Essx 5F 53
Norton in Hales. Shrp 2B 72
Norton in the Moors. Stoke 5C 84
Norton-Juxta-Twycross. Leics 5H 73
Norton-le-Clay. N Yor 2G 99
Norton Lindsey. Warw 4G 61
Norton Little Green. Suff 4B 66
Norton Malreward. Bath 5B 34
Norton Mandeville. Essx 5F 53
Norton-on-Derwent. N Yor 2B 100
Norton St Philip. Som 1C 22
Norton Subcourse. Norf 1G 67
Norton sub Hamdon. Som 1H 13
Norton Woodseats. S Yor 2A 86
Norwell. Notts 4E 87
Norwell Woodhouse. Notts 4E 87
Norwich. Norf **200** (5E 79)
Norwich Airport. Norf 4E 79
Norwick. Shet 1H 173
Norwood. Derbs 2B 86
Norwood Green. W Yor 2B 92
Norwood Hill. Surr 1D 26
Norwood Park. Som 3A 22
Norwoodside. Cambs 1D 64
Noseley. Leics 1E 63
Noss. Shet 10E 173
Noss Mayo. Devn 4B 8
Nosterfield. N Yor 1E 99
Nostie. High 1A 148
Notgrove. Glos 3G 49
Nottage. B'end 4B 32
Nottingham. Nott **200** (1C 74)
Nottington. Dors 4B 14
Notton. Dors 3B 14
Notton. W Yor 3D 92
Notton. Wilts 5E 35
Nounsley. Essx 4A 54
Noutard's Green. Worc 4B 60
Nox. Shrp 4G 71
Noyadd Trefawr. Cdgn 1C 44
Nuffield. Oxon 3E 37
Nunburnholme. E Yor 5C 100
Nuncargate. Notts 5C 86
Nunclose. Cumb 5F 113
Nuneaton. Warw 1A 62
Nuneham Courtenay. Oxon 2D 36
Nun Monkton. N Yor 4H 99
Nunnerie. S Lan 3B 118
Nunney. Som 2C 22
Nunnington. N Yor 2A 100
Nunnykirk. Nmbd 5E 121
Nunsthorpe. NE Lin 4F 95
Nunthorpe. Midd 3C 106
Nunthorpe. York 4H 99
Nunton. Wilts 4G 23
Nunwick. Nmbd 2B 114
Nunwick. N Yor 2F 99
Nupend. Glos 5C 48
Nursling. Hants 1B 16
Nursted. Hants 4F 25
Nursteed. Wilts 5F 35
Nurston. V Glam 5D 32
Nutbourne. W Sus
nr. Chichester 2F 17
nr. Pulborough 4B 26
Nutfield. Surr 5E 39
Nuthall. Notts 1C 74
Nuthampstead. Herts 2E 53
Nuthurst. Warw 3F 61
Nuthurst. W Sus 3C 26
Nutley. E Sus 3F 27
Nuttall. G Man 3F 91
Nutwell. S Yor 4G 93
Nybster. High 2F 169
Nyetimber. W Sus 3G 17
Nyewood. W Sus 4G 25
Nymet Rowland. Devn 2H 11
Nymet Tracey. Devn 2H 11
Nympsfield. Glos 5D 48
Nynehead. Som 4E 21
Nyton. W Sus 5A 26

O

Oadby. Leics 5D 74
Oad Street. Kent 4C 40
Oakamoor. Staf 1E 73
Oakbank. Arg 5B 140
Oakbank. W Lot 3D 129
Oakdale. Cphy 2E 33
Oakdale. Pool 3F 15
Oake. Som 4E 21

P

Queensferry—Rudley Green

Queensferry. *Flin* 4F 83
Queensferry Crossing.
Edin 2E 129
Queenstown. *Bkpl* 1B 90
Queen Street. *Kent* 1A 28
Queenzieburn. *N Lan* 2H 127
Quemerford. *Wilts* 5F 35
Quendale. *Shet* 10E 173
Quendon. *Essx* 2F 53
Queniborough. *Leics* 4D 74
Quenington. *Glos* 5G 49
Quernmore. *Lanc* 3E 97
Quethiock. *Corn* 2H 7
Quholm. *Orkn* 6B 172
Quick's Green. *W Ber* 4D 36
Quidenham. *Norf* 2C 66
Quidhampton. *Hants* 1D 24
Quidhampton. *Wilts* 3G 23
Quilquox. *Abers* 5G 161
Quina Brook. *Shrp* 2H 71
Quindry. *Orkn* 8D 172
Quine's Hill. *IOM* 4C 108
Quinton. *Nptn* 5E 63
Quinton. *W Mid* 2D 61
Quintrell Downs. *Corn* 2C 6
Quixhill. *Staf* 1F 73
Quoditch. *Devn* 3E 11
Quorn. *Leics* 4C 74
Quorndon. *Leics* 4C 74
Quothquan. *S Lan* 1B 118
Quoyloo. *Orkn* 5B 172
Quoyness. *Orkn* 7B 172
Quoys. *Shet*
on Mainland 5F 173
on Unst 1H 173

R

Rableyheath. *Herts* 4C 52
Raby. *Cumb* 4C 112
Raby. *Mers* 3F 83
Rachan Mill. *Bord* 1D 118
Rachub. *Gwyn* 4F 81
Rack End. *Oxon* 5C 50
Rackenford. *Devn* 1B 12
Rackham. *W Sus* 4B 26
Rackheath. *Norf* 4E 79
Racks. *Dum* 2B 112
Rackwick. *Orkn*
on Hoy 8B 172
on Westray 3D 172
Radbourne. *Derbs* 2G 73
Radcliffe. *G Man* 4F 91
Radcliffe. *Nmbd* 4G 121
Radcliffe on Trent. *Notts* 2D 74
Radclive. *Buck* 2E 51
Radernie. *Fife* 3G 137
Radfall. *Kent* 4F 41
Radford. *Bath* 1B 22
Radford. *Nott* 1C 74
Radford. *Oxon* 3C 50
Radford. *W Mid* 2H 61
Radford. *Worc* 5E 61
Radford Semele. *Warw* 4H 61
Radipole. *Dors* 4B 14
Radlett. *Herts* 1C 38
Radley. *Oxon* 2D 36
Radnage. *Buck* 2F 37
Radstock. *Bath* 1B 22
Radstone. *Nptn* 1D 50
Radway. *Warw* 1B 50
Radway Green. *Ches E* 5B 84
Radwell. *Bed* 5H 63
Radwell. *Herts* 2C 52
Radwinter. *Essx* 2G 53
Radyr. *Card* 3E 33
RAF Coltishall. *Norf* 3E 79
Rafford. *Mor* 3E 159
Raffrey. *New M* 4J 179
Ragdale. *Leics* 4D 74
Ragdon. *Shrp* 1G 59
Ragged Appleshaw. *Hants* 2B 24
Raggra. *High* 4F 169
Raglan. *Mon* 5H 47
Ragnall. *Notts* 3F 87
Raholp. *New M* 5K 179
Raigbeg. *High* 1C 150
Rainford. *Mers* 4C 90
Rainford Junction. *Mers* 4C 90
Rainham. *G Lon* 2G 39
Rainham. *Medw* 4C 40
Rainhill. *Mers* 1G 83
Rainow. *Ches E* 3D 84
Rainton. *N Yor* 2F 99
Rainworth. *Notts* 5C 86
Raisbeck. *Cumb* 4H 103
Raise. *Cumb* 5A 114
Rait. *Per* 1E 137
Raithby. *Linc* 2C 88
Raithby by Spilsby. *Linc* 4C 88
Raithwaite. *N Yor* 3F 107
Rake. *W Sus* 4G 25
Rake End. *Staf* 4E 73
Rakeway. *Staf* 1E 73
Rakewood. *G Man* 3H 91
Ralia. *High* 4B 150
Ram Alley. *Wilts* 5H 35
Ramasaig. *High* 4A 154
Rame. *Corn*
nr. Millbrook 4A 8
nr. Penryn 5B 6
Ram Lane. *Kent* 1D 28
Ramnageo. *Shet* 1H 173
Rampisham. *Dors* 2A 14
Rampside. *Cumb* 3B 96
Rampton. *Cambs* 4D 64
Rampton. *Notts* 3E 87
Ramsbottom. *G Man* 3F 91
Ramsburn. *Mor* 3C 160
Ramsbury. *Wilts* 4A 36
Ramscraigs. *High* 1H 165
Ramsdean. *Hants* 4F 25
Ramsdell. *Hants* 1D 24
Ramsden. *Oxon* 4B 50
Ramsden. *Worc* 1E 49
Ramsden Bellhouse. *Essx* 1B 40
Ramsden Heath. *Essx* 1B 40
Ramsey. *Cambs* 2B 64
Ramsey. *Essx* 2F 55
Ramsey. *IOM* 2D 108
Ramsey Forty Foot.
Cambs 2C 64
Ramsey Heights. *Cambs* 2B 64
Ramsey Island. *Essx* 5C 54
Ramsey Mereside. *Cambs* 2B 64
Ramsey St Mary's. *Cambs* 2B 64
Ramsgate. *Kent* 4H 41
Ramsgill. *N Yor* 2D 98
Ramshaw. *Dur* 5C 114
Ramshorn. *Staf* 1E 73
Ramsley. *Devn* 3G 11
Ramsnest Common. *Surr* 2A 26
Ramstone. *Abers* 2D 152
Ranais. *W Isl* 5G 171
Ranby. *Linc* 3B 88
Ranby. *Notts* 2D 86
Rand. *Linc* 3A 88
Randalstown. *Ant* 7G 175
Randwick. *Glos* 5D 48
Ranfurly. *Ren* 3E 127
Rangag. *High* 4D 169
Rangemore. *Staf* 3F 73
Rangeworthy. *S Glo* 3B 34
Rankinston. *E Ayr* 3D 116
Rank's Green. *Essx* 4H 53
Ranmore Common. *Surr* 5C 38
Rannoch Station. *Per* 3B 142
Ranochan. *High* 5G 147
Ranskill. *Notts* 2D 86
Ranton. *Staf* 3C 72
Ranton Green. *Staf* 3C 72
Ranworth. *Norf* 4F 79
Raploch. *Stir* 4G 135
Rapness. *Orkn* 3E 172
Rapps. *Som* 1G 13
Rascal Moor. *E Yor* 1B 94
Rascarrel. *Dum* 5E 111
Rasharkin. *Caus* 5F 175
Rashfield. *Arg* 1C 126
Rashwood. *Worc* 4D 60
Raskelf. *N Yor* 2G 99
Rassau. *Blae* 4E 47
Rastrick. *W Yor* 2B 92
Ratagan. *High* 2B 148
Ratby. *Leics* 5C 74
Ratcliffe Culey. *Leics* 1H 61
Ratcliffe on Soar. *Notts* 3B 74
Ratcliffe on the Wreake.
Leics 4D 74
Rathen. *Abers* 2H 161
Rathfriland. *Arm* 6F 179
Rathillet. *Fife* 1F 137
Rathmell. *N Yor* 3H 97
Ratho. *Edin* 2E 129
Ratho Station. *Edin* 2E 129
Rathven. *Mor* 2B 160
Ratley. *Hants* 4B 24
Ratley. *Warw* 1B 50
Ratlinghope. *Shrp* 1G 59
Rattar. *High* 1E 169
Ratten Row. *Cumb* 5E 113
Ratten Row. *Lanc* 5D 96
Rattery. *Devn* 2D 8
Rattlesden. *Suff* 5B 66
Ratton Village. *E Sus* 5G 27
Rattray. *Abers* 3H 161
Rattray. *Per* 4A 144
Raughton. *Cumb* 5E 113
Raughton Head. *Cumb* 5E 113
Raunds. *Nptn* 3G 63
Ravenfield. *S Yor* 1B 86
Ravenfield Common.
S Yor 1B 86
Ravenglass. *Cumb* 5B 102
Ravenhills Green. *Worc* 5B 60
Raveningham. *Norf* 1F 67
Ravenscar. *N Yor* 4G 107
Ravensdale. *IOM* 2C 108
Ravensden. *Bed* 5H 63
Ravenseat. *N Yor* 4B 104
Ravenshead. *Notts* 5C 86
Ravensmoor. *Ches E* 5A 84
Ravensthorpe. *Nptn* 3D 62
Ravensthorpe. *W Yor* 2C 92
Ravenstone. *Leics* 4B 74
Ravenstone. *Mil* 5F 63
Ravenstonedale. *Cumb* 4A 104
Ravenstown. *Cumb* 2C 96
Ravenstruther. *S Lan* 5C 128
Ravensworth. *N Yor* 4E 105
Ravernet. *Lis* 3G 179
Raw. *N Yor* 4G 107
Rawcliffe. *E Yor* 2G 93
Rawcliffe. *York* 4H 99
Rawcliffe Bridge. *E Yor* 2G 93
Rawdon. *W Yor* 1C 92
Rawgreen. *Nmbd* 4C 114
Rawmarsh. *S Yor* 1B 86
Rawnsley. *Staf* 4E 73
Rawreth. *Essx* 1B 40
Rawridge. *Devn* 2F 13
Rawson Green. *Derbs* 1A 74
Rawtenstall. *Lanc* 2G 91
Raydon. *Suff* 2D 54
Raylees. *Nmbd* 5D 120
Rayleigh. *Essx* 1C 40
Raymond's Hill. *Devn* 3G 13
Rayne. *Essx* 3H 53
Rayners Lane. *G Lon* 2C 38
Reach. *Cambs* 4E 65
Read. *Lanc* 1F 91
Reading. *Read* 201 (4F 37)
Reading Green. *Suff* 3D 66
Reading Street. *Kent* 2D 28
Readymoney. *Corn* 3F 7
Reagill. *Cumb* 3H 103
Rearquhar. *High* 4E 165
Rearsby. *Leics* 4D 74
Reasby. *Linc* 3H 87
Reaseheath. *Ches E* 5A 84
Reaster. *High* 2E 169
Reawick. *Shet* 7E 173
Reay. *High* 2B 168
Rechullin. *High* 3A 156
Reculver. *Kent* 4G 41
Redberth. *Pemb* 4E 43
Redbourn. *Herts* 4B 52
Redbourne. *N Lin* 4C 94
Redbrook. *Glos* 5A 48
Redbrook. *Wrex* 1H 71
Redburn. *High* 4D 158
Redburn. *Nmbd* 3A 114
Redcar. *Red C* 2D 106
Redcastle. *High* 4H 157
Redcliffe Bay. *N Som* 4H 33
Red Dial. *Cumb* 5D 112
Redding. *Falk* 2C 128
Reddingmuirhead. *Falk* 2C 128
The Reddings. *Glos* 3E 49
Reddish. *G Man* 1C 84
Redditch. *Worc* 4E 61
Rede. *Suff* 5H 65
Redenhall. *Norf* 2E 67
Redesdale Camp. *Nmbd* 5C 120
Redesmouth. *Nmbd* 1B 114
Redford. *Ang* 4E 145
Redford. *Dur* 1D 105
Redford. *W Sus* 4G 25
Redfordgreen. *Bord* 3F 119
Redgate. *Corn* 2G 7
Redgrave. *Suff* 3C 66
Red Hill. *Warw* 5F 61
Red Hill. *W Yor* 2E 93
Redhill. *Abers* 3E 153
Redhill. *Herts* 2C 52
Redhill. *N Som* 5A 34
Redhill. *Shrp* 4B 72
Redhill. *Surr* 5D 39
Redhouses. *Arg* 3B 124
Redisham. *Suff* 2G 67
Redland. *Bris* 4A 34
Redland. *Orkn* 5C 172
Redlingfield. *Suff* 3D 66
Red Lodge. *Suff* 3F 65
Redlynch. *Som* 3C 22
Redlynch. *Wilts* 4H 23
Redmain. *Cumb* 1C 102
Redmarley. *Worc* 4B 60
Redmarley D'Abitot. *Glos* 2C 48
Redmarshall. *Stoc T* 2A 106
Redmile. *Leics* 2E 75
Redmire. *N Yor* 5D 104
Rednal. *Shrp* 3F 71
Redpath. *Bord* 1H 119
Redpoint. *High* 2G 155
Red Post. *Corn* 2C 10
Red Rock. *G Man* 4D 90
Red Roses. *Carm* 3G 43
Red Row. *Nmbd* 5G 121
Redruth. *Corn* 4B 6
Red Street. *Staf* 5C 84
Redvales. *G Man* 4G 91
Red Wharf Bay. *IOA* 2E 81
Redwick. *Newp* 3H 33
Redwick. *S Glo* 3A 34
Redworth. *Darl* 2F 105
Reed. *Herts* 2D 52
Reed End. *Herts* 2D 52
Reedham. *Linc* 5B 88
Reedham. *Norf* 5G 79
Reedness. *E Yor* 2B 94
Reeds Beck. *Linc* 4B 88
Reemshill. *Abers* 4E 161
Reepham. *Linc* 3H 87
Reepham. *Norf* 3C 78
Reeth. *N Yor* 5D 104
Regaby. *IOM* 2D 108
Regil. *N Som* 5A 34
Regoul. *High* 3C 158
Reiff. *High* 2D 162
Reigate. *Surr* 5D 38
Reighton. *N Yor* 2F 101
Reilth. *Shrp* 2E 59
Reinigeadal. *W Isl* 7E 171
Reisque. *Abers* 2F 153
Reiss. *High* 3F 169
Rejerrah. *Corn* 3B 6
Releath. *Corn* 5A 6
Relubbus. *Corn* 3C 4
Relugas. *Mor* 4D 159
Remenham. *Wok* 3F 37
Remenham Hill. *Wok* 3F 37
Rempstone. *Notts* 3C 74
Rendcomb. *Glos* 5F 49
Rendham. *Suff* 4F 67
Rendlesham. *Suff* 5F 67
Renfrew. *Ren* 3G 127
Renhold. *Bed* 5H 63
Renishaw. *Derbs* 3B 86
Rennington. *Nmbd* 3G 121
Renton. *W Dun* 2E 127
Renwick. *Cumb* 5G 113
Repps. *Norf* 4G 79
Repton. *Derbs* 3H 73
Rescassa. *Corn* 4D 6
Rescobie. *Ang* 3E 145
Rescorla. *Corn*
nr. Penwithick 3E 7
nr. Sticker 4D 6
Resipole. *High* 2B 140
Resolfen. *Neat* 5B 46
Resolis. *High* 2A 158
Resolven. *Neat* 5B 46
Rest and be thankful.
Arg 3B 134
Reston. *Bord* 3E 131
Restrop. *Wilts* 3F 35
Retford. *Notts* 2E 86
Retire. *Corn* 2E 6
Rettendon. *Essx* 1B 40
Revesby. *Linc* 4B 88
Rew. *Devn* 5D 8
Rewe. *Devn* 3C 12
Rew Street. *IOW* 3C 16
Rexon. *Devn* 4E 11
Reybridge. *Wilts* 5E 35
Reydon. *Suff* 3H 67
Reymerston. *Norf* 5C 78
Reynalton. *Pemb* 4E 43
Reynoldston. *Swan* 4D 31
Rezare. *Corn* 5D 10
Rhadyr. *Mon* 5G 47
Rhaeadr Gwy. *Powy* 4B 58
Rhandirmwyn. *Carm* 1A 46
Rhayader. *Powy* 4B 58
Rheindown. *High* 4H 157
Rhemore. *High* 3G 139
Rhenetra. *High* 3D 154
Rhewl. *Den*
nr. Llangollen 1D 70
nr. Ruthin 4D 82
Rhewl. *Shrp* 2F 71
Rhewl-Mostyn. *Flin* 2D 82
Rhian. *High* 2C 164
Rhian Breck. *High* 3C 164
Rhicarn. *High* 1E 163
Rhiconich. *High* 3C 166
Rhicullen. *High* 1A 158
Rhidorroch. *High* 4F 163
Rhifail. *High* 4H 167
Rhigos. *Rhon* 5C 46
Rhilochan. *High* 3E 165
Rhiroy. *High* 5F 163
Rhitongue. *High* 3G 167
Rhiw. *Gwyn* 3B 68
Rhiwabon. *Wrex* 1F 71
Rhiwbina. *Card* 3E 33
Rhiwbryfdir. *Gwyn* 1F 69
Rhiwderin. *Newp* 3F 33
Rhiwlas. *Gwyn*
nr. Bala 2B 70
nr. Bangor 4E 81
Rhiwlas. *Powy* 2D 70
Rhodes. *G Man* 4G 91
Rhodesia. *Notts* 2C 86
Rhodes Minnis. *Kent* 1F 29
Rhodiad-y-Brenin. *Pemb* 2B 42
Rhondda. *Rhon* 2C 32
Rhonehouse. *Dum* 4E 111
Rhoose. *V Glam* 5D 32
Rhos. *Carm* 2D 45
Rhos. *Neat* 5H 45
The Rhos. *Pemb* 3E 43
Rhosaman. *Carm* 4H 45
Rhoscefnhir. *IOA* 3E 81
Rhoscolyn. *IOA* 3B 80
Rhos Common. *Powy* 4E 71
Rhoscrowther. *Pemb* 4D 42
Rhos-ddu. *Gwyn* 2B 68
Rhosdylluan. *Gwyn* 3A 70
Rhosesmor. *Flin* 4E 82
Rhos-fawr. *Gwyn* 2C 68
Rhosgadfan. *Gwyn* 5E 81
Rhosgoch. *IOA* 2D 80
Rhosgoch. *Powy* 1E 47
Rhos Haminiog. *Cdgn* 4E 57
Rhos-hill. *Pemb* 1B 44
Rhoshirwaun. *Gwyn* 3A 68
Rhoslan. *Gwyn* 1D 69
Rhoslefain. *Gwyn* 5E 69
Rhosllanerchrugog.
Wrex 1E 71
Rhôs Lligwy. *IOA* 2D 81
Rhosmaen. *Carm* 3G 45
Rhosmeirch. *IOA* 3D 80
Rhosneigr. *IOA* 3C 80
Rhôs-on-Sea. *Cnwy* 2H 81
Rhossili. *Swan* 4D 30
Rhosson. *Pemb* 2B 42
Rhostrenwfa. *IOA* 3D 80
Rhostryfan. *Gwyn* 5D 81
Rhostyllen. *Wrex* 1F 71
Rhoswiel. *Shrp* 2E 71
Rhosybol. *IOA* 2D 80
Rhos-y-brithdir. *Powy* 3D 70
Rhos-y-garth. *Cdgn* 3F 57
Rhos-y-gwaliau. *Gwyn* 2B 70
Rhos-y-llan. *Gwyn* 2B 68
Rhos-y-meirch. *Powy* 4E 59
Rhu. *Arg* 1D 126
Rhualt. *Den* 3C 82
Rhubha Stoer. *High* 1E 163
Rhubodach. *Arg* 2B 126
Rhuddall Heath. *Ches W* 4H 83
Rhuddlan. *Cdgn* 1E 45
Rhuddlan. *Den* 3C 82
Rhue. *High* 4E 163
Rhulen. *Powy* 1E 47
Rhunahaorine. *Arg* 5F 125
Rhuthun. *Den* 5D 82
Rhuvoult. *High* 3C 166
Y Rhws. *V Glam* 5D 32
Rhyd. *Gwyn* 1F 69
Rhydaman. *Carm* 4G 45
Rhydargaeau. *Carm* 3E 45
Rhydcymerau. *Carm* 2F 45
Rhydd. *Worc* 1D 48
Rhyd-Ddu. *Gwyn* 5E 81
Rhydding. *Neat* 3G 31
Rhydfudr. *Cdgn* 4E 57
Rhydlanfair. *Cnwy* 5A 82
Rhydlewis. *Cdgn* 1D 44
Rhydlios. *Gwyn* 2A 68
Rhydlydan. *Cnwy* 5A 82
Rhyd-meirionydd. *Cdgn* 2F 57
Rhydowen. *Cdgn* 1E 45
Rhyd-Rosser. *Cdgn* 4E 57
Rhydspence. *Here* 1F 47
Rhydtalog. *Flin* 5E 83
Rhyd-uchaf. *Gwyn* 2B 70
Rhydwyn. *IOA* 2C 80
Rhyd-y-clafdy. *Gwyn* 2C 68
Rhydycroesau. *Powy* 2E 71
Rhydyfelin. *Cdgn* 3E 57
Rhydyfelin. *Rhon* 3D 32
Rhyd-y-foel. *Cnwy* 3B 82
Rhyd-y-fro. *Neat* 5H 45
Rhydymain. *Gwyn* 3H 69
Rhyd-y-meudwy. *Den* 5D 82
Rhydymwyn. *Flin* 4E 82
Rhyd-yr-onen. *Gwyn* 5F 69
Rhyd-y-sarn. *Gwyn* 1F 69
Rhyl. *Den* 2C 82
Rhymney. *Cphy* 5E 46
Rhymni. *Cphy* 5E 46
Rhynd. *Per* 1D 136
Rhynie. *Abers* 1B 152
Ribbesford. *Worc* 3B 60
Ribbleton. *Lanc* 1D 90
Ribby. *Lanc* 1C 90
Ribchester. *Lanc* 1E 91
Riber. *Derbs* 5H 85
Ribigill. *High* 3F 167
Riby. *Linc* 4E 95
Riccall. *N Yor* 1G 93
Riccarton. *E Ayr* 1D 116
Richards Castle. *Here* 4G 59
Richborough Port. *Kent* 4H 41
Richhill. *Arm* 5D 178
Richings Park. *Buck* 3B 38
Richmond. *G Lon* 3C 38
Richmond. *N Yor* 4E 105
Rickarton. *Abers* 5F 153
Rickerby. *Cumb* 4F 113
Rickerscote. *Staf* 3D 72
Rickford. *N Som* 1H 21
Rickham. *Devn* 5D 8
Rickinghall. *Suff* 3C 66
Rickleton. *Tyne* 4F 115
Rickling. *Essx* 2E 53
Rickling Green. *Essx* 3F 53
Rickmansworth. *Herts* 1B 38
Riddings. *Derbs* 5B 86
Riddlecombe. *Devn* 1G 11
Riddlesden. *W Yor* 5C 98
Ridge. *Dors* 4E 15
Ridge. *Herts* 5C 52
Ridge. *Wilts* 3E 23
Ridgebourne. *Powy* 4C 58
Ridge Lane. *Warw* 1G 61
Ridgeway. *Derbs*
nr. Alfreton 5A 86
nr. Sheffield 2B 86
Ridgeway. *Staf* 5C 84
Ridgeway Cross. *Here* 1C 48
Ridgeway Moor. *Derbs* 2B 86
Ridgewell. *Essx* 1H 53
Ridgewood. *E Sus* 3F 27
Ridgmont. *C Beds* 2H 51
Ridgwardine. *Shrp* 2A 72
Riding Mill. *Nmbd* 3D 114
Ridley. *Kent* 4H 39
Ridley. *Nmbd* 3A 114
Ridlington. *Norf* 2F 79
Ridlington. *Rut* 5F 75
Ridsdale. *Nmbd* 1C 114
Riemore Lodge. *Per* 4H 143
Rievaulx. *N Yor* 1H 99
Rift House. *Hart* 1B 106
Rigg. *Dum* 3D 112
Riggend. *N Lan* 2A 128
Rigsby. *Linc* 3D 88
Rigside. *S Lan* 1A 118
Riley Green. *Lanc* 2E 90
Rileyhill. *Staf* 4F 73
Rilla Mill. *Corn* 5C 10
Rillington. *N Yor* 2C 100
Rimington. *Lanc* 5H 97
Rimpton. *Som* 4B 22
Rimsdale. *High* 4H 167
Rimswell. *E Yor* 2G 95
Ringasta. *Shet* 10E 173
Ringford. *Dum* 4D 111
Ringing Hill. *Leics* 4B 74
Ringinglow. *S Yor* 2G 85
Ringland. *Norf* 4D 78
Ringlestone. *Kent* 5C 40
Ringmer. *E Sus* 4F 27
Ringmore. *Devn*
nr. Kingsbridge 4C 8
nr. Teignmouth 5C 12
Ring o' Bells. *Lanc* 3C 90
Ring's End. *Cambs* 5C 76
Ringsfield. *Suff* 2G 67
Ringsfield Corner. *Suff* 2G 67
Ringshall. *Buck* 4H 51
Ringshall. *Suff* 5C 66
Ringshall Stocks. *Suff* 5C 66
Ringstead. *Norf* 1G 77
Ringstead. *Nptn* 3G 63
Ringwood. *Hants* 2G 15
Ringwould. *Kent* 1H 29
Rinmore. *Abers* 2B 152
Rinnigill. *Orkn* 8C 172
Rinsey. *Corn* 4C 4
Riof. *W Isl* 4D 171
Ripe. *E Sus* 4G 27
Ripley. *Derbs* 5B 86
Ripley. *Hants* 3G 15
Ripley. *N Yor* 3E 99
Ripley. *Surr* 5B 38
Riplingham. *E Yor* 1C 94
Ripon. *N Yor* 2F 99
Rippingale. *Linc* 3H 75
Ripple. *Kent* 1H 29
Ripple. *Worc* 2D 48
Ripponden. *W Yor* 3A 92
Rireavach. *High* 4E 163
Risabus. *Arg* 5B 124
Risbury. *Here* 5H 59
Risby. *E Yor* 1D 94
Risby. *N Lin* 3C 94
Risby. *Suff* 4G 65
Risca. *Cphy* 2F 33
Rise. *E Yor* 5F 101
Riseden. *E Sus* 2H 27
Riseden. *Kent* 2B 28
Rise End. *Derbs* 5G 85
Risegate. *Linc* 3B 76
Riseholme. *Linc* 3G 87
Riseley. *Bed* 4H 63
Riseley. *Wok* 5F 37
Rishangles. *Suff* 4D 66
Rishton. *Lanc* 1F 91
Rishworth. *W Yor* 3A 92
Risley. *Derbs* 2B 74
Risley. *Warr* 1A 84
Risplith. *N Yor* 3E 99
Rispond. *High* 2E 167
Rivar. *Wilts* 5B 36
Rivenhall. *Essx* 4B 54
Rivenhall End. *Essx* 4B 54
River. *Kent* 1G 29
River. *W Sus* 3A 26
River Bank. *Cambs* 4E 65
Riverhead. *Kent* 5G 39
Rivington. *Lanc* 3E 91
Roach Bridge. *Lanc* 2D 90
Roachill. *Devn* 4B 20
Roade. *Nptn* 5E 63
Road Green. *Norf* 1E 67
Roadhead. *Cumb* 2G 113
Roadmeetings. *S Lan* 5B 128
Roadside. *High* 2D 168
Roadside of Catterline.
Abers 1H 145
Roadside of Kinneff.
Abers 1H 145
Roadwater. *Som* 3D 20
Road Weedon. *Nptn* 5D 62
Roag. *High* 4B 154
Roa Island. *Cumb* 3B 96
Roath. *Card* 4E 33
Roberton. *Bord* 3G 119
Roberton. *S Lan* 2B 118
Robertsbridge. *E Sus* 3B 28
Robertstown. *Mor* 4G 159
Robertstown. *Rhon* 5C 46
Roberttown. *W Yor* 2B 92
Robeston Back. *Pemb* 3E 43
Robeston Wathen. *Pemb* 3E 43
Robeston West. *Pemb* 4C 42
Robin Hood. *Lanc* 3D 90
Robin Hood. *W Yor* 2D 92
Robinhood End. *Essx* 2H 53
Robin Hood's Bay. *N Yor* 4G 107
Roborough. *Devn*
nr. Great Torrington 1F 11
nr. Plymouth 2B 8
Rob Roy's House. *Arg* 2A 134
Roby Mill. *Lanc* 4D 90
Rocester. *Staf* 2F 73
Roch. *Pemb* 2C 42
Rochdale. *G Man* 3G 91
Roche. *Corn* 2D 6
Rochester. *Medw*
Medway Towns 197 (4B 40)
Rochester. *Nmbd* 5C 120
Rochford. *Essx* 1C 40
Rock. *Corn* 1D 6
Rock. *Nmbd* 2G 121
Rock. *W Sus* 4C 26
Rock. *Worc* 3B 60
The Rock. *M Ulst* 2B 178
Rockbeare. *Devn* 3D 12
Rockbourne. *Hants* 1G 15
Rockcliffe. *Cumb* 3E 113
Rockcliffe. *Dum* 4F 111
Rockcliffe Cross. *Cumb* 3E 113
Rock Ferry. *Mers* 2F 83
Rockfield. *High* 5G 165
Rockfield. *Mon* 4H 47
Rockford. *Hants* 2G 15
Rockgreen. *Shrp* 3H 59
Rockhampton. *S Glo* 2B 34
Rockhead. *Corn* 4A 10
Rockingham. *Nptn* 1F 63
Rockland All Saints. *Norf* 1B 66
Rockland St Mary. *Norf* 5F 79
Rockland St Peter. *Norf* 1B 66
Rockley. *Wilts* 4G 35
Rockwell End. *Buck* 3F 37
Rockwell Green. *Som* 1E 13
Rodborough. *Glos* 5D 48
Rodbourne. *Wilts* 3E 35
Rodd. *Here* 4F 59
Roddam. *Nmbd* 2E 121
Rodden. *Dors* 4B 14
Roddenloft. *E Ayr* 2D 117
Roddymoor. *Dur* 1E 105
Rode. *Som* 1D 22
Rode Heath. *Ches E* 5C 84
Rodeheath. *Ches E* 4C 84
Rodel. *W Isl* 9C 171
Roden. *Telf* 4H 71
Rodhuish. *Som* 3D 20
Rodington. *Telf* 4H 71
Rodington Heath. *Telf* 4H 71
Rodley. *Glos* 4C 48
Rodmarton. *Glos* 2E 35
Rodmell. *E Sus* 5F 27
Rodmersham. *Kent* 4D 40
Rodmersham Green. *Kent* 4D 40
Rodney Stoke. *Som* 2H 21
Rodsley. *Derbs* 1G 73
Rodway. *Som* 3F 21
Rodway. *Telf* 4A 72
Rodwell. *Dors* 5B 14
Roecliffe. *N Yor* 3F 99
Roe Green. *Herts* 2D 52
Roehampton. *G Lon* 3D 38
Roesound. *Shet* 5E 173
Roffey. *W Sus* 2C 26
Rogart. *High* 3E 165
Rogate. *W Sus* 4G 25
Roger Ground. *Cumb* 5E 103
Rogerstone. *Newp* 3F 33
Rogiet. *Mon* 3H 33
Rogue's Alley. *Cambs* 5C 76
Roke. *Oxon* 2E 37
Rokemarsh. *Oxon* 2E 36
Roker. *Tyne* 4H 115
Rollesby. *Norf* 4G 79
Rolleston. *Leics* 5E 75
Rolleston. *Notts* 5E 87
Rolleston on Dove. *Staf* 3G 73
Rolston. *E Yor* 5G 101
Rolvenden. *Kent* 2C 28
Rolvenden Layne. *Kent* 2C 28
Romaldkirk. *Dur* 2C 104
Roman Bank. *Shrp* 1H 59
Romanby. *N Yor* 5A 106
Romannobridge. *Bord* 5E 129
Romansleigh. *Devn* 4H 19
Romers Common. *Worc* 4H 59
Romesdal. *High* 3D 154
Romford. *Dors* 2F 15
Romford. *G Lon* 2G 39
Romiley. *G Man* 1D 84
Romsey. *Hants* 4B 24
Romsley. *Shrp* 2B 60
Romsley. *Worc* 3D 60
Ronague. *IOM* 4B 108
Ronaldsvoe. *Orkn* 8D 172
Rookby. *Cumb* 3B 104
Rookhope. *Dur* 5C 114
Rooking. *Cumb* 3F 103
Rookley. *IOW* 4D 16
Rooks Bridge. *Som* 1G 21
Rooksey Green. *Suff* 5B 66
Rook's Nest. *Som* 3D 20
Rookwood. *W Sus* 3F 17
Roos. *E Yor* 1F 95
Roosebeck. *Cumb* 3B 96
Roosecote. *Cumb* 3B 96
Rootfield. *High* 3H 157
Rootham's Green. *Bed* 5A 64
Rootpark. *S Lan* 4C 128
Ropley. *Hants* 3E 25
Ropley Dean. *Hants* 3E 25
Ropsley. *Linc* 2G 75
Rora. *Abers* 3H 161
Rorandle. *Abers* 2D 152
Rorrington. *Shrp* 5F 71
Rose. *Corn* 3B 6
Roseacre. *Lanc* 1C 90
Rose Ash. *Devn* 4A 20
Rosebank. *S Lan* 5B 128
Rosebush. *Pemb* 2E 43
Rosedale Abbey. *N Yor* 5E 107
Roseden. *Nmbd* 2E 121
Rose Green. *Essx* 3B 54
Rose Green. *Suff* 1C 54
Rosehall. *High* 3B 164
Rosehearty. *Abers* 2G 161
Rose Hill. *E Sus* 4F 27
Rose Hill. *Lanc* 1G 91
Rosehill. *Shrp*
nr. Market Drayton 2A 72
nr. Shrewsbury 4G 71
Roseisle. *Mor* 2F 159
Rosemarket. *Pemb* 4D 42
Rosemarkie. *High* 3B 158
Rosemary Lane. *Devn* 1E 13
Rosemount. *Per* 4A 144
Rosenannon. *Corn* 2D 6
Roser's Cross. *E Sus* 3G 27
Rosevean. *Corn* 3E 6
Rosewell. *Midl* 3F 129
Roseworth. *Stoc T* 2B 106
Roseworthy. *Corn* 3D 4
Rosgill. *Cumb* 3G 103
Roshven. *High* 1B 140
Roskhill. *High* 4B 154
Roskorwell. *Corn* 4E 5
Rosley. *Cumb* 5E 112
Roslin. *Midl* 3F 129
Rosliston. *Derbs* 4G 73
Rosneath. *Arg* 1D 126
Ross. *Dum* 5D 110
Ross. *Nmbd* 1F 121
Ross. *Per* 1G 135
Ross. *Bord* 3F 131
Rossendale. *Lanc* 2F 91
Rossett. *Wrex* 5F 83
Rossington. *S Yor* 1D 86
Rosskeen. *High* 2A 158
Rossland. *Ren* 2F 127
Rosslea. *Ferm* 6L 177
Ross-on-Wye. *Here* 3B 48
Roster. *High* 5E 169
Rostherne. *Ches E* 2B 84
Rostholme. *S Yor* 4F 93
Rosthwaite. *Cumb* 3D 102
Roston. *Derbs* 1F 73
Rostrevor. *New M* 8F 179
Rosudgeon. *Corn* 4C 4
Rosyth. *Fife* 1E 129
Rothbury. *Nmbd* 4E 121
Rotherby. *Leics* 4D 74
Rotherfield. *E Sus* 3G 27
Rotherfield Greys. *Oxon* 3F 37
Rotherfield Peppard. *Oxon* 3F 37
Rotherham. *S Yor* 1B 86
Rothersthorpe. *Nptn* 5E 62
Rotherwick. *Hants* 1F 25
Rothes. *Mor* 4G 159
Rothesay. *Arg* 3B 126
Rothienorman. *Abers* 5E 160
Rothiesholm. *Orkn* 5F 172
Rothley. *Leics* 4C 74
Rothley. *Nmbd* 1D 114
Rothwell. *Linc* 1A 88
Rothwell. *Nptn* 2F 63
Rothwell. *W Yor* 2D 92
Rotsea. *E Yor* 4E 101
Rottal. *Ang* 2C 144
Rotten End. *Suff* 4F 67
Rotten Row. *Norf* 4C 78
Rotten Row. *W Ber* 4D 36
Rotten Row. *W Mid* 3F 61
Rottingdean. *Brig* 5E 27
Rottington. *Cumb* 3A 102
Roud. *IOW* 4D 16
Rougham. *Norf* 3H 77
Rougham. *Suff* 4B 66
Rough Close. *Staf* 2D 72
Rough Common. *Kent* 5F 41
Roughcote. *Staf* 1D 72
Roughfort. *Ant* 1G 179
Rough Haugh. *High* 4H 167
Rough Hay. *Staf* 3G 73
Roughlee. *Lanc* 5H 97
Roughley. *W Mid* 1F 61
Roughsike. *Cumb* 2G 113
Roughton. *Linc* 4B 88
Roughton. *Norf* 2E 78
Roughton. *Shrp* 1B 60
Roundbush Green. *Essx* 4F 53
Roundham. *Som* 2H 13
Roundhay. *W Yor* 1D 92
Round Hill. *Torb* 2E 9
Roundhurst. *W Sus* 2A 26
Round Maple. *Suff* 1C 54
Round Oak. *Shrp* 2F 59
Roundstreet Common.
W Sus 3B 26
Roundthwaite. *Cumb* 4H 103
Roundway. *Wilts* 5F 35
Roundyhill. *Ang* 3C 144
Rousdon. *Devn* 3F 13
Rousham. *Oxon* 3C 50
Rousky. *Ferm* 8B 174
Rous Lench. *Worc* 5E 61
Routh. *E Yor* 5E 101
Rout's Green. *Buck* 2F 37
Row. *Corn* 5A 10
Row. *Cumb*
nr. Kendal 1D 96
nr. Penrith 1H 103
The Row. *Lanc* 2D 96
Rowanburn. *Dum* 2F 113
Rowanhill. *Abers* 3H 161
Rowardennan. *Stir* 4C 134
Rowarth. *Derbs* 2E 85
Row Ash. *Hants* 1D 16
Rowberrow. *Som* 1H 21
Rowde. *Wilts* 5E 35
Rowden. *Devn* 3G 11
Rowen. *Cnwy* 3G 81
Rowfoot. *Nmbd* 3H 113
Row Green. *Essx* 3H 53
Row Heath. *Essx* 4E 55
Rowhedge. *Essx* 3D 54
Rowhook. *W Sus* 2C 26
Rowington. *Warw* 4G 61
Rowland. *Derbs* 3G 85
Rowlands Castle. *Hants* 1F 17
Rowlands Gill. *Tyne* 4E 115
Rowledge. *Hants* 2G 25
Rowley. *Dur* 5D 115
Rowley. *E Yor* 1C 94
Rowley. *Shrp* 5F 71
Rowley Hill. *W Yor* 3B 92
Rowley Regis. *W Mid* 2D 60
Rowlstone. *Here* 3G 47
Rowly. *Surr* 1B 26
Rowner. *Hants* 2D 16
Rowney Green. *Worc* 3E 61
Rownhams. *Hants* 1B 16
Rowrah. *Cumb* 3B 102
Rowsham. *Buck* 4G 51
Rowsley. *Derbs* 4G 85
Rowstock. *Oxon* 3C 36
Rowston. *Linc* 5H 87
Rowthorne. *Derbs* 4B 86
Rowton. *Ches W* 4G 83
Rowton. *Shrp*
nr. Ludlow 2G 59
nr. Shrewsbury 4F 71
Rowton. *Telf* 4A 72
Row Town. *Surr* 4B 38
Roxburgh. *Bord* 1B 120
Roxby. *N Lin* 3C 94
Roxby. *N Yor* 3E 107
Roxhill. *Ant* 7G 175
Roxton. *Bed* 5A 64
Roxwell. *Essx* 5G 53
Royal Leamington Spa.
Warw 4H 61
Royal Oak. *Darl* 2F 105
Royal Oak. *Lanc* 4C 90
Royal Oak. *N Yor* 2F 101
Royal's Green. *Ches E* 1A 72
Royal Sutton Coldfield.
W Mid 1F 61
Royal Tunbridge Wells.
Kent 2G 27
Royal Wootton Bassett.
Wilts 3F 35
Roybridge. *High* 5E 149
Roydon. *Essx* 4E 53
Roydon. *Norf*
nr. Diss 2C 66
nr. King's Lynn 3G 77
Roydon Hamlet. *Essx* 5E 53
Royston. *Herts* 1D 52
Royston. *S Yor* 3D 92
Royston Water. *Som* 1F 13
Royton. *G Man* 4H 91
Ruabon. *Wrex* 1F 71
Ruaig. *Arg* 4B 138
Ruan High Lanes. *Corn* 5D 6
Ruan Lanihorne. *Corn* 4C 6
Ruan Major. *Corn* 5E 5
Ruan Minor. *Corn* 5E 5
Ruarach. *High* 1B 148
Ruardean. *Glos* 4B 48
Ruardean Hill. *Glos* 4B 48
Ruardean Woodside. *Glos* 4B 48
Rubane. *Ards* 3L 179
Rubery. *Worc* 3D 61
Ruchazie. *Glas* 3H 127
Ruckcroft. *Cumb* 5G 113
Ruckinge. *Kent* 2E 29
Ruckland. *Linc* 3C 88
Rucklers Lane. *Herts* 5A 52
Ruckley. *Shrp* 5H 71
Rudbaxton. *Pemb* 2D 42
Rudby. *N Yor* 4B 106
Ruddington. *Notts* 2C 74
Rudford. *Glos* 3C 48
Rudge. *Shrp* 1C 60
Rudge. *Wilts* 1D 22
Rudge Heath. *Shrp* 1B 60
Rudgeway. *S Glo* 3B 34
Rudgwick. *W Sus* 2B 26
Rudhall. *Here* 3B 48
Rudheath. *Ches W* 3A 84
Rudley Green. *Essx* 5B 54

Rudloe—Shawford

Rudloe. *Wilts* 4D 34
Rudry. *Cphy* 3F 33
Rudston. *E Yor* 3E 101
Rudyard. *Staf* 5D 84
Rufford. *Lanc* 3C 90
Rufforth. *York* 4H 99
Rugby. *Warw* 3C 62
Rugeley. *Staf* 4E 73
Ruglen. *S Ayr* 4B 116
Ruilick. *High* 4H 157
Ruisaurie. *High* 4G 157
Ruishton. *Som* 4F 21
Ruisigearraidh. *W Isl* 1E 170
Ruislip. *G Lon* 2B 38
Ruislip Common. *G Lon* 2B 38
Rumbling Bridge. *Per* 4C 136
Rumburgh. *Suff* 2F 67
Rumford. *Corn* 1C 6
Rumford. *Falk* 2C 128
Rumney. *Card* 4F 33
Rumwell. *Som* 4E 21
Runcorn. *Hal* 2H 83
Runcton. *W Sus* 2G 17
Runcton Holme. *Norf* 5F 77
Rundlestone. *Devn* 5F 11
Runfold. *Surr* 2G 25
Runhall. *Norf* 5C 78
Runham. *Norf* 4G 79
Runnington. *Som* 4E 20
Runshaw Moor. *Lanc* 3D 90
Runswick. *N Yor* 3F 107
Runtaleave. *Ang* 2B 144
Runwell. *Essx* 1B 40
Ruscombe. *Wok* 4F 37
Rushall. *Here* 2B 48
Rushall. *Norf* 2D 66
Rushall. *W Mid* 5E 73
Rushall. *Wilts* 1G 23
Rushbrooke. *Suff* 4A 66
Rushbury. *Shrp* 1H 59
Rushden. *Herts* 2D 52
Rushden. *Nptn* 4G 63
Rushenden. *Kent* 3D 40
Rushford. *Devn* 5E 11
Rushford. *Suff* 2B 66
Rush Green. *Herts* 3C 52
Rushlake Green. *E Sus* 4H 27
Rushmere. *Suff* 2G 67
Rushmere St Andrew. *Suff* 1F 55
Rushmoor. *Surr* 2G 25
Rushock. *Worc* 3C 60
Rusholme. *G Man* 1C 84
Rushton. *Ches W* 4H 83
Rushton. *Nptn* 2F 63
Rushton. *Shrp* 5A 72
Rushton Spencer. *Staf* 4D 84
Rushwick. *Worc* 5C 60
Rushyford. *Dur* 2F 105
Ruskie. *Stir* 3F 135
Ruskington. *Linc* 5H 87
Rusland. *Cumb* 1C 96
Rusper. *W Sus* 2D 26
Ruspidge. *Glos* 4B 48
Russell's Water. *Oxon* 3F 37
Russel's Green. *Suff* 3E 67
Russ Hill. *Surr* 1D 26
Russland. *Orkn* 6C 172
Rusthall. *Kent* 2G 27
Rustington. *W Sus* 5B 26
Ruston. *N Yor* 1D 100
Ruston Parva. *E Yor* 3E 101
Ruswarp. *N Yor* 4F 107
Rutherglen. *S Lan* 3H 127
Ruthernbridge. *Corn* 2E 6
Ruthin. *Den* 5D 82
Ruthin. *V Glam* 4C 32
Ruthrieston. *Aber* 3G 153
Ruthven. *Abers* 4C 160
Ruthven. *Ang* 4B 144
Ruthven. *High*
nr. Inverness 5C 158
nr. Kingussie 4B 150
Ruthvoes. *Corn* 2D 6
Ruthwaite. *Cumb* 1D 102
Ruthwell. *Dum* 3C 112
Ruxton Green. *Here* 4A 48
Ruyton-XI-Towns. *Shrp* 3F 71
Ryal. *Nmbd* 2D 114
Ryall. *Dors* 3H 13
Ryall. *Worc* 1D 48
Ryarsh. *Kent* 5A 40
Rychraggan. *High* 5G 157
Rydal. *Cumb* 4E 103
Ryde. *IOW* 3D 16
Rye. *E Sus* 3D 28
Ryecroft Gate. *Staf* 4D 84
Ryeford. *Here* 3B 48
Rye Foreign. *E Sus* 3D 28
Rye Harbour. *E Sus* 4D 28
Ryehill. *E Yor* 2F 95
Rye Street. *Worc* 2C 48
Ryhall. *Rut* 4H 75
Ryhill. *W Yor* 3D 93
Ryhope. *Tyne* 4H 115
Ryhope Colliery. *Tyne* 4H 115
Rylands. *Notts* 2C 74
Rylstone. *N Yor* 4B 98
Ryme Intrinseca. *Dors* 1A 14
Ryther. *N Yor* 1F 93
Ryton. *Glos* 2C 48
Ryton. *N Yor* 2B 100
Ryton. *Shrp* 5B 72
Ryton. *Tyne* 3E 115
Ryton. *Warw* 2B 62
Ryton-on-Dunsmore. *Warw* 3A 62
Ryton Woodside. *Tyne* 3E 115

S

Saasaig. *High* 3E 147
Sabden. *Lanc* 1F 91
Sacombe. *Herts* 4D 52
Sacriston. *Dur* 5F 115
Sadberge. *Darl* 3A 106
Saddell. *Arg* 2B 122
Saddington. *Leics* 1D 62
Saddle Bow. *Norf* 4F 77
Saddlescombe. *W Sus* 4D 26
Saddleworth. *G Man* 4H 91
Sadgill. *Cumb* 4F 103
Saffron Walden. *Essx* 2F 53
Sageston. *Pemb* 4E 43
Saham Hills. *Norf* 5B 78
Saham Toney. *Norf* 5A 78
Saighdinis. *W Isl* 2D 170
Saighton. *Ches W* 4G 83
Sain Dunwyd. *V Glam* 5C 32
Sain Hilari. *V Glam* 4D 32
St Abbs. *Bord* 3F 131
St Agnes. *Corn* 3B 6
St Albans. *Herts* 5B 52
St Allen. *Corn* 3C 6
St Andrews. *Fife* 2H 137
St Andrews Major. *V Glam* 4E 33
St Anne's. *Lanc* 2B 90
St Ann's. *Dum* 5C 118
St Ann's Chapel. *Corn* 5E 11
St Ann's Chapel. *Devn* 4C 8
St Anthony. *Corn* 5C 6
St Anthony-in-Meneage. *Corn* 4E 5
St Arvans. *Mon* 2A 34
St Asaph. *Den* 3C 82
Sain Tathan. *V Glam* 5D 32
St Athan. *V Glam* 5D 32
St Austell. *Corn* 3E 6
St Bartholomew's Hill. *Wilts* 4E 23
St Bees. *Cumb* 3A 102
St Blazey. *Corn* 3E 7
St Blazey Gate. *Corn* 3E 7
St Boswells. *Bord* 1H 119
St Breock. *Corn* 1D 6
St Breward. *Corn* 5A 10
St Briavels. *Glos* 5A 48
St Brides. *Pemb* 3B 42
St Brides Major. *V Glam* 4B 32
St Bride's Netherwent. *Mon* 3H 33
St Bride's-super-Ely. *V Glam* 4D 32
St Brides Wentlooge. *Newp* 3F 33
St Budeaux. *Plym* 3A 8
Saintbury. *Glos* 2G 49
St Buryan. *Corn* 4B 4
St Catherine. *Bath* 4C 34
St Catherines. *Arg* 3A 134
St Clears. *Carm* 3G 43
St Cleer. *Corn* 2G 7
St Clement. *Corn* 4C 6
St Clether. *Corn* 4C 10
St Colmac. *Arg* 3B 126
St Columb Major. *Corn* 2D 6
St Columb Minor. *Corn* 2C 6
St Columb Road. *Corn* 3D 6
St Combs. *Abers* 2H 161
St Cross. *Hants* 4C 24
St Cross South Elmham. *Suff* 2E 67
St Cyrus. *Abers* 2G 145
St David's. *Per* 1B 136
St Davids. *Pemb* 2B 42
St Day. *Corn* 4B 6
St Dennis. *Corn* 3D 6
St Dogmaels. *Pemb* 1B 44
St Dominick. *Corn* 2H 7
St Donat's. *V Glam* 5C 32
St Edith's Marsh. *Wilts* 5E 35
St Endellion. *Corn* 1D 6
St Enoder. *Corn* 3C 6
St Erme. *Corn* 4C 6
St Erney. *Corn* 3H 7
St Erth. *Corn* 3C 4
St Erth Praze. *Corn* 3C 4
St Ervan. *Corn* 1C 6
St Eval. *Corn* 2C 6
St Ewe. *Corn* 4D 6
St Fagans. *Card* 4E 32
St Fergus. *Abers* 3H 161
Saintfield. *New M* 4J 179
St Fillans. *Per* 1F 135
St Florence. *Pemb* 4E 43
St Gennys. *Corn* 3B 10
St George. *Cnwy* 3B 82
St George's. *N Som* 5G 33
St Georges. *V Glam* 4D 32
St George's Hill. *Surr* 4B 38
St Germans. *Corn* 3H 7
St Giles in the Wood. *Devn* 1F 11
St Giles on the Heath. *Devn* 3D 10
St Giles's Hill. *Hants* 4C 24
St Gluvias. *Corn* 5B 6
St Harmon. *Powy* 3B 58
St Helena. *Warw* 5G 73
St Helen Auckland. *Dur* 2E 105
St Helen's. *E Sus* 4C 28
St Helens. *Cumb* 1B 102
St Helens. *IOW* 4E 17
St Helens. *Mers* 1H 83
St Hilary. *Corn* 3C 4
St Hilary. *V Glam* 4D 32
Saint Hill. *Devn* 2D 12
Saint Hill. *W Sus* 2E 27
St Illtyd. *Blae* 5F 47
St Ippolyts. *Herts* 3B 52
St Ishmael. *Carm* 5D 44
St Ishmael's. *Pemb* 4C 42
St Issey. *Corn* 1D 6
St Ive. *Corn* 2H 7
St Ives. *Cambs* 3C 64
St Ives. *Corn* 2C 4
St Ives. *Dors* 2G 15
St James' End. *Nptn* 4E 63
St James South Elmham. *Suff* 2F 67
St Jidgey. *Corn* 2D 6
St John. *Corn* 3A 8
St John's. *IOM* 3B 108
St John's. *Worc* 5C 60
St John's Chapel. *Devn* 4F 19
St John's Chapel. *Dur* 1B 104
St John's Fen End. *Norf* 4E 77
St John's Town of Dalry. *Dum* 1D 110
St Judes. *IOM* 2C 108
St Just. *Corn* 3A 4
St Just in Roseland. *Corn* 5C 6
St Katherines. *Abers* 5E 161
St Keverne. *Corn* 4E 5
St Kew. *Corn* 5A 10
St Kew Highway. *Corn* 5A 10
St Keyne. *Corn* 2G 7
St Lawrence. *Corn* 2E 7
St Lawrence. *Essx* 5C 54
St Lawrence. *IOW* 5D 16
St Leonards. *Buck* 5H 51
St Leonards. *Dors* 2G 15
St Leonards. *E Sus* 5B 28
St Levan. *Corn* 4A 4
St Lythans. *V Glam* 4E 32
St Mabyn. *Corn* 5A 10
St Madoes. *Per* 1D 136
St Margaret's. *Herts* 4A 52
St Margaret's. *Wilts* 5H 35
St Margarets. *Here* 2G 47
St Margarets. *Herts* 4D 53
St Margaret's at Cliffe. *Kent* 1H 29
St Margaret's Hope. *Orkn* 8D 172
St Margaret South Elmham. *Suff* 2F 67
St Mark's. *IOM* 4B 108
St Martin. *Corn*
nr. Helston 4E 5
nr. Looe 3G 7
St Martin's. *Shrp* 2F 71
St Martins. *Per* 5A 144
St Mary Bourne. *Hants* 1C 24
St Mary Church. *V Glam* 4D 32
St Marychurch. *Torb* 2F 9
St Mary Cray. *G Lon* 4F 39
St Mary Hill. *V Glam* 4C 32
St Mary Hoo. *Medw* 3C 40
St Mary in the Marsh. *Kent* 3E 29
St Mary's. *Orkn* 7D 172
St Mary's Airport. *IOS* 1B 4
St Mary's Bay. *Kent* 3E 29
St Marys Platt. *Kent* 5H 39
St Maughan's Green. *Mon* 4H 47
St Mawes. *Corn* 5C 6
St Mawgan. *Corn* 2C 6
St Mellion. *Corn* 2H 7
St Mellons. *Card* 3F 33
St Merryn. *Corn* 1C 6
St Mewan. *Corn* 3D 6
St Michael Caerhays. *Corn* 4D 6
St Michael Penkevil. *Corn* 4C 6
St Michaels. *Kent* 2C 28
St Michaels. *Torb* 3E 9
St Michaels. *Worc* 4H 59
St Michael's on Wyre. *Lanc* 5D 96
St Michael South Elmham. *Suff* 2F 67
St Minver. *Corn* 1D 6
St Monans. *Fife* 3H 137
St Neot. *Corn* 2F 7
St Neots. *Cambs* 4A 64
St Newlyn East. *Corn* 3C 6
St Nicholas. *Pemb* 1C 42
St Nicholas. *V Glam* 4D 32
St Nicholas at Wade. *Kent* 4G 41
St Nicholas South Elmham. *Suff* 2F 67
St Ninians. *Stir* 4G 135
St Olaves. *Norf* 1G 67
St Osyth. *Essx* 4E 54
St Osyth Heath. *Essx* 4E 55
St Owen's Cross. *Here* 3A 48
St Paul's Cray. *G Lon* 4F 39
St Paul's Walden. *Herts* 3B 52
St Peter's. *Kent* 4H 41
St Peter The Great. *Worc* 5C 60
St Petrox. *Pemb* 5D 42
St Pinnock. *Corn* 2G 7
St Quivox. *S Ayr* 2C 116
St Ruan. *Corn* 5E 5
St Stephen. *Corn* 3D 6
St Stephens. *Corn*
nr. Launceston 4D 10
nr. Saltash 3A 8
St Teath. *Corn* 4A 10
St Thomas. *Devn* 3C 12
St Thomas. *Swan* 3F 31
St Tudy. *Corn* 5A 10
St Twynnells. *Pemb* 5D 42
St Veep. *Corn* 3F 7
St Vigeans. *Ang* 4F 145
St Wenn. *Corn* 2D 6
St Weonards. *Here* 3H 47
St Winnolls. *Corn* 3H 7
St Winnow. *Corn* 3F 7
Salcombe. *Devn* 5D 8
Salcombe Regis. *Devn* 4E 13
Salcott. *Essx* 4C 54
Sale. *G Man* 1B 84
Saleby. *Linc* 3D 88
Sale Green. *Worc* 5D 60
Salehurst. *E Sus* 3B 28
Salem. *Carm* 3G 45
Salem. *Cdgn* 2F 57
Salen. *Arg* 4G 139
Salen. *High* 2A 140
Salesbury. *Lanc* 1E 91
Saleway. *Worc* 5D 60
Salford. *C Beds* 2H 51
Salford. *G Man* Manchester 197 (1C 84)
Salford. *Oxon* 3A 50
Salford Priors. *Warw* 5E 61
Salfords. *Surr* 1D 27
Salhouse. *Norf* 4F 79
Saligo. *Arg* 3A 124
Saline. *Fife* 4C 136
Salisbury. *Wilts* 201 (3G 23)
Salkeld Dykes. *Cumb* 1G 103
Sallachan. *High* 2D 141
Sallachy. *High*
nr. Lairg 3C 164
nr. Stromeferry 5B 156
Salle. *Norf* 3D 78
Salmonby. *Linc* 3C 88
Salmond's Muir. *Ang* 5E 145
Salperton. *Glos* 3F 49
Salph End. *Bed* 5H 63
Salsburgh. *N Lan* 3B 128
Salt. *Staf* 3D 72
Salta. *Cumb* 5B 112
Saltaire. *W Yor* 1B 92
Saltash. *Corn* 3A 8
Saltburn. *High* 2B 158
Saltburn-by-the-Sea. *Red C* 2D 106
Saltby. *Leics* 3F 75
Saltcoats. *Cumb* 5B 102
Saltcoats. *N Ayr* 5D 126
Saltdean. *Brig* 5E 27
Salt End. *E Yor* 2E 95
Salter. *Lanc* 3F 97
Salterforth. *Lanc* 5A 98
Salters Lode. *Norf* 5E 77
Salterswall. *Ches W* 4A 84
Salterton. *Wilts* 3G 23
Saltfleet. *Linc* 1D 88
Saltfleetby All Saints. *Linc* 1D 88
Saltfleetby St Clements. *Linc* 1D 88
Saltfleetby St Peter. *Linc* 2D 88
Saltford. *Bath* 5B 34
Salthouse. *Norf* 1C 78
Saltmarshe. *E Yor* 2A 94
Saltness. *Orkn* 9B 172
Saltness. *Shet* 7D 173
Saltney. *Flin* 4F 83
Salton. *N Yor* 2B 100
Saltrens. *Devn* 4E 19
Saltwick. *Nmbd* 2E 115
Saltwood. *Kent* 2F 29
Salum. *Arg* 4B 138
Salwarpe. *Worc* 4C 60
Salwayash. *Dors* 3H 13
Samalaman. *High* 1A 140
Sambourne. *Warw* 4E 61
Sambourne. *Wilts* 2D 22
Sambrook. *Telf* 3B 72
Samhia. *W Isl* 2C 170
Samlesbury. *Lanc* 1D 90
Samlesbury Bottoms. *Lanc* 2E 90
Sampford Arundel. *Som* 1E 12
Sampford Brett. *Som* 2D 20
Sampford Courtenay. *Devn* 2G 11
Sampford Peverell. *Devn* 1D 12
Sampford Spiney. *Devn* 5F 11
Samsonslane. *Orkn* 5F 172
Samuelston. *E Lot* 2A 130
Sanaigmore. *Arg* 2A 124
Sancreed. *Corn* 4B 4
Sancton. *E Yor* 1C 94
Sand. *High* 4D 162
Sand. *Shet* 7E 173
Sand. *Som* 2H 21
Sandaig. *Arg* 4A 138
Sandaig. *High* 3F 147
Sandale. *Cumb* 5D 112
Sandal Magna. *W Yor* 3D 92
Sandavore. *High* 5C 146
Sanday Airport. *Orkn* 3F 172
Sandbach. *Ches E* 4B 84
Sandbank. *Arg* 1C 126
Sandbanks. *Pool* 4F 15
Sandend. *Abers* 2C 160
Sanderstead. *G Lon* 4E 39
Sandfields. *Neat* 3G 31
Sandford. *Cumb* 3A 104
Sandford. *Devn* 2B 12
Sandford. *Dors* 4E 15
Sandford. *Hants* 2G 15
Sandford. *IOW* 4D 16
Sandford. *N Som* 1H 21
Sandford. *Shrp*
nr. Oswestry 3F 71
nr. Whitchurch 2H 71
Sandford. *S Lan* 5A 128
Sandfordhill. *Abers* 4H 161
Sandford-on-Thames. *Oxon* 5D 50
Sandford Orcas. *Dors* 4B 22
Sandford St Martin. *Oxon* 3C 50
Sandgate. *Kent* 2F 29
Sandgreen. *Dum* 4C 110
Sandhaven. *Abers* 2G 161
Sandhead. *Dum* 4F 109
Sandhill. *Cambs* 2E 65
Sandhills. *Dors* 1B 14
Sandhills. *Oxon* 5D 50
Sandhills. *Surr* 2A 26
Sandhoe. *Nmbd* 3C 114
Sand Hole. *E Yor* 1B 94
Sandholes. *M Ulst* 2B 178
Sandholme. *E Yor* 1B 94
Sandholme. *Linc* 2C 76
Sandhurst. *Brac* 5G 37
Sandhurst. *Glos* 3D 48
Sandhurst. *Kent* 3B 28
Sandhurst Cross. *Kent* 3B 28
Sand Hutton. *N Yor* 4A 100
Sandhutton. *N Yor* 1F 99
Sandiacre. *Derbs* 2B 74
Sandilands. *Linc* 2E 89
Sandiway. *Ches W* 3A 84
Sandleheath. *Hants* 1G 15
Sandling. *Kent* 5B 40
Sandlow Green. *Ches E* 4B 84
Sandness. *Shet* 6C 173
Sandon. *Essx* 5H 53
Sandon. *Herts* 2D 52
Sandon. *Staf* 3D 72
Sandonbank. *Staf* 3D 72
Sandown. *IOW* 4D 16
Sandplace. *Corn* 3G 7
Sandridge. *Herts* 4B 52
Sandringham. *Norf* 3F 77
The Sands. *Surr* 2G 25
Sandsend. *N Yor* 3F 107
Sandside. *Cumb* 2C 96
Sandsound. *Shet* 7E 173
Sandtoft. *N Lin* 4H 93
Sandvoe. *Shet* 2E 173
Sandway. *Kent* 5C 40
Sandwich. *Kent* 5H 41
Sandwick. *Cumb* 3F 103
Sandwick. *Orkn*
on Mainland 6B 172
on South Ronaldsay 9D 172
Sandwick. *Shet*
on Mainland 9F 173
on Whalsay 5G 173
Sandwith. *Cumb* 3A 102
Sandy. *Carm* 5E 45
Sandy. *C Beds* 1B 52
Sandy Bank. *Linc* 5B 88
Sandycroft. *Flin* 4F 83
Sandy Cross. *Here* 5A 60
Sandygate. *Devn* 5B 12
Sandygate. *IOM* 2C 108
Sandy Haven. *Pemb* 4C 42
Sandyhills. *Dum* 4F 111
Sandylands. *Lanc* 3D 96
Sandy Lane. *Wilts* 5E 35
Sandylane. *Swan* 4E 31
Sandystones. *Bord* 2H 119
Sandyway. *Here* 3H 47
Sangobeg. *High* 2E 167
Sangomore. *High* 2E 166
Sankyn's Green. *Worc* 4B 60
Sanna. *High* 2F 139
Sanndabhaig. *W Isl*
on Isle of Lewis 4G 171
on South Uist 4D 170
Sannox. *N Ayr* 5B 126
Sanquhar. *Dum* 3G 117
Santon. *Cumb* 4B 102
Santon Bridge. *Cumb* 4C 102
Santon Downham. *Suff* 2H 65
Sapcote. *Leics* 1B 62
Sapey Common. *Here* 4B 60
Sapiston. *Suff* 3B 66
Sapley. *Cambs* 3B 64
Sapperton. *Derbs* 2F 73
Sapperton. *Glos* 5E 49
Sapperton. *Linc* 2H 75
Saracen's Head. *Linc* 3C 76
Sarclet. *High* 4F 169
Sardis. *Carm* 5F 45
Sardis. *Pemb*
nr. Milford Haven 4D 42
nr. Tenby 4F 43
Sarisbury Green. *Hants* 2D 16
Sarn. *B'end* 3C 32
Sarn. *Powy* 1E 58
Sarnau. *Carm* 3E 45
Sarnau. *Cdgn* 5C 56
Sarnau. *Gwyn* 2B 70
Sarnau. *Powy*
nr. Brecon 2D 46
nr. Welshpool 4E 71
Sarn Bach. *Gwyn* 3C 68
Sarnesfield. *Here* 5F 59
Sarn Meyllteyrn. *Gwyn* 2B 68
Saron. *Carm*
nr. Ammanford 4G 45
nr. Newcastle Emlyn 2D 45
Saron. *Gwyn*
nr. Bethel 4E 81
nr. Bontnewydd 5D 80
Sarratt. *Herts* 1B 38
Sarre. *Kent* 4G 41
Sarsden. *Oxon* 3A 50
Satley. *Dur* 5E 115
Satron. *N Yor* 5C 104
Satterleigh. *Devn* 4G 19
Satterthwaite. *Cumb* 5E 103
Satwell. *Oxon* 3F 37
Sauchen. *Abers* 2D 152
Saucher. *Per* 5A 144
Saughall. *Ches W* 3F 83
Saughtree. *Bord* 5H 119
Saul. *Glos* 5C 48
Saul. *New M* 5K 179
Saundby. *Notts* 2E 87
Saundersfoot. *Pemb* 4F 43
Saunderton. *Buck* 5F 51
Saunderton Lee. *Buck* 2G 37
Saunton. *Devn* 3E 19
Sausthorpe. *Linc* 4C 88
Saval. *High* 3C 164
Saverley Green. *Staf* 2D 72
Sawbridge. *Warw* 4C 62
Sawbridgeworth. *Herts* 4E 53
Sawdon. *N Yor* 1D 100
Sawley. *Derbs* 2B 74
Sawley. *Lanc* 5G 97
Sawley. *N Yor* 3E 99
Sawston. *Cambs* 1E 53
Sawtry. *Cambs* 2A 64
Saxby. *Leics* 3F 75
Saxby. *Linc* 2H 87
Saxby All Saints. *N Lin* 3C 94
Saxelby. *Leics* 3D 74
Saxelbye. *Leics* 3D 74
Saxham Street. *Suff* 4C 66
Saxilby. *Linc* 3F 87
Saxlingham. *Norf* 2C 78
Saxlingham Green. *Norf* 1E 67
Saxlingham Nethergate. *Norf* 1E 67
Saxlingham Thorpe. *Norf* 1E 66
Saxmundham. *Suff* 4F 67
Saxondale. *Notts* 1D 74
Saxon Street. *Cambs* 5F 65
Saxtead. *Suff* 4E 67
Saxtead Green. *Suff* 4E 67
Saxthorpe. *Norf* 2D 78
Saxton. *N Yor* 1E 93
Sayers Common. *W Sus* 4D 26
Scackleton. *N Yor* 2A 100
Scadabhagh. *W Isl* 8D 171
Scaddy. *New M* 5J 179
Scaftworth. *Notts* 1D 86
Scagglethorpe. *N Yor* 2C 100
Scaitcliffe. *Lanc* 2F 91
Scaladal. *W Isl* 6D 171
Scalasaig. *Arg* 4A 132
Scalby. *E Yor* 2B 94
Scalby. *N Yor* 5H 107
Scalby Mills. *N Yor* 5H 107
Scaldwell. *Nptn* 3E 63
Scaleby. *Cumb* 3F 113
Scaleby Hill. *Cumb* 3F 113
Scale Houses. *Cumb* 5G 113
Scales. *Cumb*
nr. Barrow-in-Furness 2B 96
nr. Keswick 2E 103
Scalford. *Leics* 3E 75
Scaling. *N Yor* 3E 107
Scaling Dam. *Red C* 3E 107
Scalloway. *Shet* 8F 173
Scalpaigh. *W Isl* 8E 171
Scalpay House. *High* 1E 147
Scamblesby. *Linc* 3B 88
Scamodale. *High* 1C 140
Scampston. *N Yor* 2C 100
Scampton. *Linc* 3G 87
Scaniport. *High* 5A 158
Scapa. *Orkn* 7D 172
Scapegoat Hill. *W Yor* 3A 92
Scar. *Orkn* 3F 172
Scarasta. *W Isl* 8C 171
Scarborough. *N Yor* 1E 101
Scarcliffe. *Derbs* 4B 86
Scarcroft. *W Yor* 5F 99
Scardroy. *High* 3E 156
Scarfskerry. *High* 1E 169
Scargill. *Dur* 3D 104
Scarinish. *Arg* 4B 138
Scarisbrick. *Lanc* 3B 90
Scarning. *Norf* 4B 78
Scarrington. *Notts* 1E 75
Scarth Hill. *Lanc* 4C 90
Scartho. *NE Lin* 4F 95
Scarva. *Arm* 5E 178
Scarvister. *Shet* 7E 173
Scatness. *Shet* 10E 173
Scatwell. *High* 3F 157
Scaur. *Dum* 4F 111
Scawby. *N Lin* 4C 94
Scawby Brook. *N Lin* 4C 94
Scawsby. *S Yor* 4F 93
Scawton. *N Yor* 1H 99
Scaynes Hill. *W Sus* 3E 27
Scethrog. *Powy* 3E 46
Scholar Green. *Ches E* 5C 84
Scholes. *G Man* 4D 90
Scholes. *W Yor*
nr. Bradford 2B 92
nr. Holmfirth 4B 92
nr. Leeds 1D 93
Scholey Hill. *W Yor* 2D 93
School Aycliffe. *Darl* 2F 105
School Green. *Ches W* 4A 84
School Green. *Essx* 2H 53
Scissett. *W Yor* 3C 92
Scleddau. *Pemb* 1D 42
Scofton. *Notts* 2D 86
Scole. *Norf* 3D 66
Scollogstown. *New M* 6J 179
Scolpaig. *W Isl* 1C 170
Scolton. *Pemb* 2D 43
Scone. *Per* 1D 136
Sconser. *High* 5E 155
Scoonie. *Fife* 3F 137
Scopwick. *Linc* 5H 87
Scoraig. *High* 4E 163
Scorborough. *E Yor* 5E 101
Scorrier. *Corn* 4B 6
Scorriton. *Devn* 2D 8
Scorton. *Lanc* 5E 97
Scorton. *N Yor* 4F 105
Sco Ruston. *Norf* 3E 79
Scotbheinn. *W Isl* 3D 170
Scotby. *Cumb* 4F 113
Scotch Corner. *N Yor* 4F 105
Scotch Street. *Arm* 4D 178
Scotforth. *Lanc* 3D 97
Scot Hay. *Staf* 1C 72
Scothern. *Linc* 3H 87
Scotland End. *Oxon* 2B 50
Scotlandwell. *Per* 3D 136
Scot Lane End. *G Man* 4E 91
Scotsburn. *High* 1B 158
Scotsburn. *Mor* 2G 159
Scotsdike. *Cumb* 2E 113
Scot's Gap. *Nmbd* 1D 114
Scotstoun. *Glas* 3G 127
Scotstown. *High* 2C 140
Scotswood. *Tyne* 3F 115
Scottas. *High* 3F 147
Scotter. *Linc* 4B 94
Scotterthorpe. *Linc* 4B 94
Scottlethorpe. *Linc* 3H 75
Scotton. *Linc* 1F 87
Scotton. *N Yor*
nr. Catterick Garrison 5E 105
nr. Harrogate 4F 99
Scottow. *Norf* 3E 79
Scoulton. *Norf* 5B 78
Scounslow Green. *Staf* 3E 73
Scourie. *High* 4B 166
Scourie More. *High* 4B 166
Scousburgh. *Shet* 10E 173
Scout Green. *Cumb* 4G 103
Scouthead. *G Man* 4H 91
Scrabster. *High* 1C 168
Scrafield. *Linc* 4C 88
Scrainwood. *Nmbd* 4D 121
Scrane End. *Linc* 1C 76
Scraptoft. *Leics* 5D 74
Scratby. *Norf* 4H 79
Scrayingham. *N Yor* 3B 100
Scredington. *Linc* 1H 75
Scremby. *Linc* 4D 88
Scremerston. *Nmbd* 5G 131
Screveton. *Notts* 1E 75
Scrivelsby. *Linc* 4B 88
Scriven. *N Yor* 4F 99
Scronkey. *Lanc* 5D 96
Scrooby. *Notts* 1D 86
Scropton. *Derbs* 2F 73
Scrub Hill. *Linc* 5B 88
Scruton. *N Yor* 5F 105
Scuggate. *Cumb* 2F 113
Sculamus. *High* 1E 147
Sculcoates. *Hull* 1D 94
Sculthorpe. *Norf* 2B 78
Scunthorpe. *N Lin* 3B 94
Scurlage. *Swan* 4D 30
Sea. *Som* 1G 13
Seaborough. *Dors* 2H 13
Seabridge. *Staf* 1C 72
Seabrook. *Kent* 2F 29
Seaburn. *Tyne* 3H 115
Seacombe. *Mers* 1F 83
Seacroft. *Linc* 4E 89
Seacroft. *W Yor* 1D 92
Seadyke. *Linc* 2C 76
Seafield. *High* 5G 165
Seafield. *Midl* 3F 129
Seafield. *S Ayr* 2C 116
Seafield. *W Lot* 3D 128
Seaford. *E Sus* 5F 27
Seaforde. *New M* 5J 179
Seaforth. *Mers* 1F 83
Seagrave. *Leics* 4D 74
Seaham. *Dur* 5H 115
Seahouses. *Nmbd* 1G 121
Seal. *Kent* 5G 39
Sealand. *Flin* 4F 83
Seale. *Surr* 2G 25
Seamer. *N Yor*
nr. Scarborough 1E 101
nr. Stokesley 3B 106
Seamill. *N Ayr* 5D 126
Sea Mills. *Bris* 4A 34
Sea Palling. *Norf* 3G 79
Seapatrick. *Arm* 5F 178
Searby. *Linc* 4D 94
Seasalter. *Kent* 4E 41
Seascale. *Cumb* 4B 102
Seaside. *Per* 1E 137
Seater. *High* 1F 169
Seathorne. *Linc* 4E 89
Seathwaite. *Cumb*
nr. Buttermere 3D 102
nr. Ulpha 5D 102
Seatle. *Cumb* 1C 96
Seatoller. *Cumb* 3D 102
Seaton. *Corn* 3H 7
Seaton. *Cumb* 1B 102
Seaton. *Devn* 3F 13
Seaton. *Dur* 4G 115
Seaton. *E Yor* 5F 101
Seaton. *Nmbd* 2G 115
Seaton. *Rut* 1G 63
Seaton Burn. *Tyne* 2F 115
Seaton Carew. *Hart* 2C 106
Seaton Delaval. *Nmbd* 2G 115
Seaton Junction. *Devn* 3F 13
Seaton Ross. *E Yor* 5B 100
Seaton Sluice. *Nmbd* 2G 115
Seatown. *Abers* 2C 160
Seatown. *Dors* 3H 13
Seatown. *Mor*
nr. Cullen 2C 160
nr. Lossiemouth 1G 159
Seave Green. *N Yor* 4C 106
Seaview. *IOW* 3E 17
Seaville. *Cumb* 4C 112
Seavington St Mary. *Som* 1H 13
Seavington St Michael. *Som* 1H 13
Seawick. *Essx* 4E 55
Sebastopol. *Torf* 2F 33
Sebergham. *Cumb* 5E 113
Seckington. *Warw* 5G 73
Second Coast. *High* 4D 162
Sedbergh. *Cumb* 5H 103
Sedbury. *Glos* 2A 34
Sedbusk. *N Yor* 5B 104
Sedgeberrow. *Worc* 2F 49
Sedgebrook. *Linc* 2F 75
Sedgefield. *Dur* 2A 106
Sedgeford. *Norf* 2G 77
Sedgehill. *Wilts* 4D 22
Sedgley. *W Mid* 1D 60
Sedgwick. *Cumb* 1E 97
Sedlescombe. *E Sus* 4B 28
Seend. *Wilts* 5E 35
Seend Cleeve. *Wilts* 5E 35
Seer Green. *Buck* 1A 38
Seething. *Norf* 1F 67
Sefster. *Shet* 6E 173
Sefton. *Mers* 4B 90
Sefton Park. *Mers* 2F 83
Segensworth. *Hants* 2D 16
Seggat. *Abers* 4E 161
Seghill. *Nmbd* 2F 115
Seifton. *Shrp* 2G 59
Seighford. *Staf* 3C 72
Seilebost. *W Isl* 8C 171
Seisdon. *Staf* 1C 60
Seisiadar. *W Isl* 4H 171
Selattyn. *Shrp* 2E 71
Selborne. *Hants* 3F 25
Selby. *N Yor* 1G 93
Selham. *W Sus* 3A 26
Selkirk. *Bord* 2G 119
Sellack. *Here* 3A 48
Sellafirth. *Shet* 2G 173
Sellick's Green. *Som* 1F 13
Sellindge. *Kent* 2F 29
Selling. *Kent* 5E 41
Sells Green. *Wilts* 5E 35
Selly Oak. *W Mid* 2E 61
Selmeston. *E Sus* 5G 27
Selsdon. *G Lon* 4E 39
Selsey. *W Sus* 3G 17
Selsfield Common. *W Sus* 2E 27
Selside. *Cumb* 5G 103
Selside. *N Yor* 2G 97
Selsley. *Glos* 5D 48
Selsted. *Kent* 1G 29
Selston. *Notts* 5B 86
Selworthy. *Som* 2C 20
Semblister. *Shet* 6E 173
Semer. *Suff* 1D 54
Semington. *Wilts* 5D 35
Semley. *Wilts* 4D 23
Sempringham. *Linc* 2A 76
Send. *Surr* 5B 38
Send Marsh. *Surr* 5B 38
Senghenydd. *Cphy* 2E 32
Sennen. *Corn* 4A 4
Sennen Cove. *Corn* 4A 4
Sennybridge. *Powy* 3C 46
Serlby. *Notts* 2D 86
Seskinore. *Ferm* 3K 177
Sessay. *N Yor* 2G 99
Setchey. *Norf* 4F 77
Setley. *Hants* 2B 16
Setter. *Shet* 3F 173
Settiscarth. *Orkn* 6C 172
Settle. *N Yor* 3H 97
Settrington. *N Yor* 2C 100
Seven Ash. *Som* 3E 21
Sevenhampton. *Glos* 3F 49
Sevenhampton. *Swin* 2H 35
Sevenoaks. *Kent* 5G 39
Sevenoaks Weald. *Kent* 5G 39
Seven Sisters. *Neat* 5B 46
Seven Springs. *Glos* 4E 49
Severn Beach. *S Glo* 3A 34
Severn Stoke. *Worc* 1D 48
Sevington. *Kent* 1E 29
Sewards End. *Essx* 2F 53
Sewardstone. *Essx* 1E 39
Sewell. *C Beds* 3H 51
Sewerby. *E Yor* 3G 101
Seworgan. *Corn* 5B 6
Sewstern. *Leics* 3F 75
Sgallairidh. *W Isl* 9B 170
Sgarasta Mhor. *W Isl* 8C 171
Sgiogarstaigh. *W Isl* 1H 171
Sgreadan. *Arg* 4A 132
Shabbington. *Buck* 5E 51
Shackerley. *Shrp* 5C 72
Shackerstone. *Leics* 5A 74
Shackleford. *Surr* 1A 26
Shadforth. *Dur* 5G 115
Shadingfield. *Suff* 2G 67
Shadoxhurst. *Kent* 2D 28
Shadsworth. *Bkbn* 2F 91
Shadwell. *Norf* 2B 66
Shadwell. *W Yor* 1D 92
Shaftesbury. *Dors* 4D 22
Shafton. *S Yor* 3D 93
Shafton Two Gates. *S Yor* 3D 93
Shaggs. *Dors* 4D 14
Shakesfield. *Glos* 2B 48
Shalbourne. *Wilts* 5B 36
Shalcombe. *IOW* 4B 16
Shalden. *Hants* 2E 25
Shaldon. *Devn* 5C 12
Shalfleet. *IOW* 4C 16
Shalford. *Essx* 3H 53
Shalford. *Surr* 1B 26
Shalford Green. *Essx* 3H 53
Shallowford. *Devn* 2H 19
Shallowford. *Staf* 3C 72
Shalmsford Street. *Kent* 5E 41
Shalstone. *Buck* 2E 51
Shamley Green. *Surr* 1B 26
Shandon. *Arg* 1D 126
Shandwick. *High* 1C 158
Shangton. *Leics* 1E 62
Shankhouse. *Nmbd* 2F 115
Shanklin. *IOW* 4D 16
Shannochie. *N Ayr* 3D 123
Shap. *Cumb* 3G 103
Shapwick. *Dors* 2E 15
Shapwick. *Som* 3H 21
Sharcott. *Wilts* 1G 23
Shardlow. *Derbs* 2B 74
Shareshill. *Staf* 5D 72
Sharlston. *W Yor* 3D 93
Sharlston Common. *W Yor* 3D 93
Sharnal Street. *Medw* 3B 40
Sharnbrook. *Bed* 5G 63
Sharneyford. *Lanc* 2G 91
Sharnford. *Leics* 1B 62
Sharnhill Green. *Dors* 2C 14
Sharoe Green. *Lanc* 1D 90
Sharow. *N Yor* 2F 99
Sharpenhoe. *C Beds* 2A 52
Sharperton. *Nmbd* 4D 120
Sharpness. *Glos* 5B 48
Sharp Street. *Norf* 3F 79
Sharpthorne. *W Sus* 2E 27
Sharrington. *Norf* 2C 78
Shatterford. *Worc* 2B 60
Shatton. *Derbs* 2F 85
Shaugh Prior. *Devn* 2B 8
Shavington. *Ches E* 5B 84
Shaw. *G Man* 4H 91
Shaw. *W Ber* 5C 36
Shaw. *Wilts* 5D 35
Shawbirch. *Telf* 4A 72
Shawbury. *Shrp* 3H 71
Shawell. *Leics* 2C 62
Shawford. *Hants* 4C 24

Shawforth—Sower Carr

Shawforth. *Lanc* 2G 91
Shaw Green. *Lanc* 3D 90
Shawhead. *Dum* 2F 111
Shaw Mills. *N Yor* 3E 99
Shawwood. *E Ayr* 2E 117
Shearington. *Dum* 3B 112
Shearsby. *Leics* 1D 62
Shearston. *Som* 3F 21
Shebbear. *Devn* 2E 11
Shebdon. *Staf* 3B 72
Shebster. *High* 2C 168
Sheddocksley. *Aber* 3F 153
Shedfield. *Hants* 1D 16
Shedog. *N Ayr* 2D 122
Sheen. *Staf* 4F 85
Sheepbridge. *Derbs* 3A 86
Sheep Hill. *Dur* 4E 115
Sheepscar. *W Yor* 1D 92
Sheepscombe. *Glos* 4D 49
Sheepstor. *Devn* 2B 8
Sheepwash. *Devn* 2E 11
Sheepwash. *Nmbd* 1F 115
Sheepway. *N Som* 4H 33
Sheepy Magna. *Leics* 5H 73
Sheepy Parva. *Leics* 5H 73
Sheering. *Essx* 4F 53
Sheerness. *Kent* 3D 40
Sheerwater. *Surr* 4B 38
Sheet. *Hants* 4F 25
Sheffield. *S Yor* 202 (2A 86)
Sheffield Bottom. *W Ber* 5E 37
Sheffield Green. *E Sus* 3F 27
Shefford. *C Beds* 2B 52
Shefford Woodlands.
 W Ber 4B 36
Sheigra. *High* 2B 166
Sheinton. *Shrp* 5A 72
Shelderton. *Shrp* 3G 59
Sheldon. *Derbs* 4F 85
Sheldon. *Devn* 2E 12
Sheldon. *W Mid* 2F 61
Sheldwich. *Kent* 5E 40
Sheldwich Lees. *Kent* 5E 40
Shelf. *W Yor* 2B 92
Shelfanger. *Norf* 2D 66
Shelfield. *Warw* 4F 61
Shelfield. *W Mid* 5E 73
Shelford. *Notts* 1D 74
Shelford. *Warw* 2B 62
Shell. *Worc* 5D 60
Shelley. *Suff* 2D 54
Shelley. *W Yor* 3C 92
Shell Green. *Hal* 2H 83
Shellingford. *Oxon* 2B 36
Shellow Bowells. *Essx* 5G 53
Shelsley Beauchamp.
 Worc 4B 60
Shelsley Walsh. *Worc* 4B 60
Shelthorpe. *Leics* 4C 74
Shelton. *Bed* 4H 63
Shelton. *Norf* 1E 67
Shelton. *Notts* 1E 75
Shelton. *Shrp* 4G 71
Shelton Green. *Norf* 1E 67
Shelton Lock. *Derb* 2A 74
Shelve. *Shrp* 1F 59
Shelwick. *Here* 1A 48
Shelwick Green. *Here* 1A 48
Shenfield. *Essx* 1H 39
Shenington. *Oxon* 1B 50
Shenley. *Herts* 5B 52
Shenley Brook End. *Mil* 2G 51
Shenleybury. *Herts* 5B 52
Shenley Church End. *Mil* 2G 51
Shenmore. *Here* 2G 47
Shennanton. *Dum* 3A 110
Shenstone. *Staf* 5F 73
Shenstone. *Worc* 3C 60
Shenstone Woodend. *Staf* 5F 73
Shenton. *Leics* 5A 74
Shenval. *Mor* 1G 151
Shepeau Stow. *Linc* 4C 76
Shephall. *Herts* 3C 52
Shepherd's Bush. *G Lon* 2D 38
Shepherd's Gate. *Norf* 4E 77
Shepherd's Green. *Oxon* 3F 37
Shepherd's Port. *Norf* 2F 77
Shepherdswell. *Kent* 1G 29
Shepley. *W Yor* 4B 92
Sheppardstown. *High* 4D 169
Shepperdine. *S Glo* 2B 34
Shepperton. *Surr* 4B 38
Shepreth. *Cambs* 1D 53
Shepshed. *Leics* 4B 74
Shepton Beauchamp.
 Som 1H 13
Shepton Mallet. *Som* 2B 22
Shepton Montague. *Som* 3B 22
Shepway. *Kent* 5B 40
Sheraton. *Dur* 1B 106
Sherborne. *Dors* 1B 14
Sherborne. *Glos* 4G 49
Sherborne. *Som* 1A 22
Sherborne Causeway.
 Dors 4D 22
Sherborne St John. *Hants* 1E 24
Sherbourne. *Warw* 4G 61
Sherburn. *Dur* 5G 115
Sherburn. *N Yor* 2D 100
Sherburn Hill. *Dur* 5G 115
Sherburn in Elmet. *N Yor* 1E 93
Shere. *Surr* 1B 26
Shereford. *Norf* 3A 78
Sherfield English. *Hants* 4A 24
Sherfield on Loddon.
 Hants 1E 25
Sherford. *Devn* 4D 9
Sherford. *Dors* 3E 15
Sheriffhales. *Shrp* 4B 72
Sheriff Hutton. *N Yor* 3A 100
Sheriffston. *Mor* 2G 159
Sheringham. *Norf* 1D 78
Sherington. *Mil* 1G 51
Shermanbury. *W Sus* 4D 26
Shernal Green. *Worc* 4D 60
Shernborne. *Norf* 2G 77
Sherrington. *Wilts* 3E 23
Sherston. *Wilts* 3D 34
Sherwood. *Nott* 1C 74
Sherwood Green. *Devn* 4F 19
Shettleston. *Glas* 3H 127
Shevington. *G Man* 4D 90
Shevington Moor. *G Man* 3D 90
Shevington Vale. *G Man* 4D 90
Sheviock. *Corn* 3H 7
Shide. *IOW* 4C 16
Shiel Bridge. *High* 2B 148
Shieldaig. *High*
 nr. Charlestown 1H 155
 nr. Torridon 3H 155
Shieldhill. *Dum* 1B 112
Shieldhill. *Falk* 2B 128
Shieldhill. *S Lan* 5D 128
Shieldmuir. *N Lan* 4A 128
Shielfoot. *High* 1A 140
Shielhill. *Abers* 3H 161
Shielhill. *Ang* 3D 144
Shifnal. *Shrp* 5B 72
Shilbottle. *Nmbd* 4F 121
Shilbottle Grange. *Nmbd* 4G 121
Shildon. *Dur* 2F 105
Shillford. *E Ren* 4F 127
Shillingford. *Devn* 4C 20
Shillingford. *Oxon* 2D 36
Shillingford St George.
 Devn 4C 12
Shillingstone. *Dors* 1D 14
Shillington. *C Beds* 2B 52
Shillmoor. *Nmbd* 4C 120
Shilton. *Oxon* 5A 50
Shilton. *Warw* 2B 62
Shilvinghampton. *Dors* 4A 14
Shilvington. *Nmbd* 1E 115
Shimpling. *Norf* 2D 66
Shimpling. *Suff* 5A 66
Shimpling Street. *Suff* 5A 66
Shincliffe. *Dur* 5F 115
Shiney Row. *Tyne* 4G 115
Shinfield. *Wok* 5F 37
Shingay. *Cambs* 1D 52
Shingham. *Norf* 5G 77
Shingle Street. *Suff* 1G 55
Shinner's Bridge. *Devn* 2D 9
Shinness. *High* 2C 164
Shipbourne. *Kent* 5G 39
Shipdham. *Norf* 5B 78
Shipham. *Som* 1H 21
Shiphay. *Torb* 2E 9
Shiplake. *Oxon* 4F 37
Shipley. *Derbs* 1B 74
Shipley. *Nmbd* 3F 121
Shipley. *Shrp* 1C 60
Shipley. *W Sus* 3C 26
Shipley. *W Yor* 1B 92
Shipley Bridge. *Surr* 1E 27
Shipmeadow. *Suff* 2F 67
Shippon. *Oxon* 2C 36
Shipston-on-Stour. *Warw* 1A 50
Shipton. *Buck* 3F 51
Shipton. *Glos* 4F 49
Shipton. *N Yor* 4H 99
Shipton. *Shrp* 1H 59
Shipton Bellinger. *Hants* 2H 23
Shipton Gorge. *Dors* 3H 13
Shipton Green. *W Sus* 3G 17
Shipton Moyne. *Glos* 3D 35
Shipton-on-Cherwell.
 Oxon 4C 50
Shiptonthorpe. *E Yor* 5C 100
Shipton-under-Wychwood.
 Oxon 4A 50
Shirburn. *Oxon* 2E 37
Shirdley Hill. *Lanc* 3B 90
Shire. *Cumb* 1H 103
Shirebrook. *Derbs* 4C 86
Shiregreen. *S Yor* 1A 86
Shirehampton. *Bris* 4A 34
Shiremoor. *Tyne* 2G 115
Shirenewton. *Mon* 2H 33
Shireoaks. *Notts* 2C 86
Shires Mill. *Fife* 1D 128
Shirkoak. *Kent* 2D 28
Shirland. *Derbs* 5A 86
Shirley. *Derbs* 1G 73
Shirley. *Sotn* 1B 16
Shirley. *W Mid* 3F 61
Shirleywich. *Staf* 3D 73
Shirl Heath. *Here* 5G 59
Shirrell Heath. *Hants* 1D 16
Shirwell. *Devn* 3F 19
Shiskine. *N Ayr* 3D 122
Shobdon. *Here* 4F 59
Shobnall. *Staf* 3G 73
Shobrooke. *Devn* 2B 12
Shoby. *Leics* 3D 74
Shocklach. *Ches W* 1G 71
Shoeburyness. *S'end* 2D 40
Sholden. *Kent* 5H 41
Sholing. *Sotn* 1C 16
Sholver. *G Man* 4H 91
Shoot Hill. *Shrp* 4G 71
Shop. *Corn*
 nr. Bude 1C 10
 nr. Padstow 1C 6
Shop. *Devn* 1D 11
Shopford. *Cumb* 2G 113
Shoreditch. *G Lon* 2E 39
Shoreditch. *Som* 4F 21
Shoregill. *Cumb* 4A 104
Shoreham. *Kent* 4G 39
Shoreham-by-Sea.
 W Sus 5D 26
Shoresdean. *Nmbd* 5F 131
Shoreswood. *Nmbd* 5F 131
Shorncote. *Glos* 2F 35
Shorne. *Kent* 3A 40
Shorne Ridgeway. *Kent* 3A 40
Shortacombe. *Devn* 4F 11
Shortbridge. *E Sus* 3F 27
Shortgate. *E Sus* 4F 27
Short Green. *Norf* 2C 66
Shorthampton. *Oxon* 3B 50
Short Heath. *Derbs* 4H 73
Short Heath. *W Mid*
 nr. Erdington 1E 61
 nr. Wednesfield 5D 73
Shortlanesend. *Corn* 4C 6
Shorton. *Torb* 2E 9
Shortstown. *Bed* 1A 52
Shortwood. *S Glo* 4B 34
Shorwell. *IOW* 4C 16
Shoscombe. *Bath* 1C 22
Shotesham. *Norf* 1E 67
Shotgate. *Essx* 1B 40
Shotley. *Suff* 2F 55
Shotley Bridge. *Dur* 4D 115
Shotleyfield. *Nmbd* 4D 114
Shotley Gate. *Suff* 2F 55
Shottenden. *Kent* 5E 41
Shottermill. *Surr* 3G 25
Shottery. *Warw* 5F 61
Shotteswell. *Warw* 1C 50
Shottisham. *Suff* 1G 55
Shottle. *Derbs* 1H 73
Shotton. *Dur*
 nr. Peterlee 1B 106
 nr. Sedgefield 2A 106
Shotton. *Flin* 4F 83
Shotton. *Nmbd*
 nr. Morpeth 2F 115
 nr. Town Yetholm 1C 120
Shotton Colliery. *Dur* 5G 115
Shotts. *N Lan* 3B 128
Shotwick. *Ches W* 3F 83
Shouldham. *Norf* 5F 77
Shouldham Thorpe. *Norf* 5F 77
Shoulton. *Worc* 5C 60
Shrawardine. *Shrp* 4G 71
Shrawley. *Worc* 4C 60
Shreding Green. *Buck* 2B 38
Shrewley. *Warw* 4G 61
Shrewsbury. *Shrp* 202 (4G 71)
Shrewton. *Wilts* 2F 23
Shripney. *W Sus* 5A 26
Shrivenham. *Oxon* 3H 35
Shropham. *Norf* 1B 66
Shroton. *Dors* 1D 14
Shrub End. *Essx* 3C 54
Shucknall. *Here* 1A 48
Shudy Camps. *Cambs* 1G 53
Shulishadermor. *High* 4D 155
Shulista. *High* 1D 154
Shurdington. *Glos* 4E 49
Shurlock Row. *Wind* 4G 37
Shurrery. *High* 3C 168
Shurton. *Som* 2F 21
Shustoke. *Warw* 1G 61
Shute. *Devn*
 nr. Axminster 3F 13
 nr. Crediton 2B 12
Shutford. *Oxon* 1B 50
Shut Heath. *Staf* 3C 72
Shuthonger. *Glos* 2D 49
Shutlanehead. *Staf* 1C 72
Shutlanger. *Nptn* 1F 51
Shutt Green. *Staf* 5C 72
Shuttington. *Warw* 5G 73
Shuttlewood. *Derbs* 3B 86
Shuttleworth. *G Man* 3G 91
Siabost. *W Isl* 3E 171
Siabost bho Dheas. *W Isl* 3E 171
Siabost bho Thuath.
 W Isl 3E 171
Siadar. *W Isl* 2F 171
Siadar Uarach. *W Isl* 2F 171
Sibbaldbie. *Dum* 1C 112
Sibbertoft. *Nptn* 2D 62
Sibdon Carwood. *Shrp* 2G 59
Sibertswold. *Kent* 1G 29
Sibford Ferris. *Oxon* 2B 50
Sibford Gower. *Oxon* 2B 50
Sible Hedingham. *Essx* 2A 54
Sibsey. *Linc* 5C 88
Sibsey Fen Side. *Linc* 5C 88
Sibson. *Cambs* 1H 63
Sibson. *Leics* 5A 74
Sibster. *High* 3F 169
Sibthorpe. *Notts* 1E 75
Sibton. *Suff* 4F 67
Sicklesmere. *Suff* 4A 66
Sicklinghall. *N Yor* 5F 99
Sid. *Devn* 4E 13
Sidbury. *Devn* 3E 13
Sidbury. *Shrp* 2A 60
Sidcot. *N Som* 1H 21
Sidcup. *G Lon* 3F 39
Siddick. *Cumb* 1B 102
Siddington. *Ches E* 3C 84
Siddington. *Glos* 2F 35
Side of the Moor. *G Man* 3F 91
Sidestrand. *Norf* 2E 79
Sidford. *Devn* 3E 13
Sidlesham. *W Sus* 3G 17
Sidley. *E Sus* 5B 28
Sidlow. *Surr* 1D 26
Sidmouth. *Devn* 4E 13
Sigford. *Devn* 5A 12
Sigglesthorne. *E Yor* 5F 101
Sighthill. *Edin* 2E 129
Sigingstone. *V Glam* 4C 32
Signet. *Oxon* 4H 49
Silchester. *Hants* 5E 37
Sildinis. *W Isl* 6E 171
Sileby. *Leics* 4D 74
Silecroft. *Cumb* 1A 96
Silfield. *Norf* 1D 66
Silian. *Cdgn* 5E 57
Silkstone. *S Yor* 4C 92
Silkstone Common. *S Yor* 4C 92
Silksworth. *Tyne* 4G 115
Silk Willoughby. *Linc* 1H 75
Silloth. *Cumb* 4C 112
Sills. *Nmbd* 4C 120
Sillyearn. *Mor* 3C 160
Silpho. *N Yor* 5G 107
Silsden. *W Yor* 5C 98
Silsoe. *C Beds* 2A 52
Silverbank. *Abers* 4E 152
Silverbridge. *New M* 8D 178
Silverburn. *Midl* 3F 129
Silverdale. *Lanc* 2D 96
Silverdale. *Staf* 1C 72
Silverdale Green. *Lanc* 2D 96
Silver End. *Essx* 4B 54
Silver End. *W Mid* 2D 60
Silvergate. *Norf* 3D 78
Silver Green. *Norf* 1E 67
Silverhillocks. *Abers* 2E 161
Silverley's Green. *Suff* 3E 67
Silverstone. *Nptn* 1E 51
Silverton. *Devn* 2C 12
Silverton. *W Dun* 2F 127
Silvington. *Shrp* 3A 60
Simm's Cross. *Hal* 2H 83
Simm's Lane End. *Mers* 4D 90
Simonburn. *Nmbd* 2B 114
Simonsbath. *Som* 3A 20
Simonstone. *Lanc* 1F 91
Simprim. *Bord* 5E 131
Simpson. *Pemb* 3C 42
Simpson Cross. *Pemb* 3C 42
Sinclairston. *E Ayr* 3D 116
Sinclairtown. *Fife* 4E 137
Sinderby. *N Yor* 1F 99
Sinderhope. *Nmbd* 4B 114
Sindlesham. *Wok* 5F 37
Sinfin. *Derb* 2H 73
Singleborough. *Buck* 2F 51
Singleton. *Kent* 1D 28
Singleton. *Lanc* 1B 90
Singleton. *W Sus* 1G 17
Singlewell. *Kent* 3A 40
Sinkhurst Green. *Kent* 1C 28
Sinnahard. *Abers* 2B 152
Sinnington. *N Yor* 1B 100
Sinton Green. *Worc* 4C 60
Sion Mills. *Derr* 3F 176
Sipson. *G Lon* 3B 38
Sirhowy. *Blae* 4E 47
Sisland. *Norf* 1F 67
Sissinghurst. *Kent* 2B 28
Siston. *S Glo* 4B 34
Sithney. *Corn* 4D 4
Sittingbourne. *Kent* 4D 40
Six Ashes. *Staf* 2B 60
Six Bells. *Blae* 5F 47
Six Hills. *Leics* 3D 74
Sixhills. *Linc* 2A 88
Six Mile Bottom. *Cambs* 5E 65
Sixmilecross. *Ferm* 3L 177
Sixpenny Handley. *Dors* 1E 15
Sizewell. *Suff* 4G 67
Skail. *High* 4H 167
Skaill. *Orkn* 6B 172
Skaills. *Orkn* 7E 172
Skares. *E Ayr* 3E 117
Skateraw. *E Lot* 2D 130
Skaw. *Shet* 5G 173
Skeabost. *High* 4D 154
Skeabrae. *Orkn* 5B 172
Skeeby. *N Yor* 4E 105
Skeffington. *Leics* 5E 75
Skeffling. *E Yor* 3G 95
Skegby. *Notts*
 nr. Mansfield 4B 86
 nr. Tuxford 3E 87
Skegness. *Linc* 4E 89
Skelberry. *Shet*
 nr. Boddam 10E 173
 nr. Housetter 3E 173
Skelbo. *High* 4E 165
Skelbo Street. *High* 4E 165
Skelbrooke. *S Yor* 3F 93
Skeldyke. *Linc* 2C 76
Skelfhill. *Bord* 4G 119
Skellingthorpe. *Linc* 3G 87
Skellister. *Shet* 6F 173
Skellorn Green. *Ches E* 2D 84
Skellow. *S Yor* 3F 93
Skelmanthorpe. *W Yor* 3C 92
Skelmersdale. *Lanc* 4C 90
Skelmorlie. *N Ayr* 3C 126
Skelpick. *High* 3H 167
Skelton. *Cumb* 1F 103
Skelton. *E Yor* 2A 94
Skelton. *N Yor*
 nr. Richmond 4D 105
 nr. Ripon 3F 99
Skelton. *Red C* 3D 106
Skelton. *York* 4H 99
Skelton Green. *Red C* 3D 106
Skelwick. *Orkn* 3D 172
Skelwith Bridge. *Cumb* 4E 103
Skendleby. *Linc* 4D 88
Skendleby Psalter. *Linc* 3D 88
Skenfrith. *Mon* 3H 47
Skerne. *E Yor* 4E 101
Skeroblingarry. *Arg* 3B 122
Skerray. *High* 2G 167
Skerricha. *High* 3C 166
Skerries Airport. *Shet* 4H 173
Skerton. *Lanc* 3D 97
Sketchley. *Leics* 1B 62
Sketty. *Swan* 3F 31
Skewen. *Neat* 3G 31
Skewsby. *N Yor* 2A 100
Skeyton. *Norf* 3E 79
Skeyton Corner. *Norf* 3E 79
Skiall. *High* 2C 168
Skidbrooke. *Linc* 1D 88
Skidbrooke North End.
 Linc 1D 88
Skidby. *E Yor* 1D 94
Skilgate. *Som* 4C 20
Skillington. *Linc* 3F 75
Skinburness. *Cumb* 4C 112
Skinflats. *Falk* 1C 128
Skinidin. *High* 4B 154
Skinnet. *High* 2F 167
Skinningrove. *Red C* 3E 107
Skipness. *Arg* 4G 125
Skippool. *Lanc* 5C 96
Skiprigg. *Cumb* 5E 113
Skipsea. *E Yor* 4F 101
Skipsea Brough. *E Yor* 4F 101
Skipton. *N Yor* 4B 98
Skipton-on-Swale. *N Yor* 2F 99
Skipwith. *N Yor* 1G 93
Skirbeck. *Linc* 1C 76
Skirbeck Quarter. *Linc* 1C 76
Skirlaugh. *E Yor* 1E 95
Skirling. *Bord* 1C 118
Skirmett. *Buck* 2F 37
Skirpenbeck. *E Yor* 4B 100
Skirwith. *Cumb* 1H 103
Skirwith. *N Yor* 2G 97
Skirza. *High* 2F 169
Skitby. *Cumb* 3F 113
Skitham. *Lanc* 5D 96
Skittle Green. *Buck* 5F 51
Skroo. *Shet* 1B 172
Skulamus. *High* 1E 147
Skullomie. *High* 2G 167
Skyborry Green. *Shrp* 3E 59
Skye Green. *Essx* 3B 54
Skye of Curr. *High* 1D 151
Slack. *W Yor* 2H 91
The Slack. *Dur* 2E 105
Slackhall. *Derbs* 2E 85
Slack Head. *Cumb* 2D 97
Slackhead. *Mor* 2B 160
Slackholme End. *Linc* 3E 89
Slacks of Cairnbanno.
 Abers 4F 161
Slad. *Glos* 5D 48
Slade. *Swan* 4D 31
The Slade. *W Ber* 5D 36
Slade End. *Oxon* 2D 36
Slade Field. *Cambs* 2C 64
Slade Green. *G Lon* 3G 39
Slade Heath. *Staf* 5D 72
Slade Hooton. *S Yor* 2C 86
Sladesbridge. *Corn* 5A 10
Slaggyford. *Nmbd* 4H 113
Slaidburn. *Lanc* 4G 97
Slaid Hill. *W Yor* 5F 99
Slaithwaite. *W Yor* 3A 92
Slaley. *Derbs* 5G 85
Slaley. *Nmbd* 4C 114
Slamannan. *Falk* 2B 128
Slapton. *Buck* 3H 51
Slapton. *Devn* 4E 9
Slapton. *Nptn* 1E 51
Slattocks. *G Man* 4G 91
Slaugham. *W Sus* 3D 26
Slaughterbridge. *Corn* 4B 10
Slaughterford. *Wilts* 4D 34
Slawston. *Leics* 1E 63
Sleaford. *Hants* 3G 25
Sleaford. *Linc* 1H 75
Sleagill. *Cumb* 3G 103
Sleap. *Shrp* 3G 71
Sledmere. *E Yor* 3D 100
Sleightholme. *Dur* 3C 104
Sleights. *N Yor* 4F 107
Slepe. *Dors* 3E 15
Slickly. *High* 2E 169
Sliddery. *N Ayr* 3D 122
Sligachan. *High* 1C 146
Slimbridge. *Glos* 5C 48
Slindon. *Staf* 2C 72
Slindon. *W Sus* 5A 26
Slinfold. *W Sus* 2C 26
Slingsby. *N Yor* 2A 100
Slip End. *C Beds* 4A 52
Slipton. *Nptn* 3G 63
Slitting Mill. *Staf* 4E 73
Slochd. *High* 1C 150
Slockavullin. *Arg* 4F 133
Sloley. *Norf* 3E 79
Sloncombe. *Devn* 4H 11
Sloothby. *Linc* 3D 89
Slough. *Slo* 3A 38
Slough Green. *Som* 4F 21
Slough Green. *W Sus* 3D 27
Sluggan. *High* 1C 150
Slyne. *Lanc* 3D 97
Smailholm. *Bord* 1A 120
Smallbridge. *G Man* 3H 91
Smallbrook. *Devn* 3B 12
Smallburgh. *Norf* 3F 79
Smallburn. *E Ayr* 2F 117
Smalldale. *Derbs* 3E 85
Small Dole. *W Sus* 4D 26
Smalley. *Derbs* 1B 74
Smallfield. *Surr* 1E 27
Small Heath. *W Mid* 2E 61
Smallholm. *Dum* 2C 112
Small Hythe. *Kent* 2C 28
Smallrice. *Staf* 2D 72
Smallridge. *Devn* 2G 13
Smallwood Hey. *Lanc* 5C 96
Smallworth. *Norf* 2C 66
Smannell. *Hants* 2B 24
Smardale. *Cumb* 4A 104
Smarden. *Kent* 1C 28
Smarden Bell. *Kent* 1C 28
Smart's Hill. *Kent* 1G 27
Smeatharpe. *Devn* 1F 13
Smeeth. *Kent* 2E 29
The Smeeth. *Norf* 4E 77
Smeeton Westerby. *Leics* 1D 62
Smercleit. *W Isl* 7C 170
Smerral. *High* 5D 168
Smestow. *Staf* 1C 60
Smethwick. *W Mid* 2E 61
Smirisary. *High* 1A 140
Smisby. *Derbs* 4H 73
Smitham Hill. *Bath* 1A 22
Smith End Green. *Worc* 5B 60
Smithfield. *Cumb* 3F 113
Smith Green. *Lanc* 4D 97
The Smithies. *Shrp* 1A 60
Smithincott. *Devn* 1D 12
Smith's Green. *Essx* 3F 53
Smithstown. *High* 1G 155
Smithton. *High* 4B 158
Smithwood Green. *Suff* 5B 66
Smithy Bridge. *G Man* 3H 91
Smithy Green. *Ches E* 3B 84
Smithy Lane Ends. *Lanc* 3C 90
Smockington. *Leics* 2B 62
Smoogro. *Orkn* 7C 172
Smythe's Green. *Essx* 4C 54
Snaigow House. *Per* 4H 143
Snailbeach. *Shrp* 5F 71
Snailwell. *Cambs* 4F 65
Snainton. *N Yor* 1D 100
Snaith. *E Yor* 2G 93
Snape. *N Yor* 1E 99
Snape. *Suff* 5F 67
Snape Green. *Lanc* 3B 90
Snapper. *Devn* 3F 19
Snarestone. *Leics* 5H 73
Snarford. *Linc* 2H 87
Snargate. *Kent* 3D 28
Snave. *Kent* 3E 28
Sneachill. *Worc* 5D 60
Snead. *Powy* 1F 59
Snead Common. *Worc* 4B 60
Sneaton. *N Yor* 4F 107
Sneatonthorpe. *N Yor* 4G 107
Snelland. *Linc* 2H 87
Snelston. *Derbs* 1F 73
Snetterton. *Norf* 1B 66
Snettisham. *Norf* 2F 77
Snibston. *Leics* 4B 74
Sniseabhal. *W Isl* 5C 170
Snitter. *Nmbd* 4E 121
Snitterby. *Linc* 1G 87
Snitterfield. *Warw* 5G 61
Snitton. *Shrp* 3H 59
Snodhill. *Here* 1G 47
Snodland. *Kent* 4B 40
Snods Edge. *Nmbd* 4D 114
Snowshill. *Glos* 2F 49
Snow Street. *Norf* 2C 66
Snydale. *W Yor* 3E 93
Soake. *Hants* 1E 17
Soar. *Carm* 3G 45
Soar. *Gwyn* 2F 69
Soar. *IOA* 3C 80
Soar. *Powy* 2C 46
Soberton. *Hants* 1E 16
Soberton Heath. *Hants* 1E 16
Sockbridge. *Cumb* 2G 103
Sockburn. *Darl* 4A 106
Sodom. *Den* 3C 82
Sodom. *Shet* 5G 173
Soham. *Cambs* 3E 65
Soham Cotes. *Cambs* 3E 65
Solas. *W Isl* 1D 170
Soldon Cross. *Devn* 1D 10
Soldridge. *Hants* 3E 25
Solent Breezes. *Hants* 2D 16
Sole Street. *Kent*
 nr. Meopham 4A 40
 nr. Waltham 1E 29
Solihull. *W Mid* 3F 61
Sollers Dilwyn. *Here* 5G 59
Sollers Hope. *Here* 2B 48
Sollom. *Lanc* 3C 90
Solva. *Pemb* 2B 42
Somerby. *Leics* 4E 75
Somerby. *Linc* 4D 94
Somercotes. *Derbs* 5B 86
Somerford. *Dors* 3G 15
Somerford. *Staf* 5C 72
Somerford Keynes. *Glos* 2F 35
Somerley. *W Sus* 3G 17
Somerleyton. *Suff* 1G 67
Somersal Herbert. *Derbs* 2F 73
Somersby. *Linc* 3C 88
Somersham. *Cambs* 3C 64
Somersham. *Suff* 1D 54
Somerton. *Oxon* 3C 50
Somerton. *Som* 4H 21
Somerton. *Suff* 5H 65
Sompting. *W Sus* 5C 26
Sonning. *Wok* 4F 37
Sonning Common. *Oxon* 3F 37
Sonning Eye. *Oxon* 4F 37
Sookholme. *Notts* 4C 86
Sopley. *Hants* 3G 15
Sopworth. *Wilts* 3D 34
Sorbie. *Dum* 5B 110
Sordale. *High* 2D 168
Sorisdale. *Arg* 2D 138
Sorn. *E Ayr* 2E 117
Sornhill. *E Ayr* 1E 117
Sortat. *High* 2E 169
Sotby. *Linc* 3B 88
Sots Hole. *Linc* 4A 88
Sotterley. *Suff* 2G 67
Soudley. *Shrp*
 nr. Church Stretton 1G 59
 nr. Market Drayton 3B 72
Soughton. *Flin* 4E 83
Soulbury. *Buck* 3G 51
Soulby. *Cumb*
 nr. Appleby 3A 104
 nr. Penrith 2F 103
Souldern. *Oxon* 2D 50
Souldrop. *Bed* 4G 63
Sound. *Ches E* 1A 72
Sound. *Shet*
 nr. Lerwick 7F 173
 nr. Tresta 6E 173
Soundwell. *S Glo* 4B 34
Sourhope. *Bord* 2C 120
Sourin. *Orkn* 4D 172
Sour Nook. *Cumb* 5E 113
Sourton. *Devn* 3F 11
Soutergate. *Cumb* 1B 96
South Acre. *Norf* 4H 77
Southall. *G Lon* 3C 38
South Allington. *Devn* 5D 9
South Alloa. *Falk* 4A 136
Southam. *Glos* 3E 49
Southam. *Warw* 4B 62
South Ambersham.
 W Sus 3A 26
Southampton.
 Sotn 202 (1C 16)
Southampton Airport.
 Hants 1C 16
Southannan. *N Ayr* 4D 126
South Anston. *S Yor* 2C 86
South Ascot. *Wind* 4A 38
South Baddesley. *Hants* 3B 16
South Balfern. *Dum* 4B 110
South Ballachulish. *High* 3E 141
South Bank. *Red C* 2C 106
South Barrow. *Som* 4B 22
South Benfleet. *Essx* 2B 40
South Bents. *Tyne* 3H 115
South Bersted. *W Sus* 5A 26
Southborough. *Kent* 1G 27
Southbourne. *Bour* 3G 15
Southbourne. *W Sus* 2F 17
South Bowood. *Dors* 3H 13
South Brent. *Devn* 3C 8
South Brewham. *Som* 3C 22
South Broomage. *Falk* 1B 128
South Broomhill. *Nmbd* 5G 121
Southburgh. *Norf* 5B 78
South Burlingham. *Norf* 5F 79
Southburn. *E Yor* 4D 101
South Cadbury. *Som* 4B 22
South Carlton. *Linc* 3G 87
South Cave. *E Yor* 1C 94
South Cerney. *Glos* 2F 35
South Chailey. *E Sus* 4E 27
South Chard. *Som* 2G 13
South Charlton. *Nmbd* 2F 121
South Cheriton. *Som* 4B 22
South Church. *Dur* 2F 105
Southchurch. *S'end* 2D 40
South Cleatlam. *Dur* 3E 105
South Cliffe. *E Yor* 1B 94
South Clifton. *Notts* 3F 87
South Clunes. *High* 4H 157
South Cockerington. *Linc* 2C 88
South Common. *Devn* 2G 13
South Cornelly. *B'end* 3B 32
Southcott. *Devn*
 nr. Great Torrington 1E 11
 nr. Okehampton 3F 11
Southcott. *Wilts* 1G 23
Southcourt. *Buck* 4G 51
South Cove. *Suff* 2G 67
South Creagan. *Arg* 4D 141
South Creake. *Norf* 2A 78
South Crosland. *W Yor* 3B 92
South Croxton. *Leics* 4D 74
South Dalton. *E Yor* 5D 100
South Darenth. *Kent* 4G 39
Southdean. *Bord* 4A 120
Southdown. *Bath* 5C 34
South Duffield. *N Yor* 1G 93
Southease. *E Sus* 5F 27
South Elkington. *Linc* 2B 88
South Elmsall. *W Yor* 3E 93
South End. *Cumb* 3B 96
South End. *N Lin* 2E 94
Southend. *Arg* 5A 122
Southend. *Glos* 2C 34
Southend. *W Ber* 4D 36
Southend Airport. *Essx* 2C 40
Southend-on-Sea. *S'end* 2C 40
Southerfield. *Cumb* 5C 112
Southerhouse. *Shet* 8E 173
Southerly. *Devn* 4F 11
Southernden. *Kent* 1C 28
Southerndown. *V Glam* 4B 32
Southerness. *Dum* 4A 112
South Erradale. *High* 1G 155
Southerton. *Devn* 3D 12
Southery. *Norf* 1F 65
Southey Green. *Essx* 2A 54
South Fambridge. *Essx* 1C 40
South Fawley. *W Ber* 3B 36
South Feorline. *N Ayr* 3D 122
South Ferriby. *N Lin* 2C 94
South Field. *E Yor* 2D 94
Southfleet. *Kent* 3H 39
South Garvan. *High* 1D 141
Southgate. *Cdgn* 2E 57
Southgate. *G Lon* 1E 39
Southgate. *Norf*
 nr. Aylsham 3D 78
 nr. Fakenham 2A 78
Southgate. *Swan* 4E 31
South Gluss. *Shet* 4E 173
South Godstone. *Surr* 1E 27
South Gorley. *Hants* 1G 15
South Green. *Essx*
 nr. Billericay 1A 40
 nr. Colchester 4D 54
South Green. *Kent* 4C 40
South Hanningfield. *Essx* 1B 40
South Harting. *W Sus* 1F 17
South Hayling. *Hants* 3F 17
South Hazelrigg. *Nmbd* 1E 121
South Heath. *Buck* 5H 51
South Heath. *Essx* 4E 54
South Heighton. *E Sus* 5F 27
South Hetton. *Dur* 5G 115
South Hiendley. *W Yor* 3D 93
South Hill. *Corn* 5D 10
South Hill. *Som* 4H 21
South Hinksey. *Oxon* 5D 50
South Hole. *Devn* 4C 18
South Holme. *N Yor* 2B 100
South Holmwood. *Surr* 1C 26
South Hornchurch. *G Lon* 2G 39
South Huish. *Devn* 4C 8
South Hykeham. *Linc* 4G 87
South Hylton. *Tyne* 4G 115
Southill. *C Beds* 1B 52
Southington. *Hants* 2D 24
South Kelsey. *Linc* 1H 87
South Kessock. *High* 4A 158
South Killingholme. *N Lin* 3E 95
South Kilvington. *N Yor* 1G 99
South Kilworth. *Leics* 2D 62
South Kirkby. *W Yor* 3E 93
South Kirkton. *Abers* 3E 153
South Knighton. *Devn* 5B 12
South Kyme. *Linc* 1A 76
South Lancing. *W Sus* 5C 26
South Ledaig. *Arg* 5D 140
South Leigh. *Oxon* 5B 50
Southleigh. *Devn* 3F 13
South Leverton. *Notts* 2E 87
South Littleton. *Worc* 1F 49
South Lopham. *Norf* 2C 66
South Luffenham. *Rut* 5G 75
South Malling. *E Sus* 4F 27
South Marston. *Swin* 3G 35
South Middleton. *Nmbd* 2D 121
South Milford. *N Yor* 1E 93
South Milton. *Devn* 4D 8
South Mimms. *Herts* 5C 52
Southminster. *Essx* 1D 40
South Molton. *Devn* 4H 19
South Moor. *Dur* 4E 115
Southmoor. *Oxon* 2B 36
South Moreton. *Oxon* 3D 36
South Mundham. *W Sus* 2G 17
South Muskham. *Notts* 5E 87
South Newbald. *E Yor* 1C 94
South Newington. *Oxon* 2C 50
South Newsham. *Nmbd* 2G 115
South Newton. *N Ayr* 4H 125
South Newton. *Wilts* 3F 23
South Normanton. *Derbs* 5B 86
South Norwood. *G Lon* 4E 39
South Nutfield. *Surr* 1E 27
South Ockendon. *Thur* 2G 39
Southoe. *Cambs* 4A 64
Southolt. *Suff* 4D 66
South Ormsby. *Linc* 3C 88
Southorpe. *Pet* 5H 75
South Otterington. *N Yor* 1F 99
South Owersby. *Linc* 1H 87
Southowram. *W Yor* 2B 92
South Oxhey. *Herts* 1C 38
South Perrott. *Dors* 2H 13
South Petherton. *Som* 1H 13
South Petherwin. *Corn* 4D 10
South Pickenham. *Norf* 5A 78
South Pool. *Devn* 4D 9
South Poorton. *Dors* 3A 14
South Port. *Arg* 1H 133
Southport. *Mers* 3B 90
Southpunds. *Shet* 10F 173
South Queensferry. *Edin* 2E 129
South Radworthy. *Devn* 3A 20
South Rauceby. *Linc* 1H 75
South Raynham. *Norf* 3A 78
Southrepps. *Norf* 2E 79
South Reston. *Linc* 2D 88
Southrey. *Linc* 4A 88
Southrop. *Glos* 5G 49
Southrope. *Hants* 2E 25
South Runcton. *Norf* 5F 77
South Scarle. *Notts* 4F 87
Southsea. *Port* 3E 17
South Shields. *Tyne* 3G 115
South Shore. *Bkpl* 1B 90
Southside. *Orkn* 5E 172
South Somercotes. *Linc* 1D 88
South Stainley. *N Yor* 3F 99
South Stainmore. *Cumb* 3B 104
South Stifford. *Thur* 3G 39
South Stoke. *Bath* 5C 34
South Stoke. *Oxon* 3D 36
South Stoke. *W Sus* 5B 26
South Street. *E Sus* 4E 27
South Street. *Kent*
 nr. Faversham 5E 41
 nr. Whitstable 4F 41
South Tawton. *Devn* 3G 11
South Thoresby. *Linc* 3D 88
South Tidworth. *Wilts* 2H 23
South Town. *Devn* 4C 12
South Town. *Hants* 3E 25
Southtown. *Norf* 5H 79
Southtown. *Orkn* 8D 172
South View. *Shet* 7E 173
Southwaite. *Cumb* 5F 113
South Walsham. *Norf* 4F 79
South Warnborough.
 Hants 2F 25
Southwater. *W Sus* 3C 26
Southwater Street. *W Sus* 3C 26
Southway. *Som* 2A 22
South Weald. *Essx* 1G 39
South Weirs. *Hants* 2A 16
Southwell. *Dors* 5B 14
Southwell. *Notts* 5E 86
South Weston. *Oxon* 2F 37
South Wheatley. *Corn* 3C 10
South Wheatley. *Notts* 2E 87
Southwick. *Hants* 2E 17
Southwick. *Nptn* 1H 63
Southwick. *Tyne* 4G 115
Southwick. *W Sus* 5D 26
Southwick. *Wilts* 1D 22
South Widcombe. *Bath* 1A 22
South Wigston. *Leics* 1C 62
South Willingham. *Linc* 2A 88
South Wingfield. *Derbs* 5A 86
South Witham. *Linc* 4G 75
Southwold. *Suff* 3H 67
South Wonston. *Hants* 3C 24
Southwood. *Norf* 5F 79
Southwood. *Som* 3A 22
South Woodham Ferrers.
 Essx 1C 40
South Wootton. *Norf* 3F 77
South Wraxall. *Wilts* 5D 34
South Zeal. *Devn* 3G 11
Soval Lodge. *W Isl* 5F 171
Sowerby. *N Yor* 1G 99
Sowerby. *W Yor* 2A 92
Sowerby Bridge. *W Yor* 2A 92
Sowerby Row. *Cumb* 5E 113
Sower Carr. *Lanc* 5C 96

Surlingham—Tobha Beag

Surlingham. Norf 5F 79
Surrex. Essx 3B 54
Sustead. Norf 2D 78
Susworth. Linc 4B 94
Sutcombe. Devn 1D 10
Suton. Norf 1C 66
Sutors of Cromarty. High 2C 158
Sutterby. Linc 3C 88
Sutterton. Linc 2B 76
Sutterton Dowdyke. Linc 2B 76
Sutton. Buck 3B 38
Sutton. Cambs 3D 64
Sutton. C Beds 1C 52
Sutton. E Sus 5F 27
Sutton. G Lon 4D 38
Sutton. Kent 1H 29
Sutton. Norf 3F 79
Sutton. Notts 2E 75
Sutton. Oxon 5C 50
Sutton. Pemb 3D 42
Sutton. Pet 1H 63
Sutton. Shrp
nr. Bridgnorth 2B 60
nr. Market Drayton 2A 72
nr. Oswestry 3F 71
nr. Shrewsbury 4H 71
Sutton. Som 3B 22
Sutton. S Yor 3F 93
Sutton. Staf 3B 72
Sutton. Suff 1G 55
Sutton. W Sus 4A 26
Sutton. Worc 4A 60
Sutton Abinger. Surr 1C 26
Sutton at Hone. Kent 3G 39
Sutton Bassett. Nptn 1E 63
Sutton Benger. Wilts 4E 35
Sutton Bingham. Som 1A 14
Sutton Bonington. Notts 3C 74
Sutton Bridge. Linc 3D 76
Sutton Cheney. Leics 5B 74
Sutton Coldfield, Royal. W Mid 1F 61
Sutton Corner. Linc 3D 76
Sutton Courtenay. Oxon 2D 36
Sutton Crosses. Linc 3D 76
Sutton cum Lound. Notts 2D 86
Sutton Gault. Cambs 3D 64
Sutton Grange. N Yor 2E 99
Sutton Green. Surr 5B 38
Sutton Howgrave. N Yor 2F 99
Sutton in Ashfield. Notts 5B 86
Sutton-in-Craven. N Yor 5C 98
Sutton Ings. Hull 1E 94
Sutton in the Elms. Leics 1C 62
Sutton Lane Ends. Ches E 3D 84
Sutton Leach. Mers 1H 83
Sutton Maddock. Shrp 5B 72
Sutton Mallet. Som 3G 21
Sutton Mandeville. Wilts 4E 23
Sutton Montis. Som 4B 22
Sutton on Hull. Hull 1E 94
Sutton on Sea. Linc 2E 89
Sutton-on-the-Forest. N Yor 3H 99
Sutton on the Hill. Derbs 2G 73
Sutton on Trent. Notts 4E 87
Sutton Poyntz. Dors 4C 14
Sutton St Edmund. Linc 4C 76
Sutton St Edmund's Common. Linc 5C 76
Sutton St James. Linc 4C 76
Sutton St Michael. Here 1A 48
Sutton St Nicholas. Here 1A 48
Sutton Scarsdale. Derbs 4B 86
Sutton Scotney. Hants 3C 24
Sutton-under-Brailes. Warw 2B 50
Sutton-under-Whitestonecliffe. N Yor 1G 99
Sutton upon Derwent. E Yor 5B 100
Sutton Valence. Kent 1C 28
Sutton Veny. Wilts 2E 23
Sutton Waldron. Dors 1D 14
Sutton Weaver. Ches W 3H 83
Swaby. Linc 3C 88
Swadlincote. Derbs 4G 73
Swaffham. Norf 5H 77
Swaffham Bulbeck. Cambs 4E 65
Swaffham Prior. Cambs 4E 65
Swafield. Norf 2E 79
Swainby. N Yor 4B 106
Swainshill. Here 1H 47
Swainsthorpe. Norf 5E 78
Swainswick. Bath 5C 34
Swalcliffe. Oxon 2B 50
Swalecliffe. Kent 4F 41
Swallow. Linc 4E 95
Swallow Beck. Linc 4G 87
Swallowcliffe. Wilts 4E 23
Swallowfield. Wok 5F 37
Swallownest. S Yor 2B 86
Swampton. Hants 1C 24
Swanage. Dors 5F 15
Swanbister. Orkn 7C 172
Swanbourne. Buck 3G 51
Swanbridge. V Glam 5E 33
Swan Green. Ches W 3B 84
Swanland. E Yor 2C 94
Swanley. Kent 4G 39
Swanmore. Hants 1D 16
Swannington. Leics 4B 74
Swannington. Norf 4D 78
Swanpool. Linc 4G 87
Swanscombe. Kent 3H 39
Swansea. Swan 203 (3F 31)
Swan Street. Essx 3B 54
Swanton Abbott. Norf 3E 79
Swanton Morley. Norf 4C 78
Swanton Novers. Norf 2C 78
Swanton Street. Kent 5C 40
Swanwick. Derbs 5B 86
Swanwick. Hants 2D 16
Swanwick Green. Ches E 1H 71
Swarby. Linc 1H 75
Swardeston. Norf 5E 78
Swarister. Shet 3G 173
Swarkestone. Derbs 3A 74
Swarland. Nmbd 4F 121
Swarraton. Hants 3D 24
Swartha. W Yor 5C 98
Swarthmoor. Cumb 2B 96
Swaton. Linc 2A 76
Swatragh. M Ulst 6E 174
Swavesey. Cambs 4C 64
Sway. Hants 3A 16
Swayfield. Linc 3G 75
Swaythling. Sotn 1C 16
Sweet Green. Worc 4A 60
Sweetham. Devn 3B 12
Sweetholme. Cumb 3G 103
Sweets. Corn 3B 10
Sweetshouse. Corn 2E 7
Swefling. Suff 4F 67
Swell. Som 4G 21
Swepstone. Leics 4A 74
Swerford. Oxon 2B 50
Swettenham. Ches E 4C 84
Swffryd. Blae 2F 33
Swiftsden. E Sus 3B 28
Swilland. Suff 5D 66
Swillington. W Yor 1D 93
Swimbridge. Devn 4G 19
Swimbridge Newland. Devn 3G 19
Swinbrook. Oxon 4A 50
Swincliffe. N Yor 4E 99
Swincliffe. W Yor 2C 92
Swinderby. Linc 4F 87
Swindon. Glos 3E 49
Swindon. Nmbd 5D 121
Swindon. Staf 1C 60
Swindon. Swin 203 (3G 35)
Swine. E Yor 1E 95
Swinefleet. E Yor 2A 94
Swineford. S Glo 5B 34
Swineshead. Bed 4H 63
Swineshead. Linc 1B 76
Swineshead Bridge. Linc 1B 76
Swiney. High 5E 169
Swinford. Leics 3C 62
Swinford. Oxon 5C 50
Swingate. Notts 1C 74
Swingbrow. Cambs 2C 64
Swingfield Minnis. Kent 1G 29
Swingfield Street. Kent 1G 29
Swingleton Green. Suff 1C 54
Swinhill. S Lan 5A 128
Swinhoe. Nmbd 2G 121
Swinhope. Linc 1B 88
Swinister. Shet 3E 173
Swinithwaite. N Yor 1C 98
Swinmore Common. Here 1B 48
Swinscoe. Staf 1F 73
Swinside Hall. Bord 3B 120
Swinstead. Linc 3H 75
Swinton. G Man 4F 91
Swinton. N Yor
nr. Malton 2B 100
nr. Masham 2E 98
Swinton. Bord 5E 131
Swinton. S Yor 1B 86
Swithland. Leics 4C 74
Swordale. High 2H 157
Swordly. High 2H 167
Sworton Heath. Ches E 2A 84
Swyddffynnon. Cdgn 4F 57
Swynnerton. Staf 2C 72
Swyre. Dors 4A 14
Sycharth. Powy 3E 70
Sychdyn. Flin 4E 83
Sychnant. Powy 3B 58
Sychtyn. Powy 5B 70
Syde. Glos 4E 49
Sydenham. G Lon 3E 39
Sydenham. Oxon 5F 51
Sydenham. Som 3G 21
Sydenham Damerel. Devn 5E 11
Syderstone. Norf 2H 77
Sydling St Nicholas. Dors 3B 14
Sydmonton. Hants 1C 24
Sydney. Ches E 5B 84
Syerston. Notts 1E 75
Syke. G Man 3G 91
Sykehouse. S Yor 3G 93
Sykes. Lanc 4F 97
Syleham. Suff 3E 66
Sylen. Carm 5F 45
Sylfaen. Powy 5D 70
Symbister. Shet 5G 173
Symington. S Ayr 1C 116
Symington. S Lan 1B 118
Symondsbury. Dors 3H 13
Symonds Yat. Here 4A 48
Synod Inn. Cdgn 5D 56
Syre. High 4G 167
Syreford. Glos 3F 49
Syresham. Nptn 1E 51
Syston. Leics 4D 74
Syston. Linc 1G 75
Sytchampton. Worc 4C 60
Sywell. Nptn 4F 63

T

Tabost. W Isl
nr. Cearsiadar 6F 171
nr. Suainebost 1H 171
Tachbrook Mallory. Warw 4H 61
Tackley. Oxon 3C 50
Tacleit. W Isl 4D 171
Tacolneston. Norf 1D 66
Tadcaster. N Yor 5G 99
Taddington. Derbs 3F 85
Taddington. Glos 2F 49
Taddiport. Devn 1E 11
Tadley. Hants 5E 36
Tadlow. Cambs 1C 52
Tadmarton. Oxon 2B 50
Tadwick. Bath 4C 34
Tadworth. Surr 5D 38
Tafarnaubach. Blae 4E 46
Tafarn-y-bwlch. Pemb 1E 43
Tafarn-y-Gelyn. Den 4D 82
Taff's Well. Rhon 3E 33
Tafolwern. Powy 5A 70
Tai-bach. Powy 3D 70
Taibach. Neat 3A 32
Taigh a Ghearraidh. W Isl 1C 170
Taigh Bhuirgh. W Isl 8C 171
Tain. High
nr. Invergordon 5E 165
nr. Thurso 2E 169
Tai-Nant. Wrex 1E 71
Tai'n Lon. Gwyn 5D 80
Tairbeart. W Isl 8D 171
Tairgwaith. Neat 4H 45
Takeley. Essx 3F 53
Takeley Street. Essx 3F 53
Talachddu. Powy 2D 46
Talacre. Flin 2D 82
Talardd. Gwyn 3A 70
Talaton. Devn 3D 12
Talbenny. Pemb 3C 42
Talbot Green. Rhon 3D 32
Taleford. Devn 3D 12
Talerddig. Powy 5B 70
Talgarreg. Cdgn 5D 56
Talgarth. Powy 2E 47
Talisker. High 5C 154
Talke. Staf 5C 84
Talkin. Cumb 4G 113
Talladale. High 1B 156
Talla Linnfoots. Bord 2D 118
Tallaminnock. S Ayr 5C 116
Tallarn Green. Wrex 1G 71
Tallentire. Cumb 1C 102
Talley. Carm 2G 45
Tallington. Linc 5H 75
Talmine. High 2F 167
Talog. Carm 2H 43
Talsarn. Carm 3A 46
Talsarn. Cdgn 5E 57
Talsarnau. Gwyn 2F 69
Talskiddy. Corn 2D 6
Talwrn. IOA 3D 81
Talwrn. Wrex 1E 71
Tal-y-Bont. Cnwy 4G 81
Tal-y-bont. Cdgn 2F 57
Tal-y-bont. Gwyn
nr. Bangor 3F 81
nr. Barmouth 3E 69
Talybont-on-Usk. Powy 3E 46
Tal-y-cafn. Cnwy 3G 81
Tal-y-coed. Mon 4H 47
Tal-y-llyn. Gwyn 5G 69
Talyllyn. Powy 3E 46
Talysarn. Gwyn 5D 81
Tal-y-waenydd. Gwyn 1F 69
Talywain. Torf 5F 47
Tal-y-Wern. Powy 5H 69
Tamerton Foliot. Plym 2A 8
Tamlaght. Ferm 8E 176
Tamlaght O'Crilly. M Ulst 6F 174
Tamnamore. M Ulst 3C 178
Tamworth. Staf 5G 73
Tamworth Green. Linc 1C 76
Tandlehill. Ren 3F 127
Tandragee. Arm 5E 178
Tandridge. Surr 5E 39
Tanerdy. Carm 3E 45
Tanfield. Dur 4E 115
Tanfield Lea. Dur 4E 115
Tangasdal. W Isl 8B 170
Tang Hall. York 4A 100
Tangiers. Pemb 3D 42
Tangley. Hants 1B 24
Tangmere. W Sus 5A 26
Tangwick. Shet 4D 173
Tankerness. Orkn 7E 172
Tankersley. S Yor 1H 85
Tankerton. Kent 4F 41
Tan-lan. Cnwy 4G 81
Tan-lan. Gwyn 1F 69
Tannach. High 4F 169
Tannadice. Ang 3D 145
Tanner's Green. Worc 3E 61
Tannington. Suff 4E 67
Tannochside. N Lan 3A 128
Tan Office Green. Suff 5G 65
Tansley. Derbs 5H 85
Tansley Knoll. Derbs 4H 85
Tansor. Nptn 1H 63
Tantobie. Dur 4E 115
Tanton. N Yor 3C 106
Tanvats. Linc 4A 88
Tanworth-in-Arden. Warw 3F 61
Tan-y-bwlch. Gwyn 1F 69
Tan-y-fron. Cnwy 4B 82
Tanyfron. Wrex 5E 83
Tanygrisiau. Gwyn 1F 69
Tan-y-groes. Cdgn 1C 44
Tan-y-pistyll. Powy 3C 70
Tan-yr-allt. Den 2C 82
Taobh a Chaolais. W Isl 7C 170
Taobh a Deas Loch Aineort. W Isl 6C 170
Taobh a Ghlinne. W Isl 6F 171
Taobh a Tuath Loch Aineort. W Isl 6C 170
Taplow. Buck 2A 38
Tapton. Derbs 3A 86
Tarbert. Arg
on Jura 1E 125
on Kintyre 3G 125
Tarbert. W Isl 8D 171
Tarbet. Arg 3C 134
Tarbet. High
nr. Mallaig 4F 147
nr. Scourie 4B 166
Tarbock Green. Mers 2G 83
Tarbolton. S Ayr 2D 116
Tarbrax. S Lan 4D 128
Tardebigge. Worc 4D 61
Tarfside. Ang 1D 145
Tarland. Abers 3B 152
Tarleton. Lanc 2C 90
Tarlogie. High 5E 165
Tarlscough. Lanc 3C 90
Tarlton. Glos 2E 35
Tarnbrook. Lanc 4E 97
Tarnock. Som 1G 21
Tarns. Cumb 5C 112
Tarporley. Ches W 4H 83
Tarpots. Essx 2B 40
Tarr. Som 3E 20
Tarrant Crawford. Dors 2E 15
Tarrant Gunville. Dors 1E 15
Tarrant Hinton. Dors 1E 15
Tarrant Keyneston. Dors 2E 15
Tarrant Launceston. Dors 2E 15
Tarrant Monkton. Dors 2E 15
Tarrant Rawston. Dors 2E 15
Tarrant Rushton. Dors 2E 15
Tarrel. High 5F 165
Tarring Neville. E Sus 5F 27
Tarrington. Here 1B 48
Tarsappie. Per 1D 136
Tarscabhaig. High 3D 147
Tarskavaig. High 3D 147
Tarves. Abers 5F 161
Tarvie. High 3G 157
Tarvin. Ches W 4G 83
Tasburgh. Norf 1E 66
Tasley. Shrp 1A 60
Tassagh. Arm 6C 178
Taston. Oxon 3B 50
Tatenhill. Staf 3G 73
Tathall End. Mil 1G 51
Tatham. Lanc 3F 97
Tathwell. Linc 2C 88
Tatling End. Buck 2B 38
Tatsfield. Surr 5F 39
Tattenhall. Ches W 5G 83
Tatterford. Norf 3A 78
Tattersett. Norf 2H 77
Tattershall. Linc 5B 88
Tattershall Bridge. Linc 5A 88
Tattershall Thorpe. Linc 5B 88
Tattingstone. Suff 2E 55
Tattingstone White Horse. Suff 2E 55
Tattle Bank. Warw 4F 61
Tatworth. Som 2G 13
Taunton. Som 203 (4F 21)
Taverham. Norf 4D 78
Taverners Green. Essx 4F 53
Tavernspite. Pemb 3F 43
Tavistock. Devn 5E 11
Tavool House. Arg 1B 132
Taw Green. Devn 3G 11
Tawstock. Devn 4F 19
Taxal. Derbs 2E 85
Tayinloan. Arg 5E 125
Taynish. Arg 1F 125
Taynton. Glos 3C 48
Taynton. Oxon 4H 49
Taynuilt. Arg 5E 141
Tayport. Fife 1G 137
Tay Road Bridge. D'dee 1G 137
Tayvallich. Arg 1F 125
Tealby. Linc 1A 88
Tealing. Ang 5D 144
Teams. Tyne 3F 115
Teangue. High 3E 147
Teanna Mhachair. W Isl 2C 170
Tebay. Cumb 4H 103
Tebworth. C Beds 3H 51
Tedburn St Mary. Devn 3B 12
Teddington. Glos 2E 49
Teddington. G Lon 3C 38
Tedsmore. Shrp 3F 71
Tedstone Delamere. Here 5A 60
Tedstone Wafer. Here 5A 60
Teemore. Ferm 7J 177
Teesport. Red C 2C 106
Teesside. Stoc T 2C 106
Teeton. Nptn 3D 62
Teffont Evias. Wilts 3E 23
Teffont Magna. Wilts 3E 23
Tegryn. Pemb 1G 43
Teigh. Rut 4F 75
Teigncombe. Devn 4G 11
Teigngrace. Devn 5B 12
Teignmouth. Devn 5C 12
Telford. Telf 4A 72
Telham. E Sus 4B 28
Tellisford. Som 1D 22
Telscombe. E Sus 5F 27
Telscombe Cliffs. E Sus 5E 27
Tempar. Per 3D 142
Templand. Dum 1B 112
Temple. Corn 5B 10
Temple. Glas 3G 127
Temple. Midl 4G 129
Temple Balsall. W Mid 3G 61
Temple Bar. Carm 4F 45
Temple Bar. Cdgn 5E 57
Templecombe. Som 4C 22
Temple Ewell. Kent 1G 29
Temple Grafton. Warw 5F 61
Temple Guiting. Glos 3F 49
Templehall. Fife 4E 137
Temple Hirst. N Yor 2G 93
Temple Normanton. Derbs 4B 86
Templepatrick. Ant 8J 175
Temple Sowerby. Cumb 2H 103
Templeton. Devn 1B 12
Templeton. Pemb 3F 43
Templeton. W Ber 5B 36
Templetown. Dur 5E 115
Tempo. Ferm 8F 176
Tempsford. C Beds 5A 64
Tenandry. Per 2G 143
Tenbury Wells. Worc 4H 59
Tenby. Pemb 4F 43
Tendring. Essx 3E 55
Tendring Green. Essx 3E 55
Tenga. Arg 4G 139
Ten Mile Bank. Norf 1F 65
Tenterden. Kent 2C 28
Terfyn. Cnwy 3B 82
Terhill. Som 3E 21
Terling. Essx 4A 54
Termon Rock. Ferm 2A 178
Ternhill. Shrp 2A 72
Terregles. Dum 2G 111
Terrick. Buck 5G 51
Terrington. N Yor 2A 100
Terrington St Clement. Norf 3E 77
Terrington St John. Norf 4E 77
Terry's Green. Warw 3F 61
Teston. Kent 5B 40
Testwood. Hants 1B 16
Tetbury. Glos 2D 35
Tetbury Upton. Glos 2D 35
Tetchill. Shrp 2F 71
Tetcott. Devn 3D 10
Tetford. Linc 3C 88
Tetney. Linc 4G 95
Tetney Lock. Linc 4G 95
Tetsworth. Oxon 5E 51
Tettenhall. W Mid 5C 72
Teversal. Notts 4B 86
Teversham. Cambs 5D 65
Teviothead. Bord 4G 119
Tewel. Abers 5F 153
Tewin. Herts 4C 52
Tewkesbury. Glos 2D 49
Teynham. Kent 4D 40
Teynham Street. Kent 4D 40
Thackthwaite. Cumb 2F 103
Thakeham. W Sus 4C 26
Thame. Oxon 5F 51
Thames Ditton. Surr 4C 38
Thames Haven. Thur 2B 40
Thamesmead. G Lon 2F 39
Thamesport. Medw 3C 40
Thanington Without. Kent 5F 41
Thankerton. S Lan 1B 118
Tharston. Norf 1D 66
Thatcham. W Ber 5D 36
Thatto Heath. Mers 1H 83
Thaxted. Essx 2G 53
Theakston. N Yor 1F 99
Thealby. N Lin 3B 94
Theale. Som 2H 21
Theale. W Ber 4E 37
Thearne. E Yor 1D 94
Theberton. Suff 4G 67
Theddingworth. Leics 2D 62
Theddlethorpe All Saints. Linc 2D 88
Theddlethorpe St Helen. Linc 2D 89
Thelbridge Barton. Devn 1A 12
Thelnetham. Suff 3C 66
Thelveton. Norf 2D 66
Thelwall. Warr 2A 84
Themelthorpe. Norf 3C 78
Thenford. Nptn 1D 50
Therfield. Herts 2D 52
Thetford. Linc 4A 76
Thetford. Norf 2A 66
Thethwaite. Cumb 5E 113
Theydon Bois. Essx 1F 39
Thick Hollins. W Yor 3B 92
Thickwood. Wilts 4D 34
Thimbleby. Linc 4B 88
Thimbleby. N Yor 5B 106
Thingwall. Mers 2E 83
Thirlby. N Yor 1G 99
Thirlestane. Bord 5B 130
Thirn. N Yor 1E 98
Thirsk. N Yor 1G 99
Thirtleby. E Yor 1E 95
Thistleton. Lanc 1C 90
Thistleton. Rut 4G 75
Thistley Green. Suff 3F 65
Thixendale. N Yor 3C 100
Thockrington. Nmbd 2C 114
Tholomas Drove. Cambs 5D 76
Tholthorpe. N Yor 3G 99
Thomas Chapel. Pemb 4F 43
Thomas Close. Cumb 5F 113
Thomastown. Abers 4E 160
Thomastown. Rhon 3D 32
Thompson. Norf 1B 66
Thomshill. Mor 3G 159
Thong. Kent 3A 40
Thongsbridge. W Yor 4B 92
Thoralby. N Yor 1C 98
Thoresby. Notts 3D 86
Thoresway. Linc 1A 88
Thorganby. Linc 1B 88
Thorganby. N Yor 5A 100
Thorgill. N Yor 5E 107
Thorington. Suff 3G 67
Thorington Street. Suff 2D 54
Thorlby. N Yor 4B 98
Thorley. Herts 4E 53
Thorley Street. Herts 4E 53
Thorley Street. IOW 4B 16
Thormanby. N Yor 2G 99
Thorn. Powy 4E 59
Thornaby-on-Tees. Stoc T 3B 106
Thornage. Norf 2C 78
Thornborough. Buck 2F 51
Thornborough. N Yor 2E 99
Thornbury. Devn 2E 11
Thornbury. Here 5A 60
Thornbury. S Glo 2B 34
Thornby. Cumb 4D 112
Thornby. Nptn 3D 62
Thorncliffe. Staf 5E 85
Thorncombe. Dors 2G 13
Thorncombe Street. Surr 1A 26
Thorncote Green. C Beds 1B 52
Thorndon. Suff 4D 66
Thorndon Cross. Devn 3F 11
Thorne. S Yor 3G 93
Thornehillhead. Devn 1E 11
Thorner. W Yor 5F 99
Thorne St Margaret. Som 4D 20
Thorney. Notts 3F 87
Thorney. Pet 5B 76
Thorney. Som 4H 21
Thorney Hill. Hants 3G 15
Thorney Toll. Cambs 5C 76
Thornfalcon. Som 4F 21
Thornford. Dors 1B 14
Thorngrafton. Nmbd 3A 114
Thorngrove. Som 3G 21
Thorngumbald. E Yor 2F 95
Thornham. Norf 1G 77
Thornham Magna. Suff 3D 66
Thornham Parva. Suff 3D 66
Thornhaugh. Pet 5H 75
Thornhill. Cphy 3E 33
Thornhill. Cumb 4B 102
Thornhill. Derbs 2F 85
Thornhill. Dum 5A 118
Thornhill. Sotn 1C 16
Thornhill. Stir 4F 135
Thornhill. W Yor 3C 92
Thornhill Lees. W Yor 3C 92
Thornhills. W Yor 2B 92
Thornholme. E Yor 3F 101
Thornicombe. Dors 2D 14
Thornington. Nmbd 1C 120
Thornley. Dur
nr. Durham 1A 106
nr. Tow Law 1E 105
Thornley Gate. Nmbd 4B 114
Thornliebank. E Ren 3G 127
Thornroan. Abers 5F 161
Thorns. Suff 5G 65
Thornsett. Derbs 2E 85
Thornthwaite. Cumb 2D 102
Thornthwaite. N Yor 4D 98
Thornton. Ang 4C 144
Thornton. Buck 2F 51
Thornton. E Yor 5B 100
Thornton. Fife 4E 137
Thornton. Lanc 5C 96
Thornton. Leics 5B 74
Thornton. Linc 4B 88
Thornton. Mers 4B 90
Thornton. Midd 3B 106
Thornton. Nmbd 5F 131
Thornton. Pemb 4D 42
Thornton. W Yor 1A 92
Thornton Curtis. N Lin 3D 94
Thorntonhall. S Lan 4G 127
Thornton Heath. G Lon 4E 39
Thornton Hough. Mers 2F 83
Thornton-in-Craven. N Yor 5B 98
Thornton in Lonsdale. N Yor 2F 97
Thornton-le-Beans. N Yor 5A 106
Thornton-le-Clay. N Yor 3A 100
Thornton-le-Dale. N Yor 1C 100
Thornton le Moor. Linc 1H 87
Thornton-le-Moor. N Yor 1F 99
Thornton-le-Moors. Ches W 3G 83
Thornton-le-Street. N Yor 1G 99
Thorntonloch. E Lot 2D 130
Thornton Rust. N Yor 1B 98
Thornton Steward. N Yor 1D 98
Thornton Watlass. N Yor 1E 99
Thornwood Common. Essx 5E 53
Thornythwaite. Cumb 2E 103
Thoroton. Notts 1E 75
Thorp Arch. W Yor 5G 99
Thorpe. Derbs 5F 85
Thorpe. E Yor 5D 101
Thorpe. Linc 2D 89
Thorpe. Norf 1G 67
Thorpe. N Yor 3C 98
Thorpe. Notts 1E 75
Thorpe. Surr 4B 38
Thorpe Abbotts. Norf 3D 66
Thorpe Acre. Leics 3C 74
Thorpe Arnold. Leics 3E 75
Thorpe Audlin. W Yor 3E 93
Thorpe Bassett. N Yor 2C 100
Thorpe Bay. S'end 2D 40
Thorpe by Water. Rut 1F 63
Thorpe Common. S Yor 1A 86
Thorpe Common. Suff 2F 55
Thorpe Constantine. Staf 5G 73
Thorpe End. Norf 4E 79
Thorpe Fendike. Linc 4D 88
Thorpe Green. Essx 3E 55
Thorpe Green. Suff 5B 66
Thorpe Hall. N Yor 2H 99
Thorpe Hamlet. Norf 5E 79
Thorpe Hesley. S Yor 1A 86
Thorpe in Balne. S Yor 3F 93
Thorpe in the Fallows. Linc 2G 87
Thorpe Langton. Leics 1E 63
Thorpe Larches. Dur 2A 106
Thorpe Latimer. Linc 1A 76
Thorpe-le-Soken. Essx 3E 55
Thorpe le Street. E Yor 5C 100
Thorpe Malsor. Nptn 3F 63
Thorpe Mandeville. Nptn 1D 50
Thorpe Market. Norf 2E 79
Thorpe Marriott. Norf 4D 78
Thorpe Morieux. Suff 5B 66
Thorpeness. Suff 5G 67
Thorpe on the Hill. Linc 4G 87
Thorpe on the Hill. W Yor 2D 92
Thorpe St Andrew. Norf 5E 79
Thorpe St Peter. Linc 4D 89
Thorpe Salvin. S Yor 2C 86
Thorpe Satchville. Leics 4E 75
Thorpe Thewles. Stoc T 2A 106
Thorpe Tilney. Linc 5A 88
Thorpe Underwood. N Yor 4G 99
Thorpe Waterville. Nptn 2H 63
Thorpe Willoughby. N Yor 1F 93
Thorpland. Norf 5F 77
Thorrington. Essx 3D 54
Thorverton. Devn 2C 12
Thrandeston. Suff 3D 66
Thrapston. Nptn 3G 63
Thrashbush. N Lan 3A 128
Threapland. Cumb 1C 102
Threapland. N Yor 3B 98
Threapwood. Ches W 1G 71
Threapwood. Staf 1E 73
Three Ashes. Here 3A 48
Three Bridges. Linc 2D 88
Three Bridges. W Sus 2D 27
Three Burrows. Corn 4B 6
Three Chimneys. Kent 2C 28
Three Cocks. Powy 2E 47
Three Crosses. Swan 3E 31
Three Cups Corner. E Sus 3H 27
Threehammer Common. Norf 3F 79
Three Holes. Norf 5E 77
Threekingham. Linc 2H 75
Three Leg Cross. E Sus 2A 28
Three Legged Cross. Dors 2F 15
Three Mile Cross. Wok 5F 37
Threemilestone. Corn 4B 6
Three Oaks. E Sus 4C 28
Threlkeld. Cumb 2E 102
Threshfield. N Yor 3B 98
Thrigby. Norf 4G 79
Thringarth. Dur 2C 104
Thringstone. Leics 4B 74
Thrintoft. N Yor 5A 106
Thriplow. Cambs 1E 53
Throckenholt. Linc 5C 76
Throcking. Herts 2D 52
Throckley. Tyne 3E 115
Throckmorton. Worc 1E 49
Throop. Bour 3G 15
Throphill. Nmbd 1E 115
Thropton. Nmbd 4E 121
Throsk. Stir 4A 136
Througham. Glos 5E 49
Throughgate. Dum 1F 111
Throwleigh. Devn 3G 11
Throwley. Kent 5D 40
Throwley Forstal. Kent 5D 40
Throxenby. N Yor 1E 101
Thrumpton. Notts 2C 74
Thrumster. High 4F 169
Thrunton. Nmbd 3E 121
Thrupp. Glos 5D 48
Thrupp. Oxon 4C 50
Thrushelton. Devn 4E 11
Thrushgill. Lanc 3F 97
Thrussington. Leics 4D 74
Thruxton. Hants 2A 24
Thruxton. Here 2H 47
Thrybergh. S Yor 1B 86
Thulston. Derbs 2B 74
Thundergay. N Ayr 5G 125
Thundersley. Essx 2B 40
Thundridge. Herts 4D 52
Thurcaston. Leics 4C 74
Thurcroft. S Yor 2B 86
Thurdon. Corn 1C 10
Thurgarton. Norf 2D 78
Thurgarton. Notts 1D 74
Thurgoland. S Yor 4C 92
Thurlaston. Leics 1C 62
Thurlaston. Warw 3B 62
Thurlbear. Som 4F 21
Thurlby. Linc
nr. Alford 3D 89
nr. Baston 4A 76
nr. Lincoln 4G 87
Thurleigh. Bed 5H 63
Thurlestone. Devn 4C 8
Thurloxton. Som 3F 21
Thurlstone. S Yor 4C 92
Thurlton. Norf 1G 67
Thurmaston. Leics 5D 74
Thurnby. Leics 5D 74
Thurne. Norf 4G 79
Thurnham. Kent 5C 40
Thurning. Norf 3C 78
Thurning. Nptn 2H 63
Thurnscoe. S Yor 4E 93
Thursby. Cumb 4E 113
Thursford. Norf 2B 78
Thursford Green. Norf 2B 78
Thursley. Surr 2A 26
Thurso. High 2D 168
Thurso East. High 2D 168
Thurstaston. Mers 2E 83
Thurston. Suff 4B 66
Thurston End. Suff 5G 65
Thurstonfield. Cumb 4E 112
Thurstonland. W Yor 3B 92
Thurton. Norf 5F 79
Thurvaston. Derbs
nr. Ashbourne 2F 73
nr. Derby 2G 73
Thuxton. Norf 5C 78
Thwaite. Dur 3D 104
Thwaite. N Yor 5B 104
Thwaite. Suff 4D 66
Thwaite Head. Cumb 5E 103
Thwaites. W Yor 5C 98
Thwaite St Mary. Norf 1F 67
Thwing. E Yor 2E 101
Tibbermore. Per 1C 136
Tibberton. Glos 3C 48
Tibberton. Telf 3A 72
Tibberton. Worc 5D 60
Tibenham. Norf 2D 66
Tibshelf. Derbs 4B 86
Tibthorpe. E Yor 4D 100
Ticehurst. E Sus 2A 28
Tichborne. Hants 3D 24
Tickencote. Rut 5G 75
Tickenham. N Som 4H 33
Tickhill. S Yor 1C 86
Ticklerton. Shrp 1G 59
Ticknall. Derbs 3A 74
Tickton. E Yor 5E 101
Tidbury Green. W Mid 3F 61
Tidcombe. Wilts 1A 24
Tiddington. Oxon 5E 51
Tiddington. Warw 5G 61
Tiddleywink. Wilts 4D 34
Tidebrook. E Sus 3H 27
Tideford. Corn 3H 7
Tideford Cross. Corn 2H 7
Tidenham. Glos 2A 34
Tideswell. Derbs 3F 85
Tidmarsh. W Ber 4E 37
Tidmington. Warw 2A 50
Tidpit. Hants 1F 15
Tidworth. Wilts 2H 23
Tidworth Camp. Wilts 2H 23
Tiers Cross. Pemb 3D 42
Tiffield. Nptn 5D 62
Tifty. Abers 4E 161
Tigerton. Ang 2E 145
Tighnabruaich. Arg 2A 126
Tigley. Devn 2D 8
Tilbrook. Cambs 4H 63
Tilbury. Thur 3H 39
Tilbury Green. Essx 1H 53
Tilbury Juxta Clare. Essx 1A 54
Tile Hill. W Mid 3G 61
Tilehurst. Read 4E 37
Tilford. Surr 2G 25
Tilgate Forest Row. W Sus 2D 26
Tillathrowie. Abers 5B 160
Tillers Green. Glos 2B 48
Tillery. Abers 1G 153
Tilley. Shrp 3H 71
Tillicoultry. Clac 4B 136
Tillingham. Essx 5C 54
Tillington. Here 1H 47
Tillington. W Sus 3A 26
Tillington Common. Here 1H 47
Tillybirloch. Abers 3D 152
Tillyfourie. Abers 2D 152
Tilmanstone. Kent 5H 41
Tilney All Saints. Norf 4E 77
Tilney Fen End. Norf 4E 77
Tilney High End. Norf 4E 77
Tilney St Lawrence. Norf 4E 77
Tilshead. Wilts 2F 23
Tilstock. Shrp 2H 71
Tilston. Ches W 5G 83
Tilstone Fearnall. Ches W 4H 83
Tilsworth. C Beds 3H 51
Tilton on the Hill. Leics 5E 75
Tiltups End. Glos 2D 34
Timberland. Linc 5A 88
Timbersbrook. Ches E 4C 84
Timberscombe. Som 2C 20
Timble. N Yor 4D 98
Timperley. G Man 2B 84
Timsbury. Bath 1B 22
Timsbury. Hants 4B 24
Timsgearraidh. W Isl 4C 171
Timworth Green. Suff 4A 66
Tincleton. Dors 3C 14
Tindale. Cumb 4H 113
Tindale Crescent. Dur 2F 105
Tingewick. Buck 2E 51
Tingrith. C Beds 2A 52
Tingwall. Orkn 5D 172
Tinhay. Devn 4D 11
Tinshill. W Yor 1C 92
Tinsley. S Yor 1B 86
Tinsley Green. W Sus 2D 27
Tintagel. Corn 4A 10
Tintern. Mon 5A 48
Tintinhull. Som 1H 13
Tintwistle. Derbs 1E 85
Tinwald. Dum 1B 112
Tinwell. Rut 5H 75
Tippacott. Devn 2A 20
Tipperty. Abers 1G 153
Tipps End. Cambs 1E 65
Tiptoe. Hants 3A 16
Tipton. W Mid 1D 60
Tipton St John. Devn 3D 12
Tiptree. Essx 4B 54
Tiptree Heath. Essx 4B 54
Tirabad. Powy 1B 46
Tircoed Forest Village. Swan 5G 45
Tiree Airport. Arg 4B 138
Tirinie. Per 2F 143
Tirley. Glos 3D 48
Tiroran. Arg 1B 132
Tir-Phil. Cphy 5E 47
Tirril. Cumb 2G 103
Tirryside. High 2C 164
Tir-y-dail. Carm 4G 45
Tisbury. Wilts 4E 23
Tisman's Common. W Sus 2B 26
Tissington. Derbs 5F 85
Titchberry. Devn 4C 18
Titchfield. Hants 2D 16
Titchmarsh. Nptn 3H 63
Titchwell. Norf 1G 77
Tithby. Notts 2D 74
Titley. Here 5F 59
Titlington. Nmbd 3E 121
Titsey. Surr 5F 39
Titson. Corn 2C 10
Tittensor. Staf 2C 72
Tittleshall. Norf 3A 78
Titton. Worc 4C 60
Tiverton. Ches W 4H 83
Tiverton. Devn 1C 12
Tivetshall St Margaret. Norf 2D 66
Tivetshall St Mary. Norf 2D 66
Tivington. Som 2C 20
Tixall. Staf 3D 73
Tixover. Rut 5G 75
Toab. Orkn 7E 172
Toab. Shet 10E 173
Toadmoor. Derbs 5A 86
Tobermore. M Ulst 7E 174
Toberonochy. Arg 3E 133
Tobha Beag. W Isl 5C 170

Tobha-Beag—Upper Sheringham

Tobha-Beag. W Isl 1E 170
Tobha Mor. W Isl 5C 170
Tobhtarol. W Isl 4D 171
Tobson. W Isl 4D 171
Tocabhaig. High 2E 147
Tocher. Abers 5D 160
Tockenham. Wilts 4F 35
Tockenham Wick. Wilts 3F 35
Tockholes. Bkbn 2E 91
Tockington. S Glo 3B 34
Tockwith. N Yor 4G 99
Todber. Dors 4D 22
Todding. Here 3G 59
Toddington. C Beds 3A 52
Toddington. Glos 2F 49
Todenham. Glos 2H 49
Todhills. Cumb 3E 113
Todmorden. W Yor 2H 91
Todwick. S Yor 2B 86
Toft. Cambs 5C 64
Toft. Linc 4H 75
Toft Hill. Dur 2E 105
Toft Monks. Norf 1G 67
Toft next Newton. Linc 2H 87
Toftrees. Norf 3A 78
Tofts. High 2F 169
Toftwood. Norf 4B 78
Togston. Nmbd 4G 121
Tokavaig. High 2E 147
Tokers Green. Oxon 4F 37
Tolastadh a Chaolais. W Isl 4D 171
Tolladine. Worc 5C 60
Tolland. Som 3E 20
Tollard Farnham. Dors 1E 15
Tollard Royal. Wilts 1E 15
Toll Bar. S Yor 4F 93
Toller Fratrum. Dors 3A 14
Toller Porcorum. Dors 3A 14
Tollerton. N Yor 3H 99
Tollerton. Notts 2D 74
Toller Whelme. Dors 2A 14
Tollesbury. Essx 4C 54
Tolleshunt D'Arcy. Essx 4C 54
Tolleshunt Knights. Essx 4C 54
Tolleshunt Major. Essx 4C 54
Tollie. High 3H 157
Tollie Farm. High 1A 156
Tolm. W Isl 4G 171
Tolpuddle. Dors 3C 14
Tolstadh bho Thuath. W Isl 3H 171
Tolworth. G Lon 4C 38
Tomachlaggan. Mor 1F 151
Tomaknock. Per 1A 136
Tomatin. High 1C 150
Tombuidhe. Arg 3H 133
Tomdoun. High 3D 148
Tomich. High
nr. Cannich 1F 149
nr. Invergordon 1B 158
nr. Lairg 3D 164
Tomintoul. Mor 2F 151
Tomnavoulin. Mor 1G 151
Tomsléibhe. Arg 5A 140
Ton. Mon 2G 33
Tonbridge. Kent 1G 27
Tondu. B'end 3B 32
Tonedale. Som 4E 21
Tonfanau. Gwyn 5E 69
Tong. Shrp 5B 72
Tonge. Leics 3B 74
Tong Forge. Shrp 5B 72
Tongham. Surr 2G 25
Tongland. Dum 4D 111
Tong Norton. Shrp 5B 72
Tongue. High 3F 167
Tongue End. Linc 4A 76
Tongwynlais. Card 3E 33
Tonmawr. Neat 2B 32
Tonna. Neat 2A 32
Tonnau. Neat 2A 32
Ton Pentre. Rhon 2C 32
Ton-Teg. Rhon 3D 32
Tonwell. Herts 4D 52
Tonypandy. Rhon 2C 32
Tonyrefail. Rhon 3D 32
Toome. Ant 7F 175
Toot Baldon. Oxon 5D 50
Toot Hill. Essx 5F 53
Toothill. Hants 1B 16
Topcliffe. N Yor 2G 99
Topcliffe. W Yor 2C 92
Topcroft. Norf 1E 67
Topcroft Street. Norf 1E 67
Toppesfield. Essx 2H 53
Toppings. G Man 3F 91
Toprow. Norf 1D 66
Topsham. Devn 4C 12
Torbay. Torb 2F 9
Torbeg. N Ayr 3C 122
Torbothie. N Lan 4B 128
Torbryan. Devn 2E 9
Torcross. Devn 4E 9
Tore. High 3A 158
Torgyle. High 2F 149
Torinturk. Arg 3G 125
Torksey. Linc 3F 87
Torlum. W Isl 3C 170
Torlundy. High 1F 141
Tormarton. S Glo 4C 34
Tormitchell. S Ayr 5B 116
Tormore. High 3E 147
Tormore. N Ayr 2C 122
Tornagrain. High 4B 158
Tornaveen. Abers 3D 152
Torness. High 1H 149
Toronto. Dur 1E 105
Torpenhow. Cumb 1D 102
Torphichen. W Lot 2C 128
Torphins. Abers 3D 152
Torpoint. Corn 3A 8
Torquay. Torb 2F 9
Torr. Devn 3B 8
Torra. Arg 4B 124
Torran. High 4E 155
Torrance. E Dun 2H 127
Torrans. Arg 1B 132
Torranyard. N Ayr 5E 127
Torre. Som 3D 20
Torre. Torb 2F 9
Torridon. High 3B 156
Torrin. High 1D 147
Torrisdale. Arg 2B 122
Torrisdale. High 2G 167
Torrish. High 2G 165
Torrisholme. Lanc 3D 96
Torroble. High 3C 164
Torroy. High 4C 164
Torry. Aber 3G 153
Torryburn. Fife 1D 128
Torthorwald. Dum 2B 112
Tortington. W Sus 5B 26
Tortworth. S Glo 2C 34
Torvaig. High 4D 155
Torver. Cumb 5D 102
Torwood. Falk 1B 128
Torworth. Notts 2D 86
Toscaig. High 5G 155
Toseland. Cambs 4B 64
Tosside. N Yor 4G 97
Tostock. Suff 4B 66
Totaig. High 3A 154
Totardor. High 5C 154
Tote. High 4D 154
Totegan. High 2A 168
Tothill. Linc 2D 88
Totland. IOW 4B 16
Totley. S Yor 3H 85
Totnell. Dors 2B 14
Totnes. Devn 2E 9
Toton. Notts 2C 74
Totronald. Arg 3C 138
Totscore. High 2C 154
Tottenham. G Lon 1E 39
Tottenhill. Norf 4F 77
Tottenhill Row. Norf 4F 77
Totteridge. G Lon 1D 38
Totternhoe. C Beds 3H 51
Tottington. G Man 3F 91
Totton. Hants 1B 16
Touchen-end. Wind 4G 37
Toulvaddie. High 5F 165
The Towans. Corn 3C 4
Toward. Arg 3C 126
Towcester. Nptn 1E 51
Towednack. Corn 3B 4
Tower End. Norf 4F 77
Tower Hill. Mers 4C 90
Tower Hill. W Sus 3C 26
Towersey. Oxon 5F 51
Towie. Abers 2B 152
Towiemore. Mor 4A 160
Tow Law. Dur 1E 105
The Town. IOS 1A 4
Town End. Cambs 1D 64
Town End. Cumb
nr. Ambleside 4F 103
nr. Kirkby Thore 2H 103
nr. Lindale 1D 96
nr. Newby Bridge 1C 96
Town End. Mers 2G 83
Townend. W Dun 2F 127
Townfield. Dur 5C 114
Towngate. Cumb 5G 113
Towngate. Linc 4A 76
Town Green. Lanc 4C 90
Town Head. Cumb
nr. Grasmere 4E 103
nr. Great Asby 3H 103
Townhead. Cumb
nr. Lazonby 1G 103
nr. Maryport 1B 102
nr. Ousby 1H 103
Townhead. Dum 5D 111
Townhead of Greenlaw. Dum 3E 111
Townhill. Fife 1E 129
Townhill. Swan 3F 31
Townjoy. M Ulst 3D 178
Town Kelloe. Dur 1A 106
Town Littleworth. E Sus 4F 27
Town Row. E Sus 2G 27
Towns End. Hants 1D 24
Townsend. Herts 5B 52
Townshend. Corn 3C 4
Town Street. Suff 2G 65
Town Yetholm. Bord 2C 120
Towthorpe. E Yor 3D 100
Towthorpe. York 4A 100
Towton. N Yor 1E 93
Towyn. Cnwy 3B 82
Toxteth. Mers 2F 83
Toynton All Saints. Linc 4C 88
Toynton Fen Side. Linc 4C 88
Toynton St Peter. Linc 4D 88
Toy's Hill. Kent 5F 39
Trabboch. E Ayr 2D 116
Traboe. Corn 4E 5
Tradespark. High 3C 158
Tradespark. Orkn 7D 172
Trafford Park. G Man 1B 84
Trallong. Powy 3C 46
Y Trallwng. Powy 5E 70
Tranent. E Lot 2H 129
Tranmere. Mers 2F 83
Trantlebeg. High 3A 168
Trantlemore. High 3A 168
Tranwell. Nmbd 1E 115
Trapp. Carm 4G 45
Traquair. Bord 1F 119
Trash Green. W Ber 5E 37
Trawden. Lanc 1H 91
Trawscoed. Powy 2D 46
Trawsfynydd. Gwyn 2G 69
Trawsgoed. Cdgn 3F 57
Treaddow. Here 3A 48
Trealaw. Rhon 2D 32
Treales. Lanc 1C 90
Trearddur. IOA 3B 80
Treaslane. High 3C 154
Treator. Corn 1D 6
Trebanog. Rhon 2D 32
Trebanos. Neat 5H 45
Trebarber. Corn 2C 6
Trebartha. Corn 5C 10
Trebarwith. Corn 4A 10
Trebetherick. Corn 1D 6
Treborough. Som 3D 20
Trebudannon. Corn 2C 6
Trebullett. Corn 5D 10
Treburley. Corn 5D 10
Treburrick. Corn 1C 6
Trebyan. Corn 2E 7
Trecastle. Powy 3B 46
Trecenydd. Cphy 3E 33
Trecott. Devn 2G 11
Trecwn. Pemb 1D 42
Trecynon. Rhon 5C 46
Tredaule. Corn 4C 10
Tredavoe. Corn 4B 4
Tredegar. Blae 5E 47
Trederwen. Powy 4E 71
Tredington. Glos 3E 49
Tredington. Warw 1A 50
Tredinnick. Corn
nr. Bodmin 2F 7
nr. Looe 3G 7
nr. Padstow 1D 6
Tredogan. V Glam 5D 32
Tredomen. Powy 2E 46
Tredunnock. Mon 2G 33
Tredustan. Powy 2E 47
Treen. Corn
nr. Land's End 4A 4
nr. St Ives 3B 4
Treeton. S Yor 2B 86
Trefaldwyn. Powy 1E 58
Trefasser. Pemb 1C 42
Trefdraeth. IOA 3D 80
Trefdraeth. Pemb 1E 43
Trefecca. Powy 2E 47
Trefechan. Mer T 5D 46
Trefeglwys. Powy 1B 58
Trefenter. Cdgn 4F 57
Treffgarne. Pemb 2D 42
Treffynnon. Flin 3D 82
Treffynnon. Pemb 2C 42
Trefil. Blae 4E 46
Trefilan. Cdgn 5E 57
Trefin. Pemb 1C 42
Treflach. Shrp 3E 71
Trefnant. Den 3C 82
Trefonen. Shrp 3E 71
Trefor. Gwyn 1C 68
Trefor. IOA 2C 80
Treforest. Rhon 3D 32
Trefrew. Corn 4B 10
Trefriw. Cnwy 4G 81
Tref-y-Clawdd. Powy 3E 59
Trefynwy. Mon 4A 48
Tregada. Corn 4D 10
Tregadillett. Corn 4C 10
Tregare. Mon 4H 47
Tregarne. Corn 4E 5
Tregaron. Cdgn 5F 57
Tregarth. Gwyn 4F 81
Tregear. Corn 3C 6
Tregeare. Corn 4C 10
Tregeiriog. Wrex 2D 70
Tregele. IOA 1C 80
Tregeseal. Corn 3A 4
Tregiskey. Corn 4E 6
Tregole. Corn 3B 10
Tregolwyn. V Glam 4C 32
Tregonetha. Corn 2D 6
Tregonhawke. Corn 3A 8
Tregony. Corn 4D 6
Tregoodwell. Corn 4B 10
Tregorrick. Corn 3E 6
Tregoss. Corn 2D 6
Tregowris. Corn 4E 5
Tregoyd. Powy 2E 47
Tregrehan Mills. Corn 3E 7
Tre-groes. Cdgn 1E 45
Tregullon. Corn 2E 7
Tregurrian. Corn 2C 6
Tregynon. Powy 1C 58
Trehafod. Rhon 2D 32
Trehan. Corn 3A 8
Treharris. Mer T 2D 32
Treherbert. Rhon 2C 32
Trehunist. Corn 2H 7
Trekenner. Corn 5D 10
Trekenning. Corn 2D 6
Treknow. Corn 4A 10
Trelales. B'end 3B 32
Trelan. Corn 5E 5
Trelash. Corn 3B 10
Trelassick. Corn 3C 6
Trelawnyd. Flin 3C 82
Trelech. Carm 1G 43
Treleddyd-fawr. Pemb 2B 42
Trelewis. Mer T 2E 32
Treligga. Corn 4A 10
Trelights. Corn 1D 6
Trelill. Corn 5A 10
Trelissick. Corn 5C 6
Trellech. Mon 5A 48
Trelleck Grange. Mon 5H 47
Trelogan. Flin 2D 82
Trelystan. Powy 5E 71
Tremadog. Gwyn 1E 69
Tremail. Corn 4B 10
Tremain. Cdgn 1C 44
Tremaine. Corn 4C 10
Tremar. Corn 2G 7
Trematon. Corn 3H 7
Tremeirchion. Den 3C 82
Tremore. Corn 2E 6
Tremorfa. Card 4F 33
Trenance. Corn
nr. Newquay 2C 6
nr. Padstow 1D 6
Trenarren. Corn 4E 7
Trench. Telf 4A 72
Trencreek. Corn 2C 6
Trendeal. Corn 3C 6
Trenear. Corn 5A 6
Treneglos. Corn 4C 10
Trenewan. Corn 3F 7
Trengune. Corn 3B 10
Trent. Dors 1A 14
Trentham. Stoke 1C 72
Trentishoe. Devn 2G 19
Trentlock. Derbs 2B 74
Treoes. V Glam 4C 32
Treorchy. Rhon 2C 32
Treorci. Rhon 2C 32
Tre'r-ddol. Cdgn 1F 57
Tre'r llai. Powy 5E 71
Trerulefoot. Corn 3H 7
Tresaith. Cdgn 5B 56
Trescott. Staf 1C 60
Trescowe. Corn 3C 4
Tresham. Glos 2C 34
Tresigin. V Glam 4C 32
Tresillian. Corn 4C 6
Tresimwn. V Glam 4D 32
Tresinney. Corn 4B 10
Treskillard. Corn 5A 6
Treskinnick Cross. Corn 3C 10
Tresmeer. Corn 4C 10
Tresparrett. Corn 3B 10
Tresparrett Posts. Corn 3B 10
Tressady. High 3D 164
Tressait. Per 2F 143
Tresta. Shet
on Fetlar 2H 173
on Mainland 6E 173
Treswell. Notts 3E 87
Treswithian. Corn 3D 4
Tre Taliesin. Cdgn 1F 57
Trethomas. Cphy 3E 33
Trethosa. Corn 3D 6
Trethurgy. Corn 3E 7
Tretio. Pemb 2B 42
Tretire. Here 3A 48
Tretower. Powy 3E 47
Treuddyn. Flin 5E 83
Trevadlock. Corn 5C 10
Trevalga. Corn 4A 10
Trevalyn. Wrex 5F 83
Trevance. Corn 1D 6
Trevanger. Corn 1D 6
Trevanson. Corn 1D 6
Trevarrack. Corn 3B 4
Trevarren. Corn 2D 6
Trevarrian. Corn 2C 6
Trevarrick. Corn 4D 6
Trevaughan. Carm
nr. Carmarthen 3E 45
nr. Whitland 3F 43
Treveighan. Corn 5A 10
Trevellas. Corn 3B 6
Trevelmond. Corn 2G 7
Treverva. Corn 5B 6
Trevescan. Corn 4A 4
Trevethin. Torf 5F 47
Trevia. Corn 4A 10
Trevigro. Corn 2H 7
Trevilley. Corn 4A 4
Treviscoe. Corn 3D 6
Trevivian. Corn 4B 10
Trevone. Corn 1C 6
Trevor. Wrex 1E 71
Trevor Uchaf. Den 1E 71
Trew. Corn 4D 4
Trewalder. Corn 4A 10
Trewarlett. Corn 4D 10
Trewarmett. Corn 4A 10
Trewassa. Corn 4B 10
Treween. Corn 4C 10
Trewellard. Corn 3A 4
Trewen. Corn 4C 10
Trewennack. Corn 4D 5
Trewern. Powy 4E 71
Trewetha. Corn 5A 10
Trewidland. Corn 3G 7
Trewint. Corn 3B 10
Trewithian. Corn 5C 6
Trewoofe. Corn 4B 4
Trewoon. Corn 3D 6
Treworthal. Corn 5C 6
Trewyddel. Pemb 1B 44
Treyarnon. Corn 1C 6
Treyford. W Sus 1G 17
Triangle. Staf 5E 73
Triangle. W Yor 2A 92
Trickett's Cross. Dors 2F 15
Trillick. Ferm 7F 176
Trimdon. Dur 1A 106
Trimdon Colliery. Dur 1A 106
Trimdon Grange. Dur 1A 106
Trimingham. Norf 2E 79
Trimley Lower Street. Suff 2F 55
Trimley St Martin. Suff 2F 55
Trimley St Mary. Suff 2F 55
Trimpley. Worc 3B 60
Trimsaran. Carm 5E 45
Trimstone. Devn 2F 19
Trinafour. Per 2E 143
Trinant. Cphy 2F 33
Tring. Herts 4H 51
Trinity. Ang 2F 145
Trinity. Edin 2F 129
Trisant. Cdgn 3G 57
Triscombe. Som 3E 21
Trislaig. High 1E 141
Trispen. Corn 3C 6
Tritlington. Nmbd 5G 121
Trochry. Per 4G 143
Troedrhiwdalar. Powy 5B 58
Troedrhiwfuwch. Cphy 5E 47
Troedrhiw-gwair. Blae 5E 47
Troedyraur. Cdgn 1D 44
Troedyrhiw. Mer T 5D 46
Trondavoe. Shet 4E 173
Troon. Corn 5A 6
Troon. S Ayr 1C 116
Troqueer. Dum 2A 112
Troston. Suff 3A 66
Trottiscliffe. Kent 4H 39
Trotton. W Sus 4G 25
Troutbeck. Cumb
nr. Ambleside 4F 103
nr. Penrith 2E 103
Troutbeck Bridge. Cumb 4F 103
Troway. Derbs 3A 86
Trowbridge. Wilts 1D 22
Trowell. Notts 2B 74
Trowle Common. Wilts 1D 22
Trowley Bottom. Herts 4A 52
Trowse Newton. Norf 5E 79
Trudoxhill. Som 2C 22
Trull. Som 4F 21
Trumaisgearraidh. W Isl 1D 170
Trumpan. High 2B 154
Trumpet. Here 2B 48
Trumpington. Cambs 5D 64
Trumps Green. Surr 4A 38
Trunch. Norf 2E 79
Trunnah. Lanc 5C 96
Truro. Corn 4C 6
Trusham. Devn 4B 12
Trusley. Derbs 2G 73
Trusthorpe. Linc 2E 89
Tryfil. IOA 2D 80
Trysull. Staf 1C 60
Tubney. Oxon 2C 36
Tuckenhay. Devn 3E 9
Tuckhill. Shrp 2B 60
Tuckingmill. Corn 4A 6
Tuckton. Bour 3G 15
Tuddenham. Suff 3G 65
Tuddenham St Martin. Suff 1E 55
Tudeley. Kent 1H 27
Tudhoe. Dur 1F 105
Tudhoe Grange. Dur 1F 105
Tudorville. Here 3A 48
Tudweiliog. Gwyn 2B 68
Tuesley. Surr 1A 26
Tufton. Hants 2C 24
Tufton. Pemb 2E 43
Tugby. Leics 5E 75
Tugford. Shrp 2H 59
Tughall. Nmbd 2G 121
Tulchan. Per 1B 136
Tullibardine. Per 2B 136
Tullibody. Clac 4A 136
Tullich. Arg 2H 133
Tullich. High
nr. Lochcarron 4B 156
nr. Tain 1C 158
Tullich. Mor 4H 159
Tullich Muir. High 1B 158
Tulliemet. Per 3G 143
Tulloch. Abers 5F 161
Tulloch. High
nr. Bonar Bridge 4D 164
nr. Fort William 5F 149
nr. Grantown-on-Spey 2D 151
Tulloch. Per 1C 136
Tullochgorm. Arg 4G 133
Tullybeagles Lodge. Per 5H 143
Tullyhogue. M Ulst 2C 178
Tullymurdoch. Per 3B 144
Tullynessle. Abers 2C 152
Tumble. Carm 4F 45
Tumbler's Green. Essx 3B 54
Tumby. Linc 4B 88
Tumby Woodside. Linc 5B 88
Tummel Bridge. Per 3E 143
Tunbridge Wells, Royal. Kent 2G 27
Tunga. W Isl 4G 171
Tungate. Norf 3E 79
Tunley. Bath 1B 22
Tunstall. E Yor 1G 95
Tunstall. Kent 4C 40
Tunstall. Lanc 2F 97
Tunstall. Norf 5G 79
Tunstall. N Yor 5F 105
Tunstall. Staf 3B 72
Tunstall. Stoke 5C 84
Tunstall. Suff 5F 67
Tunstall. Tyne 4G 115
Tunstead. Derbs 3F 85
Tunstead. Norf 3E 79
Tunstead Milton. Derbs 2E 85
Tunworth. Hants 2E 25
Tupsley. Here 1A 48
Tupton. Derbs 4A 86
Turfholm. S Lan 1H 117
Turfmoor. Devn 2F 13
Turgis Green. Hants 1E 25
Turkdean. Glos 4G 49
Turkey Island. Hants 1D 16
Tur Langton. Leics 1E 62
Turleigh. Wilts 5D 34
Turlin Moor. Pool 3E 15
Turnastone. Here 2G 47
Turnberry. S Ayr 4B 116
Turnchapel. Plym 3A 8
Turnditch. Derbs 1G 73
Turners Hill. W Sus 2E 27
Turners Puddle. Dors 3D 14
Turnford. Herts 5D 52
Turnhouse. Edin 2E 129
Turnworth. Dors 2D 14
Turriff. Abers 4E 161
Tursdale. Dur 1A 106
Turton Bottoms. Bkbn 3F 91
Turtory. Mor 4C 160
Turves Green. W Mid 3E 61
Turvey. Bed 5G 63
Turville. Buck 2F 37
Turville Heath. Buck 2F 37
Turweston. Buck 2E 50
Tushielaw. Bord 3F 119
Tutbury. Staf 3G 73
Tutnall. Worc 3D 61
Tutshill. Glos 2A 34
Tuttington. Norf 3E 79
Tutts Clump. W Ber 4D 36
Tutwell. Corn 5D 11
Tuxford. Notts 3E 87
Twatt. Orkn 5B 172
Twatt. Shet 6E 173
Twechar. E Dun 2H 127
Tweedale. Telf 5B 72
Tweedbank. Bord 1H 119
Tweedmouth. Nmbd 4F 131
Tweedsmuir. Bord 2C 118
Twelveheads. Corn 4B 6
Twemlow Green. Ches E 4B 84
Twenty. Linc 3A 76
Twerton. Bath 5C 34
Twickenham. G Lon 3C 38
Twigworth. Glos 3D 48
Twineham. W Sus 4D 26
Twinhoe. Bath 1C 22
Twinstead. Essx 2B 54
Twinstead Green. Essx 2B 54
Twiss Green. Warr 1A 84
Twiston. Lanc 5H 97
Twitchen. Devn 3A 20
Twitchen. Shrp 3F 59
Two Bridges. Devn 5G 11
Two Bridges. Glos 5B 48
Two Dales. Derbs 4G 85
Two Gates. Staf 5G 73
Two Mile Oak. Devn 2E 9
Twycross. Leics 5H 73
Twyford. Buck 3E 51
Twyford. Derbs 3H 73
Twyford. Dors 1D 14
Twyford. Hants 4C 24
Twyford. Leics 4E 75
Twyford. Norf 3C 78
Twyford. Wok 4F 37
Twyford Common. Here 2A 48
Twynholm. Dum 4D 110
Twyning. Glos 2D 49
Twyning Green. Glos 2E 49
Twynllanan. Carm 3A 46
Twyn-y-Sheriff. Mon 5H 47
Twywell. Nptn 3G 63
Tyberton. Here 2G 47
Tyburn. W Mid 1F 61
Tyby. Norf 3C 78
Tycroes. Carm 4G 45
Tycrwyn. Powy 4D 70
Tyddewi. Pemb 2B 42
Tydd Gote. Linc 4D 76
Tydd St Giles. Cambs 4D 76
Tydd St Mary. Linc 4D 76
Tye. Hants 2F 17
Tye Green. Essx
nr. Bishop's Stortford 3F 53
nr. Braintree 3A 54
nr. Saffron Walden 2F 53
Tyersal. W Yor 1B 92
Ty Issa. Powy 2D 70
Tyldesley. G Man 4E 91
Tyler Hill. Kent 4F 41
Tyler's Green. Essx 5F 53
Tylers Green. Buck 2A 38
Tylorstown. Rhon 2D 32
Tylwch. Powy 2B 58
Y Tymbl. Carm 4F 45
Tynan. Arm 5B 178
Ty-nant. Cnwy 1B 70
Tyndrum. Stir 5H 141
Tyneham. Dors 4D 15
Tynehead. Midl 4G 129
Tynemouth. Tyne 3G 115
Tyneside. Tyne 3F 115
Tyne Tunnel. Tyne 3G 115
Tynewydd. Rhon 2C 32
Tyninghame. E Lot 2C 130
Tynron. Dum 5H 117
Ty'n-y-bryn. Rhon 3D 32
Tyn-y-celyn. Wrex 2D 70
Tyn-y-cwm. Swan 5G 45
Tyn-y-ffridd. Powy 2D 70
Tynygongl. IOA 2E 81
Tynygraig. Cdgn 4F 57
Ty'n-y-groes. Cnwy 3G 81
Ty'n-yr-eithin. Cdgn 4F 57
Tyn-y-rhyd. Powy 4C 70
Tyn-y-wern. Powy 3C 70
Tyrie. Abers 2G 161
Tyringham. Mil 1G 51
Tythecott. Devn 1E 11
Tythegston. B'end 4B 32
Tytherington. Ches E 3D 84
Tytherington. Som 2C 22
Tytherington. S Glo 3B 34
Tytherington. Wilts 2E 23
Tytherleigh. Devn 2G 13
Tywardreath. Corn 3E 7
Tywardreath Highway. Corn 3E 7
Tywyn. Cnwy 3G 81
Tywyn. Gwyn 5E 69

U

Uachdar. W Isl 3D 170
Uags. High 5G 155
Ubbeston Green. Suff 3F 67
Ubley. Bath 1A 22
Uckerby. N Yor 4F 105
Uckfield. E Sus 3F 27
Uckinghall. Worc 2D 48
Uckington. Glos 3E 49
Uckington. Shrp 5H 71
Uddingston. S Lan 3H 127
Uddington. S Lan 1A 118
Udimore. E Sus 4C 28
Udny Green. Abers 1F 153
Udny Station. Abers 1G 153
Udston. S Lan 4H 127
Udstonhead. S Lan 5A 128
Uffcott. Wilts 4G 35
Uffculme. Devn 1D 12
Uffington. Linc 5H 75
Uffington. Oxon 3B 36
Uffington. Shrp 4H 71
Ufford. Pet 5H 75
Ufford. Suff 5E 67
Ufton. Warw 4A 62
Ufton Nervet. W Ber 5E 37
Ugadale. Arg 3B 122
Ugborough. Devn 3C 8
Ugford. Wilts 3F 23
Uggeshall. Suff 2G 67
Ugglebarnby. N Yor 4F 107
Ugley. Essx 3F 53
Ugley Green. Essx 3F 53
Ugthorpe. N Yor 3E 107
Uidh. W Isl 9B 170
Uig. Arg 3C 138
Uig. High
nr. Balgown 2C 154
nr. Dunvegan 3A 154
Uigshader. High 4D 154
Uisken. Arg 2A 132
Ulbster. High 4F 169
Ulcat Row. Cumb 2F 103
Ulceby. Linc 3D 88
Ulceby. N Lin 3E 94
Ulceby Skitter. N Lin 3E 94
Ulcombe. Kent 1C 28
Uldale. Cumb 1D 102
Uley. Glos 2C 34
Ulgham. Nmbd 5G 121
Ullapool. High 4F 163
Ullenhall. Warw 4F 61
Ulleskelf. N Yor 1F 93
Ullesthorpe. Leics 2C 62
Ulley. S Yor 2B 86
Ullingswick. Here 5H 59
Ullinish. High 5C 154
Ullock. Cumb 2B 102
Ulpha. Cumb 5C 102
Ulrome. E Yor 4F 101
Ulsta. Shet 3F 173
Ulting. Essx 5B 54
Ulva House. Arg 5F 139
Ulverston. Cumb 2B 96
Ulwell. Dors 4F 15
Umberleigh. Devn 4G 19
Unapool. High 5C 166
Underbarrow. Cumb 5F 103
Undercliffe. W Yor 1B 92
Underdale. Shrp 4H 71
Underhoull. Shet 1G 173
Underriver. Kent 5G 39
Under Tofts. S Yor 2H 85
Underton. Shrp 1A 60
Underwood. Newp 3G 33
Underwood. Notts 5B 86
Underwood. Plym 3B 8
Undley. Suff 2F 65
Undy. Mon 3H 33
Union Mills. IOM 4C 108
Union Street. E Sus 2B 28
Unstone. Derbs 3A 86
Unstone Green. Derbs 3A 86
Unthank. Cumb
nr. Carlisle 5E 113
nr. Gamblesby 5H 113
nr. Penrith 1F 103
Unthank End. Cumb 1F 103
Upavon. Wilts 1G 23
Up Cerne. Dors 2B 14
Upchurch. Kent 4C 40
Upcott. Devn 2F 11
Upcott. Here 5F 59
Upend. Cambs 5F 65
Up Exe. Devn 2C 12
Upgate. Norf 4D 78
Upgate Street. Norf 1C 66
Uphall. Dors 2A 14
Uphall. W Lot 2D 128
Uphall Station. W Lot 2D 128
Upham. Devn 2B 12
Upham. Hants 4D 24
Uphampton. Here 4F 59
Uphampton. Worc 4C 60
Up Hatherley. Glos 3E 49
Uphill. N Som 1G 21
Up Holland. Lanc 4D 90
Uplawmoor. E Ren 4F 127
Upleadon. Glos 3C 48
Upleatham. Red C 3D 106
Uplees. Kent 4D 40
Uploders. Dors 3A 14
Uplowman. Devn 1D 12
Uplyme. Devn 3G 13
Up Marden. W Sus 1F 17
Upminster. G Lon 2G 39
Up Nately. Hants 1E 25
Upottery. Devn 2F 13
Uppat. High 3F 165
Upper Affcot. Shrp 2G 59
Upper Arley. Worc 2B 60
Upper Armley. W Yor 1C 92
Upper Arncott. Oxon 4E 50
Upper Astrop. Nptn 2D 50
Upper Badcall. High 4B 166
Upper Ballinderry. Lis 3F 179
Upper Bangor. Gwyn 3E 81
Upper Basildon. W Ber 4D 36
Upper Batley. W Yor 2C 92
Upper Beeding. W Sus 4C 26
Upper Benefield. Nptn 2G 63
Upper Bentley. Worc 4D 61
Upper Bighouse. High 3A 168
Upper Boddam. Abers 5D 160
Upper Boddington. Nptn 5B 62
Upper Bogside. Mor 3G 159
Upper Booth. Derbs 2F 85
Upper Borth. Cdgn 2F 57
Upper Boyndlie. Abers 2G 161
Upper Brailes. Warw 1B 50
Upper Breinton. Here 1H 47
Upper Broughton. Notts 3D 74
Upper Brynamman. Carm 4H 45
Upper Bucklebury. W Ber 5D 36
Upper Bullington. Hants 2C 24
Upper Burgate. Hants 1G 15
Upper Caldecote. C Beds 1B 52
Upper Canterton. Hants 1A 16
Upper Catesby. Nptn 5C 62
Upper Chapel. Powy 1D 46
Upper Cheddon. Som 4F 21
Upper Chicksgrove. Wilts 4E 23
Upper Church Village. Rhon 3D 32
Upper Chute. Wilts 1A 24
Upper Clatford. Hants 2B 24
Upper Coberley. Glos 4E 49
Upper Coedcae. Torf 5F 47
Upper Cound. Shrp 5H 71
Upper Cudworth. S Yor 4D 93
Upper Cumberworth. W Yor 4C 92
Upper Cuttlehill. Abers 4B 160
Upper Cwmbran. Torf 2F 33
Upper Dallachy. Mor 2A 160
Upper Dean. Bed 4H 63
Upper Denby. W Yor 4C 92
Upper Derraid. High 5E 159
Upper Diabaig. High 2H 155
Upper Dicker. E Sus 5G 27
Upper Dinchope. Shrp 2G 59
Upper Dochcarty. High 2H 157
Upper Dounreay. High 2B 168
Upper Dovercourt. Essx 2F 55
Upper Dunsforth. N Yor 3G 99
Upper Dunsley. Herts 4H 51
Upper Eastern Green. W Mid 2G 61
Upper Elkstone. Staf 5E 85
Upper Ellastone. Staf 1F 73
Upper End. Derbs 3E 85
Upper Enham. Hants 2B 24
Upper Farmcote. Shrp 1B 60
Upper Farringdon. Hants 3F 25
Upper Framilode. Glos 4C 48
Upper Froyle. Hants 2F 25
Upper Gills. High 1F 169
Upper Glenfintaig. High 5E 149
Upper Godney. Som 2H 21
Upper Gravenhurst. C Beds 2B 52
Upper Green. Essx 2E 53
Upper Green. W Ber 5B 36
Upper Green. W Yor 2C 92
Upper Grove Common. Here 3A 48
Upper Hackney. Derbs 4G 85
Upper Hale. Surr 2G 25
Upper Halliford. Surr 4B 38
Upper Halling. Medw 4A 40
Upper Hambleton. Rut 5G 75
Upper Hardres Court. Kent 5F 41
Upper Hardwick. Here 5G 59
Upper Hartfield. E Sus 2F 27
Upper Haugh. S Yor 1B 86
Upper Hayton. Shrp 2H 59
Upper Heath. Shrp 2H 59
Upper Hellesdon. Norf 4E 78
Upper Helmsley. N Yor 4A 100
Upper Hengoed. Shrp 2E 71
Upper Hergest. Here 5E 59
Upper Heyford. Nptn 5D 62
Upper Heyford. Oxon 3C 50
Upper Hill. Here 5G 59
Upper Hindhope. Bord 4B 120
Upper Hopton. W Yor 3B 92
Upper Howsell. Worc 1C 48
Upper Hulme. Staf 4E 85
Upper Inglesham. Swin 2H 35
Upper Kilcott. S Glo 3C 34
Upper Killay. Swan 3E 31
Upper Kirkton. Abers 5E 161
Upper Kirkton. N Ayr 4C 126
Upper Knockando. Mor 4F 159
Upper Knockchoilum. High 2G 149
Upper Lambourn. W Ber 3B 36
Upperlands. M Ulst 6E 174
Upper Langford. N Som 1H 21
Upper Langwith. Derbs 4C 86
Upper Largo. Fife 3G 137
Upper Latheron. High 5D 169
Upper Layham. Suff 1D 54
Upper Leigh. Staf 2E 73
Upper Lenie. High 1H 149
Upper Lochton. Abers 4D 152
Upper Longdon. Staf 4E 73
Upper Longwood. Shrp 5A 72
Upper Lybster. High 5E 169
Upper Lydbrook. Glos 4B 48
Upper Lye. Here 4F 59
Upper Maes-coed. Here 2G 47
Upper Midway. Derbs 3G 73
Uppermill. G Man 4H 91
Upper Millichope. Shrp 2H 59
Upper Milovaig. High 4A 154
Upper Minety. Wilts 2F 35
Upper Mitton. Worc 3C 60
Upper Nash. Pemb 4E 43
Upper Neepaback. Shet 3G 173
Upper Netchwood. Shrp 1A 60
Upper Nobut. Staf 2E 73
Upper North Dean. Buck 2G 37
Upper Norwood. W Sus 4A 26
Upper Nyland. Dors 4C 22
Upper Oddington. Glos 3H 49
Upper Ollach. High 5E 155
Upper Outwoods. Staf 3G 73
Upper Padley. Derbs 3G 85
Upper Pennington. Hants 3B 16
Upper Poppleton. York 4H 99
Upper Quinton. Warw 1G 49
Upper Rissington. Glos 4H 49
Upper Rochford. Worc 4A 60
Upper Rusko. Dum 3C 110
Upper Sandaig. High 2F 147
Upper Sanday. Orkn 7E 172
Upper Sapey. Here 4A 60
Upper Seagry. Wilts 3E 35
Upper Shelton. C Beds 1H 51
Upper Sheringham. Norf 1D 78

Upper Skelmorlie—West Grafton

Upper Skelmorlie. N Ayr 3C 126
Upper Slaughter. Glos 3G 49
Upper Sonachan. Arg 1H 133
Upper Soudley. Glos 4B 48
Upper Staploe. Bed 5A 64
Upper Stoke. Norf 5E 79
Upper Stondon. C Beds 2B 52
Upper Stowe. Nptn 5D 62
Upper Street. Hants 1G 15
Upper Street. Norf
nr. Horning 4F 79
nr. Hoveton 4F 79
Upper Street. Suff 2E 55
Upper Strensham. Worc 2E 49
Upper Studley. Wilts 1D 22
Upper Sundon. C Beds 3A 52
Upper Swell. Glos 3G 49
Upper Tankersley. S Yor 1H 85
Upper Tean. Staf 2E 73
Upperthong. W Yor 4B 92
Upperthorpe. N Lin 4A 94
Upper Thurnham. Lanc 4D 96
Upper Tillyrie. Per 3D 136
Upperton. W Sus 3A 26
Upper Tooting. G Lon 3D 39
Upper Town. Derbs
nr. Bonsall 5G 85
nr. Hognaston 5G 85
Upper Town. Here 1A 48
Upper Town. N Som 5A 34
Uppertown. Derbs 4H 85
Uppertown. High 1F 169
Uppertown. Nmbd 2B 114
Uppertown. Orkn 8D 172
Upper Tysoe. Warw 1B 50
Upper Upham. Wilts 4H 35
Upper Upnor. Medw 3B 40
Upper Urquhart. Fife 3D 136
Upper Wardington. Oxon 1C 50
Upper Weald. Mil 2F 51
Upper Weedon. Nptn 5D 62
Upper Wellingham. E Sus 4F 27
Upper Whiston. S Yor 2B 86
Upper Wield. Hants 3E 25
Upper Winchendon. Buck 4F 51
Upperwood. Derbs 5G 85
Upper Woodford. Wilts 3G 23
Upper Wootton. Hants 1D 24
Upper Wraxall. Wilts 4D 34
Upper Wyche. Worc 1C 48
Uppincott. Devn 2B 12
Uppingham. Rut 1F 63
Uppington. Shrp 5A 72
Upsall. N Yor 1G 99
Upsettlington. Bord 5E 131
Upshire. Essx 5E 53
Up Somborne. Hants 3B 24
Upstreet. Kent 4G 41
Up Sydling. Dors 2B 14
Upthorpe. Suff 3B 66
Upton. Buck 4F 51
Upton. Cambs 3A 64
Upton. Ches W 4G 83
Upton. Corn
nr. Bude 2C 10
nr. Liskeard 5C 10
Upton. Cumb 1E 102
Upton. Devn
nr. Honiton 2D 12
nr. Kingsbridge 4D 8
Upton. Dors
nr. Poole 3E 15
nr. Weymouth 4C 14
Upton. E Yor 4F 101
Upton. Hants
nr. Andover 1B 24
nr. Southampton 1B 16
Upton. IOW 3D 16
Upton. Leics 1A 62
Upton. Linc 2F 87
Upton. Mers 2E 83
Upton. Norf 4F 79
Upton. Nptn 4E 62
Upton. Notts
nr. Retford 3E 87
nr. Southwell 5E 87
Upton. Oxon 3D 36
Upton. Pemb 4E 43
Upton. Pet 5A 76
Upton. Slo 3A 38
Upton. Som
nr. Somerton 4H 21
nr. Wiveliscombe 4C 20
Upton. Warw 5F 61
Upton. W Yor 3E 93
Upton. Wilts 3D 22
Upton Bishop. Here 3B 48
Upton Cheyney. S Glo 5B 34
Upton Cressett. Shrp 1A 60
Upton Crews. Here 3B 48
Upton Cross. Corn 5C 10
Upton End. C Beds 2B 52
Upton Grey. Hants 2E 25
Upton Heath. Ches W 4G 83
Upton Hellions. Devn 2B 12
Upton Lovell. Wilts 2E 23
Upton Magna. Shrp 4H 71
Upton Noble. Som 3C 22
Upton Pyne. Devn 3C 12
Upton St Leonards. Glos 4D 48
Upton Scudamore. Wilts 2D 22
Upton Snodsbury. Worc 5D 60
Upton upon Severn. Worc 1D 48
Upton Warren. Worc 4D 60
Upwaltham. W Sus 4A 26
Upware. Cambs 3E 65
Upwell. Norf 5E 77
Upwey. Dors 4B 14
Upwick Green. Herts 3E 53
Upwood. Cambs 2B 64
Urafirth. Shet 4E 173
Uragaig. Arg 4A 132
Urchany. High 4C 158
Urchfont. Wilts 1F 23
Urdimarsh. Here 1A 48
Ure. Shet 4D 173
Ure Bank. N Yor 2F 99
Urgha. W Isl 8D 171
Urlay Nook. Stoc T 3B 106
Urmston. G Man 1B 84
Urquhart. Mor 2G 159
Urra. N Yor 4C 106
Urray. High 3H 157
Usan. Ang 3G 145
Ushaw Moor. Dur 5F 115
Usk. Mon 5G 47
Usselby. Linc 1H 87
Usworth. Tyne 4G 115
Utkinton. Ches W 4H 83
Uton. Devn 3B 12
Utterby. Linc 1C 88
Uttoxeter. Staf 2E 73
Uwchmynydd. Gwyn 3A 68
Uxbridge. G Lon 2B 38
Uyeasound. Shet 1G 173
Uzmaston. Pemb 3D 42

V

Valley. IOA 3B 80
Valley End. Surr 4A 38
Valley Truckle. Corn 4B 10
Valsgarth. Shet 1H 173
Valtos. High 2E 155
Van. Powy 2B 58
Vange. Essx 2B 40
Varteg. Torf 5F 47
Vatsetter. Shet 3G 173
Vatten. High 4B 154
Vaul. Arg 4B 138
The Vauld. Here 1A 48
Vaynor. Mer T 4D 46
Veensgarth. Shet 7F 173
Velindre. Powy 2E 47
Vellow. Som 3D 20
Velly. Devn 4C 18
Veness. Orkn 5E 172
Venhay. Devn 1A 12
Venn. Devn 4D 8
Venngreen. Devn 1D 11
Vennington. Shrp 5F 71
Venn Ottery. Devn 3D 12
Venn's Green. Here 1A 48
Venny Tedburn. Devn 3B 12
Venterdon. Corn 5D 10
Ventnor. IOW 5D 16
Vernham Dean. Hants 1B 24
Vernham Street. Hants 1B 24
Vernolds Common. Shrp 2G 59
Verwood. Dors 2F 15
Veryan. Corn 5D 6
Veryan Green. Corn 5D 6
Vicarage. Devn 4F 13
Vickerstown. Cumb 3A 96
Victoria. Corn 2D 6
Victoria Bridge. Derr 3F 176
Vidlin. Shet 5F 173
Viewpark. N Lan 3A 128
Vigo. W Mid 5E 73
Vigo Village. Kent 4H 39
Vinehall Street. E Sus 3B 28
Vine's Cross. E Sus 4G 27
Viney Hill. Glos 5B 48
Virginia Water. Surr 4A 38
Virginstow. Devn 3D 11
Vobster. Som 2C 22
Voe. Shet
nr. Hillside 5F 173
nr. Swinister 3E 173
Vole. Som 2G 21
Vowchurch. Here 2G 47
Voxter. Shet 4E 173
Voy. Orkn 6B 172
Vulcan Village. Mers 1H 83

W

Waberthwaite. Cumb 5C 102
Wackerfield. Dur 2E 105
Wacton. Norf 1D 66
Wadbister. Shet 7F 173
Wadborough. Worc 1E 49
Wadbrook. Devn 2G 13
Waddesdon. Buck 4F 51
Waddeton. Devn 3E 9
Waddicar. Mers 1F 83
Waddingham. Linc 1G 87
Waddington. Lanc 5G 97
Waddington. Linc 4G 87
Waddon. Devn 5B 12
Wadebridge. Corn 1D 6
Wadeford. Som 1G 13
Wadenhoe. Nptn 2H 63
Wadesmill. Herts 4D 52
Wadhurst. E Sus 2H 27
Wadshelf. Derbs 3H 85
Wadsley. S Yor 1H 85
Wadsley Bridge. S Yor 1H 85
Wadswick. Wilts 5D 34
Wadwick. Hants 1C 24
Wadworth. S Yor 1C 86
Waen. Den
nr. Llandymog 4D 82
nr. Nantglyn 4B 82
Waen. Powy 1B 58
Waen Fach. Powy 4E 70
Waen Goleugoed. Den 3C 82
Wag. High 1H 165
Wainfleet All Saints. Linc 5D 89
Wainfleet Bank. Linc 5D 88
Wainfleet St Mary. Linc 5D 89
Wainhouse Corner. Corn 3B 10
Wainscott. Medw 3B 40
Wainstalls. W Yor 2A 92
Waitby. Cumb 4A 104
Waithe. Linc 4F 95
Wakefield. W Yor 2D 92
Wakerley. Nptn 1G 63
Wakes Colne. Essx 3B 54
Walberswick. Suff 3G 67
Walberton. W Sus 5A 26
Walbottle. Tyne 3E 115
Walby. Cumb 3F 113
Walcombe. Som 2A 22
Walcot. Linc 2H 75
Walcot. N Lin 2B 94
Walcot. Swin 3G 35
Walcot. Telf 4H 71
Walcot. Warw 5F 61
Walcote. Leics 2C 62
Walcot Green. Norf 2D 66
Walcott. Linc 5A 88
Walcott. Norf 2F 79
Walden. N Yor 1C 98
Walden Head. N Yor 1B 98
Walden Stubbs. N Yor 3F 93
Walderslade. Medw 4B 40
Walderton. W Sus 1F 17
Walditch. Dors 3H 13
Waldley. Derbs 2F 73
Waldridge. Dur 4F 115
Waldringfield. Suff 1F 55
Waldron. E Sus 4G 27
Wales. S Yor 2B 86
Walesby. Linc 1A 88
Walesby. Notts 3D 86
Walford. Here
nr. Leintwardine 3F 59
nr. Ross-on-Wye 3A 48
Walford. Shrp 3G 71
Walford. Staf 2C 72
Walford Heath. Shrp 4G 71
Walgherton. Ches E 1A 72
Walgrave. Nptn 3F 63
Walhampton. Hants 3B 16
Walkden. G Man 4F 91
Walker. Tyne 3F 115
Walkerburn. Bord 1F 119
Walker Fold. Lanc 5F 97
Walkeringham. Notts 1E 87
Walkerith. Linc 1E 87
Walkern. Herts 3C 52
Walker's Green. Here 1A 48
Walkerton. Fife 3E 137
Walkerville. N Yor 5F 105
Walkford. Dors 3H 15
Walkhampton. Devn 2B 8
Walkington. E Yor 1C 94
Walkley. S Yor 2H 85
Walk Mill. Lanc 1G 91
Wall. Corn 3D 4
Wall. Nmbd 3C 114
Wall. Staf 5F 73
Wallaceton. Dum 1F 111
Wallacetown. Shet 6E 173
Wallacetown. S Ayr
nr. Ayr 2C 116
nr. Dailly 4B 116
Wallands Park. E Sus 4F 27
Wallasey. Mers 1E 83
Wallaston Green. Pemb 4D 42
Wallbrook. W Mid 1D 60
Wallcrouch. E Sus 2A 28
Wall End. Cumb 1B 96
Wallend. Medw 3C 40
Wall Heath. W Mid 2C 60
Wallingford. Oxon 3E 36
Wallington. G Lon 4D 39
Wallington. Hants 2D 16
Wallington. Herts 2C 52
Wallis. Pemb 2E 43
Wallisdown. Bour 3F 15
Walliswood. Surr 2C 26
Wall Nook. Dur 5F 115
Walls. Shet 7D 173
Wallsend. Tyne 3G 115
Wallsworth. Glos 3D 48
Wall under Heywood.
Shrp 1H 59
Wallyford. E Lot 2G 129
Walmer. Kent 5H 41
Walmer Bridge. Lanc 2C 90
Walmersley. G Man 3G 91
Walmley. W Mid 1F 61
Walnut Grove. Per 1D 136
Walpole. Suff 3F 67
Walpole Cross Keys. Norf 4E 77
Walpole Gate. Norf 4E 77
Walpole Highway. Norf 4E 77
Walpole Marsh. Norf 4D 77
Walpole St Andrew. Norf 4E 77
Walpole St Peter. Norf 4E 77
Walsall. W Mid 1E 61
Walsall Wood. W Mid 5E 73
Walsden. W Yor 2H 91
Walsgrave on Sowe.
W Mid 2A 62
Walsham le Willows. Suff 3C 66
Walshaw. G Man 3F 91
Walshford. N Yor 4G 99
Walsoken. Norf 4D 76
Walston. S Lan 5D 128
Walsworth. Herts 2B 52
Walter's Ash. Buck 2G 37
Walterston. V Glam 4D 32
Walterstone. Here 3G 47
Waltham. Kent 1F 29
Waltham. NE Lin 4F 95
Waltham Abbey. Essx 5D 53
Waltham Chase. Hants 1D 16
Waltham Cross. Herts 5D 52
Waltham on the Wolds.
Leics 3F 75
Waltham St Lawrence.
Wind 4G 37
Waltham's Cross. Essx 2G 53
Walthamstow. G Lon 2E 39
Walton. Cumb 3G 113
Walton. Derbs 4A 86
Walton. Leics 2C 62
Walton. Mers 1F 83
Walton. Mil 2G 51
Walton. Pet 5A 76
Walton. Powy 5E 59
Walton. Som 3H 21
Walton. Staf
nr. Eccleshall 3C 72
nr. Stone 2C 72
Walton. Suff 2F 55
Walton. Telf 4H 71
Walton. Warw 5G 61
Walton. W Yor
nr. Wakefield 3D 92
nr. Wetherby 5G 99
Walton Cardiff. Glos 2E 49
Walton East. Pemb 2E 43
Walton Elm. Dors 1C 14
Walton Highway. Norf 4D 77
Walton in Gordano.
N Som 4H 33
Walton-le-Dale. Lanc 2D 90
Walton-on-Thames. Surr 4C 38
Walton on the Hill. Surr 5D 38
Walton-on-the-Hill. Staf 3D 72
Walton-on-the-Naze.
Essx 3F 55
Walton on the Wolds.
Leics 4C 74
Walton-on-Trent. Derbs 4G 73
Walton West. Pemb 3C 42
Walwick. Nmbd 2C 114
Walworth. Darl 3F 105
Walworth Gate. Darl 2F 105
Walwyn's Castle. Pemb 3C 42
Wambrook. Som 2F 13
Wampool. Cumb 4D 112
Wanborough. Surr 1A 26
Wanborough. Swin 3H 35
Wandel. S Lan 2B 118
Wandsworth. G Lon 3D 38
Wangford. Suff
nr. Lakenheath 2G 65
nr. Southwold 3G 67
Wanlip. Leics 4C 74
Wanlockhead. Dum 3A 118
Wannock. E Sus 5G 27
Wansford. E Yor 4E 101
Wansford. Pet 1H 63
Wanshurst Green. Kent 1B 28
Wanstead. G Lon 2F 39
Wanstrow. Som 2C 22
Wanswell. Glos 5B 48
Wantage. Oxon 3C 36
Wapley. S Glo 4C 34
Wappenbury. Warw 4A 62
Wappenham. Nptn 1E 51
Warbleton. E Sus 4H 27
Warblington. Hants 2F 17
Warborough. Oxon 2D 36
Warboys. Cambs 2C 64
Warbreck. Bkpl 1B 90
Warbstow. Corn 3C 10
Warburton. G Man 2B 84
Warcop. Cumb 3A 104
Warden. Kent 3E 40
Warden. Nmbd 3C 114
Ward End. W Mid 2F 61
Ward Green. Suff 4C 66
Ward Green Cross. Lanc 1E 91
Wardhedges. C Beds 2A 52
Wardhouse. Abers 5C 160
Wardington. Oxon 1C 50
Wardle. Ches E 5A 84
Wardle. G Man 3H 91
Wardley. Rut 5F 75
Wardley. W Sus 4G 25
Wardlow. Derbs 3F 85
Wardsend. Ches E 2D 84
Wardy Hill. Cambs 2D 64
Ware. Herts 4D 52
Ware. Kent 4G 41
Wareham. Dors 4E 15
Warehorne. Kent 2D 28
Warenford. Nmbd 2F 121
Waren Mill. Nmbd 1F 121
Warenton. Nmbd 1F 121
Wareside. Herts 4D 53
Waresley. Cambs 5B 64
Waresley. Worc 4C 60
Warfield. Brac 4G 37
Warfleet. Devn 3E 9
Wargate. Linc 2B 76
Wargrave. Wok 4F 37
Warham. Norf 1B 78
Waringsford. Arm 5G 179
Waringstown. Arm 4F 178
Wark. Nmbd
nr. Coldstream 1C 120
nr. Hexham 2B 114
Warkleigh. Devn 4G 19
Warkton. Nptn 3F 63
Warkworth. Nptn 1C 50
Warkworth. Nmbd 4G 121
Warlaby. N Yor 5A 106
Warland. W Yor 2H 91
Warleggan. Corn 2F 7
Warlingham. Surr 5E 39
Warmanbie. Dum 3C 112
Warmfield. W Yor 2D 93
Warmingham. Ches E 4B 84
Warminghurst. W Sus 4C 26
Warmington. Nptn 1H 63
Warmington. Warw 1C 50
Warminster. Wilts 2D 23
Warmley. S Glo 4B 34
Warmsworth. S Yor 4F 93
Warmwell. Dors 4C 14
Warndon. Worc 5C 60
Warners End. Herts 5A 52
Warnford. Hants 4E 24
Warnham. W Sus 2C 26
Warningcamp. W Sus 5B 26
Warninglid. W Sus 3D 26
Warren. Ches E 3C 84
Warren. Pemb 5D 42
Warrenby. Red C 2C 106
Warren Corner. Hants
nr. Aldershot 2G 25
nr. Petersfield 4F 25
Warrenpoint. New M 8F 178
Warren Row. Wind 3G 37
Warren Street. Kent 5D 40
Warrington. Mil 5F 63
Warrington. Warr 2A 84
Warsash. Hants 2C 16
Warse. High 1F 169
Warslow. Staf 5E 85
Warsop. Notts 4C 86
Warsop Vale. Notts 4C 86
Warter. E Yor 4C 100
Warthermarske. N Yor 2E 98
Warthill. N Yor 4A 100
Wartling. E Sus 5A 28
Wartnaby. Leics 3E 74
Warton. Lanc
nr. Carnforth 2D 97
nr. Freckleton 2C 90
Warton. Nmbd 4E 121
Warton. Warw 5G 73
Warwick. Warw 4G 61
Warwick Bridge. Cumb 4F 113
Warwick-on-Eden. Cumb 4F 113
Warwick Wold. Surr 5E 39
Wasbister. Orkn 4C 172
Wasdale Head. Cumb 4C 102
Wash. Derbs 2E 85
Washaway. Corn 2E 7
Washbourne. Devn 3D 9
Washbrook. Suff 1E 54
Wash Common. W Ber 5C 36
Washerwall. Staf 1D 72
Washfield. Devn 1C 12
Washfold. N Yor 4D 104
Washford. Som 2D 20
Washford Pyne. Devn 1B 12
Washingborough. Linc 3H 87
Washington. Tyne 4G 115
Washington. W Sus 4C 26
Washington Village.
Tyne 4G 115
Waskerley. Dur 5D 114
Wasperton. Warw 5G 61
Wasp Green. Surr 1E 27
Wasps Nest. Linc 4H 87
Wass. N Yor 2H 99
Watchet. Som 2D 20
Watchfield. Oxon 2H 35
Watchgate. Cumb 5G 103
Watchhill. Cumb 5C 112
Watcombe. Torb 2F 9
Watendlath. Cumb 3D 102
Water. Devn 4A 12
Water. Lanc 2G 91
Waterbeach. Cambs 4D 65
Waterbeach. W Sus 2G 17
Waterbeck. Dum 2D 112
Waterditch. Hants 3G 15
Water End. C Beds 2A 52
Water End. E Yor 1A 94
Water End. Essx 1F 53
Water End. Herts
nr. Hatfield 5C 52
nr. Hemel Hempstead 4A 52
Waterfall. Staf 5E 85
Waterfoot. Caus 4J 175
Waterfoot. E Ren 4G 127
Waterfoot. Lanc 2G 91
Waterford. Herts 4D 52
Water Fryston. W Yor 2E 93
Waterhead. Cumb 4E 103
Waterhead. E Ayr 3E 117
Waterhead. S Ayr 5C 116
Waterheads. Bord 4F 129
Waterhouses. Dur 5E 115
Waterhouses. Staf 5E 85
Wateringbury. Kent 5A 40
Waterlane. Glos 5E 49
Waterlip. Som 2B 22
Waterloo. Cphy 3E 33
Waterloo. Corn 5B 10
Waterloo. Here 1G 47
Waterloo. High 1E 147
Waterloo. Mers 1F 83
Waterloo. Norf 4E 78
Waterloo. N Lan 4B 128
Waterloo. Pemb 4D 42
Waterloo. Per 5H 143
Waterloo. Pool 3F 15
Waterloo. Shrp 2G 71
Waterlooville. Hants 2E 17
Watermead. Buck 4G 51
Watermillock. Cumb 2F 103
Water Newton. Cambs 1A 64
Water Orton. Warw 1F 61
Waterperry. Oxon 5E 51
Waterrow. Som 4D 20
Watersfield. W Sus 4B 26
Waterside. Buck 5H 51
Waterside. Cambs 3F 65
Waterside. Cumb 5D 112
Waterside. E Ayr
nr. Ayr 4D 116
nr. Kilmarnock 5F 127
Waterside. E Dun 2H 127
Waterstein. High 4A 154
Waterstock. Oxon 5E 51
Waterston. Pemb 4D 42
Water Stratford. Buck 2E 51
Waters Upton. Telf 4A 72
Water Yeat. Cumb 1B 96
Watford. Herts 1C 38
Watford. Nptn 4D 62
Wath. Cumb 4H 103
Wath. N Yor
nr. Pateley Bridge 3D 98
nr. Ripon 2F 99
Wath Brow. Cumb 3B 102
Wath upon Dearne. S Yor 4E 93
Watlington. Norf 4F 77
Watlington. Oxon 2E 37
Watten. High 3E 169
Wattisfield. Suff 3C 66
Wattisham. Suff 5C 66
Wattlesborough Heath.
Shrp 4F 71
Watton. Dors 3H 13
Watton. E Yor 4E 101
Watton. Norf 5B 78
Watton at Stone. Herts 4C 52
Wattston. N Lan 2A 128
Wattstown. Rhon 2D 32
Wattsville. Cphy 2F 33
Wauldby. E Yor 2C 94
Waulkmill. Abers 4D 152
Waun. Powy 4E 71
Y Waun. Wrex 2E 71
Waunarlwydd. Swan 3F 31
Waun Fawr. Cdgn 2F 57
Waunfawr. Gwyn 5E 81
Waungilwen. Carm 1H 43
Waun-Lwyd. Blae 5E 47
Waun y Clyn. Carm 5E 45
Wavendon. Mil 2H 51
Waverbridge. Cumb 5D 112
Waverley. Surr 2G 25
Waverton. Ches W 4G 83
Waverton. Cumb 5D 112
Wavertree. Mers 2F 83
Wawne. E Yor 1D 94
Waxham. Norf 3G 79
Waxholme. E Yor 2G 95
Wayford. Som 2H 13
Way Head. Cambs 2D 65
Waytown. Dors 3H 13
Way Village. Devn 1B 12
Wdig. Pemb 1D 42
Wealdstone. G Lon 2C 38
Weardley. W Yor 5E 99
Weare. Som 1H 21
Weare Giffard. Devn 4E 19
Wearhead. Dur 1B 104
Wearne. Som 4H 21
Weasdale. Cumb 4H 103
Weasenham All Saints.
Norf 3H 77
Weasenham St Peter.
Norf 3A 78
Weaverham. Ches W 3A 84
Weaverthorpe. N Yor 2D 100
Webheath. Worc 4E 61
Webton. Here 2H 47
Wedderlairs. Abers 5F 161
Weddington. Warw 1A 62
Wedhampton. Wilts 1F 23
Wedmore. Som 2H 21
Wednesbury. W Mid 1D 61
Wednesfield. W Mid 5D 72
Weecar. Notts 4F 87
Weedon. Buck 4G 51
Weedon Bec. Nptn 5D 62
Weedon Lois. Nptn 1E 50
Weeford. Staf 5F 73
Week. Devn
nr. Barnstaple 4F 19
nr. Okehampton 2G 11
nr. South Molton 1H 11
nr. Totnes 2D 9
Week. Som 3C 20
Weeke. Devn 2A 12
Weeke. Hants 3C 24
Week Green. Corn 3C 10
Weekley. Nptn 2F 63
Week St Mary. Corn 3C 10
Weel. E Yor 1D 94
Weeley. Essx 3E 55
Weeley Heath. Essx 3E 55
Weem. Per 4F 143
Weeping Cross. Staf 3D 72
Weethly. Warw 5E 61
Weeting. Norf 2G 65
Weeton. E Yor 2G 95
Weeton. Lanc 1B 90
Weeton. N Yor 5E 99
Weetwood Hall. Nmbd 2E 121
Weir. Lanc 2G 91
Welborne. Norf 4C 78
Welbourn. Linc 5G 87
Welburn. N Yor
nr. Kirkbymoorside 1A 100
nr. Malton 3B 100
Welbury. N Yor 4A 106
Welby. Linc 2G 75
Welches Dam. Cambs 2D 64
Welcombe. Devn 1C 10
Weld Bank. Lanc 3D 90
Weldon. Nptn 2G 63
Weldon. Nmbd 5F 121
Welford. Nptn 2D 62
Welford. W Ber 4C 36
Welford-on-Avon. Warw 5F 61
Welham. Leics 1E 63
Welham. Notts 2E 87
Welham Green. Herts 5C 52
Well. Hants 2F 25
Well. Linc 3D 88
Well. N Yor 1E 99
Welland. Worc 1C 48
Wellbank. Ang 5D 144
Well Bottom. Dors 1E 15
Welldale. Dum 3C 112
Wellesbourne. Warw 5G 61
Well Hill. Kent 4F 39
Wellhouse. W Ber 4D 36
Welling. G Lon 3F 39
Wellingborough. Nptn 4F 63
Wellingham. Norf 3A 78
Wellingore. Linc 5G 87
Wellington. Cumb 4B 102
Wellington. Here 1H 47
Wellington. Som 4E 21
Wellington. Telf 4A 72
Wellington Heath. Here 1C 48
Wellow. Bath 1C 22
Wellow. IOW 4B 16
Wellow. Notts 4D 86
Wellpond Green. Herts 3E 53
Wells. Som 2A 22
Wellsborough. Leics 5A 74
Wells Green. Ches E 5A 84
Wells-next-the-Sea. Norf 1B 78
Wellswood. Torb 2F 9
Wellwood. Fife 1D 129
Welney. Norf 1E 65
Welsford. Devn 4C 18
Welshampton. Shrp 2G 71
Welsh End. Shrp 2H 71
Welsh Frankton. Shrp 2F 71
Welsh Hook. Pemb 2D 42
Welsh Newton. Here 4H 47
Welsh Newton Common.
Here 4A 48
Welshpool. Powy 5E 70
Welsh St Donats. V Glam 4D 32
Welton. Bath 1B 22
Welton. Cumb 5E 113
Welton. E Yor 2C 94
Welton. Linc 2H 87
Welton. Nptn 4C 62
Welton Hill. Linc 2H 87
Welton le Marsh. Linc 4D 88
Welton le Wold. Linc 2B 88
Welwick. E Yor 2G 95
Welwyn. Herts 4C 52
Welwyn Garden City.
Herts 4C 52
Wem. Shrp 3H 71
Wembdon. Som 3F 21
Wembley. G Lon 2C 38
Wembury. Devn 4B 8
Wembworthy. Devn 2G 11
Wemyss Bay. Inv 2C 126
Wenallt. Cdgn 3F 57
Wenallt. Gwyn 1B 70
Wendens Ambo. Essx 2F 53
Wendlebury. Oxon 4D 50
Wendling. Norf 4B 78
Wendover. Buck 5G 51
Wendron. Corn 5A 6
Wendy. Cambs 1D 52
Wenfordbridge. Corn 5A 10
Wenhaston. Suff 3G 67
Wennington. Cambs 3B 64
Wennington. G Lon 2G 39
Wennington. Lanc 2F 97
Wensley. Derbs 4G 85
Wensley. N Yor 1C 98
Wentbridge. W Yor 3E 93
Wentnor. Shrp 1F 59
Wentworth. Cambs 3D 65
Wentworth. S Yor 1A 86
Wenvoe. V Glam 4E 32
Weobley. Here 5G 59
Weobley Marsh. Here 5G 59
Wepham. W Sus 5B 26
Wereham. Norf 5F 77
Wergs. W Mid 5C 72
Wern. Gwyn 1E 69
Wern. Powy
nr. Brecon 4E 46
nr. Guilsfield 4E 71
nr. Llangadfan 4B 70
nr. Llanymynech 3E 71
Wernffrwd. Swan 3E 31
Wernyrheolydd. Mon 4G 47
Werrington. Corn 4D 10
Werrington. Pet 5A 76
Werrington. Staf 1D 72
Wervin. Ches W 3G 83
Wesham. Lanc 1C 90
Wessington. Derbs 5A 86
West Aberthaw. V Glam 5D 32
West Acre. Norf 4G 77
West Allerdean. Nmbd 5F 131
West Alvington. Devn 4D 8
West Amesbury. Wilts 2G 23
West Anstey. Devn 4B 20
West Appleton. N Yor 5F 105
West Ardsley. W Yor 2C 92
West Arthurlie. E Ren 4F 127
West Ashby. Linc 3B 88
West Ashling. W Sus 2G 17
West Ashton. Wilts 1D 23
West Auckland. Dur 2E 105
West Ayton. N Yor 1D 101
West Bagborough. Som 3E 21
West Bank. Hal 2H 83
West Barkwith. Linc 2A 88
West Barnby. N Yor 3F 107
West Barns. E Lot 2C 130
West Barsham. Norf 2B 78
West Bay. Dors 3H 13
West Beckham. Norf 2D 78
West Bennan. N Ayr 3D 123
Westbere. Kent 4F 41
West Bergholt. Essx 3C 54
West Bexington. Dors 4A 14
West Bilney. Norf 4G 77
West Blackdene. Dur 1B 104
West Blatchington. Brig 5D 27
Westborough. Linc 1F 75
Westbourne. Bour 3F 15
Westbourne. W Sus 2F 17
West Bowling. W Yor 1B 92
West Brabourne. Kent 1E 29
West Bradford. Lanc 5G 97
West Bradley. Som 3A 22
West Bretton. W Yor 3C 92
West Bridgford. Notts 2C 74
West Briggs. Norf 4F 77
West Bromwich. W Mid 1E 61
Westbrook. Here 1F 47
Westbrook. Kent 3H 41
Westbrook. Wilts 5E 35
West Buckland. Devn
nr. Barnstaple 3G 19
nr. Thurlestone 4C 8
West Buckland. Som 4E 21
West Burnside. Abers 1G 145
West Burrafirth. Shet 6D 173
West Burton. N Yor 1C 98
West Burton. W Sus 4B 26
Westbury. Buck 2E 50
Westbury. Shrp 5F 71
Westbury. Wilts 1D 22
Westbury Leigh. Wilts 1D 22
Westbury-on-Severn.
Glos 4C 48
Westbury on Trym. Bris 4A 34
Westbury-sub-Mendip.
Som 2A 22
West Butsfield. Dur 5E 115
West Butterwick. N Lin 4B 94
Westby. Linc 3G 75
West Byfleet. Surr 4B 38
West Caister. Norf 4H 79
West Calder. W Lot 3D 128
West Camel. Som 4A 22
West Carr. N Lin 4H 93
West Chaldon. Dors 4C 14
West Challow. Oxon 3B 36
West Charleton. Devn 4D 8
West Chelborough. Dors 2A 14
West Chevington. Nmbd 5G 121
West Chiltington. W Sus 4B 26
West Chiltington Common.
W Sus 4B 26
West Chinnock. Som 1H 13
West Chisenbury. Wilts 1G 23
West Clandon. Surr 5B 38
West Cliffe. Kent 1H 29
Westcliff-on-Sea. S'end 2C 40
West Clyne. High 3F 165
West Coker. Som 1A 14
Westcombe. Som
nr. Evercreech 3B 22
nr. Somerton 4H 21
West Compton. Dors 3A 14
West Compton. Som 2A 22
West Cornforth. Dur 1A 106
Westcot. Oxon 3B 36
Westcott. Buck 4F 51
Westcott. Devn 2D 12
Westcott. Surr 1C 26
Westcott Barton. Oxon 3C 50
West Cowick. E Yor 2G 93
West Cranmore. Som 2B 22
West Croftmore. High 2D 150
West Cross. Swan 4F 31
West Cullerlie. Abers 3E 153
West Culvennan. Dum 3H 109
West Curry. Corn 3C 10
West Curthwaite. Cumb 5E 113
West Dean. W Sus 1G 17
West Dean. Wilts 4A 24
Westdean. E Sus 5G 27
West Deeping. Linc 5A 76
West Derby. Mers 1F 83
West Dereham. Norf 5F 77
West Down. Devn 2F 19
Westdowns. Corn 4A 10
West Drayton. G Lon 3B 38
West Drayton. Notts 3E 86
West Dunnet. High 1E 169
West Ella. E Yor 2D 94
West End. Bed 5G 63
West End. Cambs 1D 64
West End. Dors 2E 15
West End. E Yor
nr. Kilham 3E 101
nr. Preston 1E 95
nr. South Cove 1C 94
nr. Ulrome 4F 101
West End. G Lon 2D 39
West End. Hants 1C 16
West End. Herts 5C 52
West End. Kent 4F 41
West End. Lanc 3D 96
West End. Linc 1C 76
West End. Norf 4H 79
West End. N Som 5H 33
West End. N Yor 4D 98
West End. S Glo 3C 34
West End. S Lan 5C 128
West End. Surr 4A 38
West End. Wilts 4E 23
West End. Wind 4G 37
West End Green. Hants 5E 37
Westenhanger. Kent 2F 29
Wester Aberchalder.
High 2H 149
Wester Balgedie. Per 3D 136
Wester Brae. High 2A 158
Wester Culbeuchly.
Abers 2D 160
Westerdale. High 3D 168
Westerdale. N Yor 4D 106
Wester Dechmont.
W Lot 2D 128
Wester Fearn. High 5D 164
Westerfield. Suff 1E 55
Wester Galcantray. High 4C 158
Westergate. W Sus 5A 26
Wester Gruinards. High 4C 164
Westerham. Kent 5F 39
Westerleigh. S Glo 4C 34
Westerloch. High 3F 169
Wester Mandally. High 3E 149
Wester Quarff. Shet 8F 173
Wester Rarichie. High 1C 158
Wester Shian. Per 5F 143
Wester Skeld. Shet 7D 173
Westerton. Ang 3F 145
Westerton. Dur 1F 105
Westerton. W Sus 2G 17
Westerwick. Shet 7D 173
West Farleigh. Kent 5B 40
West Farndon. Nptn 5C 62
West Felton. Shrp 3F 71
Westfield. Cumb 2A 102
Westfield. E Sus 4C 28
Westfield. High 2C 168
Westfield. Norf 5B 78
Westfield. N Lan 2A 128
Westfield. W Lot 2C 128
Westfields. Dors 2C 14
Westfields of Rattray.
Per 4A 144
West Fleetham. Nmbd 2F 121
Westford. Som 4E 20
West Garforth. W Yor 1D 93
Westgate. Dur 1C 104
Westgate. Norf 1B 78
Westgate. N Lin 4A 94
Westgate on Sea. Kent 3H 41
West Ginge. Oxon 3C 36
West Grafton. Wilts 5H 35

West Green—Witcham

West Green. Hants 1F 25
West Grimstead. Wilts 4H 23
West Grinstead. W Sus 3C 26
West Haddlesey. N Yor 2F 93
West Haddon. Nptn 3D 62
West Hagbourne. Oxon 3D 36
West Hagley. Worc 2D 60
West Hall. Cumb 3G 113
Westhall. Suff 2G 67
West Hallam. Derbs 1B 74
Westhall Terrace. Ang 5D 144
West Halton. N Lin 2C 94
West Ham. G Lon 2E 39
Westham. Dors 5B 14
Westham. E Sus 5H 27
Westham. Som 2H 21
Westhampnett. W Sus 2G 17
West Handley. Derbs 3A 86
West Hanney. Oxon 2C 36
West Hanningfield. Essx 1B 40
West Hardwick. W Yor 3E 93
West Harptree. Bath 1A 22
West Harting. W Sus 4F 25
West Harton. Tyne 3G 115
West Hatch. Som 4F 21
Westhay. Som 2H 21
West Head. Norf 5E 77
Westhead. Lanc 4C 90
West Heath. Hants
nr. Basingstoke 1D 24
nr. Farnborough 1G 25
West Helmsdale. High 2H 165
West Hendred. Oxon 3C 36
West Heogaland. Shet 4D 173
West Heslerton. N Yor 2D 100
West Hewish. N Som 5G 33
Westhide. Here 1A 48
West Hill. Devn 3D 12
West Hill. E Yor 3F 101
West Hill. N Som 4H 33
West Hill. W Sus 2E 27
Westhill. Abers 3F 153
Westhill. High 4B 158
West Hoathly. W Sus 2E 27
West Holme. Dors 4D 15
Westhope. Here 5G 59
Westhope. Shrp 2G 59
West Horndon. Essx 2H 39
Westhorp. Nptn 5C 62
Westhorpe. Linc 2B 76
Westhorpe. Suff 4C 66
West Horrington. Som 2A 22
West Horsley. Surr 5B 38
West Horton. Nmbd 1E 121
West Hougham. Kent 1G 29
Westhoughton. G Man 4E 91
West Houlland. Shet 6D 173
Westhouse. N Yor 2F 97
Westhouses. Derbs 5B 86
West Howe. Bour 3F 15
Westhumble. Surr 5C 38
West Huntspill. Som 2G 21
West Hyde. Herts 1B 38
West Hynish. Arg 5A 138
West Hythe. Kent 2F 29
West Ilsley. W Ber 3C 36
Westing. Shet 1G 173
West Keal. Linc 4C 88
West Kennett. Wilts 5G 35
West Kilbride. N Ayr 5D 126
West Kingsdown. Kent 4G 39
West Kington. Wilts 4D 34
West Kirby. Mers 2E 82
West Knapton. N Yor 2C 100
West Knighton. Dors 4C 14
West Knoyle. Wilts 3D 22
West Kyloe. Nmbd 5G 131
Westlake. Devn 3C 8
West Lambrook. Som 1H 13
West Langdon. Kent 1H 29
West Langwell. High 3D 164
West Lavington. W Sus 4G 25
West Lavington. Wilts 1F 23
West Layton. N Yor 4E 105
West Leake. Notts 3C 74
West Learmouth. Nmbd 1C 120
West Leigh. Devn 2G 11
Westleigh. Devn
nr. Bideford 4E 19
nr. Tiverton 1D 12
Westleigh. G Man 4E 91
West Leith. Herts 4H 51
Westleton. Suff 4G 67
West Lexham. Norf 4H 77
Westley. Shrp 5F 71
Westley. Suff 4H 65
Westley Waterless. Cambs 5F 65
West Lilling. N Yor 3A 100
West Lingo. Fife 3G 137
Westlington. Buck 4F 51
West Linton. Bord 4E 129
Westlinton. Cumb 3E 113
West Littleton. S Glo 4C 34
West Looe. Corn 3G 7
West Lulworth. Dors 4D 14
West Lutton. N Yor 3D 100
West Lydford. Som 3A 22
West Lyng. Som 4G 21
West Lynn. Norf 4F 77
West Mains. Per 2B 136
West Malling. Kent 5A 40
West Malvern. Worc 1C 48
Westmancote. Worc 2E 49
West Marden. W Sus 1F 17
West Markham. Notts 3E 86
West Marsh. NE Lin 4F 95
Westmarsh. Kent 4G 41
West Marton. N Yor 4A 98
West Meon. Hants 4E 25
West Mersea. Essx 4D 54
Westmeston. E Sus 4E 27
Westmill. Herts
nr. Buntingford 3D 52
nr. Hitchin 2B 52
West Milton. Dors 3A 14
Westminster. G Lon 3D 39
West Molesey. Surr 4C 38
West Monkton. Som 4F 21
Westmoor End. Cumb 1B 102
West Moors. Dors 2F 15
West Morden. Dors 3E 15
West Muir. Ang 2E 145
Westmuir. Ang 3C 144
West Murkle. High 2D 168
West Ness. N Yor 2A 100
Westness. Orkn 5C 172
West Newton. E Yor 1E 95
West Newton. Norf 3F 77
West Newton. Som 4F 21
Westnewton. Cumb 5C 112
Westnewton. Nmbd 1D 120
West Norwood. G Lon 3E 39
Westoe. Tyne 3G 115
West Ogwell. Devn 2E 9
Weston. Bath 5C 34
Weston. Ches E
nr. Crewe 5B 84
nr. Macclesfield 3C 84
Weston. Devn
nr. Honiton 2E 13
nr. Sidmouth 4E 13
Weston. Dors
nr. Weymouth 5B 14
nr. Yeovil 2A 14
Weston. Hal 2H 83
Weston. Hants 4F 25
Weston. Here 5F 59
Weston. Herts 2C 52
Weston. Linc 3B 76
Weston. Nptn 1D 50
Weston. Notts 4E 87
Weston. Shrp
nr. Bridgnorth 1H 59
nr. Knighton 3F 59
nr. Wem 3H 71
Weston. S Lan 5D 128
Weston. Staf 3D 73
Weston. Suff 2G 67
Weston. W Ber 4B 36
Weston Bampfylde. Som 4B 22
Weston Beggard. Here 1A 48
Westonbirt. Glos 3D 34
Weston by Welland. Nptn 1E 63
Weston Colville. Cambs 5F 65
Westoncommon. Shrp 3G 71
Weston Coyney. Stoke 1D 72
Weston Ditch. Suff 3F 65
Weston Favell. Nptn 4E 63
Weston Green. Cambs 5F 65
Weston Green. Norf 4D 78
Weston Heath. Shrp 4B 72
Weston Hills. Linc 4B 76
Weston in Arden. Warw 2A 62
Westoning. C Beds 2A 52
Weston in Gordano.
N Som 4H 33
Weston Jones. Staf 3B 72
Weston Longville. Norf 4D 78
Weston Lullingfields.
Shrp 3G 71
Weston-on-Avon. Warw 5F 61
Weston-on-the-Green.
Oxon 4D 50
Weston-on-Trent. Derbs 3B 74
Weston Patrick. Hants 2E 25
Weston Rhyn. Shrp 2E 71
Weston-sub-Edge. Glos 1G 49
Weston-super-Mare.
N Som 5G 33
Weston Town. Som 2C 22
Weston Turville. Buck 4G 51
Weston under Lizard. Staf 4C 72
Weston under Penyard.
Here 3B 48
Weston under Wetherley.
Warw 4A 62
Weston Underwood.
Derbs 1G 73
Weston Underwood. Mil 5F 63
Westonzoyland. Som 3G 21
West Orchard. Dors 1D 14
West Overton. Wilts 5G 35
Westow. N Yor 3B 100
Westown. Per 1E 137
West Panson. Devn 3D 10
West Park. Hart 1B 106
West Parley. Dors 3F 15
West Peckham. Kent 5H 39
West Pelton. Dur 4F 115
West Pennard. Som 3A 22
West Pentire. Corn 2B 6
West Perry. Cambs 4A 64
West Pitcorthie. Fife 3H 137
West Plean. Stir 1B 128
West Poringland. Norf 5E 79
West Porlock. Som 2B 20
Westport. Som 1G 13
West Putford. Devn 1D 10
West Quantoxhead. Som 2E 20
Westra. V Glam 4E 33
West Rainton. Dur 5G 115
West Rasen. Linc 2H 87
West Ravendale. NE Lin 1B 88
Westray Airport. Orkn 2D 172
West Raynham. Norf 3A 78
Westrigg. W Lot 3C 128
West Rounton. N Yor 4B 106
West Row. Suff 3F 65
West Rudham. Norf 3H 77
West Runton. Norf 1D 78
Westruther. Bord 4C 130
Westry. Cambs 1C 64
West Saltoun. E Lot 3A 130
West Sandford. Devn 2B 12
West Sandwick. Shet 3F 173
West Scrafton. N Yor 1C 98
Westside. Orkn 5C 172
West Sleekburn. Nmbd 1F 115
West Somerton. Norf 4G 79
West Stafford. Dors 4C 14
West Stockwith. Notts 1E 87
West Stoke. W Sus 2G 17
West Stonesdale. N Yor 4B 104
West Stoughton. Som 2H 21
West Stour. Dors 4C 22
West Stourmouth. Kent 4G 41
West Stow. Suff 3H 65
West Stowell. Wilts 5G 35
West Strathan. High 2F 167
West Stratton. Hants 2D 24
West Street. Kent 5D 40
West Tanfield. N Yor 2E 99
West Taphouse. Corn 2F 7
West Tarbert. Arg 3G 125
West Thirston. Nmbd 4F 121
West Thorney. W Sus 2F 17
West Thurrock. Thur 3G 39
West Tilbury. Thur 3A 40
West Tisted. Hants 4E 25
West Tofts. Norf 1H 65
West Torrington. Linc 2A 88
West Town. Bath 5A 34
West Town. Hants 3F 17
West Town. N Som 5H 33
West Tytherley. Hants 4A 24
West Tytherton. Wilts 4E 35
West View. Hart 1B 106
Westville. Notts 1C 74
West Walton. Norf 4D 76
Westward. Cumb 5D 112
Westward Ho!. Devn 4E 19
Westwell. Kent 1D 28
Westwell. Oxon 5H 49
Westwell Leacon. Kent 1D 28
West Wellow. Hants 1A 16
West Wemyss. Fife 4F 137
West Wick. N Som 5G 33
Westwick. Cambs 4D 64
Westwick. Dur 3D 104
Westwick. Norf 3E 79
West Wickham. Cambs 1G 53
West Wickham. G Lon 4E 39
West Williamston. Pemb 4E 43
West Willoughby. Linc 1G 75
West Winch. Norf 4F 77
West Winterslow. Wilts 3H 23
West Wittering. W Sus 3F 17
West Witton. N Yor 1C 98
Westwood. Devn 3D 12
Westwood. Kent 4H 41
Westwood. Pet 5A 76
Westwood. S Lan 4H 127
Westwood. Wilts 1D 22
West Woodburn. Nmbd 1B 114
West Woodhay. W Ber 5B 36
West Woodlands. Som 2C 22
West Woodside. Cumb 5E 112
Westwoodside. N Lin 1E 87
West Worldham. Hants 3F 25
West Worlington. Devn 1A 12
West Worthing. W Sus 5C 26
West Wratting. Cambs 5F 65
West Wycombe. Buck 2G 37
West Wylam. Nmbd 3E 115
West Yatton. Wilts 4D 34
West Yell. Shet 3F 173
West Youlstone. Corn 1C 10
Wetheral. Cumb 4F 113
Wetherby. W Yor 5G 99
Wetherden. Suff 4C 66
Wetheringsett. Suff 4D 66
Wethersfield. Essx 2H 53
Wethersta. Shet 5E 173
Wetherup Street. Suff 4D 66
Wetley Rocks. Staf 1D 72
Wettenhall. Ches E 4A 84
Wetton. Staf 5F 85
Wetwang. E Yor 4D 100
Wetwood. Staf 2B 72
Wexcombe. Wilts 1A 24
Wexham Street. Buck 2A 38
Weybourne. Norf 1D 78
Weybourne. Surr 2G 25
Weybread. Suff 2E 67
Weybridge. Surr 4B 38
Weycroft. Devn 3G 13
Weydale. High 2D 168
Weyhill. Hants 2B 24
Weymouth. Dors 204 (5B 14)
Weythel. Powy 5E 59
Whaddon. Buck 2G 51
Whaddon. Cambs 1D 52
Whaddon. Glos 4D 48
Whaddon. Wilts 4G 23
Whale. Cumb 2G 103
Whaley. Derbs 3C 86
Whaley Bridge. Derbs 2E 85
Whaley Thorns. Derbs 3C 86
Whalley. Lanc 1F 91
Whalton. Nmbd 1E 115
Whaplode. Linc 3C 76
Whaplode Drove. Linc 4C 76
Whaplode St Catherine.
Linc 3C 76
Wharfe. N Yor 3G 97
Wharles. Lanc 1C 90
Wharley End. C Beds 1H 51
Wharncliffe Side. S Yor 1G 85
Wharram-le-Street.
N Yor 3C 100
Wharton. Ches W 4A 84
Wharton. Here 5H 59
Whashton. N Yor 4E 105
Whasset. Cumb 1E 97
Whatcote. Warw 1B 50
Whateley. Warw 1G 61
Whatfield. Suff 1D 54
Whatley. Som
nr. Chard 2G 13
nr. Frome 2C 22
Whatlington. E Sus 4B 28
Whatmore. Shrp 3A 60
Whatstandwell. Derbs 5H 85
Whatton. Notts 2E 75
Whauphill. Dum 5B 110
Whaw. N Yor 4C 104
Wheatacre. Norf 1G 67
Wheatcroft. Derbs 5A 86
Wheathampstead. Herts 4B 52
Wheathill. Shrp 2A 60
Wheatley. Devn 3B 12
Wheatley. Hants 2F 25
Wheatley. Oxon 5E 50
Wheatley. S Yor 4F 93
Wheatley. W Yor 2A 92
Wheatley Hill. Dur 1A 106
Wheatley Lane. Lanc 1G 91
Wheatley Park. S Yor 4F 93
Wheaton Aston. Staf 4C 72
Wheatstone Park. Staf 5C 72
Wheddon Cross. Som 3C 20
Wheelerstreet. Surr 1A 26
Wheelock. Ches E 5B 84
Wheelock Heath. Ches E 5B 84
Wheelton. Lanc 2E 90
Wheldrake. York 5A 100
Whelford. Glos 2G 35
Whelpley Hill. Buck 5H 51
Whelpo. Cumb 1E 102
Whelston. Flin 3E 82
Whenby. N Yor 3A 100
Whepstead. Suff 5H 65
Wherstead. Suff 1E 55
Wherwell. Hants 2B 24
Wheston. Derbs 3F 85
Whetsted. Kent 1A 28
Whetstone. G Lon 1D 38
Whetstone. Leics 1C 62
Whicham. Cumb 1A 96
Whichford. Warw 2B 50
Whickham. Tyne 3F 115
Whiddon. Devn 2E 11
Whiddon Down. Devn 3G 11
Whigstreet. Ang 4D 145
Whilton. Nptn 4D 62
Whimble. Devn 2D 10
Whimple. Devn 3D 12
Whimpwell Green. Norf 3F 79
Whinburgh. Norf 5C 78
Whin Lane End. Lanc 5C 96
Whinney Hill. Stoc T 3A 106
Whinnyfold. Abers 5H 161
Whippingham. IOW 3D 16
Whipsnade. C Beds 4A 52
Whipton. Devn 3C 12
Whirlow. S Yor 2H 85
Whisby. Linc 4G 87
Whissendine. Rut 4F 75
Whissonsett. Norf 3B 78
Whisterfield. Ches E 3C 84
Whistley Green. Wok 4F 37
Whiston. Mers 1G 83
Whiston. Nptn 4F 63
Whiston. S Yor 1B 86
Whiston. Staf
nr. Cheadle 1E 73
nr. Penkridge 4C 72
Whiston Cross. Shrp 5B 72
Whiston Eaves. Staf 1E 73
Whitacre Heath. Warw 1G 61
Whitbeck. Cumb 1A 96
Whitbourne. Here 5B 60
Whitburn. Tyne 3H 115
Whitburn. W Lot 3C 128
Whitburn Colliery. Tyne 3H 115
Whitby. Ches W 3F 83
Whitby. N Yor 3F 107
Whitbyheath. Ches W 3F 83
Whitchester. Bord 4D 130
Whitchurch. Bath 5B 34
Whitchurch. Buck 3F 51
Whitchurch. Card 4E 33
Whitchurch. Devn 5E 11
Whitchurch. Hants 2C 24
Whitchurch. Here 4A 48
Whitchurch. Pemb 2B 42
Whitchurch. Shrp 1H 71
Whitchurch Canonicorum.
Dors 3G 13
Whitchurch Hill. Oxon 4E 37
Whitchurch-on-Thames.
Oxon 4E 37
Whitcombe. Dors 4C 14
Whitcot. Shrp 1F 59
Whitcott Keysett. Shrp 2E 59
Whiteabbey. Ant 1H 179
Whiteash Green. Essx 2A 54
Whitebog. High 2B 158
Whitebridge. High 2G 149
Whitebrook. Mon 5A 48
Whitecairns. Abers 2G 153
Whitechapel. Lanc 5E 97
Whitechurch. Pemb 1F 43
White Colne. Essx 3B 54
White Coppice. Lanc 3E 90
White Corries. High 3G 141
Whitecraig. E Lot 2G 129
Whitecroft. Glos 5B 48
White Cross. Corn 4D 5
Whitecross. Corn 1D 6
Whitecross. Falk 2C 128
Whitecross. New M 6D 178
White End. Worc 2C 48
Whiteface. High 5E 164
Whitefarland. N Ayr 5G 125
Whitefaulds. S Ayr 4B 116
Whitefield. Dors 3E 15
Whitefield. G Man 4G 91
Whitefield. Som 4D 20
Whiteford. Abers 1E 152
Whitegate. Ches W 4A 84
Whitehall. Devn 1E 12
Whitehall. Hants 1F 25
Whitehall. Orkn 5F 172
Whitehall. W Sus 3C 26
Whitehaven. Cumb 3A 102
Whitehaven. Shrp 3E 71
Whitehead. ME Ant 7L 175
Whitehill. Hants 3F 25
Whitehill. N Ayr 4D 126
Whitehills. Abers 2D 160
Whitehills. Ang 3D 144
White Horse Common.
Norf 3F 79
Whitehough. Derbs 2E 85
Whitehouse. Abers 2D 152
Whitehouse. Arg 3G 125
Whiteinch. Glas 3G 127
Whitekirk. E Lot 1B 130
White Kirkley. Dur 1D 104
White Lackington. Dors 3C 14
Whitelackington. Som 1G 13
White Ladies Aston. Worc 5D 60
White Lee. W Yor 2C 92
Whiteley. Hants 2D 16
Whiteley Bank. IOW 4D 16
Whiteley Village. Surr 4B 38
Whitemans Green. W Sus 3E 27
White Mill. Carm 3E 45
Whitemire. Mor 3D 159
Whitemoor. Corn 3D 6
Whitenap. Hants 4B 24
Whiteness. Shet 7F 173
White Notley. Essx 4A 54
Whiteoak Green. Oxon 4B 50
Whiteparish. Wilts 4H 23
White Pit. Linc 3C 88
Whiterashes. Abers 1F 153
Whiterock. Ards 3K 179
White Rocks. Here 3H 47
White Roding. Essx 4F 53
Whiterow. High 4F 169
Whiterow. Mor 3E 159
Whiteshill. Glos 5D 48
Whiteside. Nmbd 3A 114
Whiteside. W Lot 3C 128
Whitesmith. E Sus 4G 27
Whitestaunton. Som 1F 13
White Stone. Here 1A 48
Whitestone. Abers 4D 152
Whitestone. Devn 3B 12
Whitestones. Abers 3F 161
Whitestreet Green. Suff 2C 54
Whitewall Corner. N Yor 2B 100
White Waltham. Wind 4G 37
Whiteway. Glos 4E 49
Whitewell. Lanc 5F 97
Whitewell Bottom. Lanc 2G 91
Whiteworks. Devn 5G 11
Whitewreath. Mor 3G 159
Whitfield. D'dee 5D 144
Whitfield. Kent 1H 29
Whitfield. Nptn 2E 50
Whitfield. Nmbd 4A 114
Whitfield. S Glo 2B 34
Whitford. Devn 3F 13
Whitford. Flin 3D 82
Whitgift. E Yor 2B 94
Whitgreave. Staf 3C 72
Whithorn. Dum 5B 110
Whiting Bay. N Ayr 3E 123
Whitkirk. W Yor 1D 92
Whitland. Carm 3G 43
Whitleigh. Plym 3A 8
Whitletts. S Ayr 2C 116
Whitley. N Yor 2F 93
Whitley. Wilts 5D 35
Whitley Bay. Tyne 2G 115
Whitley Chapel. Nmbd 4C 114
Whitley Heath. Staf 3C 72
Whitley Lower. W Yor 3C 92
Whitley Thorpe. N Yor 2F 93
Whitlock's End. W Mid 3F 61
Whitminster. Glos 5C 48
Whitmore. Dors 2F 15
Whitmore. Staf 1C 72
Whitnage. Devn 1D 12
Whitnash. Warw 4H 61
Whitney. Here 1F 47
Whitrigg. Cumb
nr. Kirkbride 4D 112
nr. Torpenhow 1D 102
Whitsbury. Hants 1G 15
Whitsome. Bord 4E 131
Whitson. Newp 3G 33
Whitstable. Kent 4F 41
Whitstone. Corn 3C 10
Whittingham. Nmbd 3E 121
Whittingslow. Shrp 2G 59
Whittington. Derbs 3B 86
Whittington. Glos 3F 49
Whittington. Lanc 2F 97
Whittington. Norf 1G 65
Whittington. Shrp 2F 71
Whittington. Staf
nr. Kinver 2C 60
nr. Lichfield 5F 73
Whittington. Warw 1G 61
Whittington. Worc 5C 60
Whittington Barracks. Staf 5F 73
Whittlebury. Nptn 1E 51
Whittleford. Warw 1H 61
Whittle-le-Woods. Lanc 2D 90
Whittlesey. Cambs 1B 64
Whittlesford. Cambs 1E 53
Whittlestone Head. Bkbn 3F 91
Whitton. N Lin 2C 94
Whitton. Nmbd 4E 121
Whitton. Powy 4E 59
Whitton. Bord 2B 120
Whitton. Shrp 3H 59
Whitton. Stoc T 2A 106
Whittonditch. Wilts 4A 36
Whittonstall. Nmbd 4D 114
Whitway. Hants 1C 24
Whitwell. Derbs 3C 86
Whitwell. Herts 3B 52
Whitwell. IOW 5D 16
Whitwell. N Yor 5F 105
Whitwell. Rut 5G 75
Whitwell-on-the-Hill.
N Yor 3B 100
Whitwick. Leics 4B 74
Whitwood. W Yor 2E 93
Whitworth. Lanc 3G 91
Whixall. Shrp 2H 71
Whixley. N Yor 4G 99
Whoberley. W Mid 3H 61
Whorlton. Dur 3E 105
Whorlton. N Yor 4B 106
Whygate. Nmbd 2A 114
Whyle. Here 4H 59
Whyteleafe. Surr 5E 39
Wibdon. Glos 2A 34
Wibtoft. Warw 2B 62
Wichenford. Worc 4B 60
Wichling. Kent 5D 40
Wick. Bour 3G 15
Wick. Devn 2E 13
Wick. High 3F 169
Wick. Shet
on Mainland 8F 173
on Unst 1G 173
Wick. Som
nr. Bridgwater 2F 21
nr. Burnham-on-Sea 1G 21
nr. Somerton 4H 21
Wick. S Glo 4C 34
Wick. V Glam 4C 32
Wick. W Sus 5B 26
Wick. Wilts 4G 23
Wick. Worc 1E 49
Wick Airport. High 3F 169
Wicken. Cambs 3E 65
Wicken. Nptn 2F 51
Wicken Bonhunt. Essx 2E 53
Wickenby. Linc 2H 87
Wicken Green Village.
Norf 2H 77
Wickersley. S Yor 1B 86
Wicker Street Green. Suff 1C 54
Wickford. Essx 1B 40
Wickham. Hants 1D 16
Wickham. W Ber 4B 36
Wickham Bishops. Essx 4B 54
Wickhambreaux. Kent 5G 41
Wickhambrook. Suff 5G 65
Wickhamford. Worc 1F 49
Wickham Green. Suff 4C 66
Wickham Heath. W Ber 5C 36
Wickham Market. Suff 5F 67
Wickhampton. Norf 5G 79
Wickham St Paul. Essx 2B 54
Wickham Skeith. Suff 4C 66
Wickham Street. Suff 4C 66
Wick Hill. Wok 5F 37
Wicklewood. Norf 5C 78
Wickmere. Norf 2D 78
Wick St Lawrence. N Som 5G 33
Wickwar. S Glo 3C 34
Widdington. Essx 2F 53
Widdrington. Nmbd 5G 121
Widdrington Station.
Nmbd 5G 121
Widecombe in the Moor.
Devn 5H 11
Widegates. Corn 3G 7
Widemouth Bay. Corn 2C 10
Wide Open. Tyne 2F 115
Widewall. Orkn 8D 172
Widford. Essx 5G 53
Widford. Herts 4E 53
Widham. Wilts 3F 35
Widmer End. Buck 2G 37
Widmerpool. Notts 3D 74
Widnes. Hal 2H 83
Widworthy. Devn 3F 13
Wigan. G Man 4D 90
Wigbeth. Dors 2F 15
Wigborough. Som 1H 13
Wiggaton. Devn 3E 12
Wiggenhall St Germans.
Norf 4E 77
Wiggenhall St Mary Magdalen.
Norf 4E 77
Wiggenhall St Mary the Virgin.
Norf 4E 77
Wiggenhall St Peter. Norf 4F 77
Wiggens Green. Essx 1G 53
Wigginton. Herts 4H 51
Wigginton. Oxon 2B 50
Wigginton. Staf 5G 73
Wigginton. York 4H 99
Wigglesworth. N Yor 4H 97
Wiggonby. Cumb 4D 112
Wiggonholt. W Sus 4B 26
Wighill. N Yor 5G 99
Wighton. Norf 2B 78
Wightwick. W Mid 1C 60
Wigley. Hants 1B 16
Wigmore. Here 4G 59
Wigmore. Medw 4B 40
Wigsley. Notts 3F 87
Wigsthorpe. Nptn 2H 63
Wigston. Leics 1D 62
Wigtoft. Linc 2B 76
Wigton. Cumb 5D 112
Wigtown. Dum 4B 110
Wike. W Yor 5F 99
Wilbarston. Nptn 2F 63
Wilberfoss. E Yor 4B 100
Wilburton. Cambs 3D 65
Wilby. Norf 2C 66
Wilby. Nptn 4F 63
Wilby. Suff 3E 67
Wilcot. Wilts 5G 35
Wilcott. Shrp 4F 71
Wilcove. Corn 3A 8
Wildboarclough. Ches E 4D 85
Wilden. Bed 5H 63
Wilden. Worc 3C 60
Wildern. Hants 1C 16
Wilderspool. Warr 2A 84
Wilde Street. Suff 3G 65
Wildhern. Hants 1B 24
Wildmanbridge. S Lan 4B 128
Wildmoor. Worc 3D 60
Wildsworth. Linc 1F 87
Wildwood. Staf 3D 72
Wilford. Nott 2C 74
Wilkesley. Ches E 1A 72
Wilkhaven. High 5G 165
Wilkieston. W Lot 3E 129
Wilksby. Linc 4B 88
Willand. Devn 1D 12
Willaston. Ches E 5A 84
Willaston. Ches W 3F 83
Willaston. IOM 4C 108
Willen. Mil 1G 51
Willenhall. W Mid
nr. Coventry 3A 62
nr. Wolverhampton 1D 60
Willerby. E Yor 1D 94
Willerby. N Yor 2E 101
Willersey. Glos 2G 49
Willersley. Here 1G 47
Willesborough. Kent 1E 28
Willesborough Lees. Kent 1E 29
Willesden. G Lon 2D 38
Willesley. Wilts 3D 34
Willett. Som 3E 20
Willey. Shrp 1A 60
Willey. Warw 2B 62
Willey Green. Surr 5A 38
Williamscot. Oxon 1C 50
Williamsetter. Shet 9E 173
Willian. Herts 2C 52
Willingale. Essx 5F 53
Willingdon. E Sus 5G 27
Willingham. Cambs 3D 64
Willingham by Stow. Linc 2F 87
Willingham Green. Cambs 5F 65
Willington. Bed 1B 52
Willington. Derbs 3G 73
Willington. Dur 1E 105
Willington. Tyne 3G 115
Willington. Warw 2A 50
Willington Corner.
Ches W 4H 83
Willisham Tye. Suff 5C 66
Willitoft. E Yor 1H 93
Williton. Som 2D 20
Willoughbridge. Staf 1B 72
Willoughby. Linc 3D 88
Willoughby. Warw 4C 62
Willoughby-on-the-Wolds.
Notts 3D 74
Willoughby Waterleys.
Leics 1C 62
Willoughton. Linc 1G 87
Willow Green. Worc 5B 60
Willows Green. Essx 4H 53
Willsbridge. S Glo 4B 34
Willslock. Staf 2E 73
Wilmcote. Warw 5F 61
Wilmington. Bath 5B 34
Wilmington. Devn 3F 13
Wilmington. E Sus 5G 27
Wilmington. Kent 3G 39
Wilmslow. Ches E 2C 84
Wilnecote. Staf 5G 73
Wilney Green. Norf 2C 66
Wilpshire. Lanc 1E 91
Wilsden. W Yor 1A 92
Wilsford. Linc 1H 75
Wilsford. Wilts
nr. Amesbury 3G 23
nr. Devizes 1F 23
Wilsill. N Yor 3D 98
Wilsley Green. Kent 2B 28
Wilson. Here 3A 48
Wilson. Leics 3B 74
Wilsontown. S Lan 4C 128
Wilstead. Bed 1A 52
Wilsthorpe. E Yor 3F 101
Wilsthorpe. Linc 4H 75
Wilstone. Herts 4H 51
Wilton. Cumb 3B 102
Wilton. N Yor 1C 100
Wilton. Red C 3C 106
Wilton. Bord 3H 119
Wilton. Wilts
nr. Marlborough 5A 36
nr. Salisbury 3F 23
Wimbish. Essx 2F 53
Wimbish Green. Essx 2G 53
Wimblebury. Staf 4E 73
Wimbledon. G Lon 3D 38
Wimblington. Cambs 1D 64
Wimboldsley. Ches W 4A 84
Wimborne Minster. Dors 2F 15
Wimborne St Giles. Dors 1F 15
Wimbotsham. Norf 5F 77
Wimpole. Cambs 1D 52
Wimpstone. Warw 1H 49
Wincanton. Som 4C 22
Winceby. Linc 4C 88
Wincham. Ches W 3A 84
Winchburgh. W Lot 2D 129
Winchcombe. Glos 3F 49
Winchelsea. E Sus 4D 28
Winchelsea Beach. E Sus 4D 28
Winchester. Hants 203 (4C 24)
Winchet Hill. Kent 1B 28
Winchfield. Hants 1F 25
Winchmore Hill. Buck 1A 38
Winchmore Hill. G Lon 1E 39
Wincle. Ches E 4D 84
Windermere. Cumb 5F 103
Winderton. Warw 1B 50
Windhill. High 4H 157
Windle Hill. Ches W 3F 83
Windlesham. Surr 4A 38
Windley. Derbs 1H 73
Windmill. Derbs 3F 85
Windmill Hill. E Sus 4H 27
Windmill Hill. Som 1G 13
Windrush. Glos 4G 49
Windsor. Wind 203 (3A 38)
Windsor Green. Suff 5A 66
Windyedge. Abers 4F 153
Windygates. Fife 3F 137
Windyharbour. Ches E 3C 84
Windyknowe. W Lot 3C 128
Wineham. W Sus 3D 26
Winestead. E Yor 2G 95
Winfarthing. Norf 2D 66
Winford. IOW 4D 16
Winford. N Som 5A 34
Winforton. Here 1F 47
Winfrith Newburgh. Dors 4D 14
Wing. Buck 3G 51
Wing. Rut 5F 75
Wingate. Dur 1B 106
Wingates. G Man 4E 91
Wingates. Nmbd 5F 121
Wingerworth. Derbs 4A 86
Wingfield. C Beds 3A 52
Wingfield. Suff 3E 67
Wingfield. Wilts 1D 22
Wingfield Park. Derbs 5A 86
Wingham. Kent 5G 41
Wingmore. Kent 1F 29
Wingrave. Buck 4G 51
Winkburn. Notts 5E 86
Winkfield. Brac 3A 38
Winkfield Row. Brac 4G 37
Winkhill. Staf 5E 85
Winklebury. Hants 1E 24
Winkleigh. Devn 2G 11
Winksley. N Yor 2E 99
Winkton. Dors 3G 15
Winlaton. Tyne 3E 115
Winlaton Mill. Tyne 3E 115
Winless. High 3F 169
Winmarleigh. Lanc 5D 96
Winnal Common. Here 2H 47
Winnard's Perch. Corn 2D 6
Winnersh. Wok 4F 37
Winnington. Ches W 3A 84
Winnington. Staf 2B 72
Winnothdale. Staf 1E 73
Winscales. Cumb 2B 102
Winscombe. N Som 1H 21
Winsford. Ches W 4A 84
Winsford. Som 3C 20
Winsham. Devn 3E 19
Winsham. Som 2G 13
Winshill. Staf 3G 73
Winsh-wen. Swan 3F 31
Winskill. Cumb 1G 103
Winslade. Hants 2E 25
Winsley. Wilts 5D 34
Winslow. Buck 3F 51
Winson. Glos 5F 49
Winson Green. W Mid 2E 61
Winsor. Hants 1B 16
Winster. Cumb 5F 103
Winster. Derbs 4G 85
Winston. Dur 3E 105
Winston. Suff 4D 66
Winstone. Glos 5E 49
Winswell. Devn 1E 11
Winterborne Clenston.
Dors 2D 14
Winterborne Herringston.
Dors 4B 14
Winterborne Houghton.
Dors 2D 14
Winterborne Kingston.
Dors 3D 14
Winterborne Monkton.
Dors 4B 14
Winterborne St Martin.
Dors 4B 14
Winterborne Stickland.
Dors 2D 14
Winterborne Whitechurch.
Dors 2D 14
Winterborne Zelston.
Dors 3D 15
Winterbourne. S Glo 3B 34
Winterbourne. W Ber 4C 36
Winterbourne Abbas.
Dors 3B 14
Winterbourne Bassett.
Wilts 4G 35
Winterbourne Dauntsey.
Wilts 3G 23
Winterbourne Earls. Wilts 3G 23
Winterbourne Gunner.
Wilts 3G 23
Winterbourne Monkton.
Wilts 4G 35
Winterbourne Steepleton.
Dors 4B 14
Winterbourne Stoke. Wilts 2F 23
Winterbrook. Oxon 3E 36
Winterburn. N Yor 4B 98
Winter Gardens. Essx 2B 40
Winterhay Green. Som 1G 13
Winteringham. N Lin 2C 94
Winterley. Ches E 5B 84
Wintersett. W Yor 3D 93
Winterton. N Lin 3C 94
Winterton-on-Sea. Norf 4G 79
Winthorpe. Linc 4E 89
Winthorpe. Notts 5F 87
Winton. Bour 3F 15
Winton. Cumb 3A 104
Winton. E Sus 5G 27
Wintringham. N Yor 2C 100
Winwick. Cambs 2A 64
Winwick. Nptn 3D 62
Winwick. Warr 1A 84
Wirksworth. Derbs 5G 85
Wirswall. Ches E 1H 71
Wisbech. Cambs 4D 76
Wisbech St Mary. Cambs 5D 76
Wisborough Green.
W Sus 3B 26
Wiseton. Notts 2E 86
Wishaw. N Lan 4A 128
Wishaw. Warw 1F 61
Wisley. Surr 5B 38
Wispington. Linc 3B 88
Wissenden. Kent 1D 28
Wissett. Suff 3F 67
Wistanstow. Shrp 2G 59
Wistanswick. Shrp 3A 72
Wistaston. Ches E 5A 84
Wiston. Pemb 3E 43
Wiston. S Lan 1B 118
Wiston. W Sus 4C 26
Wistow. Cambs 2B 64
Wistow. N Yor 1F 93
Wiswell. Lanc 1F 91
Witcham. Cambs 2D 64

Published by Geographers' A-Z Map Company Limited
An imprint of HarperCollins Publishers
Westerhill Road
Bishopbriggs
Glasgow
G64 2QT

www.az.co.uk
a-z.maps@harpercollins.co.uk

HarperCollinsPublishers
1st Floor, Watermarque Building, Ringsend Road, Dublin 4, Ireland

31st edition 2021

© Collins Bartholomew Ltd 2021

This product uses map data licenced from Ordnance Survey
© Crown copyright and database rights 2020 OS 100018598

AZ, A-Z and AtoZ are registered trademarks of Geographers' A-Z Map Company Limited

Northern Ireland: This is based upon Crown copyright and is reproduced with the permission of Land & Property Services underdelegated authority from the Controller of Her Majesty's Stationery Office, © Crown copyright and database right 2020 PMLPA No 100508. The inclusion of parts or all of the Republic of Ireland is by permission of the Government of Ireland who retain copyright in the data used. © Ordnance Survey Ireland and Government of Ireland.

Land & Property Services
Paper Map Licensed Partner
ORDNANCE SURVEY OF NORTHERN IRELAND

Base relief by Geo-Innovations, © www.geoinnovations.co.uk

The Shopmobility logo is a registered symbol of The National Federation of Shopmobility

A catalogue record for this book is available from the British Library.

ISBN 978-0-00-844508-9

10 9 8 7 6 5 4 3 2 1

Printed and bound in China by RR Donnelley APS Co Ltd.

INDEX TO SELECTED PLACES OF INTEREST

(1) A strict alphabetical order is used e.g. Benmore Botanic Gdn. follows Ben Macdui but precedes Ben Nevis.

(2) Places of Interest which fall on City and Town Centre maps are referenced first to the detailed map page, followed by the main map page if appropriate. The name of the map is included if it is not clear from the index entry.
e.g. Ashmolean Mus. of Art & Archaeology (OX1 2PH) .... **Oxford 200** (5D 50)

(3) Entries in italics are not named on the map but are shown with a symbol only.
e.g. *Aberdour Castle (KY3 0XA)* 1E **129**

SAT NAV POSTCODES

Postcodes are shown to assist Sat Nav users and are included on this basis.
It should be noted that postcodes have been selected by their proximity to the Place of Interest and that they may not form part of the actual postal address. Drivers should follow the Tourist Brown Signs when available.

ABBREVIATIONS USED IN THIS INDEX

Centre : Cen.   Garden : Gdn.   Gardens : Gdns.   Museum : Mus.   National : Nat.   Park : Pk.

Limited Interchange Motorway Junctions are shown on the mapping pages by red junction indicators 2

M1

Junction		
2	Northbound Southbound	No exit, access from A1 only No access, exit to A1 only
4	Northbound Southbound	No exit, access from A41 only No access, exit to A41 only
6a	Northbound Southbound	No exit, access from M25 only No access, exit to M25 only
17	Northbound Southbound	No access, exit to M45 only No exit, access from M45 only
19	Northbound Southbound	Exit to M6 only, access from A14 only Access from M6 only, exit to A14 only
21a	Northbound Southbound	No access, exit to A46 only No exit, access from A46 only
24a	Northbound Southbound	No exit Access from A50 only
35a	Northbound Southbound	No access, exit to A616 only No exit, access from A616 only
43	Northbound Southbound	Exit to M621 only Access from M621 only
48	Eastbound Westbound	Exit to A1(M) northbound only Access from A1(M) southbound only

M2

Junction		
1	Eastbound Westbound	Access from A2 eastbound only Exit to A2 westbound only

M3

Junction		
8	Eastbound Westbound	No exit, access from A303 only No access, exit to A303 only
10	Northbound Southbound	No access from A31 No exit to A31
13	Southbound	No access from A335 to M3 leading to M27 Eastbound

M4

Junction		
1	Eastbound Westbound	Exit to A4 eastbound only Access from A4 westbound only
21	Eastbound Westbound	No exit to M48 No access from M48
23	Eastbound Westbound	No access from M48 No exit to M48
25	Eastbound Westbound	No exit No access
25a	Eastbound Westbound	No exit No access
29	Eastbound Westbound	No exit, access from A48(M) only No access, exit to A48(M) only
38	Westbound	No access, exit to A48 only
39	Eastbound Westbound	No access or exit No exit, access from A48 only
42	Eastbound Westbound	No access from A48 No exit to A48

M5

Junction		
10	Northbound Southbound	No exit, access from A4019 only No access, exit to A4019 only
11a	Southbound	No exit to A417 westbound
18a	Northbound Southbound	No access from M49 No exit to M49

M6

Junction		
3a	Eastbound Westbound	No exit to M6 Toll No access from M6 Toll
4	Northbound Southbound	No exit to M42 northbound No access from M42 southbound No exit to M42 No access from M42 southbound
4a	Northbound Southbound	No exit, access from M42 S'bound only No access, exit to M42 only
5	Northbound Southbound	No access, exit to A452 only No exit, access from A452 only
10a	Northbound Southbound	No access, exit to M54 only No exit, access from M54 only
11a	Northbound Southbound	No exit to M6 Toll No access from M6 Toll
20	Northbound Southbound	No exit to M56 eastbound No access from M56 westbound
24	Northbound Southbound	No exit, access from A58 only No access, exit to A58 only
25	Northbound Southbound	No access, exit to A49 only No exit, access from A49 only
30	Northbound Southbound	No exit, access from M61 N'bound only No access, exit to M61 S'bound only
31a	Northbound Southbound	No access, exit to B6242 only No exit, access from B6242 only
45	Northbound Southbound	No access onto A74(M) No exit from A74(M)

M6 Toll

Junction		
T1	Northbound Southbound	No exit No access
T2	Northbound Southbound	No access or exit No access
T5	Northbound Southbound	No exit No access
T7	Northbound Southbound	No access from A5 No exit
T8	Northbound Southbound	No exit to A460 northbound No exit

M8

Junction		
6	Eastbound Westbound	No exit, access only No access, exit only
6a	Eastbound Westbound	No access, exit only No exit, access only
7	Eastbound Westbound	No access, exit only No exit, access only
7a	Eastbound Westbound	No exit, access from A725 Northbound only No access, exit to A725 Southbound only
8	Eastbound Westbound	No exit to M73 northbound No access from M73 southbound
9	Eastbound Westbound	No access, exit only No exit, access only
13	Eastbound Westbound	No access from M80 southbound No exit to M80 northbound
14	Eastbound Westbound	No access, exit only No exit, access only
16	Eastbound Westbound	No exit, access only No access, exit only
17	Eastbound Westbound	No exit, access from A82 only No access, exit to A82 only
18	Westbound	No exit, access only
19	Eastbound Westbound	No exit to A814 eastbound No access from A814 westbound
20	Eastbound Westbound	No exit, access only No access, exit only
21	Eastbound Westbound	No access, exit only No exit, access only
22	Eastbound Westbound	No exit, access from M77 only No access, exit to M77 only
23	Eastbound Westbound	No exit, access from B768 only No access, exit to B768 only
25	Eastbound & Westbound	Access from A739 southbound only Exit to A739 northbound only
25a	Eastbound Westbound	Access only Exit only
28	Eastbound Westbound	No exit, access from airport only No access, exit to airport only
29a	Eastbound Westbound	No exit, access only No access, exit only

M9

Junction		
2	Northbound Southbound	No exit, access from B8046 only No access, exit to B8046 only
3	Northbound Southbound	No access, exit to A803 only No exit, access from A803 only
6	Northbound Southbound	No exit, access only No access, exit to A905 only
8	Northbound Southbound	No access, exit to M876 only No exit, access from M876 only

M11

Junction		
4	Northbound Southbound	No exit, access from A406 E'bound only No access, exit to A406 W'bound only
5	Northbound Southbound	No access, exit to A1168 only No exit, access from A1168 only
8a	Northbound Southbound	No access, exit only No exit, access only
9	Northbound Southbound	No access, exit only No exit, access only
13	Northbound Southbound	No access, exit only No exit, access only
14	Northbound Southbound	No access from A428 eastbound No exit to A428 westbound No exit, access from A428 E'bound only

M20

Junction		
2	Eastbound Westbound	No access, exit to A20 only (access via M26 Junction 2a) No exit, access only (exit via M26 J2a)
3	Eastbound Westbound	No exit, access from M26 E'bound only No access, exit to M26 W'bound only
10	Eastbound Westbound	No access, exit only No exit, access only
11a	Eastbound Westbound	No access from Channel Tunnel No exit to Channel Tunnel

M23

Junction		
7	Northbound Southbound	No exit to A23 southbound No access from A23 northbound

M25

Junction		
5	Clockwise Anti-clockwise	No exit to M26 eastbound No access from M26 westbound
Spur to A21	Northbound Southbound	No exit to M26 eastbound No access from M26 westbound
19	Clockwise Anti-clockwise	No access, exit only No exit, access only
21	Clockwise & Anti-clockwise	No exit to M1 southbound No access from M1 northbound
31	Northbound Southbound	No access, exit only (access via J.30) No exit, access only (exit via J.30)

M26

Junction with M25 (M25 Jun.5)

Eastbound	No access from M25 clockwise or spur from A21 northbound
Westbound	No exit to M25 anti-clockwise or spur to A21 southbound

Junction with M20 (M20 Jun.3)

Eastbound	No exit to M20 westbound
Westbound	No access from M20 eastbound

M27

Junction		
4	Eastbound & Westbound	No exit to A33 S'bound (Southampton) No access from A33 northbound
10	Eastbound Westbound	No exit, access from A32 only No access, exit to A32 only

M40

Junction		
3	North-Westbound South-Eastbound	No access, exit to A40 only No exit, access from A40 only
7	N.W bound S.E bound	No access, exit only No exit, access only
13	N.W bound S.E bound	No access, exit only No exit, access only
14	N.W bound S.E bound	No exit, access only No access, exit only
16	N.W bound S.E bound	No exit, access only No access, exit only

M42

Junction		
1	Eastbound Westbound	No exit No access
7	Northbound Southbound	No access, exit to M6 only No exit, access from M6 N'bound only
8	Northbound Southbound	No exit, access from M6 S'bound only Exit to M6 nothbound only Access from M6 southbound only

M45

Junction with M1 (M1 Jun.17)

Eastbound	No exit to M1 northbound
Westbound	No access from M1 southbound

Junction with A45 east of Dunchurch

Eastbound	No access, exit to A45 only
Westbound	No exit, access from A45 N'bound only

M48

Junction with M4 (M4 Jun.21)

Eastbound	No exit to M4 westbound
Westbound	No access from M4 eastbound

Junction with M4 (M4 Jun.23)

Eastbound	No access from M4 westbound
Westbound	No exit to M4 eastbound

M53

Junction		
11	Northbound & Southbound	No access from M56 eastbound, no exit to M56 westbound

M56

Junction		
1	Eastbound S.E bound Westbound	No exit to M60 N.W bound No exit to A34 southbound No access from A34 northbound No access from M60
2	Eastbound Westbound	No exit, access from A560 only No access, exit to A560 only
3	Eastbound Westbound	No access, exit only No exit, access only
4	Eastbound Westbound	No exit, access only No access, exit only
7	Westbound	No access, exit only
8	Eastbound Westbound	No access or exit No exit, access from A556 only
9	Eastbound Westbound	No access from M6 northbound No exit to M60 southbound
10a	Northbound Southbound	No exit, access only No access, exit only
15	Eastbound Westbound	No exit to M53 No access from M53

M57

Junction		
3	Northbound Southbound	No exit, access only No access, exit only
5	Northbound Southbound	No exit, access from A580 W'bound only No access, exit to A580 E'bound only

M60

Junction		
2	N.E bound S.W bound	No access, exit to A560 only No exit, access from A560 only
3	Eastbound Westbound	No access from A34 southbound No exit to A34 northbound
4	Eastbound Westbound	No exit to M56 S.W bound No exit to A34 northbound No access from A34 southbound No access from M56 eastbound
5	N.W bound S.E bound	No access from or exit to A5103 S'bound No access from or exit to A5103 N'bound
14	Eastbound Westbound	No exit to A580 No access from A580 westbound No exit to A580 eastbound No access from A580
16	Eastbound Westbound	No exit, access from A666 only No access, exit to A666 only
20	Eastbound Westbound	No access from A664 No exit to A664
22	Westbound	No access from A62
25	S.W bound	No access from A560 / A6017
26	N.E bound	No access or exit
27	N.E bound S.W bound	No access, exit only No exit, access only

M61

Junction		
2&3	N.W bound S.E bound	No access from A580 eastbound No exit to A580 westbound

Junction with M6 (M6 Jun.30)

N.W bound	No exit to M6 southbound
S.E bound	No access from M6 northbound

M62

Junction		
23	Eastbound Westbound	No access, exit to A640 only No exit, access from A640 only

M65

Junction		
9	N.E bound S.W bound	No access, exit to A679 only No exit, access from A679 only
11	N.E bound S.W bound	No exit, access only No access, exit only

M66

Junction		
1	Northbound Southbound	No access, exit to A56 only No exit, access from A56 only

M67

Junction		
1	Eastbound Westbound	Access from A57 eastbound only Exit to A57 westbound only
1a	Eastbound Westbound	No access, exit to A6017 only No exit, access from A6017 only
2	Eastbound Westbound	No exit, access from A57 only No access, exit to A57 only

M69

Junction		
2	N.E bound S.W bound	No exit, access from B4669 only No access, exit to B4669 only

M73

Junction		
1	Southbound	No exit to A721 eastbound
2	Northbound Southbound	No access from M8 eastbound No exit to A89 eastbound No exit to M8 westbound No access from A89 westbound
3	Northbound Southbound	No exit to A80 S.W bound No access from A80 N.E bound

M74

Junction		
1	Eastbound Westbound	No access from M8 Westbound No exit to M8 Westbound
3	Eastbound Westbound	No exit No access
7	Northbound Southbound	No exit, access from A72 only No access, exit to A72 only
9	Northbound Southbound	No access or exit No access, exit to B7078 only
10	Southbound	No exit, access from B7078 only
11	Northbound Southbound	No exit, access from B7078 only No access, exit to B7078 only
12	Northbound Southbound	No access, exit to A70 only No exit, access from A70 only

M77

Junction with M8 (M8 Jun.22)

Northbound	No exit to M8 westbound
Southbound	No access from M8 eastbound

Junction		
4	Northbound Southbound	No exit No access
6	Northbound Southbound	No exit to A77 No access from A77
7	Northbound	No access from A77 No exit to A77

M80

Junction		
1	Northbound Southbound	No access from M8 westbound No exit to M8 eastbound
4a	Northbound Southbound	No access No exit
6a	Northbound Southbound	No exit No access
8	Northbound Southbound	No access from M876 No exit to M876

M90

Junction		
1	Northbound Southbound	No exit No Access from A90
2a	Northbound Southbound	No access, exit to A92 only No exit, access from A92 only
7	Northbound Southbound	No exit, access from A91 only No access, exit to A91 only
8	Northbound Southbound	No access, exit to A91 only No exit, access from A91 only
10	Northbound Southbound	No access from A912 Exit to A912 northbound only No exit to A912 Access from A912 southbound only

M180

Junction		
1	Eastbound Westbound	No access, exit only No exit, access from A18 only

M606

Junction		
2	Northbound	No access, exit only

M621

Junction		
2a	Eastbound Westbound	No exit, access only No access, exit only
4	Southbound	No exit
5	Northbound Southbound	No access, exit to A61 only No exit, access from A61 only
6	Northbound Southbound	No exit, access only No access, exit only
7	Eastbound Westbound	No access, exit only No exit, access only
8	Northbound Southbound	No access, exit only No exit, access only

M876

Junction with M80 (M80 Jun.5)

N.E bound	No access from M80 southbound
S.W bound	No exit to M80 northbound

Junction with M9 (M9 Jun.8)

N.E bound	No exit to M9 northbound
S.W bound	No access from M9 southbound

A1(M)

Hertfordshire Section

Junction		
2	Northbound Southbound	No access, exit only No exit, access from A1001 only
3	Southbound	No access, exit only
5	Northbound Southbound	No exit, access only No access or exit

Cambridgeshire Section

Junction		
14	Northbound Southbound	No exit, access only No access, exit only

Leeds Section

Junction		
40	Southbound	Exit to A1 southbound only
43	Northbound Southbound	Access from M1 eastbound only Exit to M1 westbound only

Durham Section

Junction		
57	Northbound Southbound	No access, exit to A66(M) only No exit, access from A66(M)
65	Northbound Southbound	Exit to A1 N.W bound and to A194(M) only Access from A1 S.E bound and from A194(M) only

A3(M)

Junction		
4	Northbound Southbound	No access, exit only No exit, access only

Aston Expressway A38(M)

Junction with Victoria Road, Aston

Northbound	No exit, access only
Southbound	No access, exit only

A48(M)

Junction with M4 (M4 Jun.29)

N.E bound	Exit to M4 eastbound only
S.W bound	Access from M4 westbound only

Junction		
29a	N.E bound S.W bound	Access from A48 eastbound only Exit to A48 westbound only

Mancunian Way A57(M)

Junction with A34 Brook Street, Manchester

Eastbound	No access, exit to A34 Brook Street, southbound only
Westbound	No exit, access only

Leeds Inner Ring Road A58(M)

Junction with Park Lane / Westgate

Southbound	No access, exit only

Leeds Inner Ring Road A64(M) (continuation of A58(M))

Junction with A58 Clay Pit Lane

Eastbound	No access
Westbound	No exit

A66(M)

Junction with A1(M) (A1(M) Jun.57)

N.E bound	Access from A1(M) N'bound only
S.W bound	Exit to A1(M) southbound only

A74(M)

Junction		
18	Northbound Southbound	No access No exit

Newcastle Central Motorway A167(M)

Junction with Camden Street

Northbound	No exit, access only
Southbound	No access or exit

A194(M)

Junction with A1(M) (A1(M) Jun.65) **and A1 Gateshead Western By-Pass**

Northbound	Access from A1(M) only
Southbound	Exit to A1(M) only

Northern Ireland

M1

Junction		
3	Northbound Southbound	No exit, access only No access, exit only
7	Westbound	No access, exit only

M2

Junction		
2	Eastbound Westbound	No access to M5 northbound No exit to M5 southbound

M5

Junction		
2	Northbound Southbound	No access from M2 eastbound No exit to M2 westbound